MW00613045

"Andrea Nicolotti's *The Shroud of Turin* is a first class historian's analysis of the fraught history of the appearance of the Shroud of Turin in the medieval period, its various travels before reaching Turin, the creation of the myth of authenticity, and the radiocarbon analysis of its medieval fabric. This is the serious historian's counterpart to *The Da Vinci Code*."

—John S. Kloppenborg, *University Professor and Chair of Religion, University of Toronto*

"Andrea Nicolotti has meticulously and proficiently reconstructed events involving the Shroud up to the present day. It is a fine book, an exemplary evidence of the value of historical research."

—Adriano Prosperi, *Professor of Modern History, Scuola Normale Superiore in Pisa and Member of the Lincean Academy in Rome*

"Andrea Nicolotti's book is a work in which the author succeeds with masterful measure and proficiency in the far from simple task of combining questions of the past with the reality of the present. In his informed use of investigative tools drawn from diverse disciplines and fields, the author deploys a refined research technique and an intellectual sensibility, in so doing revealing a rare breadth of approach."

—Pier Giorgio Zunino, *Member of the Academy of Sciences of Turin*

"This book constitutes the very best analysis of the history of the Shroud of Turin and of other competing shrouds, from antiquity to the present day. Relying on a complete reexamination of the documented evidence, this work is a masterpiece in its use of the methods of historical criticism. It is an antidote to the devotional and pseudoscientific literature put in circulation by those who believe in the authenticity of the relic."

—Fr. Pier Angelo Gramaglia, *Professor Emeritus of Patrology, Theological University of Northern Italy*

"Nicolotti's book is destined to remain for a long time the most complete historiographical assessment on the subject, but also provides some food for thought. For one whose faith is honestly understood, it ought not constitute an obstacle if the historical-archival sciences, the history of weaving, and radiocarbon dating lead to conclusions that appear to point to the unavoidable interpretation that the Shroud of Turin cannot have come to us from the funereal garb of Christ."

—Fr. Francesco Pieri, *Professor of Church History, Theological Faculty of Emilia Romagna*

"The author of this book deserves enormous credit inasmuch as he has inspected everything of significance that has been published to this point and has personally checked the documents present in the archives of the Vatican, Italy, and France, where he also sought out new documents. The book should be recommended to all those who do not wish to be deceived by the numerous current publications in defense of the authenticity of the Turin Shroud."

—Msgr. Armando Rolla, *Professor Emeritus of Holy Scripture, Pontifical Faculty of Theology in Southern Italy*

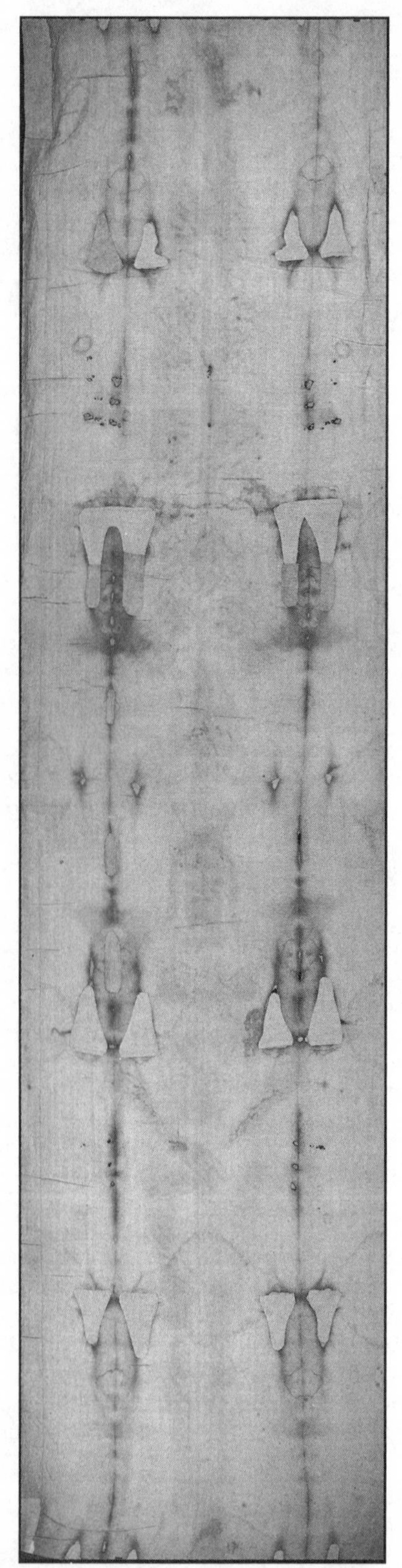

The Shroud of Turin, pre-2002 restoration

The Shroud of Turin

The History and Legends of the World's Most Famous Relic

Andrea Nicolotti
Translated by Jeffrey M. Hunt and R. A. Smith

BAYLOR UNIVERSITY PRESS

Waco, Texas 76798
Originally published in Italian as *Sindone: Storia e leggende di una reliquia controversa* by Giulio Einaudi editore S.p.A., Turin, Italy, 2015.

Cover Design by Savanah N. Landerholm
Cover image: Casella, Giovanni Andrea (17th CE), and Casella, Giacomo (17th CE), *Saint Charles Borromeo in Adoration of the Holy Shroud*. Ca. 1655. S. Carlo Church, Turin, Italy. Photo Credit: Scala / Art Resource, NY.
Book Design by Baylor University Press; layout by Scribe Inc.

The translation of this book has been funded by SEPS—Segretariato Europeo per le Pubblicazioni Scientifiche. Via Val d'Aposa 7 - 40123 Bologna (Italy). seps@seps.it / www.seps.it.

The Library of Congress has cataloged this book under ISBN 978-1-4813-1147-2.

Printed in the United States of America on acid-free paper with a minimum of thirty percent recycled content.

Contents

List of Figures

Abbreviations

AAT	Archivio Arcivescovile di Torino
ACS	Roma, Archivio Centrale dello Stato
ACT	Archivio Capitolare di Torino
ADA	Troyes, Archives départementales de l'Aube
ADC	Dijon, Archives départementales de la Côte-d'Or
AST	Archivio di Stato di Torino
ASV	Archivio Segreto Vaticano
BMB	Bibliothèque municipale de Besançon
BNF	Paris, Bibliothèque nationale de France
CICAP	Comitato Italiano per il Controllo delle Affermazioni sulle Pseudoscienze
CIELT	Centre International d'Études sur le Linceul de Turin
CSELT	Centro Studi e Laboratori Telecomunicazioni
CSICOP	Committee for the Scientific Investigation of Claims of the Paranormal (now known as CSI)
CSS	Torino, Archivio della Confraternita del SS. Sudario
ENEA	Italian National Agency for New Technologies, Energy and Sustainable Economic Development
GBEI	Grenoble, Bibliothèque municipale d'étude et d'information
STURP	Shroud of Turin Research Project

Preface

The aim of this book is to treat the history of the Shroud of Turin, from its appearance to this day. The study also seeks to summarize the history of the other burial cloths of Jesus, which, since the sixth century, have appeared in the form of relics in different places in the Christian world. After a lengthy struggle for primacy among supporters of the various shrouds, today most of those objects are generally ignored because they are scattered or overshadowed by the Shroud of Turin.

The Gospel accounts will be the starting point for reconstructing the environment in which the veneration of various shrouds was born and spread. Throughout the centuries, from late antiquity to the Middle Ages, one finds an increasing interest in the discovery and possession of relics of Jesus' passion and death. Within this broader context and in comparison with even older burial cloths, the events surrounding the Shroud of Turin come into sharper focus and receive more illumination. The history of this relic begins in the Middle Ages, when it appears in a village in France. The Shroud will then move to Chambéry, in the heart of Savoy, and finally to Turin, the new capital of the Duchy of Savoy and later of the Kingdom of Italy. The Shroud's story is fraught with adventures, whose details are often not very well known and are often misunderstood. It is a story consisting of episodes that the House of Savoy and the Church tried to hide. It is a story involving key figures of nobility, of politics, of the Church, and of science. It is a story of clashes and conflicts.

At the base of this long story is a series of careful investigations of all the most important surviving documents. One investigation was carried out at Italian archives in Turin, Rome, and the Vatican, along with several in France (Chambéry, Dijon, Troyes, Grenoble, and Paris). In the process, new documents have been discovered that illustrate some vital bits of the relic's history. The amount of material concerning the Shroud is in fact enormous, far greater than that of the other shrouds. This is not only because of the Shroud's vexing history but also because of its very fortune, as the Shroud of Turin would ultimately enjoy a reputation greater than those shrouds that had initially been more famous. This happened not only thanks to the very eloquent image it bears but also because of the powerful propaganda that was first advanced by the House of Savoy and later by the ecclesiastical authorities. In our own age, a group of authenticist scholars known as sindonologists have also made the case for authenticity. We shall consider their ideas in the last part of this book, when we treat the arguments advanced during the twentieth and twenty-first centuries. We shall see that the Shroud's history is bound to the history of sindonology, even from the first photographs of it and continuing on through its radiocarbon dating, extending even to the present day.

No general history of the Shroud has been undertaken for many years, certainly not one that is broad, thorough, and carried out with clear scientific criteria. Indeed, it would be impossible to do so and merely to leave aside the long-standing debate on the authenticity of the relic. In fact, almost every study of the Shroud has had as its main motive a position on authenticity, which fact is precisely the reason why the majority of scholars qualified to undertake such a study have preferred to steer clear of it. Even the current study will not, in fact, skirt the authenticity question, for a history that does not bother to scrutinize the origin of the object of study would be incomplete.

Even if a study of the Shroud, such as my own, is based on first-hand sources, it cannot avoid taking into account the abundant literature that already exists. Wading through the plethora of sources is a daunting task, even occasionally vexing, as the quality of the secondary research is in most cases questionable or slanted toward the clear objective of proving the relic's authenticity. Accordingly, I must devote a good deal of space to dismantling historiographical hypotheses that do not hold up under criticism. One cannot pass silently over the cases in which the sindonology has muddled the evidence; it has produced propaganda and historical-scientific fabrications, successfully influencing the *opinio communis*. The historian is called to address the issue directly, without hiding behind an artificial moderation that would only lead to reticence.

Let it be the task of others to write a history of the sincere devotion associated with the Shroud, of the theology, the literature, and the art that the Shroud has spawned. Such studies and contributions are beyond the purview of this book.

Andrea Nicolotti

Acknowledgments

The preparation of this book required four years of work, which was carried out at the Department of Historical Studies of the University of Turin, under the direction of Adele Monaci Castagno. Two research grants in the history of Christianity, coordinated by Claudio Gianotto and Paolo Cozzo, enabled this study.

I thank them for their help, as I do many others who provided bibliographic material and addressed various issues, and who also supported me morally and materially in those years even with small gestures. Among these are Joseph Accetta, Pier Giuseppe Accornero, Roberto Alciati, Aniceto Antilopi, Domenico Anzellotti, Walter Barberis, Alessandro Barbero, Marco Bella, Pierre-Marie Berthe, Corrado Bettiga, Andrea Bosco, Luciano Bossina, Patrizia Cancian, Luigi Canetti, Maria Goretti Castello, Daniela Cereia, Jean-Luc Chassel, Giovanni Cherubin, Gaetano Ciccone, Orietta Ciprotti, Cristiana Cordero, Paolo Cornaglia, Martin Davis, Vincent Debiais, Fernando J. De Lasala, Franco Faia, Roberto Falcinelli, Chiara Faraggiana di Sarzana, Anna Maria Farcito, Enzo Ferraro, Giovanni Garibotto, Bartolomeo Gariglio, Luigi Garlaschelli, Luisa Gentile, Pierangelo Gentile, Bernardo Gonella, Pier Angelo Gramaglia, Laurent Hablot, Laura Lanfranchi, Valter Laudadio, Raffaele Licinio, Antonio Lombatti, Enrique López Fernández, Angelo Luvison, Sergio Luzzatto, Tiziana Magone, Miranda Maran, Andrea Merlotti, Walter Nicolotti, Hiara Olivera, Antonio Olivieri, Sergio Pagano, Werner Paravicini, Jacques Paviot, Francesco Pieri, Valerio Polidori, Gian Marco Rinaldi, Armando Rolla,

Giovanni Sacchetti, Michele Salcito, Michelle Santelli, Xavier Serra Estellés, and Gian Maria Zaccone. I apologize here to those whom I may have forgotten. The responsibility for the judgments expressed in this work, of course, is all mine. I also thank in advance those who will, with a constructive spirit, point out to me any oversights and typographical errors, which too regularly occur in book production.

I dedicate this work to my grandmother, Teresina Concato, who unfortunately did not live long enough to see the final product, and to Gian Marco Rinaldi, who is, in my opinion, the finest scholar of the Shroud.

Introduction to the English Edition

The Italian edition of this book was well received, garnering many positive reviews in both news media and scholarly journals. The volume was also awarded two academic prizes, the Pozzale Luigi Russo Award and the Cherasco History Prize. The English edition, while maintaining the structure of the Italian edition, has been corrected at a few points and expanded to include fresh information gathered after 2015. It has also been enlarged to include, where possible, bibliography useful to English-speaking readers. Some elements that had previously been neglected or only mentioned have been added.

I would like to thank Professor John Kloppenborg for proposing this translation to Dr. Carey C. Newman, Director of Baylor University Press, who accepted the suggestion with enthusiasm. I also thank the two translators, Professors Alden Smith and Jeff Hunt, with whom I met personally to work with the translation and verify that it was fully responsive to my wishes. Every translation of ancient texts, from Old French, Greek, or Latin, has been revised directly from the original. I also want warmly to acknowledge Piergiacomo Petrioli, Diane Smith, Jamie Wheeler, Hannah Rogers, Ella Liu, and Bailey Sloan for their kind assistance with this project.

Andrea Nicolotti

Genealogical Stemma

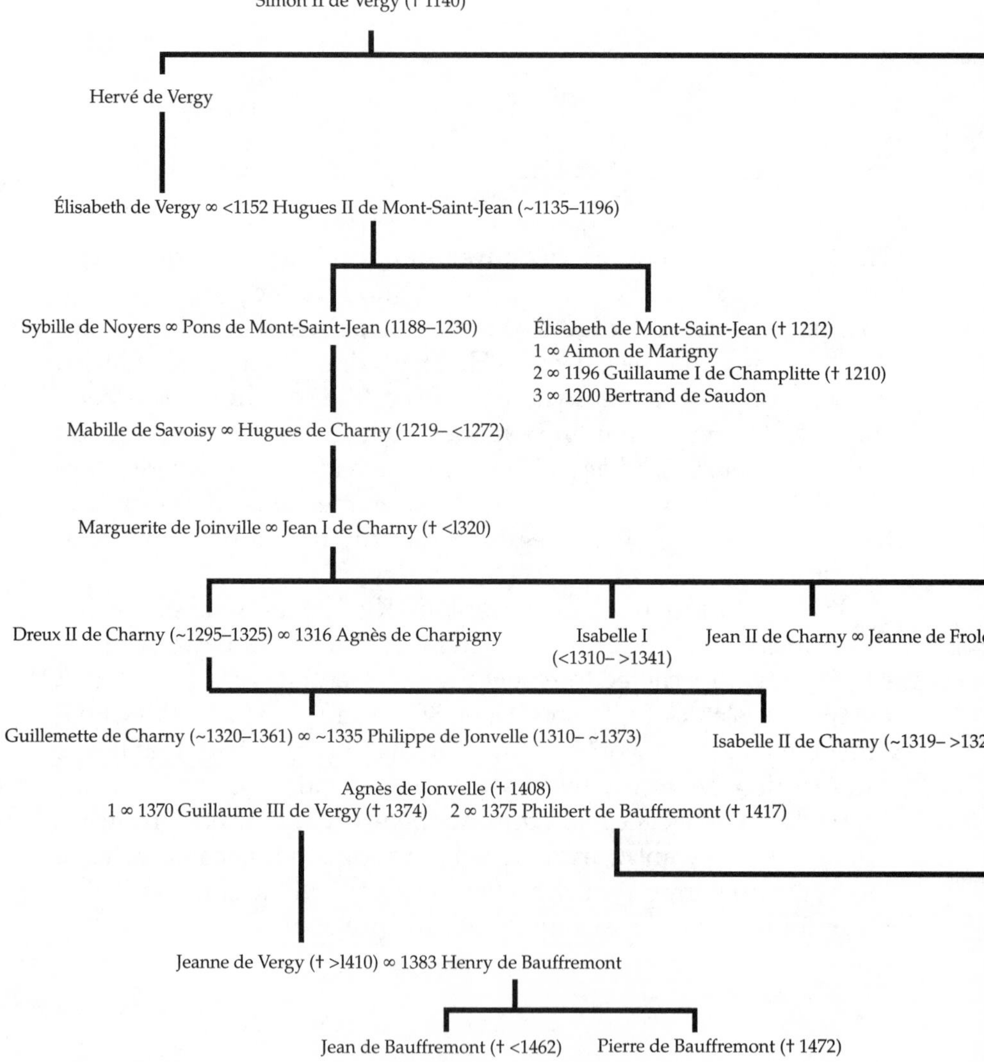

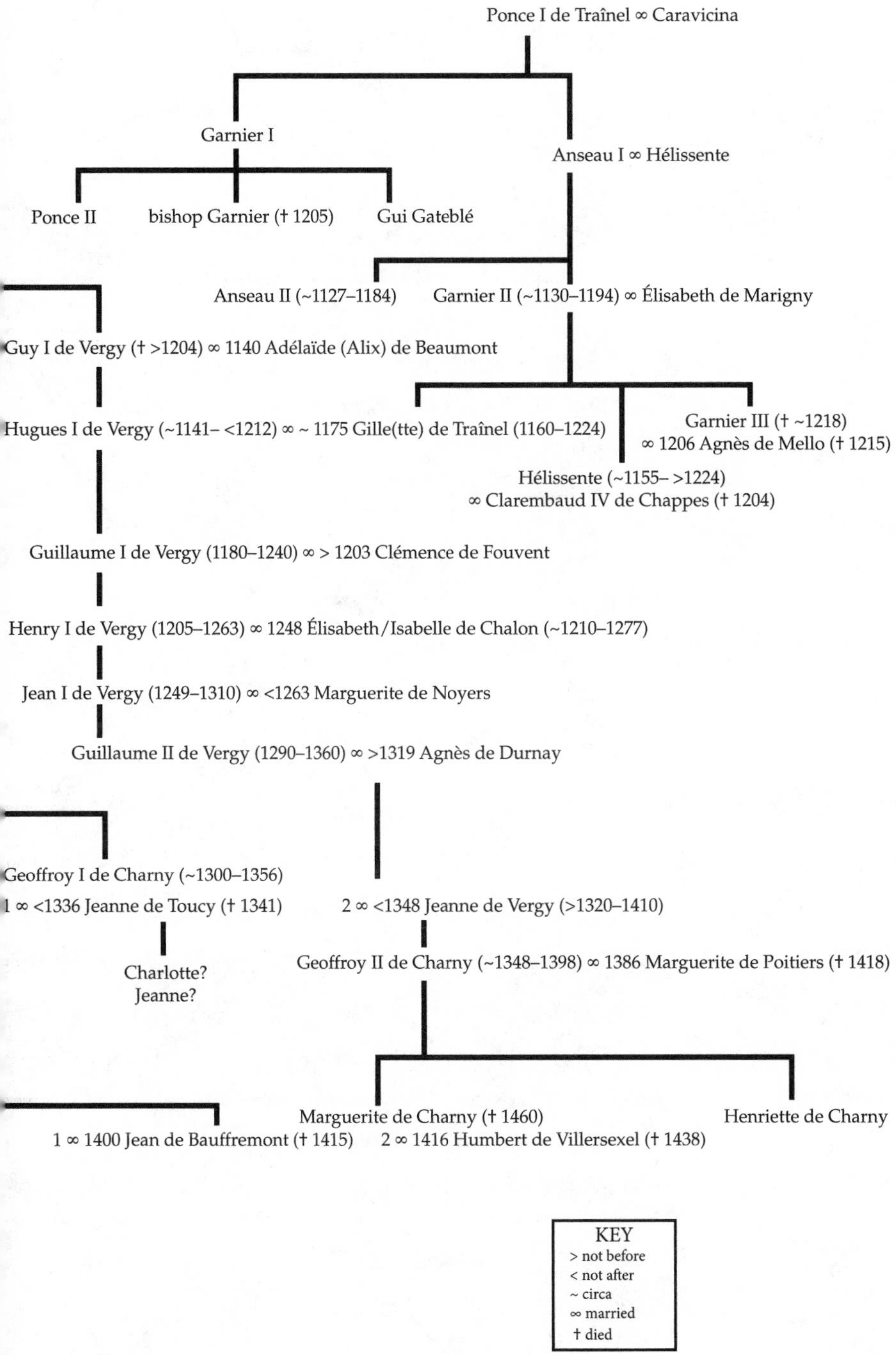

Ponce I de Traînel ∞ Caravicina
Garnier I
Anseau I ∞ Hélissente
Ponce II
bishop Garnier († 1205)
Gui Gateblé
Anseau II (~1127–1184)
Garnier II (~1130–1194) ∞ Élisabeth de Marigny
Guy I de Vergy († >1204) ∞ 1140 Adélaïde (Alix) de Beaumont
Hugues I de Vergy (~1141– <1212) ∞ ~ 1175 Gille(tte) de Traînel (1160–1224)
Garnier III († ~1218)
∞ 1206 Agnès de Mello († 1215)
Hélissente (~1155– >1224)
∞ Clarembaud IV de Chappes († 1204)
Guillaume I de Vergy (1180–1240) ∞ > 1203 Clémence de Fouvent
Henry I de Vergy (1205–1263) ∞ 1248 Élisabeth/Isabelle de Chalon (~1210–1277)
Jean I de Vergy (1249–1310) ∞ <1263 Marguerite de Noyers
Guillaume II de Vergy (1290–1360) ∞ >1319 Agnès de Durnay
Geoffroy I de Charny (~1300–1356)
1 ∞ <1336 Jeanne de Toucy († 1341)
2 ∞ <1348 Jeanne de Vergy (>1320–1410)
Charlotte?
Jeanne?
Geoffroy II de Charny (~1348–1398) ∞ 1386 Marguerite de Poitiers († 1418)
Marguerite de Charny († 1460)
Henriette de Charny
1 ∞ 1400 Jean de Bauffremont († 1415)
2 ∞ 1416 Humbert de Villersexel († 1438)
KEY
> not before
< not after
~ circa
∞ married
† died

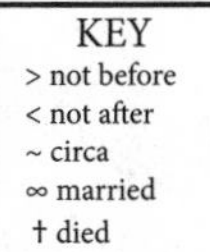

ONE

The Birth and Development of a Cult

1.1 The Fate of Jesus' Burial Cloths

1.1.1. The Most Ancient Writings

Obviously any history of Jesus' sepulchral fabrics must begin with the testimony of the ancient Gospel accounts.[1] These documents present rather detailed narrations about what happened in Jerusalem on a Friday around the year AD 30, when a man who had been sentenced to death was insulted, beaten, and scourged. Before being put on it, he was forced to carry the cross, his means of death, for the most part by himself, though in some accounts he was assisted in carrying it as he proceeded from Jerusalem to an elevated place just outside the city walls. When he arrived at that place, whose name is recorded in Scripture as Golgotha, meaning "Place of the Skull," he was crucifed. Nails were driven through his hands and, in all likelihood, also his feet. Ropes were likely also employed to hold him in place, and the wooden cross was probably fitted with some supports to help the person crucified to stay in that painful position. Left hanging to die, he is unlikely to have survived very long.

According to the Gospel accounts, few of his large number of followers were actually at his side during the crucifixion itself. A man named Joseph of Arimathea undertook the task of taking the body down from the cross and transporting it to his own nearby tomb. As one condemned to death, Jesus would not have been entitled to an honorable funeral. There would not have been the usual procession,

[1] In particular Matthew 27–28; Mark 15–16; Luke 22–24; and John 18–20, to which one can add at least the Gospel of Peter.

the songs and flautists, and the mourners to accompany the body to the cemetery. Nor is it likely a coffin or a litter would have been employed. Nonetheless, the Gospels record that the body was not thrown into a pit with the other condemned men but taken down and placed inside a rock-carved tomb, most likely on a stone bench that ran along the sides of a wall or inside a niche carved into the wall. We do not know if his body was washed first or if the funereal unctions took place.

But we do know that, according to the Synoptic Gospel accounts and also that of Peter, once the body had been taken down from the cross, Joseph wrapped it with some kind of cloth called *sindón* (σινδών).[2] At the time the word *sindón* had two meanings: a type of fine fabric, especially linen; and then, synecdochically, any object made of that fabric. The use of the Greek term *sindón* does not allow us to know if the Gospels mean to say that Jesus was wrapped up with "linen"—that is, with one or more pieces of that specific material (from which one could make bands, bandages, cloths, sheets); or with "a linen"—that is, in a single cloth lining whose shape, however, is not clarified (it may have been a long and wide cloth, a tunic, or one very long single bandage). Either translation is therefore entirely plausible: "he [Joseph] wrapped with linen" or "he wrapped it up in [a fabric made of] linen." The term *sindón* does not help us to know the form of the fabric or fabrics to which the Gospels refer, but the verbs that accompany it give us some idea about how Jesus was enshrouded. Luke and Matthew use the verb *entulísso*, which means "wrap" or "roll up." Mark, which is accepted by most scholars to be the oldest Gospel, instead uses the more restrictive *eneiléo*—that is, "wrap tightly," "envelop," "wind," "entangle." Thus, from the use of two different verbs in the Synoptic accounts, it seems possible to

[2] Matthew 27:59-60: "And having taken the body, Joseph wrapped it [in] pure *sindón* and laid it in his new sepulcher" (καὶ λαβὼν τὸ σῶμα ὁ Ἰωσὴφ ἐνετύλιξεν αὐτὸ [ἐν] σινδόνι καθαρᾷ καὶ ἔθηκεν αὐτὸ ἐν τῷ καινῷ αὐτοῦ μνημείῳ); Mark 15:46: "And he, having brought *sindón*, and having taken him down, wound him with the *sindón*, and laid him in a sepulcher" (καὶ ἀγοράσας σινδόνα καθελὼν αὐτὸν ἐνείλησεν τῇ σινδόνι καὶ ἔθηκεν αὐτὸν ἐν μνημείῳ); Luke 23:53: "And he, having taken (it) down, wrapped it in *sindón*, and laid him in a tomb" (καὶ καθελὼν ἐνετύλιξεν αὐτὸ σινδόνι καὶ ἔθηκεν αὐτὸν ἐν μνήματι); *Evangelium Petri* 24: "And he, having taken the Lord, washed and tied him with *sindón* and brought him into his own grave" (λαβὼν δὲ τὸν κύριον ἔλουσε καὶ εἴλησε σινδόνι καὶ εἰσήγαγεν εἰς ἴδιον τάφον).

conclude that, for the Gospel writers, especially Mark, the corpse of Jesus was not simply covered or clothed but rather wrapped up quite tightly.

The Gospel of John, conversely, speaks never of the *sindón* of Jesus but rather of *othónia* (ὀθόνια)—that is, of "linens," in the plural, which serve to "bind" (*déo*) the body of Jesus.[3] Though John clearly is thinking that this involves more than one cloth, he does not tell us precisely how these linens (note the plural) were used to wrap the body. Moreover, John also points out that a *soudárion* (σουδάριον)—that is, a cloth that is put on the head of the deceased—was also employed. He then enlarges on the narrative, stating that on the morning of the first day of the week (Sunday), the apostle Peter went to the tomb, which by then had been discovered to be empty, as the body of the deceased was not to be found there. Looking inside the the tomb, Peter sees only "the linen cloths lying there, and the *soudárion* that was upon his head, not lying with the linen cloths," but wrapped up in a different place or in a particular way.[4] More than this is not entirely clear, and indeed it is unwise to press the text for more information. The Gospels offer just the minimum on these details in such moments of excitement, giving scant and sometimes even somewhat contradictory information. Thus, it is not possible to consider the reports entirely objective.[5]

[3] John 19:40: "They took, therefore, the body of Jesus, and bound it by *othónia* with the spices" (ἔλαβον οὖν τὸ σῶμα τοῦ Ἰησοῦ καὶ ἔδησαν αὐτὸ ὀθονίοις μετὰ τῶν ἀρωμάτων).

[4] John 20:7. The Greek text is not at all clear: "beholdeth the linen cloths lying there, and the sudarium that was upon his head, not lying with the linen cloths, but separately [*or*: differently], having been wrapped into one place [*or*: in some place (by itself)]" (θεωρεῖ τὰ ὀθόνια κείμενα, καὶ τὸ σουδάριον, ὃ ἦν ἐπὶ τῆς κεφαλῆς αὐτοῦ, οὐ μετὰ τῶν ὀθονίων κείμενον ἀλλὰ χωρὶς ἐντετυλιγμένον εἰς ἕνα τόπον). All translations in this book, unless otherwise indicated, are my own.

[5] The critical bibliography on these few passages is noteworthy and offers a variety of conclusions that are not always reconcilable; I myself am currently conducting a study on the subject. Beyond the standard biblical commentaries, further see F. M. Braun, "Le Linceul de Turin et l'Évangile de Saint Jean," *Nouvelle revue théologique* 66 (1939): 900–935, 1025–46; A. Vaccari, "Sindone, bende e sudario nella sepoltura di Cristo," in *Secoli sul mondo: alla scoperta della Bibbia*, ed. G. Rinaldi (Turin: Marietti, 1955), 438–42; J. Blinzler, "Die Grablegung Jesu in historischer Sicht," in *Resurrexit: Actes du symposium international sur la resurrection de Jésus*, ed. É. Dhanis (Vatican City: Libreria Editrice Vaticana, 1974), 78–83; G. Ghiberti, *La sepoltura di Gesù* (Rome: Marietti, 1982), 35–54; R. E. Brown, *The Death of the Messiah* (New York: Doubleday,

The attention to the sepulchral fabrics of Jesus within these most ancient writings is at best superficial. When the discovery of the empty tomb on that famous Sunday morning is recounted, only John mentions the linen in describing what was visible within the tomb, a tomb in which the body of Jesus was no longer present. John explains that the linen and the sudarium were viewed by both Peter and John but adds nothing about their fate. Mark, by contrast, notes that some women went to the tomb, where they encountered a young man, but he does not say anything about fabrics, nor does he speak further about the tomb. Matthew neither discusses fabrics nor mentions entry into the tomb. Luke does recount the women's entry into the empty grave but is silent about the grave cloths. Later in the narrative, however, Luke does say that Peter saw linens. Yet we find in the Acts of the Apostles, also written by Luke, a later account of the events that does not include mention of the burial cloths.

Accordingly, in the Gospel accounts it does not seem that the first disciples paid particular attention to the sepulchral cloths of Jesus. It is not even proven that they spoke about the matter amongst themselves, neither did they understand that those fabrics had some role in witnessing and demonstrating the resurrection of their teacher. No one is actually named as the person who collected the linens, nor do the accounts mention that anyone even went looking for them or, much less, stored them away with the idea that they would play a commemorative role for apologetic, thaumaturgical, or cultic reasons.

The only fabrics that, according to Luke, played a significant role among the followers of Jesus were those that came into contact with the body of the apostle Paul, through which healings were carried out.[6] This important piece of information suggests that there was, in principle, no preclusion of the possibility of some eventual fabric

1994), 1242–313; P. A. Gramaglia, "I panni funerari nella tomba di Gesù (Gv 20,1–10)," *Approfondimento Sindone* 2, no. 2 (1998): 49–72; A. Nicolotti, "An Ignominious Burial: The Treatment of the Body of Jesus of Nazareth," in S. Cavicchioli and L. Provero, eds., *Public Uses of Human Remains and Relics in History* (New York: Routledge, 2020), 11–28. On the problem of contradictory sources and, more generally, on how the evangelists could avail themselves of facts, see the useful ideas of A. Destro and M. Pesce, *La morte di Gesù: Indagine su un mistero* (Milan: Rizzoli, 2014).

[6] Acts 19:11-12: "In the meantime God was working uncommon prodigies through the hands of Paul, to the point that he put upon those who were sick handkerchiefs or aprons that had been in contact with him, and their illnesses ceased, and evil spirits fled."

bearing significance; on the contrary, it actually points to a lack of interest in the cloths used to bury Jesus, which would have had to enjoy greater importance than those touched by Paul, if someone had preserved and valued them.[7] Such a comparison is, admittedly, not entirely fitting, as there is one important difference between the sepulchral fabrics and the common ones that Paul would have touched: for the Jews the cloths that had touched a corpse were impure and capable of transmitting impurity to those who touched them, which is why it was normal that one would avoid coming into contact with them at all.

Centuries later, when quite an interest in the sepulchral linen of Jesus had arisen among Christians, different authors would describe the cloths variously, referring to not a single relic but many, and often just summarizing or paraphrasing the Gospel accounts, which we have seen are themselves not easily reconcilable. When these later accounts emerge, the authors clearly do not give the impression of actually referring to any of the relics that, beginning in the Middle Ages, will become the object of veneration.[8] At the end of a long survey of historical, archaeological, and exegetical details, one must come to this conclusion: the ancients knew practically nothing about how many shrouds there were and what forms they took. We can thus only go so far as to formulate hypotheses about these subjects; we must admit that if at some point there had not emerged the need to know more, and if there had not been a shroud in Turin, probably the few lines of the Gospels that speak of those fabrics would have passed almost unnoticed. Such is the sluggish point of departure for a journey that will in fact take us on a very long quest. From here, and from this silence that will last for centuries, we must start if we want to consider the Shroud, and other shrouds as well.

For those who believe that some of the sepulchral fabrics of Jesus have been preserved and have survived to this day, it will not be easy to explain why no one mentioned them for such a long time, why no one saw the obvious value of them, and why no one ever claimed possession of them. The strongest temptation may be to go

[7] See M. Pesce, "I Vangeli e la Sindone," *MicroMega* 4 (2010): 15–26.

[8] An anthology of texts is in P. A. Gramaglia, *L'uomo della Sindone non è Gesù Cristo: Un'ipotesi storica fondata su documenti finora trascurati* (Turin: Claudiana, 1978), 45–69.

in search of texts that speak of any shroud in antiquity with such insistence that texts are "discovered" even where and when they do not exist. It is true that beyond the Gospels there were many other texts produced that speak of a shroud, "but these have served only to fire the incredulity of those capable of understanding their wording and context," as one far-from-skeptical author has stated.[9] The search for such documents has, in any case, often been conducted with excessive optimism.

Our consideration of the history of the Shroud must begin with an overview of the ancient texts that speak about the sepulchral fabrics or, according to some, demonstrate the survival of a shroud in antiquity as well as its preservation. It will always be necessary to keep in mind, too, as a vital methodological principle that, barring the existence of an established link, a reference to the survival of sepulchral cloths of Jesus in ancient Christian literature does not allow certain identification of these cloths with any relic that might turn up in later centuries. Add to this that there are in fact "other" shrouds, relics that in the medieval period were in fact in competition with the Shroud of Turin to be the sepulchral cloths of Jesus. Our analysis, therefore, will be quite detailed, useful for reconstructing a wider context that is too rarely fully taken into account. Thus, for the moment, let us consider that context before facing the history of the Turin Shroud, which we shall do in the next chapter.

1.1.2. A "Judeo-Christian" Gospel

When it comes to ancient testimonies about a shroud, the most ancient text worthy of consideration is a document known as the Gospel of the Hebrews.[10] It belongs to the category of the so-called Judeo-Christian Gospels, produced in a group of followers of Jesus who came directly from the Jewish community. Very similar to the canonical Gospel of Matthew, this Gospel is commonly dated to the second century, certainly earlier than 180. The original language may have been Aramaic, but the few surviving fragments date back

[9] T. Humber, *The Sacred Shroud* (New York: Pocket Books, 1978), 74.

[10] I deal more extensively with the Gospel of the Hebrews, the alleged Coptic Gospel of the Twelve Apostles, and the Gospel of Nicodemus, in A. Nicolotti, "Un cas particulier d'apologétique appliquée: L'utilisation des apocryphes pour authentifier le Mandylion d'Édesse et le suaire de Turin," *Apocrypha* 26 (2015): 301–31.

to a Latin translation by Jerome.[11] Let us consider one fragment of it recorded by Jerome in 392 AD:

> Also the Gospel which is named according to the Hebrews, and which was recently translated by me into the Greek and Latin languages, which Origen also often uses, relates, after the resurrection of the Saviour: "Now the Lord, when he had given *sindon* unto the servant of the priest, went unto James and appeared to him"; for James had sworn that he would not eat bread from that hour wherein he had drunk the cup of the Lord until he should see him rising from among them that sleep. And again a little afterward: "Bring ye"—saith the Lord—"a table and bread," and immediately it is added: "He took bread and blessed and brake and gave it unto James the Just and said unto him: 'My brother, eat thy bread, for the son of man is risen from among them that sleep.'"[12]

One of the goals of the compiler of this Gospel is to exalt the figure of James the Just, known as "brother of the Lord." Contrary to what is stated in the canonical Gospels (Matthew, Mark, Luke, and John), here James is recorded as the first person to view an apparition of the risen Lord. The Gospel of Hebrews also states that James drank from the chalice of the Lord, while according to the canonical Gospels he did not take part in the Last Supper. This account of the delivery of the *sindon* (i.e., of linen or cotton cloth, whose form and quantity is not specified) does not correspond to the accounts of the other

[11] On this text and, more generally, on the thorny problem of the so-called Judeo-Christian Gospels, see W. Schneemelcher, *New Testament Apocrypha*, vol. 1 (Louisville: Westminster John Knox, 1991), 134–63, 172–78; C. Gianotto, *Ebrei credenti in Gesù* (Milan: Edizioni Paoline, 2012), 173–96 and 544–46 (§ 207); A. Gregory, *The Gospel according to the Hebrews and the Gospel of the Ebionites* (Oxford: Oxford University Press, 2017). Some scholars identify the Gospel of the Jews and the Gospel of the Nazarenes.

[12] Jerome, *De viris illustribus* 2.12–13: "Evangelium quoque quod appellatur secundum Hebraeos, et a me nuper in Graecum Latinumque sermonem translatum est, quo et Origenes saepe utitur, post resurrectionem Salvatoris refert: 'Dominus autem cum dedisset sindonem servo sacerdotis, ivit ad Iacobum et apparuit ei'; iuraverat enim Iacobus se non comesurum panem ab illa hora qui biberat calicem Domini, donec videret eum resurgentem a dormientibus. Rursusque post paululum: 'Adferte,' ait Dominus, 'mensam et panem,' statimque additur: 'Tulit panem et benedixit et fregit et dedit Iacobo Iusto et dixit ei: Frater mi, comede panem tuum, quia resurrexit filius hominis a dormientibus.'"

Gospels, though there is a possible parallel to a passage from the Acts of Thomas that says, "The apostle bade his minister to set forth a table; and he set forth a stool which he found there, and spread a *sindón* upon it and set on it the bread of blessing."[13] Several features appear in both stories: the shroud, the servant, the chalice, and the bread, all suggesting some overlap between the accounts. The shroud would seem to have been a primitive tablecloth for the altar, not a sepulchral cloth per se, as it is often interpreted.

Unfortunately, the few sentences reported by Jerome do not clarify the context. It is also possible, therefore, that the shroud mentioned in the Gospel of the Hebrews is the same as that in which Jesus was buried. The Latin text, as we noted above, is only a translation. In the other writings of Jerome, however, the Hebrew *sadin*, translated as *sindón*, generally indicates fabrics that would usually be used as clothing.[14] Does the Gospel of Hebrews speak of the linen garb in which Jesus was buried, or of sheets or pieces of various shapes? It is simply not clear.

Equally difficult is determining who is meant by the description "servant of the priest." Is he the servant of James, the one spreading out the tablecloth for the bread? Or is he the servant of the high priest mentioned in the canonical Gospels on the occasion of the arrest of Jesus, who according to John was called Malchus and whose ear was cut off with a sword stroke by a follower of Jesus?[15] Or is he an ordinary servant in attendance near the sepulcher who, together with the guards, was stationed to keep watch over the tomb, according to what Matthew reports?[16] If the sepulchral context is accounted for,

13 *Acta Thomae* 49: ἐκέλευσεν δὲ ὁ ἀπόστολος τῷ διακόνῳ αὐτοῦ παραθεῖναι τράπεζαν· παρέθηκαν δὲ συμψέλλιον ὃ εὗρον ἐκεῖ, καὶ ἁπλώσας σινδόνα ἐπ' αὐτὸ ἐπέθηκεν ἄρτον τῆς εὐλογίας. I follow the interpretation proposed by A. F. J. Klijn, *Jewish-Christian Gospel Tradition* (Leiden: Brill, 1992), 85.

14 Thus P. A. Gramaglia, "Ancora la Sindone di Torino," *Rivista di storia e letteratura religiosa* 27 (1991): 90–91.

15 Matthew 26:51; Mark 14:47; Luke 22:50; John 18:10.

16 Matthew 27:62-65. Alfred Loisy, "Les origines du Nouveau Testament," *Revue du clergé français* 20 (1899): 35, has raised a relevant question: "Is not the passage about the shroud, in which Christ comes out of the tomb and consigns the shroud to its attendant, perhaps the product of a banal imagination?" Johannes Bauer, "Christliche Antike," *Anzeiger für die Altertumswissenschaft* 51 (1998): 172, notes, "this is not historical information but an invented answer to the question as to where the funerary fabric was located in which Jesus had been wrapped."

the narrative would then have an apologetic function: the delivered shroud would be proof of the effective resurrection of Jesus, tangible even in the eyes of the Jews who had condemned him, who were supposedly informed of the facts from this otherwise unidentified "servant," who is providentially present. Such a scenario is, of course, not credible, because no Jewish servant would have ever picked up a cloth that had been in contact with a corpse, much less deliver it to a priest, since the cloth would therefore have been impure and capable of contaminating whatever it touched. The account, moreover, clashes with that of the Gospel of John: if the recently risen Jesus "gave" his shroud to the servant, John and Peter could certainly not have seen it in the tomb.

In any case it seems that the community that recognized itself in this Gospel is not worried about the fact that the fabric passes through the hands of the slave of a bitter enemy of Jesus. On the other hand, inasmuch as at that period of time it was not yet even a point of consideration that a shroud might have survived somewhere, there would have been no reason to wonder what had become of it. Not even Jerome, who prepared the Latin translation of the Gospel of the Hebrews while residing in Bethlehem, makes any mention of a shroud preserved in Palestine, consistent with the other sources at the end of the fourth century in Palestine that did not know about such a relic.[17]

The phrase concerning the *sindon* in the Gospel of the Hebrews has, however, been particularly subject to speculation by those who thought they could isolate here the most ancient extrabiblical mention of what is known today as the Turin Shroud. Yet, even if we grant this strange story historical credibility and accept its sepulchral association, some difficulties arise: first of all, the contradiction with the canonical Gospels, in which the burial cloths are recorded as having remained in the tomb to be seen by those who entered after the resurrection; then, too, the fact that the risen Jesus was leaving the grave while delivering the shroud to the servant of a Jewish priest (entirely disregarding rules of purity that all Jews would have observed). How can one imagine, then, that the shroud would later have returned to the Christians? Among scholars of the Shroud, some prefer to pass

[17] See F. Puaux, "À propos du Saint-Suaire de Turin," *Revue chrétienne* 49, no. 15 (1902): 458.

over in silence the difficulties of the text,[18] yet others, on the contrary, admit that it "merely raised its own problems without helping any of those of the Shroud."[19]

Others tried to use the text but still ended up distorting its meaning. The first distortion is that of John Theodore Dodd, who suggests an error in the transmission of the text of Jerome. Dodd takes the liberty of replacing the words "servant of the priest" with the name "Peter." If Jesus had handed the shroud to Peter, one gains two advantages: the "disappearance" of the priest's uncomfortable servant and a partial agreement with the canonical Gospels. The philological justification for such violence to the text, however, is entirely fanciful. According to Dodd, someone would first have confused a supposed original Latin word *Petro* and the word *puero* ("lad" or "servant").[20] A later copyist, to help the reader, would then have had to decide to erase the word and replace it with *servo sacerdotis*, to make the reader understand that he was talking about the servant who was wounded in the ear during the arrest of Jesus.[21] There is, however, no proof whatsoever from the text for such an explanation.[22]

A second solution was proposed by Alfred O'Rahilly, who tried to make the passage compatible with the Gospel of John: "The Hebrew

[18] Thus S. Venturini, *Il libro segreto di Gesù* (Rome: Newton Compton, 2011), 92–93, argues that the identity of the priest's servant is not important, but only the news (offered by him as credible) that the shroud was "removed" and "preserved" somewhere in Palestine. That it was "preserved," however, is not written.

[19] I. Wilson, *The Turin Shroud* (London: Gollancz, 1978), 74.

[20] What happened in another manuscript of a text has nothing to do with this issue. The Codex Bobbiensis, an important fifth-century witness of the old African translation of the Bible, in a passage from the so-called shorter ending of Mark (f. 41r) states, *omnia autem quaecumque praecepta erant et qui cum puero* [i.e., *Petro*] *erant breviter exposuerunt*. Cf. J. Wordsworth, W. Sanday, and H. J. White, *Portions of the Gospels according to St. Mark and St. Matthew from the Bobbio Ms.* (Oxford: Clarendon, 1886), opening photo and p. 23.

[21] J. T. Dodd, "The Appearance of Jesus to the Priest's Servant, as Recorded in the Gospel of the Hebrews, and the Holy Shroud," *The Commonwealth* (October 1931): 189–94; taken up again by Hugh J. Schonfield in K. De Proszynski, *The Authentic Photograph of Christ* (London: Search, 1932), 54–56.

[22] It would be a curious case of *lectio facilior* changed to *difficilior*. M. Guscin, *The Burial Cloths of Christ* (London: Catholic Truth Society, 2000), 53, confused John Theodore Dodd with the much more famous Charles Harold Dodd, attributing to him this implausible theory. Guscin himself, however, rejects the hypothesis.

consonants of 'servant' (*ebed*) and 'priest' (*kohen*) would not be very different from those of 'Peter' (*Kepha*) and 'John' (*Yochanan*)"; on this reckoning, Jerome would have misread the original Hebrew of the Gospel, confusing the words.[23] Yet it is evident that neither עבד ("servant") and כיפא ("Peter"), nor כהן ("priest") and יוחנן ("John"), lend themselves to being confused in terms of script, nor is it imaginable that Jerome made such an egregious error. Neither explanation can be accepted, for the tenor of the passage of Jerome cannot so easily be called into question, as not only is the testimony of the Latin manuscripts unanimous, but Jerome's Latin also appears identical to an ancient Greek version of the same text.[24]

Equally speculative is a conjecture that views this "priest" to be one known as "John the presbyter," mentioned by Papias of Hierapolis, whose introduction to this passage would seem to come out of nowhere.[25] More interesting, but not sufficiently proven, is the hypothesis that the "priest" is the same James whose servant, as in the parallel Acts of Thomas, is said to be the one who receives the tablecloth.[26] Yet given the features of the text, there is no evidence that the story of this Gospel is credible, nor does this account alone demonstrate that any sepulchral relic of Jesus is preserved anywhere.

1.1.3. Shrouds in Ancient Christian Literature

Like the canonical texts, apocryphal texts also show little attention to the sepulchral linen of Christ. Though the Gospel of Peter describes the burial and resurrection of Jesus, it does not mention the fate of the fabrics. Some decades ago Pietro Savio drew attention to the Coptic Gospel of the Twelve Apostles, presenting it as a text of the second

[23] A. O'Rahilly, *The Burial of Christ* (Cork: Cork University Press, 1942), 59, n. 6.

[24] Traditionally attributed to Sophronius and discussed in Klijn, *Jewish-Christian Gospel Tradition*, 80.

[25] Cf. G. Zaninotto, "Mille anni di congetture," in *Il grande libro della Sindone* (San Paolo: Cinisello Balsamo, 2000), 35. On John the Presbyter, who is a different person from the apostle of the same name, and on these "presbyters" in general, see E. Norelli, *Papia di Hierapolis: Esposizione degli oracoli del Signore* (Milan: Paoline, 2005), 257–76 and 537–47. Since Papia knows of not only John but several "presbyters," one wonders why Zaninotto wants to refer to that particular John.

[26] This concept is that of C. Papini, *Sindone: Una sfida alla scienza e alla fede*, 2nd ed. (Turin: Claudiana, 1998), 28–29, which had also already been proposed by Freculphus Lexoviensis, *Chronica* 2.1.18: "Cum dedisset sindonem servo sacerdotis, ivit ad sacerdotem Iacobum, et apparuit ei."

century.[27] In it one finds, among other things, mention of the linens that wrapped Lazarus and the sepulchral cloths of Jesus, thanks to which Pilate could heal the eye of a centurion and resuscitate a dead man. Yet these texts do not in fact date back to the second century, and they are not part of the Gospel of the Twelve Apostles: the passage that concerns Lazarus is a fragment of a late homiletical text, while the other passage about Jesus is taken from a homily entitled "On the Laments of Mary," dated to the fifth or sixth century.[28] Nor can it be affirmed that "this Gospel of the Twelve Apostles or the Ebionites was probably a translation in Greek of the Gospel according to the Hebrews with heretical interpolations."[29] The relationship between the Gospel of the Hebrews, that of the Ebionites, and that of the Twelve Apostles is much more complex.[30] Their relationship is evoked inappropriately, inasmuch as the Gospel of the Twelve Apostles, which could have some relationship with that of the Ebionites (mentioned by Origen and other ancient ecclesiastical writers) has nothing to do with the Coptic texts we are considering here. Those are quite different and are much more recent.

The text of the homily certainly shows an interest in miracles and has an apologetic slant when it comes to the sepulchral cloths of Jesus, going so far as to suggest that Pilate, having become a Christian (*sic*!), is held in high esteem. Yet this late and extremely fabulous story is obviously fanciful. That said, the text itself offers a relevant piece of information: Jesus' burial cloths are no longer on this earth, because "they are brought into heaven." For this reason, the homily cannot be used to corroborate the hypothesis that these relics were known and kept somewhere on the earth: in fact, it states the exact opposite.[31]

[27] P. Savio, *Ricerche storiche sulla Santa Sindone* (Turin: SEI, 1957), 61 and 161–66.

[28] See *Clavis Apocryphorum Novi Testamenti* (Turnhout: Brepols, 1992), §§ 81.A and 74; F. Robinson, *Coptic Apocryphal Gospels* (Cambridge: Cambridge University Press, 1896), 171, 173; E. Revillout, "Les apocryphes coptes: Première partie," *Patrologia orientalis* 2 (1904): 137, 141. The Homily on the Laments of Mary is also known as the Gospel of Gamaliel.

[29] P. Baima Bollone, *Sepoltura del Messia e Sudario di Oviedo* (Turin: SEI, 1997), 75, who dates it to the beginning of the second century. He corrects himself in P. Baima Bollone, *Sindone: Storia e scienza* (Ivrea: Priuli and Verlucca, 2010), 21.

[30] Cf. Gianotto, *Ebrei credenti in Gesù*, 179–82 and 270 (§ 44).

[31] *Homilia de lamentis Mariae* (*Evangelium Gamalielis*) 11.48 (in both Coptic and Ethiopian).

Another text, thanks to which, according to Savio, "one can not doubt that the shroud and the sudarium would have been preserved," is the Gospel of Nicodemus. In this case, too, Savio ascribes the work to the second century, and Giulio Ricci dates it even before that, putting it in the first century. In reality, what we have—although it can be traced back to an older text, now lost—is a work probably written between 320 and 380.[32] In this work, rife with unlikely stories, at one point the author stages an apparition to Joseph of Arimathea of the resurrected Jesus, who mentions to him, among other things, the sepulchral linens in language similar to that of the most ancient Gospels:

> "I am Jesus, whose body you asked for from Pilate, whom you clothed with pure *sindón*, on whose face you placed the sudarium." . . . "And he took me [Joseph of Arimathea] away and showed me the place where I laid him. And the *sindónion* lay there, and also the sudarium for his face."[33]

There is practically nothing new here: the author simply refashions the Gospel of John and draws the information about the *sindón* from the other Gospels. He also uses the diminutive *sindónion* (showing he believes that the fabric was one and not many) and states precisely that the shroud was for the "face," where John instead speaks simply of the "head." Following Savio, Baima Bollone states that, according to the Coptic translation of this Gospel, "the shroud had been secured by bandages over the face of Jesus."[34] Such a deduction is, however, unfounded, for the text speaks only of a "sudarium that I had placed

[32] Savio, *Ricerche storiche*, 61–63 and 166–68 (cited from p. 63); G. Ricci, *The Holy Shroud* (Milwaukee: Center for the Study of the Passion of Christ and the Holy Shroud, 1981), XXVII. See instead *Clavis Apocryphorum Novi Testamenti*, § 62; R. Gounelle, "Un nouvel Évangile judéo-chrétien?," in *The Apocryphal Gospels within the Context of Early Christian Theology*, ed. J. Schröter (Leuven: Peeters, 2013), 357–401. D. Scavone, *The Shroud of Turin: Opposing Viewpoints* (Saint Paul: Greenhaven Press, 1989), 74, is also less than precise in the dating of these texts.

[33] *Evangelium Nicodemi* (*Gesta Pilati*) 15:6: "Ἐγώ εἰμι Ἰησοῦς, οὗ καὶ τὸ σῶμα ᾐτήσω παρὰ Πιλάτου, καὶ ἐνέδυσάς με σινδόνι καθαρᾷ καὶ σουδάριον ἐπέθηκας ἐπὶ τὸ πρόσωπόν μου. . . . Καὶ ἀπήνεγκέν με καὶ ἔδειξέν μοι τὸν τόπον ὅπου ἔθηκα αὐτόν, καὶ τὸ σινδόνιον ἔκειτο ἐν αὐτῷ, καὶ τὸ σουδάριον τὸ εἰς τὸ πρόσωπον αὐτοῦ." See also 11:3, 12:1, 15:5, in C. Tischendorf, ed., *Evangelia apocrypha*, 2nd ed. (Leipzig: Mendelssohn, 1876), 210–86.

[34] Baima Bollone, *Sepoltura del Messia*, 79.

over his face," and nowhere does any mention of bandages occur;[35] in any case, a Coptic translation in tenth-century manuscripts is not very helpful for clarification of the meaning of the original text.

The Colloquies of Zacchaeus and Apollonius, dated to 408–410, is a work that includes the following testimony of the Christian Zacchaeus: "Here the vestiges of the happy tomb still contain the indications of the cross and death, and a place marked by the present multitude attests to his ascension into Heaven, after the resurrection had been witnessed."[36] Some view this as the first testimony that indicates the preservation of linens.[37] The term *exuviae* ("traces," "spoils," "remains," "relics," and even sometimes "clothes"), however, is not sufficiently precise to clarify the author's implication. The text continues with generic references to tokens left by Christ and the apostles. Such references would seem to suggest that the author is speaking generally of what he might have seen at the Holy Sepulcher and its annexes, places in those times that were already destinations for pilgrimages. A few lines later, the document speaks of the footprints of Jesus, indicating that the author knew the tradition according to which the footprints of Christ were to have remained impressed in the ground from the moment of his ascension from the Mount of Olives.[38] Obviously at this point the reader is in the land of legend.

The fate of Jesus' sepulchral linen is bound up with other stories that are late to appear and thus largely legendary and contradictory. Isho'dad of Merv, bishop of Ḥadatha (ca. 850), in one passage writes that the linens of the sepulcher were taken away by Peter and John; yet elsewhere he states that they were returned to Joseph of Arimathea, except for one that ended up with Simon Peter, who put it

[35] M. Vandoni and T. Orlandi, *Vangelo di Nicodemo* (Milan: Istituto Editoriale Cisalpino, 1966), § 171: ⲡⲥⲟⲩⲇⲁⲣⲓⲟⲛ ⲛ̄ⲧⲁⲓⲙⲟⲣϥ̄ ⲉϫⲙ̄ ⲡⲉϥ ϩⲟ̄.

[36] *Consultationes Zacchaei et Apollonii* 1.21.13: "ecce adhuc dominicae crucis ac mortis indicia felicis sepulcri exuviae continent, et signatus a praesenti multitudine locus post resurrectionis visum caelestem testatur ascensum."

[37] See J. L. Feiertag, "Le thème littéraire des vêtements mortuaires du Seigneur depuis les témoignages des 'Apocryphes' jusqu'à ceux des récits de pèlerinage," *Apocrypha* 10 (1999): 56–73.

[38] Further on this topic, see K. Blair Moore, *The Architecture of the Christian Holy Land* (Cambridge: Cambridge University Press, 2017), 40–43; L. Canetti, *Impronte di gloria: Effigie e ornamento nell'Europa cristiana* (Rome: Carocci, 2012), 77–113.

on his head as a turban when he performed sacred ordinations.[39] The sepulchral linens are also mentioned in the Life of Saint Nino. This Georgian account of Nino's life speaks about her visit to Jerusalem during the reign of Constantine (306–337), including information she gathered about the fate of Jesus' burial cloths:

> And they found the linen early in Christ's tomb, whither Pilate and his wife came. When they found it, Pilate's wife asked for the linen, and went away quickly to her house in Pontus, and she became a believer in Christ. Some time afterwards, the linen came into the hands of Luke the Evangelist, who put it in a place known only to himself. Now they did not find the sudarium, but it is said to have been found by Peter, who took it and kept it, but we know not if it has ever been discovered.[40]

Nino, considered to be the apostle of Georgia, is mentioned (without name) for the first time in the fifth century;[41] but the reference to relics of the tomb and their transferal into Pontus (northern Turkey) appears only in the Life of Saint Nino, which is cobbled together from "stories attributed to fantastic authors, invented according to the most banal formulas of literature of the imagination."[42] In fact, the story—a sort of novel or saga—is attested from manuscripts that are not earlier than the tenth century and that, in various forms, show numerous alterations. Its late drafting explains also why Pilate and his wife are presented in an extremely favorable light.

It should be noted, too, that the fate of the sepulchral linens is never the same in the texts cited above. Thus, none of them is useful to ascertain any historically accurate fact about the survival of these fabrics. Rather, all bear witness to the birth of a later, often romantic, and fanciful interest in these and other physical objects related to the life of Jesus.

39 M. Dunlop Gibson, *The Commentaries of Isho'dad of Merv*, vol. 1 (Cambridge: Cambridge University Press, 1911), 208 and 280–81.

40 M. Wardrop and J. O. Wardrop, "Life of St. Nino," *Studia Biblica et Ecclesiastica* 5 (1903): 11.

41 Rufinus Aquileiensis, *Historia Ecclesiastica* 10.11.

42 P. Peeters, "Les débuts du christianisme en Géorgie d'après les sources hagiographiques," *Analecta bollandiana* 50 (1932): 50.

1.2. Medieval Shrouds and Sudariums

1.2.1. Relics in the Holy Land

At the time of increased fervor in the search for relics in the Holy Land, no one ever claimed to have found burial cloths. We do, however, have accounts of the first relic seekers, beginning with Helena, the mother of the emperor Constantine, whose quest would lead to the discovery of the cross. None are recorded as seeking burial cloths. The same can be said for the first reports written by the pilgrims who visited the places associated with Jesus:[43] the author of the *Itinerarium Burdigalense*, who visited the Holy Land and left a description of his visit in the year 333, does not speak of burial cloths. The pilgrim Egeria, who resided in Jerusalem from 381 to 384, does not mention such cloths either, even though she had witnessed the honors paid to various other relics, including the column of the scourging, the *titulus* of the cross, and the cross itself (along with other outlandish objects, such as the ring of Solomon and the oil horn with which the kings of Israel were consecrated).

With the passage of time, despite the criticism of some bishops like Augustine, Gregory of Nyssa, and John Chrysostom, the turnout of pilgrims to Jerusalem was constantly rising. As a result, there was a large transference of relics to the West. The various travelogues clearly reveal the progressive increase in such "discoveries" in Palestine, both in terms of holy places supposedly linked to biblical personalities and in terms of the objects connected with those personalities and places. Dated to approximately 500, the *Breviarius of Jerusalem* refers also to new relics beyond what had been mentioned in previous sources. These include the chalice of the Last Supper, the tray on which the head of John the Baptist was placed, the spear that pierced Jesus' side, the crown of thorns, the sponge soaked with vinegar given to him just before his death, and the reed that held the sponge. Shortly after the *Breviarius*, the *De situ terrae sanctae*, written

[43] On these pilgrimages to the Holy Land, see E. D. Hunt, *Holy Land Pilgrimage in the Later Roman Empire AD 312–460* (Oxford: Clarendon, 1982); P. Maraval, *Lieux saints et pèlerinages d'Orient* (Paris: Cerf, 1985); A. Graboïs, *Le pèlerin occidental en Terresainte au moyen âge* (Paris: De Boek, 1998); J. Wilkinson, *Jerusalem Pilgrims before the Crusades* (Warminster: Aris and Phillips, 2002); C. Morris, *The Sepulchre of Christ and the Medieval West: From the Beginning to 1600* (Oxford: Oxford University Press, 2005).

by the archdeacon Theodosius in circa 530, describes a large number of incredible places and objects: the mat of the paralytic who was healed by Jesus, a stone on which Christ left an imprint of his shoulders, and one on which the Madonna sat down to rest after falling from her donkey. Until that time, however, it had never occurred to anyone "to discover" the burial cloths of Jesus.[44]

The first testimony, in fact, to the burial garments will not occur until we find mention in an anonymous pilgrim from Piacenza who made a trip to Palestine between 551 and 637 (most likely between 560 and 570):

> On that bank of the Jordan there is a cave in which there are chambers with seven virgins who had been sent there as children. When one of them dies, she is buried in the same chamber. Another chamber is dug out and another girl is sent, so that the number remains unchanged. They have some people who ever wait outside for them. We entered fearfully in that place to pray but did not see anyone's face. The sudarium that had been placed upon the Lord's forehead is said to be in that the same place.[45]

The anonymous author from Piacenza, however, would seem to lack sufficient acumen and to harken rather easily to disparate oral traditions. Among the strangest relics one finds in this text are the abecedary of Jesus and the tree trunk on which he sat when he was in school with other children, the jug from which he drank, a stone on which he had climbed that preserved his footprints, the stones cast to murder Saint Stephen, the bones of the children butchered

[44] *Inventio* is a technical term that designates the discovery of relics; in this case the paronomasia upon the English "invention" is fitting. The sources are mentioned and examined by Gramaglia, *L'uomo della Sindone*, 13–19; also idem, "Le reliquie palestinesi e i panni funerari di Gesù," *Approfondimento Sindone* 4, no. 1 (2000): 13–50.

[45] *Itinerarium Anonymi Placentini* 12: "In illa ripa Iordanis est spelunca, in qua sunt cellulae cum septem virgines, quae ibi infantulae mittuntur, et dum aliqua ex ipsis mortua fuerit, in ipsa cellula sepelitur et alia cellula inciditur et mittitur illic alia infantula, ut numerus stet, et habent foris, qui eis permanent. In quo loco cum timore magno ingressi sumus ad orationem, faciem quidem nullius videntes. In ipso loco dicitur esse sudarium, qui fuit in fronte Domini." On this work (once wrongly attributed to Saint Antoninus Martyr of Piacenza), see C. Milani, *Itinerarium Antonini Placentini* (Milan: Vita e Pensiero, 1977). The text has been transmitted in two versions, a shorter original and a longer one that is a Carolingian revision, stylistically improved.

by Herod, and the cup the apostles used for the celebration of the Eucharist. The reports of the shroud, in particular, are indirect, as the pilgrim speaks with oblique language, such as "they say," and does not record first-hand observation. Still, they are important because we finally have a record of nascent interest in one of Jesus' sepulchral linens (the sudarium that was the linen used on Jesus' head). It is interesting to note that the anonymous author, at another point in his account, uses the term *sindon* to indicate the garments in which the faithful immersed themselves in the consecrated waters of the Jordan.[46]

In 614 the Persians, led by Khosrow II, conquered Jerusalem; Khosrow pillaged the city, seizing many relics. Among the most famous of those relics, the majority of which were lost, was that of the cross; that relic would, in 628, be recovered by the Byzantine emperor Heraclius I. Sophronius, the patriarch of Jerusalem († 638), in his work *Anacreontica* left us an inventory of the relics that remained in the city after the looting, a list that reveals that many indeed had been lost. Some of these later reappear, though often in a completely different form, while others were replaced with new relics.[47]

Of what remained in Jerusalem after the sack, Adomnan, abbot of the Island of Iona (west of Scotland), provides a written report in 680–688 based on what a Frankish bishop named Arculf had told him. For almost a year (ca. 680), Arculf is supposed to have resided in Jerusalem, when the city was under Muslim sway. Adomnan reports that in the Holy City Arculf had seen with his own eyes "the sacred sudarium of the Lord which was placed upon his head in the sepulcher." Arculf adds what he says the residents of Jerusalem had told him: initially the sudarium had been stolen from Christ's tomb by a Jew who believed in Christ. This Jew then passed it on to his son and his descendants until the fifth generation. The sudarium, like a lucky talisman, was said to have miraculously enriched all those who possessed it. When the line of descent came to an end, the shroud is said to have passed into the hands of some unbelieving Jews, who, owing to their possession of it, also became rich.

[46] *Itinerarium Anonymi Placentini* 11: "omnes descendunt in fluvio pro benedictione induti sindones."

[47] See Gramaglia, *L'uomo della Sindone*, 39–42; idem, "Reliquie cristiane a Gerusalemme sotto il dominio arabo," *Approfondimento Sindone* 5, no. 1 (2001): 3–39.

At a certain point, however, the believing Jews, wanting to obtain their relic again, generated a dispute in the city. The caliph Mu'awiya († 680), however, decided to bring it to a conclusion by subjecting the sudarium to a trial by fire. The sudarium, once it had been placed upon a pyre, was unharmed by the flames and then floated up in the air, falling into the hands of the faction of Jewish believers. They then placed it

> in a casket of the church, wrapped in another linen cloth. Our brother Arculf saw it one day taken out of the casket, and amid the multitude of the people that kissed it, he himself kissed it in an assembly of the church; it measures about eight feet in length.[48]

The *sudarium* that would have been placed on Jesus' head and face (also called *linteum, linteolum* and *linteamen*) must be distinguished here, as in the Gospel of John, from the *linteamina* that wrapped the other parts of the body in the tomb and of which Adomnan speaks elsewhere.[49] The size specified here (ca. 8 ft by the ancient measurement; i.e., slightly less than 2.5 m long) suggests a garment that would have been wrapped around the head several times;[50] one cannot, as some do, say that it was therefore the Turin Shroud, which in any case is almost twice as long. The same Arculf provides a measurement of 7 ft for the sepulchral cave area of Jesus' tomb—that is, space enough

[48] Adomnanus, *De locis sanctis* 1.9.1–16: "De illo quoque sacrosanto Domini sudario quod in sepulchro super capud ipsius fuerat positum. . . . In scrinio ecclesiae in alio involutum linteamine condunt. Quod noster frater Arculfus alia die de scrinio elevatum vidit et inter populi multitudinem illud osculantis et ipse osculatus est in ecclesiae conventu, mensuram longitudinis quasi octonos habens pedes" (M. Guagnano, ed., *Adomnano di Iona: I luoghi santi* [Bari: Edipuglia, 2008]). An English translation is that of J. R. MacPherson, *The Pilgrimage of Arculfus in the Holy Land* (London: Palestine Pilgrims' Text Society, 1889).

[49] Adomnanus, *De locis sanctis* 1.2.10: "in quo Dominicum corpus linteaminibus involutum conditum quievit."

[50] To reconcile the size of this shroud with the Shroud of Turin, one cannot call into question the measurement known as the "liprando foot," which was 0.414 m and was in use in northern Italy. That measurement owes its legendary origin to King Liutprand, who, at the time of Arculf, was not even born (so A. Tonelli, "Verso l'ostensione della Sindone," *Rivista dei giovani* 14 [1933]: 535; and P. Baima Bollone and P. P. Benedetto, *Alla ricerca dell'uomo della Sindone* [Milan: Club degli Editori, 1978], 58).

to hold a recumbent man.[51] Bede the Venerable, in resuming this account at the beginning of the eighth century, while having never set foot in the Holy Land, tells a story clearly dependent on that of Arculf, also specifying the measurement of the shroud.[52] None of these sources speaks of a shroud that enveloped the body, let alone an imprinted image of Christ. It should be noted that, contrary to what the anonymous man of Piacenza stated, according to Arculf the sudarium was not on the bank of the Jordan but in Jerusalem. Had it been moved, or is this a new one?

The account of Adomnan, in addition to being quite imaginative, is also a bit inconsistent: on the one hand, he claims that the sudarium had remained hidden for a long time and had been found only three years earlier, but on the other, he tells a story that does not leave room for it disappearing and being hidden.

Adomnan reports that Arculf, or someone on his behalf, also knew of other unlikely relics: the stone that sealed the tomb, the chalice of the Last Supper, the sponge that held the vinegar, the spear, the cross, the remains of the oak of Abraham, the twelve stones of Galgal, the earth that Christ walked upon that preserved his footprints, the stone containing the inexhausable water with which Jesus was washed at birth, and a fabric, embroidered by Mary, bearing the images of Jesus and the apostles.[53] Scholars wonder whether a pilgrim ever in fact existed behind the figure of Arculf, or if he is merely a literary fiction. Either of the two possibilities must also

[51] Adomnanus, *De locis sanctis* 1.2.10: "cuius longitudinem Arculfus in septem pedum mensura mensus est manu." Today the bench of the Holy Sepulcher of Jerusalem measures 2 × 0.93 m and rises 0.66 m from the ground.

[52] Bede the Venerable, *De locis sanctis* 4: "sudarium capitis Domini. . . . Quod mane mox totus populus summa veneratione salutabat et osculabatur; habebat autem longitudinis octo pedes" (P. Geyer, ed., *Itinera Hierosolymitana saeculi III–VIII* [Vindobonae: Tempsky, 1898], 307.23 and 308.15–17). In one of the manuscripts of Arculf, *cubitos* appears instead of *pedes* (which would thus almost double the size). An English translation is A. G. Holder and W. Trent Foley, *Bede: A Biblical Miscellany* (Liverpool: Liverpool University Press, 1999), 1–25.

[53] M. G. Siliato, *Sindone: Mistero dell'impronta di duemila anni fa* (Casale: Piemme, 1997), 115, invents the notion that this red and green *linteamen* of the Madonna is "the first pictorial copy of the Shroud."

take into account the obvious activity of literary reworking by the Scottish abbot.[54]

Shortly after 730, John of Damascus proffers a list of objects from Palestine that he deems worthy of veneration:

> We venerate things through which and in which God redeemed us, both before the coming of the Lord and during the period of his incarnation, like Mount Sinai and Nazareth, the manger in Bethlehem and the grotto, the holy Golgotha, the wood of the cross, the nails, the sponge, the reed, the sacred and saving spear, the clothing, the tunic, the linen cloths (*sindónas*), the wrappings (*spárgana*), the holy tomb, the source of our resurrection, the stone that sealed the tomb, the holy mount of Zion, and also the Mount of Olives, the sheep gate pool [pool of Bethesda] and the blessed precinct of Gethsemane.[55]

Though this list is helpful for understanding what the opinion of John of Damascus was vis-à-vis the cult of relics, it offers no precise information about the actual preservation or permanent residence of these objects in Jerusalem.

The case of Epiphanius Hagiopolita is different. Between the end of the eighth century and the beginning of the ninth, he offers this description of Jerusalem:

> In the middle of the Holy City is the Holy Sepulcher of the Lord, and close to the sepulcher is the Place of the Skull; Christ was crucified there. It has a height of thirty-six steps; that is stairs. Under the place of the crucifixion there is a church, known as the sepulcher of Adam; and in the midst of these is the Garden of Joseph;

[54] Cf. N. Delierneux, "Arculfe, sanctus episcopus gente Gallus: Une existence historique discutable," *Revue belge de philologie et d'histoire* 75 (1997): 911–91; Guagnano, *Adomnano di Iona*, 37–40 and 67–74.

[55] John of Damascus, *Orationes de imaginibus tres* 3.34: προσκυνοῦμεν κτίσματα, δι' ὧν καὶ ἐν οἷς ἐνήργησεν ὁ θεὸς τὴν σωτηρίαν ἡμῶν εἴτε πρὸ τῆς τοῦ κυρίου παρουσίας, εἴτε μετὰ τὴν ἔνσαρκον αὐτοῦ οἰκονομίαν, ὡς τὸ Σιναῖον ὄρος καὶ τὴν Ναζαρέτ, τὴν φάτνην τὴν ἐν Βηθλεὲμ καὶ τὸ σπήλαιον, τὸν Γολγοθὰ τὸν ἅγιον, τοῦ σταυροῦ τὸ ξύλον, τοὺς ἥλους, τὸν σπόγγον, τὸν κάλαμον, τὴν λόγχην τὴν ἱερὰν καὶ σωτήριον, τὴν ἐσθῆτα, τὸν χιτῶνα, τὰς σινδόνας, τὰ σπάργανα, τὸν τάφον τὸν ἅγιον, τὴν πηγὴν τῆς ἡμῶν ἀναστάσεως, τὸν λίθον τοῦ μνήματος, τὴν Σιὼν τὸ ὄρος τὸ ἅγιον, τὸ τῶν ἐλαιῶν αὖθις ὄρος, τὴν προβατικὴν καὶ Γεθσημανῆς τὸ ὄλβιον τέμενος. English translation of A. Louth, *Saint John of Damascus: Three Treatises on the Divine Images* (Crestwood: St Vladimir's Seminary Press, 2003).

> and to the north of the garden one finds the prison where Christ was locked up along with Barabbas; between the prison and the place of the crucifixion is the door of holy Constantine, in which the three crosses were found; and above the door there is a sanctuary; there lies the cup where Jesus drank the vinegar and the gall; and it is like an emerald, covered with silver; in the same place lies the basin of marble where the Christ washed the feet of his disciples; there lies the spear, the sponge, the reed, the crown of thorns, and the pure shroud (*sindóne*), modeled on the blanket (*sindón*) that the apostle Peter saw in heaven; it tells of each animal depicted, on the one side those intended for consumption and on the other side those not destined for consumption, everything profane and impure; they say this was shown by the archangel Gabriel.[56]

It seems that the depiction of animals lies precisely on this *sindóne* preserved as a relic, which the author is trying to describe; this would mean that it is not a burial shroud but a fabric that refers to the biblical story of the sheet that Peter saw in heaven.[57] If instead it were a funeral cloth, which would accord with the sequence of the relics of

[56] Epiphanius Hagiopolita, *Enarratio Syriae, Urbis Sanctae, et sacrorum ibi locorum* 1–2: μέσον δὲ τῆς ἁγίας πόλεως, ἔστιν ὁ ἅγιος τάφος τοῦ κυρίου· καὶ πλησίον τοῦ τάφου, ἔστιν ὁ τόπος τοῦ κρανίου· ἔνθα ἐσταυρώθη ὁ Χριστός· ἔχων τὸ ὕψος βαθμούς, ἤτοι σκαλία λς· ὑποκάτω δὲ τῆς σταυρώσεως, ἔστιν ἐκκλησία, τοῦ Ἀδὰμ ὁ τάφος· καὶ μέσον αὐτῶν, ἔστιν ὁ κῆπος τοῦ Ἰωσήφ· καὶ πρὸς βορρὰν τοῦ κήπου, ἔστιν ἡ φυλακή, ὅπου ἦν ὁ Χριστὸς ἀποκεκλεισμένος· καὶ ὁ Βαραβάς· καὶ μέσον τῆς φυλακῆς καὶ τῆς σταυρώσεως, ἔστιν ἡ πύλη τοῦ ἁγίου Κωνσταντίνου· ἐν ᾧ εὑρέθησαν οἱ τρεῖς σταυροί· καὶ ἐπάνω τῆς πύλης, ἔστι τὸ ἱερόν· ἔνθα κεῖται τὸ ποτήριον, ὁποῦ ἔπιεν ὁ Χριστὸς τὸ ὄξος καὶ τὴν χολήν· ἔστι δὲ ὡς χαλίκιν πράσινον, ἐνδεδυμένον ἀσίμιν· εἰς δὲ τὸν αὐτὸν τόπον κεῖται τὸ λεκάνιον, ὁποῦ ἔνιψεν ὁ Χριστὸς τοὺς πόδας τῶν μαθητῶν αὐτοῦ· ἔστι δὲ μαρμάνινον· ἔνθα κεῖται ἡ λόγχη καὶ ὁ σπόγγος καὶ ὁ κάλαμος· καὶ ὁ στέφανος ὁ ἐξ ἀκανθῶν· καὶ ἡ σινδόνη ἡ καθαρὰ· εἰς τύπον τῆς σινδόνος· ἣν εἶδε Πέτρος ὁ ἀπόστολος ἐν τῷ οὐρανῷ· ἔχουσα πᾶν ζῶον ἱστορισμένον· εἰς τὸ ἓν μέρος τὰ δαπανώμενα· καὶ εἰς τὸ ἓν μέρος τὰ μὴ δαπανώμενα· πὰν κοινὸν καὶ ἀκάθαρτον· ἣν λέγουσι δειχθῆναι παρὰ Γαβριὴλ τοῦ ἀρχαγγέλου (H. Donner, ed., "Die Palästinabeschreibung des Epiphanius Monachus Hagiopolita," *Zeitschrift des Deutschen Palästina-Vereins* 87 [1971]: 67–68). See Acts 10:11-12.

[57] Thus A.-M. Dubarle, *Histoire ancienne du Linceul de Turin*, vol. 1 (Paris: Œil, 1985), 135–36. The episode is recounted in Acts 10:11-12: "[Peter] saw the sky opened up, and an object like a great sheet coming down, lowered by four corners to the ground, and there were in it all kinds of four-footed animals and crawling creatures of the earth and birds of the air."

the passion, it would be one proof of the preservation of this relic in Jerusalem.

More or less in the same period, in the year 808, a report sent to Charlemagne specified that in the Constantinian Basilica of the Holy Sepulcher—three connected buildings then comprised this structure that covered the area between Golgotha and Jesus' tomb—there were to be two priests involved with the safekeeping of the chalice of the Lord, and two near the cross and the shroud.[58]

It can therefore be affirmed that the existence in Jerusalem of relics believed to be Jesus' funerary garb was, at least by the ninth century, taken for granted, albeit with some uncertainties concerning their form and place of conservation. The next phase in the history of relics of the Holy Land was their systematic but often unmonitored transference, whether true or presumed, to other places. The typology of Palestinian relics that were rediscovered and then transferred puts a strain on modern sensibilities: to take but a few examples, we may cite the bathing vessel of the baby Jesus, his cradle, his diaper, his footprints, his foreskin, his umbilical cord, his baby teeth, the tail of the donkey on which he entered Jerusalem, the dishware of the Last Supper, the column of the scourging, his blood, the relics of the bodies of the grandparents of Jesus and of the Magi, and even the milk of the Madonna and her wedding ring. It is easy to see how any and all objects related to Christ's death and resurrection could hardly be left out of that list.[59] Moreover, the movement of Jerusalem's relics, whether bought, stolen, or falsified, reached its peak at the time of the Crusades.[60]

[58] *Commemoratorium de casis Dei vel monasteriis*, 77: "presbyteri . . . ad sanctam crucem et sudarium II" (T. Tobler, ed., *Descriptiones Terrae Sanctae ex saeculo VIII, IX, XII et XV* [Leipzig: Hinrichs, 1874]).

[59] There is a brief exposition in F. Molteni, *Memoria Christi: Reliquie di Terrasanta in Occidente* (Florence: Vallecchi, 1996). For a first introduction to the motivations that lay at the root of the desire to collect relics, see the essays in M. Bagnoli et al., eds., *Treasures of Heaven: Saints, Relics, and Devotion in Medieval Europe* (New Haven: Yale University Press, 2010).

[60] Cf. J. Durand, "Reliquie e reliquiari depredati in Oriente e a Bisanzio al tempo delle crociate," in *Le crociate: L'Oriente e l'Occidente da Urbano II a San Luigi, 1096–1270*, ed. M. Rey-Delqué (Milan: Electa, 1997), 378–89; A. Benvenuti, *Reliquie e soprannaturale al tempo delle crociate* (Milan: Electa, 1997), 355–61.

1.2.2. Relics in Europe

The Carolingian era, even as it peeked through the doors of the ninth century, was already and would prove further to be an age of intense trafficking in relics: the abbot Paschasius Radbertus succinctly states that "never before have so many and so great miracles occurred at one time by the relics of saints since the beginning of the world, for everywhere the saints in this kingdom and those brought here begin to excite each other to song, like cocks at cock-crow."[61] And a legend grew up around the figure of Charlemagne himself, making him the recipient of the relics that were coming from the Holy Land. One can easily follow a steady progression in the details: the *Vita Karoli*, written by Einhard in about 828, tells us for the first time that Charles had sent ambassadors with some gifts to Jerusalem, receiving in return from the caliph Hārūn al-Rashīd many gifts of great value: "dresses, spices and other riches of the oriental lands."[62] No relics are yet mentioned. In the *Annales regni Francorum* such simple gifts become relics from Jesus' tomb, sent to France by the patriarch of Jerusalem;[63] certainly there could not have been the shroud among them, as the one mentioned in 808 would still have been in its place. But, over the years, the magnification of the deeds and legends reported about the Carolingians increased to such a point as to give rise, from the end of the tenth century, to the notion that Charlemagne had made a trip to Jerusalem, or even personally led a crusade.[64] Documentary basis for this crusade never existed, and in the last years of the eleventh century we find even the falsification of some letters of the patriarch of Jerusalem and the Byzantine emperor Constantine V. Some, to prove the authenticity of certain relics, composed fantastical narratives about their origin,

[61] Paschasius Radbertus, *De vita Walae* 2.1.

[62] Einhard, *Vita Karoli Magni* 16: "revertentibus legatis suos adiungens inter vestes et aromata et ceteras orientalium terrarum opes ingentia illi dona direxit."

[63] *Annales regni Francorum*, anno 799: "Monachus quidam de Hierosolimis veniens benedictionem et reliquias de sepulchro Domini, quos patriarcha Hierosolimitanus domno regi miserat, detulit" (F. Kurze, ed., *Annales regni Francorum* [Hanover: Hahn, 1895], 108).

[64] Cf. C. Rossi, "Le Voyage de Charlemagne: Le parcours et les reliques," *Critica del testo* 2, no. 2 (1999): 619–53; M. Gabriele, *An Empire of Memory: The Legend of Charlemagne, the Franks, and Jerusalem before the First Crusade* (Oxford: Oxford University Press, 2011).

both in Latin and in the vernacular. The acquisition of various relics is ascribed to this nonexistent journey of Charlemagne: the body of Saint Andrew; drops of the blood of Christ; pieces of the cross, of the sepulcher, and of the crown of thorns, which would come to obtain such great importance as an object granting validity to the French royal house. In the third quarter of the twelfth century a poetic composition surfaces in which Charlemagne is portrayed asking that some relics be sent from the patriarch of Jerusalem, who is clearly depicted as ready and willing to give them to him. Here, at last, a certain piece of the shroud appears, which the patriarch promises that he will not let him miss:

> You shall have them in abundance: you shall have at once the arm of Saint Simeon, and I shall have the head of Saint Lazarus brought to you, and some of Saint Stephen's blood, one of God's martyrs. . . . Part of Jesus' sudarium which covered his head, when he was placed and laid down in his tomb. . . . You will have one of the nails that pierced his feet, and the holy crown that God wore on his head; and you will have the chalice that he blessed; I shall also happily give you the silver dish—it is inlaid with gold and with precious stones—and you will have the knife that God held when eating, some hairs from Saint Peter's beard and from his head . . . some of the virgin Mary's milk, with which she suckled Jesus when he first came down to earth to be among us, and some cloth from the holy tunic which she wore.[65]

Now the fantasy has become utterly unbridled. A poem about the destruction of Rome, dated to the first half of the thirteenth century, tells how "the shroud in which Jesus was wrapped"—perhaps a long cloth, rather than a small shroud—was kept in St. Peter's Basilica in Rome until, during the sack of the city (August 23, 846), it was stolen by the mythical Saracen king Fierabras and brought to Spain, and then subsequently recovered by Charlemagne.[66]

[65] *Le voyage de Charlemagne à Jerusalem et à Constantinople* (C. Rossi Bellotto, ed., *Il viaggio di Carlo Magno a Gerusalemme e a Costantinopoli* [Alessandria: Dell'Orso, 2006], ll. 162–189). Translation from S. Gaunt and K. Pratt, *The Song of Roland and Other Poems of Charlemagne* (Oxford: Oxford University Press, 2016); the translation is slightly modified here because it is at one point less than precise.

[66] *La destruction de Rome*, vv. 26–27 and 1271–81 (L. Formisano, ed., *La destruction de Rome* [Florence: Sansoni, 1981]). Some texts concerning Charlemagne are commented on by R. Baum, "Reliquie e letteratura," in F. Navire, *Storia*

In another story, purportedly written at the time of Charles the Bald (but actually seemingly composed between the end of the eleventh and the beginning of the twelfth centuries), it is said that the objects acquired in the East by Charlemagne were brought to the imperial city of Aachen (Aix-la-Chapelle). Among the various relics were the crown of thorns, a fragment of the cross, the blouse of the Madonna, the swaddling cloths of baby Jesus, and Saint Simeon's arm; the sudarium of Christ also appears (not just a piece, but the intact whole). That Charles received a cloth and kept it in Aachen is mentioned in several other sources, but there is disagreement about the date of the acquisition. Did he obtain it in Jerusalem as a gift of the patriarch? Did he receive it at Constantinople from the hands of the emperor?[67] Recognizing the unlikelihood of both possibilities, one seventeenth-century scholar proposed a seemingly credible solution, namely that the relics were sent to Charles from Saint Irene, mother of the Byzantine emperor Constantine VI.[68]

In addition, it has been proposed that after the death of Charlemagne, the relics became part of the heritage of the monastery of St. Cornelius "ad Indam" (Kornelimünster), in the vicinity of Aachen, built by Charlemagne's son, Louis the Pious. Later the cloth would have been transferred to the royal abbey Saint-Corneille in Compiègne by Charles the Bald.[69] That transference, which occurred between 860 and 877, is recorded in a declaration of Philip I of France,

della Santissima Sindone di Torino: Dal Manoscritto dell'abate Giuseppe Pasini (Bonn: Romanistischer Verlag, 2013), IX–XXIV.

[67] H. Bloch, *Annales Marbacenses qui dicuntur* (Hanover: Hahn, 1907), 13: Charlemagne receives from the emperor various relics, including the *sudarium Domini*, and places them in Aachen (source of 1238); this is confirmed by Vincent of Beauvais († 1264): H. Gering, *Islendzk æventyri*, vol. 2 (Halle: Verlag der Buchhandlung des Waisenhauses, 1883), 345, ll. 100–103.

[68] Cf. J. Langelle, *Histoire du Saint Suaire de Compiègne* (Paris: Coignard, 1684), 27–35.

[69] *Descriptio qualiter Karolus magnus clavum et coronam Domini a Constantinopoli Aquisgrani attulerit qualiterque Carolus Calvus hec ad S. Dionysium retulerit* (ca. 1080): Charlemagne (f. 10r) "saccum de bubalino tergore factum in quo spineam coronam et clavum ac frustum crucis sudariumque Domini cum aliis reliquiis, nam sanctissime virginis Marie camisiam et cinctorium unde Dominum puerum in cunabulis cinxerat et brachium sancti Symeonis simul insuerat, quiete deportans collo suo suspensum, Ligmedon venit"; the emperor then deposits the relics in Aachen (f. 12r) until the time when Charles the Bald (f. 15v) "sudarium Domini Cumpennii dimisit quod castrum ad instar Constantinopolis facere moliebatur"

dated to 1092; in it, however, a *sudarium* is not mentioned, but rather a *linteamen* or *sindon* that enveloped the body of the Lord, which shows that either the two terms were interchangeable or that the relic had by then been separated into two pieces.[70] Yet this should not astonish us, since in the centuries to come things would become even more confused: in fact, it is said that both the shroud and the sudarium were transferred to Compiègne, while the linen that wrapped Jesus on the cross at the moment of death would remain in Aachen. From an initially small fragment, then, a total of three complete relics developed, one of which is not even mentioned in the Gospels.[71]

Despite the transfer to Compiègne, in 1359 the "pure shroud" was still considered part of the heritage of the monastery of St. Cornelius. A letter sent to the pope that year stated that, despite the destruction of the monastery that occurred in 1310, the shroud had been relocated to the new abbey along with the other relics.[72] Indeed, there are still preserved today at Aachen in the St. Cornelius monastery cloth relics that are clearly of late manufacture; these are the towel with which Jesus dried the disciples' feet, the shroud, and the sudarium. The last of these is made of very thin fabric measuring 4 × 6 m, folded sixteen times. It is sewn onto a precious frame of embroidered cloth. The shroud itself, made of linen and measuring 1.80 × 1.05 m, is worked and decorated with floral and cross-shaped motifs. To explain the presence of the shroud in both Aachen and Compiègne it is claimed

---

(F. Castets, ed., "Iter Hierosolymitanum, ou voyage de Charlemagne à Jérusalem et à Constantinople," *Revue des langues romanes* 36 [1892]: 417–74).

[70] See E. Morel, *Cartulaire de l'Abbaye de Saint-Corneille de Compiègne*, vol. 1 (Montdidier: Champion, 1904), 53: "linteamen . . . in quo dominicum corpus in sepulchro iacuisse perhibetur, quod sindonem secundum Evangelistam nominamus." Also, Hugues de Fleury in 1108 says that Charles the Bald bedecked his town of Compiègne with the "preciosa Domini nostri Iesus [*sic*] Christi sindone" (Hugo Floriacensis, *Liber qui modernorum regum Francorum continet actus* 1.1, in *Monumenta Germaniae Historica: Scriptores*, vol. 9, ed. G. D. Waitz [Hanover: Hahn, 1851], 377).

[71] See P. von Beeck, *Aquisgranum* (Aquisgrani: Hulting, 1620), 173 and 169; *Trésor d'Aix-la-Chapelle ou courte description des saintes reliques* (Aix-la-Chapelle: Vlieckx, 1839), 9.

[72] H. Disselnkötter, "Die mittelalterlichen Zeugnisse über die großen Heiligtümer zu Aachen," *Annalen des Historischen Vereins für den Niederrhein insbesondere das alte Erzbistum Köln* 121 (1932): 13–16; also published by Savio, *Ricerche storiche*, 89–90, n. 24.

that these are the same relic divided in two,[73] but the sources do not refer to any division of the garment. Evidently the shrouds/ sudariums began to multiply in an uncontrollable manner. From some less-than-congruous descriptions of the sixteenth and seventeenth centuries, it appears that the reliquary of the so-called Saint Seigne at Compiègne contained two linens, one large (the shroud) and one small (the sudarium).[74] There was a total of four fabrics, therefore: two at Compiègne and two more in Aachen. Compiègne's relic came to an uncertain end: according to some it was lost during the French Revolution; according to others, it survived until 1840, when a clumsy maid, wanting to restore its pristine whiteness, reduced it to pulp by immersing it in a whitening bath. The coexistence of these relics in two important religious centers of the Carolingian tradition has not prevented other cities from boasting possession of the same objects.[75] In Arles an inventory of the year 1152 mentions, in addition to various relics pertaining to Christ, the Madonna, and the apostles, "a linen cloth that hangs on the throne of the church when the church is prepared for a festival; [the throne is] on the altar, and this cloth is sewn onto another fabric decorated in gold: our Lord Jesus Christ was enveloped in this linen cloth." In 1690 all these relics were still there, kept in the metropolitan Church of St. Trophimus, including a "part of the cloth in which our Lord was buried."[76] Subsequently they were dispersed because of the French Revolution, a fate that many relics of this sort endured.

In the thirteenth century, another shroud appeared in the Cistercian abbey of Cadouin. There are no attestations to the holy shroud of Cadouin before 1214, when it appears that Simon IV de Montfort, the leader of the crusade against the Albigensians, procured a fixed revenue for the abbey to pay for a lighted lamp to burn perpetually,

[73] See J. Kleinermanns, "Die evangelischen Heiligtümer," *Aus Aachens Vorzeit* 10, no. 12 (1906): 145–56; 1, no. 4 (1907): 23–45; 5, no. 17 (1907): 65–79 (the author believes the relics are authentic).

[74] See E. Morel, "Le Saint Suaire de Saint-Corneille de Compiègne," *Bulletin de la Société historique de Compiègne* 11 (1904): 134, 185, 195–96.

[75] G. Ciccone and C. Sturmann, in *La sindone svelata e i quaranta sudari* (Livorno: Donnino, 2006), 73–126, have collected information on most of the relics here described.

[76] J. H. Albanés and U. Chevalier, *Gallia christiana novissima*, vol. 3, *Arles* (Valence: Imprimerie valentinoise, 1901), § 2524; G. Duport, *Histoire de l'Église d'Arles* (Paris: Cavelier, 1690), 304.

day and night, in front of the relic. Official propaganda taken from a text of a parchment that was exhibited in the abbey tells the story about the shroud having been found in the East by the bishop of Le Puy-en-Velay, who had been papal legate during the First Crusade (1095–1099). The shroud, having been delivered by the bishop at the moment of his death to a priest, who in turn entrusted it to a friar, would eventually (and fortuitously) arrive in France, namely at the Church of Brunet, near Cadouin. Yet when the monks of Cadouin learned that the Church of Brunet had been burned and that the relic had miraculously survived the fire, they seized the shroud and transported it to their abbey in roughly 1117 (two years after the abbey was founded).[77] According to a later version of this tale, the bishop—who in that account is specified as Adhémar de Monteil—instead would have found the shroud in Antioch, together with the spear of Longinus, the Roman soldier who pierced Jesus' side. Inasmuch as the canons of Le Puy-en-Velay did not want to accept the authenticity of the relic, the priest of Brunet, once the church's fire was under way, himself turned the shroud over, according to this account, to the monks of Cadouin.[78] From there the relic did not travel any farther, save for a stay in Toulouse between 1392 and 1463, during which sojourn it was also in Paris (1399–1402) for a short time. King Charles VI had the shroud brought there as a treatment for his mental illness.[79] In 1643 Jean de Lingendes, bishop of Sarlat, after having examined the relic and its accompanying documentation presented to him by monks, had to declare that the relic

[77] Thus the *Pancharta Caduniensis*, which was affixed within the abbey and declared the identification of the shroud of Cadouin with that described by the Anonymous Pilgrim of Piacenza and by Arculf; ed. in *Recueil des historiens des croisades: Historiens occidentaux*, vol. 5, pt. 1 (Paris: Imprimerie Nationale, 1886), 299–301. The story is resumed and expanded in J. Tarde, *Les chroniques de Jean Tarde* (Paris: Oudin, 1887), 52–57.

[78] *Chronica Albrici monachi Trium Fontium*, in *Monumenta Germaniae Historica: Scriptores*, vol. 23, ed. P. Scheffer-Boichorst (Leipzig: Hiersemann, 1925), 637.38–638.10, 824.15–26.

[79] Cf. M. Fournié, "Une municipalité en quête de reliques: Le saint suaire de Cadouin et son dépôt à Toulouse à la fin du Moyen Âge," *Mémoires de la Société Archéologique du Midi de la France* 71 (2011): 127–62; Fournié, "Dévotions à Toulouse au XVe siècle autour du Saint Suaire de Cadouin-Toulouse," *Annales du Midi* 282 (2013): 269–86.

> was truly the holy and venerable shroud that had straightaway been put on the divine head and on the holy body of our Redeemer and Savior Jesus Christ. No greater assurance of this truth could be found and, as it was stained with the blood of Jesus Christ and is consecrated by contact with his body, there is no more august or more precious relic in the world, not even if one should find one more certain and better attested than this.[80]

This is an unequivocal declaration of authenticity. Further proof came from the great number of miracles attributed to it, including the resurrection of more than sixty dead people, which had made it by far the most famous French shroud.[81]

Fortunately, this shroud did not go missing during the French Revolution. This shroud is a linen measuring 1.35 × 2.95 m, with bands decorated in polychrome silk on the two short sides, and with stains presumed to be caused by blood and funerary ointments. In the modern period, some historians began to make known their reservations about the possibility of it being dated to the time of Christ, as they recognized some Kufic script woven in the decoration of the fabric. These historians' opinions were initially underestimated.[82] Yet in 1933 the inscription style was confirmed, and, among other things, the name of the Fatimid caliph al-Musta'lī († 1101) was discernible. It was understood then that the shroud's origin was not only medieval but even Egyptian and Islamic. At that point, Georges-Auguste Louis, bishop of Périgueux, ordered that from then on the relic be withdrawn from veneration, and he abolished the pilgrimage that kept beckoning thousands of the faithful to return each year.[83] The same embarrassing event occurred with the alleged

[80] A. Carles, *Histoire du Saint-Suaire de Cadouin*, 4th ed. (Toulouse: Sistac et Boubée, 1879), 62. See also J. B. Mayjonade, "Le Saint-Suaire de Cadouin," *Revue des sciences ecclésiastiques* 67 (1893): 48–63.

[81] See E. Guichard, *Histoire du St. Suaire et du Sacré Bandeau de Iesu-Christ* (Paris: Bessin, 1644); M. Fournié, "Les miracles du suaire de Cadouin-Toulouse et la folie de Charles VI," *Revue d'histoire de l'Église de France* 99 (2013): 25–52.

[82] Still in 1929 the sindonologist Noël Noguier de Malijay considered it authentic, perhaps embroidered by the Virgin Mary (*Le Saint-Suaire de Turin ou le Saint Linceul* [Paris: Spes, 1929], XII–XIII).

[83] See J. Francez, *Un pseudo-linceul du Christ* (Paris: Desclée De Brouwer et Cie, 1935); G. Wiet, "Un nouveau tissu fatimide," *Orientalia* 5 (1936): 385–88; J. Maubourguet, "Le Suaire de Cadouin," *Bulletin de la Société historique et archéologique du Périgord* 63 (1936): 348–63; *Les pérégrinations du Suaire de Cadouin* (Le Buisson-de-Cadouin:

veil of Saint Anne, mother of the Madonna, preserved in Provence in the Church of Apt. This veil is a richly woven fabric decorated with Islamic inscriptions similar to those on the shroud mentioned above.[84] This unhappy story reveals just how untrustworthy legends about the origins of the relics could be, even when they seemed to be supported by relatively ancient documentation and were "confirmed" by the repetition of numerous miracles achieved by the relics' intercession.

Another famous medieval holy shroud is that of Carcassonne, the so-called Saint Cabouin. It is mentioned in a document of 1397—that is, in the first of the surviving registers of a religious society, known as a confraternity, dedicated to the cult of the relic, which evidently existed previously. The story surrounding this shroud is that it was transported to France in 1298 by two friars of the Augustinian order who came from the East and had obtained the relic from a Jewish family. We know that in 1402 there was a trial against the Augustinians of Carcassonne undertaken by the Cistercians of Cadouin, who believed that the relic of Carcassonne was only an illegally removed part of their own older shroud. The case was won by the Augustinians. Another adversity that the relic had to endure was a test of fire. This occurred in the first half of the sixteenth century when Martin de Saint-André, bishop of Carcassonne, tried to burn a piece of it to verify the shroud's authenticity. He undertook this trial thrice, and each time the shroud miraculously escaped the flames. When the Augustinian monastery became the property of the state, the shroud was moved to the hospital church, where it was hidden during the French Revolution, and at the end of the nineteenth century it was brought to the cathedral, where its cult continued throughout the first half of the twentieth century. In 1963 the relic was moved to a room adjacent to the cathedral, and it is still located there: it consists of a rectangular piece of silk taffeta of about 40 × 80 cm sewn to a larger piece of silk. Carbon-14 (C14) dating has established that the

---

Association les Amis de Cadouin, 1997); G. Cornu, "Le 'suaire' de Cadouin, pièce de tirāz fatimide," *Archéologie islamique* 8–9 (1999): 29–36. See also the documentation collected at www.amisdecadouin.com, along with various articles.

[84] Cf. Francez, *Un pseudo-linceul du Christ*, 25–34; G. Marçais and G. Wiet, "Le Voile de Sainte Anne d'Apt," *Monuments et mémoires de la Fondation Eugène Piot* 34 (1934): 177–94.

silk dates to the years between 1220 and 1475 (but a terminus ante quem of 1397, as noted above, has been established for it).[85]

Another shroud (or sudarium) is housed in the cathedral of Cahors. Called Sainte Coiffe because it is shaped like a cap made of overlapping layers of fabric, this sudarium is said to have covered the head from the brow to the nape of the neck and to have buttoned under the chin, leaving the face uncovered. With regard to the object's provenance, conjectures are bizarre: some have said it was brought from the Holy Land at the beginning of the twelfth century by the bishop-crusader Géraud de Cardaillac; others instead have evoked the names of Pepin the Short or Charlemagne, who supposedly would have given it to Aymat, bishop of Cahors; and he, to test its authenticity, allegedly placed it on the head of a dead man, who thereby was immediately resuscitated. Or again, Saint Martial, bishop of Limoges, has been mentioned, as has Saint Géry, bishop of Cambrai, or even the legendary Saint Veronica together with her husband, Saint Amadour, who in the first century are said to have brought the relic to France.

As is often the case, the lengthy silence of historical sources is justified, given the subterfuge surrounding the concealment of the Sainte Coiffe, for it is said to have long remained hidden within a wall (this is the same subterfuge, we shall see later, that occurs in the case of the Shroud of Turin). In 1580, upon the conquest of Cahors by the Huguenots, all the relics are said to have been destroyed, save the sudarium, which was rescued and taken to Luzech; the altar of the church was removed and ended up decorating a garden of the castle of Cénevières. The marble of the altar was allegedly found in 1634 in the castle. That same marble preserved the following inscription: "On 27 July of the year 1119, Callixtus II, Pontifex Maximus, dedicated the altar of the sudarium of the head of Christ." This would be the oldest document attesting to the existence of a sudarium in Cahors, were it not for the fact that the owner of the castle lost this, too.[86]

[85] Cf. T. Bouges, *Histoire du Saint Suaire de Notre Seigneur Jésus-Christ gardé en l'église des Pères Augustins de la ville de Carcassonne* (Toulouse: Robert, 1722); D. Cardon, "Un Saint Suaire en soie: Le Saint Cabouin de Carcassonne," *Bulletin du CIETA* 70 (1993): 101–10; M. Fournié, "Le Saint Suaire de Carcassonne au Moyen Âge," *Bulletin de la Société d'Études Scientifiques de l'Aude* 110 (2010): 67–76.

[86] Cf. J. Gary, *La Sainte Coiffe: Notice sur le Saint Suaire de Cahors* (Cahors: Delsaud, 1892), which summarizes all previous sources.

The veneration of the Sainte Coiffe, which was returned to Cahors in 1585 and escaped the French Revolution, continued uninterruptedly through the first half of the twentieth century. When the object was finally recognized as dating to the eleventh century, however, it was transferred to a chapel of the cloister, in a small collection of religious art. For a certain period it was also placed in a security deposit box in a bank. In recent years the pseudo-relic has regained a little notoriety thanks to the sindonologist Robert Babinet, who believes he has identified a perfect correspondence between the bloodstains of the Coiffe and those of the Shroud of Turin. To support the idea that the sudarium was present in Constantinople until 1204 and thereafter at Cahors—one may well wonder why among so many sudariums Babinet regards only that of Constantinople to be authentic—Babinet rejects as false the report of the dedication of the altar in 1119. Instead, he brings into play the Templars and the Holy Grail, and thus invents a transfer from Constantinople to Cahors.[87] This way of dealing with sources and relics follows a cliché that, as we shall see, was also used to authenticate other relics that otherwise would not have merited any attention. It is curious that the new bishop of Cahors, Laurent Camiade, decided to resume the exhibitions of the relic, beginning in 2015. Beginning in 2019 the reliquary was relocated to the cathedral for display.

Not all the shrouds and all the sudariums were in France (below we shall consider the shroud of Besançon, dating to the sixteenth century). A linen of Christ could also perhaps be found much far from France: for example, in the Hovhannavank monastery in the village of Ohanavan in Armenia. In his *Geographia*, Vardan Areveltsi († 1271) in fact affirms that in that monastery was "the relic of the holy Precursor [Saint John the Baptist], the cloth of Christ, the holy nail of the right hand and the holy right hand of the Protomartyr [Saint Stephen]." The information is also reported on an Armenian map prepared in Constantinople in 1691, five centuries later: "There is [a relic] of the cloth of Christ, the holy nail of the right hand, the right hand of the Protomartyr and [a relic] of the hair of the Mother of the Lord."[88] It is not clear what this "cloth" (*varšamak*) is—whether

[87] R. Babinet, *Le témoin secret de la résurrection* (Paris: Godefroy, 2001).

[88] Texts are cited and translated in G. Uluhogian, *Un'antica mappa dell'Armenia* (Ravenna: Longo, 2000), §§ 267–68. M. Eordegian, "The Holy Shroud in Armenian

it was the shroud itself or one of the legendary fabrics upon which Christ pressed his face (e.g., the Veil of Veronica or the Mandylion). From the map we understand that the relic was not whole.

We now turn our attention back to Europe, where one of the shrouds presumed to have been placed on the face of Jesus is preserved in Mainz. A quite late legend tells that it was donated to Saint Bilhild († 734) by the noble Cunigunde; but since Cunigunde was born after Bilhild's death, others later surmised that, instead of Cunigunde, the author intended to submit the name of Chimnechild, wife of Saint Sigebert, king of Austrasia († 656). This shroud was said to have been divided into two parts: one part ended up in the monastery of Altenmünster, of which Bilhild was the founder, and every year on the day after Easter it was put on display; the other part ended up in the cathedral of Mainz, for Rigibert, bishop of Mainz, was thought to have been an uncle of the saint.[89] The half that was at the monastery, which was closed in 1781, was then transferred to the Church of St. Emmeran in Mainz. After the bombing of the church that occurred in 1945, it was moved to the eastern crypt of that city's cathedral;[90] the other part is in the chapel of the castle of Aschaffenburg.[91] The

Manuscripts and Literature," in *Sindone 2000: Congresso mondiale*, ed. E. Marinelli and A. Russi, vol. 2 (San Severo: Gerni, 2002), 383–88, asserts that the presence of the relic is not able to be confirmed. This article, however, does not meet minimum scientific criteria.

[89] See N. Serarius, *Moguntiacarum rerum libri quinque* (Moguntiae: apud Balthasarum Lippium, 1604), 72 and 283; J. G. von Eckhart, *Commentarii de rebus Franciae orientalis* (Würzburg: sumptibus almae Universitatis Iuliae, 1729), 225–26; I. Gropp, *Collectio novissima scriptorum et rerum Wirceburgensium* (Frankfurt: ex officina Weldmanniana, 1741), 783; J. H. Dielhelm, *Rheinischer Antiquarius* (Frankfurt am Main: Stock and Schilling, 1739), 398; J. Brand, *Officia propria sanctorum patronorum aliorumque ecclesiae et dioecesis Limburgensis* (Frankfurt am Main: typis Andreae, 1830), 257; F. Falk, "Die Heiligthümer in der Schloßkapelle zu Aschaffenburg," *Der Katholik* 60, no. 2 (1880): 191–202.

[90] See T. Jung, *Geschichte und Andacht vom heiligen Schweißtuch unseres Herrn Jesu Christi, das sein heiliges Haupt im Grabe bedeckt hat, und wovon ein Teil in der Pfarrkirche St. Emmeran, Mainz, aufbewahrt und verehrt wird* (Mainz: St. Emmeran, 1934); C. Feussner, "Mainzer Wallfahrten in Geschichte und Gegenwart," in *Pilger und Wallfahrtsstätten in Mittelalter und Neuzeit*, ed. M. Matheus (Stuttgart: Steiner, 1999), 106–11.

[91] Inv.-Nr. Asch.T0049 (Aschaffenburg inventory number); cf. *Aschaffenburg Castle: Official Guide* (Munich: Bayerische Verwaltung der staatlichen Schlösser, 1997), 53–54.

fabric is linen, probably of the twelfth century, embellished with decorations in the form of diamonds with blunt corners. The diamonds are red and elaborated with geometric designs in blue. To the side there are two dark lines and a band that runs parallel containing a zig-zag pattern with the same shades of red and blue that appear on the diamonds. The half in Aschaffenburg is stitched onto a complete decorated fabric of the sixteenth century. The cathedral also holds another shroud made of finer white silk.

In Germany, according to a missive written around 1085 by Bishop Benzo of Alba, Constantine X must have sent a fragment of the shroud of Christ to the emperor Henry IV.[92] And in November 1353, Charles IV of Luxembourg asked the pope for permission to bring another piece of the Lord's shroud to Prague. The shroud itself had been obtained from some Alemannian church.[93]

Rome, too, could certainly not be without a shroud. On an altar of the papal Basilica of St. John Lateran, together with other significant relics (the rods of Moses and Aaron, some of the loaves and fish that Jesus multiplied, the towel of the Last Supper, the tunic and the purple mantle of Jesus, a little blood that flowed from his side, his foreskin and umbilical cord) there was, attested at least from the twelfth century, the "sudarium that was on his head." This cloth, to which Marco Polo[94] probably alludes, is mentioned in the list of relics provided by the *tabula magna Lateranensis*, a mosaic inscription on the wall of the ambulatory near the entrance door of the sacristy, commissioned by Pope Nicholas IV (1288–1292), as well as in another list drawn up by Onofrio Panvinio († 1568). In 1543 John Calvin noted the irony of the coexistence of this sudarium in several churches, including the Lateran. Today the relic is no longer in existence, and its disappearance is unaccounted for; in 1656 Cesare Rasponi speaks of

[92] Benzo Albensis, *Ad Henricum IV imperatorem*: "Basileus autem Constantinus misit tibi signa similia, videlicet de sudario Domini, de cruce, simulque de corona spinea" (H. Seyffert, ed., *Sieben Bücher an Kaiser Heinrich IV* [Hanover: Hahn, 1996], 152).

[93] *Monumenta Vaticana res gestas Bohemicas illustrantia*, vol. 2 (Pragae: typis Gregerianis, 1907), § 196: "de sudario Domini."

[94] M. Polo, *Il Milione* 59: "in the same mountain [of Chingitalas] there is a vein of the substance from which asbestos is made. . . . These threads were then spun and made into cloth. . . . And I may add that they have at Rome a large sheet of this material, which the Grand Kaan sent to the Pope to make a wrap for the holy sudarium of Jesus Christ."

Lateran relics as if they are objects of the past, but in 1723 the literary figure Giovanni Mario Crescimbeni still maintains that at the papal altar of the basilica there is "the sudarium sprinkled with blood," which had covered the face of Christ in the tomb.[95]

1.2.3. Relics in Constantinople

The capital of the Roman Empire, Constantinople, certainly could not lack for precious relics that could rival those of the West; indeed, for the possession of relics from Jerusalem, the "new Rome" far outstripped the ancient one and could well bill itself as the "new Jerusalem." The period in which the most important transfers of these objects occurred followed closely upon an iconoclastic crisis that, beginning in 843, saw the reemergence of the legitimacy of veneration of icons. Some witnesses affirm the presence in Byzantium of the sepulchral cloths of Jesus; others, however, never mention it.[96]

A letter sent by Emperor Constantine VII Porphyrogenitus clarifies what relics pertaining to Christ's passion he possessed in the year 958: the beams and the placard of the cross, the spear, the reed, the blood escaped from his side, the garment, "the sacred bands, the theophoric *sindón* and the remaining marks of his undefiled passion."[97] In the middle of the tenth century, therefore, Constanti-

[95] Ioannes Diaconus, *Descriptio Lateranensis ecclesiae*, in *Codice topografico della città di Roma*, vol. 3, ed. R. Valentini and G. Zucchetti (Rome: Istituto Storico Italiano per il Medio Evo, 1953), 337: "sudarium quod fuit super caput eius" ("the sudarium that was placed upon his head"); *Le cose maravigliose dell'alma città di Roma* (Rome: Accolto, 1570), 4v: "il sudario che gli fu posto sopra la faccia nel sepolcro" ("the sudarium that was placed upon his face in the tomb"); O. Panvinio, *Le sette chiese romane* (Rome: Blado, 1570), 186; J. Calvin, *Traité des reliques* (Geneva: Labor et Fides, 2000), 38–39; C. Rasponi, *De basilica et patriarchio Lateranensi* (Rome: Lazzeris, 1656), 46; G. M. Crescimbeni, *Stato della SS. chiesa papale lateranense nell'anno 1723* (Rome: S. Michele a Ripa Grande, 1723), 94. See also Savio, *Ricerche storiche*, 86–88.

[96] One example is John the Geometer, who never speaks of "the image of Christ visible in his shroud," contrary to the affirmation made by Baima Bollone (*Sindone: Storia e scienza*, 29) as well as J. L. Carreño Etxeandía, *La Sindone: Ultimo reporter* (Alba: Paoline, 1977), 93; and P. C. Pappas, *Jesus' Tomb in India* (Fremont: Jain, 1991), 125.

[97] Constantinus VII Porphyrogenitus, *De contionibus militaribus* 8: τῶν ἱερῶν σπαργάνων, καὶ τῆς θεοφόρου σινδόνος καὶ τῶν λοιπῶν τοῦ ἀχράντου πάθους αὐτοῦ συμβόλων (R. Vari, ed., "Zum historischen Exzerptenwerke des Konstantinos Porphyrogennetos," *Byzantinische Zeitschrift* 17 [1908]: 83).

nople claimed to possess the sepulchral linen of Jesus in the form of the bands and the *sindón*. During the Byzantine age, the prevailing notion was that Jesus was in the tomb wrapped in bands twisted around his body. Iconography suggests this understanding, as well as the fact that on Easter Day dignitaries of the empire appeared "wrapped with splendid scarves (*lóroi*), in imitation of the burial bands of Christ."[98] The *lóros* was a long, narrow scarf, adorned with precious stones, that was worn by turning it around the body. Some fragments of these relics, including those of the *sindón*, are preserved there because they were placed inside a precious Constantinopolitan reliquary of the ninth century, removed during the Fourth Crusade and today preserved in Limburg an der Lahn.[99]

The emperor gathered the relics of the passion and death of Christ within the Chapel of the Virgin of the Pharos inside his Bucoleon palace. The heritage of this small and precious chapel was not the result of a casual collection, but rather of an intentional project to gather the relics of Christ, as if the imperial palace were a small Jerusalem that replaced the original, which had by then fallen into the hands of the infidels.[100] We thus have numerous testimonies about the relics preserved at the Church of the Virgin of the Pharos. There is a Greek text of the second half of the eleventh century, rendered into Latin by an anonymous translator. In it, it is said that there are many relics in the Church of the Virgin of the Pharos, including Christ's crown of thorns, the robe, the scourge, the reed, the sponge, the nails,

[98] Constantinus VII Porphyrogenitus, *De cerimoniis aulae Byzantinae* 2.52: λαμπροφοροῦσι τοῖς λώροις, εἰς τύπον τῶν ἐνταφίων Χριστοῦ σπαργάνων ἑαυτοὺς ἐνειλίττοντες (J. J. Reiske, ed., *De cerimoniis aulae Byzantinae*, vol. 1 [Bonn: Weber, 1829], 766).

[99] Cf. A. Ginnasi, "La stauroteca di Limburg an-der-Lahn," *ACME* 62, no. 1 (2009): 97–130.

[100] See the studies in J. Durand and B. Flusin, eds., *Byzance et les reliques du Christ* (Paris: Association des amis du centre d'histoire et civilization de Byzance, 2004); B. Flusin, "Construire une nouvelle Jérusalem: Constantinople et les reliques," in *L'Orient dans l'histoire religieuse de l'Europe: L'invention des origines*, ed. M. A. Amir-Moezzi and J. Scheid (Turnhout: Brepols, 2000), 51–70; M. Bacci, "Relics of the Pharos Chapel: A View from the Latin West," in Восточнохристианские реликвии: *Eastern Christian Relics*, ed. A. M. Lidov (Moscow: Progress-Traditsija, 2003), 234–48; H. A. Klein, "Sacred Relics and Imperial Ceremonies at the Great Palace of Constantinople," in *Visualisierungen von Herrschaft: Frühmittelalterliche Residenzen—Gestalt und Zeremoniell*, ed. F. A. Bauer (Istanbul: Yayinlari, 2006), 79–99.

the spear, the blood, the belt, the shoes, and finally "the linen and the sudarium of the tomb."[101] A letter probably written by Robert I, Count of Flanders, around 1106, falsely dated 1092 and attributed to the Byzantine emperor Alexios I Komnenos, more generally refers to "the linens found in the tomb after the resurrection."[102] In about 1150 an anonymous English pilgrim refers only to "the sudarium that was on the head" of Christ, without mentioning other linens.[103] In 1171 Amalric I, king of Jerusalem, was admitted to the most inaccessible parts of the imperial palace to venerate "the relics of the saints and the most precious witnesses of the sacrifice of our Lord Jesus Christ, that is, the cross, the nails, the spear, the sponge, the reed, the crown of thorns, the *sindon*, and the sandals."[104]

In another account, an anonymous visitor to Constantinople around 1190 found himself in some difficulty: in the chapel he saw "part of the linen with which Joseph of Arimathea was deemed worthy to wrap the crucified body of Christ," but he could not accept that the entire *sindon* was kept in the tomb, because he knew well that "the *sindon*, and also part of the crown of Christ, are in Gaul, in Compiègne, the gift of Charles the Bald."[105] That same visitor does

[101] Anonymus (Mercati), *De sanctuariis et reliquiis urbis Constantinopoleos* 1: "lintheamen et sudarium sepulture eius" (K. N. Ciggaar, ed., "Une description de Constantinople traduite par un pèlerin anglais," *Revue des études byzantines* 34 [1976]: 245). The list of relics added as an appendix to the itinerary of Nikulás of MunkaÞverá depends on Anonymous of Mercati; cf. R. Simek, "Die zwei Häupter Johannes des Täufers: Byzantinische Reliquien in altnordischen Handschriften," *Skandinavisztikai Füzetek* 5 (1992): 25–38.

[102] P. Riant, *Alexii I Comneni ad Robertum I epistula spuria* (Geneva: Fick, 1879), 17: "linteamina, post resurrectionem eius inventa in sepulchro"; cf. E. Joranson, "The Problem of the Spurious Letter of Emperor Alexius to the Court of Flanders," *American Historical Review* 55, no. 4 (1950): 811–32; C. Sweetenham, *Robert the Monk's History of the First Crusade* (Aldershot: Ashgate, 2005), 215–22.

[103] *Relliquiae Constantinopolitanae*: "sudarium quod fuit super caput eius" (P. Riant, ed., *Exuviae sacrae Constantinopolitanae*, vol. 2 [Geneva: Fick, 1878], 211).

[104] Guillelmus Tyrensis, *Historia rerum in partibus transmarinis gestarum* 20.23: "sanctorum etiam reliquias, dispensationis quoque domini nostri Iesu Christi preciosissima argumenta, crucem videlicet, clavos, lanceam, spongiam, arundinem, coronam spineam, sindonem, sandalia" (R. B. C. Huygens, ed., *Guillaume de Tyr. Chronique* [Turnhout: Brepols, 1986]).

[105] *Descriptio Sanctuarii Constantinopolitani*: "Item pars linteaminum, quibus crucifixum Christi corpus meruit involvere iam dictus Arimathensis Ioseph, in supradicta capella imperiali continetur. Syndon enim, pars quoque corone Christi,

not raise many doubts and prefers not to deny the authenticity of any of the relics, exploiting the fact that the sources often speak of *sindon*, *sudarium*, linens, and sepulchral bands interchangeably, as if they were synonymous.

The most romantic description of the Constantinopolitan relics of the passion of Christ is that of Nicolaus Mesarites, dating to July 1200. Nicolaus had custody of the sacred objects of the Church of the Virgin of the Pharos; in one of his discourses, he extols the church's sacredness by comparing it to the ark of the covenant of the Solomonic Temple and lists a series of ten relics, comparing them to the tablets of the Ten Commandments. Among those he mentions "the burial cloths (*sindónes*) of Christ: they are of linen, of a cheap material readily accessible, still smelling of perfume, exempt from corruption, since they wrapped the indescribable, naked corpse sprinkled with myrrh after the passion."[106] For Mesarites, *sindón* is therefore synonymous with "sepulchral fabric" and can be used in the plural, as there was more than a single linen preserved in Constantinople.

Soon, however, the city would suffer an unforeseen disaster: on April 13, 1204, the crusaders, who should have gone to free Jerusalem, entered Constantinople, putting it to the sword and setting it ablaze. The imperial palaces were sought out immediately and fell subject to the fury of the crusaders, who carried out their sack of the city for three days, pillaging everything they found, including the relics. The sepulchral linens of Jesus kept in the Church of the Virgin of the Pharos were, however, preserved from looting and became the personal property of the new Latin emperor, who at least initially tried not to allow the contents of the church to be dispersed or to be subject to the constant, frenetic transference of relics to the West.[107]

---

ex Karoli Calvi dono, habetur Carropoli Gallie" (Riant, *Exuviae sacrae Constantinopolitanae*, 217).

[106] Nicolaus Mesarites, *Seditio Ioanni Comneni* 13: ἐντάφιοι σινδόνες Χριστοῦ · αὗται δ'εἰσὶν ἀπὸ λίνου, ὕλης εὐώνου κατὰ τὸ πρόχειρον, ἔτι πνέουσαι μύρα, ὑπερτεροῦσαι φθορᾶς, ὅτι τὸν ἀπερίληπτον νεκρὸν γυμνὸν ἐσμυρνημένον μετὰ τὸ πάθος συνέστειλαν (A. Heisenberg, ed., *Die Palastrevolution des Johannes Komnenos* [Würzburg: Stürzt, 1907]).

[107] See the synthesis of K. Krause, "Immagine-reliquia: Da Bisanzio all'Occidente," in *Mandylion: Intorno al Sacro Volto da Bisanzio a Genova*, ed. G. Wolf, C. Dufour Bozzo, and A. Calderoni Masetti (Milan: Skira, 2004), 209–35.

Still, ultimately, nothing could curb the West's desire for relics, and pieces of the shroud and sudarium of Christ reached Europe. We know that already in 1205 Nivelon de Quierzy, bishop of Soissons, gave the abbey of St. Mary in his city a relic from the shroud,[108] and that in the same year Konrad von Krosigk, bishop of Halberstadt, brought into his diocese a portion both of the sudarium and of the shroud.[109] The knight Robert de Clari donated to the abbey of Corbie one of the fragments of the burial cloth of Christ from the Church of the Virgin of the Pharos no later than 1206 and, afterward, two more.[110] Clairvaux also had a section of the shroud, brought back by the monk Hugues at some point during the reign of Emperor Henry (1206–1216).[111]

The bulk of the relics of the passion and the tomb, however, remained in Constantinople, even if they were violently fragmented, as Abbot Nicolaus of Otranto attests. He had occasion to attend to a dispute between Latins and Greeks held in Constantinople in 1206 and recalls the devastation of the city that had been carried out in 1204 by the crusaders: "[They] entered as thieves into the storehouse (*skeuphylakion*) of the Grand Palace where the holy things where kept—that is, the precious pieces of wood, the crown of thorns, the sandals of the Savior, the nail and the bands, that we later also saw with our own eyes."[112] Nicolaus wrote both in Latin and in Greek, and in this passage he used both languages to designate the sepulchral linens, using the terms *fasciae* and *spárgana* and confirming the Byzantine tradition that regarded the linen of Jesus to have had the shape of bands. The next year, Nicolaus Mesarites also

[108] See Riant, *Exuviae sacrae Constantinopolitanae,* 67 and 190: "de sindone munda."

[109] *Gesta episcoporum Halberstadensium,* in *Monumenta Germaniae Historica: Scriptores,* vol. 23, ed. L. Weiland (Hanover: Hahn 1874), 120, ll. 43–44: "de syndone eiusdem [Domini] et de sudario."

[110] Cf. Riant, *Exuviae sacrae Constantinopolitanae,* 176: "del suaire nostre Seigneur"; and 198: "de sudario Domini in duobus locis."

[111] Cf. Riant, *Exuviae sacrae Constantinopolitanae,* 193: "de sindone."

[112] Nicolaus Hydruntinus, *Tractatus de communione*: ἐν τῷ σκευοφυλακίῳ τῷ τοῦ μεγάλου παλατίου λῃστρικῶς εἰσφρησάντων ἐν οἷς τὰ ἅγια ἀπέκειντο ἤγουν τὰ τίμια ξύλα ὁ ἀκάνθινος στέφανος τὰ τοῦ Σωτῆρος σανδάλια ὁ ἧλος καὶ σπάργανα ἅτινα καὶ ἡμεῖς ὕστερον αὐτοψεὶ ἐθεασάμεθα ("in scevofilacium magni palacii tanquam latrones intrantes ubi sancta posita erant scilicet pretiosa ligna spinea corona Salvatoris sandalia clavus et fascia que et nos postea oculis nostris vidimus"). My transcription is from Nicolaus' autograph codex (Bibl. Vat., Pal. gr. 232, f. 106r).

confirmed that "the *othónia* and the sudariums" of Christ still remained in Constantinople.[113]

Some years later, however, Emperor Baldwin II found himself running short of funds and agreed to enter into negotiations about selling relics to Louis IX, king of France, who also desired to own the most precious artifacts of Christianity. Between 1242 and 1248, Louis built in Paris the sumptuous Sainte-Chapelle, a church for his own royal palace that was supposed to become the reliquary for the sacred objects that he intended to obtain from Constantinople. The Byzantine emperor had direct access to the Church of the Virgin of the Pharos and its surrounding buildings; King Louis, too, could now pass directly from his palace to the chapel. The relics, once obtained, were placed inside an impressive wooden reliquary known as the *Grande châsse*.[114]

We know of a document of 1247 by which Emperor Baldwin of Constantinople oversaw the bestowal of various of his relics upon Louis, an event that had already happened. Among these were "part of the shroud with which the body [of Christ] was wrapped in the tomb."[115] From this "part" of the sudarium—or of the actual shroud, if one prefers, for, as we have seen, the two terms are used virtually as synonyms—other fragments were then removed, one donated in 1248 by Louis to the Church of Toledo, another to Vézelay in 1267.[116]

113 Nicolaus Mesarites, *Epitaphius in Ioannem* 27: αἱ ὀθόναι καὶ τὰ σουδάρια (A. Heisenberg, ed., *Der Epitaphios des Nikolaos Mesarites* [Munich: Bayerische Akademie der Wissenschaften, 1923]). There is no reason to claim that Nicolaus had seen the Shroud at Athens (so Siliato, *Sindone*, 239).

114 Cf. J. Durand and M. P. Laffitte, eds., *Le trésor de la Sainte-Chapelle* (Paris: Réunion des musées nationaux, 2001). On the *Grande châsse*, see also R. Branner, "The Grande Châsse of the Sainte-Chapelle," *Gazette des Beaux-Arts* 77 (1971): 5–18. In general, C. Hediger, ed., *La Sainte-Chapelle de Paris: Royaume de France ou Jérusalem céleste?* (Turnhout: Brepols, 2007); M. Cohen, *The Sainte-Chapelle and the Construction of Sacral Monarchy* (Cambridge: Cambridge University Press, 2014).

115 S. J. Morand, *Histoire de la Ste-Chapelle Royale du Palais* (Paris: Clousier-Prault, 1790), *Pièces justificatives*, 8: "partem sudarii quo involutum fuit corpus eius in sepulchro." Transcribed and translated in A. Nicolotti, *From the Mandylion of Edessa to the Shroud of Turin: The Metamorphosis and Manipulation of a Legend* (Leiden: Brill, 2014), 190–91.

116 Cf. Riant, *Exuviae sacrae Constantinopolitanae*, 138 and 155; on Toledo, see M. Solé, "Sobre el fragmento 'de syndone qua corpus ejus sepultum jacuit in sepulchro' regalado por S. Luis, rey de Francia, a la catedral de Toledo," in *La Sindone e la scienza: Bilanci e programmi*, ed. P. Coero-Borga, 2nd ed. (Turin: Edizioni Paoline,

Although the relic was not whole, William Durand, in the last decade of that same century, wrote that he saw simply "the *sindon*" in the chapel of the king of France in Paris.[117] In 1451 Antonio Astesano, too, describing Sainte-Chapelle, states that "the sacred shrouds" were preserved in it, or at least "part of them."[118] Between 1534 and 1573 another inventory speaks of a fragment "of the shroud of the Lord."[119] Among the periodic inventories of the chapel's patrimony, one particular description of the shroud's container from 1740 has come down to us:

> A reliquary, almost square in shape, from nine to ten thumb measurements in length and width, closed at the top with four rock crystals, with inlay and embedded gold, with sides and back of gilded silver, adorned with enamel bas-reliefs; and on the back the tomb of our Lord is depicted in bas-relief. In this reliquary there are relics, with this inscription: *De Sindone Domini*.[120]

Following the French Revolution, the set of relics of Sainte-Chapelle was dismantled and stored in boxes: one part was lost or put up for sale, while the rest was sent to the foundry to be made into ingots of precious metal. Most of the relics were lost forever; only descriptions remain, and in some cases images.[121] For this reason, the greater part of the burial linens of Jesus that were in Constantinople no longer exists. What remained of them, except for later forgeries, were the fragments that were sent to several European churches first by the Latins, after the conquest of 1204, subsequently by Louis

---

1979), 391–93; C. Barta and D. Duque, "The Sindone Sample from Constantinople in Toledo," *Revue internationale du Linceul de Turin* 21 (2001): 34–37 (to be used with caution; it is useful for the textile description of the fragment—i.e., linen with plain weave, which fails to include a provenance from the Shroud of Turin).

117 Guillelmus Durandus, *Rationale divinorum officiorum* 6.80.10: "cum sindone qua corpus fuit involutum."

118 Antonio Astesano, *Epistolae heroicae* 3.124–26: "Illic esse ferunt etiam sudaria sacra, illa quibus Christum tumulandum, impulsus amore, involvit Ioseph, partem aut (ne fallar) eorum."

119 A. Vidier, "Le trésor de la Sainte-Chapelle," in *Mémoires de la Société de l'Histoire de Paris et de l'Île-de-France* 35 (1908): 193: "De sindone Domini."

120 Vidier, "Trésor de la Sainte-Chapelle," 295–96. Inasmuch as a thumb measurement in the eighteenth century corresponded to 2.7 to 2.8 cm, the envelope must have measured around 24 to 28 cm.

121 Cf. Durand and Laffitte, *Trésor de la Sainte-Chapelle*.

of France. These are not the only occasions on which such transfers took place: even at the beginning of the fifteenth century Manuel II Palaiologos donated a piece "of a holy shroud of our Lord," which would end up in the collegiate Church of Saint-Pierre of Lille;[122] it is not known from what source he obtained it. As is so often the case, here again it is simpler not to raise too many questions: as we have seen, the ancient world was full of shrouds, bands, and sudariums kept in different places and in competition among themselves. Thus, one should keep in mind that it is self-deception to imagine that all fragments were passed down in a regular manner and were of secure provenance.

One could also add to this list all of the fragments of fabrics kept in other cities, including those of Aix-en-Provence, Aosta, Bourg-en-Bresse, Brescia, Cambrai, Chartres, Clermont-Ferrand, Cologne, Dijon, Einsiedeln, Figeac, Florence, Fontainebleau, Halberstadt, Hanover, Laon, Lyon, Livorno, Lorch, Milan, Le Mont-Dieu, Reims, Rome, Sant Feliu de Guíxols, Toledo, Toulouse, and Vézelay, to name but a few.[123] Each of them possesses a relic derived from the burial garments of Jesus, and behind each a traditional story has been formed, with tales of miracles that occurred based on the relics; these miracles, however, are ultimately a topos. Such topoi are derived from apologetic literature and would seem never to be lacking even for those relics that are later proved to be false and are subsequently removed from the typical itineraries of the faithful who might wish to venerate them.

1.2.4. The Blachernae Fabric

Robert de Clari, a knight of Picardy who took part in the Fourth Crusade, after returning to his homeland wrote an account of the conquest of Constantinople.[124] At one point in his report this passage appears:

> And among those others there was another church which was called My Lady Saint Mary of Blachernae, where there was the

[122] C. P. Serrure, *Voyages et ambassades de messire Guillebert de Lannoy* (Mons: Hoyois, 1840), 44: "d'un saint suaire nostre Seigneur."

[123] See Ciccone and Sturmann, *Sindone svelata*, 114–26.

[124] Translated with notes by A. M. Nada Patrone, *Roberto di Clari: La conquista di Costantinopoli* (Genoa: Istituto di Paleografia e Storia medievale, 1972).

> *sydoines* where our Lord had been wrapped, which every Friday raised itself upright, so that one could see the form of our Lord there; and no one, either Greek or French, ever knew what became of this *sydoines* when the city was taken.[125]

Among the dozens of relics mentioned in the documents of the time, this description in particular has attracted interest because it speaks of a sepulchral fabric revealing a "form of our Lord." The object, therefore, recalls the characteristics of another famous relic of our own time, the famous Shroud of the cathedral of Turin.

Whether it is the same sepulchral fabric is a hypothesis that cannot be verified historically, as there is no documented relationship between the two objects, for the Turin Shroud appeared about a century and a half later in France, without reference to that of Constantinople. Further, the identity of the two shrouds should be ruled out if the result of the radiocarbon dating of the Turin Shroud is taken into account, for that analysis places the shroud of Turin's origin to a later period. Hypothetically speaking, if the two relics were not precisely the same object, they could well have been two competing relics, like the other shrouds and the sudariums we discussed previously, united by the fact that they each bore an image. It is the opinion of this author, however, that the report of Robert de Clari on the Constantinopolitan relic is for various reasons simply unreliable, as I have demonstrated elsewhere.[126] According to Robert, this *sydoines* ("cloth") was in the Basilica of the Blachernae. That church, located in the northwestern part of Constantinople overlooking the estuary known as the Golden Horn, was connected to a homonymous imperial palace. As its name indicates, the church was dedicated to Saint Mary and was the most renowned place of Marian worship in the city. From inside the basilica a smaller building could be accessed,

[125] R. de Clari, *La conquête de Constantinople*, §92: "Et entre ches autres en eut un autre des moustiers que on apeloit medame Sainte Marie de Blakerne, ou li sydoines, la ou Nostres Sires fu envolepés, i estoit, qui cascuns des venres se drechoit tous drois, si que on i pooit bien veir le figures nostre Seigneur, ne ne seut on onques, ne Griu, ne Franchois, que chis sydoines devint quant le vile fu prise" (P. Lauer, ed., *La conquête de Constantinople* [Paris: Champion, 1924], 90). The English translation is that of Peter Dembowski.

[126] I have honed this argument in every way possible in A. Nicolotti, "Una reliquia costantinopolitana dei panni sepolcrali di Gesù secondo la Cronaca del crociato Robert de Clari," *Medioevo greco* 11 (2011): 151–96.

a type of chapel for reliquaries commissioned by Emperor Leo I (457–474), in this case to house a relic of Mary.[127] Apart from Robert, no source among those describing that church and its relics speaks of a sepulchral fabric of Christ, as all insist on the notion that the chapel exclusively housed relics of the Madonna. It is in fact difficult to understand why this cloth would have been kept in a Marian sanctuary and not in the Chapel of the Virgin of the Pharos, which was part of the other imperial palace, that of Bucoleon, on the other side of the city, where we know that all the relics of the passion and death of Christ were stored. We have already seen that all the lists of the relics of Constantinople, both before and after 1204, place the sepulchral linens of Jesus only in the Church of the Virgin of the Pharos and not at Blachernae. It is thus not possible that the citizens of Constantinople could imagine that the same relic was in two different churches at the same time. The report of Robert, therefore, isolated and in conflict with other sources, points to the fact that, as some have suggested, he may not have actually observed the relic directly. Indeed, Robert never actually claims to have "seen" the relic.[128]

Further, on which Friday could he have seen the cloth having "raised itself upright" or could he have heard the account of someone who had enjoyed a view of it? Perhaps in 1203, in the period, before the sack of 1204, when the Latin crusaders had time to visit the monuments of the city?[129] But this is incompatible with the fact that in his chronicle Robert places the story of his visit to the city only after the narration of the events of the city's sack (chaps. 82–92), not before. When the crusaders entered Constantinople on April 12, 1204, it was a Monday; the next day Henry of Hainaut took possession of the

[127] On this sanctuary, R. Janin, *La géographie ecclésiastique de l'Empire byzantin*, pt. 1a, vol. 3, *Les églises et les monastères* (Paris: Institut français d'études byzantines, 1969), 161–71; A. M. Schneider, "Die Blachernen," *Oriens* 4, no. 1 (1951): 82–120; G. P. Majeska, *Russian Travelers to Constantinople in the Fourteenth and Fifteenth Centuries* (Washington: Dumbarton Oaks, 1984), 333–37; C. Mango, "The Origins of the Blachernae Shrine at Constantinople," in *Radovi XIII Međunarodnog Kongresa za starokršćansku arheologiju*, ed. N. Cambi and E. Marin, vol. 2 (Split: Archeološki muzej and Pontificio Istituto di Archeologia Cristiana, 1998), 61–75.

[128] Cf. E. von Dobschütz, *Christusbilder: Untersuchungen zur christlichen Legende* (Leipzig: Hinrichs, 1899), 77.

[129] As recounted by Geoffroy de Villehardouin, *La conquête de Constantinople*, §192.

palace, preventing it from being looted by soldiers.[130] The Church of the Blachernae wound up in the hands of the Latin clergy accompanying the crusader expedition, passing directly to the dependencies of the Holy See;[131] under these conditions it is impossible to think that the Byzantine clergy could continue their own ceremonies the following Friday according to the ancient customs. Robert himself, moreover, declared that "no one, neither Greek nor French, ever knew what became of this *sydoines* when the city was taken," meaning that the crusader knew nothing specific about the fate of this object.

It is necessary to ask a more fundamental question: is Robert de Clari in fact a credible source? He was an uncultured man who had a tendency to accept unquestioningly the possibility of the strangest relics (for example, he takes for granted that the tears of the Madonna are still visible on the marble table where Christ was deposed from the cross). He was not a historian by profession, and he did not write reports daily but observed events as he traveled. Only after returning home did he decide to compose his account of the crusade. Despite the accuracy of some of his stories, the interval of time that passed between the events and the writing of the report certainly offers a basis for many errors that modern historians have not failed to list. In the case of the Blachernae burial fabric, was there or was there not an eyewitness? Was the strangeness of his report and the mistaken fruit it bore due to a defect in his memory or to an unreliable story of one of his sources?

Some have proposed that the "shroud" of Blachernae was in fact an *epitáphios*—that is, a large and embroidered cloth that depicts the body of Christ dead and positioned for burial.[132] It is a liturgical object very well known today in the devotion of Christians following the Byzantine rite, used on Good Friday during the procession commemorating the burial of Christ. It should, however, be noted that this liturgical tradition is rather late, and the rite of the *epitáphios* did not yet exist in Constantinople at the time of the Fourth Crusade. If

[130] Cf. A. Carile, *Per una storia dell'impero latino di Costantinopoli*, 2nd ed. (Bologna: Patron, 1978), 154 and 159–61; De Villehardouin, *La conquête de Constantinople*, §250.

[131] On the fate of the Constantinopolitan churches sought by the Latin clergy, cf. R. Janin, "Les sanctuaires de Byzance sous la domination latine (1204–1261)," *Revue des études byzantines* 2 (1944): 134–84.

[132] This hypothesis, among others, has been proposed by Ciccone and Sturmann, *Sindone svelata*, 180.

the cloth in question was a liturgical veil, it is easier to believe that it would have been called an *aér*, which was used to cover the offerings on the altar and had a role in the procession for the transfer of gifts during the eucharistic liturgy. This veil could measure as much as 2.5 m and in the late twelfth century began to be decorated with the figure of the dead Christ, naked and stretched out. Certainly the *aér* is at the origin of the rite of the *epitáphios*, but, unlike the latter, its use was not limited to Good Friday. It is therefore possible that in 1203–1204 Robert de Clari saw or heard of a large sheet depicting the dead body of Jesus, unknown to the Western liturgical tradition and therefore easy to get confused with something else.[133]

Even if the *aér-epitáphios* could provide an explanation of Robert's description, much still remains unclear, such as when, in Robert's account, the fabric "every Friday raised itself upright so that one could see the form of our Lord there." This is a precise description, so precise that it reveals the particular misunderstanding into which the knight must have fallen.

One should recall that no source confirms the existence of a sepulchral cloth of Jesus at Blachernae; rather, the most famous relic of Blachernae was a dress of Mary, which was sometimes described as her funerary fabric.[134] Perhaps it is not that surprising that Robert and his source confused the fabric of Mary with that of Jesus:[135] even in recent times some sindonologists have supposed that at Blachernae were the burial cloths of Christ, discovered in Jerusalem by Pulcheria and brought to Constantinople after 436. Such a scenario, however, arises from the misunderstanding of a report of Nicephorus Callistus, who was speaking of the swaddling cloths of the Madonna.[136]

[133] P. Johnstone, *Byzantine Tradition in Church Embroidery* (London: Alec Tiranti, 1967), 26, who regards the veil as having hung on the walls of the church; S. Ćurčić, "Late Byzantine Loca Sancta? Questions Regarding the Form and Function of Epitaphioi," in *The Twilight of Byzantium*, ed. idem (Princeton: Princeton University Press, 1991), 251–72, believes that such veils also functioned as coverings spread upon on the tombs.

[134] Different traditions on Marian relics are described by J. Wortley, "The Marian Relics at Constantinople," *Greek, Roman, and Byzantine Studies* 45 (2005): 171–87.

[135] As suggested by J. Ebersolt, *Sanctuaires de Byzance* (Paris: Leroux, 1921), 45.

[136] See A. Loth, *La photographie du Saint Suaire de Turin* (Paris: Oudin, 1910), 101–2; R. W. Hynek, *La passione di Cristo studiata dalla scienza medica moderna*, 2nd ed. (Milan: Vita e Pensiero, 1938), 13; A. S. Barnes, *The Holy Shroud of Turin* (London: Burns Oates & Washbourne, 1934), 51; E. A. Wuenschel, "The Holy Shroud of Turin:

If—as we have seen—modern scholars can confuse different cloths, even more so can we accept that a crusader made such a mistake. Yet of greatest interest is what happened at Blachernae every Friday: in that sanctuary there was a venerable icon of Mary in a prayerful position, called the Blachernitissa, that every Friday was the subject of a miracle known as "the habitual miracle." Every week, at the time of Friday's vespers, the silk veil that covered the icon of the Virgin is said to have risen alone and remained miraculously suspended aloft, completely revealing the image of the Madonna to the eyes of all; it would then come back down to cover the icon at three o'clock on Saturday afternoon. This well-known miracle, "during which the curtain of the icon suddenly rises, as if moved by a whisper,"[137] is described in numerous sources beginning in the eleventh century: Michael Psellos, some Western travelers, William of Malmesbury, Jean Beleth, the First Chronicle of Novgorod, Gautier de Coincy (a contemporary of Robert de Clari), and others.[138]

I believe there is a close relationship between the veil of the "habitual miracle" and the *sydoines* of Robert de Clari: both stories are set in the Church of Blachernae; both take place every Friday (not just on Good Friday, as one scholar has proposed);[139] both concern a fabric; both describe a fabric that "raised itself upright" to make an image visible (the image of the Marian icon and that of Christ). Robert could have heard about the miracle that took place every Friday at the Church of Blachernae, which was also famous in the West for the "shroud" of Mary and for the "shroud" that hung before her icon. The habitual miracle involved the prodigious lifting of a veil so that the underlying image of Mary would be visible; Robert speaks of a veil and of an image, but does not say anywhere that

Eloquent Record of the Passion," *American Ecclesiastical Review* 93 (1935): 447; P. Barbet, *La passion de N.-S. Jésus-Christ selon le chirurgien*, 10th ed. (Paris: Médiaspaul, 1982), 29; cf., however, Nicephorus Callistus, *Historia ecclesiastica* 14.2 and 15.14.

137 Michael Psellus, *De miraculo in Blachernais patrato* 136 (E. A. Fisher, ed., *Michaelis Pselli orationes hagiographicae* [Stuttgart: Teubner, 1994]).

138 Virtually all the sources are collected by V. Grumel, "Le 'miracle habituel' de Notre Dame des Blachernes à Constantinople," *Échos d'Orient* 30 (1931): 129–46, which is augmented by Nicolotti, *Una reliquia costantinopolitana*.

139 According to B. Frale, *I Templari e la sindone di Cristo* (Bologna: il Mulino, 2009), 111 (English translation: *The Templars and the Shroud of Christ* [New York: Skyhorse, 2012]). The possibility is already excluded in P. F. Dembowski, "À propos of 'cascuns des venres' in Robert de Clari," *Shroud Spectrum International* 1, no. 4 (1982): 37–38.

the image of Jesus was above the veil: though Robert says that the *sydoines* in fact "raised itself upright, so that one could see the form of our Lord there," he does not specify exactly where such a figure was. It could also stand behind. The story naturally prompts us to think of a shroud with a figure on it, but this is because we in the modern period are influenced by the Shroud of Turin.

Everyone therefore knew that there was a miraculous fabric at Blachernae: the veil that uncovered the Marian icon and the veil that was part of the Madonna's cloths were both miraculous. The veil hanging in front of the icon was decorated with images. Perhaps the crusader was relating it to a precious liturgical veil that represented, even figuratively, the shroud of the dead Christ. Had he seen it in some church? Could the fact that he speaks of the "form of our Lord" be related to the fact that the icon of the Blachernitissa, according to some sources, also contained the image of Christ on his mother's lap? It seems possible that the fusion of some or all of these elements of different origins may have caused Robert or his source to create a distorted miraculous account,[140] as he had also done, for example, for two relics preserved in another church.[141] On the other hand, it would be very strange if in that church every Friday there was a special exposition of a relic of Christ: in fact, the day was already occupied by the Marian functions linked to the habitual miracle and a great weekly procession that started from Blachernae and ended at Chalcoprateia, a place in which another relic of Mary's clothing was kept.

As for the Picard term *sydoines*, which modern translators normally make to mean "shroud," it does not need definitely to refer to a funerary garment: in the French of the twelfth and thirteenth centuries, *sydoines* (with its graphic variants *sydoine*, *sidone*, *sindoine*, *sidonne*, etc.)[142] meant not only "shroud" or "funerary cloth" but also "cloth," "fabric," or "cloth dress" in general. It is also interesting to

[140] John Wortley is even more convinced: "[Robert] certainly seems to have confused it with the 'customary miracle'" ("Marian Relics," 187, n. 41); the same goes for B. Milland-Bove, "Miracles et interventions divines dans la Conquête de Constantinople," in *Miracles d'un autre genre*, ed. B. Milland-Bove and O. Biaggini (Madrid: Casa de Velázquez, 2012), 90–91.

[141] Cf. Nicolotti, *From the Mandylion of Edessa*, 109–12.

[142] Cf. A. Tobler and E. Lommatzsch, *Altfranzösisches Wörterbuch*, vol. 9 (Wiesbaden: Steiner, 1973), col. 627; W. Wartburg, *Französisches etymologisches Wörterbuch*,

note that at that time three Western writers used the Latin word *sindon* or the French *sydoyne* to designate the veil hanging in front of the Blachernitissa icon:[143] this detail, too, may have confused Robert in composing his account.

Ultimately, I think we can exclude the notion that at Blachernae there was a burial cloth of Jesus with the image of his body. There is no need to imagine that the Byzantines built an easel to hoist up a shroud and present it to the people, as some sindonologists claim, because Robert's *sydoines* was nothing but a cloth, with or without an image, that was hanging in front of a painting, and that it was famous for, each Friday, "raising itself upright" miraculously. My opinion, which in the past has also been held by others, is not, in any case, of vital importance for the reconstruction of the history of the Shroud of Turin: even if the Blachernae was really a funerary fabric, known only to Robert and unknown to everyone else, there is "no evidence that this lost *sydoines* which Robert de Clari would therefore never have been able to see, is actually the same relic as the Shroud."[144] The latter shroud, in fact, beyond the fact that it is a more recent manufacture, will make its appearance only 150 years later and in an entirely different location; and when there will be inquiries about its provenance, no one will make reference to the city of Constantinople. To conclude, I take as my own the words of Michele Pellegrino, formerly cardinal of Turin and a serious scholar of history and Christian literature: "I know of no proven link between this shroud and the one existing before 1300 in Constantinople."[145]

1.2.5. The Sudarium of Oviedo

The Sudarium of Oviedo deserves a more detailed treatment than others, in no small part owing to the great and ever-increasing fame that it has enjoyed. Preserved in the Cathedral of San Salvador of the

vol. 11 (Basel: Zbinden, 1964), 641; F. Godefroy, *Dictionnaire de l'ancienne langue française*, vol. 7 (Paris: Bouillon, 1892), 417.

143 Cf. Nicolotti, *Una reliquia costantinopolitana*, 191.

144 J. P. Martin, "Notes sur le manuscrit de Bruxelles de Garin le Lorrain," in *Convergences médiévales*, ed. N. Henrard et al. (Brussels: De Boeck and Larcier, 2001), 325–26. Even the sindonologist Gino Zaninotto has wed himself to this interpretation: "La S. Sindone a S. Maria delle Blakerne nel 1204: Un'ipotesi debole," in *Quattro percorsi accanto alla Sindone*, ed. D. Repice (Rome: Radicequadrata, 2011), 89–113.

145 E. Hauser, "The Riddle of the Shroud," *Reader's Digest* 108 (1976): 53.

Spanish city of Oviedo,[146] this artifact is attested from the last quarter of the eleventh century and is made available to the faithful as an object of veneration three times per annum (fig. 1.1). This artifact is a linen cloth with dimensions of about 83 × 53 cm, woven using a plain weave, with small holes, upon which are visible some traces of red spots. This relic, along with many others, was part of the patrimony enclosed inside a holy ark made of oak wood. This ark is covered with finely worked silver and gilt plates, decorated with rich iconographic trappings and inscriptions.

The veneration of the Sudarium along with the other relics in the ark is the culmination of a process that started in the eighth and ninth centuries, the period in which the city of Oviedo was founded. It should therefore be understood in the light of the joint efforts of the city's clergy and the royal political regime, who joined forces to transform their city into a center of worship as well as an obligatory stop for pilgrims en route to Santiago de Compostela.[147]

The first document that speaks of our Sudarium is dated March 14, 1075. It describes the solemn opening of the ark in the cathedral of Oviedo in the presence of King Alfonso VI of León, in the midst of his court and numerous clergy. In the city of Toledo, the document states, several relics brought from various places had been placed in the ark, in order to save them from the advance of the Muslim forces in the eighth century. According to this account, the ark afterward arrived in Oviedo, where it remained closed for a long time, forgotten and hidden in the cathedral. To justify this long stay of the ark without anyone opening it, the document explains that once, at the time of the episcopate of Ponce de Tabérnoles (ca. 1025–1035), there was an attempt to look within it, but when that took place the ark sent out a blinding light causing all to desist from any further attempts. This time Alfonso and his court, however, after engaging in a period of hard fasting and prayer, were able to complete the business without damage. Later the document goes on to record the presence of about

[146] I have expounded upon the content of this section in greater depth in A. Nicolotti, "El Sudario de Oviedo: Historia antigua y moderna," *Territorio, sociedad y poder* 11 (2016): 89–111.

[147] Cf. M. S. Beltrán Suárez, "Los orígenes y la expansión del culto a las reliquias de San Salvador de Oviedo," in *Las peregrinaciones in Santiago de Compostela y San Salvador de Oviedo en la Edad Media*, ed. J. I. Ruiz de la Peña Solar (Oviedo: Principado de Asturias, 1993), 37–55.

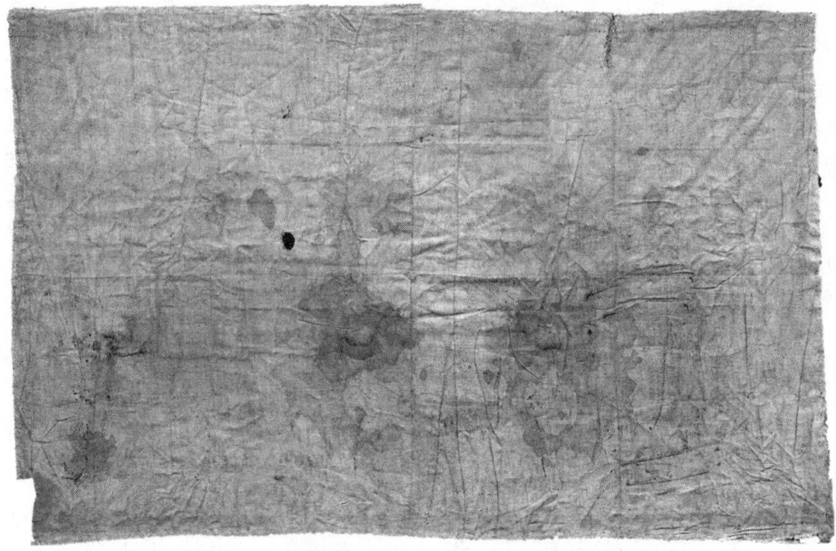

FIGURE 1.1. The Sudarium of Oviedo

thirty relics that were found inside the ark. Among these was a fragment of the wood of the cross, some of the blood of Christ, a portion of the bread of the Last Supper, a fragment of the tomb, another of the holy land that Christ walked upon, a piece of the clothing and some of the milk of the Madonna, and a piece "of the clothing of the Lord that was divided by lot, and of his sudarium."[148]

This document is problematic because it is preserved not in its original manuscript form but only in two copies of the thirteenth century. Several elements have cast doubt on its complete authenticity.[149] Yet, be that as it may, there are also other sources to testify that

[148] "De vestimento Domini sorte partito et de sudario eius." Image of the parchment, with transcription and translation, can be found in M. J. Sanz Fuentes and M. Calleja Puerta, *Litteris confirmentur* (Oviedo: Cajastur, 2005), 261–70. Many texts useful for our discussion have been transcribed in F. J. Fernández Conde and R. Alonso Álvarez, "Los catálogos de las Reliquias de la Catedral de Oviedo," *Territorio, Sociedad y Poder* 12 (2017): 55–81.

[149] Historians "are agreed in considering the account of the certificates corresponding to the opening of the ark to have been completely falsified in the scriptorium of Oviedo": R. Alonso Álvarez, "El obispo Arias y la apertura del Arca Santa de Oviedo," *Mediaevalia* 17 (2014): 92.

toward the end of the eleventh century, news of the existence of relics transferred to Oviedo circulated in Spain. An example is a letter sent by Osmundo de Astorga to Ida of Boulogne between 1082 and 1096; that letter indicates, for the first time, that relics arrived from Jerusalem.[150] Most likely the ark, which had never been mentioned earlier, was kept in the treasury of the cathedral that is today known as the *Cámara Santa*, before 1102, when Bishop Pelagius placed a relic of Saint Eulalia inside it.[151] From scrutiny of an inscription on the precious silver covering of the ark, which was donated by King Alfonso VI, one can date the ark itself to be around 1075.[152] The same inscription mentions some relics contained inside, among which are a piece "of the clothing [of Christ] that was divided by lot" and part "of the sudarium."[153]

[150] B. de Gaiffier, "Sainte Ide de Boulogne et l'Espagne," *Analecta Bollandiana* 86 (1968): 71–72.

[151] In an interpolation of that same Pelagius in *Chronica Alfonsi III*: "Deinde capsellam istam in aliam capsam maiorem argenteam que ibi dederat rex dominus Adefonsus, filius Fredenandi regis et Sancie regine, et posuit eam in thesauro"; in J. Prelog, ed., *Die Chronik Alfons' III* (Frankfurt am Main: Lang, 1980), 90.

[152] According to J. Harris, "Redating the Arca Santa of Oviedo," *Art Bulletin* 77 (1995): 82–93, the ark would have been built no earlier than 1120; this possibility is denied, however, by R. Alonso Álvarez, "Patria uallata asperitate moncium: Pelayo de Oviedo, el arca de las reliquias y la creación de una topografía regia," *Locus amoenus* 9 (2007–2008): 21–22. I. G. Bango Torviso, "La renovación del tesoro sagrado a partir del concilio de Coyanza," *Anales de historia del arte* 21, no. 2 (2011): 11–67, posits the year engraved on the ark to be 1072; its transcription is, however, uncertain because the silver is damaged. The terminus ante quem seems to be 1077, because Alfonso is called *princeps* and not yet *rex* or *imperator*; R. Walker, "Becoming Alfonso VI: The King, His Sister and the Arca Santa Reliquary," *Anales de historia del arte* 21, no. 2 (2011): 391–412, accepts this dating. A general description of the ark can be found in E. Fernández González, "El Arca Santa de Oviedo y sus precedentes," in *Alfonso VI y su legado*, ed. C. Estepa Díez et al. (León: Instituto Leonés de Cultura, 2012), 311–43. In 1934 the ark suffered serious damage due to a bomb attack that destroyed the whole chapel: cf. M. P. García Cuetos, "Cámara Santa de la catedral de Oviedo: De la destrucción a la reconstrucción," *Restauración & rehabilitación* 53 (2001): 54–60.

[153] "De vestimento illius quod per sortem divisum est . . . atque sudario." Transcription of Manuel Gómez-Moreno, in J. Manzanares Rodríguez, *Las joyas de la Cámara Santa* (Oviedo: Tabularium Artis Asturiensis, 1972), 21; see also the transcription of D. Rico Camps, "La inscripción histórica del Arca Santa de Oviedo," *Territorio, Sociedad y Poder* 12 (2017): 52–53. Some old transcriptions, which are erroneous, reported also "de sindone dominico"; in reality "de sepulcro dominico" was written in the text.

The person most responsible for the creation of the legend was in fact Pelagius, who in 1101 became bishop of Oviedo and incorporated into his writings a good deal of information about the provenance of these relics. Pelagius was the author of a *Liber testamentorum ecclesiae Ovetensis*, a cartulary—that is, a compedium of church records that he composed at different times between 1109 and 1130 and preserved in an original richly illuminated manuscript. This volume comprises several documents, many of them spurious or heavily interpolated—a situation not uncommon in such cartularies—that are chiefly concerned with presumed donations or privileges granted to the cathedral or diocese of Oviedo, along with other pages of a more general, historical-antiquarian nature. Pelagius was also the author of other collected writings (*Corpus Pelagianum*), which included a *Liber chronicum*, consisting of a collection of preexisting chronicles that the bishop had reworked and manipulated in a consistently heavy-handed fashion, as has already been explained. The corpus also included a *Chronicon regum Legionensium*, written entirely by Pelagius.[154]

Because of the numerous falsifications that he effected, Pelagius came to be dubbed "El fabulero," "the story teller," who was in fact known for "his lack of rigor and his ability to tell a story beyond the limits of good sense, especially when it involves exalting the grandiosity of his own episcopal seat."[155] That same author put his hand to a powerful ideological work that would provide historical and

[154] On the works and intentions of Pelagius, cf. F. J. Fernández Conde, "La obra del obispo ovetense D. Pelayo en la historiografía española," *Boletín del Real Instituto de Estudios Asturianos* 25, no. 73 (1971): 249–91; idem, *El Libro de los Testamentos de la catedral de Oviedo* (Rome: Pontificia Università Gregoriana, 1971), 50–69; R. Alonso Álvarez, "El obispo Pelayo de Oviedo (1101–1153): Historiador y promotor de códices iluminados," *Semata* 22 (2010): 331–50; idem, "El Corpus Pelagianum y el Liber testamentorum ecclesiae Ouetensis: Las 'reliquias del pasado' de la catedral de Oviedo y su uso propagandístico en la obra del obispo Pelayo de Oviedo," in *Texte et contexte: Littérature et histoire de l'Europe médiévale*, ed. M. F. Alamichel (Paris: Houdiard, 2011), 519–48; idem, "La obra histórica del obispo Pelayo de Oviedo y su relación con la Historia legionensis (llamada silensis)," *e-Spania* 14 (2012), https://journals.openedition.org/e-spania/21586; in relation to the relics, idem, "Patria uallata asperitate moncium," 17–29.

[155] F. J. Fernández Conde, "Las reliquias y el Sudario de la Cámara Santa de Oviedo," in *Castilla y el mundo feudal*, ed. M. I. del Val Valdivieso and P. Martínez Sopena, vol. 3 (Valladolid: Junta de Castilla y León, 2009), 560.

propagandistic legitimacy to the supremacy of the bishop's seat of Oviedo, whose religious and political importance was waning and whose independence was then threatened by the nearby dioceses of Braga and Toledo. Propaganda about relics, moreover, was intended to make the cathedral of Oviedo an important stop on the route of pilgrims.

The story told by Pelagius in the *Liber testamentorum* goes something like this: while Sisebut reigned over the Visigoths (612–621), an ark full of relics, manufactured by some of the "disciples of the apostles," left Jerusalem after the devastation wrought by Khosrow II of Persia. This ark was then transported to Africa by a certain priest named Philip, presbyter of Jerusalem and companion of Jerome (an impossibility, as Jerome had lived two centuries earlier). After the subsequent conquest of the region, the ark had to be transported to Toledo by Fulgentius of Ruspe, which is impossible, as Fulgentius died in 532.[156] The ark remained in Toledo at the period in which the bishop Ildefonsus ruled (657–667) until the end of the kingdom of Roderic, the last king of the Visigoths (710–712), who fell during the Muslim invasion. Accordingly, Bishop Julian took the box to Asturias in northern Spain (which is also impossible, as Julian died well before the reign of Roderic).[157] The ark was kept for a while in a tent, as was the case with the biblical ark of the covenant in its tabernacle. Alfonso II († 842), who made Oviedo the capital of his kingdom in the manner of a Solomonic king, had several churches built there, among which was the Church of the Savior and its annexed Chapel of St. Michael, known as the *Cámara Santa*, where he arranged for the ark to be kept.[158] The story ends with the long list of relics contained

[156] In fact, to save the credibility of the story, one must replace Fulgentius of Ruspe with Fulgentius of Écija, brother of Isidore of Seville.

[157] To correct the error, the historian Rodrigo Jiménez de Rada actually exchanged the name of Julian for that of Urban, who was a bishop of Toledo at that time (*De rebus Hispaniae* 4.3: "Ab aliquibus dicitur quod a Iuliano pontifice Toletano et Pelagio principe reliquiarum arca et sanctorum scripta ab ecclesia Toletana in Asturias sunt translata, stare non potest").

[158] The *Cámara Santa* consisted of an upper floor where the relics were kept (St. Michael's Chapel) and a lower crypt (that of St. Leocadia). As there is no previous documentary evidence, most historians believe that the chapel was built only after the death of Alfonso II (e.g., F. de Caso et al., *La Catedral de Oviedo*, vol. 1, *Historia y restauración* [Oviedo: Nobel, 1999], 56); E. López Fernández, "Las Reliquias y la Cámara Santa de la Catedral de Oviedo en las Fórmulas de donación desde el siglo

in the ark, a prestigious assortment of objects: among these was a small amount of the blood of Christ, a piece of the cross, a bit of the tomb, a piece of the crown of thorns, a portion of Jesus' tunic, a piece of Jesus' swaddling cloths, and portions of the bread of the Last Supper and of the miracle of the multiplication of the loaves, together with a part "of the shroud of the Lord"; further on in the document, too, a part "of the sudarium of the Lord" is mentioned.[159]

Leaving aside the improbability of all of this, differences immediately arise between this story and that of the document of 1075; among other things, in the earliest source, it is said that the relics at Toledo were taken from surrounding regions and placed "into a certain ark" (*in quadam archa*), though there is no mention of its provenance from Jerusalem or of the origin of the ark in apostolic times. Pelagius tells the story of the relics also in that part of the *Corpus Pelagianum* that treats the *Adelfonsii Tertii Chronica* (a work of the tenth century). The text is largely identical to that of the *Liber testamentorum*, but with some changes. The priest Philip is no longer called Jerome's companion, and it is also reported that the ark was escorted by other denizens of Jerusalem as it was transported through the Mediterranean. Moreover, it is said that Fulgentius transported the ark from Africa not to Toledo but to Cartagena and that only many years later did the relics arrive in Toledo. Their arrival in Asturias is associated no longer with Julian alone but also with Pelagius, king of Asturias and paladin of anti-Islamic response (as a consequence, the ark assumes the role of protector of Spain). There is reference to it being kept in a tent before entering Oviedo; mention is also made

---

IX al siglo XIII y en otros testimonios de la época," *Studium Ovetense* 31 (2003): 157–214, places the construction a few decades earlier. On the *Cámara* in general, see L. Arias Páramo, *La Cámara Santa de la catedral de Oviedo* (Gijón: Trea, 1998). For the other relics preserved there, cf. M. P. García Cuetos, "Los Reyes de Asturias: La Cámara Santa de la catedral de Oviedo," in *Maravillas de la España medieval*, ed. I. G. Bango Torviso, vol. 1 (Valladolid: Junta de Castilla y León, 2001), 205–14.

159 M. J. Sanz Fuentes, ed., *Liber testamentorum Ecclesiae Oventesis* (Barcelona: Moleiro Editor, 1995), 456–61 ("de sindone Domini" and "de sudario Domini"). The part that interests us is reproduced and examined by P. Henriet, "Oviedo, Jérusalem hispanique au XIIIe siècle," in *Pèlerinages et lieux saints dans l'Antiquité et le Moyen Âge*, ed. B. Caseau et al. (Paris: Association des Amis du Center d'Histoire et Civilization de Byzance, 2006), 235–48.

of it having been kept in caves. It is interesting to note that here the sudarium is missing from the list of relics.[160]

Brief information about the wandering of the ark can also be found in the *Historia Silense*, written around 1115 near León or Sahagún: there it is said that from Jerusalem the ark came directly to Seville on one ship, then stayed in Toledo for a hundred years, until it was put to sea again and came to a port of Asturias near Gijón; finally it arrived at Oviedo at the behest of King Alfonso II, without any bishop being mentioned.[161] It should be noted here that locating documents of the period that connect Alfonso II with the ark turns out to be an undertaking that is "little less than impossible."[162]

A short account called "of Valenciennes," of the first third of the twelfth century and written for the use of pilgrims, describes these stages for the journey of the ark: Africa, Cartagena, Toledo, and finally Oviedo.[163] A later revision (the report of "Osma," dated to the first half of the thirteenth century) adds Seville before Toledo.[164] Lucas de Tuy (between 1232 and 1239) instead tells that the ark, after having remained in Toledo for seventy-five years (i.e., from 636), was transferred to Asturias in the same year in which the Arabs invaded Spain (711); then, in 828, it was brought to Oviedo by Pelagius, king of Asturias.[165] Variant traditions reveal that the legend was still far from having assumed a definite shape.

Three other manuscripts from the twelfth to thirteenth centuries reveal an even more complex revision of the legend:[166] it is said

160 Cf. Prelog, *Die Chronik Alfons' III*, 76–92. See also the edition of M. Guscin, *La historia del Sudario de Oviedo* (Oviedo: Ayuntamento de Oviedo, 2006), 202–8.

161 See J. Pérez de Urbel, ed., *Historia Silense* (Madrid: Escuela de Estudios Medievales, 1959), 63–64 and 138–39.

162 M. Calleja Puerta, "Las reliquias de Oviedo en los siglos VIII-IX," in *Ciclo de Conferencias Jubileo 2000*, ed. idem et al. (Oviedo: Real Instituto de Estudios Asturianos, 2004), 135.

163 D. de Bruyne, "Le plus ancien catalogue de reliques d'Oviedo," *Analecta bollandiana* 45 (1927): 93–96 (Valenciennes, Bibliothèque Municipale, MS 99).

164 Cf. M. Calleja Puerta, "La traslación del Arca Santa a la catedral de Oviedo según el manuscrito número 8 de la catedral de Burgo de Osma," *Memoria Ecclesiae* 36 (2011): 213–21.

165 Lucas Tudensis, *Chronicon mundi* 4.14, ed. E. Falque (Turnhout: Brepols, 2003).

166 See C. Kohler, "Translation de reliques de Jérusalem à Oviedo," *Revue de l'Orient Latin* 5 (1897): 6–12; A. Rucquoi, "Un milagro de Santiago en Oviedo (Ms. Cambrai 804)," *Compostellanum* 58 (2013): 393–415; one should also consult Guscin, *Historia del Sudario de Oviedo*, 211–25.

that the holy ark, having been constructed in Jerusalem, had been entrusted to the waves of the sea at the port of Jaffa, without a boat to carry it. Pursued by two holy men, Julian and Seranus (this is the same story that is told about the relics of James, which would have been followed by Athanasius and Theodorus), the ark was divinely guided, stopping in African Carthage, not Spanish Cartagena. To avoid it falling into enemy hands, it was then taken to Toledo at the time of Ildefonsus, bishop of Toledo, even though Carthage remained free throughout Ildefonsus' episcopate; to protect it from the invasion, it was moved to the top of the mountain called Monsacro, where it remained for forty-five years. Monsacro is a mountain near Oviedo that from prehistoric times was considered a sacred place and was later Christianized; it is possible that when Pelagius spoke of "caves" he thought of those of Monsacro. Here King Alfonso II sent other relics of saints from all over Spain, and he added them to those of Julian and Seranus and to the other collections during the movement of the ark. Ultimately, the ark came to give a certain luster to the city of Oviedo, which had itself recently been embellished with new and impressive buildings. For the occasion of its return to Oviedo, the box was inserted within a larger and more precious ark, though the legs of the older box were allowed to protrude from the new one. Finally, it was placed in the Chapel of St. Michael.

This story is interspersed with and enriched by miraculous episodes and devotionals, including the account of an exorcism, all of which are absent from previous versions. It also contains the story of the opening of the ark by Alfonso VI and Abbot Álvaro, who lost his sight after doing so,[167] and of the discovery of twelve boxes of relics therein. In the list of relics, however, again no sepulchral cloth appears, an absence not surprising at that time because, unlike today, funerary relics made of cloth were not then given the particular sort of preeminence that other objects in the ark were granted.

The legend of Oviedo's ark, by then already rather confusing and contradictory, came to be blended with another, borne of the aforementioned story of Osmundo de Astorga in the eleventh century, which spoke of a maritime expedition by seven Christians to acquire

[167] On this Álvaro, cf. M. Calleja Puerta, "La Catedral de Oviedo como centro de conservación de documentos en la alta Edad Media," *Estudos em homenagem ao professor doutor José Marques*, vol. 4 (Porto: Universidade do Porto, 2006), 188–91.

relics from Jerusalem. That story mentions relics that had been divided between Astorga and Oviedo.[168] The seven characters, taken from still another legend, were none other than the seven *viri apostolici* sent by Saint Peter and Saint Paul to evangelize Spain. Osmundo's story was attested for the first time in the sixteenth century: Saint Turibius, bishop of Astorga (beginning of the fifth century), is said to have been responsible for the transfer of relics (though there is no mention of an ark) from Jerusalem to a place between Galicia and Asturias, and for the placement of part of them in a chapel near Monsacro known as Santa María de Monsacro.[169] We speak no longer of the summit of the mountain but only of a chapel, no trace of which, however, remains.[170]

Leaving the mixture of legends to return to the relics, it is notable that Pelagius and the accounts of Valenciennes and Osma speak not only of a relic "of the sudarium" but also "of the shroud." In fact, in the cathedral of Oviedo is preserved not only the relic of the Sudarium but also part of a shroud that consists of a piece of cloth encased in a silver frame, which measures about 25 square cm and is free of stains and impressions. The Sudarium is presented as being intact, or almost intact, even though the texts speak of a relic "from the sudarium" (*de sudario*), suggesting a section taken from it.[171] Finally, it should be noted that during the restoration of the ark in the modern era, remains of an older ark were not discovered inside the medieval one, let alone one dating back to the first or second centuries.

The Sudarium was only one of many relics in the ark and was considered less important than others; it was in fact ignored for about four hundred years, between the twelfth and the sixteenth centuries,

[168] Cf. de Gaiffier, "Sainte Ide de Boulogne," 71–72; F. J. Fernández Conde, *La Iglesia de Asturias en la Alta Edad Media* (Oviedo: Instituto de Estudios Asturianos, 1972), 164–65.

[169] See A. Molinier and C. Kohler, *Itinera Hierosolymitana et descriptiones Terrae Sanctae*, vol. 2 (Geneva: Fick, 1885), 119.

[170] Further on Monsacro and its relation to the relics, cf. F. J. Fernández Conde and M. C. Santos del Valle, "Toponimia y tradiciones del Monsacro," *Lletres asturianes* 23 (1987): 99–112; M. P. García Cuetos, "El culto a las reliquias en Asturias: La Cámara Santa y el Monsacro," in *Religion and Belief in Medieval Europe*, ed. G. de Boe and F. Verhaege (Zellik: Institut voor het Archeologisch Patrimonium, 1997), 241–54.

[171] See D. Leone, *El Santo Sudario en España* (Barcelona: Borrás, 1959), 164. It is displayed a few meters from the Sudarium.

in all documents referring to the relics of Oviedo: the inventories of 1305 and 1385 are silent about it, as are the deed of the founding of the Confraternity of the *Cámara Santa* (1344), the privileges of 1465, the bull of Martin V of 1421, the books of the chapter, and especially the *buletas*—that is, the notices marked out for the pilgrims that contained a list of the relics preserved in the city. Only starting in the middle of the sixteenth century does the Sudarium reappear, first in the chapter registers, then also in the *buletas*.[172]

Despite these confusing origins, the relics contained in the ark—and for a certain period the Sudarium itself—were the object of lay veneration, even if it has been discontinued.[173] Oviedo was in those days a station on the pilgrim's journey to Santiago de Compostela; in modern times, however, interest in these relics, in part because of doubts about their authenticity, waned. Yet the situation radically changed in 1966 when the Roman sindonologist Msgr. Giulio Ricci drew attention to the Sudarium (ignoring all the other relics of the ark and even the piece of shroud, since it is not made of the same material as that of Turin and therefore, according to him, could not be authentic). In his opinion, the colored spots present on the Sudarium, which are almost symmetrical, perfectly matched the bloodstains appearing on the front of the man's face on the Shroud of Turin. He thus deduced that the Sudarium, after having been folded in two, had been placed on top of the Shroud that in the tomb enveloped the face of Christ and was tied to the neck with a band, without, however, surrounding the whole head.[174]

The explanation is farfetched, because the contact between the blood and the piece of cloth, especially if between the blood and the fabric there are other layers of fabric, cannot precisely reproduce the spots beneath with "perfect correspondence in measurements";

[172] Cf. E. López Fernández, *Historia de un silencio: El Santo Sudario de Oviedo a través de los siglos* (Granda: Madú, 2009), 58–155.

[173] These were also the object of periodic inspections: cf. E. López Fernández, "Las reliquias de San Salvador de Oviedo en los libros de acuerdos del cabildo," *Studium Ovetense* 37 (2009): 99–132.

[174] G. Ricci, *L'uomo della Sindone è Gesù*, 2nd ed. (Rome: Studium, 1969), 161–66; see also, for a summary, Ricci, *Holy Shroud*, 137–43. The history of the "sindonological" rediscovery of the Sudarium up to 2008 is narrated by E. López Fernández, *El Santo Sudario de Oviedo* (Granda: Madú, 2004), 87–110; idem, *Historia de un silencio*, 234–58.

furthermore, on the corresponding area of the Shroud the stains are not the same, and their proximity should have given them even greater intensity, which is not the case. In addition, as has already been noted, the design of the stains posited by Ricci in 1966 "is a simple and capricious arabesque pattern, lacking any correspondence to the spots on the Sudarium."[175] Later Ricci completely changed his interpretation, advancing the notion that the Sudarium was placed directly on the face of Christ, not in the tomb but instead only during the short time of the transport of the corpse from the cross to the grave; and at the same time he expanded his guesswork as to the points of contact between the fabric and the face.[176]

From the moment Ricci proposed his hypothesis, certain sindonologists commenced a series of studies employing the same methodology used for the Shroud of Turin (we will consider those methods later) in order to demonstrate the authenticity of the discovery. In 1977 Ricci obtained permission to excise some threads and small pieces of fabric, some of which he sent to Max Frei-Sulzer for a palynological examination (looking for pollen characteristic of Jerusalem); two years later, using adhesive tape, Frei-Sulzer himself proceeded to make further superficial withdrawals. In 1985 Pierluigi Baima Bollone began his series of studies. He was allowed to extract samples using adhesive tape and to take new photographs. He also removed seven threads for examination under a microscope.[177] The Centro Español de Sindonología, founded in 1987, then took charge of the research on the Sudarium.[178] In 1994 this institute coordinated the first international congress on research on the Sudarium, organized on the model of previous sindonological congresses.[179] The explanation of

[175] J. M. Fernández Pajares, "El Santo Sudario de Oviedo y su pretendida relación con la Sábana Santa de Turín," *Boletín del Instituto de Estudios Asturianos* 66 (1969): 3–25 (cited from p. 23). The author, nevertheless, considers the Sudarium to be authentic.

[176] G. Ricci, *La Sindone contestata difesa spiegata* (Rome: Collana Emmaus, 1992), 257–74.

[177] Cf. Baima Bollone, *Sepoltura del Messia*, 168–206.

[178] First results appeared in G. Heras Moreno, J. D. Villalaín Blanco, and J. Izquierdo Gómez, "El Sudario de Oviedo y la Síndone de Turín," in *La datazione della Sindone*, ed. T. Ladu, 2nd ed. (Cagliari: n.p., 1991), 443–90.

[179] J. M. Rodríguez Almenar and J. Chirivella Garrido, eds., *El sudario del Señor: Actas del I Congreso Internacional sobre el Sudario de Oviedo* (Oviedo: Cabildo de la Catedral de Oviedo, 1996). More informative are J. Briansó Augé, *El Santo*

how the stains were formed was then further changed: the Sudarium was then suggested to be the fabric that was on Jesus' head while he hung on the cross and remained in place for the journey from Golgotha to the tomb. It was then replaced by the Shroud and was left "wrapped in a place by itself" as the Gospel of John recounts (20:7).

The pseudoscientific method used for explaining the origin of the stains is, in any case, interesting. It takes its initial assumptions as true instead of demonstrating them; that is, it assumes that the Sudarium was wrapped around the head of the crucified corpse. Spanish scholars have gone so far as to conjecture the position of the head on the cross at the time of death (bent forward by 70°, and 20° toward the right, with reference to the verticality) and the position of the fabric on the head, which was wrapped in an unusual way, because the Sudarium would have been folded over upon itself (as the symmetry of the spots requires). Ultimately the Sudarium would have been knotted above the head and affixed with pins or stitches. Those same scholars suggest, moreover, that while the corpse was in a vertical position on the cross, its right arm was raised, and that later the crucified man was placed facedown upon his right side for roughly forty-five minutes with his forehead resting upon a hard surface. Then the corpse was transported to the tomb: the shape of the stains would mean that someone on this occasion had placed his left hand on the fabric over the nose of the corpse of Christ, trying to stop the flow of blood and other fluid through the nose and mouth, strongly pressing upon those orifices; even the position of the fingers of this hand is described through the analysis of presumed fingerprints. Finally, before the body was wrapped in a shroud (that of Turin) the Sudarium would have been separated from the body and placed in contact with aloe and myrrh.

According to sindonologists, there are four principal stains, presumed to be from blood and fluid, identified on the Sudarium. One was allegedly formed at the time of the deposition from the cross, and the other three as a consequence of the movements undergone by the corpse afterward. Other stains would have formed differently—for example, following contact with blood in the hair or with other

---

Sudario de la Catedral de Oviedo (Llanera: Ayuntamiento de Oviedo, 1997); and J. M. Rodríguez Almenar, *El Sudario de Oviedo* (Pamplona: Ediciones Universidad de Navarra, 2000); in English, along the same lines, M. Guscin, *The Oviedo Cloth* (Cambridge: Lutterworth, 1998); and J. Bennett, *Sacred Blood, Sacred Image: The Sudarium of Oviedo* (Littleton: Libri de Hispania, 2001).

wounds. The sindonologists of Oviedo have sought to demonstrate this thesis by manufacturing some anthropomorphic experimental mannequins. One is in the form of a tilting head furnished with a system of pipes that allow the exit of liquids from the nose. The sindonologists have thus been able to carry out experiments that recreated spots on test shrouds similar to those found on the relic. Such an outcome is, of course, not surprising, because when one knows the result at which one wants to arrive, it is a simple matter to find a method to produce it; the possibility that the marks did not come from the body of a crucified man, in fact, is not even taken into consideration. A geometric comparison between the smudged spots and the imprint of the Shroud would eventually lead to the belief that both fabrics had touched the same face, that of Jesus of Nazareth (given the presumed authenticity of both relics, of course). Three medical sindonologists[180] established that on some threads taken from the Sudarium there was human blood belonging to the AB group, traces of DNA, and even some traces of lipstick presumed to belong to the wife of the dictator Francisco Franco.

In April of 2007 the second international congress on the Holy Sudarium took place, under the aegis of the Centro Español de Sindonología.[181] At this meeting, Enrique López Fernández, canon of Oviedo, historian, biblicist, and author of several historical studies on the cathedral of Oviedo and its treasure, caused quite a stir simply by reminding the assembly of the documented absence of any reference to the Sudarium before the late Middle Ages. He expounded upon the impossibility of attributing historical value to the contradictory stories about the provenance of the ark from Jerusalem, and the lack of documentation on the existence and veneration of the Sudarium for four centuries (the twelfth through the sixteenth). This presentation served only to produce a strong reaction on the part of those present, who were intent on supporting the contrary view.[182] A group of researchers of the Instituto Nacional de Toxicología y

[180] Pierluigi Baima Bollone, José Delfín Villalaín Blanco, and Carlo Goldoni.

[181] J. M. Rodríguez Almenar and I. Villar Revilla, eds., *Oviedo relicario de la cristiandad: Actas del II Congreso Internacional sobre el Santo Sudario* (Oviedo: n.p., 2009).

[182] The same story is told from one point of view (e.g., López Fernández, *Historia de un silencio*, 249–50; López Fernández confirmed it with greater detail in personal conversations with me) or from a conflicting point of view (so M. Guscin, "The

Ciencias Forenses conducted tests that yielded unexpected results: the alleged bloodstains did not reveal the presence of either blood or DNA, contrary to what had been claimed before.[183]

The only conclusive exam performed on the material, by scientists who are not sindonologists, was C14 dating. Between 1990 and 1992 three independent datings of three different fragments of the Sudarium were made in C14 laboratories in Tucson and Toronto: all three fragments were dated between the sixth and ninth centuries AD, with the highest probability being in the eighth century.[184] In 2007 a new carbon dating examination provided the same results.[185] But as in the case of the Shroud of Turin, those who support the authenticity of the Sudarium simply ignore this evidence, insisting on the other "studies" that—as an expert on the matter has stated well—"do not purport to do anything other than to confirm what is already certain from the opening hypothesis."[186] Yet the reasons adopted for rejecting the results of the C14 analysis are impressive for their inconclusiveness.[187]

Second International Conference on the Sudarium of Oviedo," *British Society for the Turin Shroud Newsletter* 65 [2007]: 37).

183 A. Alonso et al., "El ADN del Sudario de Oviedo," in Rodríguez Almenar and Villar Revilla, *Oviedo relicario de la cristiandad*, 167–73.

184 Cf. M. Moroni, "La radiodatazione del Sudario di Oviedo," *Collegamento pro Sindone* (March–April 1999): 29–36. The author, however, is a sindonologist and consequently does not regard the results as reliable. It should be added that in October 1977 part of the fabric taken from Giulio Ricci had been transported to the United States to the chemist and microscopist Walter McCrone (whose work will be discussed below); the material was to have undergone the radiocarbon test at the Lawrence Berkeley Laboratory in California. It remained in Berkeley until 1984, where it was available to McCrone and physicist Richard Muller. Later, because Berkeley was not technologically equipped to develop the accelerator that would be used for dating and on which, in those years, Muller was working, the material, already transformed by Muller into CO2 in the gaseous state, was closed within two ampoules and was sent to the laboratory in Tucson, Arizona. But the laboratory found that the ampoules had not been hermetically sealed, and thus the samples turned out to be useless. The episode is recounted by Paul Damon in a letter reproduced by Guscin, *Oviedo Cloth*, 77–78. The description of the facts provided by Guscin in this book is incorrect, however, as he was not aware of the first dating attempt at the time of the C14 test and confused it with the subsequent dating attempt. See H. D. Sox, *File on the Shroud* (Sevenoaks: Coronet, 1978), 122–25; also R. Falcinelli, "Análisis sobre la tela de protección del Sudario de Oviedo," in Rodríguez Almenar and Villar Revilla, *Oviedo relicario de la cristiandad*, 639–40.

185 F. Montero Ortego, "Otros estudios de carácter químico y biológico," in Rodríguez Almenar and Villar Revilla, *Oviedo relicario de la cristiandad*, 159–66.

186 Fernández Conde, *Reliquias y el Sudario*, 564.

187 See C. Barta Gil, "Datación radiocarbónica del Sudario de Oviedo," in Rodríguez Almenar and Villar Revilla, *Oviedo relicario de la cristiandad*, 137–55. The author,

Those who deal with the Sudarium's history make no effort to analyze critically; they simply accept as true the legendary report of the apostolic origin of the relics and their journey to Oviedo. They neglect every difficulty and mask every contradiction, attributing value to the falsifications invented by Pelagius. They thus transform the Sudarium "into the protagonist of a novel whom we could qualify as curious, willing to sin in a benevolent fashion."[188] The usual procedure in these cases is that, when a legendary report coincides with the thesis that one wants to demonstrate, one accepts it; when a report opposes the thesis, it is discarded, accused of being mere fantasy. Thus, even radiocarbon dating is considered erroneous because it contrasts with legendary medieval tales, which are treated as if they were credible and sufficient to demonstrate the Jerusalemite and subapostolic origin of the ark.[189] It is not by chance that the authenticators of the Sudarium are the same people who deal with the Shroud of Turin: later in this book, all their "scientific" procedures will be seen to be of exactly equal value.

---

however, a sindonologist, believes that the results of the four dates are unacceptable because they stand in contrast to the evidence of the Sudarium: in fact, it would have been wrapped about the head of a crucified man (which has not been demonstrated) and must necessarily be ancient, since the punishment of crucifixion was no longer used after the Constantinian era (which is false: see M. G. Castello, *Questioni tardoantiche: Storia e mito della svolta costantiniana* [Rome: Aracne, 2010], 151–263). Furthermore, the presence of wrinkles in the Sudarium is said to be an indication of the fact that it was tied to the head of the crucified man (which has not been demonstrated); and as early as the fifth century, Nonnus of Panopolis wrote that the sudarium of Jesus had been knotted to the hair, which is said to "prove" that Nonnus knew the Sudarium of Oviedo (which is pure fantasy). Previously someone had tried to attribute the alleged C14 "rejuvenation" of the Sudarium to the effects of the bomb explosion that in 1934 destroyed the *Cámara Santa*; a similar such excuse was used to devalue the C14 dating of the Shroud. But the dating of one of the protective fabrics of the Sudarium, which dates to the sixteenth century and in 1934 was in contact with the relic, turned out to be perfectly accurate.

[188] Fernández Conde, *Reliquias y el Sudario*, 551.

[189] This is what Guscin, for example, does in his *Historia del Sudario de Oviedo*. He also draws on documents prior to those mentioned above, such as Canon V of the Council of Braga of 675, in which an order is issued that during processions the relics are not to be worn around the bishop's neck, but carried by deacons inside an ark; I do not see how one can think that such a general provision, addressed to all bishops, is an allusion to the ark of Oviedo (cf. p. 175).

TWO

The Shroud of Lirey-Chambéry-Turin

2.1. Origins

2.1.1 A Long Sheet of Cloth

Let us now consider the history of the Shroud that is today preserved in Turin. Though it is not the first chronologically, its fame has overshadowed all others. The Shroud is a linen sheet now measuring 4.42 × 1.13 m. It is composed of two pieces of cloth joined by a seam on their longer sides. On the larger piece, measuring 1.05 m in width, there is a double monochromatic image that shows the front and back of a man, aligned so that the heads of the images meet at the center of the cloth. The image of the man bears marks from flagellation and crucifixion, with various red spots corresponding to blows. The other piece is a thin strip only 8 cm wide and 3.88 m in length. This second piece (a sidestrip) is not as long as the first and is aligned in such a way that it does not extend all the way to either end, being 38 cm short on one end and 16 cm short on the other. The measurements down to the millimeter are approximate since the tension in the fabric is variable.[1]

The finished edges of the two long sides, technically known as selvages, are visible, but on the short sides, there are no discernible initial or final bands to indicate the beginning or end of the fabric. Such an arrangement reveals that originally the fabric was a little longer and, therefore, that it was shortened at the two ends, or, more likely, that it was part of a fabric that was much longer (and perhaps

[1] Measurements in M. Flury-Lemberg, *Sindone 2002: Preservation* (Turin: ODPF, 2003), 121.

also wider). In that case, the linen would not have been made especially to be a shroud but would have been sold as part of a large fabric that was priced according to length; what is now the Shroud would have been cut (from a roll?) to obtain the desired length. Although the Shroud is often described as a "sheet," its length, which exceeds 4 m, is not comparable to a sheet meant for a bed. Some have hypothesized that the fabric was originally woven in the medieval period to serve as an altar cloth;[2] the suggestion is possible, but there is no evidence beyond the hint provided by the Latin word *sindon*, which was sometimes used to denote the outer cloth over an altar.[3] The same homonym must be considered very carefully when one looks for occurrences of the Shroud in the liturgy.[4]

A gap in the fabric at one of the corners on the side where the smaller band was attached is due to a cut made in 1973 to provide a sample for textile expert Gilbert Raes (from whom comes the name "Raes' corner"). This gap was further enlarged in 1988 to acquire a portion of the fabric for radiocarbon testing.

[2] Cf. Papini, *Sindone: Una sfida*, 19.

[3] For the ninth century, see Amalarius, *De ecclesiasticis officiis* 3.19: "Sindone, quam solemus corporale nominare" (at that time the corporal was of considerable size, like a tablecloth). Beginning in the seventh century the corporal was likened to Jesus' shroud: for an example, see J. Quasten, ed., *Expositio antiquae liturgiae Gallicanae* (Monasterii: Aschendorff, 1934), 19–20: "Corporalis vero palla ideo pura linia est super quam oblatio ponitur, quia corpus Domini puris linteaminibus cum aromatibus fuit obvolutum in tumulo."

[4] Cf. P. Tomatis, "La Sindone nella liturgia," in *La Passione di Gesù e la Sindone*, ed. N. Ciola and G. Ghiberti (Vatican City: Lateran University Press, 2014), 61–62, who claims that "well before the extraordinary and most unusual sheet of the Shroud appeared in France in the mid-fourteenth century, a presence of the Shroud is attested in the liturgy." In support he cites the *oratio super sindonem* typical of the Ambrosian and Gallican liturgies—so-called because it was recited at the point when the fabric specifically called a *sindon* was spread over the altar—and two fabrics typical of the Byzantine liturgy, the *antimension* and the *epitaphion*. The proposition is true, but only, however, on a symbolic level; in fact, it was completely traditional that some objects and liturgical acts were ideally associated with something else. For example, in the Byzantine rite, the knife used to cut the bread of the Eucharist represented the spear that pierced Jesus' ribs. These were symbolic references completely independent of the belief that somewhere was preserved or not the original object that was being recalled (in this case, a shroud or spear). Therefore, generally speaking, this argument cannot be used to demonstrate the existence of a "shroud" relic in the time when these liturgical objects or these prayers came into use.

Two scorch marks, which appear as black lines, and a series of vaguely triangular holes caused by burns, run lengthwise down the fabric. The damage is believed to have occurred in a fire that broke out in Chambéry in 1532. In addition to the scorch marks already mentioned, other, smaller holes are visible, roughly circular in shape (known as poker holes) and grouped together. This pattern appears on the Shroud four times; from the positions of the repeated pattern we understand that the cloth deteriorated after the material had been folded over twice, forming four overlapping layers. They are known to have existed before the fire of 1532, since they were already documented on a painted copy of the Shroud that dates to 1516 and is preserved in the Church of Saint-Gommaire at Lierre. Apart from some fanciful explanations,[5] it is generally thought that these holes were due to some accidental contact with something extremely hot (like coals from incense) or with a corrosive liquid, perhaps initially reddish in color.[6] The latter possibility would explain why both the painting from 1516 and other later reproductions represent these holes not as black burns but rather as red spots, like those of blood.[7]

One can also see on the sheet two symmetrical series of rings—one large, the other small—that were caused by contact with a liquid. Contrary to what was once thought, the larger series of rings was not due to an attempt to put out the fire in 1532; rather, the effort to douse the flames is believed to be the cause of the other series of rings, which is smaller and corresponds to the position of the burns.

[5] Cf. J. Leysen, "Le St. Drap de Turin à la lumière des visions d'Anne Catherine Emmerick," *Sindon* 23 (1976): 30–31, thinks that they are marks caused by the nails and thorns of Jesus' crown. The article is absurd. Moreover, Emmerick's account of the passion is incompatible with the reality of the Shroud of Turin (cf. Nicolotti, *From the Mandylion of Edessa*, 168–69, n. 89). For some supporters of the false hypothesis that the Shroud passed through Besançon and was stolen, the holes were due to a sudden fire in 1350 and were later colored red by the thieves to make them look like drops of blood and deceive observers; see Tonelli, *Verso l'ostensione della Sindone*, 472–80, 543–44; A. Cojazzi, "Nuovi contributi sulla Santa Sindone," *Rivista dei giovani* 14 (1933): 674–75.

[6] Cf. D. Raffard de Brienne, *Dizionario della Sindone* (Turin: Elledici, 1998), 76; and M. Flury-Lemberg, "Die Leinwand des Turiner Grabtuches zum technischen Befund," *Sindon* 13 (2000): 26–27.

[7] For example, A. Paleotti, *Esplicatione del sacro Lenzuolo ove fu involto il Signore*, 2nd ed. (Rossi: Bologna, 1599), illustrated table; and likewise the copy of the Shroud in Inzago.

The fiber used for the Shroud was flax (*linum usitatissimum*). The threads, which are unbleached and made of a single yarn, were spun with the spindle running clockwise, so that their fibers twist to the right, corresponding to the shape of the letter Z (this is called "Z-twist"). The current color—certainly the fabric has darkened with age—is similar to Pantone number 16-1326 (Prairie Sand). The average thickness of the fabric is 0.38–0.39 mm; its average weight is 225–235 g per square meter. Each square centimeter of fabric contains an average of thirty-eight warp threads and twenty-six weft threads. In technical terms the weaving of the Shroud fabric is defined as a warp-direction chevron twill, three up and one down, generally composed of straight series of forty-one threads and reverse series of thirty-nine threads, totaling a repeat of eighty threads and four picks. The sequence of chevrons results in a mirrored pattern of stripes commonly referred to as "herringbone."[8]

The linen tends to retain indications of folding. Countless folds and wrinkles are visible on the Shroud, mostly caused by compression forced on the fabric from the ill-conceived practice of rolling it around a cylinder, a method adopted as early as the sixteenth century and in use until 1998. Some indications remain that allow one to intuit the various methods of folding that were used over time. At least four different practices were adopted at various points.[9]

[8] Textile studies of the Shroud are various, but of unequal value. Among those undertaken by those who have actually viewed the cloth, I recommend at least G. Raes, "Rapport d'analyse," in *La S. Sindone: Ricerche e studi della commissione di esperti nominata dall'Arcivescovo di Torino*, supplement, *Rivista diocesana torinese* (January 1976): 79–83 (English translation: "Analysis report," in *Report of Turin Commission on the Holy Shroud* [pro manuscripto, London: Screenpro Films, 1976]); G. Vial, "Le Linceul de Turin: Étude technique," *Bulletin du CIETA* 67 (1989): 11–24; idem, "À propos du linceul de Turin," *Bulletin du CIETA* 69 (1991): 34–35; idem, "À propos du Linceul," *Montre-nous ton visage* 10 (1993): 28–30; Flury-Lemberg, "Die Leinwand des Turiner Grabtuches," 21–43; P. Vercelli, *La Sindone nella sua struttura tessile* (Cantalupa: Effatà, 2010) (very weak in its discussion of history). The work of Gabriel Vial is particularly reliable; Vial was a member of the Centre International d'Étude des Textiles Anciens and curator of the Ancient Textile Museum in Lyon. E. Delorenzi, "Osservazioni sui rappezzi e rammendi della S. Sindone," in *S. Sindone: Ricerche e studi*, 107–20 (English translation: "Observations on the Patches and Darns in the Holy Shroud," in *Report of Turin Commission on the Holy Shroud*), describes well the condition of the Shroud before the 2002 restoration.

[9] Cf. Flury-Lemberg, "Die Leinwand des Turiner Grabtuches," 26–30 and plates 5–14; idem, *Sindone 2002*, 39–48; compare with A. Guerreschi and M. Salcito, "Études

As for the origin of the fabric, the historical documentation currently available does not date to a period before the 1350s. From the perspective of the history of weaving techniques—investigation into which is complex, and so I provide only the conclusions[10]—the manufacture of a fabric like that of the Shroud required the use of a horizontal treadle loom with four shafts. Knowledge of treadle looms came, perhaps from China, in the eleventh century AD or a little before, and the loom with four shafts was probably introduced by the Flemish in the thirteenth century.[11] This explains why up to the present time no fabric similar in technique to the Shroud has ever been found in all of antiquity. Moreover, the oldest comparable example currently identified dates to the second half of the fourteenth century.[12] It must be added that the yarn twist of the Shroud (Z-twist) is the exact opposite of that used in ancient and medieval Palestine (S-twist): therefore, the Shroud could not have been of Palestinian origin.[13]

The interval thus established by the synthesis of historical and technological evidence—dating approximately between the turn of the twelfth century and the middle of the fourteenth century at the

---

sur les brûlures et les halos présents sur le Suaire," *Revue Internationale du Linceul de Turin* 29 (2007): 30–45 (unreliable for all the historical explanations aside from their consideration of the folds). On the disagreement about the method of folding adopted in 1532, the year of the fire, I will say more below.

[10] I spent months surveying all the scientific literature on the matter, consulted various experts on the history of textiles, and checked one by one all the examples of ancient cloth that are wrongly said to be similar to that of the Shroud. The results of my research can be found in A. Nicolotti, "La Sindone di Torino in quanto tessuto: Analisi storica, tecnica, comparativa," in *Non solum circulatorum ludo similia: Miscellanea di studi sul cristianesimo del primo millennio*, ed. V. Polidori (Rome: Amazon KDP, 2018), 148–204. The sindonological literature on the topic is vast, but unfortunately almost always unusable: see, for example, the conclusions of G. M. Rinaldi, "Le fonti di Emanuela Marinelli per il tessuto della Sindone," http://sindone.weebly.com/articoli.html.

[11] Cf. W. Endrei, *L'évolution des techniques du filage et du tissage du moyen âge à la révolution industrielle* (Paris-La Haye: Mouton, 1968), 82–85.

[12] Cf. D. King, "A Parallel for the Linen of the Turin Shroud," *Bulletin du Cieta* 67 (1989): 25–26.

[13] The best and most recent work on this issue is O. Shamir, "A Burial Textile from the First Century CE in Jerusalem Compared to Roman Textiles in the Land of Israel and the Turin Shroud," *SHS Web of Conferences* 15, no. 10 (2015): 1–14 (and erratum). Sindonologists have recently proposed that the Shroud came from India, after having affirmed the contrary for decades, in a sorry attempt to circumvent the problem.

latest—has found further clarification and confirmation through radiocarbon dating performed in 1988. This analysis established a date (of the material, not the image) between 1260 and 1390.[14] If the current Shroud is physically the same as that of which the medieval sources speak, the dating narrows to 1260–circa 1355.

2.1.2 Geoffroy de Charny

The first documents to speak of the Shroud, which date to the second half of the fourteenth century, concern a rural church built at the expense of the French knight Geoffroy de Charny. Near the end of the thirteenth century, the village of Charny, in the Côte-d'Or region of France, was a fief of the noble Jean, who belonged to a cadet branch of the lords of Mont-Saint-Jean and was married to Marguerite de Joinville. His sons were named Jean, Dreux, and Geoffroy; Geoffroy was born in about the year 1300.[15] He likely had a sister named Isabelle.[16] It is known with certainty that in 1315, Jean and Dreux accompanied Louis of Burgundy during his expedition to Morea, and they were quite probably followed by the young Geoffroy. He later became the heir of the lordship of Charny; a document from April 20, 1336, secures his presence in France and describes him as the husband of Jeanne de Toucy-Bazarnes,[17] from whom he

[14] Cf. P. E. Damon et al., "Radiocarbon Dating of the Shroud of Turin," *Nature* 337 (1989): 611–15.

[15] Bibliography on Geoffroy: A. Piaget, "Le Livre Messire Geoffroi de Charny," *Romania* 26 (1897): 394–97; A. Perret, "Essai sur l'histoire du Saint Suaire du XIVe au XVIe siècle," *Mémoires de l'Académie des sciences, belles-lettres et arts de Savoie* 4 (1960): 53–61; P. Contamine, "Geoffroy de Charny (début du XIVe siècle-1356)," in *Histoire et société: Mélanges offerts à Georges Duby*, ed. M. Balard, vol. 2 (Aix-en-Provence: Publications de l'Université de Provence, 1992), 107–21; R. W. Kaeuper and E. Kennedy, *The Book of Chivalry of Geoffroi de Charny* (Philadelphia: University of Pennsylvania Press, 1996), 3–18; A. Lombatti, "Geoffroy de Charny (ca. 1300–1356): Il cavaliere della Sindone," *Studi medievali* 53, no. 1 (2012): 213–58.

[16] In 1320 Isabelle was called *damoiselle* and daughter of the Lord of Charny; in 1341 she was called *madame* and sister of "mon seigneur Gyeffroy de Charny." It seems likely to me the reference is to our Geoffroy (A. Longnon, *Documents relatifs au comté de Champagne et de Brie, 1172–1361*, vol. III [Paris: Imprimerie Nationale, 1914], 168F and 284M).

[17] It is unclear whether Geoffroy had a daughter by Jeanne de Toucy. According to some, her name was Charlotte, and about 1350 she married Bertrand de Chasan, Lord of Écutigny and Missery; according to others she was Jeanne, later called Jeanne de Nuars (Nuère): cf. M. Lainé, *Archives généalogiques et historiques de la*

had acquired the lordship and the castle of Pierre-Perthuis (Yonne), which he established as his primary residence.

Though of modest origins by the standards of nobility, during the Hundred Years' War the knight Geoffroy found a way to make himself known as "the most stalwart and valorous man of all,"[18] becoming a figure of the highest level on the side of the French king. From 1337 we find Geoffroy among the participants in the military campaigns of Gascony and Honnecourt, at Tournai and Amiens, and in Hainaut and Flanders—always in the service of Raoul I de Brienne, Count d'Eu († 1345).[19] At Morlaix in 1342, during one of these very conflicts, he was taken prisoner by the English and confined in Goodrich Castle in Herefordshire; he did not remain in England for long, since he was suddenly permitted to return to France to gather the funds needed to pay his ransom.

In the spring of 1344, a crusade against the Turks began. On October 28 of that year, the crusaders seized the harbor of Smyrna; on January 17 in the following year, however, they were attacked, and the highest-ranking among them were killed. Humbert II, Dauphin of Viennois, raised sails from Marseilles on September 3, 1345, heading another expedition sent to aid the crusaders. After a lengthy stay at Negroponte, he arrived at Smyrna at the beginning of the summer of 1346.[20] We know with certainty that Geoffroy was also in Smyrna, though it is not clear whether he arrived with the first expedition

---

noblesse de France, vol. 5 (Paris: chez l'auteur, 1836), 155; A. Pissier, "Notice historique sur Menades," *Bulletin de la Société des sciences historiques et naturelles de l'Yonne* 78 (1924): 269; G. de Soultrait, *Inventaire des titres de Nevers de l'abbé de Marolles* (Nevers: Fay, 1873), col. 160.

[18] As Jean Froissart describes him: J. A. Buchon, ed., *Les Chroniques de Jean Froissart*, vol. 3 (Paris: Verdière, 1824), 187, § 351: "le plus prud'homme de tous les autres et le plus vaillant."

[19] On Raoul I, see E. Lebailly, "Raoul d'Eu: Connétable de France et seigneur anglais et irlandais," in *La Normandie et l'Angleterre au Moyen Âge*, ed. P. Bouet and V. Gazeau (Caen: Crahm, 2003), 239–48.

[20] On the crusades in Smyrna during these months, see C. Faure, "Le dauphin Humbert II à Venise et en Orient," *Mélanges d'archéologie et d'histoire* 27 (1907): 509–62; U. Chevalier, "La croisade du dauphin Humbert II (1345–1347)," *Bulletin de la Société d'archéologie et de statistique de la Drôme* 54 (1920): 38–76; P. Lemerle, *L'Émirat d'Aydin, Byzance et l'Occident* (Paris: Presses universitaires de France, 1957), 180–203; C. M. Setton, *The Papacy and the Levant (1204–1571)*, vol. 1 (Philadelphia: American Philosophical Society, 1976), 184–209.

or the second.[21] Probably on this occasion Geoffroy made a stop in Brindisi; a painting in a church provides evidence of his passage.[22] Philippe de Mézières recounts that the knight was in Smyrna in the year 1346 "or around then," along with Edward of Beaujeu, Jean I le Meingre, Thomas de Voudenay, and Jean de Saintré. The reports, however, are not entirely precise, and it is not certain whether they refer to 1345 or 1346.[23] We know that Edward of Beaujeu was already in Smyrna in 1345; less is known of the others, as their names do not appear on a list of individuals who accompanied Humbert en route to Smyrna in that same year.[24] A document I discovered reveals that on June 30, 1346, the pope accepted a petition presented to him, evidently some time before, by the bishop and chapter of Patras together with Geoffroy and Philippe de Jonvelle (who married the daughter of Geoffroy's brother Dreux).[25] By then Geoffroy could have already been in Smyrna (whether he arrived with the first expedition or followed Humbert on the second) and perhaps could have also already returned to France, passing through Patras on his way. In any case, on August 2 he was at Port-Sainte-Marie (Lot-et-Garonne).[26] Humbert II, however, withdrew to Rhodes.

At the siege of Aiguillon, Geoffroy fought under the command of John, Duke of Normandy, son of King Philip VI of Valois and

[21] According to G. Demay, *Inventaire des sceaux de la collection Clairambault à la Bibliothèque Nationale*, vol. 1 (Paris: Imprimerie Nationale, 1885), n. 2226, in September of 1345, Geoffroy was in Sens and therefore could not have been in the expedition with Humbert. If one examines the photograph of the original document, however, the year is practically illegible and seems out of place relative to the increasing order (from oldest to more recent) in which the *pièces* were collected (BNF, MS Clairambault 29, p. 2133, pièce 63). If the BNF permitted the examination of all its manuscripts on site, instead of keeping a good number of them enclosed in a warehouse only to sell pictures of them at a high price, perhaps I could have resolved the question with a lens or a Wood's lamp.

[22] Cf. M. Semeraro, "Una committenza di Goffredo I di Charny, il 'cavaliere della Sindone,' in Santa Maria del Casale," *Rivista di storia della Chiesa in Italia* 72 (2018): 405–33.

[23] Philippe De Mézières, *La chevalerie de la Passion de Jésus-Christ*, BNF, MS Arsenal 2251, ff. 13r–v; M. A. Brown, ed., *Philippe de Mézières' "Order of the Passion"* (Ph.D. diss., University of Nebraska, 1971); also cited by Lombatti, *Geoffroy de Charny*, 232.

[24] Cf. U. Chevalier, *Choix de documents historiques inédits sur le Dauphiné* (Montbeliard: Hoffmann, 1874), 96–104.

[25] ASV, reg. suppl. 11, f. 75.

[26] BNF, MS Français 27167 (Pièces originales 683), Dossier Charny en Bourgogne, n. 15992, pièce 5.

future heir to the throne. On March 18, 1347, Geoffroy was awarded the privilege of carrying the *oriflamme* (the royal standard of France) into battle at the head of the troops. By that time the king had made him a member of his permanent council, and, beginning in October of 1348, he provided him with a residence in Paris.[27]

In the meantime, Aimery de Pavie was holding the city of Calais on behalf of the king of England, Edward III. Geoffroy prepared a plan to reconquer the city and obtained a promise from Aimery to deliver the city over to him after a payment of 20,000 gold écus. Word of this arrangement reached Edward, however, who then had the garrison at Calais reinforced in secret and set an ambush for his enemy. During the night of December 31, 1349, and into the wee hours of the next day, when the French, led by Geoffroy, breached the walls as per the agreement, they came upon Edward and his troops waiting for them. Those not killed were taken prisoner, and Geoffroy himself, at the king's expense, was taken to London personally by the knight to whom he surrendered, John de Potenhale. On December 20, Edward granted Guillaume Buynet, Geoffroy's servant, safe conduct to France to gather funds to pay for his release; the ransom amounted to 12,000 gold écus, acquired thanks to the contribution of the new king of France, John II the Good. Yet not even a second imprisonment could stop Geoffroy, who, after being freed, in early June of 1351 took part in the battle of Ardres, this time victoriously. In June of 1352, at Saint-Omer, there arose an opportunity for revenge against the traitor Aimery de Pavie; Geoffroy captured him, decapitated him, and had him quartered and displayed the remains on the city gates.

For a while Geoffroy was able to live far from the battlefield and to attend sessions of the king's council in Paris. But in the middle of August 1356, the conflict resumed, and the knight, having again joined with royal troops, reached Poitiers in the following month. On September 19, a tremendous battle took place, resulting in a disastrous defeat for the French (image 4). The English captured the French king, while his *oriflamme*-bearer Geoffroy—Lord of Lirey, Savoisy, Montfort, and Pierre-Perthuis—fighting to the end alongside John II the Good, perished. He was first buried in the cemetery of the Franciscan order in Poitiers; then, in 1371, his body was taken to Paris and interred in

[27] For the house, see J. Viard, *Documents parisiens du règne de Philippe VI de Valois (1328-1350)* (Paris: Champion, 1900), 326–27.

the Church of the Celestines, along with other illustrious servants of the fatherland.

The courageous Geoffroy was not only a warrior but also a writer: his extant works, a *Livre de chevalerie* (Book of Chivalry) in prose, a *Livre Charny* in verse, and some *Demandes pour la jouste, le tournois, et la guerre* (Questions for the Joust, Tournaments, and War), are all dedicated to feats of arms and the qualities a good knight ought to possess.[28] Geoffroy also had a role in a chivalrous order founded on January 6, 1352, at the behest of King John the Good as a response to the founding of the Order of the Garter by Edward III. It was known as the *Ordre des chevaliers de Nostre Dame de la Noble Maison* (Order of the Knights of Our Lady of the Noble House), or, more famously, as the *Ordre de l'Étoile* (Order of the Star) because of the star on a red background fastened onto a knight's garb in reference to the star of Bethlehem followed by the three kings. The order was short-lived, since after the defeat at Poitiers, it set itself on the path of decadence, surviving for a few decades for purely honorific purposes.[29] This is as much as is known of the life of one who passed into history not only as a noble soldier but also as "the Knight of the Shroud."

2.1.3 The Collegiate Church of Lirey

Around the middle of the fourteenth century, Lirey, about 15 km from Troyes, was a village under the jurisdiction of the parish of Saint-Jean-de-Bonneval.[30] At a certain point, Geoffroy de Charny, who was lord of the place, decided to build a chapel there. It is not known when exactly he settled upon this decision, but we know when he took the first step to move the project forward. In the first few months of 1343, in fact, he requested from the French king an

[28] Kaeuper and Kennedy, *Book of Chivalry*; M. A. Taylor, *A Critical Edition of Geoffroy de Charny's "Livre Charny" and the "Demandes pour la joute, les tournois et la guerre"* (Ph.D. diss., University of North Carolina, 1977).

[29] Described in B. J. Dacier, "Recherches historiques sur l'établissement et l'extinction de l'Ordre de l'Étoile," *Mémoires de l'Académie des Inscriptions et Belles-Lettres* 39 (1777): 662–88; D. J. D. Boulton, *The Knights of the Crown* (Woodbridge: Boydell, 2000), 167–210; see also Y. Renouard, "L'Ordre de la Jarretiére," *Le Moyen Âge* 55 (1949): 281–300.

[30] Still useful is the description of the town provided by A. Roserot, *Dictionnaire historique de la Champagne méridionale (Aube) des origines à 1790*, vol. 2 (Langres: Imprimerie Champenoise, 1945), 796–801.

amortization of 140 livre tournois, in the form of land or an annual revenue, so he could invest them in the construction of a vicarage in Lirey "for the salvation of his own soul, and that of his wife and their forebears" and make provision for five chaplains who would live there.[31] The written request is not extant, but we can glean the tenor of it from the positive response signed by King Philip VI in June at Châteauneuf-sur-Loire.[32] This act established a mortmain: that provision established that a chapel be built at Geoffroy's expense to be an inalienable ecclesiastical possession, not subject to taxation. This document repudiates those authors who have in the past maintained that Geoffroy had promised to construct the church in fulfillment of a vow made to the Virgin Mary during his second imprisonment in 1350, after which he would be set free by two angels.[33]

The construction of the church dragged on. In the meantime, in the years from 1344 to 1346, we know that Geoffroy asked the pope for some indults that did not pertain to his chapel.[34] Finally, on April 16, 1349, the knight sent forth a petition to Clement VI in which he affirmed that he had a church built in honor of the Annunciation of Mary and instituted there five canons with a revenue of 30 livre tournois each. He asked that the church be elevated to collegiate status—that is, that of an institution with a chapter of canons—and

[31] The amortization had to be authorized by the king because the goods transferred to the designated institution were no longer subject to taxation and therefore constituted a loss in revenue for fiscal authorities.

[32] Cf. Savio, *Ricerche storiche*, 97, n. 12.

[33] This explanation was already proposed by N. Camuzat, *Promptuarium sacrarum antiquitatum Tricassinae dioecesis* (Augustae Trecarum: Moreau, 1610), 410v–412r; and by N. Des Guerrois, *La Sainctеté chrestienne, contenant les vie, mort et miracles de plusieurs saincts de France* (Troyes: Jacquard, 1637), 373r–375v. Jean Ragon provides the same explanation in a historical manuscript from around 1640, partially edited by A. F. Arnaud, *Voyage archéologique et pittoresque dans le département de l'Aube et dans l'ancien diocèse de Troyes* (Troyes: Cardon, 1837), 115–16. The explanation is again offered by F. Cognasso, "Da Gerusalemme a Costantinopoli, a Lirey, a Chambéry," in *Torino e la Sindone*, ed. C. Moriondo and D. Piazza (Turin: Alfeda, 1978), 55. On the contrary J. Du Teil, *Autour du Saint Suaire de Lirey*, 2nd ed. (Paris: Picard, 1902), 1–2, n. 1, later taken up by D. C. Scavone, "Geoffroy's Vow and the Church at Lirey," *Sindon* 1 (1989): 129–32, who tries to save the legend by shifting Geoffroy's vow to his first imprisonment in 1342.

[34] Cf. Savio, *Ricerche storiche*, 108–9, nn. 34–36 (an indult for a portable altar, a plenary indulgence *in articulo mortis*, permission to perform liturgical celebrations in places under interdict and during the night).

that he be granted the right of patronage over it for himself and his descendants. Geoffroy also requested that the five canons be able to elect a sixth member as their dean, and that a hundred-days' indulgence be granted to whoever had visited the church during the feasts of the Virgin Mary or made an offering in her favor. Ten days later, on April 26, he sent a second petition requesting that the offerings collected in the church be permitted to be used for the chapter, thereby establishing some amount of compensation for the rector of the parish church in Saint-Jean-de-Bonneval. Geoffroy further asked that he be allowed to add a cemetery to the church for himself, his kin, the canons, and all those who desired burial there.[35]

His obligations in the war, however, forced Geoffroy to postpone his plans temporarily: only in 1351, after his return from his long imprisonment in England, was he able to resume work on his collegiate church. In September of that year, the new king of France added another 60 livre to the amortization that had already been granted in 1343, exempting it from taxation as well. The fact that the document announcing the grant refers to the chapel as *fundata vel fundanda* (founded or about to be founded) leads one to believe that the structure did not yet exist or was not completed.[36] Again, on February 20, 1353, demonstrating how little had been done, Geoffroy asked the abbot of Montier-la-Celle, Aymeric Orlhuti, the benefice collector of Saint-Jean-de-Bonneval, for permission to build a church in Lirey on payment of an annual revenue of 6 livre and four hectares of grassland.[37]

The real foundation would be celebrated with a deed dated June 20, 1353. The new chapel, a simple wooden structure, was dedicated to the Trinity and the Annunciation of Mary, and for its maintenance Geoffroy was obliged to pay 260 livre tournois each year (which some months later increased by a further 62 livres and 10 sols).[38] The collegiate church had six canons, under revenue and in residence, chosen by the Lord of Lirey, and the dean at least had to be

[35] Cf. U. Chevalier, *Autour des origines du suaire de Lirey* (Paris: Picard, 1903), docs. A and B.

[36] ADA, 9 G 1.

[37] According to A. Prévost, "L'ancienne collégiale de Lirey," *Revue de Champagne et de Brie* 11 (1899): 809, but the document has not been identified.

[38] From earnings on the gates of Troyes that Geoffroy enjoyed, which were also amortized by the king in a decree dated to October of 1353. In the same year, the

a priest. Two masses had to be performed in the church each day, and the office had to be in accordance with the custom in Troyes, always in memory of the dead from Charny's families, especially Geoffroy's deceased wife, Jeanne de Toucy.[39] We know the names of two clergymen closely connected with Geoffroy, and who, though not counted among the canons of Lirey, certainly assisted in the foundation of the church: Jean Nichole, Geoffroy's chaplain, presbyter of Autun and canon of four collegiate churches, who was at his side on the day of the church's founding; and Guillaume de Bazarnes, of the house of De Toucy, canon and cantor of the Church of Reims. Sixty years of age and suffering from eye disease, he retired to Lirey at the request of his brother-in-law Geoffroy in 1354.[40]

The foundation of a church by a member of the laity, who selected the clergy who would pray for him and his family, was at the time a common enough occurrence, and the institution of patronage existed for precisely this situation. The patronage system regulated the rights and responsibilities of benefactors who constructed churches and funded their activities; the issue of patrons designating clerics was particularly delicate as it was in substance a diminishment of ecclesiastical authority and therefore often a source of conflict. In the case of the collegiate church in Lirey, the matter was settled by the new pope, Innocent VI, to whom on January 30, 1354, Geoffroy sent more requests, all of which would be approved. Some reiterated appeals from five years earlier, while others were new. For example, the pope granted that the dean elected by the chapter would have to be approved by the bishop of Troyes and that the legacies of canons who died without a will would become property of the collegiate church. At the same time, the annual stipend for the canons was set at 30 livres and the one-hundred-days' indulgence was increased to a year and forty days—a typical figure that recalls the indulgences of the patriarchal Roman basilicas. The indulgence was available

king gave up the proceeds from an income of a further 100 livres donated by Geoffroy: ADA, 9 G 1.

[39] Cf. Camuzat, *Promptuarium sacrarum antiquitatum*, 412r–420v.

[40] As is known from the acceptance of an entreaty from Geoffroy dated January 30, 1354: Savio, *Ricerche storiche*, 113–15, n. 1. Jean was a canon of Notre-Dame de Beaune, Notre-Dame de Provins, Sainte-Agnès de Beaune, and Notre-Dame *in Castro de Mariaux*. Guillaume was the brother of Jeanne de Toucy, Geoffroy's first wife.

to the church's benefactors and any who came to the church on the four major feast days of the Virgin Mary (Nativity, Annunciation, Purification, and Assumption), to which Christmas, Easter, the Feast of the Ascension, and Pentecost were added some months later.[41]

All that was left to Geoffroy was to specify what income was owed to the collegiate church; he did so on October 16 in a document signed in the church itself, listing the funds in minute detail and providing also a list of names that included Dean Robert de Caillac and some other canons who had been installed in the church.[42] The procedure for electing a dean is well known from a document of May 20, 1356: he had to be elected by the canons and was then immediately presented to the Lord of Lirey, who asked the bishop of Troyes for the dean's canonical investiture.[43] Eight days later, from his castle in Aix-en-Othe, Henry de Poitiers, bishop of Troyes, could definitively affirm the establishment of the collegiate church. This confirmation arrived less than four months before Geoffroy's death.[44] None of these documents makes any mention of a shroud.

2.1.4 The Nebulous Appearance of the Shroud

From 1353, then, the village of Lirey, fief of Geoffroy de Charny, in the diocese of Troyes, was enriched with a small church equipped with a chapter.[45] In the same year Henry de Poitiers was made bishop of Troyes, becoming at the same time both captain and governor of the city and distinguishing himself as a capable military leader. Troyes' circumstances in the second half of the fourteenth century were quite difficult, as was the case throughout France, since the population that had survived the devastating Black Death was burdened with heavy

[41] Cf. Savio, *Ricerche storiche*, 102–3, n. 21 (Geoffroy's entreaty); 103–4, n. 23 (letter from the pope to Geoffroy); 104, n. 23 (papal bull); 104–5, n. 24 (grant of indulgences); ASV, Reg. Aven. 147, ff. 542r–543r (three letters from the pope to the canons). The grant of indulgences is dated August 3: Savio, *Ricerche storiche*, 103, n. 21 (request); 105, n. 25 (concession).

[42] ADA, 9 G 1; summarized in Prévost, *L'ancienne collégiale de Lirey*, 906–7. The canons are Guillaume de Bragelogne, Renaud de Savoisy, Henri de Oisilly, Jean de Lisines, and Robert de Saint-Vinnemer. All are priests.

[43] Cf. Camuzat, *Promptuarium sacrarum antiquitatum*, 420v–422r.

[44] Cf. Camuzat, *Promptuarium sacrarum antiquitatum*, 422v.

[45] In addition to the bibliography already cited, see Ciccone and Sturmann, *Sindone svelata*, 23–71, which also provides an Italian translation of various documents.

taxation. Beginning in 1290 important and costly expansions were added to the city cathedral at the expense of the chapter. On June 25, 1354, the bishop, Henry, confirmed the creation of a confraternity of Saint Peter to accelerate the completion of the work, and he granted indulgences to whoever made donations to the confraternity or the cathedral.[46]

In this period, a shroud turns up in the small collegiate church. The fabric, as has already been said, was recent, but it is impossible to know whether it was produced there or somewhere else; Troyes was very well known for its fabrics.[47] Unfortunately, no document exists to clarify definitively when, how, and by whom the relic was transferred to Lirey. In order to reconstruct this first period, it is necessary to rely on retrospective writings, the most detailed of which, dating to 1389, is the work of Pierre d'Arcis-sur-Aube, bishop of Troyes from 1377 to 1395. Pierre recounts that around the year 1355, Robert de Caillac, dean of canons of Lirey, had obtained a long fabric that bore the image of the mangled body of Christ. He exhibited this fabric to the faithful—for a price—leading them to believe that it was Jesus' authentic burial linen. The relic's fame soon spread, due also to some misleading incidents of miraculous healing that occurred during the exhibition of the cloth.

The bishop Henry de Poitiers was anxious to investigate the happenings taking place in the region under his episcopal control; after an investigation aided by theologians and trusted advisors—according to the account of Pierre d'Arcis, Henry's successor—Henry was able to uncover the fraud perpetrated by the dean. The shroud was a simple fabric on which a skilled forger had artificially depicted the beaten body of Christ. The forger, moreover, was identified, and he confirmed the bishop's suspicions. The dean and his accomplices, upon seeing their deception come to light, were compelled to stop exhibitions of the fabric, and they removed it before the bishop could confiscate it. It seems that they took it beyond the diocese, but precisely where cannot be known. Perhaps it made its way to one or the other of lands owned by Charny, such as Savoisy or Montfort.

[46] ADA, G 3868.

[47] See H. Liébert, *L'Industrie à Troyes à la fin du Moyen Âge (XIV et XVème siècles)* (Ph.D. diss., Faculté des lettres, Paris, 1950), 39–61.

No written sources contemporary to the event are extant. Among documents surviving from around the same time are some concerning the collegiate church in those years, the first chronologically being a large parchment granting an indulgence that was written not long after the incident of the forged shroud. On June 5, 1357, twelve bishops, who were at the time residents of the pontifical court in Avignon, signed a bull in which they indicated the conditions for profiting from an indulgence at Lirey. These conditions were indeed very favorable, inasmuch as it was only necessary for the faithful—properly penitent and having confessed their sins—to visit the collegiate church on one of about fifty particular religious feast days, including the octaves, or to participate in liturgies that were performed in the collegiate church or perform them themselves. They could also go there for a funeral, pray for the dead, follow the one carrying the Eucharist or the holy oil, or visit the relics (unfortunately, no list is provided).[48] The faithful could also pray for the bishop of Troyes and the Duke of Burgundy, or for the memory of the founders of the chapel and their close relatives, or perform works of religious piety, or make offerings or wills in favor of the church. Since there were twelve signatory bishops and each granted an indulgence of forty days, the total comes to 480 days for one act alone.[49] The cardinal Guy de Boulogne would later add another forty days.[50]

One might wonder whether the granting of all these indulgences, especially those signed by as many as twelve bishops, was not a visible sign of a particular interest of the highest ecclesiastical authorities in the small rustic church on account of the precious relic it held, or whether the numerous indulgences were a way to repay in some measure the collegiate church, which, after being prohibited by the bishop from displaying the Shroud, certainly suffered from

[48] Therefore Wilson, *Turin Shroud*, 168, is incorrect when he speaks of a "complete list of the relics in the Lirey collegiate church, derived from a letter signed by twelve bishops." Unfortunately, the error has been picked up by some other authors, including C. Foley, "The Besançon Cloth," *Sindon* 1 (1989): 64–65; V. Saxer, "Le Suaire de Turin aux prises avec l'histoire," *Revue d'histoire de l'Église de France*, 76 (1990): 26; Papini, *Sindone: Una sfida*, 46; J. Nickell, *Inquest on the Shroud of Turin*, 2nd ed. (Amherst: Prometheus, 1998 [1983]), 11.

[49] Cf. Chevalier, *Autour des origines du suaire de Lirey*, doc. E. The document's large size allowed for it to be read by the public and affixed to the door of the church.

[50] ADA, I 17 n. 8.

a sudden, severe dearth of images and pilgrimages. Anyone knowledgeable of the customs of the time, however, knows that similar indulgences were nothing special but rather business as usual. Forty days of indulgence was the maximum that a bishop could grant.[51] Yet to bypass this limitation there arose the custom of combining the indulgences of multiple bishops into a single concession, thereby producing—as in this case—a "collective letter," often signed by twelve prelates, a reference to the number of the apostles. For those bishops of dioceses situated in the East or in southern Italy, who at the time were living at the pontifical curia, the granting of collective indulgences such as this was also a means of financial support, since a monetary contribution was expected from those who received the indulgences. We have many examples of indulgences operating in this way, all of which are similar to indulgences granted to Lirey.[52] Thus, to obtain so many indulgences, there was no need to have any special relic; on the contrary, the accumulation of indulgences in Lirey continued even after the Shroud was removed from the church, and in the first half of the seventeenth century reached the considerable figure of 5,118 days.

2.1.5 Clash of the Titans

In the 1350s, the first part of the story came to an end, and for more than thirty years nothing more was known of the Shroud of Lirey. Perhaps it was being kept hidden in the Charny family home or perhaps somewhere else. The craftsman of the relic did not dare to replicate the shrouds: one can easily imagine that after the bishop's intervention he would have devoted much attention to his work. Henry de Poitiers was a soldier whom history remembers as a "bishop-captain" and as a "good warrior who acted with strength"[53]: such a man had to be taken seriously. The key players,

[51] As established in the Fourth Lateran Council, can. 62.

[52] Cf. H. Delehaye, "Les lettres d'indulgences collectives," *Analecta Bollandiana* 44 (1926): 342–79; 45 (1927): 7–123, 323–44; 46 (1928): 149–57, 287–343, with hundreds of examples; H. Enzensberger, "Quoniam ut ait Apostolus: Osservazioni su lettere di indulgenza nei secoli XIII e XVI," *Studi Medievali e moderni* 1 (1999): 57–100.

[53] J. A. Buchon, *Les Chroniques de sire Jean Froissart*, vol. 1 (Paris: Société du Panthéon Littéraire, 1853), 404; for a description of Henry de Poitiers, see A. Prévost, *Le diocèse de Troyes: Histoire et documents*, vol. 2 (Dijon: Union typographique, 1924), 5–14; Ciccone and Sturmann, *Sindone svelata*, 36–37.

in the meantime, changed. In 1358 the dean Robert de Caillac died; Simon Frère was elected in his place and, two years later, Guillaume de Bragelogne. The young Geoffroy II de Charny, son of the deceased Geoffroy I, founder of the collegiate church, came of age in the 1370s and inherited his father's fiefs and freed himself from the guardianship of Aymon de Genève, the second husband of his mother, Jeanne de Vergy. Ironically, he would later marry Marguerite de Poitiers, the niece of the late bishop Henry. The bishopric of Troyes moved from Jean Braque (1370–1375) to Pierre de Villiers (1376–1377); in 1377 the bishopric fell to the aforementioned Pierre d'Arcis, who governed the diocese until his death in 1395. In those years, too, work on the cathedral of Troyes continued, but with poor results. On August 13, 1365, the cathedral tower fell, and in 1389, on Christmas day, part of the nave; soon after, part of the transept collapsed. The reconstruction resumed thanks to extraordinary donations from the bishop, the canons, the king, the pope, and some of the city's nobles.[54]

At a certain point, something happened that again concerned the Shroud. Geoffroy II, after distinguishing himself in numerous battles in France and Scotland, became a knight banneret (*chevalier banneret*)—that is, the head of a company of knights who served under his own banner. In 1389 he qualified as one of the king's chamberlains.[55] In that same year Pierre de Thury, a cardinal with the title of St. Susanna who also served as apostolic legate to the king of France, happened while on certain business to be passing through the ecclesiastical region of Sens, to which the diocese of Troyes belonged (perhaps in the course of a journey to Paris, where he arrived around April 6).[56] He met Geoffroy, who took the opportunity to bring to the cardinal's attention a petition regarding the Shroud, which was still unable to be exhibited because of measures taken by the late bishop of Troyes. The only solution for Geoffroy was to have the current bishop, Pierre d'Arcis, rescind the prohibition or to have the order countered by a cleric of higher rank, like Pierre de Thury. Geoffroy then explained to the cardinal that in the collegiate church of Lirey

[54] Cf. S. Murray, *Building Troyes Cathedral* (Bloomington: Indiana University Press, 1987), 18–42.

[55] BNF, MS Français 27167 (Pièces originales 683), Dossier Charny en Bourgogne, n. 15992, pièce 24.

[56] According to G. Mollat, "Clément VII et le suaire de Lirey," *Le correspondant* 210 (1903): 255.

his own deceased father "had a place made with reverence for a certain figure or representation of our Lord Jesus Christ's shroud, offered to him in generosity."[57] He added that because of war and pestilence, and "also by the order of the ordinary of the place and for certain other reasons," such a figure or representation had been later transferred and kept hidden in a more secure location. This admission of Geoffroy confirms for us that the late bishop of Troyes did intervene some years before, but the knight prefers to leave the details vague. Geoffroy then asked the cardinal for permission to reinstate the object in the church "for the honor of the aforementioned church, for the devotion of the people, and for the enhancement of divine worship." The cardinal accepted the request and in a letter to Geoffroy authorized him

> to have stationed and positioned the aforementioned figure or representation in the aforementioned Church of St. Mary, in an adequate place, honorable and decorous, without the need to seek or obtain permission from the bishop of the diocese or from anyone else.

Consequently, the Shroud was brought back to the church from the place where it had been hidden, and the chapter of canons resumed exhibitions. The collegiate church soon became a destination for pilgrims once again.

These acts were not all well received by the ordinary, Pierre d'Arcis. Convinced of the correctness of the measures taken against the Shroud by his predecessor Henry de Poitiers, and probably annoyed by having his authority circumvented, the bishop intervened heavily. First, on the occasion of a synod convened in the diocese of Troyes,[58] he ordered all the diocesan clergy to omit any reference to the Shroud in their preaching, regardless of whether they intended to speak well of it or not.[59] Later he enjoined the dean of Lirey, under penalty of excommunication, to cease exhibitions immediately. The bishop did not consider his injunction to be in conflict with cardinal Pierre de Thury's authorization, since the cardinal did not grant Geoffroy

[57] "Quamdam figuram sive repraesentationem sudarii Domini nostri Iesu Christi sibi liberaliter oblatam."

[58] In the diocese of Troyes at least two synods were celebrated each year.

[59] Cf. Prévost, *Diocèse de Troyes*, 2:10–11.

permission to *exhibit* the Shroud for veneration but rather granted him permission only to *place* it in the church.

The dean—at that time a man named Nicole Martin—refused to obey and continued the exhibitions, appealing to the pope in the meantime. Geoffroy II made an appeal as well. In 1389 Clement VII, previously known as Robert de Genève, was the pope of Avignonese obedience. After being consulted, he decided in favor of the canons and rendered void Pierre d'Arcis' act of excommunication. To this decision he added what was lacking in the cardinal's authorization—that is, the explicit authorization to perform exhibitions for the people's devotion. At this point, silence was imposed on the bishop about the prohibitions he had promulgated. All of this is thoroughly explained in a letter from the pope to Geoffroy II de Charny dated July 28, 1389.[60]

In the meantime, Geoffroy also turned to the French king, from whom he obtained royal safeguard, which he considered an authorization to continue exhibitions despite the bishop's prohibition. In response, at the very time the pope was deciding in Geoffroy's favor, Bishop Pierre also made an appeal to the king, whom he served as an advisor, seeking an annulment of the royal safeguard. The bishop's reasons, as expressed before Parliament, were as follows: in the collegiate church of Lirey "there was a certain handmade cloth, rendered skillfully (*artificialiter*) in respect to figure and likeness, and as a tribute to the sacred shroud in which the most precious body of our Lord Jesus Christ was wrapped," and "to the aforementioned church the people of Champagne and the surrounding regions flowed each day in abundance to adore that cloth, without fear of committing idolatry." Geoffroy—the bishop continues—persevered in having the Shroud shown "with torches lit and the priests robed in sacerdotal vestments, as if it were a matter of the true shroud of Christ." In such a way, seeing such solemnity, all are led to believe erroneously "that that is the true shroud of Christ, and led into deception and irreverence toward the Holy Mother Church and the orthodox faith."

[60] Cf. Chevalier, *Autour des origines du suaire de Lirey*, doc. H (written on July 28 and delivered on August 3). Neither what Geoffroy wrote nor what the dean and cardinal wrote have survived; only the pope's response survived, which, however, as was customary, incorporated and summarized the text of the petition to which it responded and therefore provides a context.

The parliament and the king were convinced that the bishop's arguments were sound and decided to revoke the safeguard granted previously. On August 4, 1389—just as soon as the pope had decided exactly the opposite—Charles VI wrote to the bailiff of Troyes and ordered him to confiscate the Shroud and transfer it to one of the churches of Troyes or, in any case, to a secure location in the custody of the king until a new arrangement could be made.[61]

At the time, the bailiff of Troyes was Jean de Venderesse, Lord of Marfontaine. On August 15, the Feast of the Assumption, at the request of the bishop and on the authority of the royal letter, Jean went to Lirey to execute the order. Matters suddenly proved very complicated, however, as Jean himself reports in a colorful and vivid account written upon his return to Troyes:

> We came to the city and the collegiate church of Our Lady of Lirey in the diocese of Troyes, and there in the church's tribune we found the dean and some of the canons of it [the collegiate], who were in the tribune. They were preparing, as it seemed, to exhibit the aforementioned cloth to the people outside the church. They asked why we had ascended to that place, and we responded that we had come to see the cloth. They said that while we remained there, they would not show the cloth; but if we wanted to go outside with the people, we would see it quite soon. We were informed by someone that the cloth was in a reliquary, and we saw the torches that they would light to show it, so it was said, and the people below said that they were expecting to see it soon. But since, due to the church's layout, if we had left and gone outside, the cloth could have been carried away, we did not want to leave that place. Then, in the presence of the dean, the canons, and several other individuals, Huguenin de Nantuse, presenting himself as procurator of my lord the bishop with power of attorney, which he promptly displayed to us, showed us again the letter [of the king] transcribed above and asked several times that we enforce it and put it into action immediately; by virtue of that letter, transcribed above, we commanded the dean, in the name of our king, to get the cloth that was in the church, the one mentioned in the letter, and hand it over to us. The dean responded that it was not in his power to hand the cloth over. Since at the far

[61] Letter to the bailiff of Troyes, also containing the bishop's reasons: U. Chevalier, *Étude critique sur l'origine du St. Suaire de Lirey-Chambéry-Turin* (Paris: Picard, 1900), doc. A.

end of the tribune there was a small closet, called "treasure," with several locks, where it was customary to put the relics, vestments, ornaments, and books of the church, the procurator of my lord the bishop was saying and affirming that the cloth was there, while the dean objected to the contrary, telling us to attend to what we were doing, and that inside the closet there were several relics, vestments, ornaments, books, money and many other things belonging to the church. The dean only had one key to the "treasure," which had several locks, as was said, and therefore he was unable to open it. The procurator, in the name of the aforementioned, asked us many times that the "treasure" be opened, broken and busted by force, and was saying that we had to do so. The dean, for his part, was saying the opposite, that the cloth was not there, and the procurator in his turn contradicted him. Because of the dispute between the two parties and given that it was afternoon, time for lunch, in doubt that in the time that we were at lunch the cloth would be stolen and carried away by the dean and the canons, at the request of the procurator we placed a seal on the door of the "treasure" using our seal and appointed two royal sergeants, namely Adenot d'Aubruissell and Jean de Beaune, to keep watch to see that the seal was not broken. And during lunchtime they remained in the church to watch over the door on our orders and at the procurator's request. Afterward, at about the time of vespers, the dean asked us insistently several times to remove the seal on the "treasure" in order to put the relics safely in order, as was fitting, as well as the vestments and other objects of the church, and also to take out some money and other necessary things of which they had great need and necessity for the church; he was also saying that the cloth was not there. Furthermore, that dean and the canons were making a number of appeals against my lord the bishop to the Holy See of Rome in regard to this case, as he kept saying, asking us to allow the door to be opened immediately. The procurator of my lord the bishop was opposed to it, always maintaining the opposite position, on behalf of and in the name of my lord the bishop, and he was saying that on no account should we remove our seal from the "treasure" if the dean did not open it widely and completely. The dean claimed that he was unable to open it by himself because he had only one key to the "treasure," and that the men of the lord of Lirey had the other, without whom he could not open it, and would have been unable to do so by himself. We proposed in response that if he wanted to send someone to look for or to be given the other key, we would order two sergeants to watch over the seal until

> he brought the other key; then we would take our seal from the door. To that the dean responded that he did not know when or at what time the one who had care of the other key on behalf of the lord of Lirey might come, and he kept asking that the seal be removed. Nevertheless, because of the dispute between the parties, we said that we would take some time, until the next day, to consider the matter; but since the dean felt he had been greatly offended, according to him, by the fact that the "treasure" was and remained sealed, and by the fact that we had told him earlier that by compulsion we would put the material goods of the church in the hands of our king if he did not hand over the cloth, the dean made an appeal against us, and the canons of the church who were present, together with the dean, did so also, on behalf of and in the name of the dean and the canons of the church. On account of the appeal thus interposed, we did not proceed further in this matter, but held firm in that state.[62]

The bailiff, therefore, could not carry out the order given to him, but had to limit himself to putting the Shroud under guard in the name of the king, by placing seals on the "treasure" in the presence of Nicole Martin, priest and dean of the collegiate church, and of the canons Jean Boigney, Jacques Colardot, and Thiebault Goutey.[63] This treasure, then, was a closet for sacred accoutrements that, according to a common use at the time, was protected by doors with several locks to discourage thieves.[64] The canons say that the Charny family was responsible for one of the keys; the person charged with keeping it for the family evidently avoided coming to open it that day.

Twenty days later, on September 5, the bailiff Jean de Venderesse wrote at the bishop's request to his first sergeant Jean de Beaune, ordering him to bring the contents of some letters to the notice of the canons.[65] The sergeant carried out his orders that same day: showing the letters and reporting verbally, he repeated that the Shroud had been put in the king's hands. The sergeant then went to the castle of Lirey to inform Geoffroy de Charny of the decree; but Geoffroy was

[62] Chevalier, *Étude critique*, doc. B.

[63] Cf. Chevalier, *Étude critique*, doc. C. Francesco Cognasso erroneously affirms that the king's envoy broke open the coffer containing the Shroud and found it empty (*Da Gerusalemme a Costantinopoli*, 56).

[64] Cf. P. Dor, *Les reliquaires de la Passion en France du Ve au XVe siècle* (Amiens: Cahmer, 1999), 141–46.

[65] Cf. Chevalier, *Étude critique*, doc. E.

gone, and in his place the squire Jacquemon de Montfort received the notice.[66]

The appeal to the pope, however, had just brought about a decision in favor of the canons. Despite the king's support, Pierre d'Arcis suddenly found his hands tied: he decided, then, sometime between August 1389 and the early days of 1390, to write a long letter to the pontiff in which he explained his view on the whole matter. It is the document cited above, which has become known as the Memorandum of Pierre d'Arcis, and it is worthwhile to read it in its entirety, since it is rich in valuable evidence.

> *The truth about the cloth of Lirey, which for a long time previously was exhibited, had been exhibited, and now again was exhibited, concerning which I intend to write to our lord the Pope, in the manner written below and as briefly as I am able.*
>
> Behold, I kiss with devotion the blessed feet, with all the promptness that submission owes. Most Blessed Father, the greater cares, which above all concern danger for souls and which, on account of the power of some, it is impossible for the weak to provide for properly, must be brought to the Holy apostolic See, so that by its caring providence all matters may be settled advantageously, to the praise of God and the well-being of the subjects. Therefore a dangerous and, by its example, destructive matter, which recently occurred in the diocese of Troyes, I have deemed fit to be brought to the ears of Your Holiness, so that, by the providence of Your same Holiness, who does not cease diligently to watch over the interests of your subjects and to keep them from harm, it might be resolved with a swift remedy to the praise of God, the honor of the Church, and the well-being of your subjects. Since indeed, Most Blessed Father, a short while ago in the diocese of Troyes, the dean of a certain collegiate church, specifically in Lirey, deceitfully and wickedly, inflamed with the fire of avarice and cupidity, not from devotion but for gain, arranged to have in his church a certain cloth, cunningly portrayed, on which was portrayed in a subtle manner the double image of a single man, that is to say his front and back; [the dean] falsely asserted and pretended that this was the very shroud in which our Savior Jesus Christ was enrobed in the sepulchre, and on which shroud there had remained the impression of the whole likeness of the Savior

[66] Report of the sergeant to the bailiff: Chevalier, *Étude critique*, doc. F.

himself with the wounds that he bore; much more than throughout the kingdom of France, this matter has been so widely disseminated throughout the whole world, so that people have flowed from all parts of the world. For the purpose of drawing in those very people, so that by cunning cleverness gold might be extorted from them, miracles were fabricated there by certain men induced to this by the reward, who pretended to be healed during an exhibition of the aforementioned shroud, which was believed by all to be the shroud of the Lord. In attending to this matter, Lord Henry de Poitiers, of good memory, at the time the bishop of Troyes, struck by the persuasiveness of many prudent men, since it was his duty in the exercise of his ordinary jurisdiction, took it upon himself to investigate promptly the truth of this matter: many theologians and other learned men assured him that this could not in fact be the shroud of the Lord, because it had the imprinted likeness of the Savior himself, since the Holy Gospel makes no mention of an impression of this sort, while, however, if it had been true, it is not likely that the holy evangelists would have kept silent or omitted it, nor that it would have remained secret or hidden up to this time. And finally, first by cleverness and care, and then by the gathering of information pertaining to this, he at last discovered the deception, and how [the image on] that cloth had been artificially portrayed. It was even proved by the artist who had portrayed it that it was made by work of a man, not miraculously wrought or bestowed. Therefore, after consulting in timely counsel with many learned men, both theologians and those skilled in law, and determining that he ought not and could not dismiss the matter nor conceal it, as required by his office he chose to proceed against the aforementioned dean and his accomplices for the purpose of rooting out that error. They, seeing their malice had been uncovered, hid and suppressed the noted cloth so that it could not be found by the Ordinary himself; and afterward they kept it concealed for 34 years or so, until this year. Now, however, with premeditated fraud and a view to personal gain, the current dean of that church, as it is said, suggested to Lord Geoffroy de Charny, knight, temporal lord of the place, that he see to it that the cloth be relocated to the church, so that pilgrimage to the church would be renewed and the church would be enriched by the proceeds. This knight, at the suggestion of that dean, who was following in the footsteps of his predecessor, approached Lord Cardinal de Thury, Your Holiness' nuncio and legate in the regions of France. He remained in silence about the fact that at the time it was claimed that the cloth was the shroud of the Savior, and that it bore impressed upon it the likeness of the Savior, and that the Ordinary had assailed against this fact, seeking the extirpation of an error to which it had given rise, and that for fear of the Ordinary the cloth had been hidden, and even transported outside the diocese, as it is said. He disclosed to the aforementioned Lord Cardinal that the cloth was a representation or figure of the shroud, to which many were led in devotion, which cloth previously had been held in the stated church with great veneration and had been frequently visited with greatest devotion, but because of the kingdom's wars and for other reasons, and at the command of the Ordinary of the place, it had been located for a long time at a safe distance and preserved in safe custody. [Geoffroy] requested that he be permitted to place in the church the representation or figure of the shroud, to which many were drawn by devotion and were desiring to view, so that it could there be displayed and shown to the people and venerated by the faithful. The Lord Cardinal, not assenting to the entire request, but likely for a particular purpose, and therefore in this he acted wisely, granted to the supplicant by apostolic authority that without permission from the Ordinary of the place or anyone else, he could place or locate the representation or figure of the Lord's shroud in the aforementioned church or in a suitable place elsewhere. On the pretext of this letter, the aforementioned cloth was displayed and frequently shown to the people in the aforementioned church on solemn days and feast days, and otherwise, openly, with the greatest solemnity, even greater than when the Body of our Lord Jesus Christ was shown there, namely with two priests garbed in albs with stoles and maniples, very reverently, with torches lit and in a high, elevated place built especially for this alone. Of course in public it was not claimed to be the true shroud of Christ; nevertheless in private it is asserted and proclaimed, and so it is believed by many, and especially because previously, as stated above, it was said to be the true shroud of Christ, and in a certain contrived way of speaking recently invented in the church it is not called the shroud, but rather the sanctuary, which sounds the same in the ears of the people who are not at all discerning in such matters. A multitude of people flows to the place as often as the cloth is exhibited or is expected to be exhibited, since they believe—but rather, in truth, are erring—that it is the true shroud; and a rumor is going around among the people that it was approved by the apostolic See through the letter of the aforementioned Lord Cardinal. Furthermore, I, Most Blessed Father, seeing so great an inducement to sin renewed among the people and an error of this sort growing in its danger to and deception of souls, and considering that the dean of the church was not content with the bounds set by the Lord Cardinal's letter, which nevertheless had been obtained by suppressing the truth and suggesting falsehood, as was already said, and wishing as much as was in my power to oppose the dangers to souls and to destroy and root out such a detestable error from the flock entrusted to me, having again made timely consultation about this matter with many learned men, I prohibited the dean, under penalty of excommunication *latae sententiae,* from exhibiting or showing the aforementioned cloth to the people until otherwise might be determined in this matter. But he, disobedient, having recourse to an appeal, going against the prohibition, persevered in exhibiting it as before; even the knight himself supported and defended this sort of practice, holding that cloth in his own hands on a certain solemn day and exhibiting it publicly to the people with the solemnity that I already mentioned; thanks to a safeguard of the king, he had the cloth kept in his possession with the right of exhibition and he had me notified of that safeguard. And so, under the protection afforded by both his appeal and the safeguard, that error is defended, maintained, and grows strong in contempt of the Church and as a stumbling block to the people and a danger to souls. On these matters I am unable to intervene because of the aforementioned facts that obstruct me; rather more it is asserted and defended to the dishonor of my predecessor, who pursued this matter during his tenure, and to my dishonor, who desires to attend to this matter in a proper and prudent manner—oh what grief! Rather, supporting this, they cause it to be spread among the people that I pursue this matter out of envy or cupidity and avarice, and so that I might seize the cloth, just as at other times my predecessor had been so accused; some even say that I proceed in this matter too tepidly and that the fact that it is tolerated is a mockery. And even though with earnestness and humility I urged and requested that the already-mentioned knight cease and refrain from exhibitions of the cloth for a time, until Your Holiness was consulted and made a determination, he did not care to do so, but in fact, unbeknownst to me, he had it reported to Your Holiness that which he had reported to the aforementioned Lord Cardinal, and that I, refusing to comply with the letter of the Lord Cardinal himself, and disregarding the appeals, would not cease to move ahead with prohibitions and sentences of excommunication against those showing the cloth itself and against the people who frequented that place to venerate it. But, with all due respect to him who reported this, in proceeding in the aforementioned manner against the ones exhibiting the cloth and those venerating it, in no way did I contravene the letter, although obtained through deception, of the aforementioned Lord Cardinal, in which he had not granted that the cloth could be shown to the people or even venerated, but only that it could be placed and located in the already-mentioned church or elsewhere in a suitable place. Because they were not content with the concession of the Lord Cardinal, therefore I proceeded against them by right of the Ordinary, not without much counsel, as was incumbent upon me because of my position, with a view to removing the stumbling block and rooting out this sort of error, believing that it would not be without great blame if, with closed eyes, I were to allow such things to pass by. But, looking to my own security in this matter, always relying on the counsel of learned men, it was necessary that I have recourse to the secular branch, especially when I considered that the knight himself had begun to put the case in the hands of a secular power, as was mentioned, by having the cloth remain in his possession and by having the right to exhibit and to display it to the people because of the safeguard of the king, which seems rather absurd; I saw to it that that cloth be placed in the king's hands, always seeking that goal, that at least while I brought the account of the matter to Your Holiness' attention, in the meantime there might be a suspension of the aforementioned exhibition, which I obtained gently and without any difficulty when the whole council of the king's Parliament was fully informed concerning the superstitious invention of this shroud and its abuse, and concerning the aforementioned error and stumbling block. And everybody knowing the merits of the case is amazed that I am impeded by the Church in this sort of prosecution, I, who ought to be helped vigorously, but rather ought to be punished severely if I were negligent or remiss in this matter. But nevertheless the aforementioned knight, forestalling me and, as is said, referencing the matters which were stated above, at last obtained from Your Holiness a letter, in which it is said in fact, having confirmed the letter of the aforementioned Lord Cardinal and from certain knowledge, that it is granted to the knight that, notwithstanding any prohibitions and appeals, it might be permitted that the cloth be exhibited and shown to the people, and venerated by the faithful, imposing on me perpetual silence, as it is reported, since I was unable to have a copy of the letter. But inasmuch as a canon requires me not to allow anyone to be deceived by worthless fabrications[67] or false documents on account of lucre, I am sure that the letter has been obtained through the suggestion of falsehood and the suppression of the truth, because otherwise it would not have been obtained without having summoned or listened to me, especially since the presumption ought to have been in my favor, that unless I had a motive I would have been unwilling to impede a business of this sort without cause or to disturb anyone in their prudent and otherwise well-ordered devotion. I am firmly confident that Your Holiness will uphold with equanimity that I resist the aforementioned exhibition, with the aforementioned issues in mind, until I receive different instructions from Your Holiness, once you have been informed more fully in the truth of the matter. Therefore, Most Blessed Father, may Your Holiness vouchsafe to direct the gaze of your consideration to the aforementioned and provide for these matters in such a way that this sort of error and stumbling block and detestable superstition be utterly rooted out both through action and restriction by the providence of Your Holiness, in such a way that that cloth neither as a shroud, nor a "sanctuary," nor as a representation or figure of the Lord's shroud, because the Lordly shroud was not made such, nor by any other contrived way or name be exhibited to the people or even venerated. But as a sign of reproaching superstition let it be condemned publicly after having revoked the aforementioned letter obtained through deceit, rather, declaring the letter void, [lest by chance the grudging persecutors of the Church and the invidious detractors that irreverently offend the governance of the Church eventually say that against the scandals and errors a stronger and more advantageous solution is found in the secular court than the ecclesiastical one].[68] For now I offer myself prepared in readiness to inform you adequately and without hesitation through public opinion and otherwise about everything I alleged above with a view to my justification and exoneration of conscience concerning this sort of deed, which is very close to my heart, and indeed I would have personally come before the presence of Your Holiness to set forth my complaint properly, if the strength of my body had allowed, certain that I am not able to

[67] Here the transcription of Chevalier, *variis figmentis*, must be corrected to *vanis figmentis*, an expression that appears in the text of canon 62 of Fourth Lateran Council.

[68] This part has been deleted in one of the two manuscripts. It can be conjectured that, at a later date, the author considered it too imprudent.

> express fully or sufficiently enough in writing the weight of the scandal, the reproach of the Church and ecclesiastical jurisdiction, and the danger to souls; nevertheless, I do what I am able, so that I may deserve to be excused chiefly before God, relinquishing what is left to the disposition of Your Holiness. May the Almighty see fit to preserve you auspiciously and for a long time as one useful and necessary to the guidance of His Holy Church. Written [etc.].[69]

The publication of this text at the end of the nineteenth century by the canon Ulysse Chevalier provoked heated reactions both from those who believed that they had finally found proof that the Shroud was not authentic and from sindonologists who quickly went to work to mitigate or nullify the importance of Chevalier's text. Before one draws any conclusions, then, it is necessary first to clear the field of many objections raised regarding the authenticity of this document and its contents,[70] and to clear away the accusations directed against Bishop Pierre d'Arcis, who has been characterized as "petty," author of a "slanderous libel," and driven by his interest in "prestige and money."[71] Certainly one cannot say that he was prejudiced against the worship of relics, since the city of Troyes was full of them: in the Church of St. Stephen there were already two fragments of a blood-stained shroud, preserved there since 1161, and in the treasure of the cathedral was the dish from Jesus' Last Supper, brought from Constantinople after the sack of 1204, along with relics of the cross,

[69] Chevalier, *Étude critique*, doc. G.

[70] For example, A. Eschbach, *Le Saint Suaire de notre Seigneur vénéré dans la cathédrale de Turin* (Turin: Marietti, 1913), 93–105, makes every attempt to demonstrate the falsehood or at least the inconsistency of the document; B. Bonnet-Eymard, "Study of Original Documents of the Archives of the Diocese of Troyes in France with Particular Reference to the Memorandum of Pierre d'Arcis," in *History, Science, Theology, and the Shroud*, ed. A. Berard (Amarillo: Man in the Shroud Committee, 1991), 233–60, with observations that are often erroneous or specious, believes that the Memorandum is a "miserable rough draft" devoid of any guarantee of authenticity, of unknown provenance, redacted by an anonymous cleric in the service of Pierre d'Arcis, written in bad faith, and never sent to the pope; and so he goes after modern "modernist" clerics who have attributed and continue to attribute value to it.

[71] G. M. Pugno, *La Santa Sindone che si venera a Torino* (Turin: SEI, 1961), 91; G. Sanna Solaro, *La S. Sindone che si venera a Torino illustrata e difesa* (Turin: Bona, 1901), 92; L. Fossati, *La Santa Sindone* (Turin: Borla, 1961), 94.

part of the head of Saint Philip, the arm of Saint James, and the whole body of Saint Helena.[72]

First, the source: currently, the original Memorandum sent to the pope has not been found, but two exemplars preserved by the sender survive: one a draft, the other a fair copy. The two manuscripts, today preserved at the Bibliothèque Nationale de France, certainly come from the archive of the diocese of Troyes, as evidenced by the fact that both are marked with two identifying shelf marks that coincide with those found in an index dating to 1519, which lists the documents present at the time in the episcopal archive.[73]

It has been proposed that the text was redacted in a form that was incomplete or unfit to be sent to the pope. The document does in fact begin without the customary *intitulatio*—that is, it begins without announcing the name of the sender—and it also lacks an *inscriptio*, which indicates the recipient; lastly, the manuscript is undated. But the fact that the *intitulatio* and *inscriptio* are not solemnly expressed should not be too astounding, given that it is a private letter;[74] the former, then, could have been added to the top of the original that was intended to be sent, while the latter was not necessary, as the recipient was clear.[75] The text ended with the word *scriptum*, commonly used to introduce a formula for dating; evidently the formula had to be completed later, in the physical copy to be delivered to the pope.

[72] Cf. C. Lalore, *Inventaires des principales églises de Troyes*, vol. 2 (Troyes: Dufour-Bouquot, 1893), 3 and 13 (inventory from 1319); H. d'Arbois de Jubainville, *Histoire des ducs et des comtes de Champagne*, vol. 3 (Paris: Durand, 1861), 181 and 344; C. Nioré, "Le vase de la cène dans l'ancien trésor de la cathédrale de Troyes," *Mémoires de la Société académique du Département de l'Aube* 32 (1895): 217–50.

[73] Cf. Chevalier, *Étude critique*, docs. I and J. Therefore, Emmanuel Poulle is wrong to accuse Chevalier of lacking evidence for it: "He even claims, without any proof, it was once taken from the episcopal archives" ("Le linceul de Turin victime d'Ulysse Chevalier," *Revue d'histoire de l'Église de France* 92 [2006]: 349). E. A. Wuenschel, *Self-portrait of Christ: The Holy Shroud of Turin* (Esopus: Holy Shroud Guild, 1954), 65, says of the Memorandum that "there exists only a late copy," which is false.

[74] Cf. A. Pratesi, *Genesi e forme del documento medievale* (Rome: Jouvence, 1987), 76–77; F. de Lasala and P. Rabikauskas, *Il documento medievale e moderno* (Rome: Pontificia Università Gregoriana, 2003), 51–52. To use Josef Blinzler's words, one can say that if we eliminated any historical testimony not presented according to standard protocol, our ancient history books would be full of empty pages ("Noch einmal: Zum Prozeß um das Turiner Grabtuch," *Benediktinische Monatsschrift* 32 [1956]: 236).

[75] "Most blessed father" can only be the pope, as the context immediately reveals.

Therefore, all of this is insufficient to cause the extant text to be considered unpresentable: with the addition of a few elements to indicate the sender and the date, it could essentially have been sent as it was. Pierre d'Arcis, moreover, was a jurist and had been an advisor at the Châtelet (a tribunal of Paris) and a lawyer at Parliament; he certainly knew how to draw up a document.

One of the two copies, the fair copy, has a name written on the back, *Magistro Guillelmo Fulconis* ("to the master Guillelmo Fulconis"). This man is certainly to be identified with Guillaume Foulques de Villebichot (Guillelmus Fulconis de Villabicheto), who was at the time *procurator* to the papal curia of Avignon.[76] The procurators of the Curia served as intermediaries and operated at the Holy See on behalf of a client—in this case the bishop Pierre d'Arcis—who was unable to act directly, either because of the geographic distance or because of the complexity of the matters to be considered. The bishop, then, was intending to send the text to his procurator so that he would present it to the pope. The procurators functioned as intermediaries but did not have the power to intervene in documents that came to them: if, then, Pierre d'Arcis had his Memorandum sent to Guillaume, and he presented it to the pope, we can be almost certain that it did not undergo substantial modifications in regard to its content. A later paraphrase of the document in French could raise some doubt,[77] since it expresses certain concepts differently than the original Latin, which could lead one to think that a different recension of the text was in circulation; it seems, however, that everything can also be explained by an imperfect rendering by the paraphraser.[78] In any

[76] On him, see P.-M. Berthe, *Les procureurs français à la cour pontificale d'Avignon* (Paris: École des Chartes, 2014), 579–82. The identification proposed by Zaccone must be corrected, specifically his assertion that "Villabicheto" refers to "Villeblovin" (or better, "Villeblevin"). For this error, see G. M. Zaccone, *La Sindone: Storia di una immagine* (Milan: Paoline, 2010), 112.

[77] Cf. Chevalier, *Étude critique*, doc. H.

[78] G. M. Zaccone, "The Shroud from the Charnys to the Savoys," *Sindon* 13 (2000): 399, notes these two discrepancies: in one case the subject is inverted ("the current dean of that church suggested to Geoffroy de Charny" becomes "the current dean of that church suggested by Geoffroy de Charny"); also, the end of the letter "is presented with different nuances and without such an explicit request." All things considered, the differences seem negligible to me. The first could be a simple error in translation, the second a hasty summary. I noticed these other differences as well: where the Latin says "it is not likely that the holy evangelists would have kept silent

case, the bishop's archive in Troyes has no alternate versions of the document, and it is difficult to imagine that the bishop would have wanted to preserve a version containing a text that was later modified, without preserving as well a copy of the definitive text.

Unfortunately, we do not have proof of the delivery to the procurator, and therefore to the pope, either; two points lend support to the two transfers: the first is that one of the two manuscripts of the Memorandum bears on its reverse the wording "copy of the letter sent by the Bishop of Troyes to our lord the Pope"; the second point is that the pope had to have received this information, because otherwise the tenor of the measures he took afterward is inexplicable. Discussion on this point, in any case, is partly otiose, since the historical value of this document lies in its content. Its consignment (or not) to the pope, either in this form or as a version lightly retouched on the advice of the procurator, is to us a question of less importance. In fact this document furnishes us with the actual thought of the bishop unimpeded by discretion or due caution.

In short, Pierre d'Arcis holds the dean of the collegiate church of Lirey, Robert de Caillac, responsible for his actions aimed at having the Shroud in his church and reaping economic benefits from it. This cloth (*pannum*) was cunningly portrayed (*artificiose depictum*; the verb *depingo* ought be understood as not necessarily "to paint" but also in general "to portray," "to depict," "to color," "to draw," "to embroider," or "to adorn" with any technique) in a subtle manner (*subtili modo*). The intervention of the bishop Henry de Poitiers was due to the fact that this cloth attracted too many people, enticed by the relic and by false miracles staged for them. Henry also posed the question of the Shroud's authenticity to many experts and theologians, who determined that the appearance of a shroud with an image inside

---

or omitted it, nor that it would have remained secret or hidden up to this time," the French paraphrase says "none of the Evangelists made mention of this effigy, which they would not have omitted and which would not have remained hidden from the bishops until this time"; and again, where the Latin says "without permission from the Ordinary of the place or anyone else," the French paraphrase is contradictory, saying "with the permission of the Ordinary," which can only be an error. Many points are summarized only briefly, because the French text is half as long as the Latin. However, when the French quotes Latin excerpts literally, it renders for us a text identical to the one we have. The evidence for postulating a different source seems to me insufficient.

cannot be reconciled with the silence of the Gospels and the entirety of the venerable ecclesiastical tradition.

The bishop also undertook an investigation that succeeded in uncovering the fraud, the craftsman, and the technique used: therefore "it was even proved by the artist who had portrayed it that it was made by work of a man."[79] The name of this forger is not mentioned, and further supporting documentation has not come down to us (assuming it existed); on the basis of this absence various defenders of the relic maintain that Pierre d'Arcis lied.[80] At the beginning of the previous century, someone claimed to have found this name in a certain document, but the report has not been verified.[81] Certainly one

[79] Bonnet-Eymard, *Study of Original Documents*, 239–40, manipulates the text to the point of translating it as "it was even proved, thanks to the artist who had reproduced it, that it was made by human hand," as if he were talking about a painter who had copied the Shroud onto another cloth. The translation is mistaken, as Béné has also noticed: C. Béné, "Une nouvelle interpretation du 'mémoire' de Pierre d'Arcy?," *La lettre mensuelle du Cielt* 30 (1992): 2–3.

[80] For example, F. Cognasso, "La S. Sindone di Torino e la tradizione storica medievale," in *La Santa Sindone nelle ricerche moderne: Risultati del convegno nazionale di studi sulla Santa Sindone tenuto a Torino nel 1939*, 2nd ed. (Turin: Lice-Berruti, 1950), 139–40; A. Koch, "Zum Prozeß um das Turiner Grabtuch," *Stimmen der Zeit*, 157 (1956): 412–13; G. Pisanu, "La storia e la Sindone di Torino," in Ladu, *Datazione della Sindone*, 231–35. A passage of F. de Mély, review of *Le portrait de N.-S. Jésus Christ*, by A. Loth, "Le portrait de N.-S. Jésus-Christ," *La chronique des arts et de la curiosité* 29 (September 8, 1900): 304, could have made it seem that a written acknowledgment of the artist existed, but it was a misunderstanding.

[81] In two letters written to the canon Ulysse Chevalier on February 1 and 7, 1902, the priest Arthur Prévost, historian of the diocese of Troyes, claims to have known from a certain source that the duke Pierre Eugène of Bauffremont, while conducting research on the Charny family documents preserved in archives of the department of Seine-et-Oise, had come across the name of the Shroud's painter. The duke informed Umberto I, king of Italy, who asked him to stay silent and keep it to himself (GBEI, R9089). I went to research the Charny family documents, which were later transferred to the archives of the department of Dijon. A cursory examination of the collection did not permit me to find anything like it, but a more in-depth search is needed. In general, those documents pertain to a later period and to other possessions of the Charny family apart from Lirey. The possibility that the quantity of documents has diminished since the duke's time cannot be ruled out, but there is currently no way to confirm Prévost's claim; we do know by other means, however, that the Duke of Bauffremont was studying the question in those years, and that Chevalier had heard about the possibility that the duke had discovered the document even before Prévost confirmed it for him. See the

cannot say—as some have—that Pierre d'Arcis was not in a position to know the particulars of an investigation undertaken in the past by Henry de Poitiers. Even before becoming bishop, since 1373, he lived in Troyes, having been appointed treasurer and vicar general of the bishop Jean Braque; a mere seven years separated Henry de Poitiers' death and the beginning of Pierre d'Arcis' bishopric; many of his canons were already in service in Henry's time (for example, Guillaume de Creney, the keeper of the seals). Pierre d'Arcis, therefore, had a means of informing himself on everything, even of hearing from the witnesses themselves.

The result of Henry's investigation was proceedings against the dean and the canons, which resulted in the concealment of the relic for thirty-four years "or so" (*vel circa*). This timeframe is very problematic. It is important to know what the bishop meant by that "or so": was he uncertain about the number of years or, more likely, of months? *Vel circa* is an expression that is encountered in many documents of the period, and it cannot be intended as an indication of the author's ignorance of the facts. If the Memorandum was written in the second half of the year 1389, after subtracting thirty-four years one comes to the year 1355; hypothetically, granted that the bishop counted the years by following the French calendar, which followed Easter-style method of calculation, one could extend the date when the Shroud began to be concealed up to April 23 of what for us today is 1356.[82] If the Memorandum was written in the early days of 1390 (allowing for the pope to have responded quickly by letter on January 6), using modern reckoning instead, one could include the whole of 1356, so that the Shroud may have ceased to be displayed at any point during this year. The uncertainties involved in calculating a date make it impossible to know definitively whether, according to Pierre d'Arcis, the exhibitions of the Shroud began when Geoffroy I de Charny was still alive (that is, before September 19, 1356). It should be noted that the bishop never names Geoffroy I and attributes all responsibility for the fraud to the dean and the canons. If the dean and the

epistolary documentation in A. Nicolotti, *Il processo negato* (Rome: Viella, 2015), 46–48.

[82] The current method, named "Circumcision-style," has the year begin on January 1. The French method, named "Easter-style," made Easter the beginning of the year, and therefore, for some of the early months, the date is a year behind the modern calculation.

canons were in fact solely responsible, it would not be important to know whether Geoffroy was alive or not at the time, since the dean Robert de Caillac was able to perform exhibitions without consulting him. At the time, in fact, Geoffroy was regularly absent from Lirey. According to the bishop, it was only the dean who induced Geoffroy II to reestablish the Shroud in the church, by intervening with the cardinal de Thury and obtaining permission to do it. Both the text of the papal bull of 1389 and the Memorandum of Pierre d'Arcis lead us to understand that the cardinal consented to the transfer of the Shroud for the worship of the faithful but was not informed of the reasons why it had been removed in the past, nor did he authorize exhibitions in which people were led to believe that the cloth was the true shroud of Christ.

The bishop denounced the performance of exhibitions in an elevated place with candles and vestments, as well as the encouragement of the popular conviction that the cloth was the true shroud of Christ, a notion instilled by instead calling the object a *sanctuarium*: the term was adopted—alongside the French variant *sanctuaire*—to indicate relics, especially those that had come into contact with the bodies of martyrs. *Sanctuaire* and *Sain(c)t-Suaire* ("Holy Shroud") do not differ markedly in pronunciation. The dean and Geoffroy responded to the prohibition against performing exhibitions with an appeal and a royal safeguard. Pierre d'Arcis was annoyed by the fact that they took their case directly to the pope without even consulting him, and because they accused him of opposing the cardinal's letter; he, on the contrary, believed that he had in no way disregarded the cardinal's orders by his own instruction allowing the placement of the Shroud in the church, but not its solemn exhibition. The bishop was convinced that the cardinal had consented to the dean's request because he was ill-informed and unaware of what was actually happening in the collegiate church. Evidently, he was displeased as well that the pope had listened to the requests of the dean and Geoffroy and fulfilled them without asking his opinion—and also without notifying him by providing a copy of the letter sent to Geoffroy.

Pierre felt the need to justify himself for having recourse to the king and to Parliament when he convinced them to seize the Shroud, saying that he did it only after the dean and Geoffroy had already requested and obtained the intervention of secular power.[83] We can imagine that this turn to secular authority, invoked to resolve an ecclesiastical question, left the pope more than a little annoyed, and that, also for that reason, he resolved to decide in favor of the collegiate church of Lirey without consulting the bishop and acted discourteously in neglecting to notify him of his decision. The bishop, for his part, also believed that the pope's decision was made without a full understanding of the facts and declared that he was confident that he acted appropriately in impeding the exhibitions, which, in his opinion, were being performed solely for the sake of lucre and to the detriment of the faithful. His was an opposition that was necessary, he would have us understand, for reasons pertaining simultaneously to doctrinal and pastoral order.[84] He was not alone: the canon of the Fourth Lateran Council of 1215, which is quoted by the bishop in the Memorandum, obligated the clergy to remain vigilant, so that the people who went to the churches to venerate the relics "were not deceived by worthless fabrications or false documents, as is practiced in very many places for lucre," an exercise very widespread at the time.[85]

For Clement VII (Robert de Genève), the situation was bound to prove very complicated. On the one hand there were the weighty requests from one of his own bishops, who had obtained the support of the king and Parliament. On the other hand, there were the canons of Lirey and their influential protector Geoffroy II. Moreover, he had to contend also with the embarrassment of familial connection: Aymon de Genève—Geoffroy II's stepfather and the second husband of his mother, Jeanne de Vergy—was in fact the pope's uncle.[86] We do not

[83] In this sense Zaccone, "Shroud from the Charnys to the Savoys," 399–400, according to whom the document can also be understood as a sort of defensive memory.

[84] On which reasons Zaccone lingers: Zaccone, *Sindone: Storia di una immagine,* 113–16.

[85] *Concilium Lateranense IV,* constitutio 62.

[86] That is, an uncle according to the custom in Brittany, or, as we would say, a second cousin. Aymon was the grandson of Amadeus II, Count of Geneva; that same Amadeus was the great-grandfather of the pope. Therefore, the pope's father was Aymon's first cousin. Many authors identify Aymon as the pope's uncle because, according to a particular practice for defining familial relationships (*oncle à la manière de Bretagne*), sometimes also used in Italy, first cousins of a parent are simply called "uncles."

know whether Clement examined the issue more closely by listening to other witnesses, but we know his decision, which was promulgated in a document on January 6, 1390. In part it pleased the canons and Geoffroy by confirming the decision of the cardinal legate and granting authorization to continue the exhibitions. In part it pleased the bishop, insisting forcefully on prohibition against performing solemn exhibitions in which the relic was treated as authentic and not simply as a devotional representation.

His papal bull of 1390 can be divided into two parts. The first part is simply the word-for-word reprisal of the bull of July 28, 1389, with the exposition (*narratio*) of the facts up to that point. The second part, however, contains new instructions on performing exhibitions of the Shroud, thereby also offering an implicit response to the objections contained in the Memorandum of Bishop Pierre d'Arcis (which, therefore, had to be known to the pope). To complicate the matter further, two versions of the bull existed, created some time apart. The first version was written in January, while the second, written in June, is shorter and was corrected in certain points, granting the canons more freedom. The dual texts of this bull have provoked endless discussions: perhaps the pope had an afterthought? Perhaps he desired to encourage the worship of the relic? Perhaps the first version of the bull was only a draft, and was never sent? Answers to these questions can only come from a careful examination of the manuscripts.

Fortunately, the text of the bull, in both versions, is preserved at the Vatican in the Avignon registers, in which documents issued by the pope were transcribed from either a draft or the original. An overview of the register reveals that the bull was dated January 6, 1390, and that a month later, on February 6, it was probably sent to its recipients (or to whoever their proxies were). Almost three months later, however, something led the Holy See to modify certain details in the text, a practice that was not unusual.[87] On May 28, the text was corrected by order of Giovanni Moccia da Napoli, *secretarius* of the pope;[88] then, two days later, on May 30, the bull was sent again in its corrected form, and was corrected on the register as well, where traces of the pen and the additions made on that occasion remain

[87] In that same register, I counted sixteen other corrected bulls.

[88] On Moccia, see A. Coville, *La vie intellectuelle dans les domaines d'Anjou-Provence de 1380 à 1435* (Paris: Droz, 1941), 369–93.

visible. Similar corrections were also made to another bull that retained the same content but was addressed to officials in Langres, Autuns, and Châlons.[89] The recipients likely had to arrange for the substitution of the old version with the new one: the papal register records the delivery date of the first version, which was then erased and replaced with the second version's delivery date. Today, originals of the two final versions are preserved,[90] while we have only a contemporary copy of the first versions.[91] It is probable that the originals of the first version were lost, since they were substituted with the new corrected originals. In any case, some example of the first version must have been circulated, as evidenced by the fact that in 1624 Jean-Jacques Chifflet cited in one of his books an excerpt of that version of the letter.[92]

At this point, since the edition of this papal text has in the past generated much discussion, it will be helpful to translate the bull, indicating clearly its modifications. The left-hand column contains the text of the first version. On the right is the second, corrected version (the document is only divided where the two versions differ):

[89] Here are the ends of the two documents. ASV, Reg. Aven. 261, f. 259r: "Datum Avinione VIII idus ianuarii anno duodecimo. +—+ ~~T(radit)a XIII VIII idus februarii anno XII°. H(enricus) Monachi. R(ubricata)~~. Exp(edita) V ~~idus~~ kalendas iunii anno XII°. R(aymundus) de Valle. T(radit)a et correcta III kalendas iunii anno XII°. H(enricus) Monachi. R(ubricata)." ASV, Reg. Aven. 261, f. 259v: "Datum Avinione VIII idus ianuarii anno duodecimo. + ~~T(radit)a VIII idus februarii anno XII. H(enricus) Monachi. R(ubricata). Exped(ita)~~ + T(radit)a et correcta III kalendas iunii anno XII. H(enricus) Monachi. R(ubricata)." The deleted lines matched the first version of the text and were struck through with the stroke of a pen; two corrections to errors in dating have also been made (which I have indicated with a double strikethrough). *Datum* indicates the date of the issue; *expedita* marks the date on which the letter was put in writing and prepared; *tradita* (*parti*) means "delivered to the recipient" or whoever was acting as a stand-in at the pontifical court; *rubricata* means "noted in the index of delivered letters." The signs of the cross sometimes mark out a blank space for inserting the name of the *rescribendarius*; sometimes, on the contrary, they stand in place of the *expedita*. The names of the papal officials are Raymond Duval, in charge of making the text, and Henry Moine, responsible for the delivery (cf. X. Serra Estellés, *Los registros de súplicas y letras pontificias de Clemente VII de Aviñón* [Rome: Iglesia Nacional Española, 1988], 122, 132, 125 [including n. 101], and 165–66).

[90] ADA, I 19 n. 3 and 4 (original parchments).

[91] BNF, MS Lat. 10410, f. 113r–v. The same handwriting is used at the papal court. Are we perhaps dealing with a copy made by the chancellery from minutes or a register?

[92] J.-J. Chifflet, *De linteis sepulchralibus Christi Servatoris crisis historica* (Antwerp: Apud Balthasarem Moretum, 1624), 102.

> Clement, a bishop, servant of the servants of God, for the future remembrance hereof. The prudent foresight of the Apostolic See sometimes modifies what has been granted by it, and it decides and prescribes concerning those things as the condition of matters and the times require, and it observes that it is beneficially profitable in the Lord.

The subsequent portion comes from the bull of 1389; afterward it continues as follows:

> Therefore, as concerns this sort of method of exhibition, we want to remove any chance of error and idolatry, being concerned to make provision for a suitable remedy, and by the tenor of the present document, through apostolic authority, we establish and ordain, whenever it happens hereafter that the already-mentioned figure or representation is shown to the people, the aforementioned dean and chapter, and other ecclesiastical persons showing this figure or representation and present during this sort of exhibition,

for as long as the exhibition itself continues by no means on that account should they wear cloaks, surplices, albs, copes, or any other ecclesiastical garb or paraments, nor may they perform other	they may not perform any of the

> solemnities that are customarily performed during exhibitions of relics; and that for this reason torches, flambeaux, or candles should on no account be lit

	for solemnity

> nor are any lights to be used in that place. When showing the aforementioned figure, when a major crowd of people will have gathered there,

	at least each time that it happens that in that very place a sermon should be given,

he should preach publicly to the people and say in a loud, intelligible voice, stopping any deception, that the aforementioned figure or representation

is not the true shroud of our Lord Jesus Christ, but a sort of depiction or painting made as a figure or representation of the shroud	they display not as the true shroud of our Lord Jesus Christ, but as a figure or representation of the aforementioned shroud

that is said to have been that of our Lord Jesus Christ himself. We decree that in the case that our will, decree, and this order are not observed, our aforementioned letter and its effect are null and void. Let no one then at all be permitted to infringe upon this expression of our will, decree, ordinance, and mandate or in reckless abandon to contradict this document. But if anyone presumes to attempt it, let him know that he will incur the indignation of Almighty God and his blessed apostles Peter and Paul. Given in Avignon, on the eighth day before the Ides of January, in the twelfth year of our pontificate.[93]

In 1386, at Rippingale, in the diocese of Lincoln, something similar to the case of Lirey happened: the bishop conducted an investigation and discovered that some of his faithful had constructed a statue, called the Jurdon Cross, and had begun to worship it, claiming that it was a source of miracles. In that case the bishop's actions were repudiated by the pope, who dismissed all objections and, in 1392, authorized in addition the construction of a chapel in honor of the object.[94] For Lirey, however, matters did not unfold in quite the same

[93] Chevalier, *Autour des origines du suaire de Lirey*, doc. J (the first version appears in the text; the second version in the apparatus); I have verified it in the register of Avignon and in the original of the ADA. Chevalier has been accused many times of having maliciously produced an edition that masked the corrections of the second version (most recently, for reasons I agree with only in part, by Poulle, "Linceul de Turin"); Chevalier himself had already attempted to respond to this accusation (*Autour des origines du suaire de Lirey*, 12–14). My synopsis resolves the root of the problem.

[94] Cf. D. M. Owen, "Bacon and Eggs: Bishop Buckingham and Superstition in Lincolnshire," in *Popular Belief and Practice*, ed. G. J. Cuming and D. Baker (Cambridge: Cambridge University Press, 1972), 141.

way. The substance of the papal action is clear: by changing course from his 1389 decision, the pope in part became subject to Pierre d'Arcis' complaints and imposed some limitations on the canons; one could rightly call the decision "diplomatic."[95] Without forbidding exhibitions, "to remove any chance of error and idolatry," he forbade the clergy from wearing solemn liturgical dress on those occasions. Then he ordered the priests to speak to the faithful in a loud voice, "stopping any deception," that the ceremony to which they were attending was not the exhibition of the true shroud of Christ. In a very similar bull, he later instructed the officials of Langres, Autuns, and Châlons to keep watch over the enforcement of his instructions.[96] The pope, who may have been a little annoyed, addressed a brief notice to the bishop, in which he urged him not to impose further obstacles to the enforcement of his order, under threat of excommunication.[97]

Without substantial modification of his decision, about five months later, the text of the bull was corrected. If, in the first version, the pope clarified what garb the clergy should not wear, in the second he only specified that the exhibitions of the Shroud could not occur with the solemnity afforded to relics: the prohibition against wearing any type of choir dress or any paraments forced the canons to perform exhibitions clothed in ordinary garb, which evidently seemed too restrictive. The second version, then, specified that a public announcement by the canons had to be made as part of every sermon that usually accompanied this sort of liturgy. The most significant change comes in the final section. In the first version, the canons were obligated to announce clearly that the Shroud was not the true shroud of Christ but its "depiction" (*pictura*) or "painting" (*tabula*). One might suppose that someone made the pope aware that the terms *pictura* and *tabula* were not the most suitable for describing the object as it was in reality. Moreover, the phrase "it is not the true shroud of the Lord" was replaced with "they display [it] not as the true shroud of the Lord," as if the pope wanted to use language that was less direct. Leaving, however, the reference to idolatry, not recalling the prohibition of solemn exhibitions and continuing to pretend the priest would proclaim that the exhibition did not concern the

[95] Koch, *Zum Prozeß*, 414.
[96] Cf. Chevalier, *Autour des origines du suaire de Lirey*, doc. K (corrected version).
[97] Cf. Chevalier, *Étude critique*, doc. N.

true shroud of Christ, the pope in substance maintained his position: the Shroud was a "figure or representation" of the shroud, not the authentic shroud.

The *litterae communes* (public letters) of Clement VII have been preserved well enough, but his private correspondence has been lost entirely,[98] for which reason we do not know whether or not there was any private correspondence or some negotiation conducted to modify the text. In any case, it is erroneous to infer from the second version, from May, that the pope, having realized the inconsistency of Pierre d'Arcis' accusations, did not want to take a position on the relic's authenticity but only wanted to advise prudence and that, personally, he was hesitant or, rather, convinced of its authenticity.[99] The inadmissibility of the latter position is evident in the fact that, in addition to everything else, he did not withdraw the order to "stop any deception." Therefore in modern times Clement has come under heavy fire from some who believe in the authenticity of the Shroud and who accuse him of having signed "old papers, smeared with squabbles, stamped with concerns"[100] in adopting a measure "founded only on ridiculous reasons"[101] and carrying out an "act of weakness and complaisance."[102]

Immediately after the corrected version of the bull was sent, Clement VII granted a year and forty days' indulgence to whoever, being penitent and confessed, would visit the church of Lirey—the church, not the Shroud specifically—and make donations during certain religious holidays, and he struck whoever stole alms from the

[98] Cf. R. C. Logoz, *Clément VII (Robert de Genève): Sa chancellerie et le clergé romand au début du Grand Schisme* (Lausanne: Payot, 1974), 217.

[99] As Poulle claims: Poulle, "Linceul de Turin," 350, 353–54. For me the observations of the one who discovered the Vatican documents, Msgr. Guillaume Mollat, remain valid (*Clément VII et le suaire de Lirey*, 257–58). There is no value in the considerations of J.-B. Rinaudo and C. Gavach, *Le linceul de Jésus enfin authentifié?* (Paris: François-Xavier de Guibert, 2010), 70–71, who did not understand anything about the question and who in addition attribute to Poulle the discovery of manuscripts known for more than a century.

[100] G. Intrigillo, *Sindone: L'istruttoria del secolo* (Cinisello Balsamo: San Paolo, 1998), 31.

[101] G. Re, *La Santissima Sindone: Racconto storico popolare* (Turin: Paravia, 1903), 21.

[102] E. Colomiatti, "De l'authenticité du Saint Suaire de Turin," *Revue des sciences ecclésiastiques* 80 (1899): 418.

church with censure, a measure that could only be absolved by the Holy See.[103] This action could perhaps signify that the pope wanted to compensate the canons, at least in part, for the damage eventually caused by the enforcement of his restrictive decisions, or that he desired to strike a conciliatory chord with them and with Geoffroy II, who was the stepson of his father's first cousin. One cannot conclude, however, that this new document indicates implicitly that the pope took a position on the authenticity of the cloth, since the phrasing used in granting indulgences, though mentioning the presence in the church of the "figure or representation of the shroud," follows the traditional formula for granting indulgences to churches dedicated to Mary (the collegiate church had already obtained many indulgences in January 1354, without mention of any shroud).

We must remember that the appearance of this shroud in Lirey did not cause difficulties for the popes because of the presence of other similar relics in different places. As soon as he had resolved the matter in Lirey, in 1394, Clement VII had to settle a question on the ownership of the holy shroud of Cadouin (another fabric of considerable size).[104] Some years later, in 1405, Benedict XIII of Avignon granted various privileges to a chapel in Toulouse, where the shroud of Jesus (which afterward was the one in Cadouin, the long Islamic linen) "is said to be preserved."[105] As Patrick Geary has aptly written, "the multiplicity of bodies or identical relics of saints was a constant phenomenon that only occasionally caused serious disputes or disagreements."[106]

The matter in Lirey was therefore resolved temporarily. Geoffroy II de Charny, who, like his father, spent little time in Lirey, left for the Barbary Crusade with a group of knights sent by Philip II the Bold, Duke of Burgundy, in the summer of 1390.[107] The following year he went to Prussia.[108] Nearly everyone today confuses our

[103] Cf. Chevalier, *Autour des origines du suaire de Lirey*, doc. L.

[104] Cf. J. Dupuy, *L'estat de l'église du Périgord depuis le christianisme*, vol. 2 (Perigueux: Dalvy, 1629), 123–24.

[105] Cf. Savio, *Ricerche storiche*, V, n. 1.

[106] P. J. Geary, *Furta sacra: Thefts of Relics in the Central Middle Ages* (Princeton: Princeton University Press, 1978), 64.

[107] Cf. J. Kervyn De Lettenhove, ed., *Œuvres de Froissart: Chroniques*, vol. 14 (Brussels: Devaux, 1872), 225.

[108] Cf. W. Paravicini, *Die Preußenreisen des europäischen Adels*, vol. 2 (Sigmaringen: Thorbecke, 1995), 196, n. 29.

Geoffroy II with another Geoffroy de Charny, the bailiff of Caux and Mantes-la-Jolie, but the bailiff was a bastard son and served the Duke of Burgundy as *maître d'hôtel*. It is not impossible that this *bâtard* could have been an illegitimate son of Geoffroy I.[109]

In 1396 Geoffroy, Lord of Montfort, Savoisy, and Lirey, appears among those who accompanied John the Fearless, Count of Nevers, to the Crusade of Nicopolis.[110] On September 25, 1396, the troops suffered a tremendous defeat at Nicopolis, where whoever was not killed was taken prisoner. Only a few were set free, after paying a ransom, and were able to return to France at the beginning of 1398. It seems that our Geoffroy was one of those who did not return.[111] This unfortunate outcome precludes what is usually asserted, that Geoffroy was buried at the abbey of Froidmont. The effigy on this tomb, dated May 22, 1398, bears the name Geoffroy. Indeed, the stone is reproduced in nearly every book on the Shroud, since it portrays the figure of the knight wearing armor.[112] However, the Geoffroy de Charny buried in Froidmont is recorded there as "Lord of Thury-sous-Clermont," not of Montfort, and the noble coat of arms depicted on his chest is certainly not that of our Geoffroy.[113] It remains unclear whether Geoffroy the bailiff and Geoffroy, Lord of Thury, were the same person or, rather, relatives.

[109] ADC, B1465, f. 80v: "Messire Geuffroy bastart de Charny, chevalier, bailly de Caux et maistre d'ostel." The error occurs again in M. G. Dupont-Ferrier, *Gallia regia ou état des officiers royaux des bailliages et des sénéchaussées de 1328 à 1515*, vol. 2 (Paris: Imprimerie nationale, 1942), § 5871; vol. 4, 1954, § 14847.

[110] Cf. A. S. Atiya, *The Crusade of Nicopolis* (London: Methuen, 1934), 144 and 147.

[111] The claim was made by the historian Alexis Salazard, who in the eighteenth century gathered various reports from documents preserved at the Chamber of Audit of Dijon, which are today in part lost: BNF, MS Bourgogne 26, f. 288: "Charny, Gieffroy de, chevalier, seigneur de Montfort, mourut au voyage d'Hongrie où il fut avec le conte de Nevers" ("Charny, Gieffroy de, knight, lord of Montfort, died on the voyage from Hungary where he was with the count of Nevers").

[112] The tombstone is now lost, though the design can be found in BNF, Estampes, Réserve Pe 3, f. 16 (Gaignières 3898): https://gallica.bnf.fr/ark:/12148/btv1b6907040j.item.

[113] They differ in that the escutcheon on the tomb contains a bend, a typical means of identifying different or bastard branches of a family (it is a "brisure"). The coat of arms of Geoffroy the bailiff, a bastard, also contains this same brisure (cf. Demay, *Inventaire des sceaux*, 235, § 2229). The coat of arms belonging to Geoffroy of Montfort and Lirey does not have any brisures.

2.1.6 Pilgrimage Badges

Up to this point we have dealt with written descriptions of the Shroud of Lirey. But some iconographic representations have come down to us as well. In the second half of the fourteenth century, the town of Lirey—documents tell us—became a destination for pilgrims because of the Shroud. It was customary that pilgrims, once they reached their destination, bought an object to put around their neck, on their clothes, or on their hat as a memento and testimony of their pilgrimage. Some of these mementos were natural objects (like the seashell of Santiago de Compostela or the palm of Jerusalem); others were manufactured. To the latter category belonged certain insignia, particular to each sanctuary, in the form of a plaque or medallion made from lead, tin, or an alloy of the two. The metal was formed using two stone dies (three, if a pin were added to the back), into which the melted metal was poured; symmetrical holes made on the stones caused them to line up precisely, and small channels were carved on the mold for the excess metal to run out. The engravings bore, in mirrored form, the design that would then be formed on the plaque. The insignia were produced in a series, and the rights belonged to the church, which then made a profit from their sale.[114]

We are fortunate enough to have a medallion and a schistose stone mold belonging in fact to the collegiate church in Lirey. The medallion was found in 1855 in Paris, in the River Seine near the Pont au Change (fig. 2.1);[115] the mold was found in 2009 in the region of Gadouille, at the border of the town of Machy, which is between 3 and 4 km from the collegiate church of Lirey (fig. 2.2).[116]

[114] On these objects, see D. Bruna, *Enseignes de plomb et autres menues chosettes* (Paris: Le Léopard d'Or, 2006).

[115] Paris, Musée National du Moyen Âge, CL 4752 (45 × 62 mm). Cf. M. Prinet, "Une image du Saint Suaire," *Procès-verbaux et mémoires—Académie des sciences de Besançon* (1923): 165–71; D. Bruna, *Enseignes de pèlerinage et enseignes profanes* (Paris: Réunion des musées nationaux, 1996), 61–62 (with faulty details on the history of the relic); *D'azur et d'argent: L'art du blason en Champagne*, exhibition catalog (Troyes: Amis des archives de l'Aube, 2000), § 37.

[116] Private property of Alain Hourseau, who describes it in his book *Autour du Saint Suaire et de la collégiale de Lirey (Aube)* (Paris: BoD, 2012), 233–37. I criticized some aspects of this book in *Rivista storica italiana* 125, no. 3 (2013): 890–99. Based on the dimensions of the stone, the dimensions of the medallion would have been 70 × 62 mm.

FIGURE 2.1 Pilgrimage badge of Lirey (Aube), between 1355 and 1410

FIGURE 2.2 Mold for a pilgrimage badge of Lirey (Aube), between 1355 and 1410, mirror image

FIGURE 2.3 Exhibition of the Roman Veil of Veronica

The survival of these objects is truly fortunate, since both depict an exhibition of the Shroud. They are currently the oldest existing representations of the Shroud, although broken and incomplete.

At the center of the image there are two clerics clothed in copes who, during an exhibition, spread out the Shroud while supporting it with their hands. Only on the stone mold are their heads visible, which are uncovered and tonsured. In the following centuries, representations based on this same model almost always depict the heads covered with a miter, because the exhibitions were performed by bishops and no longer by the canons of Lirey. On the Parisian medallion, the upper part of which is missing, it is impossible to tell whether on the sides there were two columns forming part of the structure of the church, or rather two decorated posts of an altar or chest in which the Shroud was preserved (perhaps a coffer such as is mentioned in a document of 1418, to which I will return later). The mold of the second medallion, being less damaged, shows us instead an architectural feature, specifically a gothic cornice composed of three twisted columns that support two pointed arches. The room is elevated, and from there the Shroud is shown to the gathered people, whom the report of the bailiff of Troyes and the Memorandum of Pierre d'Arcis mention. Perhaps a specially constructed wooden stand was carried out with equipment similar to that used in Rome for the Veil of Veronica (fig. 2.3). Just under the Shroud, two shields with heraldic coats of arms on them are visible, which perhaps also hung from the parapet of the balcony. The shields on the stone are separated by an image of Christ's face, while on the metal artifact they are separated by an empty and open tomb from which protrudes a cross adorned with a crown. On the metal piece, devices used in Jesus' torture are also visible (the *arma Christi*), such as the scourge. At the bottom center of the stone are the words "SVAIRE IhV" ("shroud of Jesus"); on either side of the stone, under the coats of arms, appear two letters that are difficult to identify because they are damaged: on the left is "V" (vocalic or consonantal), or else "E" or "C"; and on the right "C" or "O." Is it therefore difficult to tell whether the writing is entirely in French or rather a combination of French and Latin.[117] We cannot even exclude the possibility that we are dealing

[117] There are various possibilities: for example, *Vergy—Suaire Ihesu—Charny* (initials of the surnames below the coats of arms); or, mixing French and Latin, *est*

with decorative motifs, not letters, or perhaps the Greek letters alpha and omega (A and Ω). On the shroud depicted on the mold, one can see a herringbone pattern, which is usually interpreted as the precise representation of a type of weaving of the relic. That is possible, but it could also be a simple decorative motif that perhaps was intended to evoke generally the design of a fabric. On the cloth that pattern is recognizable only if one examines it very closely, for at a distance of 2 m the pattern is no longer perceptible; each chevron shape in the herringbone pattern is formed by two strips, each of which measures 11 mm in length. The benefit of reproducing on the medallion the exact woven pattern, enlarged beyond actual proportions, as a means of identification, is therefore difficult to understand. It should be noted, too, that the twill pattern carved on the stone of the medallion is an incorrect representation of the original, since it does not go in the right direction (it is horizontal instead of vertical).

On the metal artifact the body of the man depicted on the Shroud is visible, both front and back, with the limbs being quite noticeable. On the dorsal image of the figure on the mold some swellings are perceptible at the level of the loins and feet. They are difficult to interpret, and it has been proposed to view them as a representation of the drops of blood or burn marks. On the stone, which is more damaged, the feet of the man are just barely discernible.

The coats of arms on the shields deserve some elaboration. The one with three shields pertains to the de Charny family (gules, three Escutcheons, two and one, Argent), the other, with three flowers, to Jeanne de Vergy (gules, three Cinquefoils, two and one, Or, in a border, Argent).[118] The position of the coats of arms changes between the artifacts: on the Machy mold, the coat of arms of the de Charnys is on the left (one must recall that, for a coat of arms, left and right are reversed in respect to the viewer); on the Paris medallion, it is on the right. Since the right is the preeminent side, if the coat of arms of

---

suaire Ihesu Crist; ecce suaire Ihesu Christi (the reading that I initially preferred).

118 There is no agreement of the color of the bordure (argent, sable, or azure): cf. J.-L. Chassel, *Sceaux, armes et emblemes de la maison de Vergy* (L'Étang-Vergy: Amis de Vergy, 1976), 17. In heraldry, the bordure is a band of contrasting tincture forming a border around the edge of the shield; it is often used as a way of distinguishing identical coats of arms that belong to the members of the same family (cadency), such as when there is a need to indicate a distinct branch of a particular family (in this case the cadet branch of the family Vergy, lords of Mirebeau).

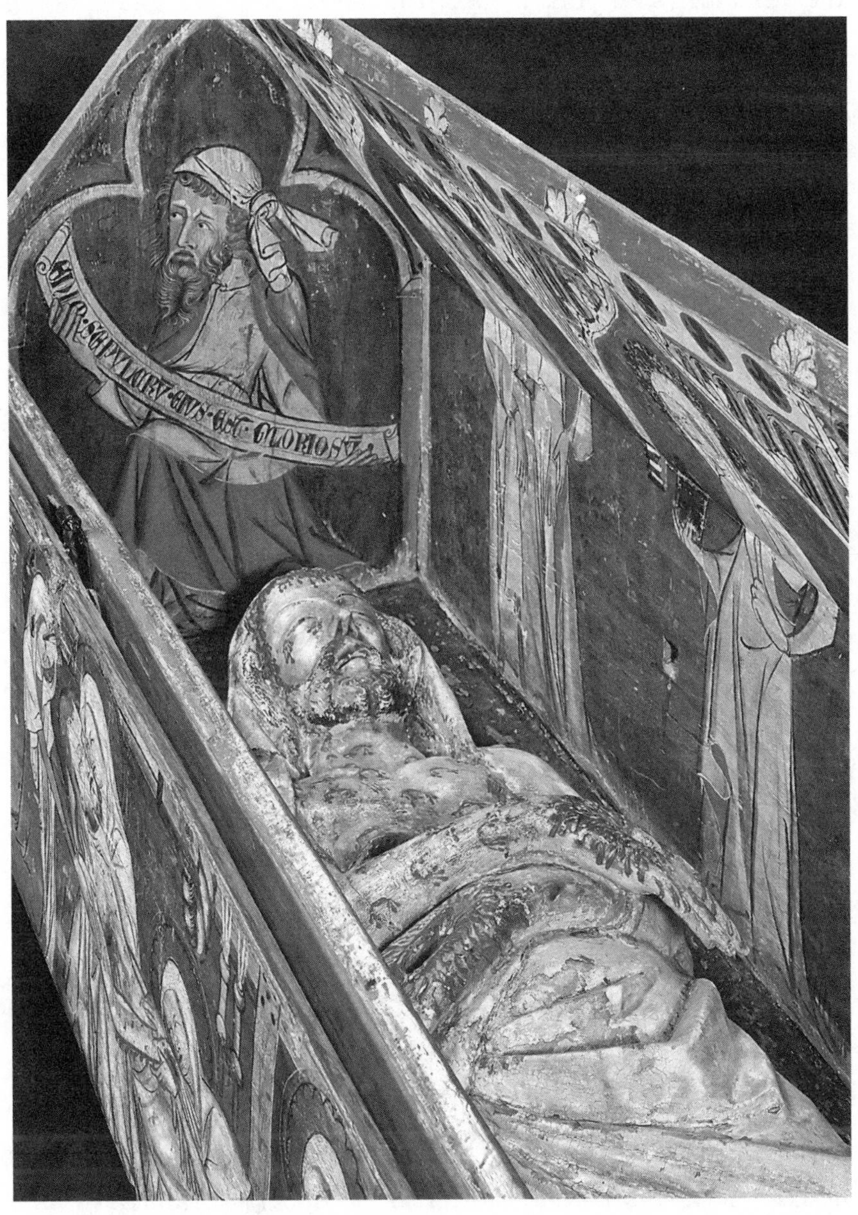

FIGURE 2.4 Tomb for the Easter grave of Maigrauge Monastery, circa 1330

the de Charnys pertains to Geoffroy I, one could presume that the medallion was made before the death of the Lord of Lirey (September 19, 1356) and that the mold dates from a time when he was already deceased, since he then lost his position of prominence in favor of his wife Jeanne.[119] That interpretation, however, is not secure: it is true that the position on the right was generally reserved for men, except for certain cases in which the positions were reversed to emphasize the eminence of the wife over her husband. But it is equally true that this practice was not always used and that there are known instances of women who continued to have their coats of arms depicted on the left even after the death of their husbands or who placed their own heraldry on the right despite not being widows.[120]

One cannot even exclude entirely the possibility that the coat of arms of the de Charnys refers not to Geoffroy I but rather to his son Geoffroy II, who had inherited the heraldry and lordship of Lirey from his father; he could have continued to place his coat-of-arms alongside his mother's. The rules of heraldry at that time were still not strictly codified. As a result, I believe that the positions of the two shields does not provide a sufficient basis to establish with complete certainty the chronological priority of one or the other of the objects, and I think that the combination of the heraldry of the de Charnys and the Vergys can lead only to the conclusion that both objects may date back to the period of the first exhibitions (ca. 1355), even if the period of the second exhibitions (ca. 1389) cannot be excluded entirely.[121]

[119] Alain Hourseau indicates this possibility, suggested to him by Ian Wilson, but causes confusion by considering "right" and "left" from the perspective of the observer, and not in respect to the images represented, as heraldic practice requires: that leads him to a conclusion exactly opposite of what is in fact the case. It must be added that the presence of both coats of arms of the two spouses should not lead one to think that the exhibitions happened before Geoffroy's death (as asserted by F. Barbesino and M. Moroni, *Lungo le strade della Sindone* [San Paolo: Cinisello Balsamo 2000], 70), since widows had the right to retain their husbands' coat of arms, at least until they were eventually remarried (as is rightly noted by A. Lombatti, *Sfida alla Sindone* [Pontremoli: Centro editore, 2000], 181).

[120] For a variety of examples, see C. Schleif, "Men on the Right—Women on the Left," in *Women's Space: Patronage, Place, and Gender in the Medieval Church*, ed. V. Chieffo Raguin and S. Stanbury (Albany: State University of New York Press, 2005), 207–49.

[121] For the reasons expressed above, I cannot consider Wilson's theory that suggests the mold originates from the period of the first exhibitions in the mid-fourtheenth century and the Paris badge from the end of that century: I. Wilson,

According to Marcello Semeraro, it is quite probable that the Paris badge dates from the period of the first exhibitions, though there is more uncertainty regarding the mold.[122] It is in any case impossible that they were made after the death of Jeanne de Vergy, in November or December of 1410.

2.1.7 What Did the Shroud Mean to People Centuries Ago?

Geoffroy II described the Shroud of Lirey as a "figure or representation" of the shroud of Christ. Cardinal de Thury characterized it in the same way, allowing it to be kept in the church but not, by doing so, authorizing any act of veneration befitting relics. The pope did likewise, permitting that such a "figure or representation" be displayed as such, while avoiding any deception and any solemnity. Whoever reads these words recognizes immediately that they are referring to not an original but a copy. Moreover, in their appeals neither Geoffroy nor the canons ever sought to characterize the Shroud as an authentic relic.[123] What they asked of the cardinal and the pope was not the authentication of a relic but permission to display the "figure or representation" of a relic. The terminology used does not allow much room for misunderstanding; the words *figure* and *representation* could refer to any reproduction of a sacred image. At issue here is the "figure or representation" not of the image of Jesus but of his shroud: the object being represented, to which the term "figure or representation" refers, is not the body of Christ but rather his shroud, including the image.[124] Three clergymen of Lieges understood

---

"A (Very Tangled) Tale of Two Pilgrim Badges," *British Society for the Turin Shroud Newsletter* 86 (2017): 18–26.

122 Semeraro, "Una committenza."

123 Even sindonologist Werner Bulst thinks that "the ancient owners (and Clement VII with them) did not regard the cloth as the true shroud of Jesus": *The Shroud of Turin* (Milwaukee: Bruce, 1957), 15.

124 According to Poulle, "Linceul de Turin," 350, it is on the contrary clear that the expression *figura seu repraesentatio sudarii* must be translated "image or representation that appears on the sheet" (that is, the form of the crucified man imprinted on the fabric), and that the pope, in using this phrasing, implied that the relic was authentic. It is clear to me that this is not the case. The pope, first of all, forbade the canons to treat the Shroud as authentic; he would have contradicted himself by implying its authenticity. Clement spoke of a *figura sive representatio sudarii Domini nostri Ihesu Christi liberaliter oblata* ("figure or representation of our Lord Jesus Christ's shroud, offered to him in generosity"; that is, the image on the Shroud is

properly when in 1449 they read these documents: "within them it is said expressly that the linen is not the true shroud of Jesus Christ, but only a representation and a figure."[125]

King Charles and Pierre d'Arcis substantially affirm something similar: the Shroud is a "handmade cloth, rendered skillfully in respect to figure and likeness, and as a tribute to the sacred shroud" in which the body of Jesus was wrapped, or a "cloth cunningly portrayed." They were unable to find any fault in the characterization of the object advanced by its guardians —at least officially—but they were opposed to the practice of solemn exhibitions.

Therein lies the heart of the problem: the accusation directed against the canons by the two bishops of Troyes and King Charles was not that of displaying a "representation" of the shroud but of displaying it fraudulently as if it were an authentic relic. The church's preservation of a simple artistic representation would not have provoked any protest, as long as the object could be interpreted as a painting, a sacred image intended for the edification of the faithful. The canons understood this distinction well, as did Geoffroy II. In fact, they never described the object to the pope as an authentic relic. We know, however, that in Lirey the Shroud was shown solemnly to a gathering of people, in a ritual array with the solemnity typical of the exposition of a relic, which they probably called a *sanctuarium*. Taking such measures would have been unacceptable for a simple reproduction. Therefore, the accusation made against the canons is fitting: that they encouraged more or less implicitly, in practice, the veneration of an object that was undeserving of it.

Putting the issue of the object's authenticity before the pope could have been risky; perhaps that explains Geoffroy and the canons

---

not what is offered but rather the Shroud itself), a *figura* that was later transferred, placed in the church, and shown during exhibitions (always the Shroud, not the image). On August 4, King Charles spoke of a *pannus manufactus et in figuram vel similitudinem ac commemoracionem sacri Sudarii . . . artificialiter depictus* ("handmade cloth, rendered skillfully in respect to figure and likeness, and as a tribute to the sacred shroud"). The bishop thought that they ought not display that cloth "neither as a shroud, nor a 'sanctuary,' nor as a representation or figure of the Lord's shroud, because the Lordly shroud was not made such." And even Clement wrote that the "aforementioned figure or representation is not the true shroud of our Lord." Accordingly, we cannot accept the translation of Poulle.

[125] C. Zantfliet, "Chronicon," in *Veterum scriptorum et monumentorum amplissima collectio*, ed. E. Martène, vol. 5 (Montalant: Paris, 1729), col. 462.

resorting, on an official level, to terminology that did not support the authenticity of the Shroud but rather denied it. We can certainly agree that the language of the petition sent to the pope by those in possession of the Shroud attempted to avoid, officially, the problem of authenticity by shifting most of the attention to the question of the legitimacy of the worship of images.[126] The attempt notwithstanding, the pope's response does not overlook the central issue: the figure or representation could be displayed, he said, only if it was presented for what it was, namely, a copy and not a relic. Consequently, the exhibitions were bound to an ironclad framework that did not allow room for misunderstandings. Different terminology (e.g., "Holy Shroud,") began to be used only in the forties of the following century, when the Shroud was no longer in Lirey; at that point the old terminology used in the fourteenth century was largely pushed aside, and the Shroud began to be treated by everyone as a true and proper relic.

The various positions can, then, be summarized thus: Geoffroy and the canons officially speak of a copy of the shroud, but in practice they showed it as if it were authentic, and they encouraged veneration of it. The bishop did not want such a copy to be shown, and he denounced the double-dealing of the canons. The pope, while condemning any action that would encroach upon the worship of relics, treated it as a copy and permitted it to be shown only as a simple sacred image.

It remains to consider what those who had charge of the relic actually thought of it: did they regard it as authentic but avoid making that claim on an official level, so as not to incur a possible censure? Or did they know that it was a fake but were not disposed to put an end to the exhibitions, which brought fame and proceeds to their collegiate church? Or perhaps their positions were more nuanced, and for some the problem of authenticity could have been of lesser importance than the catechetical function that the Shroud could perform?[127] The answer cannot be determined with certainty, nor is it possible to suppose what the thoughts were of those who had charge of the relic before the period of the documents. One certainly

[126] According to Zaccone, "Shroud from the Charnys to the Savoys," 401–4.

[127] On forgeries it is useful to read U. Eco, *Fakes and Forgeries*, in idem, *The Limits of Interpretation* (Bloomington: Indiana University Press, 1994), 174–202.

cannot deny that the Shroud was not only an object of devotion for the collegiate church but also a powerful means of enrichment, as was acknowledged several times by both the canons and those interacting with them.

To establish the views that were held regarding the Shroud at the time of its appearance is certainly of interest. Bishops and popes in the past have declared the authenticity of numerous relics that were later acknowledged to be spurious, but for the Shroud the case is idiosyncratic, as the exact opposite happened. Both the bishop and the pope intervened to limit the veneration of an object that, according to them, ought not to have been considered a relic; later, on the contrary, many moderns have shown a propensity to recognize the authenticity of that same relic that others from the medieval period deemed a fake. It is a rare case, if not the only one of its kind.

2.1.8 Shrouds, Relics, Liturgy, and Theology

Let us set aside, for a moment, the question of authenticity to consider a fertile field of investigation that concerns itself with examining relics in the fuller context of devotion and the interest they garnered in the past. In the late Middle Ages the emergence of individuality and subjectivity becomes more pronounced and noticeable, as does the search for visual and physical contact with the sacred, phenomena that increase in the veneration of relics on the one hand and of eucharistic species on the other.[128] The former, in particular, in this period reached a fever pitch that caused a sharp increase in the quest for relics of any kind, often with little regard for the sanctity of the objects or the dignity of cadavers.[129] With the increasing demand for relics came a substantial growth in the relic industry, to the benefit of whoever engaged in the exchange and commerce of relics, including fakes. Relics were made even more desirable by the conviction that they also had a thaumaturgical and apotropaic function that extended to the whole of the city that hosted them, that they acted

[128] Cf. G. J. C. Snoek, *Medieval Piety from Relics to the Eucharist: A Process of Mutual Interaction* (Leiden: Brill, 1995).

[129] The case of Elizabeth of Thuringia is emblematic. Her still-fresh corpse was raided for relics, as reported by Caesarius Heisterbacensis, *Vita Sanctae Elyzabeth Lantgraviae* 30, ed. A. Hilka, *Die Wundergeschichte des Caesarius von Heisterbach* (Bonn: Hanstein, 1937).

as a sort of rampart or palladium that was integrated into the city's defense system. Crusades were always accompanied by the search for new relics or the theft of relics (one might think of the sack of Constantinople and the transfer of hundreds of relics into the West); certain pleas and limitations imposed by ecclesiastical authorities failed to curb the phenomenon, and these authorities themselves not infrequently were involved in what they were trying to stop. The desire of monasteries, bishops, and cities for powerful celestial protectors could result in actions that were, strictly speaking, illegal from the canonical point of view but were nonetheless theologically justified by the need to ensure that relics be venerated in a dignified manner. The theft of relics was known as *sancta rapina* or *laudabile furtum*.[130]

Once obtained, the relics were transferred into cities and churches and solemnly placed on altars and in reliquaries. Sometimes the items were accompanied by sigils and documents that certified any recent relocations; on other occasions their provenance was not known or had to be kept hidden, since confirmation was unavailable. In many cases, accounts indicate that relics were acquired thanks to some noble, king, pilgrim, or crusade. There were also instances in which the relics were "rediscovered" where they had always been, thereby confirming that they had remained hidden or forgotten for a long time. The display of relics, whether continuous or intermittent, created centers of pilgrimage with political and economic importance due to the wealth of the travelers who not only provided for a location's economic stability but also gave many offerings to the owners of the relics.[131] It was against the immorality of exploiting relics for monetary gain that Boccaccio unleashed his fierce satire in his story from the *Decameron* of Brother Cipolla, who enriched

[130] See the classic Geary, *Furta sacra*. For a general overview, J. Bentley, *Restless Bones: The Story of Relics* (London: Constable, 1985); Molteni, *Memoria Christi*; C. Freeman, *Holy Bones, Holy Dust: How Relics Shaped the History of Medieval Europe* (New Haven: Yale University Press, 2011); P. George, *Reliques: Le quatrième pouvoir* (Nice: Éditions romaines, 2013).

[131] On this aspect of this topic see also N. Herrmann-Mascard, *Les reliques des saints: Formation coutumière d'un droit* (Paris: Klincksieck, 1975), 271–312; and C. Buenacasa Pérez, "La instrumentalización económica del culto a las reliquias: Una importante fuente de ingresos para las iglesias tardoantiguas occidentales (ss. IV–VIII)," in *Santos, obispos y reliquias*, ed. C. Bosch Jiménez (Alcalà: Universidad de Alcalà, 2003), 123–40.

himself by exploiting the credulity of the faithful and by convincing them that he had at his disposal improbable relics, like the feather of the archangel Gabriel and the coals on which Saint Lawrence was roasted;[132] Erasmus of Rotterdam would later do the same in his delightful dialogue where he portrays a pilgrim always on the hunt for new relics to venerate.[133]

All things considered, relics were lucrative; this was true from an economic point of view, certainly, but it would be reductive to obscure the religious value that the faithful accorded them. It was that value that compelled them to make long pilgrimages to be close to relics, to be able to see, touch, kiss, and venerate them. To see and touch the objects were two indispensable acts, and the religious authorities put in place a series of features aimed at bringing them about. In some cases, the very structures of the ecclesiastical buildings were designed for the display of relics; in other cases elevated platforms were built, albeit often with perishable materials. The *Heiltumsstuhl* of Nuremberg is a famous example of such a structure; structures for display were also built for the Shroud in Lirey and in Turin, where in the post-Rennaisance period it was shown on richly adorned balconies and pavilions.

Efforts to obtain immediate contact with the object of veneration, visually and tangibly near those who worshipped and prayed, increasingly led to modifications to the structure of reliquaries to render the relics more perceptible. At first, there were simple coffers or objects that reproduced the anatomical shape of the relics they held; these containers were always rather richly adorned with narrative and demonstrative images. At the same time, the use of transparent materials and perforated walls allowed people to see their contents, just as in the case of the monstrance for the bread of the Eucharist. Between the reliquary and the relic, a relationship came to be established similar to that which existed between the relic and the body; the reliquary was not only an accessory but a true and proper *ornamentum* that rendered the salvific value of its contents visually

[132] G. Boccaccio, *Decameron* 6.10, with the title "Brother Cipolla promises to show the feather of the angel Gabriel to some peasants; finding in place of which coals that he says were those on which St. Lawrence was roasted."

[133] Desiderius Erasmus, *Peregrinatio religionis ergo*; English translation: *A Pilgrimage for Religion's Sake*, in *Collected Works of Erasmus: Colloquies* (Toronto: University of Toronto Press, 1997), 619–74.

comprehensible.[134] This phenomenon, however, only partly concerns the Shroud, which had to be removed from its coffer and unfolded to be seen; its reliquary was merely a precious case, and the relic was visible during exhibitions, when the reliquary was emptied and set aside, or when, in more recent times, the relic is removed from its case and is put in a panel for viewing. Today the frame of the Shroud used during the displays—whose form is in no way traditional—has in any case responded to the need for viewing, as it has been provided with glass to make the object visible.

The worship of the Shroud took shape at a particularly propitious moment for the veneration of an image-relic from Jesus' tortured body. In the middle of the fourteenth century, there came about a particular devotion centered on Christ's passion and on the contemplation of the five wounds from the nails of the cross and the spear and those from the crown of thorns. The literature, even in the vulgar tongue, concentrated on painful aspects of the passion and the cross by creating hymns, sequences, antiphons, sermons, treatises, and poems that invited people to contemplate the suffering and human physicality of Jesus' body. Artistic representations of *Christus patiens*, human and suffering, grew exponentially, largely replacing those of Christ glorious and triumphant over death. The art yielded bloody representations that displayed the tangible results of the passion, some of which had a specific liturgical use, such as the coffins constructed according to the canons of Gothic art and displayed in churches, meant to represent Christ's death;[135] one might consider the Easter tomb of Maigrauge Abbey (in Fribourg, Switzerland). That tomb, which dates from this period, is a decorated sarcophagus in which was placed a statue of the dead and wounded Christ (fig. 2.4).[136] In general, various aspects of devotion, influenced primarily by

[134] On this issue, see Canetti, *Impronte di gloria*; on reliquaries, for a brief discussion see V. H. Elbern, "Reliquiario," in *Enciclopedia dell'arte medievale*, ed. A. M. Romanini (Rome: Istituto della Enciclopedia Italiana, 1998), 892–910; M. Bagnoli, ed., *Treasures of Heaven: Saints, Relics and Devotion in Medieval Europe* (London: British Museum, 2010).

[135] Cf. J. E. A. Kroesen, *The "Sepulchrum Domini" through the Ages: Its Form and Function* (Leuven: Peeters, 2000), especially 53–108. Cardini and Montesano recognize the characteristics of a Gothic work of art in the Turin Shroud: F. Cardini and M. Montesano, *La Sindone di Torino oltre il pregiudizio* (Milan: Medusa, 2015), 99.

[136] Fribourg, Musée d'art et d'histoire, n. inv. MAHF 1995–38.

Franciscan mysticism (which was nurtured by the memory of Saint Francis' stigmata), could find in the Shroud of Lirey both an outlet and a justification.[137] Given its location in war-torn, economically depressed France, the Shroud assumed a very particular value. One should not even underestimate the influence of the celebration of the Jubilee in Rome in the years 1330 and 1350; on those occasions the exhibition of the Veronica, with its imprint of the suffering face of Christ, played a central role. Each pilgrim, who—as Petrarch says—"comes to Rome, following his desire, to look upon the image of Him, whom he hopes to see again up in heaven,"[138] went to venerate the Veronica inside the Basilica of St. Peter. From images that come a little later we can get an idea of the similarity between the system of exhibition for the Veronica and that of the Shroud (fig. 2.3). An indirect indication of a connection between the two objects can be gathered from the fact that the terms *sudarium* and *suaire* were interchangeably attributed by contemporaries to both the Veil of Veronica and the Shroud of Lirey: a less than fortunate choice, if one retains ancient evangelical terminology as a touchstone, but one that is consistent with the usage of the time.[139] It has also been hypothesized that the tolerance shown by Clement VII of Avignon in 1389–1390 in regard to exhibitions of the Shroud must be read in light of the strife between the two simultaneously reigning popes; in a time of schism, Clement would have had some interest in encouraging the veneration of the Shroud to the detriment of the veneration of the Veronica, which in that same year was displayed in Rome for the Holy Year of 1390, in the territory subject to the pontiff with whom he was competing.[140] On November 27, 1389, the pope declared the excommunication of all the people from the regions faithful to him who should make a pilgrimage to Rome to venerate the relics of the apostles. One can

[137] Cf. A. L. Mayer, "Das Grabtuch von Turin als typisches Beispiel spätmittelalterlicher Schaudevotion," *Archiv für Liturgiewissenschaft* 4, no. 2 (1956): 348–64; Perret, "Essai sur l'histoire du Saint Suaire," 71–77; O. Celier, *Le signe du linceul: Le Saint Suaire de Turin: De la relique à l'image* (Paris: Cerf, 1992), 197–237.

[138] F. Petrarch, *Canzoniere* 16: "Movesi il vecchierel canuto et biancho" ("Grizzled and white the old man leaves").

[139] Noted by U. Chevalier, "Autour des origines du Suaire de Turin," *L'université catholique* 41 (1902): 433–37.

[140] Cf. Ciccone and Sturmann, *Sindone svelata*, 48.

also note that the pontificate of Clement also saw the flowering of veneration of other shrouds in French territory.[141]

As regards a model or prototype that could have encouraged belief in a sepulchral fabric of Jesus that bore images of his tortured body, currently no precedent comparable to the Shroud of Lirey has been discovered. Other remains of shrouds of Christ existed, but none of them with images. The sole exception would be that of the cloth that, according to Robert de Clari, was found in Constantinople in the years 1203–1204, but I have already said that I do not consider the report credible.[142]

An interesting parallel does exist, however: "an image called a 'sudarium' (*sudario*) in the vulgar tongue, which depicts the face of Jesus Christ," which a noble, Pietro Pipino, son of the count of Minervino Murge, presented on July 20, 1333, to the bishop of Tertiveri (Foggia) so that he would grant an indulgence to whoever venerated it, to which condition the bishop assented.[143] From that exchange we have confirmation of the use of the term *sudario* in relation to cloths depicting the image of Christ, in this case only his face. We are not told whether this was the face of the living Jesus (as on the Veronica) or of the dead Jesus (as on the Shroud). The text is also interesting because, in the same period, it uses some terms that also occur in documents on the Shroud of Lirey ("shroud" [*sudarium*], "image" [*ymago*], and "to represent" [*represento*]).

An important line of inquiry is provided by the tradition, well rooted not only in France but throughout Europe, of preserving a cloth in the church for the purpose of representing the shroud of Christ; that cloth was used in the very widespread practice of showing a cloth during a liturgical ceremony of a theatrical nature at Easter time that put on stage the discovery of the empty tomb in Jerusalem

141 Cf. M. Fournié, "Les suaires méridionaux du Christ, des reliques 'clémentines'? Éléments d'enquête," in *Église et État, Église ou État? Les clercs et la genèse de l'État moderne*, ed. C. Barralis et al. (Paris: Publications de la Sorbonne, 2014), 417–32.

142 I refer again to Nicolotti, *Una reliquia costantinopolitana*, 151–96. Assuming, however, that I am wrong, one would then have to conclude that worship for a shroud bearing an image was recognized for the first time in Constantinople in the first years of the thirteenth century.

143 "Quamdam ymaginem vulgariter dictum Sudarium quod representat faciem Iesu Christi": published in J. M. Martin, "Un document épiscopal sur la vénération du Saint Suaire en Italie au XIVe siècle," in *Les prélats, l'Église et la société—XIe-XVe siècles*, ed. F. Beriac (Bordeaux: CROCEMC, 1994), 135–41.

by the women. The possible dependency on this sacred representation (sometimes called the "Mystery") of the appearance of shrouds to be later venerated as relics has been evidenced numerous times since the Enlightenment. One of the more convincing supporters of this theory was the Parisian canon Nicolas-Sylvestre Bergier (1718–1790), confessor of the royal family and academic of Besançon:

> Sheets or shrouds, which are shown in many churches, are unable to have been used in the burial of the Savior, especially since the fabric of these shrouds is a fairly modern work. It is likely that in the twelfth and thirteenth centuries, when the custom of representing the Mysteries in churches was introduced, it represented, on Easter, the resurrection of Jesus Christ. The hymn *Victimae paschali* was sung, in which Mary Magdalene says: "I have seen the tomb of the living Christ, the glory of the risen, the angelic witnesses, the shroud, and the clothes." At the word "shroud," a cloth imprinted with the figure of the buried Jesus Christ was shown to the people. These cloths or shrouds, kept in treasures of the churches since they always served the same purpose, were later taken to be the linens that were used for the burial of our Savior; that is why they are found in many different churches, in Cologne, Besançon, Turin, Brioude, etc., and there is conviction that they were brought from Palestine during the Crusades. It does not follow from this that these shrouds are undeserving of respect, or that the worship directed toward them is superstitious. They are old images of the buried Jesus Christ, and it seems certain that more than once God has rewarded with benefits the faith and piety of the faithful who honor these commemorative signs of the mystery of our redemption.[144]

Bergier's opinion is significant because it comes from a clergyman of vast culture, who at the time was reported to be an illustrious defender of the Christian faith (his apologetic writings against Voltaire, Rousseau, and Holbach are famous). In this passage he attempts to reconcile the falsity of the relics with the legitimacy of their veneration, by framing the veneration within the category of worship of images. In regard to the information that Bergier had, we know that this sort of sacred drama is affirmed well before the twelfth century; its origin must be sought in France in the first half of the

[144] N.-S. Bergier, *Encyclopédie méthodique: Théologie*, vol. 3 (Paris: Panckoucke, 1790), 539–40.

tenth century. What concerns us more, among the different attested typologies, is the dramatization of the *Quem quaeritis*, a dialogue in which characters—clerics in costume—staged the discovery of the empty tomb and showed symbolically to the people gathered in the church the shroud left behind by the risen Christ.[145] We have significant evidence that the use of a simple liturgical cloth in the *Quem quaeritis* could have fostered its transformation into a relic, object of worship, since that is what happened in the sixteenth century with the shroud of Besançon: the case of this shroud demonstrates that the lines between fiction and reality could at times be quite blurred.[146] The theatrical scene could be rendered more realistic by the construction of a true representation of a tomb that could be permanent, built into the walls of the church, or more commonly moveable, such as a large wooden sarcophagus with an openable cover. Within the tomb was placed a statue of the dead Christ that later would be carried on Easter Day, leaving in the tomb only a shroud (that sometimes would be used later as the altar cloth). Sometimes mannequins with moveable limbs were used: normally they were nailed to the cross, but on Holy Friday they could be taken down, with the arms being folded to carry them to the tomb and to make them assume the position of a cadaver laid out for burial. We have different examples of sarcophagi and of the mannequins of Christ used or being thus positioned. Some have characteristics comparable to the Christ of the Shroud (crossed hands, bloody wounds, and facial features).[147] It should not be forgotten that at the time, painted cloths, especially those used to cover crucifixes,

[145] Cf. B. D. Berger, *Le drame liturgique de Pâques* (Paris: Beauchesne, 1976); C. C. Flanigan, *Liturgical Drama and Dramatic Liturgy: A Study of the "Quem queritis" Easter Dialogue and Its Cultic Context* (Ph.D. diss., Washington University, 1981); and especially J. Drumbl, *"Quem Quaeritis": Teatro sacro dell'alto Medioevo* (Rome: Bulzoni, 1981), to be supplemented by A. Davril, "L'origine du 'Quem quaeritis,'" in *Requirentes modos musicos*, ed. D. Saulnier (Solesmes: Abbaye Saint-Pierre, 1995), 119–36. A brief description of some of these representations can be found in A. Carénini, "La Sindone nel dramma liturgico di Pasqua e i misteri della Passione," in *Sindone: Immagini di Cristo e devozione popolare*, ed. A. Carénini and P. Grimaldi (Turin: Omega, 1998), 73–89.

[146] C. Freeman, "The Origins of the Shroud of Turin," *History Today* 64, no. 11 (2014): 38–48, believes that this is the origin of the Shroud of Turin. Similar considerations can be found in H. Farey, "Towards a Medieval Context for the Turin Shroud," *British Society for the Turin Shroud Newsletter* 85 (2017): 15–25.

[147] Cf. Kroesen, *Sepulchrum Domini*.

statues, and other liturgical furnishings with fabrics, already existed and were stained or embroidered with images bearing reference to the subject they were intended to veil.[148]

All of these elements—the search for and trade in relics, their exhibitions, the change in people's feelings toward them, the practice of pilgrimage, the acts of devotion centered largely on Christ's passion, the mysticism about the holy wounds of Jesus, the worship of the Roman Veronica, the Easter ceremony, the liturgical shrouds, and the decorated coverings—provide excellent grounds for explaining and justifying the emergence of worship of a shroud that appeared in France in the middle of the fourteenth century. That argument's sole deficiency would be a contemporary example that corresponds perfectly to the situation in Lirey. For now, it seems that the Shroud of the French collegiate church is an unprecedented relic. As the creation of the *Quem quaeritis* can be attributed to the reformist Odo of Cluny, abbot of Fleury, the rise of worship of a Shroud with image seems, for the moment, to be a novelty of the collegiate church of Lirey.

2.2. Passage of the Shroud's Ownership

2.2.1 The Shroud Leaves Lirey

At the death of Geoffroy II de Charny, the lordship of the town of Lirey was inherited by Marguerite, his daughter and therefore the granddaughter of Geoffroy, the founder of the collegiate church.[149] Marguerite married Jean de Bauffremont, who died in the battle of Agincourt in 1415; she then married Humbert de Villersexel, Count de la Roche-en-Montagne, Lord of Saint-Hippolyte (Doubs) and Orbe (Vaud). It should be noted that despite the partial homonym, the De la Roche-en-Montagne have nothing to do with the De la Roche-sur-l'Ognon, lords of Ray and Athens, who, from the eighteenth century, some have wanted to connect with the arrival of another shroud in the city of Besançon.

[148] Cf. J. T. Micklethwaite, *The Ornaments of the Rubric* (London: Longman, 1897), 52; W. H. S. J. Hope and E. G. C. F. Atchley, *English Liturgical Colours* (London: S.P.C.K., 1918), 58; attention has been drawn to this question in H. Farey, *The Medieval Shroud*, pro manuscripto, 2018, https://independent.academia.edu/HughFarey.

[149] For an unsurpassed presentation of events concerning the Shroud in these years up to 1578, see Perret, "Essai sur l'histoire du Saint Suaire," 49–121.

In 1418, in the midst of the Hundred Years' War, Champagne was controlled by Burgundian gangs and was in the grip of devastation from the conflict, as well as from civil war. Even the clergy and French ecclesiastical structures, since the middle of the previous century, had fallen into a condition of extreme decay and material and spiritual impoverishment.[150] One can easily understand why, in that year, the canons of Lirey, fearing for the safety of their treasures, decided to secure the Shroud and numerous other precious objects by entrusting them to the custody of Count Humbert. In a document dated July 6, 1418, he undertook to protect the treasures from possible raids and to return them to the canons when peace was restored.

The document regarding the delivery of the objects speaks of "a cloth on which appears the figure or representation of the shroud of our lord Jesus Christ"; the terminology used is the same as in the papal documents and thus demonstrates that, at least in writing, the Shroud continued to be presented not as an authentic relic but only as a representation. The use of this terminology is significant, since this document was not a public communication that prompted special caution but a private agreement between Humbert and the canons. The document specifies that the cloth was kept in a coffer (*coffre*) bearing the Charny coat of arms.[151] To read the list of other relics in the collegiate church's possession is interesting; among the items listed are a fragment of the cross, a hair and piece of Mary's clothing, a relic of Saint Lawrence, and oil gathered from a miraculous image of Mary kept in Saydnaya, north of Damascus.[152]

Humbert stated that he wanted to keep the Shroud in Montfort castle (in the region of Montigny-Montfort, Côte d'Or), 70 km from Lirey.[153] We do not know whether it ever made it there, nor for how long; we do know, however, that soon afterwards the Shroud ended

[150] Largely described by H. Denifle, *La désolation des églises, monastères et hôpitaux en France pendant la guerre de cent ans*, 3 vols. (Paris: Picard, 1897–1899).

[151] Cf. Lalore, *Inventaires des principales églises*, 263: "Ung drap ou quel est la figure ou répresentation du suaire nostre seigneur Jesu-Crist, lequel est en ung coffre armoyé des armes de Charny."

[152] On which see M. Bacci, "A Sacred Space for a Holy Icon: The Shrine of Our Lady of Saydnaya," in *Иеротопия: Создание сакрадьных пространств в Византии и Древней Руси*, ed. A. M. Lidov (Moscow: Indrik, 2006): 373–87.

[153] Sanna Solaro, *S. Sindone che si venera a Torino*, 29, thought that by "Montfort" another castle near Saint-Hippolyte (Doubs) was meant, but he does not make very clear where or why.

up more than 230 km from Lirey, in Saint-Hippolyte (Doubs), the chief town of Humbert's seigniory. A tradition attested in the seventeenth century affirms that in the Church of Saint-Hippolyte, in a chapel called *des Buessarts*, the double image of the man of the Shroud was painted on a wall, and that each year at the Doubs river, the Shroud was shown in a meadow that afterward was called *Pré du Seigneur* ("Meadow of the Lord," which is believed to be identical with the place today called *Clos Pascal*).[154] It is also reported that there was a field there nicknamed *du mauvais conseil* ("of the bad counsel"), the place where Marguerite de Charny made the decision, which was approved by broad agreement, not to return the Shroud to the canons of Lirey. Some think that a record of this period in the Franche-Comté remained in the Church of Saint-Léger de Chaux-lès-Châtillon in the town of Les Terres-de-Chaux, about 6 km from Saint-Hippolyte. In that church, at the end of the 1990s, following a restoration, a series of medieval frescoes was discovered, among which can be made out the depiction of a cloth with the face of Jesus at its center, and a nobleman carrying what seems to be a reliquary in his hands; it is commonly said that they are images depicting the Shroud and Humbert de Villersexel, a claim that is possible but not proven.[155]

During this period when the Shroud was removed from Lirey and the diocese of Troyes, exhibitions continued. It is difficult to believe that Humbert and Marguerite carried out their own exhibitions of the Shroud by presenting it as just any "figure or representation"; the relic was likely offered to the faithful for veneration as if it were authentic.

Humbert de Villersexel died on August 22, 1438, without having produced a male heir by Marguerite de Charny. His possessions, therefore, in accordance with his will from May 5, 1437, passed to his niece's husband, François de la Palud, Lord of Varambon.[156] In

[154] Cf. Chifflet, *De linteis sepulchralibus*, 107–8.

[155] Images of the frescoes are in G. Barbet, *Othon de la Roche: Chroniques sur l'étonnante histoire d'un chevalier Comtois devenu Seigneur d'Athènes* (Besançon: Fortis, 2012), 36–37. De Vregille doubts that the images depict the Shroud: B. de Vregille, "Du Saint-Suaire de Lirey, Chambéry et Turin au Saint-Suaire de Besançon," *Barbizier* 28 (2004): 19–24.

[156] In 1432, François married Jeanne de La Petite-Pierre, daughter of Gillette de Villersexel, Humbert's sister. On François, see S. Guichenon, *Histoire de Bresse et de Bugey*, pt. 3 (Lyon: Huguetan, 1650), 292–95 (who instead of "Jeanne" mistakenly

the seventeenth century, Chifflet reported that the Varambon family kept a cypress coffer that contained a small box with the Charny coat of arms, which he believed contained the Shroud while it was entrusted to the family of the lords of Villersexel.[157]

After Humbert's death, the Shroud remained in the hands of the widow Marguerite, who considered it a family possession and, breaking her word, did not allow it to be returned to the canons of Lirey. For the second time in the course of a century, the Shroud therefore became the object of opposing claims. In May of 1443, the canons, led by the dean Pierre Sauvageot, lodged a complaint before the Parliament of Dôle, confident in the letter signed by Humbert in 1418 that bore the promise of restitution. For her part, Marguerite did not deny the authenticity of the document but held that it could not pertain to all the objects kept in the collegiate church at the time, "at least as regards the holy Shroud, which was obtained by the late Sir Geoffroy de Charny, my grandfather." She added as well that the collegiate church of Lirey and the castle of the place were not secure enough to keep the cloth. To avoid a trial, on May 8, the opposing parties agreed to the following conditions: Marguerite had to return immediately the objects that the chapter of Lirey had placed in the safekeeping of her deceased husband twenty-five years earlier. The sole exception to this arrangement was made for the Shroud, for which she received an extension of another three years before it had to be returned, along with payment to the canons of an annual fee of 12 francs to be used for repairs to the church and "as compensation for the benefits and alms that because of the precious jewel, the holy Shroud, could reach and come to the church of Lirey." One sees therefore how possession of the Shroud also brought quantifiable economic benefits. Marguerite herself bore the cost of a journey to Dôle made by three canons, and she added some vestments as a gift. There was, however, a condition: in the event that on the next feast day of Saint John the Baptist (June 24) the lordship of Lirey should transfer to François de la Palud, the return of the Shroud would necessarily also happen forthwith. Charles de Noyers, Marguerite's

---

writes "Marguerite," and is followed by many others); J. Paviot, "François de la Palud, seigneur de Varambon, un encombrant seigneur du XVe siècle," in *Hommes, cultures et sociétés à la fin du Moyen Âge*, ed. P. Gilli and J. Paviot (Paris: Université Paris-Sorbonne, 2012), 257–92.

[157] Chifflet, *De linteis sepulchralibus*, 107–8.

stepbrother, was made guarantor of the fulfillment of the terms. In the document laying out these conditions, for the first time the Shroud was called a "Holy Shroud."[158] At this point, on the day after the agreement was reached, the Parliament of Dôle and Philip III of Burgundy also put an agreement in writing, noting that François de la Palud was not satisfied with the conditions; for the moment the relics—excluding the Shroud—had to be deposited temporarily in the Franciscan church of Dôle until Pentecost, when they would be returned to the canons.[159]

At the end of the established three-year term, May 8, 1446, the Shroud was not returned. The canons repeated their request, this time before the authorities of Besançon. Marguerite persisted in saying that the collegiate church of Lirey was too run-down to be able to guarantee the safety of the Holy Shroud and asked for another extension. Thus, the canons and Marguerite came to a new agreement, which was signed on July 18, 1447: the Shroud would remain in Marguerite's possession for two more years, to be returned the canons on October 28, 1449. In the meantime, she would make annual payments to the chapter that had been increased to 15 francs, and a payment of 50 francs for procedural expenses and other tasks.[160]

Nothing came of the promise. On November 6, 1449, the dean and three canons of Lirey appealed to Antoine Guerry, provost of Troyes, against Charles de Noyers, stepbrother of Marguerite and her representative. Once again an agreement was reached for a three-year extension, still relying upon payments to the chapter amounting to 50 livre tournois, intended to fund repairs to the collegiate church and the residence of the canons, with a deadline of October 28, 1452.[161] This time as well, for the fourth time, Marguerite did not keep her promise to return the Shroud.

In the meantime, Marguerite continued to move from one place to another, taking the Shroud with her and collecting offerings by performing traveling exhibitions.[162] We know of at least one such instance in 1449, since it was reported by a contemporary, the monk

[158] Chevalier, *Étude critique*, doc. R.
[159] Chevalier, *Étude critique*, doc. S.
[160] Chevalier, *Étude critique*, doc. T.
[161] Chevalier, *Étude critique*, doc. V.
[162] Trips involving traveling displays of relics, specifically intended to garner offerings, were quite common: cf. P. Héliot and M. L. Chastang, "Quêtes et voyages

Corneille de Santvliet. Marguerite had come to Belgium, to Chimay (Hainaut), to display the Shroud—which Corneille determined to be "rendered with admirable artifice"—drawing a large crowd for the event. The event provoked the curiosity of the bishop of Liège, Jean de Heinsberg, who immediately sent two professors of Holy Scripture to investigate the case and to prevent the faithful from "further fluctuating in credulity in this matter." The professors were Jean de Bruxelles, abbot of the Cistercian Aulne monastery, and Henri Bakel, canon of Liège. Marguerite, compelled by the two clergymen to show them the documentation in her possession to prove the legitimacy of the relic, provided three bulls from Clement VII and the document from Cardinal-Legate Pedro de Luna (?),[163] from which the two experts confirmed that the Shroud was not the authentic linen of Christ but only a representation of it; and so Marguerite could not continue with her exhibitions.[164]

We know that in the same year (1449), on July 6, Marguerite entered the city of Mons, farther north, always keeping the Shroud with her.[165]

2.2.2 The Shroud Sold to the House of Savoy

In this period some events occurred that brought the Dukes of Savoy into play. François de la Palud—heir of Humbert de Villersexel, the late husband of Marguerite de Charny—in those years was in the service of the Duke of Savoy, Amadeus VIII, who in

de reliques au profit des églises françaises du Moyen âge," *Revue d'histoire écclésiastique* 59 (1964): 789–822; 60 (1965): 5–32.

[163] The chronicler wrote "Petrus de Luna," which would be Pedro Martínez de Luna, the future Benedict XIII of Avignon; we therefore ought to consider that even this cardinal intervened in the debate and issued a document that has not survived. On the contrary, modern commentators believe, rightly, I think, that the author has confused Pedro de Luna with Pierre de Thury, who we know granted a pardon to Geoffroy II.

[164] Cf. Zantfliet, *Chronicon*, coll. 461–63. Santvliet also copies one of the documents, the papal bull of July 28, 1389. Cf. G. Monchamp, "Liège et Rome à propos de l'authenticité du Saint-Suaire de Turin," *Leodium* 2 (1903): 6–12.

[165] Upon her arrival with "the Holy Shroud of our Lord" the city of Mons gave her a good quantity of wine: cf. M. A. Arnould, "Sur le séjour du Saint-Suaire en Hainaut au XVe siècle," *Annales du Cercle archéologique de Mons* 68 (1974): 192–94. On the Shroud's time in Belgium, see A. Nicolotti, "Le Saint Suaire de Turin en Belgique . . . à Liège?," *Trésor de Liège—Bulletin trimestriel* 47 (2016): 13–18.

1424 granted him confirmation of the fiefs of Varambon and Bouligneux.[166] In March of 1431, however, François committed an ill-conceived act in which he violated a peace treaty and without Amadeus' authorization sacked the city and territory of Trévoux, capital of the Dombes, which at the time was dependent on the Duke of Bourbon. This quite reckless act created difficulties for his patron, Amadeus, who punished François by confiscating his possessions in Savoy, Varambon, and Bouligneux.[167] Three years later they were restored to him, on February 11, 1434;[168] in the meantime, however, François had moved his residence to lands controlled by the Duke of Burgundy, far from Savoy. Perhaps his desire to keep his distance from Savoy explains why, once possession of his territories was restored, François decided to dispose of them by making an exchange with Marguerite de Charny: he gave her the Savoyard fiefs of Varambon and Bouligneux, along with 4,000 gold écus, in exchange for some Burgundian fiefs that belonged to Marguerite, specifically Beaumont-sur-Vingeanne, Montfort (Montigny-Montfort), Savoisy, Thury (Côte-d'Or), and the land of Tonnerre (in a deed dated November 24, 1435).[169]

The peace with Savoy did not last long. In 1439 Amadeus VIII left the crown to his son Louis and took up the papal tiara under the name Felix V. In those years one of the favorites of the Savoyard court was Jean de Compey, Lord of Thorens; this Jean, in turn, was hated by a good number of other nobles, among whom was François de la Palud. On August 29, 1446, during a hunting party organized by Duke Louis, Jean de Compey was attacked by two nobles and suffered a serious injury to his face. The two aggressors, to escape the anger the duke felt toward whoever had made an attempt on his favorite's life, sought refuge at Varambon in François' castle.

[166] AST, Protocolli ducali serie rossa, no. 72, ff. 209r–212r (October 26, 1424).

[167] Cf. A. C. de Lateyssonnière, *Recherches historiques sur le département de l'Ain*, vol. 4 (Bourg: Martin-Bottier, 1843), 298–301; J. H. Costa de Beauregard, *Souvenirs du règne d'Amédée VIII* (Chambéry: Puthod, 1859), 67–113, 228–35.

[168] AST, Protocolli ducali serie rossa, no. 73, ff. 569r–571v.

[169] Edited by A. Nicolotti, "Marguerite de Charny, François de La Palud e Ludovico di Savoia: Due documenti inediti," *Bollettino storico-bibliografico subalpino* 116, no. 1 (2018): 191–209, doc. 1. The tenor of the exchange is also confirmed by Guichenon, *Histoire de Bresse et de Bugey*, pt. 2, 15, who adds that the trade was approved by Duke Louis on May 6, 1436.

The leaders of the Savoyard states and Amadeus VIII, who were preoccupied with the consequences of a possible clash among powerful members of the nobility, tried to promote a reconciliation between those nobles and the duke. On March 2, 1447, Amadeus issued a decree of reconciliation among the parties, forcing his son Louis to sign, even if Jean de Compey wanted to decline any compromise. But reconciliation was only a temporary delusion, and vengeance did not have to wait. Amadeus died in January of 1451, and soon after, on the following April 17, Louis felt free to prepare a case against the conspirators at Pont-de-Beauvoisin, which resulted in a series of heavy sentences. Naturally, François de la Palud did not escape unscathed, but was banished and deprived of his knighthood and the Collar of Savoy and of his goods and offices. The following May 19, Louis additionally ordered the castle of Varambon to be razed; only the chapel was spared from destruction.[170] Bouligneux was also confiscated and given to others.[171]

François took refuge in Burgundy and put himself in the service of Duke Philip, and together with the other persecuted families, he sent requests for help to Philip himself and Charles VII, the king of France. The latter, already ill-disposed toward the Duke of Savoy for other reasons, openly took a position in favor of the exiles and forced Louis to be more reasonable. After inducing him to go to Cleppé in France, on October 27, 1452, he persuaded him to sign a treaty by which he was obliged to restore to the prescribed nobles their goods and offices within three months' time. But Louis began to do anything to avoid complying with his promise.[172]

[170] AST, Protocolli ducali serie rossa, no. 96, f. 101.

[171] AST, Protocolli ducali serie rossa, no. 96, f. 273 (June 18, 1451). However, another document indicates that Bouligneux was in the possession of Marguerite in October of 1454: A. Nicolotti, "The Acquisition of the Shroud by the House of Savoy: Documentary Evidence," in *The Shroud at Court: History, Usages, Places and Images of a Dynastic Relic*, ed. P. Cozzo, A. Merlotti, and A. Nicolotti (Leiden: Brill, 2019), 48, doc. 6.

[172] On the event, see also Guichenon, *Histoire de Bresse et de Bugey*, pt. 1 (Lyon: Huguetan, 1650), 79–82; F. dal Pozzo, *Essai sur les anciennes assemblées nationales de la Savoie, du Piémont, et des pays qui y sont ou furent annexés* (Paris: Ballimore, 1829), 89–113; J. H. Costa de Beauregard, *Familles historiques de Savoie: Les seigneurs de Compey* (Chambéry: Puthod, 1844), 43–61 (documents on 96–108); L. Lecestre, *Le Jouvencel par Jean de Bueil*, vol. 1 (Paris: Renouard, 1887), CLXXXI–CXCIV; G. Du Fresne de Beaucourt, *Histoire de Charles VII* (Paris: Picard, 1881–1891), vol. 5:

Marguerite de Charny, while her husband's heir was dealing with all these difficulties, travelled through France with the Shroud. On September 13, 1452, she found herself in Burgundy, where she performed an exhibition in the castle of Germolles (Mellecey). About 60 km away, in Mâcon, François de la Palud was living under the protection of Duke Philip. In February of 1453, Marguerite was in Geneva, where she resided at the expense of Louis' court. The meeting between Marguerite and the House of Savoy happened, therefore, at a crucial moment: Louis was seeking at all costs to avoid the shame of restoring goods and fiefs to François, and Marguerite, in François' absence, decided to negotiate with the duke without concerning herself with that nephew-in-law with whom she was on anything but good terms.[173] On March 22, 1453, Marguerite therefore granted to Louis her rights to Varambon in exchange for the castellany of Miribel, near Lyon; on the same day,[174] she also yielded the credit of 4,000 écus, which she was claiming from François; in exchange for the fief she also achieved for herself an annual payment of 100 florins to be earned from the revenues of the castellany of Montluel.[175]

Here a difficulty arises. François had given Varambon to Marguerite in 1435, as we said. The transfer was in effect for a certain period, as evidenced by a document of 1436 in which François is described as "Lord of Montfort and Beaumont-sur-Vingeanne, known as Varambon." In 1440 he himself still signed documents as François "called Varambon," as though the lordship of Varambon no longer

---

168–73, 178–81, 298; vol. 6: 65–71; F. Gabotto, "Giovanni di Compey signore di Thorens," *La nuova rivista: Pubblicazione settimanale di politica, scienze, lettere ed arti* 5 (1883): 218–20, 234–36, 244–45, 257–58, 267–69; F. C. Uginet, "Compey, Jean de," in *Dizionario Biografico degli Italiani*, vol. 27 (Rome: Istituto della Enciclopedia Italiana, 1982): 689–92; A. Barbero, *Il ducato di Savoia* (Rome: Laterza, 2002), 163–83.

[173] The idea that Marguerite went to the Duke of Savoy to beseech François' freedom from the Turks is farfetched (Pugno, *Santa Sindone che si venera a Torino*, 91).

[174] The day was not March 26, as some have mistakenly transcribed.

[175] The documents in Turin that pertain to Marguerite were first identified in 1908 by Giovanni Sforza, director of the Archivio di Stato of Turin, after an investigation conducted at the request of Baron Antonio Manno (CSS, Fondo Pia, 3.1.1.213). They were briefly described by Zaccone, "Le investiture feudali nei domini del Duca di Savoia a favore di Marguerite de Charny contessa De La Roche (1453–1455)," *Sindon* 27, no. 34 (1985): 21–41; I edited them in full together with commentary in Nicolotti, "Acquisition of the Shroud."

belonged to him.[176] Nevertheless, in 1446, when the conspirators fled to the castle of Varambon, it was clearly under François' control, and certainly in 1451 Louis would not have had it destroyed if it had not belonged to François. In fact, in a judicial act from August 13, 1446, a few days before the attempt on Jean de Compey's life, François was called "count de la Roche, lord of Villersexel and Varambon,"[177] and in other documents dated 1448, 1450, and 1451 he had the title "Lord of Varambon."[178] This must mean that the fief was not under Marguerite's control, but rather François', who for some reason had returned to Savoy.[179] Evidently the exchange of 1435 either lasted a short time or had been withdrawn, cancelled, or modified at least in part.

At present the details are elusive, but one thing is certain: Louis believed—whether rightly or wrongly—that he could negotiate with Marguerite as if she were the owner of the fief of Varambon. If the 4,000 écus that François promised to Marguerite in 1435 had never been paid, as it seems from the contract between Louis and Marguerite, could the sale have been considered null and void? Perhaps Louis, by virtue of the sentence against François that he himself had issued in 1451, considered Marguerite the legitimate holder of the fief? She was treated as such; I have found a contract of surety, dated January 11, 1448, in which different Lords of Bresse, among them Jean de Compey, guaranteed that Marguerite keep the fiefs of Varambon and Bouligneux under the dominion of the Duke of Savoy, and that at her death she would not leave them to others who

176 A document from November 7, 1440, in fact, was signed "François de la Palud, dit Varembon, comte de la Roche et seigneur de Villerssexel" (cited in Paviot, "François de la Palud," 274, n. 129).

177 *Recueil sur l'histoire de Savoie*: Paris, Bibliothèque de l'Arsenal, MS 3712, f. 14v.

178 Cf. R. Biolzi, *Avec le fer et la flamme: La guerre entre la Savoie et Fribourg (1447–1448)* (Lausanne: Université de Lausanne, 2009), 224; Guichenon, *Histoire de Bresse et de Bugey*, pt. 4, 148–50; É. Pérard, *Recueil de plusieurs pièces curieuses servant à l'histoire de Bourgogne* (Paris: Cramoisy, 1664), 588–91; Paviot, "François de la Palud," 290–92. Paviot's article records certain names of François that sometimes appear to be incoherent and that need to be studied in depth.

179 This is also confirmed by the fact that on May 9, 1445, he granted his own possessions of Burgundy to Jean bâtard de Vergy. Cf. S. Guichenon, *Histoire de Bresse et de Bugey*, pt. 3, 293. The same year Louis of Savoy made him a knight.

were not subjects of the duke.[180] In short, it seems that in practice Varambon was in François' hands, whereas some, at that very time, recognized Marguerite as its owner.[181]

It is possible that Louis, by recognizing Marguerite as the true owner of Varambon and taking control of both the castellany and the credit still owed to her, intended to deprive François of the possibility of regaining it. One must remember that the duke was compelled against his will to promise to restore François' confiscated possessions. Yet he could bypass that obstacle if Varambon should be recognized as Marguerite's property, for, in that case, François could no longer expect its return. Louis, in turn, could then acquire the rights to the city from Marguerite, as he in fact did, thereby becoming its new, legitimate owner and definitively preventing its return to François. At the same time, the purchase allowed him to damage François and avoid the humiliation of François' reinstatement. In this way we may better understand why Marguerite granted the duke the rights of the fief of Varambon, even if they may not have been hers to give.[182] It is interesting to see how in these Savoyard documents from 1453 François de la Palud, not by mere chance, was described as "the ex-lord of Varambon."

In that same period, it would seem that this dispute about the Shroud is likely to have been settled.[183] A document from February 25, 1453, reveals that Louis ordered a payment of 60 francs and 10 gold écus to be made to his advisor, Louis François des Allymes; 10 francs

[180] Edited by Nicolotti, "Marguerite de Charny, François de La Palud e Ludovico di Savoia," doc. 2.

[181] In the same year, 1448, François spent a period of convalescence in Varambon: cf. E. Pibiri, *En voyage pour Monseigneur: Ambassadeurs, officiers et messagers à la cour de Savoie* (Lausanne: Société d'histoire de la Suisse romande, 2011), 474.

[182] Also P. Masson, *Elogia serenissimorum ducum Sabaudiae* (Paris: Quesnel, 1619), 99, brings together, albeit confusingly, François de la Palud with Marguerite de Charny and the House of Savoy by way of the Shroud: "That which makes the Marquis de la Palud immortal in the remembrance and memory of the living is the gift offered to Louis from the hands of the distinguished lady Marguerite de Charny, namely, the Holy Shroud."

[183] Perret has examined the essential documents: Perret, "Essai sur l'histoire du Saint Suaire," 82–91; W. Zurbuchen, "Le Saint Suaire à Genève en 1453," *Bulletin de la Société d'histoire et d'archéologie de Genève* 16 (1978): 255–84; Zaccone, "Investiture feudali"; E. Pibiri, "L'acquisition du Saint Suaire par la Maison de Savoie en 1453: De nouveaux textes," *Rivista di storia della Chiesa in Italia* 57 (2003): 155–64.

and 10 gold écus were used to pay the squire and the cost of food for the countess Marguerite, who at that time was to be journeying to Geneva to handle some matters only described as "confidential" (*pro nonnullis secretis agibilibus*), while the remaining 50 francs were for the dean and the chapter of Lirey.[184] Since the amount earmarked by the duke for the chapter coincided exactly with the amount they were claiming from Marguerite,[185] it is clear that the duke's intervention served to settle the countess' debt, so as to hold off and further delay the return of the Shroud, which was owed to them. The payments Louis made to provide fully for Marguerite's expenses during the whole of her trip to Geneva—more than 150 florins in all—show the duke's particular concern for Marguerite, who had at least two things that interested Louis: the rights to the fief of Varambon and the Shroud, which in those days was shown at least three times in Geneva (on two occasions in the presence of Annabella of Scotland, the fiancée of the son of Duke Louis). One of the exhibitions occurred on February 26, the day after the aforementioned payment by Louis, from a platform specially built on the wall of the convent of the Dominicans; there was another exhibition, between March 17 and 19, with Marguerite's permission, as usual, which shows that the transfer of ownership of the relic had not yet occurred.[186]

It is difficult to establish the exact day on which the Shroud was given to Louis. In documents from March 22, 1453—in which the duke enfeoffed Marguerite for life with the castellany of Miribel and provided the annuity from the revenues of the castellany of Montluel in exchange for the transfer of her rights over Varambon—Marguerite was called "generous, our kinswoman, and most dear," and was made the object of numerous expressions of praise that acknowledge, though they do not specify, "numerous, praiseworthy services

[184] Cf. Pibiri, "Acquisition du Saint Suaire," 162–63.

[185] Since the time of John II the Good, the franc had become synonymous with the livre tournois.

[186] Cf. Zurbuchen, "Saint Suaire à Genève," 266–73. In 1985 Gian Maria Zaccone ("Investiture feudali," 41, n. 67) was questioning whether the "Countess of Villars" mentioned in the documents edited by Zurbuchen could with any certainty be identified as Marguerite de Charny, bearing a title that belonged to her husband, Humbert de Villersexel (formerly called "Villars-Seyssel"). The same documents also mention a "Lord of Allymes" whom Zurbuchen was unable to identify; since Eva Pibiri has revealed the relationship between Marguerite de Charny and Louis François des Allymes, there is no longer room to doubt the identity of the countess.

rendered to us up to now through her" (*multa et laudabilia obsequia per eam nobis hactenus impensa*). It should be noted that Miribel and Montluel are two castellanies tied directly to Louis François des Allymes, the one who had taken care of Marguerite in Geneva and who had taken part in at least one of the exhibitions of the Shroud. It may be possible to pinpoint the link between Marguerite and the Duke of Savoy in the person of Louis François. One might also find in those laconically described "confidential matters" and "services rendered" a vague reference—with all due caution[187]—not only to the negotiations concerning the fief of Varambon but also to those over the transfer of the Shroud. That transfer, undeniably, did not happen free of charge, though it is not explicitly mentioned in the documents.

Many authors have therefore considered March 22, 1453, to be the precise date of the transfer of ownership of the relic;[188] others suppose, instead, that the Shroud was physically handed over a few days after March 25 (Palm Sunday), on which day an exhibition took place in Geneva at the chapel of the noble Jean de Rolle.[189] At present, establishing an unequivocal date is impossible, since the above-cited legal transactions between Marguerite and Louis on March 22 regard only an enfeoffment in return for the transfer of land and the establishment of an annuity in return for the transfer of a debt.

The content of an archival document that I discovered in the course of my research is critical for this discussion. It records that on March 29 Louis gave Marguerite 10,000 gold écus and established for her an annual pension of 1,000 florins of a lighter weight.[190] This time Marguerite did not have to give anything in exchange; through his donation the duke affirmed that he wanted to compensate her "for the close, sincere affection and the exceptional kindness she always showed toward us" (*intimam et sinceram affectionem et benevolentiam*

[187] The *obsequia* that a vassal renders to his sovereign are often indicated in documents of the time, without this constituting a special case for Marguerite.

[188] Beginning with E. F. Pingone, *Sindon evangelica* (Turin: Bevilaqua, 1581), 29, followed by S. Guichenon, *Histoire généalogique de la royale maison de Savoye*, vol. 1 (Lyon: Barbier, 1660), 95 and 513.

[189] The Chapel of St. Catherine, later called Chapelle de Brandis, near the current Place du Molard and demolished in 1889 (photograph in C. L. Perrin, *Les vieux quartiers de Genève* [Geneva: Georg, 1904], 44–45).

[190] Nicolotti, "Acquisition of the Shroud," doc. 5. The pension was to be received annually on the feast day of Saint Michael from incomes of the castellany of Châteauneuf-en-Valromey.

singularem quam erga nos semper gesserit). Perhaps this sum was payment for the Shroud? The sale of the Shroud is never given as a specific reason for these transactions, but this does not mean that this sale was not recognized by both parties; it is likely that reference to the Shroud was deliberately omitted so as not to leave written traces of an illicit transfer. Louis knew well that trading in relics was illegal, and he knew just as well that various legal judgments had acknowledged that the right to possess the Shroud resided with not Marguerite but rather the collegiate church of Lirey.

As for François de la Palud, in the end he won anyway. In October of 1452, as noted above, Louis had promised the king of France that he would restore to all the condemned nobles, including François, the possessions they held prior to sentencing. He did not do so at that time. The king—to whom the nobles had once again appealed[191]—pressed him to the point of forcing him, compelling him to sign a new agreement on July 2, 1454; and finally, on September 30, 1454, Louis sent the letters patent allowing the agreement he made with the king to be carried out. He ordered the already-promised restitution of goods and titles, even those that in the meantime had been given to others, promising to pay François de la Palud the amount of 12,000 écus to compensate him for the destruction of his castle, to be paid in three annual installments of 4,000 écus.[192] As the last act of the event, on March 27, 1455, in Chambéry, Jean de Compey reconciled (at least formally)[193] with his attackers. In substance it seems that Louis' attempts to avoid François' reinstatement were useless, and his business with Marguerite de Charny must have been frustrated to some degree. But Louis' resistance continued until the end, since even on July 2, 1455, François was able to say that he had been deprived of his possessions in Savoy, which evidently had not been physically returned to his control.[194]

On April 11, 1455, a new document informs us that Louis had to give Marguerite de Charny the fief of Flumet as a substitute for

[191] *Suplication et requeste faicte au roy par les nobles de Savoye*: BNF, MS Français 18983, f. 49 (no. 41).

[192] The text of the measures taken was published by Guichenon, *Histoire de Bresse et de Bugey*, pt. 4, 28–30.

[193] But only three days later, on March 31, Jean would kill a member of the league, Pierre de Menthon.

[194] Cf. Guichenon, *Histoire de Bresse et de Bugey*, pt. 3, 294.

Miribel, which was taken away from her.[195] According to documents dating from August 13, 1455, moreover, it seems that Marguerite must have received 600 florins from Antoine de la Palud, François' brother. The reason is that more than two years prior, Marguerite had left him in charge of the fiefs of Varambon and Bouligneux for a period of six years.[196] Therefore, Antoine had had use of those fiefs up to that time. What was the significance, therefore, of the sale of Varambon to the duke? Was it withdrawn or annulled? In July of that year, François found himself in Mâcon once more, under Burgundy's protection, since new conflicts had arisen between himself and Louis;[197] François died the following year. But in his will of November 6, 1456, he would bequeath both Varambon and Bouligneux to his son, Philibert Philippe, and he would mention Montfort as property of which he was disposing, having obtained it in exchange with Marguerite: therefore, the act of 1435, at least in part, had remained in force, or there had been new agreements.[198]

"The transfer [of the Shroud] absolutely could not have been a transaction free of charge, but was certainly, on the contrary, sold for a price."[199] In short, something like a sale or trade took place, however disguised. On this matter there was no longer doubt even before I found a nearly contemporary document in which the word "to sell" is used explicitly.[200] This fact should not overshadow the religious piety that, other reasons aside, must have driven the ducal couple

[195] Nicolotti, "Acquisition of the Shroud," doc. 8. There is also another act dated November 20, 1454, in which Louis granted to Marguerite the land of Clermont as a fief in exchange for that of Miribel (idem, "Acquisition of the Shroud," doc. 7). Zaccone, "Investiture feudali," 34, thinks that evidently this decision was soon withdrawn or was not ever put into effect. According to Perret, "Essai sur l'histoire du Saint Suaire," 87, the transfer of Flumet must also have been withdrawn since Louis could not have it, inasmuch as it had already been granted to Guillaume de la Fléchère. There also exists a document of October 27, 1456, in which François de Bonivard is called castellan of Flumet (AST, Protocolli ducali serie rossa, no. 96, f. 133).

[196] Nicolotti, "Acquisition of the Shroud," doc. 9.

[197] Cf. Guichenon, *Histoire de Bresse et de Bugey*, pt. 3, 294–95.

[198] But it turns out that in 1471 Beaumont-sur-Vingeanne and Bouligneux still needed to be redeemed. Pérard, *Recueil de plusieurs pièces curieuses*, 599–600, 605.

[199] Zaccone, "Investiture feudali," 28.

[200] BNF, MS Duchesne 61, f. 116r: "ung reliquiaire qu'on appelloit le saint suaire lequel elle [i.e., Marguerite] vandit au feu duc de Savoye." The document is undated but dates to the second half of the fifteenth century.

to acquire the Shroud. While they were alive, both, especially the duchess, bore witness to the fact. Moreover, Louis was a descendant of Saint Louis, king of France, and could not have failed to recognize the prestige that the French crown had attained following the acquisition of Jesus' crown of thorns and all the other relics brought over from Constantinople after the Fourth Crusade. The significance of acquiring the relic is demonstrated by the fact that the *Chronica latina Sabaudiae,* written between 1487 and 1489, records the acquisition of the Shroud from Marguerite as the only thing worthy of mention in the whole of Duke Louis' life.[201]

Marguerite de Charny thus sold the Shroud, disregarding the rights of the Lirey chapter, which continued to claim it. On May 30, 1457, she, who had already been excommunicated, was newly condemned and excommunicated by the curia of Besançon; it was decreed that every Sunday and every feast day in the church her condemnation be remembered publicly, and that whenever she came to a city, religious services were to be suspended until she left.[202] The decree of condemnation was issued even to officials in Lyon and Troyes, with the justification that Marguerite had not returned the Shroud and had not paid the fees owed—with the exception of that fee financed at the time by the Duke of Savoy.[203] It is interesting to see that by now the Shroud is called *sudarium seu sanctuarium,* that is, "shroud or relic," even by officials of the curia; that is precisely the definition that, seventy years before, according to the bishop Pierre d'Arcis, some were improperly using to describe the cloth, thereby passing it off as a relic. But by this point, there was no one who took offense at it anymore.

The duke, for his part, had no intention of losing the Shroud to anyone; protected and fearless due to his high rank, on May 1, 1455, he had already made the canon Jean Renguis custodian of the relic. Marguerite, on the contrary, remained stricken by the worst censures and turned to Charles de Noyers, her stepbrother, to attempt a new agreement with the church of Lirey before the provost of Troyes. On January 19, 1459, Charles pledged to pay the chapter 800 gold ducats,

201 "Chronica latina Sabaudiae," in *Monumenta Historiae Patriae: Scriptorum tomus I* (Turin: e Regio Typographeo, 1840), col. 616. The author is Étienne Morel, abbot of Ambronay and bishop of Saint-Jean-de-Maurienne.

202 Cf. Chevalier, *Étude critique,* doc. W.

203 Cf. Chevalier, *Étude critique,* doc. Z.

the amount already owed, to which he added a further 300 livre; all of the money would have to be paid by October 1. He asked in exchange for the withdrawal of the censures and for renunciation of any claim to the Shroud by the canons. Charles further pledged to obtain from the pope and the bishop of Troyes written permission for Marguerite to divest herself of the relic. If the money were not sent on the agreed-upon day, the excommunication would have to apply also to Charles himself.[204]

At this point it was already indisputable that the relic was not in Marguerite's possession; in the document signed on that occasion it is recognized that the Shroud "is the most beautiful and notable jewel of the aforementioned church and that, long ago, it was taken from the aforementioned church by the aforementioned lady or by someone on her behalf, and afterward she divested herself of it."[205] In short, by now it was well known even in Lirey that Marguerite had sold the Shroud. The canons agreed to have the excommunication revoked once they received the money that was promised, but it never happened, and on about July 22, 1460, Marguerite de Charny died excommunicated and without absolution. On April 20, she had left the lands of Lirey to her godson and cousin Antoine Guerry des Essarts, and in the same year she had designated Guillaume de Roussillon, Lord of Bouchage, and his wife, Béatrix de Poitiers, as heirs of her possessions.[206]

Once again the canons remained disappointed and decided to turn directly to the House of Savoy, the new keepers of the relic. The canons Nicolas de la Rothière and Jean Larrecier therefore went to Louis, equipped with three letters and the full powers assigned them by the chapter and Louis Raguier, bishop of Troyes; they reminded the duke that Geoffroy de Charny gave to the collegiate church "a most holy Shroud, which depicts the effigy of our Savior and Redeemer Jesus Christ," which brought visits and earnings to the church; they therefore demanded the return of the cloth or equivalent monetary compensation.

[204] ADA, I 19 n. 2A.

[205] Chevalier, *Étude critique*, XXXVII.

[206] According to P. Anselme, *Histoire généalogique et chronologique de la maison royale de France*, vol. 8 (Paris: Compagnie des libraires associés, 1733), 203, on October 24, 1455, Marguerite had already granted him the lordships of Roffey, of Ligny-le-Châtel en Tonnerrois, and what she held in Ricey.

On February 6, 1464, in Paris, an agreement was reached: the canons accepted an annuity of 50 gold Savoyard francs of a lighter weight to be collected every year in perpetuity on the feast day of Saint Andrew from proceeds of the castle and district of Gaillard, in Upper Savoy. In exchange Louis asked only for the celebration of a monthly mass on his behalf.[207] On the following May 23, Louis wrote to the chapter to ask for the remission of excommunication for the now-deceased Marguerite and her secretary and guarantor, Philibert Thibault.[208]

But not even this debt was honored, since Louis died in 1465 without ever having paid what he promised. A new appeal by the canons followed, which was presented on May 14, 1473, to Yolande of Valois, regent duchess, by Marc de Vaudrey, protonotary apostolic, canon, and archdeacon of Besançon, and Hugues Mergey, *maître ès arts*; the canons' request was to finally obtain the owed annuity, with eight years of arrears or, alternatively, to get the Shroud back.[209] And again, between 1472 and 1482, the canons wrote to King Louis XI of France to ask for economic support, telling of the whole matter and lamenting that nothing had been granted them, neither the Shroud nor the money promised by Savoy.[210] But it was completely useless. From a document datable to the sixteenth century (before 1578), it turns out that the canons still remembered the wrong they had suffered because of the "perfidious woman who handed over and, as they say, sold the Shroud to the Duke of Savoy."[211] In 1691, a dean of Lirey made the last, anachronistic attempt to inquire about the current ownership of the castle of Gaillard, hoping to be able to get some income by virtue of the agreement from 1464.[212]

One can now understand why, in 1900, the canon who first published all these documents stated the following: "The annals of the Shroud of Turin are a long violation of the two virtues so frequently urged in our holy Books: justice and truth."[213]

207 Cf. Chevalier, *Étude critique*, doc. Z.

208 Cf. Chevalier, *Étude critique*, doc. AA.

209 Cf. Chevalier, *Étude critique*, doc. BB.

210 Cf. Chevalier, *Autour des origines du suaire de Lirey*, doc. M. The king's response (idem, *Autour des origines du suaire de Lirey*, doc. N) is incomplete.

211 Chevalier, *Étude critique*, doc. GG.

212 ADA, I 19 n. 1A.

213 Chevalier, *Étude critique*, 42.

2.2.3 Who Was the Owner of the Shroud?

At this point it is necessary to take a step back and try to understand who first procured the Shroud, who decided to preserve it and display it in the collegiate church of Lirey, and who was its legitimate owner. The answer is not self-evident, since the existing documents that speak of the Shroud are relatively late and sometimes contradictory.

The view most widely held today is that the Shroud was acquired by Geoffroy I de Charny before 1356, the year he died. His son, Geoffroy II, asserts as much in 1389, when he said that someone had "generously offered" it to his father (*liberaliter sibi oblatam*).[214] Marguerite de Charny confirmed this in 1443, when she stated that it "was obtained by the late Sir Geoffroy de Charny" (*fut conquis par feu messire Geoffroy de Charny*).[215] Assuming that Geoffroy II and Marguerite were speaking truthfully, and that the Shroud came into Geoffroy I's possession before his death, we must still establish when it was placed in the collegiate church of Lirey. None of the documents that concern the founding or approval of the collegiate church mentions the Shroud, but that does not seem to me to be adequate grounds for excluding a priori the possibility that the Shroud was there, since in those documents there was never a cogent reason to mention it. The fact that on May 28, 1356, Henry de Poitiers, bishop of Troyes, approved the measures for the founding of the collegiate church could lead one to think that up to that point there had not yet been any reason for friction due to the Shroud, or, on the contrary, that the matter was already resolved.

Only later, in 1464, did the canons of Lirey claim before the Duke of Savoy that Geoffroy I had "given and bestowed" (*dedit et largitus est*) the Shroud to the collegiate church.[216] Some years later they made

[214] Chevalier, *Autour des origines du suaire de Lirey*, 31.

[215] Chevalier, *Étude critique*, XXIII. In the past this passage has been a source of misunderstanding, since various individuals have translated *conquis* as "won" and *feu* as "fire," thinking about a "fire" of battle (a crusade, a war with the Turks or others); for example, Chifflet, *De linteis sepulchralibus*, 105–6; Von Dobschütz, *Christusbilder*, 74; P. de Gail, *Histoire religieuse du Linceul du Christ* (Hauteville: Parvis, 1974), 136. But actually, in this case, *feu* means "late," because Geoffroy was dead, and the verb *conquérir* can be used in the general sense of "to obtain something by effort," without necessarily referring to a military context. How Geoffroy would have gotten the relic, therefore, Marguerite does not tell us.

[216] Chevalier, *Étude critique*, XL.

the same assertion before Louis XI,[217] and then again in the sixteenth century.[218] Where Geoffroy got the Shroud is never mentioned, which might lead one to think that it was unknown or that no one wanted to be accountable for a provenance that was doubtful, illegal, or fraudulent.

It is necessary to distinguish carefully between the several scenarios that the different passages make possible; Geoffroy could have obtained (or had made) the Shroud during his lifetime and could have placed it in his church immediately or even later, after he had kept it for himself for an initial period of some length. The collegiate church could have received it either before or after his death. Finally, the placement of the Shroud in the church, at whatever point it happened, does not oblige us to think that exhibitions began immediately. In fact, some think that the Shroud appeared in the collegiate church after Geoffroy I's death, or at least that the exhibitions did not begin before that point, which would have provoked the anger of the bishop of Troyes.[219] The Memorandum of Pierre d'Arcis, as we have seen, says that the first conflict between the canons and the bishop of Troyes happened in 1355 "or so." But in contrast to the others, Pierre never drew Geoffroy I into the matter and attributed to the dean of the canons the responsibility for "having arranged to have in his church a certain cloth, cunningly portrayed."[220]

One can reconcile the two perspectives on how the Shroud came to the collegiate church of Lirey by imagining that Geoffroy obtained the Shroud from someone or procured it for himself, and that afterward the canons made sure to keep it for themselves. Or rather that Geoffroy, after having decided to have a chapel built, appointed someone, like the dean, to procure all the necessary furnishings for the church, including relics, just as he would have appointed someone to

[217] Chevalier, *Autour des origines du suaire de Lirey*, 39.

[218] Chevalier, *Étude critique*, LIX. Papini, *Sindone: Una sfida*, 53, thinks that in this text the canons affirm that they received the Shroud after Geoffroy's death; I believe that Papini mistranslated due to bad punctuation in the Latin edition of the text (which I checked in the manuscript).

[219] For example, F. Chamard, *Le Linceul du Christ: Étude critique et historique* (Paris: Oudin, 1902), 49, n. 1; Wilson, *Turin Shroud*, 72–73 and 167–68; A. Legrand, *Le Linceul de Turin* (Paris: Desclée De Brouwer, 1980), 35; Saxer, "Suaire de Turin," 27; P.-É. Blanrue, *Miracle ou imposture? L'histoire interdite du "suaire" de Turin* (Brussels: Epo, 1999), 85–93.

[220] Chevalier, *Étude critique*, VII.

build the church. It is useful to bear in mind in this regard that in the years 1354–1356, Geoffroy spent almost all of his time far from Lirey, normally next to the king of France, and certainly did not have time to busy himself with the furnishing of his collegiate church. In this way it may be that the dean was able to acquire (or commission) the Shroud on his own, as Pierre d'Arcis claimed, and it would not even be in apparent contrast with the sources that speak of a gift made by Geoffroy to the collegiate church; since the whole construction of the church and the acquisition of the furnishings was financially supported by Geoffroy, one could rightfully say that the Shroud, like everything else, was a gift from Geoffroy. And this is true also for all the other relics deposited in the church and itemized in 1418. But was Geoffroy advised regarding everything that the dean did? Was he approving his decisions?

In short, a definitive answer cannot be given. The documents are late and were redacted in a time of conflict in which the parties had some interest in supporting one or another version of the facts. I believe that in any case one cannot deny that someone of the de Charnys, at a certain point in the second half of the fourteenth century, was involved in acquiring or keeping the relic. This is demonstrated by the fact that in 1418, the Shroud was kept in the collegiate church in a coffer bearing the coat of arms of the family, and that the same coat of arms, along with that of the Vergys, was appearing on medallions made as mementos of exhibitions. The presence of the coats of arms alone, however, is not a certain indication of ownership; the de Charnys could have also limited themselves to providing a reliquary incised with their coat of arms, without being the owners of its contents.[221]

In any case, we ought not to confuse the simple possession of the Shroud by the de Charnys or the canons with its liturgical worship in the form opposed by the bishops. Geoffroy or someone acting on his behalf could have donated or procured for the collegiate church a representation of the shroud without claiming that it was being shown because it was authentic, a stance that later the canons themselves might have adopted independently, thereby inviting an accusation from Pierre d'Arcis. In fact, it is good to keep separate—as the biblical scholar Raymond E. Brown advised—the deliberate intention

[221] Cf. Chevalier, *Étude critique*, XXII.

to deceive on the part of a hypothetical forger and the possibility that someone intended to create an image of the dead body of Christ for the purpose of honest devotion, at least initially.[222]

Without knowing with absolute certainty when the Shroud was placed in the collegiate church, or by whom,[223] the question of the object's ownership is not easy to resolve. The canons were agreed in believing that it had been given to the collegiate church and that it ought to have remained there; according to them, Marguerite was falsely claiming that the Shroud belonged to her as the Lady of Lirey and because she found it among the goods inherited from her father, Geoffroy II, and those inherited from her late husband, Humbert.[224] But on none of the numerous occasions in which it was mentioned in legal proceedings was Marguerite able to prove that she was the owner of the relic, which she would certainly have done if she had had a certificate for it. Marguerite tried to claim possession of the relic by presenting it as an object belonging to her grandfather, but the tribunal did not agree with her; evidently the court was either unconvinced of the veracity of her claim or believed that Geoffroy I had left the Shroud to the canons, granting them the right of ownership.[225] If Marguerite was granted extensions, it was not because of her right of ownership, but through the concession of the canons, and because she insisted that the chapter was not able to guarantee adequate protection for the precious relic. Each extension, moreover, was granted after a promise of payment and must have been simply intended as an agreement for temporary custody. Therefore, the subsequent transfer of the Shroud to the Savoys was certainly illegal.

Gian Maria Zaccone postulates that particular private agreements existed between Geoffroy I and the canons regarding the ownership of the Shroud, although perhaps not publicly divulged "also

[222] R. E. Brown, "Brief Observations on the Shroud of Turin," *Biblical Theology Bulletin* 14, no. 4 (1984): 146; the idea was already proposed by Chevalier, *Autour des origins du Suaire de Turin*, 436–37; and by H. Thurston, "À propos du Saint Suaire de Turin," *Revue du clergé français* 33 (1902): 155–60.

[223] It is false that the bull of Clement VII attests that Geoffroy I performed an exhibition of the Shroud at least once (M. Tosatti, *Inchiesta sulla Sindone* [Casale Monferrato: Piemme, 2009], 80).

[224] Cf. Chevalier, *Étude critique*, LX.

[225] Therefore, I cannot follow Du Teil, *Autour du Saint Suaire de Lirey*, 3–4, according to whom Geoffroy I had entrusted his relic merely to the care of the canons.

because Geoffroy's own right of ownership was not very clear."[226] Even assuming that Geoffroy truly did possess the Shroud, in fact, we know not where or how or by what more or less legitimate right he acquired it. Zaccone rightly recalls that the relationship between the chapter of Lirey and the de Charnys was governed by the norms of the *ius patronatus,* which was a system of privileges and obligations belonging to the family of a *patronus,* who, like Geoffroy, assumed the duty of constructing and maintaining an ecclesiastical structure and also subsidizing the personnel who served there. Among the various rights of the *patronus,* some of which were honorific, the most important was the ability to choose the clerics who would serve under the auspices of his patronage. The patron could not control all the religious ornaments held in the church, but he could make use of his rights for their protection and safekeeping, so that they did not become dilapidated.[227] Given this ability one can understand why Humbert and Marguerite were able to transfer the Shroud into the lands they possessed to guarantee its safety and safekeeping, which was among the patron's responsibilities. This explains, too, why Marguerite, when she was before the tribunal, so insisted on the fact that the collegiate church was not a safe place to keep the relic.

For the patron, as for anyone else, the sale of relics was in any case prohibited. Marguerite's legal situation regarding the Shroud was anything but clear, and the prohibition against trading in relics explains quite well why the Shroud was given to the House of Savoy without the usual bill of sale that would mention it explicitly.[228] It also explains why subsequent historians of the House of Savoy sought to blot out this indecorous account, by saying that the Shroud came into the duke's possession as a gift according to the will of heaven.

[226] Zaccone, "Investiture feudali," 26.

[227] Cf. C. Gagliardi, *Commentarium de iurepatronatus* (Naples: ad signum anchorae, 1850); P. Thomas, *Le droit de propriété des laïques sur les églises et le patronage laïque au moyen Âge* (Paris: Leroux, 1906).

[228] Both Zaccone and Zurbuchen are in agreement on this: Zaccone, "Investiture feudali," 28; Zurbuchen, "Saint Suaire à Genève," 279. Therefore it is not true that "the Shroud was handed over by Marguerite of Charny, by deed of notary (after obtaining the Brief of Assent from the Pope), to Anne of Lusignan, wife of Duke Louis" (Ricci, *Holy Shroud,* XXXVII).

2.2.4 *A Relic of Noble Lineage*

Veneration of the Shroud was initially private, as was the veneration of other relics in the personal chapel of the Duke of Savoy.[229] All the relics, along with other objects needed at court, accompanied the duke in all his transitions from one home to another and were transported by a long caravan of mules. In the words of one court historiographer, the dukes "had the Holy Shroud brought with them to protect them from any sort of misfortune."[230] The chaplain Jean Renguis had in his care not only the Shroud but also all the other sacred ornaments of the "walking chapel," including relics, sacred furnishings, vestments, and portative organs and altars. It is possible—albeit not yet demonstrated—that for a period the Shroud was kept in Geneva in a chapel of the Franciscan convent of Rive, which was closely linked to the Savoy dynasty; this would explain why, deviating from tradition, the duke and the duchess were buried in that convent, and earlier (1461) they had had a "chapel of the Lord's tomb" built there.[231] At certain points the relics were placed in the ducal chapel of Chambéry, capital of the duchy;[232] on February 24, 1466, for example, when the new duke Amadeus IX and his wife, Yolande, wrote to Pope Paul II, they reported that in their ducal chapel "among other things, one of the shrouds of our Lord Jesus Christ and many other relics are preserved honorably and fittingly" (the expression "one of the shrouds" is noteworthy).[233]

The time was approaching, however, to find a more permanent place for the Shroud. On April 21, 1467, the pope granted to Amadeus and Yolande the rights of a collegiate church for their chapel dedicated to Mary and Saints Paul and Maurice, which they had built in the castle of Chambéry by 1408; after the pope's intervention it became a mother-church for the whole bailiwick of Savoy, under the direct control of the Holy See and freed from the local bishop's

[229] A good presentation on the history of the relic up to its transfer to Turin can also be found in Perret, "Essai sur l'histoire du Saint Suaire."

[230] Guichenon, *Histoire généalogique*, 613.

[231] This hypothesis is that of L. Ripart, "Le Saint Suaire, les Savoie et Chambéry," in Cozzo, Merlotti, and Nicolotti, *Shroud at Court*, 64–67.

[232] Cf. R. Brondy, *Chambéry: Histoire d'une capitale vers 1350–1560* (Lyon: Presses Universitaires de Lyon, 1988).

[233] Savio, *Ricerche storiche*, 249: "inter alia unum ex sudariis Domini nostri Ihesu Christi et quamplures alie venerabiles reliquie sint honorifice et decenter reposita."

influence. It had a dean named by the duke, twelve canons, six priests, six child cantors, two teachers, four clerics, and an organist.[234] By 1472 the chapel was officially designated "holy." On June 6, 1483, an inventory of the precious objects kept in the chapel was drawn up; the most important was the Shroud, which was wrapped in a red silk cloth and placed in a box covered with crimson velvet, completely studded with silver-gilt nails, and sealed by a lock with gilded key. In the same coffer, in addition to the Shroud, there were also other relics.[235] In 1498, in Turin, the box was described as "a coffer covered in crimson velvet, with silver-gilt roses and silver corners."[236]

The relic became the palladium of the House of Savoy. It was the sacred object to which they turned in times of difficulty to obtain help and protection, and the devotion of three women in particular contributed to the growth of its veneration: Claudine de Brosse of Brittany, wife of Duke Philip II; Philiberta of Savoy, their daughter; and Margaret of Austria, wife of Duke Philibert II. In this period the chapel of Chambéry was being prepared to become the permanent home of the Shroud; we have the document for the relic's solemn transfer within the city of Chambéry to the ducal chapel from the church of the convent of St. Francis, where it was at that time. The document is dated June 15, 1502, and it reports that the "silver-gilt box" was placed "in a certain cabinet in the chapel itself, built into the walls and opposite the high altar itself," protected by iron doors with four locks. Two keys were left with the duke, one was given to the canons, and the fourth was given to Antoine de Roussillon,

[234] Cf. A. de Jussieu, *La Sainte-Chapelle du château de Chambéry* (Chambéry: Perrin, 1868), 36–38, 161–67; Savio, *Ricerche storiche*, 251–58. On Sainte-Chapelle in general, see A. Perret, *La Sainte-Chapelle du château ducal de Chambéry* (Lyon: Publications de la Société des amis de la Sainte-Chapelle, 1967); J. B. Scott, *Architecture for the Shroud* (Chicago: University of Chicago Press, 2003), 39–54; M. Santelli, *La Sainte-Chapelle du château des ducs de Savoie à Chambéry* (Chambéry: Société savoisienne d'histoire et d'archéologie, 2003); C. Guilleré and A. Palluel-Guillard, *Le château des ducs de Savoie: Dix siècles d'histoire* (Chambéry: Altal éditions, 2011), 63–67, 83–89, 170–73, 220–24; L. Gruaz, "Sainte-Chapelle du Château des ducs de Savoie," in *Dictionnaire d'histoire et de géographie ecclésiastiques* 32 (2019): coll. 1451–59.

[235] Cf. A. Fabre, *Trésor de la Sainte Chapelle des ducs de Savoie au Château de Chambéry* (Lyon: Schuring, 1875), 55 and 90.

[236] P. Vayra, *Inventari dei castelli di Ciamberì, di Torino e di Ponte d'Ain, 1497–1498* (Turin: Paravia, 1883), § 943.

president of the ducal Chamber of Audit.[237] Still today one can see the wall's hollowed-out space, once occupied by the cabinet, which was located in the apse of the chapel, 1.5 m from the back of the current altar, which stands approximately where the medieval one did.[238] The opening in the wall measures about 165 cm in length, 50 cm in height, and 60 cm deep, and it cannot be reached without using a ladder or the mezzanine level, since its bottom is about 2.5 m above the current floor.[239] The position is not unusual; cabinets in walls behind the altar used for the preservation of relics were not rare in this period.[240]

At this point, the Duke of Savoy—as the Byzantine emperor of Constantinople had already done with the Chapel of the Pharos, and as the king of France had done with the Sainte-Chapelle of Paris—attached a private chapel to his residence and enriched it with the presence of a dynastic relic. The Sainte-Chapelle of Paris presents an apt parallel,[241] since what happened in Savoy can be interpreted as a revival of what Louis IX had done to ensure his possession and the most worthy placement of Christ's crown of thorns, which he acquired at a very high cost from the Latin emperor

[237] Cf. de Jussieu, *Sainte-Chapelle*, 219–22. As for the location of the relic, the exact words are "in quodam armario in ipsa capella et infra menia ipsius e contra ipsum magnum altare constructo." Some think that the Shroud was in the sacristy on the side of the chapel: L. G. Piano, *Comentarii critico-archeologici sopra la SS. Sindone di N.S. Gesù Cristo*, vol. 2 (Turin: Bianco, 1833), 196; Sanna Solaro, *S. Sindone che si venera a Torino*, 42; G. Donna d'Oldenico, "Da Chambéry a Torino," in Moriondo and Piazza, *Torino e la Sindone*, 81. Even if *contra* sometimes means "about," "nearby" (a bit like the French *contre*), it seems to me that the translation "opposite" is preferable for two reasons: for the more restrictive meaning of "contra" when preceded by "e," and because the sacristy is a room on the side of the church; why speak of a place inside the walls near the high altar, if a separate room is meant?

[238] The current altar dates to the eighteenth century.

[239] I made the measurements. Others offer more ample dimensions, because instead of accounting for the usable internal space, they measure the opening, which is larger.

[240] Cf. Dor, *Reliquaires de la Passion*, 120–21.

[241] On these sorts of chapels, see C. Billot, "Les saintes chapelles (XIIIe-XVIe siècle): Approche comparée des fondations dynastiques," *Revue d'histoire de l'Église de France* 73, no. 191 (1987): 229–48; L. Gaffuri, "La Sainte-Chapelle tra Parigi e Chambéry: Un emblema 'replicabile' della sacralità di corte (XV secolo)," *Reti Medievali Rivista* 17, no. 1 (2016): 1–10.

of Constantinople.[242] The mere possession of relics so precious had more than a religious value; it was seen as a sign of divine benevolence, a tangible indication of protection that God guaranteed to the city and the owner who possessed them, and, ultimately, a true instrument for legitimizing political power.[243] The acquisition of the Shroud by the House of Savoy should be interpreted as an aspect of the process of the construction of its identity as a royal dynasty and self-legitimization: the search for relics of the passion of Christ was not a secondary aspect, because in medieval Christianity such relics were strictly associated with the idea of sovereignty. All the great ruling houses possessed important relics of the passion, although prior to the acquisition of the Shroud, the Savoy dynasty possessed merely a few small fragments of the cross. The purchase of the Shroud allowed the dukes of Savoy to exhibit their christological royalty.[244]

In the years preceding, the Shroud had been far from stationary. Among its peregrinations, Yolande of Valois took it to Piedmont in 1476; it also was probably exhibited at Rivoli and Pinerolo in 1478, at Savigliano in 1488, at Vercelli on Good Friday of 1494, and at Turin on Good Friday of 1495.[245] We know that scaffolding adorned with very rich tapestries was built for the exhibition at the castle of Rivoli on Good Friday or Holy Saturday of 1478.[246] But even after its transfer to

[242] On this, see C. Mercuri, *Corona di Cristo corona di re* (Rome: Edizioni di Storia e Letteratura, 2004); French revised translation: *Saint Louis et la couronne d'épines: Histoire d'une relique à la Sainte-Chapelle* (Paris: Riveneuve, 2011).

[243] The bibliography is ample: here I note only E. Bozóky, *La politique des reliques de Constantin à Saint Louis* (Paris: Beauchesne, 2006).

[244] I have elaborated on this in A. Nicolotti, "I Savoia e la Sindone di Cristo: Aspetti politici e propagandistici," in *Cristo e il potere: Teologia, antropologia e politica*, ed. L. Andreani and A. Paravicini Bagliani (Florence: SISMEL—Edizioni del Galluzzo, 2017), 247–81.

[245] Cf. G. Lanza, *La Santissima Sindone del Signore che si venera nella R. Cappella di Torino* (Turin: Roux Frassati, 1898), 53–55; G. Donna d'Oldenico, "La Sindone nella politica dei Duchi di Savoia e nella considerazione di S. Carlo Borromeo zelatore della prima ricerca critico esegetica," *Verbanus* 5 (1984): 222; idem, "Da Chambéry a Torino," 74–77.

[246] Cf. S. Cordero di Pamparato, "La prima esposizione della Sindone in Piemonte," *L'Italia reale-Corriere* 25, no. 41 (February 11–12, 1898); P. Caffaro, *Notizie e documenti della chiesa pinerolese*, vol. 4 (Pinerolo: Chiantore-Mascarelli, 1899), 28–30, n. 2; M. C. Daviso di Charvensod, *La duchessa Iolanda (1434–1478)* (Turin: Paravia, 1935), 178 and 185, n. 23; E. Biagi, "La Sindone venne a Pinerolo," *L'eco del Chisone*, April 1, 1982, 3; L. Gaffuri, "The First Exhibitions of the Shroud in Piedmont and

Sainte-Chapelle, the Shroud could still travel. For example, Antoine de Lalaing—Lord of Montigny, later knight of the Order of the Golden Fleece, Count of Hoogstraten, and minister—reports that on Good Friday of 1503 at Bourg-en-Bresse, Philibert of Savoy and his wife, Margaret of Austria, arranged a showing of the Shroud for Philip I of Habsburg, who was passing through that city on his return from a trip to Spain. At the exhibition, which occurred both publicly and privately, two homilies on the passion were delivered, one for the nobles and one for the crowd gathered in the plaza of the covered market. Antoine provides a lovely description of the image of the man on the cloth, concluding that on that occasion, to see whether the Shroud was authentic or not, "it was boiled in oil, put in the fire, and washed and bleached several times; but it could not blot out nor remove the aforementioned impression and figure."[247] For decades this account was generally dismissed by sindonologists because the examination of the current Shroud excludes the possibility of it having undergone this ordeal; according to many sindonologists, Lalaing's assertion was the result of a rumor.[248] There are two possibilities: either the current Shroud is not the same as the one displayed in 1503, or Lalaing is unreliable. If we accept the second explanation, we have a good example of how care is needed when dealing with sources that speak of relics; we ought to consider how, in some cases, such sources have been blindly believed by the same people who, in other cases, rush to delegitimize them.

Another instance in which the Shroud was removed from Chambéry was when it resided in the castle of Billiat under the care of Claudine de Brosse, probably for three years, until 1506. Claudine

---

Yolande of Valois, Duchess of Savoy," in Cozzo, Merlotti, and Nicolotti, *Shroud at Court*, 89–103.

[247] Ed. M. Gachard, *Collection des voyages des souverains des Pays-Bas*, vol. 1 (Brussels: Hayez, 1876), 286: "On l'a boulit en huille, bouté en feu, lavé et buet par pluseurs fois: mais on n'a peut effachier ne oster ladicte imprimure et figure." On this exhibition, see A. Chagny, "An Exposition of the Holy Shroud in the Market Place of Bourg-en-Bresse," *Shroud Spectrum International* 37 (1990): 3–8.

[248] G. Zaninotto, "Ma la Sindone non fu bollita nell'olio," in Ladu, *Datazione della Sindone*, 293–307; M. Centini, "L'ordalia di Bourg en Bresse," in Ladu, *Datazione della Sindone*, 381–90. See also R. Souverain, "Réflexions sur l'ordalie supposée de Bourg-en-Bresse en 1503," *La lettre mensuelle du CIELT* 25 (1992): 4–6, on the mistaken hypothesis that boiling oil can alter the results of the radiocarbon dating of the fabric.

paid great devotion to the relic, believing it capable of averting plague and political crises;[249] at her death in 1513, she was buried in the Sainte-Chapelle of Chambéry a few meters from the Shroud.[250]

2.2.5 *Public Veneration of the Shroud*

For a certain period the cult of the Shroud had remained more or less tied to the ceremonies and sacred representations of the Easter triduum.[251] By now it was time that the Shroud, which had found a place worthy of it, be granted the dignity of official, public veneration. Again having received a home of its own, something it had lost when it had left Lirey, in Chambéry the relic found itself in a fecund environment for establishing its worship; in this period, moreover, a particular sensibility flourished in regard to artistic representations and meditations on the passion and death of Jesus, which were favored in the preaching by friars of the mendicant orders. A Dominican friar, Antoine Pennet—confessor of the Duke of Savoy, professor of theology, and prior of the convent of Plainpalais in Geneva—was in all likelihood the author of the first liturgical text dedicated to the Holy Shroud.

"Rejoice, o good, happy Savoy, in granting the joys of the Shroud to the world; rejoice, ye entire mother Church."[252] So begins the antiphony of first vespers of the Shroud, with praise of the Savoyard duchy and the whole Church. Pennet chose to focus his entire liturgy on the theme of the passion and burial of Christ, drawing inspiration for the readings of the Office from Thomas Aquinas' *Catena aurea*. In accordance with the allegorical spirit of the period, Pennet sought out each passage of Scripture in which there was mention of linens, veils, wraps, and shrouds, and applied it to the relic; he investigated nearly every prophetic allusion, such as Joseph's clothes, Aaron's tunic, the cloak of Elijah, the fleece of Gideon, the scarlet cord of Rahab, and Noah's covering.

[249] Cf. Perret, "Essai sur l'histoire du Saint Suaire," 95–96. One should avoid J. Chaveyron, "Le Saint Suaire a-t-il été à Billat [*sic*]?," *Le Bugey* 14 (1974–1975): 837–40, 943–44.

[250] This tomb, of which minimal traces have been found, no longer exists.

[251] See Gaffuri, "First Exhibitions," 90–93.

[252] "Gaude felix leta Sabaudia, Syndonis dans mundo gaudia. Gaude tota mater Ecclesia."

The right to approve a new liturgical text belonged to the pope, and the circumstances were more than favorable for this step. The condemnations of the bishops of Troyes and the limitations imposed in the past by Clement VII were by this time forgotten. On the contrary, in a treatise written in 1462 by Francesco della Rovere—published after he became pope under the name Sixtus IV—there was an explicit mention of the Savoyard Shroud that, in a way, authenticated it.[253] By finding a theological basis in this very text on the blood of Christ—which dealt with the thorny issue of whether divine blood remained on earth after the resurrection—the Duke of Savoy tried to convince the pope of the benefit of venerating the Shroud. To that end he sent a postulator, Louis de Gorrevod de Challant, a person of the highest rank, to present the case in Rome. He was bishop of the Savoyard diocese of Saint-Jean-de-Maurienne, and he was quite familiar with the Shroud. Among other things, in the already-mentioned exhibition of 1503 in Bourg-en-Bresse, he had been one of the three prelates who held it in their hands to show it to the nobles and the people. Louis' mission was to get Pope Julius II to accept the petition that Charles II, Duke of Savoy, and Claudine de Brosse, his mother, had sent on May 9, 1506. In that petition, the Savoys informed the pope that they were keeping the Shroud at Sainte-Chapelle in a silver box and that the relic was drawing crowds of the faithful and generating numerous miracles, especially during exhibitions. Therefore, Charles proposed the creation of a liturgical holiday to be celebrated every May 4—that is, the day after the Feast of the Finding of the True Cross. In the same petition, Charles included a proposed text that could be used in the celebration of the Office and in the Mass of the Holy Shroud; the text was written, in fact, by Antoine Pennet. In the text, Charles requested the approval for the entire territory of his duchy, asking moreover for permission to establish a confraternity with five hundred members in Sainte-Chapelle and for a grant of indulgences.[254]

[253] F. della Rovere, *De sanguine Christi*, quoted from a 1473 edition in Chevalier, *Étude critique*, doc. CC: "the shroud in which the body of Christ was wrapped when it was taken down from the cross, looked after with great devotion by the dukes of Savoy and stained with the blood of Christ."

[254] Savio, *Ricerche storiche*, 207–32. The history of the liturgy of the Shroud from its beginnings up to today is outlined by E. M. Vismara, "La liturgia della Sindone," in *Santa Sindone nelle ricerche moderne*, 171–92; A. Nocent, "La liturgia della Santa

The pope accepted all these requests and had a bull of approval drawn up in which he reproduced the text of the liturgy, limiting himself to some minimal retouching. He did not show any doubt about the authenticity of the relic and encouraged its adoration with these words:

> If we adore and venerate the holy cross on which our Lord Jesus Christ hung and by which we were redeemed, it seems certainly fitting and proper that we ought also to venerate and adore the shroud on which are clearly seen the remains of Christ's humanity with which his divinity was joined, namely the remains of his true blood.[255]

Beginning in 1506, therefore, the Shroud had its own liturgy, and its veneration enjoyed papal approval.[256] In 1514 Leo X confirmed the Office for all of Savoy, and in 1582, Gregory XIII extended the Office to all the Savoyard domains, even toward the mountains.[257] Afterward, both the liturgical reform of Council of Trent and certain flaws in the text prompted a revision; we know that the text was emended several times, although we do not know the precise time of each change. In 1595 some readings were modified, and between 1592 and 1598 the texts of the mass were reformed.[258] Some theologically questionable phrases were corrected; for example, the expression "by virtue of the Holy Shroud" (*per virtutem Sanctae Sindonis*), which occurs in the Introit and Postcommunion of the mass and which could cause suspicion of idolatry toward the relic, was suppressed.[259] For the same

---

Sindone," in Ladu, *Datazione della Sindone*, 417–28; R. Savarino, "Lo sviluppo della liturgia ufficiale," in *Guardare la Sindone: Cinquecento anni di liturgia sindonica*, ed. G. M. Zaccone and G. Ghiberti (Cantalupa: Effatà, 2007), 205–26.

[255] Savio, *Ricerche storiche*, 232–45 (the citation is on p. 234).

[256] The manuscript text (different from that of the bull) is in Turin, Biblioteca Nazionale, MS E.IV.13 (*Officium et Missa Sanctissimae Sindonis*), with a miniature that depicts Pennet offering his composition to the duke. The printed edition is *Officium cum missa Sancte Syndonis sudarium Christi vulgariter nuncupate* (Geneva: Jean Belot, 1506–1507).

[257] The brief of Gregory XIII is reproduced in *L'ostensione della S. Sindone* (Turin: Bona, 1931), table LXVI.

[258] The interval between 1592 and 1598 is proposed by E. Demaria, *I canti per la messa della Sindone* (Torino: Astra Media, 2015): 19–22.

[259] The excessive zeal of the panegyrists of the Shroud can be seen, for example, even in an attempt to rewrite the Latin prayer of the Hail Mary replacing the Madonna with the Shroud: "Hail Holy Shroud, full of grace and glory, the Lord is

reason, the verse "we adore thy Holy Shroud" (*tuam Sanctam Sindonem adoramus*) was changed to "we venerate thy Shroud" (*tuam Sindonam veneramur*), even if the same Pope Julius II had explicitly spoken of the cult of adoration and had been followed by others.[260] The hymns of the Office were revised and corrected by Cardinal Giovanni Bona and approved on January 21, 1673. A better redactor could not have been chosen; Bona was known for his erudition in spiritual, patristic, and liturgical matters and was famous for his best-known work, then recently published, the *Rerum liturgicarum libri*. In the end, the result was a liturgical formulary that was well thought out theologically and that remained unchanged until the twentieth century.[261] Naturally the creation of a liturgy of the Shroud immediately favored the composition of music dedicated to it.[262]

In the meantime, in Chambéry, once the Office was approved, the worship of the Shroud was favored in every way; for his part, the pope guaranteed indulgences to whoever visited Sainte-Chapelle on the feast of May 4 or participated in an exhibition of the Shroud. In December of 1508, Margaret of Austria, widow of Duke Philibert II

---

with you; blessed are you among all the icons, and blessed the fruit who rested in you, Jesus. Holy Shroud, God's rest, be with us sinners now, and in the hour of our death. Amen" ("Ave Sancta Sindon gratia, et gloria plena, Dominus tecum, benedicta tu inter omnes imagines, et benedictus fructus qui in te requievit, Iesus. Sancta Sindon, requies Dei, adesto nobis peccatoribus nunc, et in hora mortis nostrae. Amen"): I. Loffredo, *Il tabernacolo del riposo di Dio: Discorso panegirico sopra la santa Sindone* (Turin: Cavaleri, 1652), 6.

260 For example, E. Quarantotto, *La Sacra Sindone* (Verona: Angelo Tamo, 1624), 11–12: "The Most Holy Shroud merits being honored by the faithful with adoration of latria . . . after it directly touched the body, with which the divine nature was united by a hypostatic or personal union, and [the Shroud] received it not only in the form of a corpse, but at the same time touched it, having been shaped by the blessed and triumphal soul."

261 It can be read, for example, in *Officium Sacratissimae Sindonis D.N.I.C. in dioecesibus subalpinis et alibi recitandum* (Augustae Taurinorum: Marietti, 1867) (Office); *Missae Sanctorum in archidioecesi Taurinensi celebrandae* (Taurini: Marietti, 1903), 27*–28* (Mass).

262 Cf. M. T. Bouquet-Boyer, *Itinerari musicali della Sindone* (Turin: Centro Studi Piemontesi, 1981); idem, "Musica e musicisti intorno alla Sindone," in *Il potere e la devozione*, ed. V. Comoli and G. Giacobello Bernard (Milan: Electa, 2000), 110–13. According to A. Walters Robertson, "The Man with the Pale Face, the Shroud, and Du Fay's Missa 'Se la face ay pale,'" *Journal of Musicology* 27, no. 4 (2010): 377–434, in 1452–1453 Guillaume Dufay composed his mass *Se la face ay pale* in honor of the Shroud, but the author offers no proof, only suppositions.

and, at the time, regent of the Netherlands, commissioned a new and more lavish coffer for the relic: a masterpiece of Flemish gold work by Liévin Van Lathem, trusted goldsmith of the duchy, which cost more than 12,000 gold écus. The coffer—which was sent on August 10, 1509—was made of silver, gilded in many places, and engraved with images. The pure silver to be cast, which the duchess sent to the goldsmith, weighed around eight kilograms.[263]

In 1514, the bishop Louis de Gorrevod, who served as intermediary between the duke and the pope on the matter of the liturgy, also established the feast day of the Shroud at his own expense in the cathedral of Geneva, and in 1532 he instituted an annuity for the cleric who served that day at Saint-Jean-de-Maurienne. The nascent Confraternity of the Holy Shroud of Chambéry was led by the noble Jean de la Forest, dean of Sainte-Chapelle and at the same time canon of Geneva, protonotary apostolic, abbot of Payerne, prior of Nantua, provost of Montjoux, and almoner of Savoy; of course, Duke Charles was also a member of the confraternity.

Meanwhile, the House of Savoy continued its efforts to increase their prestige in the ecclesiastical sphere as well. The marriage of Philiberta of Savoy to Giuliano de' Medici, son of Lorenzo the Magnificent and brother of Pope Leo X, helped strengthen connections with the papacy. In June 1515, four months after the marriage, the pope permitted the elevation of Sainte-Chapelle to the status of a metropolitan church, which would be the seat of an archbishop appointed by the House of Savoy. The dean Jean de la Forest was immediately promoted to the episcopal dignity, a move that, as it turned out, would be quite ephemeral, since the following year the pope, yielding to the insistences of the king of France, had to revoke his order and restore Chambéry to the jurisdiction of the diocese of Grenoble. Philiberta, however, never withdrew her support for the cause of the

[263] Heinrich Cornelius Agrippa von Nettesheim records the price in his funeral discourse for the duchess: E. Münch, *Margaretha von Oesterreich, Oberstatthalterin der Niederlande*, vol. 1 (Leipzig: Scheible, 1833), 300. The quantity of silver comes from a receipt published in M. Bruchet, *Marguerite d'Autriche, Duchesse de Savoie* (Lille: Danel, 1927), 140, n. 6 ("33 marcs, 11 estrelins et 20 grains d'argent"); the description of the coffer comes from its own notification of delivery and from a letter from the canons: idem, *Marguerite d'Autriche*, 360–61 and 371. On the goldsmith, see A. Princhard, "Liévin Van Lathem," *Revue de la numismatique belge* 5 (1855): 369–78.

Shroud, to which she was deeply devoted, wanting at her death to be taken from Billiat to Chambéry to be buried in Sainte-Chapelle.

The chapel, of course, befitted the dignity of its owners and the Shroud. Built in various phases beginning in 1408, it was steadily enlarged and embellished thanks to the work of talented architects, sculptors, and painters. Between 1521 and 1527 the grand stained-glass windows in the apse were installed, which, along with the statues, marble tombs, rich paintings, and sacred furnishings, made Sainte-Chapelle a small jewel worthy of the lavish celebrations it hosted.[264] The management of the ducal chapel was entrusted to a grand almoner accompanied by a series of chaplains, clerics, and cantors.[265] The Shroud was always in its place, behind the high altar, enclosed in the cabinet with iron doors and four locks. The duke held one key,[266] the city council held another, the Chamber of Audit had the third, and the chapter of the collegiate church had the fourth. The relic was generally shown at least twice per year, on the Shroud's own feast day, May 4, and on Good Friday, but could also be exhibited on other festive occasions. As for the location of the exhibition, it is generally thought to have been the walkway that runs all the way around Sainte-Chapelle and goes through the buttresses.[267] By way of a door located in the apse, on the left when facing the altar (still visible today, but walled off), one can access a ladder, which connected with the path outside. In that location, the exhibition could be performed at a height of about seventeen meters above the ground level of the plaza below. I have not yet, however, found contemporary sources that confirm this striking hypothesis.

We know that the castle plaza was sometimes used as a theater for exhibitions; for example, in 1521, in the presence of Edmond de Saulieu, abbot of Clairvaux, the Shroud was carried in procession

264 I say "small" since the chapel measures only 22.5 × 13 m.

265 Cf. P. Cozzo, "Il clero di corte nel Ducato di Savoia fra XVI e XVII secolo," in *L'affermarsi della corte sabauda*, ed. P. Bianchi and L. C. Gentile (Turin: Zamorani, 2006), 361–86.

266 We have an epistolary exchange between the duke and city council of Chambéry, datable to the years 1513–1528, which shows us that when the duke left the city he took the key with him: F. Mugnier, *Lettres des princes de la Maison de Savoie à la ville de Chambéry* (Chambéry: Ménard, 1888), 68–69.

267 The current walkway can be found in the same place but has been architecturally modified and surrounded by a railing that, since 1959, has replaced the merlons and machicolations that were there previously.

into a room in the castle "where a scaffolding was made outside the windows to show it to the people who stood below."[268] But generally the place designated was the point where the external walls of the city entered the *promenade de Verney*; this "walkway" was a rectangular pedestrian area embellished with six rows of trees; only part of the area remains today, having been transformed into a park by the same name. The *promenade* was situated below the walls where the Palais de Justice currently stands, not far from the ancient convent of St. Dominic; thus, the pilgrims, processing along the tree-lined path, could see the Shroud being displayed from a covered platform built over the bleachers without having to assemble inside the city walls. This spot was about five hundred meters from the castle, and the relic had to be brought there in procession.[269]

[268] M. Harmand, "Relation d'un voyage à Rome," *Memoires de la Société d'agriculture, des sciences, arts et belles-lettres du département de l'Aube* 15 (1849–1850): 228: "Apres loffice, trois evesques revestuz prindrent le S. Suaire, enveloppe en soye rouge, et le porterent en procession en une chambre ou lon avoit fait un eschaffault dehors les fenestres, pour le monstrer au peuple qui estoit en bas. Quant vint sur les dix heures Monseigneur levesque de Belley, commandataire ou monastere de Haulte Combe, et Monseigneur de Sainct Claude, sortirent sur cest eschaffault et illec desployarent le precieux S. Suaire."

[269] Cf. F. Mugnier, "Les registres des entrées à l'audience du sénat de Savoie," *Mémoires et documents publiés par la Société savoisienne d'histoire et d'archéologie* 37 (1898): 367. In August of 1561: "Feste Assomption Nostre Dame. A dix heures du matin fut monstré le précieux St. Suaire de N. S. Jesuscrist par le bon playsir et commandement de S. A., sur la galerie nouvellement faicte sur les murailles de ceste ville regardant contre les Vernays. Et y avoit grande assemblée de peuple pour icelluy voir et vénérer." Two days later, on Sunday, August 17, an exhibition took place in the castle plaza. The exhibition in Verney also finds mention in a manuscript by a certain Salins, quoted by J. Fodéré, *Narration historique, et topographique des convens de l'Ordre S. François, et monastères S. Claire* (Lyon: Rigaud, 1619), 921–22: "Ledict convent de S. Dominique, aboutit aux murailles de la ville, qui seroit une grande commodité, pour porter asseurément le precieux reliquaire du S. Suaire, les iours qu'on le monstre dessus la place du Vernay, en faisant un couvert sus lesdictes murailles, au lieu qu'à present on le porte depuis la S. Chappelle, le tour est fort long, incommode, et perilleux." Perret, "Essai sur l'histoire du Saint Suaire," 105, quotes an imprecise French translation of the report of the pilgrimage of the cardinal Luigi d'Aragona, which asserts that the Shroud was shown "du haut des murs du château, ou du côté d'une prairie qui s'etend hors de la ville" ("from the top of the castle walls, or on the side of a meadow which extends outside the city"). The original Italian text, however, says only "da sopra li mura del castello verso una certa prateria che vi e fora della terra" ("from above the castle walls toward a certain meadow that is outside the land") (A. Chastel, *Luigi d'Aragona: Un cardinale del Rinascimento*

Among the illustrious pilgrims who wanted to admire the Shroud in these years, in addition to the abbot of Clairvaux, were the princess Clara Gonzaga, the rulers of France Anne of Brittany and Francis I (who left on foot from Lyon in May of 1516),[270] the constable of Bourbon, and the cardinal Luigi d'Aragona in 1518.[271] Johannes Justus von Landsberg († 1539) provides a lovely description of the Shroud and his impressions in one of his sermons.[272] The chronicles of the time speak with a wealth of detail about exhibitions in which the Shroud, held by three bishops, was shown to the people from above, while a private exhibition on the high altar of Sainte-Chapelle was reserved for distinguished guests. The city in the days of the exhibitions was all abuzz, and even from its earlier days had been polished to a shine for the welcoming of pilgrims.[273] This period represents the apogee of worship of the Shroud as a prestigious personal relic of the House of Savoy and an object venerated by crowds of devoted faithful. Even the memory of the humble collegiate church of Lirey has, by this time, vanished. One can well imagine what the sudden loss of the precious relic at this point would have meant for Chambéry and the House of Savoy.

---

in viaggio per l'Europa [Rome: Laterza, 1987], 248); I think that the chronicler, who could not attend the public exhibition, has confused the city walls with those of the castle (it would not make sense to display it from the walls of the castle *toward* the meadow).

270 Also noted by G. Paradin, *Chronique de Savoye* (Lyon: Ian de Tournes, 1561), 395–96; and G. Mollat, "Deux pèlerinages au Suaire de Chambéry-Turin," *Revue de l'art chretien* 47 (1904): 157–59, who also reports the description of the Shroud made by the ambassador from Ferrara.

271 Cf. Bruchet, *Marguerite d'Autriche*, 140. Luigi d'Aragona (as one reads in Chastel, *Luigi d'Aragona*, 248–49) was able to touch the Shroud, but it seemed to him that it was made neither of linen nor silk; one of the manuscripts of the account of his pilgrimage (Biblioteca Nazionale di Napoli, MS XIV E 35, f. 89r, olim 173) also contains a sixteenth-century drawing of the Shroud; it is reproduced in A. R. Casper, "Painting as Relic: Giambattista Marino's Dicerie Sacre and the Shroud of Turin," in *Art and Reform in the Late Renaissance: After Trent*, ed. J. M. Locker (New York: Routledge, 2018), 287.

272 J. J. Landsberg, "Homilia LVI in passione Christi," in *D. Joannis Justi Lanspergii Cartusiani opera omnia*, vol. 3 (Montreuil: typis Cartusiae Sanctae Mariae de Pratis, 1889), 119–20.

273 The context is described well by Perret, "Essai sur l'histoire du Saint Suaire," 95–106.

2.2.6 *The Tragic Fire*

During the night of December 3, 1532, a fire broke out among the wood stalls of Sainte-Chapelle (someone afterward would speak of a fire maliciously caused by Protestants,[274] but no proof exists; others mention a lit candle that was forgotten). We know that, above all, the fire damaged the area of the chancel and the stained glass but did not cause the brickwork or façade to collapse, though in the past some have made claims to the contrary.[275] It was understood immediately that the relic was in great danger, and there was neither the time nor a way to gather all four keys needed to open the cabinet of the relic. We do not have reports from the time to indicate how matters proceeded, only late accounts, not without celebratory exaggerations. The first chronologically is that of the Lombard Jesuit Francesco Adorno, who, in 1578, forty-six years after the fire, recorded what was evidently reported to him on his journey to Turin:

> It is truly most grand, what happened about 40 or 50 years ago: when the chapel in which this most miraculous Shroud was placed was burning with a fire so great that not only did it consume everything, but the stone turned to rubble; and the silver coffer, in which it was kept, was indeed damaged by fire; the sacred Shroud, which was in it, was burned in some places, but when the fire reached the outline of the sacred image of the Lord, it stopped there, nor in any place was his image damaged by it, as is clearly seen today.[276]

Three years later, Emmanuel-Philibert de Pingon, historian of the House of Savoy, in his book dedicated to the Shroud described the events of that night as follows:

[274] L. Martinenghi echoes this accusation in *Canzoni, sonetti et sestine in lode della Sacra Sindone conservata in Turino* (Brescia: Borelli, 1590): 5: "Thee, O Shroud, the faithless people dared to put to the fire; ah, babarous heart, poorly believing the faith!"

[275] For example, de Jussieu, *Sainte-Chapelle*, 20–23; and Santelli, *Sainte-Chapelle du château*, 32, 39, deny it.

[276] [F. Adorno], *Lettera della peregrinatione di monsig.re ill.mo cardinale di S. Prassede arcivescovo di Milano, per visitare la sacra Sindone di N. Signore Iesu Christo, a Turino* (Venice: n.p., 1578), 2.

> On December 3, the feast day of the saint virgin Barbara, just around midnight, the chapel of the castle in which the Shroud was placed caught fire because of flames[277] of unknown origin. Everyone rushed to it, but the most conscientious of all, Philibert de Lambert, archivist and advisor to the duke, summoned a blacksmith by the name of Guillaume Pussode and two Franciscans. With undaunted spirit they went through the midst of the flames, they broke the white-hot chancel railings attached to the high altar and the locks, and pulled out the Shroud; but by then the silver coffer had melted, and they carried it out intact, while all around the fire receded. Once the flames had spread, and the fire was advancing, the marbles and columns were consumed; but the nature of the fire was defeated by the faith of the pious men, itself stronger than the fire, and by the power of divine will. The blaze receded; those who, it was thought, would have been burned, were drenched as if by fresh dew. The men themselves were amazed by it, as we believe once happened to those Hebrew lads. Truly we saw this happen in the presence of all—in fact I was present then—and we were astounded. Not long after, the Shroud was presented publicly, completely unharmed except for some small traces of burns left in the folds—though outside the area of the cloth bearing the sacred image—as eternal testimonies of the miracle.[278]

The reports are more characteristic of hagiography than a chronicle of an event. Adorno exaggerates the scale of the fire and claims that the Shroud's coffer was completely in flames. Pingon goes so far as to compare the three Savoyards to the three Hebrew youths who passed unharmed through the fire in the burning furnace in the age of Nebuchadnezzar.[279] Pingon, in particular, is credited as an eyewitness of the miraculous sight, but one must not forget that at the time of the fire he was not yet eight years old.

No other eyewitness account is known. In 1596, when the Milanese patrician Giovanni Tonso wrote the official biography of Emmanuel Philibert of Savoy (which brought him an annual pension of 500 écus), he did no more than paraphrase Pingon, though he omitted the Old Testament comparison and did not mention the receding flames or the heavenly dew, but still insisted on the theme of the miraculous:

277 *Acris sacellum* is a printing error for *arcis sacellum*.
278 Pingone, *Sindon evangelica*, 22.
279 Daniel 3:8-94.

> Since a part of the linen had begun to catch fire, it was indeed strange that it was not immediately burned completely and that the linen, although nothing is more suited to catching fire straightaway, resisted the force of so great a fire, while in the same place and at the same time the wooden beams, iron, and marble burned. This could not have happened but for a divine will that desired it be so.[280]

Along the same lines, in 1606, Giuseppe Cambiano di Ruffia, a high official in the Savoyard artillery, wrote:

> It seems that, by a hidden judgment, God wanted to preserve that holy relic for the pious and Catholic House of Savoy; as was seen also likewise three years before the wars began in these states, when it was saved miraculously from the fire, though it so blazed in the Holy Chapel of Chambéry, full of waxes and votives, that the free-stones were consumed by it, the iron box where the relic lay, entirely enflamed and scorching hot, only some corners of the cloth were burned, without damaging where the figure of our Lord is, as one sees; and it was a wonder that a blacksmith who went to open the box and look to save it, as soon as he touched it with his hammer, it opened and a religious man, taking it up, saved it without any of them feeling any harm in so great a fire; and this was almost a harbinger of the wars that followed soon after.[281]

In April of 1609, the noble Florisel de Claveson passed through Chambéry, and when he put an account of his journey into writing, he told of the event of the fire while certainly having Pingon's book in front of him. Significantly, this document provides the name of one of the two Franciscans, Maurice Gand.[282] In 1662, François Capré, master of the Chamber of Audit, added further details: the two friars who threw themselves into the flames along with Philibert de Lambert were two Franciscans from the monastery of Saint-François.

[280] G. Tonso, *De vita Emmanuelis Philiberti Allobrogum Ducis* (Turin: apud Dominicum Tarinum, 1596), 209.

[281] G. Cambiano, "Historico discorso al serenissimo Filippo Emanuele di Savoia," in *Monumenta Historiae Patriae*, coll. 1113–14.

[282] J. C. Dubé, ed., *Florisel de Claveson: Voyage d'Italie (1608–1609)* (Moncalieri: CIRVI, 2001), 313–15.

> They broke the iron chancel railing of the high altar and, having gotten rid of all the burning locks, they brought before the eyes of the entire court and the people who hurried there the Holy Shroud, which had remained whole, though the silver coffer, richly adorned, given by Margaret of Austria, Duchess of Savoy, was by that point melted.[283]

But this report, in addition to being late, is mistaken at least in part, since from an expense report from 1534 that I found we learn that the duke gave nine arm-lengths of Franciscan grey cloth "to the guardian father of St. Mary of Egypt for the pain that was suffered in saving the precious Holy Shroud on the night of the fire."[284] The friars, then, are not the Conventuals of Saint-François (that church today is the city cathedral) but rather the Observants of Sainte-Marie-l'Égyptienne, a different convent that arose elsewhere.

Immediately after the fire, the customary exhibitions were interrupted. The following Good Friday, April 10, 1533, passed without a showing of the Shroud. Neither was it exhibited on its own feast day, May 4. It seems that at that point, many people in the city were convinced that the Holy Shroud had disappeared. Contemporaneous and impartial witnesses confirm it, specifically two pilgrims who were passing through Chambéry. The first was Greffin Affagard, Lord of Courteilles and knight of the Holy Sepulchre.

> Some say that it was burned; in fact, we have seen the results and effects of the fire set in the chapel. Others were saying that the duchess took it to bring it to Spain and that, to hide her actions, she had a fire set in the chapel. Whatever the case, since then it has no longer been shown.[285]

The second witness is Guillaume de Pierrefleur, a Swiss memorialist who reports that on May 4, 1533, the date of the customary annual exhibition,

[283] F. Capré, *Traité historique de la chambre des comptes de Savoye* (Lyon: Barbier, 1662), 399.

[284] "[A]u pere gardien de Saincte Marie Egiptiaque pour la peyne qu'il a prise à saulver le precieux sainct suayre la nuyt de l'incendie"; now published by P. Cancian, "Sulle tracce della Sindone nella documentazione finanziaria di casa Savoia," *Bollettino Storico-Bibliografico Subalpino* 115, no. 2 (2017): 442.

[285] J. Chavanon, ed., *Relation de Terre Sainte (1533–1534)* (Paris: Lecoffre, 1902), 6.

> The precious Holy Shroud ought to be shown; but all were disappointed, since it was not shown. The reason, as one had to be given, was that while the lord Duke of Savoy was visiting his own lands, as I already mentioned, the lady of Savoy desired to withdraw, unbeknownst to her husband, to his town of Portugal, from which she had come, that is, from its royal house; and about this it was said that among other treasures [that she took with her] there was the precious Holy Shroud. The aforementioned lady was pursued and traced back to the town by the lord duke's people. Another reason is that this year the Sainte-Chapelle of Chambéry, in which the Holy Shroud was kept, was burned, and it was said that it had remained burned.[286]

Evidently both authors, who wrote without knowing each other, reported from the same two explanations gleaned directly from the inhabitants of Chambéry: that the Duchess Beatrice of Portugal (1504–1538), wife of Duke Charles, took the relic away, or that it was burned. Neither speaks of the miracle of its rescue.

It seems to me that the first explanation becomes comprehensible if one examines the duchess' movements in those months. Beatrice spent very little time in Chambéry, since she lived her whole life on the slopes of Piedmont. However, she lived in the Savoyard capital for almost a year between the summer of 1531 and that of 1532 and then moved to Turin, never again to return to Chambéry. When the fire broke out, Beatrice had already been in Turin for about four months. In February of 1533, she reached Bologna, where she was reunited with Charles. On that occasion it was decided that she would return to Spain with their son, Louis, following the emperor Charles V, a trip that had already been planned the year before. The official reason was to visit her sister, Isabella, wife of the emperor; the unofficial reason was to create even closer ties to Charles V, who was at the time strongly opposed to the king of France. Therefore, on April 8, Beatrice sailed on an imperial ship on the way to Madrid. But soon, being pregnant, she felt poorly due to the choppy sea and had to postpone her journey and disembark at Sanremo, in order then to head to and settle in the Savoyard city of Nice. The young Louis, however, continued the journey to Spain and remained there to be educated with

[286] L. Junod, ed., *Mémoires de Pierrefleur* (Lausanne: La Concorde, 1933), ch. 63. After this passage, the author reports, however, on the survival and restoration of the cloth that occurred in 1534.

the prince of Spain, only to die three years later.[287] Word of Beatrice's departure through imperial lands certainly reached Chambéry, as well as of her sudden change of plan involving Nice. Such a change could have led to the rumor that the lady had tried secretly to abandon the duchy, taking with her, among other things, the Shroud, which she stole during her stay at Chambéry, but that she had been "pursued and brought back to the country by the lord duke's men." On the other hand, Beatrice, who with this action had further angered the king of France, was already not well regarded by the people of Chambéry precisely because of her pro-imperial and anti-French policy.[288]

The other explanation had greater traction outside the city—that is, that the Shroud was no longer shown because it must have been completely burned. Even François Rabelais speaks of it in his *Gargantua*, written in 1534, when he recounts how some men, after suffering a misfortune, dedicated themselves to the Shroud of Chambéry—uselessly, since "three months later it was burned so much that not a bit of it could be saved."[289] In Geneva, Antoine Froment, a Protestant pastor, recounts that between January and February of 1534, some Catholics were claiming that a possessed woman in Chambéry was saying that the Shroud had burned, and that later she was set free thanks to exorcisms performed in the name of that very relic.[290] A few years later Michel Roset, while recalling the fire in Chambéry, seems to take for granted that the relic had not been spared.[291] Certainly it is not surprising to hear these words from the mouths of Genevan Protestants, who forcefully opposed

[287] Cf. A. Segre, "Documenti di storia sabauda dal 1510 al 1536," *Miscellanea di storia italiana* 39 (1903): 72.

[288] To identify all of Beatrice's movements as determined from her correspondence, see G. Fornaseri, *Beatrice di Portogallo duchessa di Savoia* (Cuneo: SASTE, 1957).

[289] F. Rabelais, *Gargantua* 27: "mais il bruslae troys moys après si bien qu'on n'en peut salver un seul brin."

[290] A. Fromment, *Actes et gestes merveilleux de la cité de Genève* (Geneva: Revilliod, 1854), 85: "Voyre iusques à Chambéry qui donnoit entendre que une demoyselle estoit demonyacle, laquelle avoil ces troys dyables au corps; pour confirmer le Sainct Suayre, qui avoit esté bruslé; et en la vertu de ce Suayre les coniurant, les firent sourtir hors du corps de ceste femme."

[291] M. Roset, *Les chroniques de Genève* (Geneva: Georg, 1894), 167: "Le quatrième de décembre la chappelle de Chambéry brulla, en laquelle estoit l'ydole nommée Sainct Suayre." This work was finished in 1562.

the worship of relics; and only a few years earlier even Erasmus of Rotterdam had emphasized the inconsistency of such worship insofar as it was not accompanied by a true faith of the heart.[292]

In April of 1533, Clement VII sent a letter to the aforementioned Louis de Gorrevod, who in the meantime had become a cardinal. There Clement VII writes:

> We have learned that previously, after the church known as the Holy Chapel of the castle of Chambéry, in the diocese of Grenoble, where the cloth known as the shroud of our Savior—as is piously believed—had been housed, had burned, the aforementioned cloth survived due to a certain swift rescue from the fire, with the help of divine grace.

Furthermore, in the case that it was true, he asked Louis to make the relic's survival known to all the faithful, who otherwise might think that it must have been completely destroyed by the fire and therefore might grow tepid in their devotion toward it. He ordered that a seemly place be found for the relic and that whatever damage it sustained in the fire be repaired by some nuns chosen by the cardinal himself.[293] From this letter it is very clear that the pope had already been informed of everything—the rescue of the Shroud, the accounts of its destruction, and the fact that it was damaged and in need of repair.

In this letter there first appears the cautious wording *ut pie creditur*—that is, "as is piously believed." The pope says the belief that Jesus was wrapped in the Shroud of Savoy is pious; that does not

[292] Desiderius Erasmus, *Enchiridion militis christiani* (1503), ed. W. Welzig, *Ausgewählte Schriften*, vol. 1 (Darmstadt: Wissenschaftliche Buchgesellschaft, 1967), 204: "Do you gape at a tunic or a sudarium that is said to have been Christ's and while asleep do you read the divine oracles of Christ? You believe that if you have at home a small piece of the cross, it is a thing greater than the greatest that you possess, but that is nothing if you keep enshrined in your heart the mystery of the cross."

[293] Chevalier, *Autour des origines du suaire de Lirey*, doc. O. There is confusion between the different editions, so some date the act to April 8, 1534 (Guichenon, *Histoire généalogique*, 2:497; and Capré, *Traité historique*, 402). That is a mistake, because both speak of "the tenth year of his pontificate," which is 1533, not 1534. The editions that rely on the document preserved at ASV use the date April 23; those based on the document preserved at AST date it to April 28.

necessarily indicate that Clement VII did not believe in the authenticity of the relic, but simply that he adopted a cautious position.[294]

The Savoyard cardinal was in no hurry; in fact, he let an entire year pass without doing anything. The pope, for his part, showed no doubt as to what the outcome of the inquiry would be. On March 21, 1534, still *before* the inquiry, he offered a plenary indulgence to whoever would attend the next exhibition of the Shroud, which would take place only *after* the cardinal's inquiry.[295] Finally, on April 15, 1534, as recounted in a meticulous procès-verbal,[296] Louis de Gorrevod went to the castle of Chambéry and the tower, popularly known as the *grotta thesauri*—where the court archives were housed[297]—where the Shroud had been placed. He took the relic to Sainte-Chapelle and spread it out on a table for sworn identification by himself and the witnesses. There were twelve witnesses, three of whom were bishops; there was also Philibert de Lambert, the relic's savior, described as "keymaster" of that "tower of the treasure" where the Shroud was being kept.[298] All the witnesses stated:

[294] For a long time, on the basis of an authentic but incorrectly attributed text (also republished by Chevalier, *Autour des origines du suaire de Lirey*, doc. Q), it was thought that in 1670 the Sacred Congregation of Indulgences had revived the phrase *ut pie creditur* and had allowed an indulgence to be obtained not because one venerated the Shroud as if it were authentic but rather for contemplating the suffering of Christ's crucifixion, especially the moment of his death and burial, thereby emphasizing the fruits of meditation more than the persuasion of authenticity. In reality this was what the *relator* of the congregation wanted, according to his own recollection, which was later rejected. Cf. E. A. Wuenschel, "Un'altra pretesa decisione di Roma contro l'autenticità della Sindone," *Sindon* 7 (1961): 13–34.

[295] AST, Savoia per paesi per A e B, file 4, no. 9.

[296] The better edition, but not without errors, is in Guichenon, *Histoire généalogique*, 2:497–99.

[297] The north tower, which has fortunately survived the numerous destructions suffered by the castle, is still today known as *tour de la trésorerie* and rises a few meters from Sainte-Chapelle. The Latin name *grotta* or *crota* and the corresponding French *crote* are not necessarily meant in the sense of "cave" but can also indicate a space surmounted by a vault. The *tour de la trésorerie* is precisely formed by two superimposed levels, both with vaulted ceilings.

[298] Claude d'Estavayer, bishop of Belley; Pierre Farfein, auxiliary bishop of Geneva; Pierre Meynard, auxiliary bishop of Maurienne and Tarentaise; Jean Count of Gruyère; Pierre de Lambert, president of the Chamber of Audit of Savoy; Hugues de la Balme, Lord of Tiret and first majordomo of the duke; Jean Oddinet, majordomo of the duke; Jacques de Seyturier, Lord of Marsonnas, majordomo of the duke; Philibert de Nancuise, Lord of la Grange; Jean-François du Pont, Lord of

> It is the same cloth as the Holy Shroud . . . which before the fire we ourselves often saw, touched, and held in our hands, and showed to the people, although in the two folds, right and left, one can see in twelve places a certain darkening from the effect of the fire, and in some of these places a slight mutilation from the effect of the fire; also in the same darkening a split, but this occurs outside the image and imprint of the sweat of Christ's body.[299]

At the end, the Shroud—the cardinal's report continued—was taken back to the tower. The following day it was transferred from the tower to the monastery of Sainte-Claire-en-Ville and spread out on another table for a second sworn identification. This time the document was signed by twenty-three witnesses, including nobles and clerics.[300]

What happened inside the monastery, beyond the notary's document, can be determined from a good report that the same sisters of the Order of Saint Clare put in writing as a record of the event.[301] They received the Shroud at 8 am, brought by a solemn procession with a large train of people. After the identification, the relic was entrusted to five nuns, who took charge of the restoration.[302] A wooden frame

---

Villaret; François de Luyrieux, squire to the duke; Philibert de Lambert, keymaster of the tower of the treasure. The two Lamberts, Pierre and Philibert, were brothers.

[299] Guichenon, *Histoire généalogique*, 498.

[300] François de Luxembourg, Viscount of Martigues, son of Louise of Savoy; Jean de la Chambre, Viscount of Maurienne; Guillaume de Poitiers, Baron of Miolans and Lord of Sérignan; Sébastien de Montbel, Count of Entremont; Charles de la Chambre, Baron of Meximieux; Alexandre de Viry, Lord of Sallenôves; Claude de Ballaison, Lord of Avanchy; Bernard de Menthon, governor of the Genevois; Claude de Mareste, Lord of Loissey and bailiff of Bugey; Sibuet de la Balme, Lord of Ramasse; Philibert de la Baume, Lord of Perrex; Antoine de Villette, Lord of la Cous; Pierre de Morny, abbot of Saint-Sulpice; Charles Rossi, commendatory prior of San Giorgio near Chambéry; Guillaume de Veigy, canon and official of Geneva; Barthélemy de Montferrat, preceptor of the commandery of Les Échelles; Pierre de Bellegarde, dean of the church of Sallanches; Eynard de Villette, prior of Bourget; Guillaume d'Oyonnax, dean of Cerdon; Jacques de Passier, doctor of law, vicar-general of Maurienne, archdeacon of Tarentaise; Claude Gruet, canon of Geneva and apostolic protonotary; Geoffroy Boisson, canon of Maurienne and apostolic protonotary; Claude Volon, secretary to the bishop of Grenoble.

[301] Chevalier, *Autour des origines du suaire de Lirey*, doc. P; English translation in D. Crispino, "The Report of the Poor Clare Nuns," *Shroud Spectrum International* 2 (1982): 19–27.

[302] Louise de Jargin, abbess (written "Gergin" in Latin documents from Turin; it cannot be "Vergin," as certain transcriptions suggest); Bertrande Passina, vicar; Péronette Rosset, sacristan; Marie de Berre; and Colette Bochette.

with a Holland cloth stretched over it was brought in; the Shroud was laid over this and attached with tacks all around in order to reinforce it (thereby hiding one of its sides). Afterward, using linen taken from the corporals of the altar, the nuns patched the larger burns. Everything occurred under the watch of the nobles, the clerics, and a crowd hardly held back by guards, among unceasing prayers. After fifteen days, on April 30, the duke returned to the monastery to examine the Shroud and "to mandate how it was to be wrapped in violet taffeta." I have found the expense report for the cloth acquired in that period: Holland cloth, white silk, taffeta, and violet silk for the Shroud; black velvet to cover its box and to line the stick around which it had to be wrapped; and finally white satin to be put in the middle of that same box.[303] Finally, on May 2, with a new, imposing procession, accompanied by the flourish of trumpets and the ringing of bells, the Shroud was returned to the duke, wrapped on a roller along with a red silk cover. In that way, according to the nuns, "it was taken to the castle with great solemnity; and we would remain poor orphans of Him who had so kindly visited us with his holy image." Thus concludes the valuable account, which also contains the first detailed description of the image of the man with his wounds, described individually, all of which can still today be seen on the Shroud of Turin. It is impossible not to see multiple influences in this description, including biblical and spiritual literature, mystic visions, and liturgical texts to which the nuns were accustomed.[304]

At the end of the restoration work, the relic was again placed in its niche behind the high altar. Since the niche is considerable in size, one might wonder whether it was enlarged on that occasion to accommodate the fabric, which required more space than was needed previously, since it was no longer kept folded but rather rolled; the large size can also be explained by the fact that originally, the cabinet was used to hold not only the Shroud but also other relics.

All the ceremony surrounding the Shroud's return, however, was not enough. Some were convinced that the return of the relic was staged and that this Shroud of 1534 was nothing but a false replacement, since the true relic had to have been destroyed in the fire two years earlier. In 1543 John Calvin wrote as much in clear words:

[303] Now published by P. Cancian, "Sulle tracce della Sindone," docs. 1 and 2.
[304] Identified by Zaccone: *Sindone: Storia di una immagine*, 161–64.

> They have shown that they have painters available, since whenever a shroud was burned, a new one was found the next day. It was said to be the same as before, which miraculously was saved from the fire. But the painting was so fresh that lying would have been pointless, had there been eyes there to see it.[305]

From then until now, there has been no lack of those who thought that the actual Shroud kept in Turin was a fraudulent reproduction of the one that burned in 1532,[306] painted, necessarily, on an old fabric made about two centuries earlier, the use of which provided an impression of antiquity. Neither the House of Savoy nor the city of Chambéry, it was said, would have accepted the loss of so venerated an object, so weighted with religious and political significance, and with such a capacity for drawing envy, pilgrims, and money. There is no dearth of historical accounts of cloth relics luckily saved from flames, as if it were a *topos* more than an exceptional occurrence. On June 10, 1194, for example, a fire almost completely destroyed the cathedral of Chartres. The people were in fear over the fate of an important relic, the tunic of the Virgin Mary, and many thought that, if it had been destroyed, there would have been no point in rebuilding the church. Then—according to a source from about 1210—on a feast day the intact relic was shown to the people; it was said that during the fire, some had placed it safely in the crypt, where the fire had been unable to reach due to the intervention of Mary herself.[307] Also, in Aachen, in 1310, doubt arose as to whether the shroud there had burned in a fire, but in 1359 the monks wrote to the pope, assuring him that the relic was safe;[308] the same thing happened at Cadouin in 1117, when the church where the holy shroud was kept caught fire, but it was immediately made known that the relic remained miraculously unharmed.[309] When in the sixteenth and seventeenth centuries the clergy of Besançon had to fabricate an ancient history

305 Calvin, *Traité des reliques*, 41.

306 Vigorously affirmed by, for example, F. Puaux, "Le Saint-Suaire de Turin," *Le Matin*, April 25, 1902, 2; and A. C. Coppier, "Le Saint-Suaire de Turin: Une peinture de Sodoma," *Mercure de France* 959 (1938): 335–43.

307 *Miracula Beate Marie Virginis in Carnotensi ecclesia facta* 1; A. Thomas, ed., "Les miracles de Notre-Dame de Chartres," *Bibliothèque de l'École des Chartes* 42 (1881): 505–50.

308 Cf. Savio, *Ricerche storiche*, 88–90.

309 *Pancharta Caduniensis* 3; ed. in *Recueil des historiens des croisades*, 300.

for their new shroud in order to justify its survival of a blaze that in 1350 had devastated the cathedral, they contrived that it had miraculously escaped the flames. In sum, one could rightfully question how it was that things always turned out so well for the relics. Beyond these specific examples, many cases are known in which relics that were destroyed or stolen were replaced with duplicates. This fact was not unknown even among people at the time, and the whole effort put into certifying the survival of the Shroud of Chambéry in a very solemn and unassailable manner was not accidental; it was intended to allay any suspicion regarding its authenticity. But to those who remained unconvinced, this effort seemed an indication of culpability rather than a guarantee.

Today it is right to wonder whether there is in fact some cause to consider that those suspicions were well founded. First of all, one could ask why the oldest sources ignored the account of the relic's timely rescue from the flames, and why so much time was allowed to pass before the Shroud was again shown to the people; it could have been done immediately to quash any growing rumors. Instead, months passed before the pope instructed the cardinal Louis to certify the survival of the relic (and we have already seen that that happened only after contacts between the two parties had already intervened), and another year passed before the cardinal complied with the request. Why was there such a delay, which served only to feed suspicions? Some thought that the time was used to find an old cloth, two centuries old and similar enough, and a forger of sufficient skill to make a new shroud that resembled the one that had been destroyed. The addition of artfully fabricated burns would have been necessary because it was unthinkable to show the people a pristine shroud, since everyone knew that it had in some way been damaged by the fire; a potential false shroud had necessarily to bear signs of the fire, but at the same time had to safeguard the visibility of the central image (or it would have become useless). The preservation of the image, certainly, would have increased, not diminished, the devotion of the faithful. Nor was this an isolated case; as recently as four years before the chapel of Chambéry burned, for example, there was an even more severe fire in the city of Forlì, from which only a woodcut on paper of the Virgin Mary could be saved miraculously from the flames; it immediately became an object of worship throughout the whole city. The miracle of sacred images set upon by fire and burned only on edges that lack painting is very widespread, persisting even in the modern era.[310]

There is, however, another explanation for the delay in displaying the Shroud; both at the time of the fire and for the whole period that followed, up until the spring of 1534, Duke Charles II was residing outside Chambéry, engaged as he was in managing the increasing difficulties of the duchy. We know that at least from October 27, 1532, both the duke and the duchess were in Turin and preparing to leave for Bologna.[311] I have found two of Charles' writings, dated November 26 and December 1, 1532, that confirm his presence in Turin.[312] Beatrice, for her part, would never again return to Chambéry. Their arrival in Bologna is dated to January 30, 1533. Both returned to Turin on February 16, and they reunited in Nice in early June. On November 25, 1533, when Philip of Savoy, Duke of Nemours, died in Marseille, Duke Charles II was absent and had to be represented at the funeral. Only from the second half of February 1534, therefore, was Charles able to inspect personally the damage to the chapel and the Shroud in Chambéry; one might think that it was necessary to await his return before making any decision in regard to these damages, a possibility that could also explain Louis de Gorrevod's long delay.[313]

What should be made of the thirty-five sworn testimonies? Might one perhaps think that the time between the fire and the inquiry was sufficient to render the two shrouds—the true one and the replacement—indistinguishable in everyone's memories. Or was the duke perhaps able to influence the witnesses? Regarding this possibility it is noteworthy that all those who took part in the sworn identifications of the Shroud were closely connected to the House of Savoy, beginning with the papal legate, Cardinal Louis

[310] As a single example, there is the image of the Immaculate Madonna preserved in Ivrea (Turin), which, some say, in 1859 remained unharmed despite being thrown into a fire.

[311] That day, in fact, they had a meeting with the Venetian ambassador Marino Giustinian: *I diarii di Martino Sanuto*, vol. 57 (Venice: Videntini, 1902), coll. 201–2.

[312] AST, Protocolli ducali serie rossa, no. 166, ff. 73 and 67.

[313] For an overview of these years, with much information on the duke's movements, see A. Segre, "La politica sabauda con Francia e Spagna dal 1515 al 1533," *Memorie della Reale Accademia delle Scienze di Torino* 50 (1901): 249–348; idem, "Documenti di storia sabauda," 1–295.

de Gorrevod, the same man who at least since 1503 had come into contact with the Shroud many times, had held it in his own hands during exhibitions, and had supported the approval and diffusion of its veneration. His brother Laurent, governor of Bresse, was favored by the duke and was an associate of Margaret of Austria; in fact Laurent, on August 10, 1509, delivered the new coffer for the Shroud that Margaret had commissioned into the hands of the canons of Chambéry.[314] The noble Louis, from the time he was young, thanks to the political support he enjoyed, was able to accumulate prestigious and beneficial appointments. Already canon of Geneva and abbot of Ambronay and Saint-Pierre de Bessua, at the age of only twenty-six he was named bishop of Saint-Jean-de-Maurienne. As prince of the Holy Roman Empire and almoner to the Duke of Savoy, in 1501 he blessed the wedding between Duke Philibert II and Margaret; and when in 1515 the pope, at the insistence of the duke, created a new diocese at Bourg-en-Bresse, Louis was elected bishop of this territory as well. He took part in the Fifth Council of the Lateran as the duke's delegate; in 1528 in Sainte-Chapelle, he held the future Duke Emmanuel Philibert at his baptism in place of his godmother Margaret, who did not cease to press the pope and various kings until in 1530 she secured the cardinalship for her protégé; and some months later he was selected as papal legate *a latere* for all matters in the lands of the duchy. Therefore Louis, clearly, could not have been the most suitable person to conduct an investigation independent of the House of Savoy, since he truly owed everything to that family.

The thirty-five witnesses were all connected to the Savoys by a web of relationships based on subjection, political interest, financial dependence, favors, and family bonds. The bishop Claude d'Estavayer was the first chancellor of the Most Holy Order of the Annunciation, abbot of Hautecombe, and confidant to the duke; Pierre Farfein was the duke's confessor. It should be emphasized that at the time, due to an act issued by Pope Nicholas V in 1451, the archbishops, bishops, abbots, and many priors in Savoy were appointed by the same duke, and they were practically always scions of noble families.[315] Among

314 Cf. A. Chagny, *Correspondance politique et administrative de Laurent de Gorrevod*, vol. 1 (Mâcon: Protat, 1913), 67–68.

315 On the Savoyard episcopate, see F. Meyer, "Les évêques de Savoie et la cour (XVIe–XVIIe siècles)," in Bianchi and Gentile, *Affermarsi della corte sabauda*, 387–405.

the other signatories there appeared ducal officials, court stewards, and squires; they were all individuals close to Charles II. Even the monastery of Sainte-Claire-en-Ville owed its foundation to the generosity of Yolande of Valois. No one was a stranger to that world.

One has to wonder, however, whether the cardinal could have acted differently in choosing witnesses to question; the answer is no, because the identification of the Shroud had necessarily to be asked of individuals who had previously seen it closely and touched it, and certainly that identification could not be entrusted to strangers. Those who had had the privilege of such familiarity with the Shroud were, for one reason or another, all favored by the duke.

What of the fire? Many authors, including modern ones, insist on a miraculous occurrence:

> Whoever considers the results of that terrible blaze, namely the complete destruction of the closets and furnishings, the ruin of the chapel, the melted metal, and considers that therein only one cloth was saved, cannot in truth attribute it to a natural cause.[316]

The extent of the damage caused by the fire, as described above, provides another reason for skeptics to think that the Shroud did not survive the fire. Some have even attempted to reproduce experimentally the conditions to which the fabric had to have been subjected during the fire in order to prove what would have happened at the time, even if the unknown variables are too numerous to be able to manage this in a precise way. Neither the intensity of the fire nor the specific location of the initial outbreak is known. Also unknown are the exact shape, thickness, and quantity of iron present in the doors of the closet embedded in the wall, where the coffer with the Shroud was kept. Some aspects of the fire, however, can be gauged. The broken stained glass in the apse indicates that the fire was not minimal in size; the windows must have been broken quite early, since glass has a low resistance to heat and is among the first things to succumb to it. The fire need not however have been very large, since of the three windows in the apse, the one on the left was completely destroyed, the one on the right was

[316] [G. Melano], *Notizie storiche ragguardanti alla Santissima Sindone* (Turin: Fodratti, 1842), 29.

partially destroyed, and the center window was best preserved.[317] In a fire, the ambient temperature can surpass 1,000 degrees Celsius (1,832 degrees Fahrenheit). Savoyard authors recount that at the time of the rescue, the Shroud's silver box was melting, and silver, as we know, melts at 962°C (1,763°F). However, among silversmiths, pure silver is never used, but rather silver mixed with other metals (chiefly copper), which lower its melting point slightly. Some parts could also have been welded together with tin, which melts at 232°C (450°F). Even descending to this threshold, however, the temperature is still very high; linen begins to turn yellow at only 120°C (248°F),[318] for which reason even exposure alone to a temperature of 150°C (302°F) would have indelibly darkened the fabric, rendering the image of the crucified man indiscernible. At 300°C (572°F), then, the cloth would have been lost. But can we be sure of the temperature that the inside of the coffer reached? Unfortunately, its dimensions, its thickness, and the amount of air in the coffer with the Shroud are unknown, as is the sort of heat exposure it underwent; it is therefore impossible to know how hot the inside of the coffer could have become even if we knew the external temperature. If the coffer was a wooden box covered in silver, and not a purely metal box, we would have to conclude that the fabric had dual safeguards. The ignition temperature of wood is about 250°C (482°F) and depends on numerous factors, even if prolonged contact with hot surfaces can trigger a carbonizing process at much lower temperatures.

All of these uncertainties notwithstanding, today, as in Pingon's time, among supporters of the Shroud's authenticity are those who can explain the relic surviving the fire only by invoking divine intervention, since they are convinced that under such circumstances

[317] Cf. M. Roques, "Vitraux du XVIe siècle en Savoie et en Dauphiné," in *Actes du quatre-vingt-septième congrès national des sociétés savantes: Section d'archéologie* (Paris: Imprimerie nationale, 1963), 343; idem, *Les apports néerlandais dans la peinture du sud-est de la France* (Bordeaux: Institut d'histoire de l'art médiéval, 1963), 223–26; Conservation régionale des monuments historiques, *Chambéry, Savoie, les vitraux de la Sainte-Chapelle* (Lyon: Direction régionale des affaires culturelles de Rhône-Alpes, 2000); Santelli, *Sainte-Chapelle du château*, 73–90.

[318] Cf. M. Bona et al., *Manuale di tecnologia tessile* (Rome: ESAC, 1981), 66.

a normal linen fabric would have certainly been destroyed.[319] The same circumstances lead others to think that it necessarily must have been destroyed. An interesting hint comes from the burn marks visible on the Shroud of Turin, which are of two types: two long parallel scorch marks that run longitudinally over the length of the fabric, and a series of gaps in the fabric that repeat in pairs along the scorch marks, but that diminish in size from the center to either side. Thanks to the symmetry of these burns it is possible to attempt to deduce how the Shroud was folded at the time of the fire; probably the cloth was folded over itself symmetrically six times, forming an approximately 37 × 30 cm "packet" of forty-eight overlapping linen layers.[320] The two long parallel scorch marks could have been formed through contact or proximity to a heat source (a side of the coffer, for example). The large gaps, however, could not have been caused because "a drop of melting silver burned right through the Shroud's many folds,"[321] as has long been claimed, since a drop leaves a hole and would not produce those elongated burns vaguely triangular in shape (with a maximum size of about 28 cm). It is better to think in terms of a red-hot object that dropped obliquely onto the fabric (perhaps a bar that broke off from the lid of the coffer and fell on the linen, or a white-hot rod used by the hypothetical forger). Whatever the cause, it should be noted that heat source damaged only one of the four sides, sparing the others. The largest part, which had to have

319 Cf. A. Tamburini, "L'incendio di Chambéry: Un contributo minore alla ricerca sindonica," *Collegamento pro Sindone* (January–February 1995): 28–40; M. Cappi, *La Sindone dalla A alla Z* (Padova: Il Messaggero, 1997), 89 (citing Gogliardo Capelli); idem, "L'incendio di Chambéry," *Il Telo* 2, no. 4 (1998): 11–13.

320 For the system of folding, see A. Tonelli in G. Enrie, *La Santa Sindone rivelata dalla fotografia*, 2nd ed. (Turin: Sei, 1938), 28–29; and J. Tyrer, "The Foldings of the Shroud in 1532," *Shroud Spectrum International* 31 (1989): 11–13. A variant that excludes the sixth fold, but without an entirely clear reason for it, is proposed by Guerreschi and Salcito, "Études sur les brûlures," 30–45: the result would be sixteen overlaying layers of cloth on one side and thirty-two layers on the other (the last fold was not symmetrical), with the whole forming a "packet" measuring about 75 × 30 cm. The system proposed by Flury-Lemberg, "Die Leinwand des Turiner Grabtuches," 41, is mistaken from the second fold; the author later changed this in idem, "Die Leinwand mit dem ungemalten Christusbild: Spuren ihrer Geschichte," in *Das Christudbild: Zu Herkunft und Entwicklung in Ost und West*, ed. K. Dietz et al. (Würzburg: Echter Verlag, 2016), 187.

321 R. A. Wild, "Shroud of Turin," in *New Catholic Encyclopedia*, vol. 13 (Gale: Thomson, 2003), 96.

rested on the bottom of the coffer, as well as the top section of the folded cloth, did not suffer even a slight darkening relative to the rest of the fabric, as, on the contrary, one would expect if these layers had been the most exposed to the heat compared to the others folded inside (but one could object that even the external layers were protected by other fabrics that covered them). In any case, everything happened as painlessly as possible; out of all the six exposed sides of the folded cloth, damage occurred to the only *one* that precluded harm to the part of the sheet with the image of the man; if one of the other five sides had been damaged by the heat, or if the heat source had shifted a few centimeters further, the image of the crucified man would have suffered irreparable damage. If we are not faced with the work of a skilled forger who attentively calculated the geometry of the folds, the Shroud suffered limited damage thanks to a number of extremely favorable and fortuitous circumstances, which certainly could invoke the miraculous.

Here is my conclusion: there are some good reasons to lead one to at least suspect a substitution, and these are worth putting forth, but currently suspicions of substitution remain unproven. Therefore, in the absence of cogent proofs, from here on I will assume that the Shroud of Turin is the same as that which existed before the fire of 1532. The traditional hagiographic reconstruction of the event, as it seems to me, should be heavily scaled back; if the current Shroud is truly the same as the one in the fire, it is highly improbable that its preservation occurred in the impossible conditions recounted in the histories of courtiers (high flames, the need to approach the closet, to break the doors, and to reach a higher location), and the fire—at least during the rescue—was far less serious than they would have us believe.

2.2.7 The Shroud in Flight

Only two years had passed after the triumphal resumption of exhibitions when the Shroud again had to leave Chambéry. In 1536, in fact, the king of France, Francis I, by then hostile to Charles II of Savoy because of his alliance with the emperor, decreed the military occupation of the duchy. Charles was on the Italian side of his duchy and had the relic transferred to Turin in the summer of 1535; it is thought to have come through the Col d'Arnas or that of the

Collerin, passing through Lago della Rossa, Balme, and Voragno (on the outside wall of whose parish church remains a contemporary fresco depicting an exhibition in which the cardinal De Gorrevod very likely takes part).[322] Soon, however, the advance of the French overwhelmed even Turin, which fell into enemy hands without even an attempt at resistance, while the duke took shelter in Vercelli. And so began a new period of pilgrimage for the relic: on April 24, 1536, Beatrice reached Milan, bringing the Shroud with her, and Charles also arrived on the following day. On Sunday, May 7, both Charles and Beatrice performed an exhibition in the presence of three bishops from a stage mounted on the ravelin in front of Sforza Castle, during which, it is claimed, three possessed individuals were healed.[323] Later, at an unspecified date, an exhibition was held in Orzinuovi (Brescia).[324] In March of 1537, it was Nice's turn, where the people sought safety for the city from the invading French by holding a procession in which they all walked barefoot, wearing sackcloth and with ashes sprinkled on their heads, and held an exhibition on Good Friday from the battlements of Fort Saint-Elme.[325]

In fact, the castle of Nice was chosen as the site for negotiations desired by Pope Paul III, which it was hoped would put an end to the conflict; the duke, the king of France, the pope, and the emperor Charles V would all have taken part. Paul III, therefore, asked the duke Charles II for the temporary use of his castle, in order that he might take up residence there and conduct the negotiations. However, between April and May of 1538, when the various parties were already en route, the people of Nice feared that their arrival in the city and use of the castle would turn into a dispossession, and they urged the duke to deny them the use of the castle, making him go back on his word. François-Noël de Bellegarde, ducal ambassador

[322] Cf. G. Donna d'Oldenico and G. C. Sciolla, *Gli affreschi di Voragno ed il passaggio della Sindone in Val di Lanzo* (Lanzo: Società storica delle Valli di Lanzo, 2010); C. Cargnino and G. G. Massara, *Testimonianze sindoniche in Haute Maurienne, nelle valli di Lanzo e nella Piana di Ciriè* (Lanzo: Società storica delle Valli di Lanzo, 2000).

[323] Cf. A. Grossi, "L'ostensione milanese della Sindone: 7 maggio 1536," *Aevum* 87, no. 3 (2013): 783–806, which can be supplemented slightly by Segre, "Documenti di storia sabauda," 128, n. 3.

[324] Mentioned by D. Codagli, *L'historia orceana* (Brescia: Borella, 1592), 165.

[325] The dating of Good Friday to March 29, 1537, is incorrect (Perret, "Essai sur l'histoire du Saint Suaire," 111, who picks it up from Goffredo Casalis), because on that year Good Friday fell on the thirtieth of the month.

to the emperor, wrote that the primary reason that he counselled against yielding the castle was the presence of the Holy Shroud, since God willed that it come into the possession of the House of Savoy and that it must not be surrendered to any other.[326] In this period there were some expenditures for the coffer containing the Shroud—namely, repairs and locks for the doors, according to the expense report I tracked down.[327]

Charles II was living through the worst period of his reign as duke: while he was in Genoa, news reached him of his wife Beatrice's death in Nice on January 8, 1538. On June 18, 1538, Charles V and Francis I reached an agreement, but the signed ten-year truce—which in reality would last only four years—did not restore to Savoy its lost lands. At the end of August 1543, Nice fell to the French, but the castle held out.[328] Vercelli became for all intents and purpose the new capital of the duchy, and from that year the Shroud also found a home there, being placed on the altar of the old sacristy of the Cathedral of St. Eusebius. The Shroud remained there while Charles II moved from one city to another, seeking a solution to the political crisis. On September 17, 1553, the duke died, by then abandoned by everyone and robbed of his jewelry by his own household servants. His natural successor was his third son, Emmanuel Philibert.[329]

Charles' death left an open opportunity for the French, who, on November 18, entered and sacked Vercelli under the command of Charles de Cossé, Count of Brissac. His soldiers succeeded in seizing

[326] Cf. A. Segre, "Documenti ed osservazioni sul Congresso di Nizza (1538)," *Rendiconti della Reale Accademia dei Lincei—Scienze morali* 10 (1901): 89: "Premièrement pour le service de Dieu quest le S.te Suaire que repose dedans et quel a pleu à Dieu le faire tomber entre les mains de la Maison et quil croit que ledict reliquaire leur aide à conserver et quil ne vouldroit tant quil plairoit à Dieu labandonner ny sen fier pour estre tel relicaire à nul aultre vivant tant quil plaira a Dieu."

[327] "Pour fere rabiller la petite serrure d'argent qu'il fallust rompre qu'estoit au coffre du Sainct Suayre . . . pour accoustrer le couffre où a faillust remectre le Sainct Suayre et y fere une serrure d'Allemaigne"; now published by Cancian, "Sulle tracce della Sindone," 447.

[328] For a description of the events of these years, see A. Segre, "Carlo II di Savoia: Le sue relazioni con Francia e Spagna e le guerre piemontesi dal 1536 al 1545," *Memorie della Reale Accademia delle Scienze di Torino* 52 (1903): 135–222.

[329] Charles' last years are described by A. Segre, "Appunti sul ducato di Carlo II di Savoia tra il 1545 ed il 1550," *Rendiconti della Reale Accademia dei Lincei—Scienze morali* 9 (1900): 134–55; idem, "Appunti di storia sabauda dal 1546 al 1553," *Rendiconti della Reale Accademia dei Lincei—Scienze morali* 12 (1903): 202–27.

the duke's possessions, among which was a famous horn that was considered very valuable because it was thought to have belonged to a unicorn. The Shroud, though sought after, escaped the raid, even if it is unclear how it happened because of contradictions in the accounts. The canon Giovanni Battista Modena (who was not even born when all this took place) claimed that another canon, by the name of Giovanni Antonio Costa, who was charged with the protection of the relic, feigned a lack of hostility toward the French in order to earn their trust and to pass unnoticed. He then found a way to carry the coffer containing the Shroud outside the cathedral, concealing it under his canonical hood and then hiding it in his own home. An eyewitness, the basketmaker Giovannino Morra, instead told a different story, saying that the Shroud itself miraculously prevented the soldiers from approaching the altar where it lay by making them back away, in a manner reminiscent of how the soldiers, attempting to arrest Christ, backed away and fell before him,[330] and that it was afterward hidden in the home of a certain Sir Claudio, probably a priest. Perhaps the witness confused the canon Claudio Costa (though in 1553 he was already dead) with Giovanni Antonio Costa, his grandson? Or is the reference to a certain Claude Vyosse, a singer of the ducal musical chapel?[331] The official version—recounted in a message sent to the duke by his majordomo Cristoforo Duc just after the sack—was that "the Holy Shroud was saved through a miracle, since all wanted it at all costs and remained all night to have it, and were unable to open the doors, a miracle!"[332] Also, according to the official Giuseppe Cambiano di Ruffia, the Shroud was saved from the soldiers' raid because "such fear took hold of them that there was no one bold enough to touch it."[333] François Capré said that the Count of Brissac "was never able to approach the Holy Shroud, being

[330] John 18:6.

[331] See D. Silano, "Chi ha (veramente) salvato la Sindone a Vercelli nel 1553," *Bollettino storico vercellese* 92 (2019): 77–104.

[332] The sources are edited and discussed in G. Ferraris, "La S. Sindone salvata a Vercelli," in *Atti del I convegno regionale del Centro Internazionale di Sindonologia*, ed. Reale Confraternita del SS. Sudario (Turin: a cura dei Quaderni Sindon, 1960), 11–57.

[333] Cambiano, *Historico discorso*, col. 1113. For a similar account, see I. Baldi, *Discorso intorno a' misteri della santa croce, nel giorno di sua inventione, dove anche si ragiona a lungo della sacra Sindone* (Turin: n.p., 1605), 52.

seized by so great a fright that he was forced to withdraw."[334] Finally, Giuseppe Pasini asserted that the hands of the soldiers "remained retracted by a sudden paralysis."[335] Other authors, however, recount a third version of the story: François de Boyvin du Villars, the Count of Brissac's secretary, and Agostino Bucci, a Savoyard, assert that due to his devotion, the count wanted to spare the relic since it was a holy object, and the friar François Victon maintains in addition that the count ordered that it be returned to its original place after the soldiers had already taken it.[336] In conclusion, the one thing that is certain is that the Shroud did not leave Vercelli; everything else is confusion and propaganda.

Finally, in 1557, at the battle of St. Quentin, imperial troops overcame the forces of the French, allowing Emmanuel Philibert, at the head of a triumphant army, to reclaim his territories. The arrival of the victorious duke at Vercelli with his consort Margaret on November 7, 1560, was celebrated with a public exhibition at the Piazza Maggiore from the home of the Confraternity of Saint Nicholas. With the return of peace, on April 15, 1561, the duke signed the order for the almoner Jacques Lambert to transfer the Shroud to Chambéry, "where its ancient home was"; the relic arrived on the evening of June 3 and was placed in the convent of Sainte-Marie-l'Égyptienne, then solemnly transferred to Sainte-Chapelle the next day.[337] Two exhibitions were immediately granted, one on August 15 from the walls and the other on August 17 in the Piazza Castello.[338]

A new displacement led the relic to Annecy, where on May 5, 1566, Jacques of Savoy, Duke of Nemours, was wed to Anna d'Este; the

334 Capré, *Traité historique*, 398.

335 Navire, *Storia della Santissima Sindone di Torino*, 85.

336 F. de Boyvin, *Mémoires sur les guerres démeslées tant en Piedmont qu'au Montferrat et Duché de Milan*, 2nd ed. (Lyon: Rigaud, 1610), 356; A. and D. F. Bucci, *Il solenne battesimo del serenissimo prencipe di Piemonte Filippo Emanuelle primogenito figliuolo di Carlo Emanuele duca di Savoia* [. . .] *celebrato in Turino l'anno 1587* (Turin: Antonio de' Bianchi, 1587), 24v–25r; F. Victon, *Histoire ou bref traité du S. Suaire de N.S. Iesus Christ* (Paris: Cramoisy, 1634), 65–67.

337 AST, Savoia per paesi per A e B, file 4, no. 11 (the duke's order and report of the arrival). An edited version of the order is in Pugno, *Santa Sindone che si venera a Torino*, 191–92, n. 176.

338 Cf. G. Pérouse, "Chambéry et Emmanuel-Philibert," in *Lo Stato Sabaudo al tempo di Emanuele Filiberto*, ed. C. Patrucco, vol. 1 (Milan: Miglietta, 1928), 334–35; Mugnier, "Registres des entrées," 365, 367.

Shroud was displayed between July 17 and July 23 to distinguished visitors, among whom the most notable were the princes Catherine and Henry, Duke of Guise, sons from Anna's first marriage, and Antoinette de Bourbon-Vendôme, Duchess of Guise, and her two sons, Louis and Charles de Lorraine, both of whom were cardinals. Françoise de Sionnaz also participated in the exhibition. At the time she was carrying in her womb the little Francis de Sales, the future saint who would come to have a particular devotion to the Shroud.[339]

Apart from this brief transfer, in this period the Holy Shroud once again had a stable home in Chambéry, where it was enclosed in a reliquary protected by iron doors.[340] We have a beautiful miniature from approximately 1520 that depicts an exhibition where the relic is held in the hands of three bishops (the one in the center is always the most illustrious),[341] and another miniature from 1559 on a similar theme, portraying an exhibition in front of an altar, probably that of Sainte-Chapelle itself.[342] A later image (1579) shows us instead a public exhibition, also from the period at Chambéry.[343] The method of performing exhibitions, therefore, remained the same as in the Shroud's days in Lirey, as the pilgrims' medallions attest.

The situation in Sainte-Chapelle, however, must not have been the best; the archbishop of Vercelli, who visited Sainte-Chapelle in 1576, described the church as semi-abandoned. Even the third miter for the bishops to wear during exhibitions was missing.[344] Evidently it was a period of decline: the only truly significant presence was the relic, which the canons proudly had depicted on their capitular

[339] Cf. A. Ducis, "Le Saint Suaire à Annecy et la naissance de saint François de Sales," *Revue savoisienne* 24 (1883): 33–35, 77, 86–87, 101–4; A. Pedrini, "Francesco di Sales e la Sindone," *Palestra del clero* 65, no. 7 (1986): 479–94.

[340] Cf. J. Delexi, *Chorographia insignium locorum* (Chambéry: per Franciscum Pomarum, 1571), 23r.

[341] This miniature appears in a Book of Hours belonging to Johann von Erlach, illuminated by the master of Claudius of France. It was sold by Christie's in 2016. Photographs are available on the Christie's website. See www.christies.com.

[342] Found in a prayer manual described in A. Griseri, "La Sindone: Un piedistallo per il ritratto del duca," in *Arte d'Occidente: Temi e metodi*, ed. A. Cadei et al., vol. 3 (Rome: Edizioni Sintesi informazione, 1999), 1113–18. Image reproduced on the cover of Cozzo, Merlotti, and Nicolotti, *Shroud at Court*.

[343] Reproduced in B. Barberis and G. M. Zaccone, *La Sindone e il suo museo* (Turin: Utet, 2010), 148.

[344] Cf. Pugno, *Santa Sindone che si venera a Torino*, 192–96, n. 178.

seal being held by the saints Maurice and Lazarus, protectors of the House of Savoy.[345]

2.2.8 Charles Borromeo and the Shroud's Transfer to Turin

The reform of the duchy enacted by Emmanuel Philibert led to a shift in the center of political activity to Piedmont and raised Turin to the rank of capital.[346] Its new designation, accompanied by strong population growth, made it the subject of an intense effort to restructure and augment the city, the results of which were most evident in the rise of a fortified citadel and the construction of a ducal palace suited to the needs of a capital. All of this was accompanied by the implementation of very particular political, artistic, and religious cultures. From 1505, the new capital, Turin, had a new cathedral, built by Cardinal Domenico della Rovere (who lived, however, in Rome, while being at once bishop of Turin, Tarentaise, Corneto, and Geneva). In 1513 Leo X freed the diocese from the jurisdiction of the metropolis of Milan, and Giovanni Francesco della Rovere was the first to bear the title of archbishop.[347] At this point it was obvious that Emmanuel Philibert had it in mind to transport all of the duchy's most sacred objects to Turin. In 1576 he had the bones of his predecessor Amadeus VIII, the antipope Felix V, transferred to the city; and he had by then begun to think about the Shroud, the most precious dynastic relic. The duke was certainly prompted by his own veneration of the holy relic, but he did not ignore the benefit he would receive from bringing to the capital an object that provoked the most fervent expressions of worship. In fact, "the people in a fervor of devotion—the duke was saying—are held in check much more than those who live for nothing, and so are more obedient

[345] Described in A. Lange, "Le Saint-Suaire sur le sceau du chapitre de la Sainte-Chapelle de Chambéry au XVIe siècle," *Sindon* 21 (1975): 12–17.

[346] See P. Cozzo, "De Chambéry à Turin: Le transfert de la capitale du duché de Savoie au XVIe siècle," in *Les capitales de la Renaissance*, ed. J.-M. Le Gall (Rennes: Presses universitaires de Rennes, 2011), 165–77. On Turin throughout this period, see G. Ricuperati, ed., *Storia di Torino*, vol. 3, *Dalla dominazione francese alla ricomposizione dello Stato (1536–1630)* (Turin: Einaudi, 1998).

[347] A profile of all the bishops of Turin beginning from the sixteenth century is provided by G. Tuninetti and G. D'Antino, *Il cardinal Domenico Della Rovere costruttore della cattedrale e gli arcivescovi di Torino dal 1515 al 2000* (Cantalupa: Effatà, 2000).

to their prince."[348] It was not by chance that in the years to come a significant boost was given to the veneration of the two members of the House of Savoy declared "Blessed," Amadeus IX and Margaret of Savoy, Marchioness of Monferrato. In the medieval period as well as in modern times, physical proximity to a precious relic conferred proof of a special divine favor toward whoever possessed it; that benevolence served as confirmation of the legitimacy of temporal power that descended from God himself.

In its last year in Chambéry the Shroud had been used as a weapon against evil spirits and as an effective tool of anti-Protestant propaganda: it is said that in May 1578 it was placed upon the head of a woman who, as a result of her Calvinist baptism, was possessed by a legion of demons. Coming into contact with the Shroud obtained her liberation and conversion to Catholicism.[349] Nevertheless, devotion to the Shroud had not become widespread, remaining primarily linked to elites and incapable of competition with other, more widely followed devotions that were supported by the Catholic Reformation.[350] This situation, however, is not surprising, as a relic possessed by an individual "is not a means to build a common identity, but rather an opportunity to underline an individual uniqueness, a personal distinction, to claim for oneself a particular supernatural protection that distinguishes that person from other members of society."[351]

A pretext for ordering the transfer of the relic to Turin was provided to the duke by Charles Borromeo, the highly esteemed archbishop of Milan. In the years 1576–1577, his city had been afflicted by a terrible plague, and when the contagion began to wane, the cardinal Borromeo—who had already demonstrated his interest in relics of the

[348] F. Barbaro, "Relazione della corte di Savoia," in *Le relazioni degli ambasciatori veneti al Senato durante il secolo decimosesto*, ed. E. Alberi, ser. 2, vol. 5 (Florence: Società editrice fiorentina), 80: "La gente infervorata di divozione è molto più frenata di quella che vive a caso, e in conseguenza è più obbediente al suo principe."

[349] Cf. A. Grossi, "Un carteggio inedito di san Carlo Borromeo (1578–79): La Sindone e l'esorcismo di una calvinista," *Aevum* 89, no. 3 (2015): 687–720.

[350] Cf. F. Meyer, "Centre dynastique, religiosité et mémoire urbaine: Chambéry et le Saint Suaire du XVIe au XVIIIe siècle," in Cozzo, Merlotti, and Nicolotti, *Shroud at Court*, 75–88.

[351] F. Carlà, "Exchange and the Saints: Gift-Giving and the Commerce of Relics," in *Gift Giving and the 'Embedded' Economy in the Ancient World*, ed. F. Carlà and M. Gori (Heidelberg: Winter Verlag, 2014), 412–13.

passion by escalating the worship of the Holy Nail in Milan—made a vow to visit the Shroud in a pilgrimage of thanksgiving.[352] The Duke of Savoy, aware of the holy bishop's intentions,[353] decided to have the Shroud brought to Turin to spare his distinguished and, by now, no longer young guest a tiresome journey over the Alps. The move was in truth a pretext, because the duke already had it in mind to transfer the relic to Turin.[354]

At the time, the dean of the Sainte-Chapelle of Chambéry was Pierre de Lambert, bishop of Saint-Jean-de-Maurienne. He was the one who received the unwelcome order for the transfer of the relic, which was physically entrusted to Louis Milliet de Challes, first president of the Savoyard Senate, and to the canon Neyton, cantor of Sainte-Chapelle. Probably the wooden casket displayed today in the Museum of the Shroud of Turin, stripped of its covering of tortoiseshell or mother-of-pearl, was the one used on the occasion of the Shroud's transfer.[355] Some think that during the transfer, the precious treasure was taken through Little St. Bernard Pass, Aosta, Ivrea, and Ciriè. Others say that it was transported through the Lanzo Valleys. Certainly, it made a stop at the castle of Lucento, at the city gates, where it remained for three days. Afterward, on September 14, 1578, the feast of the Exaltation of the Holy Cross, the arrival of the relic in Turin on a carriage was celebrated by a solemn procession accompanied by the firing of cannons. The site chosen to house the Shroud was a chapel a few steps from the ducal palace, originally dedicated to Saint Mary of the Snow and known as Saint Mary of the Nativity, but in the last few years renovated by Emmanuel

[352] The Shroud during the crisis of the Savoyard duchy became famous even in Milan: cf. C. Debiaggi, "Sull'origine della devozione di San Carlo Borromeo verso la S. Sindone," *Studi Piemontesi* 37, no. 2 (2008): 423–27.

[353] Their correspondence is edited by G. Galbiati, *I duchi di Savoia Emanuele Filiberto e Carlo Emanuele I nel loro carteggio con San Carlo Borromeo* (Milan: Biblioteca Ambrosiana, 1941); see also G. Gentile, "Il viaggio della Sindone," *Rivista Museo Torino* 8 (2015): 8–11.

[354] See Donna d'Oldenico and Sciolla, *Affreschi di Voragno*, 64, n. 5.

[355] In Altessano, hamlet of Venaria Reale, there is a copy of this casket, made in the nineteenth century but still fashioned with the sheets of mother-of-pearl and the silver lock: see L. Fossati, "Urne e reliquiari nella storia della Sacra Sindone," *Collegamento pro Sindone* (September–October 1998): 11–21; (November–December 1998): 28–41, to be completed with C. Arnaldi di Balme, ed., *La Sindone e la sua immagine: Storia, arte e devozione* (Turin: Sagep, 2018), 16–17 (with photographs).

Philibert and renamed in honor of Saint Lawrence, on whose feast day, August 10, in 1557 the duke won his victory in the Battle of St. Quentin. It was a small, Romanesque church (torn down in the 1630s) that rose against the wall in the region between the Palatine Gate and the Bastion Verde, not to be confused with the current Church of Saint Lawrence in Piazza Castello, the work of Guarino Guarini, completed in 1780.[356]

Cardinal Borromeo organized every detail of his pilgrimage, attending closely to the choice of biblical literature on which to meditate in prayer during the journey from Milan to Turin. He left with a dozen others in attendance and in four days arrived at the city gates, after passing through various locales—Trecate, Novara, Vercelli, Cigliano, Chivasso—always being well received by the clergy and local population. On October 9, the duke and the archbishop left to go meet him, and having received him with six other bishops, they conducted him to the ducal palace with all due pomp. It was said that Borromeo was very tired when he arrived in Turin with blisters on his feet; a barber who attempted to help by cutting them did nothing more than make them more painful. During the private exhibition, in which the cardinal of Vercelli also participated, the distinguished guest wanted to kiss the relic and touch it with his hands repeatedly while it was spread on a table, and he asked for the opportunity to examine it in detail.

The public exhibition of the Shroud was scheduled for the following day, after the solemn celebration in the cathedral, but the influx of people was such that in the end the ceremony had to be moved to the Piazza Castello and a stage had to be prepared in a great hurry. Two cardinals and nine bishops took part in the exhibition; the critical moment in the ceremony was immortalized, almost as in a photograph, in a famous engraving by Giovanni Testa (fig. 2.5). Once returned to the cathedral, the relic was arranged on another stage, and the celebration of the Forty Hours' Devotion began. A sermon was planned for every hour, two of which were delivered by Borromeo. The duke assisted devotedly in all the celebrations. Given the continual arrival of new pilgrims, a second exhibition had to be performed

[356] Cf. S. Klaiber, "The First Ducal Chapel of San Lorenzo: Turin and the Escorial," in *Politica e cultura nell'età di Carlo Emanuele I*, ed. M. Masoero, S. Mamino, and C. Rosso (Florence: Olschki, 1999), 329–43.

FIGURE 2.5 Giovanni Testa, Exhibition of the Shroud after its transfer from Chambéry to Turin in 1578, presided over by Charles Cardinal Borromeo

in the plaza on the morning of October 14. Two days later the cardinal left Turin to return to Milan, but not before he had made a stop at the Sacred Mount of Varallo. It is necessary also to remember the famous Italian poet Torquato Tasso among those who attended the exhibition. For detailed information on all of these events we are indebted to the pen of the Jesuit Francesco Adorno, confessor of Charles Borromeo; to the reports of the ambassadors present in Turin; and to the account by Emmanuel-Philibert de Pingon.[357] At the end of the exhibition, the city, elevated in prestige and in the moral authority of a new capital, bade farewell to Borromeo.[358] The cardinal was so pleased that he returned two more times to visit the Shroud, in 1582 and 1584.[359]

[357] [Adorno], *Lettera della peregrinatione* (a rare edition, whose existence even recently has been erroneously denied); republished from a manuscript, with commentary, by P. Savio, "Pellegrinaggio di San Carlo Borromeo alla Sindone in Torino," *Aevum* 7, no. 4 (1933): 433–54; for the Latin version, see G. A. Guarneri, *Epistola qua peregrination ab ill.mo et rev.mo card.li S. Praxedis suscepta exponitur* (Bergomi: per Cominum Venturam, 1579), later inserted in Pingone, *Sindon evangelica*, 65–85. On the ideological differences at the heart of the two reports of Francesco Adorno and Philibert Pingon, see M. Guglielminetti, "Due testimonianze del pellegrinaggio di san Carlo alla Sindone," in *Il volto di Cristo*, ed. E. Corsini et al. (Turin: Theleme, 1999), 117–27. Savio's article contains the testimonies of the ambassadors in the footnotes; additionally, see Mollat, *Deux pèlerinages*, 159–60.

[358] On this period, Donna d'Oldenico, "Sindone nella politica dei Duchi di Savoia," 215–67.

[359] For a description of St. Charles' three visits to the Shroud, see G. P. Giussani, *Vita di s. Carlo Borromeo*, Stamperia della Camera Apostolica, Rome 1610, 334–44, 434–36, 479. The exhibition of 1582 is narrated by Agostino Cusano: L. Fossati and

One can well understand that after this success, the duke had no intention of depriving himself and Turin of the precious relic; on the contrary, he sought to enrich the treasure that already existed, and in 1591 the remains of the martyr Saint Maurice were brought in from the abbey of St. Maurice, Agaunum, after a promise of substantial revenue and economic privileges for the Swiss who were deprived of the relics. We know that in 1579, certainly in response to urgent requests coming from Chambéry, the duke pledged to return the Shroud after he had time to display it for veneration by all the cities of Piedmont;[360] naturally, he did not keep this promise, a fact that must have saddened the canons of Saint-Chapelle no less than the canons of Lirey had been saddened almost two centuries before. Alongside politico-religious concern of a dynastic sort, Charles Borromeo's interest is indicative of a new, particular pastoral style that, through solemn exhibitions, homiletics, the publication of books, and catechesis, established itself fully as part of the Counter-Reformation and favored the veneration of the Shroud as an instrument of piety and the edification of the faithful.[361] This period also saw the establishment of theological positions that clarified the role of the Shroud in relation to the legitimacy of the veneration of the images.[362] The Shroud's good fortune would continue for the whole of the baroque period, until the second half of the eighteenth century, during the Enlightenment, when the exhibitions underwent a drastic reduction and practically took place only during events concerning the House of Savoy. Its arrival at Turin ushered in the beginning of a new life for the Shroud.

L. De Blasi Zaccaria, eds., "Carlo Borromeo a Torino: L'ostensione della Sindone del 1582 in uno scritto inedito," *Studi Piemontesi* 16 (1987): 429–36. One often reads that Borromeo also went to see the Shroud in 1581, but an analysis of his letters excludes this possibility: see Baldassarre Oltrocchi in G. P. Giussani, *De vita et rebus gestis Sancti Caroli Borromei*, ex Typographia Bibliothecae Ambrosianae, Milan 1751, coll. 580–82.

360 Cf. Perret, "Essai sur l'histoire du Saint Suaire," 116.

361 Cf. G. Gentile, "Il contributo di Carlo Borromeo e l'epoca barocca," in Zaccone and Ghiberti, *Guardare la Sindone*, 128–60.

362 An example is in S. Maiolo, *Historiarum totius orbis omniumque temporum pro defensione sacrarum imaginum adversus Iconomachos libri* (Rome: in aedibus populi Romani, 1585), 14–17.

THREE

The Shroud in Piedmont

3.1. The Early Days of the Shroud in Turin

3.1.1. A Triumphal Cult

Within the context of its new and definitive residence at Turin, the Shroud straightaway came to be seen not only as a relic to which one could offer personal devotion but also as a tangible sign of protection from heaven granted to the ducal house that possessed it. And the ducal house, for its part, acted in such a way as to ensure this situation, establishing itself as a family chosen by heaven to guard the most famous relic of Christianity and, on that basis, legitimizing its own claim to appear as a sovereign family superior to others.

For the conservation of the Shroud a new ark was prepared consisting of a wooden box chiseled in the form of a cuboid covered with precious metal and decorated with stones; depictions of angel heads; and sixteen large oval medallions on which the instruments of the passion are portrayed. It would remain in this condition until 1998.[1]

On April 12, 1582, Gregory XIII, at the request of the duke, extended the solemnity of the Feast of the Shroud (May 4) also to the ducal lands on the Italian side of the Alps and granted a plenary indulgence to all the confessed and communicated faithful who were in attendance at the exhibition.[2] The Shroud could also be shown in correspondence with events that involved the members of the House of Savoy, such as, for example, in 1587 when the baptism

[1] Photographs are in Barberis and Zaccone, *Sindone e il suo museo,* 218–19.

[2] Savio, *Ricerche storiche,* 302–5.

of Prince Philip Emmanuel was performed,[3] or during periods of calamity—wars, natural disasters, or epidemics, whether among men or animals—when the House of Savoy organized propitiatory ceremonies in which the Shroud played a leading role. On the first Sunday in Lent of 1599, for example, there was a solemn procession against the plague, during which the bodies of the saints and the most famous relics of the city were carried: in addition to the Shroud, the bodies of Saint Secundus and Saint Maurice and the relics of Saint Catherine, along with those of the cross and of the crown of thorns, were also present.[4] In 1632, as an expression of thanks for the cessation of the plague of 1630, a silver votive plaque, paid for by the city of Turin, was deposited at the Chapel of the Shroud after a procession.[5]

This was the time of solemn exhibitions at Turin, on the occasions when the city was adorned in a scenic fashion: "it is the theater that the royal court adopted for the lavish ceremonies with which, by means of the relic, the Savoy dynasty is celebrated."[6] The center of the exhibition was the Piazza Castello, which overlooks the ducal palace and the castle (the current Palazzo Madama), a medieval building that incorporated the gate of the ancient decumanus (east/west Roman street). A stage surmounted by a canopy was built in the middle of the square or in front of the castle gate, in the same position in which used to be erected temporary gazebos and kiosks for parties, carousels, weddings, and other entertainments of a nonreligious nature. There was never a shortage of decorations, shields, and crests, including the banners of the ruling house. The authorities and the general public took their places in the square in hierarchical order, eager for the exhibition of the artifact. Then the relic was carried in a procession onto the stage, and, supported by bishops, immediately behind whom the members of the House of Savoy were positioned, it was opened and displayed to those celebrating nearby, while the muskets were firing in the air. The privilege of carrying the

[3] Described by D. F. Bucci, *Il solenne battesimo del prencipe di Piemonte Filippo-Emanuele*, 2nd ed. (Turin: Bevilacqua, 1588), 33v–34v.

[4] Described by A. Cornuato, *Breve relatione della processione solenne fatta in Torino la prima domenica di Quaresima con assistenza di S.A. Serenissima per la preservatione et liberatione d'essa città dalla peste* (Turin: Bianchi, 1599).

[5] Cf. L. Fossati, *La Sacra Sindone: Storia di una secolare devozione* (Leumann: Elledici, 2000), 152–57. Today the plaque is preserved in the Royal Palace.

[6] P. Cozzo, *La geografia celeste dei duchi di Savoia* (Bologna: il Mulino, 2006), 65–66.

processional canopy that surmounted the Shroud was often reserved for the most influential ambassadors—those of Venice, Spain, and France—while the papal nuncios participated in the exhibition, holding the relic in their hands. In some cases, the very presence in the city of an ambassador, a sovereign, or a prelate who was considered important could be reason for organizing an exhibition of the relic. If, however, the Duke of Savoy was not able to attend the exhibition, either because of illness or mourning for a member of the House of Savoy, he simply cancelled it.[7]

An engraving of 1613 by Antonio Tempesta presents the way in which, at the time, the shroud was shown to the people.[8] At the foot of the stage depicted on the engraving, many people stretch their hands upward as if in anticipation of something, and some church officials allow rosaries to fall from above. These rosaries have evidently been placed upon the sacred linen. It is said that during the exhibition of 1621, Vincenzo Giliberti, general of the Order of the Theatines, as he was preaching to the crowd, was injured by a rosary chain tossed from below that struck him in the face. For the exhibition of 1613, Francis de Sales, bishop of Geneva, was in Turin and took an active part in the celebrations. Francis himself tells us that, while holding the Shroud in his hands to show it to the people, the sweat from his face fell onto the linen relic. Maurice of Savoy, the twenty-year-old son of Charles Emmanuel I, Duke of Savoy, was at that time already cardinal and had held that office since the age of fifteen. When he attended the exhibition in which Francis de Sales participated and saw the relic nearly soiled, he became irritated. Francis, however, merely replied, "our Lord was not so delicate, Who poured out his sweat and blood only to mix them with our own."[9]

Sermons and panegyrics pronounced by the best preachers accompanied the exhibitions; many of these have survived, and some have very original titles (such as "The Shield," "Sacred Rainbow,"

[7] And so it happened, for example, on May 4, 1650, when Charles Emmanuel II had been ill with measles; in 1662 the same thing happened for the illness of the Royal Madama Christine of Bourbon, and the following year for the death of the Duchess of Parma, Margaret Yolande of Savoy: see Savio, *Ricerche storiche*, 313, 319.

[8] Reproduced in Comoli and Giacobello Bernard, *Potere e la devozione*, 60.

[9] *Œuvres de Saint François de Sales*, vol. 16, *Lettres, 1613–1615* (Lyon: Vitte, 1910), 177–79.

"God the Painter," "The Deformity That Arouses Love," "The Triumphal Bed for the Prince's Rest"). The most famous preacher to try such a topic was Paolo Segneri, but the most prolific writer was the inquisitor of Turin, Camillo Balliani.[10] In these panegyrics, the praise directed to the sacred relic was always joined to the exaltation and legitimizing of the House of Savoy, sometimes reaching unheard-of levels of adulation that verged on heterodoxy. The Shroud was proposed as proof of the superiority of the House of Savoy over all the other princes, the demonstration of the special affection of God for them, the guarantee of their faith, the protection of the territory, the legitimacy of their dominion, the eternity of their duchy, and the force of their army.[11]

There were not many people, however, whom the preacher's voice could reach, and the greater part of the faithful who were packed into the square could do nothing other than gaze upon the exposed Shroud from a distance. Yet this was not possible for everyone, owing to the overcrowding of the city: we know of pilgrims who were not even able to get close to the square and had to content themselves with spiritually participating from afar, without the experience of seeing

[10] P. Segneri, *Panegirici sacri* (Bologna: Monti, 1664), 245–59; C. Balliani, *Ragionamenti sopra la Sacra Sindone di N. S. Giesù Christo* (Turin: Pizzamiglio, 1627); cf. G. M. Zaccone, "Contributo allo studio delle fonti edite sulla Sindone nei secoli XVI e XVII," in *La Sindone: Nuovi studi e ricerche*, ed. P. Coero-Borga and G. Intrigillo (Cinisello Balsamo: Paoline, 1986), 59–60.

[11] A panegyric that seems to me to be of great significance is that of G. Buonafede, *Regalo di Dio alla real corona di Savoia: Panegirici sacri a i misterij della S. Sindone di N. Sig. Giesù Christo* (Asti: Giangrandi, 1654), where among other things we can read: "This Shroud is to remain in your hands until the end of the world, and then the angels of paradise will receive it from your hands in order to return it to God. . . . Just as you received it as a gift to enjoy forever, until the end of the world, without fear that it be taken from you by anyone, your kingdom will endure as long as will the Shroud. And the Shroud will last with you until the end of the world. Therefore it is a gift, but at the end of the world you will return it to God in order that it be placed in the temple of heaven for all eternity. Therefore it is a pledge. O happy house of Savoy, which, endowed by so great a pledge, is glorified by this sacred gift. Fortunate house it is that has these treasures in common with heaven. This house will not perish, but, more blessed than that of Obed-Edom, will go on prospering until the end of the world" (78–80; translation of John Beldon Scott). I have collected the proofs of propagandistic uses of the Shroud in the modern age in Nicolotti, "I Savoia e la Sindone di Cristo"; see also L. Giachino, "Syndonic Panegyrics in the 17th Century," in Cozzo, Merlotti, and Nicolotti, *Shroud at Court*, 185–213.

it. For them the Shroud's mere presence was more important than viewing the relic. The moment when the Shroud was shown from the balcony could be inferred from the firing of cannons and the sound of music in the distance. When Giovanni Antonio Panighetti—who later received the title Servant of God—came with some family members to the gates of the city to assist with the exhibition of 1775, his entry was impeded due to the excessive crowd that had already thickened; without losing heart, they all turned back toward Monte dei Cappuccini where, a kilometer and a half away, they audibly lifted up their prayers as they kneeled and looked toward Piazza Castello: "We do not need," he said, "to see with our eyes the Holy Shroud. Faith is enough for us."[12]

By means of posted invitations, the dukes invited their own subjects and pilgrims to the Feast of the Shroud.[13] The firing of cannons and evening lights transformed Turin into a true festival town. The exhibitions of the seventeenth century are estimated to have had between forty thousand and sixty thousand participants. Pilgrims would try to find a place from which to view the Shroud wherever they might best do so: in the square, in windows, on balconies, and even from roofs. Not surprisingly, accidents thus also sometimes occurred, as when in 1647 during an exhibition in the cathedral some people died because of the size of the crowd and the heat.[14] The public authorities issued a series of regulations for each exhibition to limit the influx of pilgrims and to ensure public safety.[15] These regulations also concerned the owners of the houses that overlooked Piazza Castello, providing instruction as to how to build wooden bleachers in front of their houses to accommodate the pilgrims. The

[12] A. Vaudagnotti, *Il ciabattino santo di Moncalieri: Vita di Giovanni Antonio Panighetti da Varzo*, 2nd ed. (Turin: Sacro Cuore, 1932), 164–65. On the importance of showing and seeing, see A. Casper, "Display and Devotion: Exhibiting Icons and Their Copies in Counter-Reformation Italy," in *Religion and the Senses in Early-Modern Europe*, ed. W. de Boer and C. Göttler (Leiden: Brill, 2013), 43–62.

[13] One, of 1674, is reproduced in *Ostensione della S. Sindone*, plate LXIX; another, of 1684, is in Scott, *Architecture for the Shroud*, plate 5.

[14] Savio, *Ricerche storiche*, 312.

[15] An ordinance of 1722 is reproduced in *Ostensione della S. Sindone*, plate LXXI. On the role of the city in the organization of the exhibitions, see D. De Franco, "Turin and the Holy Shroud: Supplies of Wheat and Management of Public Order during the Ostensions (XVII–XVIII Centuries)," in Cozzo, Merlotti, and Nicolotti, *Shroud at Court*, 167–84.

bleachers, once joined together, were open only at the passages of the roads, forming almost a sort of amphitheater. To get a seat in the bleachers one had to pay for a ticket, as a 1737 provision reminds us:

> Inasmuch as His Majesty has deigned to allow the owners of the houses that are situated around the respective squares, in which the exhibition of the Most Holy Shroud is to be made, to build bleachers for the greater convenience of the visitors, they [the homeowners] themselves are expected to provide what is necessary for the construction, and are expected to begin their construction on the day that we decide, thus forbidding any and every master carpenter under penalty at our judgment to put his hand to the same [i.e., building bleachers] unless receiving due instruction from us. We reserve the right to visit those bleachers that have been built, and to set the ticket price, as well as the number of people who can occupy each series of these bleachers so as to prevent arguments between them, which could arise from lack of this measure.[16]

At the behest of Charles Emmanuel II, beginning in the year 1656, immunity for any crime for the space of fifteen days was guaranteed to the pilgrims, and the soldiers who should fail to respect such a privilege would receive the sentence "of three strokes of the lash, to be given them publicly."[17]

When, in 1659, two blocks of buildings that were obstructing the current Piazzetta Reale were removed, an imposing walkway was built along the façade of the ducal palace, dividing Piazzetta Reale from Piazza Castello; this terrace of masonry and arches, which acted as a guard station and a link between the two side wings of the palace, was enlarged at its center into an octagonal platform that began to be used as a place to carry out the exhibitions of the Shroud, eliminating the need for a stage to be built in the middle of the square each time. A beautiful painting by Pieter Bolckmann shows us one of these exhibitions.[18] On the central platform a covered pavilion ("pinnacolo") was sometimes installed from which the Shroud was displayed

[16] The ordinance of Pietro Eugenio d'Angennes, chief of police, dated to March 31, 1737; cf. the edition of Lanza, *Santissima Sindone del Signore*, 76–78.

[17] *Leggi e costituzioni di Sua Maestà da osservarsi nelle materie civili e criminali* (Turin: Valetta, 1723), bk. 1, ch. 2, p. 5, § 10.

[18] Reproduced in Scott, *Architecture for the Shroud*, plate 10.

from either side to allow everyone to see it. Because a gallery (*Grande galleria*), now demolished, connected the palace with the castle (the current Palazzo Madama), the Shroud could be moved and shown both from the pavilion and from the castle without it ever actually being brought into the square. Despite the fact that there was a plan to build a permanent covered pavilion on the walkway, the work never came to fruition; in some exhibitions, but not all, there were sumptuous temporary pavilions. Sometimes, after the exhibition proper, fireworks were launched from the same pavilion.[19]

Devotion to the relic was not limited solely to the moment of the exhibition, and it was reignited by the massive diffusion of images of the Shroud that chiefly began in the second half of the seventeenth century. The apostolic nuncio to the House of Savoy tells us that the Lenten preacher of 1650, Stefano Pepe, of the Theatine order, was the one who started a "new devotion" surrounding the Shroud, exhorting that "all shops and homes and also street corners ought to keep a depiction of the Holy Shroud and have a lamp to light it."[20] An image was immediately painted on the facade of what was then the municipal building. Two of the four frescoes that adorned Piazza San Carlo are still visible at the corners of Alfieri and Santa Teresa Streets. There is no need here to expound upon the proliferation of prints, paintings, frescoes, votive chapels, facsimiles, ex-votos, banners, coins, medals, and ribbons bearing the emblem of the Shroud. The image of the relic, which is the palladium of the House of Savoy, was also placed on the personal combat armor of that house's sovereign. A military standard with a radiant image at its center of the Shroud supported by the Madonna and angels, surrounded by the inscription *Protector noster aspice Deus et respice in faciem Christi tui* ("Behold, o God our

[19] Cf. M. Viale Ferrero, "Gli apparati per le ostensioni della S. Sindone," *Bollettino della Società Piemontese di Archeologia e Belle Arti* 32–34 (1978–1980): 79–93; Cozzo, *Geografia celeste*, 229–30; especially cf. Scott, *Architecture for the Shroud*, 219–48. For the displays put on at Turin from the moment of the transfer until the year 1700, we refer to the descriptions furnished by the apostolic nuncio published in Savio, *Ricerche storiche*, 307–32. A list with descriptions of the displays in this period can be found in Pugno, *Santa Sindone che si venera a Torino*, 211–53 (with many documents); and in Fossati, *Sacra Sindone*, 128–91. With particular attention to the ceremonial, F. Varallo, "The Shroud in the Ceremonial Policy of the House of Savoy between the End of the 16th Century and the 18th Century," in Cozzo, Merlotti, and Nicolotti, *Shroud at Court*, 238–71.

[20] Savio, *Ricerche storiche*, 313.

protector, and look on the face of thy Christ"; Psalm 83:10), is adorned with the crest of the city of Turin; the standard was put in place during the clashes between the two factions in the civil war—the "principisti" and "madamisti"—who contended for power over the Duchy of Savoy after the death of Victor Amadeus I in 1637.[21] During the siege of Turin in 1706, the clairvoyant Serafina Brunelli claimed to have seen the Shroud take the shape of a rock and encompass the city, like a wall of defense, against the French.[22] An interesting print of 1684, which celebrated the wedding of Victor Amadeus II of Savoy to Anne Marie d'Orléans, figuratively represents the close link between the Duchy of Savoy and the Shroud: the image of Turin, in fact, is surrounded by the figures of the dukes and the Shroud, which is portrayed as being waved like a banner by an angel who is engaged in protecting both. The military character of the image is emphasized by the presence of the Constantinian inscription *in hoc signo vinces* ("in this sign you will conquer"). All around the image a series of panes tells of miraculous episodes in the history of the relic.[23]

In 1598, twenty years after the Shroud arrived in Turin, the Royal Confraternity of the Most Holy Shroud came into being. Beyond its religious activity, the confraternity was also distinguished by its commitment to caring for the poor. Through its own efforts and with the help of an endowment of the monarch, in the middle of the eighteenth century the confraternity built the Pazzerelli Hospital in Turin, and, in 1764, a new church was dedicated to the Most Holy Shroud. This confraternity still exists and is fully functioning.[24] A homonymous confraternity had previously been founded, in 1522 in

[21] The standard is located today in Turin, in the Sala Cateriniana of the Church of St. Dominic. It was blessed on September 2, 1640. See A. Merlotti, "La reliquia, lo stendardo, la chiave: La Santa Sindone nella Guerra civile (1638–1642)," *Studi Piemontesi* 45, no. 2 (2016): 413–21 (with picture).

[22] Cf. D. Bolognini and E. Ciferi, "L'assedio di Torino negli scritti di Serafina Brunelli," in *Memorie e attualità dell'assedio di Torino del 1706 tra spirito europeo e identità regionale*, ed. G. Mola di Nomaglio et al. (Turin: Centro Studi Piemontesi, 2007), 902–4.

[23] Reproduced in G. M. Zaccone, ed., *L'immagine rivelata* (Turin: Centro Studi Piemontesi, 1998), 108.

[24] Cf. *Storia della Confraternita del SS. Sudario e Vergine B.ma delle Grazie eretta in Torino l'anno 1598* (Turin: n.p., 1825); also, B. Barberis and M. Boccaletti, *Nel nome della Sindone: La Confraternita del SS. Sudario dalla fondazione (1598) ad oggi* (Cantalupa: Effatà, 2006).

Ciriè. In 1537 a Company of Savoyards and Piedmontese had been gathered at Rome under the title "The Holy Shroud," established as an "arch-confraternity" in 1597. This blanket organization had its headquarters in the Church of the Holy Shroud ("Santo Sudario"), the religious reference point of the Savoyan subjects who resided in Rome. After the Roman Veronica shroud was said to have disappeared in 1527, a new alternative cult centered on the Turin Shroud was able to be formed for the Romans.[25] The confraternity of Ciriè would seem to have gone extinct at some point in the seventeenth century, and that of Rome at the end of the nineteenth century.

A second restoration of the Shroud is worthy of mention, for which on December 18, 1595, papal authorization was requested: it was necessary in fact to adjust some parts of the Shroud that were damaged in the fire of 1532, "which, with lapse of time and with folding and unfolding, have become so extensive that they have great need of mending as soon as possible."[26]

3.1.2. Poetry and Literature Touching upon the Shroud

In literature in particular, the Shroud of Turin remained a permanent fixture as a source of poetic inspiration. This inspiration manifests itself in different compositions in Latin, beginning with those appended to the treatise of the historian Pingon, as well as others in

[25] Cf. G. Croset-Mouchet, *La Chiesa ed Arciconfraternita del SS. Sudario dei piemontesi in Roma* (Pinerolo: Lobetti-Bodoni, 1870); P. Cozzo, "Una chiesa sabauda nel teatro del mondo: La chiesa del Santo Sudario dei piemontesi a Roma da fondazione a cappella palatina," *Ricerche di storia sociale e religiosa* 30 (2002): 91–111; idem, "Il Santo Sudario dei Piemontesi: Identità e rappresentazione di una 'nazione' ambigua (secoli XVI–XVII)," in *Identità e rappresentazione: Le chiese nazionali a Roma, 1450–1650*, ed. A. Koller and S. Kubersky-Piredda (Rome: Campisano, 2015), 495–510; M. Tabarrini, "Carlo Rainaldi e i Savoia a Roma: La chiesa del Santo Sudario," in *Architetture di Carlo Rainaldi nel quarto centenario della nascita*, ed. S. Benedetti (Rome: Gangemi, 2012), 296–321; A. Serra, "Accesi di devoto affetto verso questa meravigliosa reliquia: The Roman Archconfraternity of the Most Holy Shroud's Devotional Choices and Strategies of Cult Promotion," in Cozzo, Merlotti, and Nicolotti, *Shroud at Court*, 214–37; on the fortune of the Shroud iconography in Rome, P. Caretta, "Se bene è nella città di Torino, nondimeno in qualche parte ne gode Roma: Some Considerations on the (Mis)fortune of Savoyard Iconography in Papal Rome," in Cozzo, Merlotti, and Nicolotti, *Shroud at Court*, 272–96.

[26] ASV, Segr. Stato Savoia, b. 33, f. 433r: "che con la lunghezza del tempo et col piegare e spiegare si sono tanto allargate che hanno gran bisogno di esser quanto prima accommodate."

French, Piedmontese, and Italian.[27] Among the last of these are certain memorable passages consecrated to the relic within a composition by Giovan Battista Marino dedicated at the end of 1608 to Charles Emmanuel I of Savoy. In this work the theme of the relic reached its fullest development, as it was said to have been painted with the blood of Christ as an instrument and a sign of the legitimacy of the family that would, by divine will, come to possess it as a powerful palladium, a defense from the enemy:

> And it was a fatal law, carved in heaven above in golden characters, perhaps from God, that the sacred impression of the wounds, formed on a white cloth, through which wounds from five broad channels His life poured in a bloody stream, was entrusted to no other hand on earth [than that of the Savoyard family]. O high treasure of an infinite price! O home loved by Heaven beyond every other! It was not a lowly work wrought by earthly hand, nor was it a flawed product of an obscure master. O image, whose painter was the lifeless Christ, whose brushes were nails and whose paint was the blood. This Shroud is a commemoration of love and a divine pledge such as to make the angels of Heaven envious, so that they would long to weave the veil out of the threads of such a noble linen, would long to weave robes, when spreading their wings in the highest orbits they assume a form visible to mortals. Among ancient memories let the lover of Hylas [Heracles] take pride in the pelt of the Nemean lion;[28] let [Jason] boast to have cultivated the soldiers like sprouts to win the precious thread of the golden fleece.[29] But let the possessor of the consecrated and blessed filaments call himself much happier than these. Elijah, a man of lively zeal and compassionate affection, left here as heir

[27] For a brief review of the poetic compositions in Latin, Italian, French, and Piemontese, cf. G. Gasca Queirazza, "Devozione alla Santa Sindone," *Studi Piemontesi* 27, no. 1 (1998): 3–4. For the seventeenth century, also in prose, cf. M. L. Doglio, "'Grandezze e meraviglie' della Sindone nella letteratura del Seicento," in Comoli and Giacobello Bernard, *Potere e la devozione*, 17–28. For a specific case, cf. A. Maggi, "The Word's Self-Portrait in Blood: The Shroud of Turin as Ecstatic Mirror in Emanuele Tesauro's Baroque Sacred Panegyrics," *Journal of Religion* 85, no. 4 (2005): 582–608. See also S. Grossmann, "The Sovereignty of the Painted Image: Poetry and the Shroud of Turin," in *From Rome to Eternity: Catholicism and the Arts in Italy, ca. 1550–1650*, ed. P. M. Jones and T. Worcester (Leiden: Brill, 2002), 179–222.

[28] Nemean lion, which Heracles killed during his first labor and whose pelt he used as a coat.

[29] Jason sowed the teeth of a dragon, which sprouted into an army of soldiers.

> of his own mantle his beloved [Elisha], when, entirely engulfed in flames, he was snatched up to heaven in an unusual way. The Redeemer left the bloody sheet to his beloved [the duke] on earth when he departed. The affectionate Jew [Veronica] had obtained previously the face of the eternal Sun, darkened with blood and sweat, received in a delicate veil, while He was running to the next sunset. He [the duke] is obtaining the likeness of the entire body, marked by scourges and suffering. So, with the favor of the guardian cloth, may he also live secure and content, because, when the bloody shade is unveiled, it puts greater fear into the barbarians than the eagles and dragons of the Roman standards do with their horrid and dim aspects. For no other reasons does it please me to believe that Heaven chose him [the duke] for such high fortune, if only because he could defend the triumphal flag against Parthian and Thracian, and, if so ordained among all the Kings, could become the standard bearer of the holy banner.[30]

Giovan Battista Marino will resume these very themes in a more developed prose form in the *Dicerie sacre* (*Sacred Discourses*) of 1614, one of which is entitled *La pittura* (*The Painting*) and dedicated to Charles Emmanuel I, Duke of Savoy. In it, the exaltation of the relic is a recurrent theme: "this venerable image, both with respect to the 'Painter,' and with respect to what is painted, is admirable. It is admirable because of the Painter, who is God, because of the painting, which is a divine form, and because of the thing painted, which is entirely divinity." Encomium is another recurrent theme: "to enrich the furnishing of his Church with an inestimable piece, it is enough that He left on earth this mysterious fabric adorned by his own hand, not with material and fleeting colors, but with immortal and divine hues, whose keeper you are, Most Serene Sire. . . . It seems to me excessive to remind you how remarkable a privilege of your Most Serene House to be destined to possess so notable a relic, adored by men, envied by the Angels, a peculiar sign and pledge of the immense love of God." The argument that the poet makes about the Palladium runs thus:

> And if the whole universe could be made safe beneath so faithful a defense, just how much more can and must the city of Turin be held secure, preserved by such a powerful guardian? If the

[30] G. B. Marino, *Il ritratto del serenissimo Don Carlo Emanuello Duca di Savoia* (Turin: n.p., 1608), vv. 197–204; ed. G. Alonzo (Rome: Aracne, 2011), 106–7.

colored arch of the rainbow, placed among the clouds of heaven, was the proof of God's peace with men, why shouldn't this veil, so well depicted, placed among the mountains of the earth, give us an indication of the friendship of God with the citizens of Turin? If the doorframes marked with the Lamb's blood were exempt from the anger of the Angel of Death,[31] why wouldn't the doors of Turin, which enclose the bloody remains of this salutary victim, be free of any scourge? If the scarlet cord hanging from the window of Rahab was a sign for her house to be spared in the sack of Jericho,[32] why wouldn't this bandage, dipped in the blood of Christ, keep Turin safe from the wrath of disrespected Heaven? If the doctoral purple, placed by Ulpian the jurist against the onslaught of armed soldiers who were pursuing the Emperor Severus, checked their audacity and caused them, out of reverence for him, to desist from their temerity,[33] why wouldn't this purple mantle, tinged with that holy color, about which I reasoned earlier, on its own authority be able to defend Turin from the arms of all who might wish to overrun it? If the statue of Pallas [Athena] placed in the temple of Ilium was a defense for the fortresses of Troy against the swords of the Greeks,[34] why won't this portrait of the true God, displayed in the center square of Turin, be a shelter against the ranks of the barbarians? If the image of the Mother, transferred by Aladdin to the profane mosque,[35] was a fateful guardian for the walls of Jerusalem, why wouldn't the image of the Son, carried to the sacred church of Charles, not guard Turin from all injuries and enemy snares? If the shield on which Jupiter was carved, believed to be celestial by Numa Pompilius, had the power to keep Rome from any misfortune,[36] why wouldn't this implement, wrought by the Maker of Heaven and painted with his true portrait, not have power to protect Turin from any adversity? If Demetrius did not want Rhodes to be consumed by fire, though he was able to

[31] Exodus 12:7, 13.

[32] Joshua 2:18.

[33] According to the *Historia Augusta*, Ulpian frequently protected Severus Alexander from the soldiers' ill will by sheltering him under his own purple robe (Aelius Lampridius, *Alexander Severus* 51).

[34] The Palladium, a statue on which the safety of Troy was said to depend.

[35] According to Torquato Tasso, *Gerusalemme liberata* 2, Aladdin, the Saracen king of Jerusalem, had stolen an image of the Virgin from a Christian church and set it up in a mosque, after being told by a sorcerer that the Virgin would then forsake the Christian army and favor the Muslims.

[36] The Ancile was a sacred shield kept in the Temple of Mars, which fell from heaven during the reign of Numa Pompilius, the second king of Rome.

> destroy and conquer it, in order not to burn the Bacchus of Protogenes, and did not mind losing the battle in order to avoid losing the painting,[37] why would the sword of divine Justice not forgive Turin for having regard for this glorious painting, made not by human hands, but by the very hand of God? Accordingly, o Turin, live in safety while taking refuge under the protection of such a shield. Have no fear that the injuries of Fortune prevail against you or the assaults of the enemies offend you. For I speak not only of the weapons of worldly armies and the gathering of the infernal forces, but in fact of the avenging lightning bolts of the arm of God in his wrath, for these will render you respect, while those vengeful weapons, in turn, will return blunted and dull.[38]

The same Charles Emmanuel I was the author of verses about the Shroud, some still unpublished,[39] and he sustains the theme of the Shroud as a painting wrought with blood:

> O cloth, or rather, O printed book in which wonderful and at the same time prodigious blood can be seen with amazement and contentment. You are the lofty and marvelous gift of God that opens Heaven to us. In this sworn pact His torment has been written, with such blood-red ink, with efficacious marks.

Emphasizing at some length the mixture of the blood of Christ and the cry of the Madonna, he writes:

> And staining the white linen a thousand times with precious and rare pearls that, alas, go pouring out from her eyes, she is

[37] According to Aulus Gellius, *Noctes Atticae* 15.31, during the siege of Rhodes, when Demetrius Poliorcetes was told that the Ialysus of Protogenes (sometimes considered to be a painting of Bacchus) was in a part of the town exposed to attack, he changed his plan of operations.

[38] G. B. Marino, *Dicerie sacre del Cavalier Marino* (Turin: Pizzamiglio, 1614); G. Pozzi, ed., *Dicerie sacre* (Turin: Einaudi, 1960), 73–201 (quotes from 89, 87, 189, 175–76). See also M. Fumaroli, "De l'icone en negatif a l'image rhetorique: Les autoportraits du Christ," in *L'immagine di Cristo dall'acheropita alla mano d'artista dal tardo Medioevo all'età barocca*, ed. C. L. Frommel and G. Wolf (Vatican City: Biblioteca Apostolica Vaticana, 2006), 441–48; E. Ardissino, "Le Dicerie sacre del Marino e la predicazione di primo Seicento," in *Marino e il Barocco, da Napoli a Parigi*, ed. E. Russo (Alessandria: Edizioni dell'Orso, 2009), 165–83; F. Giunta, "La 'Pittura' di Giovan Battista Marino: Note sull'adorazione della Sacra Sindone tra Cinque e Seicento," *Studi e problemi di critica testuale* 95 (2017): 127–48.

[39] AST, Storia della Real Casa cat. III, manuscripts of Carlo Emanuele I, no. 15.3.

> embroidering the cloth all around with quilting sown by her suffering, having distributed the drops to form a beautiful work, encircling it with the ruby drops of that blood whereby the sorrowful image was wrought.[40]

And he does not fail to touch upon the militaristic theme:

> Cloth, yes, but in fact it is a broad and sacred banner, under which the Christian ought to wage war. It is the famous labarum of the cross [the Chi Rho], a source of awe in the face of insane barbarian rage. That cloth, which you gave us in the Great Judgment, is a faithful banner, secure and victorious against the wicked and proud Enemy, that it might serve as a sign, that it might serve as pledge, so that such a furious devourer (alas!) not ruin us on that great day; but let it be as when there was a colored sign and the household was saved.[41]

Another item of curiosity is a poem, also by Charles Emmanuel, in which the author tries to identify the presence of the signs of the zodiac at various points on the cloth and the image.[42]

The reading of these texts reminds us that here, as in previous writers, the image of the Shroud was considered to have been the result of its being in contact with a body dripping with blood, sweat, and spices. A famous miniature by Giovanni Battista della Rovere (approx. 1625–1630) represents the way in which, at the time, it was thought that the body of Christ had been wrapped at the foot of the cross and afterwards had left vestiges.[43] It was believed that it was there, and not inside the tomb, that Jesus had imprinted the image on the fabric. Three hundred years later that notion had to be abandoned, as the idea that the image was produced by simple contact between the skin and the canvas came to be seen as a geometric impossibility. But to tell the truth many in the sixteenth and seventeenth centuries had already realized the difficulty and had to postulate

[40] M. Guglielminetti, "Carlo Emanuele I scrittore," in Ricuperati, *Storia di Torino*, 3:662–63.

[41] L. C. Bollea, ed., "Le idee religiose e morali di Carlo Emanuele I duca di Savoia," *Rivista d'Italia* 10, no. 7 (1907): 930. The final line here is a reference to the lintels stained with blood to avert the Angel of Death during the Passover.

[42] Cf. S. Mamino, "Carlo Emanuele I e lo Zodiaco della Sindone," in Comoli and Giacobello Bernard, *Potere e la devozione*, 29–46.

[43] Photograph in Scott, *Architecture for the Shroud*, plate 4.

that God himself had painted the image in a supernatural way, using blood as color but making it settle on the fabric in an unnatural way so as to avoid deformity, because if it had been stained in a natural way, the stains on the cloth would have been geometrically malformed.[44]

3.1.3. The Construction of a Legend and Theological/Exegetical Reflection

During the sixteenth century the history of the Shroud undergoes a radical process of suppression and subsequent reconstruction. This reconstruction was engendered by the Savoyard dynasty's acquisition of the Shroud and, what is more, its transfer to Turin; all of this overshadowed the troubled vicissitudes of the preceding two centuries and left space for new, peaceful, admirable, and glorious events that obscured the Shroud's time in Lirey. As early as 1518 there was a warning sign. When the cardinal Luigi d'Aragona went to Chambéry, he was told of the relic's origin, namely that the Savoys had taken possession of it during a military expedition with the brothers Godfrey of Bouillon and Baldwin of Boulogne. In this explanation, based on the legendary participation of Humbert II, Count of Savoy, in the First Crusade, they obtained it from a woman who had sold it in exchange for the liberation of her husband from imprisonment (perhaps an unrecognizable distortion of the events of Marguerite de Charny).[45] Such examples of legend found a very powerful means of amplification in publications that abundantly flourished in the sixteenth and seventeenth centuries.[46]

In 1578 Francesco Adorno, on the occasion of Charles Borromeo's visit to Turin, presented two possible "traditions" for the acquisition of the Shroud.[47] The first tradition posits that the Shroud was left to the Savoys by Charlotte of Lusignan, queen of Cyprus, cousin and wife of

[44] This aspect is considered in greater depth in A. Casper, "Made Not Begotten: The Shroud of Turin as Divine Artifice," in idem, *The Shroud of Turin as Art, Icon, and Relic in Early Modern Italy*, in preparation.

[45] Cf. Chastel, *Luigi d'Aragona*, 249.

[46] Cf. Zaccone, *Contributo allo studio delle fonti edite*, 35–73, who reviews 111 publications.

[47] [Francesco Adorno], *Lettera della peregrinatione di Monsignore illustrissimo cardinale di S. Prassede, arcivescovo di Milano: Per visitare la sacra Sindone di Nostro Signore Giesù Christo a Turino* (Milan: per Pacifico Pontio, 1578), 1.

Louis of Savoy count of Geneva, who died in 1487. Yet this is an impossible account, given that the Shroud had been venerated a century before that time in Lirey. The second account suggests that the Shroud was donated by the grand master of the Hospitallers to that Duke of Savoy who saved Rhodes from the siege of the Turks. This explanation was formulated on the basis of the false legend, widespread at the time, that one of the Amadeuses of Savoy had been in Rhodes and had saved the Shroud.[48] Thus, the incorrect notion that the Shroud came to Savoy from the East became more and more widespread.

Borromeo's pilgrimage and the relic's transfer to Turin also provided the opportunity for writing the first book focused on the Shroud. The client was the garment's owner, the Duke of Savoy, and the author was Emmanuel-Philibert de Pingon (1525–1582), Baron of Cusy and court historian.[49] The book was begun in 1578 and was printed with the title *Sindon evangelica* ("The Shroud of the Gospel") in 1581 exclusively on the order of Charles Emmanuel I, who had to overcome the hesitation of the author, as Pingon was evidently not yet satisfied with the result obtained and refused to publish the work.[50] The author dedicated the work to the two sons of the aristocrat of Chambéry who had dragged the Shroud from the flames a few decades before: both were bishops, one from Nice, the other from Saint-Jean-de-Maurienne. The book came out at the same time as another of his writings, *Arbor gentilitia* ("Family tree"), in which the legitimization of the Savoy dynasty passed through the creation of an illustrious but spurious Saxon genealogy.[51]

Pingon's work has been widely criticized since the nineteenth century because, apart from its obviously encomiastic character, it is lacking in method, is often inaccurate, is disordered and uncritical, and is "rife more with the vagaries of civic or national mythology than

[48] Hence the incorrect interpretation of the motto of the House of Savoy, F.E.R.T., as *fortitudo eius Rhodum tenuit* ("his strength conquered Rhodes").

[49] A Pingon biobibliographical reference can be found in R. Quaglia, *Filiberto Pingone*: *La Sindone dei Vangeli* (London: Lulu, 2010), XX–XXXIII; see also M. Lucianaz, "Sulle vicende editoriali del trattato Sindon evangelica," *Sindon* 12 (1999): 19–31.

[50] Pingon, *Sindon evangelica*.

[51] Pingon, *Inclytorum Saxoniae, Sabaudiaeque principum arbor gentilitia* (Turin: Bevilaqua, 1581); cf. L. Ripart, "Le mythe des origines saxonnes des princes de Savoie," *Razo* 12 (1992): 147–61.

with serious historiographical intentions."[52] Pingon, who enjoyed free access to documents of the ducal archives, was a keen researcher of manuscripts, coins, medallions, and ancient epigraphs. He collected a great deal of material "but with little critical rigor and with a predisposition to trust falsifications and legends," when he was not making them up himself.[53] In spite of such flaws, his work is a touchstone that mirrors both knowledge about the Shroud at that time and the growing importance that the relic came to assume in its new location in Turin. Unfortunately, however, Pingon was also responsible for the propagation of a largely misleading history of the relic: he believes that, after the death of Jesus, the Shroud remained in the Holy Land and that at the time of the First Crusade it passed into the hands of the Christian kings of Jerusalem. The kingdom of Jerusalem and of Cyprus between the eleventh and fifteenth centuries was an appanage of the House of Lusignan and came into the hands of Louis of Savoy count of Geneva in 1458 thanks to his aforementioned marriage to Charlotte of Lusignan.

The account maintaining that the Shroud remained in the East until this time superseded all other legends pertaining to shrouds that had arrived in the West previously (of which we have already spoken) and rendered those legends useless for constructing a history for our Shroud. According to Pingon, the precious relic arrived in Chambéry after the fall of Constantinople (1453) at the hands of the Ottoman Turks commanded by Mehmed II. At that time Louis I reigned over Savoy with his wife, Anne of Cyprus (Lusignan), the aunt of Charlotte. It is at this point that Pingon brings on stage, as it were, Marguerite de Charny, transforming her into a noblewoman from Greece:

> While nothing remained safe in Greece, Asia or Syria, and all were fleeing the cruelty of the most outrageous tyrant, an illustrious

[52] V. Castronovo, *Samuel Guichenon e la storiografia del Seicento* (Turin: Giappichelli, 1965), 94. See also A. Barbero, "Filiberto Pingone storico e uomo di potere," in *Imagines ducum Sabaudiae*, ed. M. Gattullo (Savigliano: L'artistica editrice, 2009), 9–13.

[53] M. L. Doglio, *La letteratura a corte*, in Ricuperati, *Storia di Torino*, 3:620. In the library of Pingon there were some manuscripts to which he added some false notes of possession ascribed to his ancestors; cf. *Il teatro di tutte le scienze e le arti: Raccogliere libri per coltivare idee in una capitale di età moderna* (Turin: Centro Studi Piemontesi, 2011), 64–65.

> noblewoman, by the name of Margaret of Carni, having gathered the luggage, in the midst of which she had placed this exceptional Shroud, decided to change her environs by leaving Greece and relocating to France. It turns out that she was descended from the kings of Jerusalem based on the fact that in the *History of Cyprus* she is called "of Jerusalem," married to Hector of Lusignan, the son of Philip: the circumstances fit all the details. I think that she is called "of Carni" because she was the ruler of Carina, a city of Ionia in Asia Minor, or of the Aeolian Carne, or even from Carne, which is a citadel of Phoenicia, located near Mount Lebanon. Others say that it is Burgundian because in that place there was a family of her illustrious name, and from there she moved to Asia or was conducted to France from Asia. When the "carna" arrived in Italy and with long journeys passed over the Alps, she was welcomed to Chambéry (i.e., the palace of the dukes of Savoy) by Duke Louis and Duchess Anne of Cyprus, with every honor, as was appropriate to a highly important noblewoman and relative. Finally, she gave them the most holy gift of the Shroud.[54]

The information offered above, however, is far from accurate. As far as regards this Margaret, the wife of Hector of Lusignan, the author refers to a work by Stefano of Lusignan, which actually describes quite another Margaret, called Zorzalemi.[55] The other etymologies, too, are unreliable. Marguerite de Charny was French, as Charny was the name of a French town, with no connection to Greece.

In the modern era, those looking for a believable story to give credence to the Shroud have tried to salvage something from this story, assuming that Pingon confused Marguerite de Charny with Agnès de Charpigny, a woman of the nobility of Vostitsa in Achaia, the wife of Dreux de Charny, brother of Geoffroy I (and therefore aunt of Marguerite).[56] Agnès is, however, not Marguerite, and she was in

[54] Pingon, *Sindon evangelica*, 17.

[55] Stefano di Lusignano, *Chorograffia et breve historia universale dell'isola di Cipro* (Bologna: Benaccio, 1573), 79r.

[56] The idea had been presented by Du Teil, *Autour du Saint Suaire de Lirey*, 19–28; and was later reprised by B. Bonnet-Eymard, "Les témoignages historiques surabondent," *La contre-réforme catholique au XXe siècle* 271 (1991): 23; and by N. Currer-Briggs, *The Shroud in Greece* (London: British Society for the Turin Shroud, 1988). Also Zaccone, "Shroud from the Charnys to the Savoys," 390–97, devotes particular attention to this Greek trail, taking the hypothesis of Du Teil as his point of departure. Those who reject this explanation are A.-M. Dubarle, *Histoire ancienne du linceul de Turin*, vol. 2 (Paris: Guibert, 1998), 67; and D. C. Scavone, "Did Geoffroy I

any case already dead by 1453. Further, why would the Shroud have been in Vostitsa, in Achaia? If the relic had then been the property of Dreux and Agnès, it would have passed not to the lower branch of the family tree represented by Geoffroy de Charny but rather to their daughter Guillemette, their only heir. In 1359 or shortly before, the Greek fiefdom of Vostitsa was given to Marie of Bourbon, when Geoffroy was already dead, and Agnès de Jonvelle inherited what remained. In short, this line of inquiry renders the events even more unlikely than they already have appeared.[57]

But let us return to Pingon. On the same page where the above citation from the *Sindon evangelica* appears, the author reproduces the image of a coin depicting an angel that raises the Shroud as a trophy, which Louis must have minted in 1453 to celebrate the acquisition of the relic. That coin, although it has been reprinted many times in books dedicated to the Shroud, has never been discovered. Rather than a coin, it was probably a commemorative medallion, perhaps made after 1453, whose model was reproduced subsequently.

In his book Pingon also gives the date and place of the cession of the Shroud to the Savoys. The place of the delivery of the Shroud is wrong, since it was not Chambéry but Geneva. The date, however, would be correct—March 22, 1453—if there were not a printing error in Pingon's book. There it is written as 1452, not 1453; furthermore, in 1452 Marguerite was abroad.[58]

---

de Charny Obtain the Present Turin Shroud on the Smyrna Campaign of 1346" (2005), 7–11, www.shroud.com/pdfs/scavone2.pdf.

[57] Initially the Baron Du Teil believed that the Shroud had been taken by Geoffroy de Charny on his voyage to Cyprus. He had later elaborated on this "Greek theory" after having discovered that Dreux de Charny, the older brother of Geoffroy I, had been married to Agnès de Charpigny, the Lady of Vostitsa. Du Teil had been informed of this relationship by a friend, the duke Pierre Eugène of Bauffremont, a descendant of a Henry de Bauffremont who at the end of the fourteenth century had inherited the de Charny lordship by marrying Jeanne de Vergy, whose great grandfather was Dreux de Charny. But neither Bauffremont nor Du Teil had ever been able to find information about the provenance of the Shroud from Greece amidst the papers of the family, and in 1902–1903 they wrote to the Baron Manno stating that they were hoping to trace whence it came (specifically in Venice or in the Vatican). Their investigations, however, were fruitless (AST, Archivi privati, Manno, envelope 24, inserts 38 and 49; envelope 68, inserts 135 and 169/6; envelope 28, insert 74; CSS, Fondo Pia, 3.1.1.166 and 176).

[58] As regards the date, it is a question of the printing error, for in the same book, on p. 29 and in the illustration on p. 19, the author writes the year correctly.

With Pingon, the history of the sale of the Shroud to the Savoys assumes the traits of the "golden legend." Pingon sets aside—whether from ignorance or deliberate omission—the clashes in Lirey, the prosaic purchase of the Shroud by Louis of Savoy, the complaints of the religious officials, and the court decisions and excommunications, and he instead tells us a devotional story about a gift given by the will of heaven. Pingon tells of a certain Marguerite de Charny who was about to leave from Chambéry with the Shroud as her own precious relic enclosed in a golden box mixed in with her luggage, and he mentions some thieves who, due to the negligence of the Greek servants, managed to steal it. These thieves, afterward, once they had recognized the value of the cloth, decided to divide it in half. The hands of the one holding the scissors, however, were contorted with paralysis and were unable to cut the garment.[59] The other thief then tried to wash away the image from the fabric, but when he did so it became so brilliant that it blinded him. Meanwhile the duke and Marguerite sent a herald to announce solemn punishments for anyone who might try to acquire the stolen fabric, and a reward for anyone who should return the stolen item. At this point the thieves repented and returned the Shroud. Louis, given the importance of the relic, insistently asked Marguerite to give it to him, taking advantage of her kinship with his wife, Anne of Cyprus; Marguerite, however, was unwilling to separate herself from her treasure and instead prepared to leave Chambéry again. But when she left the city (through Porte de Maché, as will be specified in later books) the mule carrying the box with the Shroud dug in his hooves, revealing that he did not want to continue. Interpreting this as a mark of divine will, Marguerite had to yield and give the relic to the dukes of Savoy.

The notion of a sacred object that does not want to move, whether because of its weight or immobility, is a theme that is common to many miraculous stories that emphasize the idea of divine will in the preservation of an object. In that same year (1453) Turin also becomes the scene of a powerfully propagandized event that is the basis of the elaboration of the legend of the resounding "eucharistic miracle": a consecrated host, enclosed in a sacred golden vessel,

[59] In 1518 a variant on the story was recorded, according to which at the command of two brothers of the House of Savoy a tailor was sought to cut the Shroud with scissors, and he was rendered blind (Chastel, *Luigi d'Aragona*, 249).

stolen by sacrilegious hands, escapes from the booty of thieves and rises high in the sky, before the eyes of all. And in that place, half a century later, Charles Emmanuel I, Duke of Savoy, laid the foundation stone of the current Basilica of Corpus Domini. Also, in this case the legend—later recognized as invented—speaks of a mule that is no longer willing to move from the place where the miracle will occur.[60] Ever since the biblical story of the donkey of Balaam, such an account of a humanized animal had been a topos in literature dealing with supernatural themes: animals guide the lost, speak, disobey their master, and kneel before sacred objects.

Pingon's account is both quite imaginative and entirely practical in that it emphasizes how the Shroud and House of Savoy are two inseparable realities not left to the vagaries of history but rather dependent upon the will of heaven. That same will performed miracles through the holy relic: Pingon tells of four of them, in Latin prose and Phalaecian hendecasyllables. The first is dated to May 1533, when the young girl Fusina, daughter of William of Chambéry, falls ill to a half-paralysis; the second occurs in the following year, when a man is saved from a fall in the river thanks to the invocation of the Shroud; the third is the healing of some demoniacs in 1535; the last one occurs in 1581, when a mute regains the ability to speak.[61]

The author assures the reader that there was an eyewitness for all of these events. In sum, Pingon's book is not only the first significant example of a history of the Shroud composed in an encomiastic manner and with a sense of the miraculous, but it also is remarkable for its inclusion of poetry, as noted above. Pingon's poem, too, is followed by seventeen celebratory works by thirteen different authors, all in Latin.

[60] On the birth of the story, see F. Cognasso, "La tradizione storica del miracolo di Torino del 1453," *Bollettino Storico Bibliografico Subalpino* 51 (1953): 157–64; and R. Savarino, "Documenti e fonti storiche sul miracolo e la chiesa del Corpus Domini," in *La basilica urbana del Corpus Domini: Il miracolo di Torino*, ed. R. Savarino et al. (Turin: Allemandi, 2004), 17–35. A commission of the diocese expressly charged to examine the sources concluded that "the traditional account of the miracle does not offer proof of a verified historical event" ("Relazione al Consiglio presbiterale diocesano sul miracolo del SS. Sacramento," *Rivista diocesana torinese* 59 [1977]: 208–11).

[61] Pingon, *Sindon evangelica*, 31–34.

To offer greater access to these stories to those who did not know Latin, six years later Agostino Bucci, a doctor and orator in the Savoy court, wrote a brief treatise about the Shroud, thoroughly dependent on the work of Pingon, for the occasion of the display of the Shroud that accompanied the baptism of Philip Emmanuel, prince of Piedmont. Within it, not merely by chance, he dedicated ample space to the eucharistic miracle of 1453.[62] In this way, with only a few exceptions, Pingon's history became the official history of the Shroud. The miracle of the mule and the events involving the Greek matron were also repeated in 1596 by Giovanni Tonso, biographer of Emmanuel Philibert, Duke of Savoy, and then by Alfonso Paleotti, archbishop of Bologna, in 1598; by Giovanni Botero in 1603; by Prospero Bonafamiglia, Knight of Saints Maurice and Lazarus, in 1606 (in a book that was also translated into Spanish); by Innocenzo Baldi in the same year; by Jacques Gaultier in 1616; by Eugenio Quarantotto in 1642; by François Victon in 1634; and finally, by Michele Berod in 1648.[63]

This string of authors dependent on Pingon persists without interruption until a French author takes up the history of the Shroud and brings the focus of research again upon the original documents, which results in a completely different interpretation. Jean-Jacques Chifflet (1588–1660), a seventeenth-century physician, antiquarian, and archaeologist of Besançon, paid particularly careful attention to the history of shrouds, publishing in 1624 a treatise entirely dedicated to the sepulchral linen of Jesus.[64] Chifflet was distinguished from the

[62] Bucci, *Solenne battesimo del serenissimo prencipe*, 21r–29r; reedited with commentary by A. Nicolotti, "Breve trattato di Agostino Bucci sulla Sindone di Torino," *Segusium* 53 (2014): 77–98.

[63] Tonso, *De vita Emmanuelis Philiberti*, 209; Paleotti, *Esplicatione del sacro Lenzuolo*, 9–10; G. Botero, *Seconda parte de' prencipi christiani, che contiene i prencipi di Savoia* (Turin: Tarino, 1603), 511–13; Baldi, *Discorso intorno a' misteri*, 57; P. Bonafamiglia, *La sacra historia della Santissima Sindone di Christo Signor nostro* (Rome: Zannetti, 1606), 15–21; idem, *La sacra historia de la Sanctissima Sávana de Christo nuestro Senor* (Turin: Cavaleris, 1607), 13–19; J. Gaultier, *Tabula chronographica status ecclesiae catholicae a Christo nato ad annum MDCXIV* (Lyon: Cardon, 1616), 719–20; Quarantotto, *Sacra Sindone*, 28–29; Victon, *Histoire ou bref traité*, 50–58; M. Berod, *Le prerogative della Santissima Sindone in compendio* (Rome: stamperia della Reverenda Camera Apostolica, 1648), 20–23.

[64] Chifflet, *De linteis sepulchralibus*; it was also issued in a French summary, the work of André de Campans Parisien, with the title *Hierothonie de Jésus-Christ, ou discours des saincts suaires de Nostre Seigneur* (Paris: Cramoisy, 1631).

Savoyard historians in one essential way: he lived in a city where there was another shroud that claimed to be authentic. Yet this was not a problem for him, for he managed the delicate balancing act of considering them both "authentic."

Chifflet created for the shroud of his own town, Besançon, a story that called the First Crusade into question. He had no difficulty in recounting the hardly honorable past of the Turin Shroud. First, he refutes the historical reconstructions of Adorno and Pingon; then, indicating that he is in possession of the relevant documents (some of which Nicolas Camuzat had already published),[65] he goes on to narrate the particulars of the entire story clearly: Geoffroy de Charny, the foundation of the collegiate church in Lirey, the first exhibitions, the prohibition of Henry de Poitiers, the appeal to Cardinal de Thury, the intervention of the sovereign, the excommunication of Pierre d'Arcis, the bull of Clement VII of Avignon, the delivery of the relic to Humbert de Villersexel, the escape of Marguerite, the attempts of the canons to get back the relic, its arrival in the Sainte-Chapelle of Chambéry, and the fire of 1532.[66] Of all this Chifflet is well informed, but regarding the sale of the Shroud he admits that he lacks reliable reports. He speaks of a rumor according to which Marguerite supposedly went to the House of Savoy (to Chambéry, he believes, having been given that false impression by Pingon) to demand the release of a certain prisoner of the Greeks, the Turks, or someone else.[67] Some said that it was her husband, Humbert—a story that had already been told to to the cardinal Luigi d'Aragona, in Turin—but Chifflet recognizes it is not possible. Others say François de la Palud; yet this, too, is impossible, although behind this distorted account one might be able to glimpse a faded reference to François, who was not Marguerite's husband but rather her husband's heir, not a prisoner but rather an exile deprived of property.[68] For what follows, Chifflet does nothing but paraphrase Pingon. All that remains of his book is an attempt to support the authenticity of all burial relics in circulation in Europe.

Accordingly, after 1624, revisions to Pingon's story began. Agaffino Solaro di Moretta, advisor to Maurice, cardinal of Savoy and bishop

[65] Camuzat, *Promptuarium sacrarum antiquitatum*, 410v–425v.

[66] Chifflet, *De linteis sepulchralibus*, 89–107, 111–26.

[67] Chifflet, *De linteis sepulchralibus*, 108–10.

[68] Such is the reading of G. M. Zaccone, "Sindone di Torino e Sindone di Besançon: Appunti per una ricerca parallela," *Sindon* 9–10 (1996): 113.

of Fossano, had almost finished a book dedicated to the Shroud when he died in 1625. The book was published posthumously, with an interesting addition: the original historical part, written by the bishop, depended on Pingon, but the person who took charge of the publication after Solaro's death wanted to insert in the text a valuable corrective note by the Jesuit Pierre Monod, historian of the House of Savoy. Monod, asserting that he has consulted books and sources more reliable than Pingon, refutes the opinion of Pingon and Solaro regarding the coming of Marguerite from Greece; he thus conveys in summary fashion the true history of the Shroud, from Geoffroy de Charny up to the transfer to the House of Savoy; yet from that point on he perpetuates the false story of the arrival of Marguerite in Chambéry and of the theft of the Shroud and of its miracles.[69] In 1639 Agostino Calcagnino does the same thing in his book on the Mandylion of Genoa.[70] In 1660 Samuel Guichenon, historiographer of the Savoy court, would also confirm that the woman's origin was not Eastern but in fact French.[71] Similarly, two years later, François Capré, the master of the Chamber of Audit of Savoy, also did not fail to recount the events in Lirey. Capré denied the idea that Marguerite was from the East and again proposed the date of 1452 for the transfer of the relic, a date that originated from a minor printing error, as we discussed previously. For the rest he continued to follow Pingon. However, he admitted that when he consulted the ducal documents of the time he had not found any reference to the version of the story that he had recounted.[72] The legacy of Pingon is also noticeable in the writing of the Paduan abbot Giuseppe Pasini, who came to the University of Turin to teach Sacred Scripture and oriental languages and immediately was instructed by King Victor Amadeus II to write a history of the Shroud (which, however, would never be published). As far as concerns the ancient portion of the relic's history, Pasini offers

[69] A. Solaro, *Sindone evangelica, historica e theologica* (Turin: Cavaleriis, 1627), 69–75; Monod himself, years before, had followed Pingon: P. Monod, *Recherches historiques sur les alliances royales de France et de Savoye* (Lyon: Pierre Rigaud, 1621), 86–90.

[70] A. Calcagnino, *Dell'imagine edessena* (Genoa: Ferroni, 1639), 405–22.

[71] Guichenon, *Histoire généalogique*, 1:513.

[72] Capré, *Traité historique*, 394–96. But still in 1683 there were those who told the story of an Eastern Marguerite coming from Cyprus: O. Rinaldi, *Continuatione degli Annali ecclesiastici che comincia dall'anno MCXCVIII* (Rome: Masotti e Chellini, 1683), 604.

an account of the Shroud from its preservation by Nicodemus until, in 1187, the Christians abandoned Jerusalem and took it with them, among many other relics. Then, without clarifying how it happened, Pasini recounts the transfer to Geoffroy de Charny and, as Capré had already, from here on follows Chifflet for the events until 1453, and Pingon from that date onward.[73]

In essence, therefore, historians generally were content to accept the story of Pingon, perhaps—but not always[74]—correcting only the part that concerned the events of the Shroud when it was in the hands of the Charny family. We thus find complete freedom for the historian who chose to treat the centuries that preceded this period: from the preservation of the Shroud in the hands of Saint Mary or Nicodemus, to the age of the Crusades, when there is nothing on the Shroud except for "the darkling shadow of profound silence," each writer could dubiously advance "very forceful conjectures" as he saw fit.[75]

But the history of the Shroud is not the only aspect of the relic subject to reevaluation: between 1590 and 1630 we see the publication of two treatises that deal with other themes pertaining to the relic. For example, the archbishop of Bologna Alfonso Paleotti (1531–1610), obeying the command of the Madonna conveyed to him in 1590 by the mystic Giovanni Francesco Parenti of Bolsena, provided the first careful description of the Shroud, enriched with numerous, erudite quotations from the Scriptures and the works of the fathers and mystics of the Church. The work, after a good deal of research by the author, was published in 1598, even though some "risky" parts, insofar as they were nontraditional, seemed to ecclesiastical censors to be unbecoming: for example, Paleotti claims that there were four, not three, nails of the cross, that Christ's wrists and not his palms were pierced, and that his teeth had been broken by beatings. The visionary mystic Giovanni Francesco let Alfonso

[73] See the edition of Navire, *Storia della Santissima Sindone di Torino*, 53–118.

[74] For example, the eighteenth-century copyist of the report of the Poor Clares of Chambéry (1534) relates that, after the Fourth Crusade, the Franks left the Shroud to the Lusignan, and in the middle of the fifteenth century Charlotte of Lusignan came to Savoy accompanied by Princess Marguerite de Charny, her relative; Chevalier, *Autour des origines du suaire de Lirey*, doc. P. Instead F. Avondo, *Per la Santissima Sindone esposta al pubblico culto* (Turin: Derossi, 1775), 34–41, repeats the account of Pingon with a minimal mention in a note of the French events.

[75] Solaro, *Sindone evangelica*, 75 and 77.

know that the devil had taken action so that his book "would declare falsehood and would not sell"; yet the Virgin Mary herself, appearing to the archbishop with the book in her hand, assured that the pope would grant a reprint amended in the above points, not because they were wrong, but because the people were not ready to accept them: the truth would be restored "in its own time." Thus in 1599 the book came out in a second modified edition, with two completely rewritten chapters.[76] The intent of the work, which was written in the vernacular, is purely spiritual and edifying: the description of each wound of Christ provides a powerful catechetical and pastoral means to induce meditation on the passion. The work was a great editorial success and was translated into Latin with lengthy annotations by Daniele Mallonio. The book would also be produced in this annotated form in French and German, clearly intended for a learned audience.[77]

The second volume that is worthy of note is the aforementioned posthumous treatise of Agaffino Solaro.[78] The main purpose of that work, which bridges the gap left by Pingon and Paleotti, is a theological reflection on the Shroud treating the legitimacy of the worship of the blood of Christ, the kind of adoration that should be offered to the relic, the cult of icons, and, finally, the providential connection of the Shroud with the House of Savoy. Solaro is also noted for an innovative theory that explains how the image was impressed upon the canvas. Unlike the other authors, Solaro believes that the image is not due to the contact with the bloody body of Christ after its deposition from the cross but the result of a miracle that came to pass entirely at the moment of the resurrection. Owing both to its approach and to its content, Solaro's work is still of interest today. The part that is perhaps most dated is that in which Solaro employs

[76] Paleotti, *Esplicatione del (sacro) Lenzuolo*, 1598 and 1599 editions. Cf. M. Fanti, "Genesi e vicende del libro di Alfonso Paleotti sulla Sindone," in *La Sindone: Scienza e fede*, ed. L. Coppini and F. Cavazzuti (Bologna: Clueb, 1983), 369–79 (p. 373 cited here). For the second edition of the book, we have two modern anastatic reprints.

[77] A. Paleotti and D. Mallonio, *Iesu Christi crucifixi stigmata Sacrae Sindoni impressa* (Venice: apud Baretium, 1606); idem, *Tableau de mortification tiré sur l'histoire miraculeuse des stigmates de Iésus Christ* (Paris: Foucault, 1609); idem, *Beschreibung der h. Leinwath oder Grabtuchs Christi* (Augsburg: Christoff Mang, 1607).

[78] Solaro, *Sindone evangelica*; cf. G. M. Zaccone, "Un manuale del Seicento del vescovo di Fossano Agassino [*sic*] Solaro di Moretta sulla Sindone," in *In sequela Christi*, ed. O. Aime, G. Ghiberti, and G. Tuninetti (Cantalupa: Effatà, 2003), 669–91.

all his energies to refute the criticisms of the Protestants, especially those of the Calvinists. Sebastian Valfrè, later beatified, was largely inspired by this treatise, once it had been opportunely expurgated of the most controversial parts. Based on it, he would write his own treatise, which he used for the spiritual education of the two daughters of Victor Amadeus II, Marie Adélaïde and Maria Luisa.[79]

3.1.4. The Copies and the Shroud of Besançon

The Shroud of Chambéry-Turin—the only one to have borne the image of the body of the crucified Christ—had become famous throughout Europe from the time it came into the possession of the House of Savoy. In various cities there were chapels and churches dedicated to the Holy Shroud. Moreover, there were copies painted on cloth in circulation, many copied from the original with the same dimensions. So far, more than fifty have been discovered. We know that one copy, not yet identified, was made by the Flemish painter Bernard van Orley on behalf of Margaret of Austria.[80] Another was produced in 1502, again for Margaret, and was sent to Brescia to the Augustinian mystic Laura Mignani, sister-in-law of Elisabetta Gonzaga; it still existed at the end of the eighteenth century.[81] The oldest surviving copy among those that bear a date is from 1516 and is preserved in the Church of Saint-Gommaire in Lierre, Belgium; in the past it was attributed to Albrecht Dürer or identified with that of Orley, yet the evidence of such identification is not sufficiently convincing.[82] Two life-size copies in Noalejo, Spain, dated 1527, are thought to have been transported by Mencía de Salcedo, lady-in-waiting of Isabella of Portugal, queen of Spain. Some believe that

[79] Cf. G. M. Zaccone, "Una composizione del Beato Sebastiano Valfré sulla Sindone," *Studi Piemontesi* 13, no. 2 (1984): 379–86.

[80] Bill of sale published in J. J. Altmeyer, "Marguerite d'Autriche gouvernante des Pays-Bas," *Revue belge* 15 (1840): 48: "Une belle painture faicte à remembrance du Sainct Souaire sur taffetas blancq."

[81] Cf. C. Doneda, *Notizie istoriche del monastero di Santa Croce di Brescia* (Brescia: Bossini, 1764), 125–26. Some have regarded this copy to be the same as that of Bernard van Orley.

[82] Cf. A. Thiéry, *Une copie du suaire de Turin exécutée en 1516 et actuellement dans les archives de l'église Saint-Gommaire à Lierre* (Louvain: Nova et vetera, 1912); A. M. Colombo, "La più antica copia della Sindone: L'esemplare di Lier," in *La Sindone nei secoli nella collezione di Umberto II* (Turin: Gribaudo, 1998), 218–20 (with photograph).

others were made before the fire of 1532, but there is no evidence.[83] In addition, at the very time the Shroud was in Chambéry, after the fire, Spanish copies appeared in Madrid (1567), Guadalupe and Navarrete (1568), and Alcoy (1571).[84] It continued to be reproduced after its transfer to Turin. A copy donated by the Duke of Savoy to Charles Borromeo dates to 1581 and is located in Inzago; others are in Toledo (before 1587), Puebla de los Angeles (1595), Ripalimosani (1595–1601), Plasencia (1612), Lisbon (1620), and Torres de la Alameda (1620). In the years following, the number of these replicas increased exponentially.[85] Some of these shrouds bear an inscription with the date and place of production, but others lack such identifying features. Often copies were sent upon request to monarchs, princes, ambassadors, and prelates. These could be considered true relics simply because, after they had been painted, they were put in contact with the original (the last time such spiritual transference occurred was 1978). Sometimes it was said that the image of the copy was miraculously replicated, without human intervention, just by contact. That a copy was not considered merely an artistic handicraft is confirmed by the fact that when Emmanuel Philibert made a copy for his cousin Philip II of Spain, he wanted the painter to work bareheaded, kneeling and

[83] It is said that the copy preserved in the monastery of the Mother of God at Xabregas (today in the National Museum of Lisbon) was a gift of the emperor Maximilian I († 1519) to his cousin Eleanor of Viseu (see J. de Belém, *Crónica seráfica da Santa Província dos Algarves* [Lisbon: no Mosteiro de São Vicente de Fora, 1755], 27); some date it to 1507 (Leone, *Santo Sudario en España*, 178–81). There is no proof, however, that the report is authentic (see F. de Mély, "L'histoire d'un suaire: Le Saint Suaire d'Enxobregas," *Revue Archéologique* 40 [1902]: 55–61).

[84] Cf. A. Pérez de Tudela Gabaldón, "Copies of the Holy Shroud for the Court of King Philip II of Spain (1527–1598)," in Cozzo, Merlotti, and Nicolotti, *Shroud at Court*, 313–34.

[85] Thores (1621), Logroño (1623), Summit (1624), Rome (1626), Moncalieri (1634), Castillo de Garcimunoz (1640), Turin (1643), and others. Although incomplete, see L. Fossati, "Le copie della Sacra Sindone a confronto con l'originale," *Sindon* 3 (1991): 33–56; idem, "Le copie della Santa Sindone a grandezza naturale," www.shroud.it/FOSSAT10.PDF; cf. also F. Molteni, ed., *La memoria di Cristo: Le copie della Sindone* (Siena: Santa Maria della Scala, 2000); also, P. Cozzo, "'Et per maggior divotione vorrebbe che fusse della medesima grandezza et che avesse tocato la istessa santa Sindone': Copie di reliquie e politica sabauda in età moderna," *Annali di Storia moderna e contemporanea* 16 (2010): 397–410.

surrounded by candles and priests in prayer.[86] The study of these copies is interesting because it can give us an idea of how the Shroud appeared when they were made; one must pay close attention, however, as the replicas are often not very faithful reproductions. For example, many depict a band around the waist that in the original is not there and was not visible at the time.[87] The copies of the Shroud, in addition to being intended for devotional purposes, were also used as an instrument by the Savoy to establish relations with the other European princes and sovereigns. The offering of these artifacts and their distribution was not indiscriminate but responded to obvious political and diplomatic reasoning. It is no coincidence that many pictorial copies are found in the Iberian Peninsula and in the domains of the House of Habsburg: during the sixteenth century the Savoy had found in the Habsburgs the main supporters of their policy of ascent and the most faithful allies against French expansionism; this alliance saw its greatest expression in the marriage of Charles Emmanuel I to Catherine Michelle of Habsburg. Further, the contacts between the House of Savoy and Bavaria—an ever-increasing geopolitical reality—were accompanied by a marked increase in signs of devotion to the Shroud in Munich and Bavaria and reached an apex in the marriage of Henriette Adelaide of Savoy and Ferdinand Maria of Bavaria. The promotion of the cult of the Shroud, with the aim of implanting it in lands in which other analogous cults existed and were already well established, reveals itself to be a complex exportation of a dynastic devotion.[88]

A shroud similar to that of Turin, perhaps one of its undated copies, appeared in the city of Besançon in the first quarter of the sixteenth century and also became famous, as if it were the original, to the point that it could compete with that of the Savoy. The history of this shroud is very informative because it reveals how relatively

[86] The account of Bonafamiglia, *Sacra historia della Santissima Sindone*, 25–27. Similarly, when in 1616 the canon Pietro Strozzi had to make a copy of the Vatican Veronica, he did not begin his work without having first confessed and taken the sacrament.

[87] Already Avondo, *Per la Santissima Sindone*, 31–32, assures us that such a band is not on the original.

[88] Cf. Cozzo, "'Et per maggior divotione,'" 397–410; idem, "Idiomi del sacro fra Savoia e Impero (secoli XVI–XVII)," in *Stato sabaudo e Sacro romano impero*, ed. M. Bellabarba and A. Merlotti (Bologna: il Mulino, 2014), 271–96.

easy it was at the time to create a new relic and spread its cult by convincing the faithful of its authenticity. We only have descriptions and images of the Besançon shroud, for it was destroyed during the French Revolution (fig. 3.1).[89] This replica, which measured around 2.50 × 1.30 m, consisted of two pieces of cloth sewn lengthwise bearing the image only of the frontal part of Christ's body. The imprint of the body was yellow and was visible on both sides of the fabric. Unlike the Turin Shroud, that of Besançon showed no traces of the wounds from Christ's scourging but only the principal five wounds. Unlike the other shrouds and copies of which we have spoken that were scattered around Europe, this one did not yet exist in the Middle Ages, and the story behind it was invented only in modern times.

We know that from the eleventh century, every year at Easter in St. John's Cathedral at Besançon, there was a sacred representation called the *jeu* or *mystère de la résurrection*. One part of this show was an enactment of the discovery of the empty tomb of Jesus and the "shroud" found in the tomb. As already mentioned, this type of sacred representation spread throughout Europe from the tenth century on. We also know that in the middle of the thirteenth century in Besançon some of the acting roles were undertaken by children dressed as angels, and by three canons who personified the three Marys at the tomb, dressed in white, with their heads covered by veils. One of them displayed to the faithful the shroud that had been left in the tomb, as a testimony to the resurrection; it was the size of an amice—that is, of that liturgical vestment of white cloth that surrounds the neck and shoulders of priests. As it was of rather small

[89] Cf. P. C. Guibard, "L'ostension du Saint-Suaire," *Annales Franc-Comtoises* 4, no. 7 (1867): 321–26; also, J. Gauthier, "Notes iconographiques sur le Saint Suaire de Besançon," *Proces-verbaux et memoires—Academie des sciences, belles-lettres et arts de Besançon* (1883): 288–327; idem, "Le Saint Suaire de Besançon et ses pèlerins," *Mémoires de la Société d'émulation du Doubs* 7 (1902): 164–85; J. Guillaume, "Le Saint-Suaire de Besançon," *La revolution française* 43 (1902): 5–16; P. Vignon, *Linceul du Christ*, 2nd ed. (Paris: Masson, 1902), 135–54 (English translation: *The Shroud of Christ* [Westminster: Constable, 1902], 61–76); idem, *Le Saint Suaire de Turin*, 2nd ed. (Paris: Masson, 1939), 105–8; [A. Blanchet], *Un document sur le Saint-Suaire de Besançon, 1439–1794* (n.p., 1909); M. Spinelli-Flesch, "Le saint suaire de Besançon," *Barbizier* 28 (2004): 27–51; V. Marcelli, "Les images du saint suaire de Besançon," *Barbizier* 28 (2004): 53–102; de Vregille, *Du Saint-Suaire de Lirey*, 17–25; idem, "L'apparition du Saint-Suaire," in *La cathedrale Saint-Jean de Besançon*, ed. B. de Vregille et al. (Besançon: Renaissance du Vieux Besançon, 2006), 59–60.

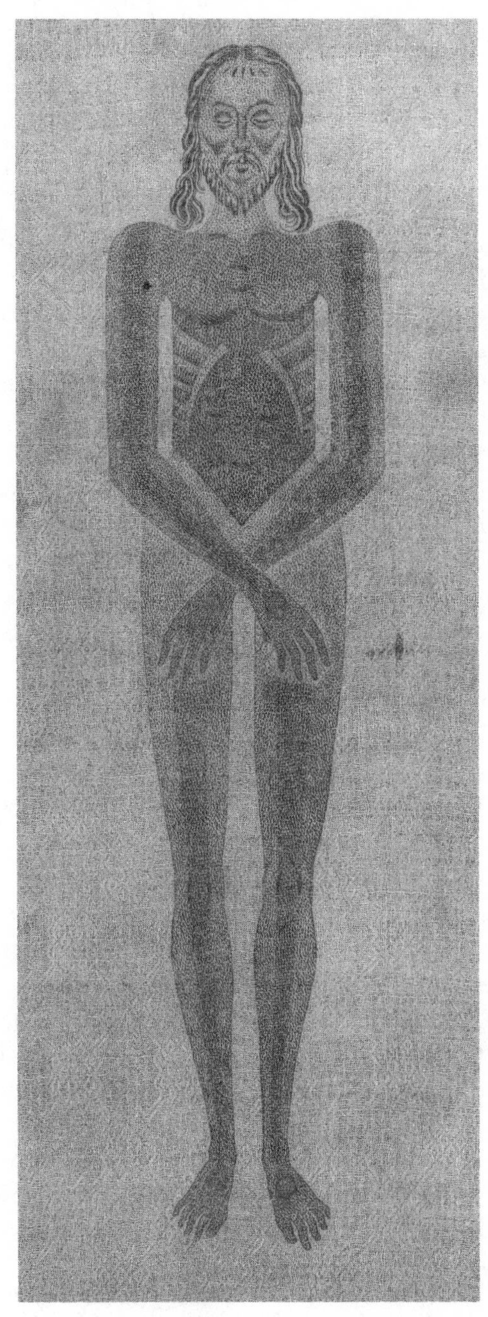

FIGURE 3.1 Pierre de Loisy (?),
Copy of the Besançon Shroud

dimensions, only one canon was required to show it.[90] The demonstration took place only once per year and was not accompanied by any exhibition of relics.

In Besançon, after the year 1500, the *mystère* fell into disuse. In 1519 there was some discussion of restoring it, but nothing came of the proposal; in March 1523, however, a canon was sent to Dijon to retrieve the theatrical text (along with the music to perform it) to stage it again. This time, however, the production took place no longer at St. John's Cathedral but in the competing Cathedral of St. Stephen. Thus, there was need of a new cloth to be used as a representation of the shroud. Among the recorded deliberations of the metropolitan chapter of that year, where the planning of the next Easter *mystère* was discussed, mention was made of a "sudarium or shroud that used to be put on display"—referring therefore to the practice of undertaking the sacred representation— and instructions were given for it to be enclosed in a casket specially made and closed with three locks.

Accordingly, from the date of August 8, 1523, things change, for on that day it was established that on the occasion of the Easter holidays, of the Ascension, and of the discovery of the body of Saint Stephen, that shroud "could henceforth be revered and shown with the utmost devotion, with all due honor and reverence."[91] From then on, the cloth became the object of pilgrimages, and a terrace was later built outside the church to show it to the people, who were so numerous that they could not be contained within the church building. About thirty thousand pilgrims took part in the ceremony of 1533, and in 1544 a confraternity dedicated to the holy relic was established.

This point bears repeating: the shroud of Besançon with the image of Christ did not exist before 1523. It is never mentioned in the municipal or ecclesiastical records. No historian had ever spoken of it, and the liturgical books show that there is no trace of its veneration before the sixteenth century.[92] The shroud previously used for the staging of the *mystère* had no particular distinction, for it had never

[90] BMB, MS 98, f. 40; W. Lipphardt, ed., *Lateinische Osterfeiern und Osterspiele*, vol. 1 (Berlin: De Gruyter, 1975), 112–13 (manuscript is dated to slightly before 1253).

[91] The texts of the deliberations of the chapter are published by Gauthier, "Notes iconographiques," 290–92.

[92] See, for example, S. Legendre, *Nos decanus et capitulum Ecclesie Bisuntine: Le chapitre cathédral de Besançon, un corps social et son insertion dans l'État bourguignon (1404–1477)* (Ph.D. diss., Université de Franche-Comté de Besançon, 2011); also

received any act of veneration nor did it draw a crowd; a white veil that had only a symbolic value could not attract the faithful.

No contemporary document helps us understand precisely how it was possible for a cloth used for a theatrical representation to be transformed so quickly into a cloth that would be exhibited for veneration. What was the provenance of this shroud, which was now quite different from that of the thirteenth century? In 1573 it was spoken of for the first time as more than just any white cloth. Rather, it was now referred to as a painted linen with the image of the body of the dead Christ, like the Shroud of Lirey-Chambéry, which, at the time, had already become rather famous. The shroud of Besançon itself was, in all probability, simply a copy of that of Lirey-Chambéry-Turin, or a copy of a copy, or possibly a copy of a hypothetical model common to them both. For several years, starting from 1418, the Shroud of Lirey was kept at Saint-Hippolyte, not far from Besançon; for a time, Marguerite de Charny took it with her on her peregrinations throughout Europe, and by the sixteenth century it was located permanently in Chambéry. Most likely someone considered using a sheet painted with an image of Jesus, as on the already famous Shroud of Lirey, for the renewed holy exhibition of the Church of Saint Stephen rather than the simple white amice that was used in the Church of Saint John. It is because of such an evocative painting that soon the interest in the *mystère* gave way to veneration of the object per se.

However, like that of Lirey, the shroud of Besançon did not have a history, and it was therefore necessary to invent one.[93] Whence could that relic that had never been mentioned in the most ancient documents have come? It had not appeared in the ancient chronicles of the city and even in 1523 was still considered only an accessory useful for the staging of the paschal mystery. Louis Gollut made mention of it having arrived in the city in the fifth century, at the

R. Jurot, *L'ordinaire liturgique du diocèse de Besançon* (Fribourg: Éditions universitaires de Fribourg, 1999), 157–58.

[93] One cannot, therefore, say that in the Middle Ages there were two shrouds competing with one another—as does, for example, F. Cardini, "La Sindone: Note storiche," *Vita e pensiero* 72 (1989): 194—because that of Besançon did not yet exist, at least as a relic.

time of the bishop Celidonius.[94] In 1609 a canon of Besançon, François d'Orival, recounted a story that the shroud had been given to Emperor Honorius by the patriarch of Jerusalem; in 454 the empress Eudocia, wife of Theodosius II, then sent it via ambassadors to the bishop of Besançon, and in the presence of Galla Placidia, including also the arm of Saint Stephen, the head of Saint Agapitus, the bodies of the martyrs Epiphanius and Isidore, a piece of Christ's robe, and the comb and some hair of the Virgin Mary.[95] A few years after François, Pierre Despotots proposed the date of 447 for the transfer of the shroud.[96] Jacques Gaultier proposed an earlier date, 417, then later changed it to 439.[97] It is clear from the documents that in Besançon the veneration of the arm of Saint Stephen and the other strange relics mentioned by François had begun in the Middle Ages, well before that of the shroud: the shroud, therefore, was added to the preexisting relics only in the modern age.[98]

In 1624 the historian Jean-Jacques Chifflet rejected all these proposals and advanced the theory that in the first years of the twelfth century a canon of the Church of Saint Stephen bought the shroud in Palestine during the First Crusade.[99] A theory attested for the first time in 1714 by the Jesuit Pierre-Joseph Dunod[100] and revived in 1750 by his nephew François-Ignace Dunod de Charnage[101] had greater success: the shroud was taken from the emperor of Constantinople during the Fourth Crusade (1204) by the knight

[94] Cf. L. Gollut, *Les mémoires historiques de la république séquanoise et des princes de la Franche-Comté de Bourgougne* (Dole: Dominique, 1592), 52.

[95] F. d'Orival, *Le Sainct-Suaire de Besançon: Antiquité, miracles et vénérations d'icelluy*, BMB, MS Chiflet 4, ff. 168v–169v.

[96] P. Despotots, "Recueil de plusieurs choses mémorables appartenant à la cité selon le temps qu'elles sont passées," *Mémoires et documents inedits pour servir à l'histoire de la Franche-Comté* 7 (1876): 286.

[97] J. Gaultier, *Table chronographique de l'estat du christianisme depuis la naissance de Jésus iusque à l'année MDCXII* (Lyon: Roussin, 1613), 281; idem, *Table chronographique* [. . .] *iusque à l'année MDCLXXII* (Lyon: Arnaud & Borde, 1673), 381.

[98] In fact, a medieval hymn that lists the presumed relics brought to Besançon by Theodosius does not mention the shroud. Cf. G. M. Dreves, *Analecta hymnica Medii Aevi*, vol. 10 (Leipzig: Reisland, 1891), § 221.

[99] Chifflet, *De linteis sepulchralibus*, 52–54.

[100] *Dissertation sur le Saint-Suaire de Besançon*, BMB, MS 826, ff. 1–49.

[101] F.-I. Dunod de Charnage, *Histoire de l'église, ville et diocèse de Besançon*, vol. 1 (Besançon: Daclin, 1750), 408; taken up later by J. Richard, *Histoire des diocèses de Besançon et de Saint-Claude*, vol. 1 (Besançon: Cornu, 1847), 444.

Othon de la Roche-sur-l'Ognon, who afterward sent it to France to his father Pons in the family castle at Rigney in France (23 km from Besançon); in 1206 Pons finally donated it to the bishop of Besançon, Amédée de Dramelay (a transaction quite impossible, as Pons had already died in 1203).

This theory, entirely invented, is based on glaring falsifications of preexisting documents. That Pierre-Joseph Dunod was the author of this theory and that his work dated back to 1714 has been unknown until now; my detailed autopsy of the contents of manuscript 826 in the Municipal Library of Besançon provides a path to the author's identity and to the authentic sources that Dunod deliberately distorted.[102]

But how could these authors explain the centuries-old silence of the sources up to 1523? In this regard a fire in the cathedral during Lent in the year 1350 that is supposed to have destroyed all the documents must be called into question—fires are always a panacea for historians of relics who have a dearth of documents![103] In fact, in March of that year, probably on the sixth of the month, a fire broke out that caused much damage to both cathedrals in Besançon;[104] obviously the claim was made that during the fire the documents demonstrating the authenticity of the shroud went up in smoke, but the shroud itself was saved. Chifflet tells us that to preserve it from the fire, someone cast it into a hidden corner of the church (his French translator specifies that a canon did it, and then forgot to go and get it back!).[105] Although for a time everyone thought it was destroyed, a few years later the shroud would be found intact, emanating a divine light from the place where it was hidden and attracting the attention of the priests. Two excellent painters were then summoned who, having examined the image carefully, ascertained that it was made not with pigments or with human artifice but with blood and unguents. And from then on the relic would show its

[102] My own study on this topic has been published with an edition of the manuscript and a commentary: A. Nicolotti, *Le Saint Suaire de Besançon et le chevalier Othon de la Roche* (Vy-lès-Filain: Éditions Franche-Bourgogne, 2015).

[103] The sources say 1349 because according to that region's medieval reckoning the new year began at Easter.

[104] Cf. P. Gresser, *Calamités et maux naturels en Franche-Comté aux XIVe et XVe siècle* (Besançon: Cêtre 2008), 258–65.

[105] Chifflet, *Hierothonie de Jesus-Christ*, 48.

authenticity by healing the sick and even resurrecting the dead.[106] Beyond these fantastic events, Chifflet's book goes on to report all sorts of miracles.

But how long did the supposed blunder of the shroud's misplaced status continue after the fire? Chifflet said that it lasted only "a few years," yet the canon François d'Orival, in 1609, had written that the discovery of the relic had happened "around the year 1517," almost two centuries later. This is understandable, because he knew well that no documents, even those written after the fire, ever mentioned the shroud before the sixteenth century, and thus it was more convenient to maintain that it had remained hidden until then.[107]

How did the faithful of Besançon behave in the face of the coexistence of two famous shrouds, one in their city and one in Turin? Jean-Jacques Chifflet managed to declare them both authentic: that of Turin would have served to wrap the body of Christ deposed from the cross and to carry it to the tomb; that of Besançon, in turn—which for him is the sudarium of the Gospel of John—would then have covered only the front part of the body as it lay in the tomb.[108] This identification of the sudarium will later attract some criticism.[109] Chifflet's account explains why there are many signs of blood on the Shroud of Turin, while on that of Besançon there are only the signs of the five major wounds: the corpse, removed from the first shroud, would have been washed before being put into the second.

That shroud then remained in the Church of Saint Stephen until 1668, when it was transferred to the Cathedral of Saint John. It was presented as a source of glory for the city of Besançon, which was initially a center of the Habsburg tradition and later, in the sixteenth century, came under Spanish rule. Unlike Turin, however, Besançon did not have a single structured dynasty that could support an ideological and propagandistic infrastructure able to make Besançon's shroud competitive with other relics of Christ. In Spain the Savoy had already spread the cult of the Shroud of Turin, of which there were

[106] Chifflet, *De linteis sepulchralibus*, 66–71.

[107] D'Orival, *Le Sainct-Suaire de Besançon*, f. 172v.

[108] Chifflet, *De linteis sepulchralibus*, 40–49, 145–50.

[109] Cf. F. Quaresmio, *Historica theologica et moralis Terrae Sanctae elucidatio*, vol. 2 (Antverpiae: Moret, 1639), 529–40, in particular 537. The author—a Franciscan of the Holy Land—considers that it is possible that four fabrics simultaneously wrapped Jesus in the tomb: those of Besançon, Turin, Mainz, and Compiègne.

also several copies. After Besançon's annexation to France in 1676, the importance of the shroud of that city met a slow decline.[110] Exhibitions continued until, in March 1794, revolutionaries took control of the church and, rummaging through the archives, found a thick, perforated paper that could be used to make the drawing of the figure of Jesus (known as a *poncis*) and identified it—wrongly or rightly—as the model with which the canons periodically renewed the color of the imprint of the shroud. Some priests of Besançon, among those who had adhered to revolutionary ideals, confessed that they had long ago been convinced of the spuriousness of the relic. Sent to the National Convention of Paris, the Besançon shroud was judged to be a fake and was thus destined for destruction: the order was given to tear it up and make of it some bandages. We do not know exactly what happened to it after it was made into fabric, as in any case it was taken out of circulation.[111] Such was the inglorious end of one of the most famous image-bearing shrouds ever fashioned. Its adventures, however, are quite useful to illustrate how easy it was to invent a relic and to give it a story.

3.1.5. A New Chapel in Turin

Upon its arrival in Turin, the Lirey-Chambéry Shroud had been stored in the ancient chapel of St. Lawrence, near the north wall of the city. Later the duke had it moved "into a chapel next to his rooms, richly decorated,"[112] built in 1578–1580 on the noble floor of the ducal palace, in an area not far from the cathedral. In 1610, when the sacred linen was transferred to the cathedral, this chapel was converted into a wardrobe of the prince Victor Amadeus I. It seems we should abandon the idea, widespread even today, that the Shroud was kept in a circular room, with Ionic columns, probably a small temple with the accoutrements of a thermal bath, that was demolished in 1891.[113]

[110] Cf. P. Cozzo, "Le mille e una sindone," *MicroMega* 4 (2010): 63.

[111] The minutes of the period are published by J. Guillaume, *Études revolutionnaires: Première série* (Paris: Stock, 1908), 198–212. See also V. Petit, "À la recherche du Suaire perdu de Besançon: Enquête patrimoniale, enjeux identitaires," *Revue d'Histoire Ecclésiastique* 111 (2016): 92–114.

[112] Letter from the bishop of Mondovì of May 10, 1586; Savio, *Ricerche storiche*, 308.

[113] Cf. for example, Klaiber, "First Ducal Chapel," now refuted by new documentation presented by P. Cornaglia, "Museum versus Chapel of the Holy Shroud:

It was housed there only temporarily, until a new building could be constructed that would "accommodate a more dignified preservation of the Holy Shroud, which is not possible presently in the small chapel of the palace."[114] Cardinal Borromeo, eager to make a connection, even a visual one, between the Shroud and the local church, wished that the relic be placed inside the cathedral. He sent his architect, Pellegrino Tibaldi, to the duke to advise him of this proposition. The duke, however, had the idea of building a church and a monastery in the Piazza Castello specifically for the Shroud, and he commissioned Tibaldi to prepare a prospectus, which was afterward never executed. Meanwhile, between 1584 and 1587 the Shroud was kept in a wooden building inside the cathedral, above the high altar—which at the time receded further than the current one—consisting of four columns; these bore a balcony and a round temple surmounted by a dome supported by four seraphs, beneath which was the box that housed the relic; between 1607 and 1609 this structure was replaced by a construction more durable, designed by Carlo di Castellamonte, with a base of stone and four columns in Frabosa marble, featuring a wooden superstructure and a balcony. Everything would be demolished in 1685 to make room for the new chapel; on May 23 of that year the relic was moved to the ducal palace and then, on June 9, to the Chapel of Saints Stephen and Catherine, in expectation of its final location.[115]

The initial design of the duke was not able to be realized, but it remained his intention to create a new space for the Shroud that, by virtue of its being located between the ducal palace and the cathedral, would demonstrate the exclusive bond between the relic and the ruling house. In the early years of the seventeenth century several projects were undertaken, then abandoned, including those of Ascanio Vitozzi and Carlo di Castellamonte for an elliptical chapel to be erected at the back of the cathedral, behind the presbytery, with

---

The Octagonal Hall of the Palace of Victor Amadeus I, Duke of Savoy and King of Cyprus," in Cozzo, Merlotti, and Nicolotti, *Shroud at Court*, 335–53.

[114] Letter from the bishop of Mondovì of September 22, 1582; Savio, *Ricerche storiche*, 308.

[115] In addition to the general bibliography, see C. B., "L'antico coro del Duomo di San Giovanni," *Il Duomo di Torino* 2, no. 4 (1928): 9–17. The Chapel of Saints Stephen and Catherine stood at the end of the left aisle, where one of the two staircases now provides access the Shroud Chapel.

access to the nave of the church and also to the dukal palace, with a balcony to be used for the exhibitions. We know that Duke Charles Emmanuel I already in 1620 had clear ideas about his Sainte-Chapelle building: he envisioned a large chapel united with but, at the same time, distinct from the cathedral where the bodies of Saint Maurice and other saints could be placed to "guard" the Shroud in special side chapels; at the time he still lacked two bodies, but he was counting on them being taken from some abbeys.[116] The purpose is clear: make the chapel the attractive centerpiece of his own sacred collecting, on the model of the great sovereigns of the past. The presence of all the relics and the privileged bond shared with the most important dynastic relic was coming to fruition.

In the middle of the 1650s, just after the foundation of the new chapel had been finished, Amedeo di Castellamonte[117] and Bernardino Quadri were entrusted with a new project; but as for the work already underway, strong doubts arose about whether the building being constructed, a circular chapel, could support the planned dome. At this point, on May 19, 1668, Charles Emmanuel II appointed as the new architect of the chapel the Theatine friar Guarino Guarini, who gave the work its definitive shape. The chapel, which was finished in 1683, the year of the death of Guarini, has a circular plan and is raised above the foot traffic of the church so as to be in direct communication with the second story of the adjacent ducal palace and connect, concretely and symbolically, the Savoy family with its relic. The passage between the nave of the cathedral and the chapel is secured by two dark marble steps, giving the sensation of "ascending on earth," as Guarini himself wrote. From the nave of the cathedral one could admire the proscenium that opened on the chapel (at that

[116] Cf. G. Claretta, "Inclinazioni artistiche di Carlo Emanuele I di Savoia e de' suoi figli," *Atti della Società di Archeologia e Belle Arti per la Provincia di Torino* 5 (1887): 351–52.

[117] On the work of Carlo and Amedeo di Castellamonte in relation to the Shroud, see P. Cozzo, "Nella scia del 'pegno celeste': L'orizzonte della sacralità sindonica nell'opera di Carlo e Amedeo di Castellamonte (Chambéry, Torino, Roma)," in *Carlo e Amedeo di Castellamonte 1571–1683, ingegneri e architetti per i duchi di Savoia*, ed. A. Merlotti and C. Roggero (Rome: Campisano, 2016), 129–40; T. Wilke, "Planning Process of the di Castellamonte's Chapel of the Holy Shroud," in Merlotti and Roggero, *Carlo e Amedeo di Castellamonte*, 141–52. On the projects of Vitozzi, see T. Wilke, "Newly Found Plans for the Chapel of the Holy Shroud," *Studi Piemontesi* 46, no. 1 (2017): 75–85.

FIGURE 3.2 Jean Fayneau, based on a design by Guarino Guarini, cutaway drawing of the Chapel of the Holy Shroud in Turin

time the irritating split window, which was commissioned much later by Charles Felix in 1825, had not yet been installed): inside is a triumph of contrasts between light and shadow, brightness and dark (thanks to the use of precious Frabosa black marble), with a dome full of ascending arches and large windows ending in a telescoped and slender point (fig. 3.2). In the middle, on the dark floor in which bronze stars are set, reflecting the light that comes from above, a monumental baroque altar stands out, the work of Antonio Bertola. Construction of this piece began on October 18, 1687. The complex and allusive structure of the chapel reveals the emphasis that Guarini put on the use of geometry and light as a means to define divine architecture. A large reliquary in the form of a marble arch surmounts the altar, locked behind grating and plate glass; at its sides hang four large silver lamps that are perpetually lit. The Shroud was finally placed in its new home on the first of June, 1694.[118] We can infer from an engraving of that period what the faithful, crowded in the cathedral, could have seen of the various exhibitions that were made on the raised balustrade of the chapel that overlooked the nave (fig. 3.3).

The construction of the new chapel completely defined the sacred space of the relic and placed it in large part into a relationship with the court and the ducal palace. According to the plans of the years

[118] On the Turinese chapels of the Shroud, cf. N. Carboneri, "Vicenda delle cappelle per la Santa Sindone," *Bollettino della Società Piemontese di Archeologia e Belle Arti* 18 (1964): 95–109; L. Tamburini, *Le chiese di Torino dal Rinascimento al Barocco*, 2nd ed. (Turin: Angolo Manzoni, 2002), 254–68; M. Momo, *Il Duomo di Torino: Trasformazioni e restauri* (Turin: Celid, 1997), 67–114; J. B. Scott, "La cappella reliquiaria di Guarini e l'ostensione della Sindone," *Sindon* 11 (1999): 37–74; idem, "La cappella del Guarini," in *Sindone: Cento anni di ricerca*, ed. B. Barberis and G. M. Zaccone (Rome: Istituto poligrafico e Zecca dello Stato, 1998), 135–53; G. Dardanello, "La cappella della Sindone," in *I trionfi del Barocco*, ed. H. A. Millon (Milan: Bompiani, 1999), 461–66; idem, "Progetti per le prime cappelle della Sindone a Torino," in Masoero, Mamino, and Rosso, *Politica e cultura nell'età di Carlo Emanuele I*, 345–63; L. Tamburini, "I luoghi della Sindone," in Comoli and Giacobello Bernard, *Potere e la devozione*, 89–96; G. Dardanello, S. Klaiber, and H. A. Millon, eds., *Guarino Guarini* (Turin: Allemandi, 2006), 59–87, 291–307, 323–28; S. Albrecht, "Die Planungsgeschichte der Kapelle des Grabtuchs Christi in Turin: Ein neuer Zeichnungsfund," *Marburger Jahrbuch für Kunstwissenschaft* 37 (2010): 183–208; Cornaglia, "Museum versus Chapel of the Holy Shroud." On the altar, cf. E. Olivero, "L'altare della SS. Sindone e il suo autore," *Il Duomo di Torino* 2, no. 7 (1928): 6–11. In general, on the places of conservation and exhibition of the Shroud, one should always consult the excellent work of Scott, *Architecture for the Shroud*.

FIGURE 3.3 Bartolomeo Giuseppe Tasnière, after Giulio Cesare Grampin, Reconstruction of the exhibition of the Shroud from the Chapel of the Holy Shroud in the Turin Cathedral of May 4, 1703

1659–1667, the chapel was to become the magisterial Church of Saints Maurice and Lazarus (to whom a Savoyard order of knights was dedicated) and reliquary of the remains of Saint Maurice and of the Blessed Amadeus IX of Savoy. Christine of France, the duke's mother and former regent (*Madame Royale*), also thought of establishing a monastery of Mauritian nuns. The duke desired to take the chapel out from under the authority of the diocesan ordinary, so as to put it under that of the great prior of the Order of Saints Maurice and Lazarus, which would have carried out episcopal functions in it. The goals mentioned above, including completely uncoupling the chapel from the authority of the archbishop and the chapter of the cathedral, provoked long discussions pertaining to the issue of jurisdiction. The duke could never complete all his plans, but, starting from 1730, he managed to impose on the chapel the authority of the grand court almoner (chosen from among the finest names of the Savoyard patriciate and inspired by the homonymous figure of the courts of Madrid and Lisbon).[119] Under his authority, as in a very small diocese constituted only by members of the court, there was a palatine clergy, whose formation took place in the Basilica of Superga, newly built on the hill outside the city, the seat of a congregation of the same name. The tensions between the duke, the archbishop, the palatine clergy, and the chapter were reflected outwardly in the complex and delicate organization of the religious ceremonial court, which required the drafting of meticulous orders of protocol.[120]

3.2. Between the Eighteenth and Nineteenth Centuries

3.2.1. The Peak and the Decline

In May of 1706, during the War of the Spanish Succession, the Franco-Spanish soldiers surrounded Turin and began the famous siege that would last 117 days. The head of the Savoyard engineers, who worked for the fortification of the citadel of Turin, was Bertola, the designer of the altar of the Shroud.

[119] Cf. A. Merlotti, "I regi elemosinieri alla corte dei Savoia, re di Sardegna (secc. XVIII–XIX)," in *La corte en Europa: Política y religión (siglos XVI–XVIII)*, ed. J. Martínez Millán, M. Rivero Rodríguez, and G. Versteegen, vol. 2 (Madrid: Polifemo, 2012), 1025–58.

[120] Cf. M. T. Silvestrini, "La Chiesa, la città e il potere politico," in Ricuperati, *Storia di Torino*, 3:1179–88.

In the wake of certain ducal family members leaving the city on June 16, the Shroud was brought to Genoa. We know the stages of this journey: Cherasco (where a public exhibition was performed), Mondovì, Ceva, Garessio, Ormea, Pieve di Teco, Oneglia, and then, by sea, Savona and Genoa. After the victory of the Piedmontese, which occurred on September 7, the relic was carried back through Savona, Saliceto, and Cherasco, arriving in Turin on October 2, 1706.[121] We have some iconographic testimonies of this journey, because the route of the Shroud was preserved in frescoes that depicted it on walls in some of the places that it passed through. The practice of painting the Shroud on the facades of houses, doors, and intersections reached its apogee in the seventeenth and eighteenth centuries. In reality, only in a few cases do these paintings testify to a genuine passage of the relic through that place; instead, they generally respond to other needs. They in fact document devotion, recall an exhibition that took place in Turin, mark a stage of approach along the pilgrims' path, or even serve as apotropaic symbols.[122]

For the House of Savoy, a new period opened up after the victory, which had as its first tangible result the acquisition of the crown of the kingdom of Sicily, later exchanged for that of Sardinia, thereby transforming the Duke of Savoy into a king. In 1722 and 1737, the exhibitions, celebrated on the occasion of two royal marriages, rose to new heights in terms of the organization of the display; the exhibition of 1722 involved a pavilion designed in classical style by Filippo Juvarra,[123] while that of 1737 was a triumph of baroque architecture (fig. 3.4). The coincidence of secular and religious festivities provided

[121] Cf. M. D. Fusina, "Le peregrinazioni della Sindone durante l'assedio di Torino (1706)," *Bollettino della Società per gli studi storici, archeologici ed artistici della provincia di Cuneo* 67 (1972): 151–57; L. Bagnara, "1706: Viaggio dei Savoia da Torino a Genova con la 'Sacra Sindone,'" *La Casana* 3 (1999): 22; B. Taricco, *Arte sacra a Cherasco* (Peveragno: Basegrafica, 2000), 83–86.

[122] Several have occupied themselves with the study of these frescoes: G. Terzuolo, "La sacralizzazione del territorio: I luoghi della Sindone," in Carénini and Grimaldi, *Sindone: Immagini di Cristo*, 167–209; S. Giriodi, *Le altre Sindoni: Guida agli affreschi sindonici in Piemonte* (Marene: Blu edizioni, 2010); G. Scalva, ed., *Presenze sindoniche nelle Valli di Lanzo e nel Canavese* (Turin: Nautilus, 2010). See also M. D. Fusina, "La diffusione della iconografia della Sindone in Piemonte," *Studi Piemontesi* 1 (1972): 97–103.

[123] Visible in a woodcut reproduced in *Sindone nei secoli*, 101.

an opportunity to adorn the whole city with remarkable decorations and lighting, meticulously described by contemporaries.[124]

The exhibitions are thus described in a publication of the period, intended to encourage pilgrims and travelers to visit Turin:[125]

> Once the day set for such a ceremony has arrived, the cathedral is adorned with superb tapestries of velvet with gold fringe and background, and chandeliers hanging from all arches, and golden arms extending from the walls, bearing double torches, and the royal chapel of the Most Holy Shroud more richly decorated with finest silver and an infinite number of lights. His Majesty processes there in the morning, dressed in royal cloak, with the great collar of the Supreme Order, wrought entirely of diamonds, accompanied by the whole court into the cathedral; and he is seated there on a majestic throne under a magnificent canopy and has beside him His Royal Highness the Duke of Savoy and next to him the other princes of the Blood and the knights of the Supreme Order of the Most Holy Annunciation; from his royal chapel he attends to the office, assisted by the grand almoner, and is served by the masters of court ceremonies. So mass is sung pontifically, with His Majesty receiving all the honors that ceremonial royalty demands. After the mass is said, everyone processes to the Chapel of the Shroud. Having come there, the king puts aside the great cloak and dons the red dress of the Order of Saints Maurice and Lazarus. Then he delivers the four keys that open the sacred tomb where the venerable ark is kept, and, lowered by four canons, it is placed on a table decorated with rich tapestry; it is covered with a blanket embellished with priceless jewels. Next, incense is lit and the prayer is said by the celebrant cardinal. While those actions are performed in church, in the pavilion where the Shroud will be put on display two masses are celebrated for all the those watching in the two squares, which is also done on the loggia behind the royal castle that looks back on the district of Po. In the meantime, the solemn procession begins, at front of which is a group of

124 See the fine illustrated publication of that period: *La sontuosa illuminazione della città di Torino per l'augusto sposalizio delle reali maestà di Carlo Emmanuele re di Sardegna e di Elisabetta Teresa principessa primogenita di Lorena con l'aggiunta della pubblica esposizione della Santissima Sindone* (Turin: Giovanni Battista Chais, 1737).

125 On the role of the voyage and of the pilgrimage, and on the show that the city offered to those who had determined to visit the Shroud, see C. Roggero Bardelli, "Sguardi sulla Sindone di Pellegrini e viaggiatori in età moderna," in Comoli and Giacobello Bernard, *Potere e la devozione*, 57–74.

FIGURE 3.4 Antoine Herisset, *The Exhibition of 1737*

trumpeters and others with similar instruments. Then comes the clergy, the magnificent silver cross preceding them; two heralds follow, one of the Supreme Order, the other of the Order of Saints Maurice and Lazarus, dressed in their own garb and solemn uniforms. Next comes the royal chapel's musical corps, followed by the canons dressed with copes, with torches lit, behind whom come the bishops, sixteen of them on this last occasion, with copes and miters, flanked by the knights of the Grand Cross of Saints Maurice and Lazarus, after which come the knights of the Supreme Order of the Most Holy Annunciation with their clothes and large gold necklaces, with lighted torches in their hands, followed by the most eminent cardinal with his entire ecclesiastical court. Along with the cardinal comes the most precious treasure box, accompanied by incense and borne by four most dignified canons wearing tunicles, under the aforementioned rich and superb canopy, which is itself borne to the door of the great hall of the Swiss guards by His Majesty, by his Royal Highness the Duke of Savoy, by his Royal Highness the Duke of the Chablais and by the Most Serene Highness the prince of Carignano. There, four knights of the Supreme Order take turns bringing it to the queen's parade room, and from here it is carried by four Knights Grand Cross to the place set for the pavilion. Behind the sacred relic comes His Majesty with all the royal family, followed by princes and princesses of the Blood with lit torches in their hands, and then by all the knights and ladies of the court, and by all the magistrates dressed in uniform. Once the procession has arrived on the loggia, they all disburse to the windows of the galleries that look upon the pavilion, so that they, too, can adore the Holy Linen. Finally the box, having arrived in the middle of the pavilion, is placed on a table covered with very rich tapestry; after which His Majesty orders that the seals, which they found intact, be recognized, a public act duly carried out by the first secretary of state of His Majesty for internal affairs. Thereupon the lid is removed by the deacons and they draw forth with all veneration the Most Holy Shroud. In meantime, the preacher who gave the homily that year in the cathedral makes a short speech to that great group of people to excite them to reverence and veneration of the most holy relic. After the speech, the cardinal, together with all sixteen bishops, takes the Sacred Linteus and displays it outside the loggia for the public adoration. This exhibition is accompanied by sound of musical instruments and the firing of cannons, as well as the rumble of the military instruments of the Swiss guards and sentries of the King's Gate, that stand in order at the foot of the pavilion, and those of a regiment of infantry and bodyguards, lined up in order on horseback in the middle of these squares, with sword in hand and flags displayed. After the Most Holy Shroud has been displayed from the one side of the pavilion to the other, it is brought to the loggia of the royal castle that looks towards the other square and the districts of the Po and the Accademia, also covered with a new façade; and there also, with the same order as noted above, it is shown to the public. In the middle of this square an infantry battalion and a company of His Majesty's mounted bodyguards are lined up with swords in their hands. After the holy relic is displayed, it is placed in its usual case which is closed with His Majesty's customary seals. With the same accompaniment and on the same street, it is then brought back to the royal chapel.[126]

Upon the recognition of the authenticity of the Shroud by the pontiffs, there were no more doubts, and it even found its way into the most famous treatise written by Benedict XIV, which regulates the

[126] G. G. Craveri, *Guida de' forestieri per la real città di Torino* (Turin: Rameletti, 1753), 30–34. There are descriptions of the exhibitions much more detailed than this, under the form of official reports, such as those of 1684 and 1775 included in Scott, *Architecture for the Shroud*, 344–51. See also Piano, *Comentarii critico-archeologici*, 1:390–95; also, G. Biraghi and M. B. Pollone, "Le cerimonie della Sindone," in *Storia illustrata di Torino*, ed. V. Castronovo, vol. 11 (Milan: Elio Sellino, 1994), 3001–20.

process of beatification and canonization.[127] Thus, after 1466,[128] it was customary that the exhibitions were accompanied by the granting of plenary indulgences by the popes. Inasmuch as the opportunity to gain an indulgence had a deadline, it was periodically renewed, until in 1743 this concession was granted in perpetuity.[129] Some claim that Clement VIII granted to Catherine Michelle of Habsburg, Duchess of Savoy, that a recitation of the prayer known as the "collect," taken from the liturgy of the Mass of the Shroud, would obtain the liberation of a soul from purgatory each time it was said; but the report is false.[130] Rather, in 1699 it was established that the recitation of that prayer, at any time of the year, would produce a hundred days of indulgence. In English translation (which was later printed on holy cards), with the indulgence granted by Pius IX of September 16, 1859,[131] it reads thus:

> O Lord, who in the most Holy Shroud, which enfolded Thy adorable Body on being taken down from the cross, hast left manifestations of Thy presence here below and evident tokens of Thy love, by the merits of Thy holy passion and out of regard for this venerable linen which served for Thy burial, mercifully grant, we beseech Thee, that in the resurrection we also may share in that glory, in which Thou shalt reign for eternity. Amen.

A new era, however, now opened for the Shroud: in 1697 the ancient tradition of the annual display of May 4 had fallen into disuse, and already a few years before had been foregone, for various practical reasons. The Shroud's transfer to the new chapel designed by Guarini coincided with the end of a custom that was centuries old.[132]

[127] Prospero Lambertini, *De servorum Dei beatificatione et beatorum canonizatione* 2.2.31.17–18.

[128] Cf. Savio, *Ricerche storiche*, 249.

[129] There is a list in Piano, *Comentarii critico-archeologici*, 1:427–30; some indulgences bound to the Chapel of the Shroud are conserved or transcribed in AAT, 1.3.3 and in AAT, Fondo dei cappellani palatini, 19 (from 1699 to 1934).

[130] L. Fossati, *Sacra Sindone*, 159, reproduces a printing with the text of the prayer and the promise of indulgence; but various pronouncements of the Holy Office declare it to be false (*Archivio storico della Congregazione per la Dottrina della Fede*, St., st. H 3 d 5; St. st. H 3 p 2; St. st. H 3 g 6).

[131] This same prayer will garner, even in 1934, five hundred days of indulgence, if recited during the year, and a plenary indulgence for the day of the Feast of the Shroud on May 4.

[132] Other dates of alleged exhibitions, reported in some modern publications, are incorrect. For a description of the exhibitions in this period, see A. Merlotti, "The

From then on, the relic was almost exclusively exhibited publicly on the occasion of family events of the reigning dynasty (for example, the wedding of Charles Emmanuel IV and Marie Clotilde of Bourbon in 1775) or for visits by eminent personalities (such as privately for Emperor Joseph II of Habsburg-Lorraine in 1769). From 1697 until the end of the monarchy in 1946, there were only ten public exhibitions: 1722 (wedding), 1737 (wedding), 1750 (wedding), 1775 (wedding), 1815 (visit of the pope), 1842 (wedding), 1868 (wedding), 1898 (wedding), 1931 (wedding), 1933 (Holy Year). From the eighteenth century, therefore, the Shroud's strong presence in the urban landscape was lost. It remained only a court relic, whose veneration by the people was rare.

In the second half of the century a sharp decline in the literature inspired by the Shroud corresponded to the lower frequency of public displays. The year 1798 marks the end of the ancient Piedmontese regime. The century would close with the French republicans conquering Piedmont and with the abdication of Charles Emmanuel on December 8 of that year. Exiled to Sardinia, he chose on that occasion not to flee with his dynastic relic but to leave it in the custody of the archbishop of Turin; the transfer was sealed by a brief greeting ceremony, in which the king, after having venerated the relic without unfolding it, enclosed it with the seals of the archbishop instead of the usual royal seals. Only after the departure of the king was the relic shown to a delegation of people. The five keys to the railings that protected the reliquary—three in the possession of the king and two held by his guardian chaplain—all remained available to the archbishop, who kept only one for himself and distributed the other four to others.

The French looted the chapel and took possession of the gold and silver, sending them piecemeal to the mint or to France. Written requests for the sacred furnishings addressed by the occupants to the chaplain Carlo Antonio Brillada have been preserved, stating that "citizen Brillada" could save only a crucifix and some crystal candlesticks, which could not be melted.[133] The Shroud, however,

---

Holy Shroud between the Court of Savoy and the City of Turin: The Ostensions from Seventeenth to Nineteenth Centuries (1630–1831)," in Cozzo, Merlotti, and Nicolotti, *Shroud at Court*, 124–66. In 1697 there were sixty thousand participants at the exhibition, in an era when the total population of Turin was about forty-three thousand: cf. Scott, *Architecture for the Shroud*, 390, n. 1.

[133] Cf. Lanza, *Santissima Sindone del Signore*, 133–35.

would remain in the hands of its guardian. From the architectural point of view, too, the public space of the Shroud would come to be heavily reshaped. In 1801 the gallery connecting the Royal Palace with the castle, through which the Shroud was transported when put on display on the side of the castle that faced the Po, was demolished. Add to this that there would be a fire in 1811 caused by fireworks for the marriage of Napoleon's son. That fire damaged the walkway on which the pavilion facing the Royal Palace was built. The walkway was removed and replaced a few years later by the current railing of Pelagio Palagi. With these two interventions the era of the great spectacular exhibitions of the square ended. With the risk of a transfer to Paris avoided,[134] the Shroud was removed from its box only in 1804 for a private exhibition for Pope Pius VII, who traveled from Turin to crown Napoleon. Seven cardinals were present at the event, as were two archbishops and six bishops.[135]

The exile of the Savoys lasted until 1814. On their return they wanted to celebrate their restoration and the end of the Napoleonic era with a solemn *Te Deum* in the cathedral and with private veneration of the Shroud, and on May 21 of the following year they displayed the Shroud from the balcony of the castle (Palazzo Madama, which by then had a new facade) after having carried it through the square at ground level, as in earlier times.[136] This public exhibition of 1815 was the first public display with a pope present.[137] Another exhibition occurred in 1822 from inside the chapel, on the occasion of the inauguration of Charles Felix—the last celebration for the inauguration of a reign and the last exhibition of the relic from the top of the chapel balustrade (in 1825 a large partition window was placed between the chapel and the

[134] Piano speaks about this in *Comentarii critico-archeologici*, 1:331.

[135] Cf. *Sacratissimae Sindonis Taurinensis legalis recognitio anni 1799 una cum verbali anni 1804 facto coram SS.mo D.N.D. Pio papa VII* (Prato: Botta and Paravia, 1804); M. Grosso, "Il soggiorno a Torino di papa Pio VII e la privata esposizione della Sindone del 13 novembre 1804," *Sindon* 9 (1965): 24–29.

[136] One can see what would have been the course of the parade in the table reproduced in *Sindone nei secoli*, 117.

[137] Cf. *Narrazione della solennità celebrata in Torino il di 21 maggio dell'anno 1815 nella quale la santità di Pio VII espose alla pubblica venerazione la SS. Sindone* (Turin: Domenico Pane, 1815); AAT, Fondo dei cappellani palatini, 44, pp. 26–32. There was no public exhibition in 1814, as erroneously claimed by some authors (whom I had initially trusted).

nave of the church below).[138] On May 4, 1842, under the reign of Charles Albert, the Shroud's final exhibition in Piazza Castello occurred on the occasion of the wedding of Vittorio Emanuele to Marie Adélaïde of Habsburg-Lorraine; the relic was displayed on each of the four sides of Palazzo Madama for ten minutes, once in the morning and again in the afternoon. Among those present were Don John Bosco and Silvio Pellico, who has left a brief recollection of it.[139] It was also an opportunity to publish for the first time a text of meditation for the exhibition, addressed to the laity.[140] In the years immediately following, the Chapel of the Shroud served as a kind of Pantheon for the House of Savoy, and between 1843 and 1850 Charles Albert had four funeral monuments in marble sculpted, which were positioned around the altar of the Shroud (Emanuel Philibert, Prince Thomas Francis, Charles Emmanuel II, and Amadeus VIII).[141]

In 1868 there was another exhibition that lasted four days (April 24–27), on the occasion of the wedding of Umberto to Margherita of Savoy;[142] that same year saw the first attempt at an exhibition in the modern sense, as the Shroud was put on display for three days in a single frame placed above the main altar of the cathedral,

138 Described in AAT, Fondo dei cappellani palatini, 44, pp. 33–46.

139 Cf. C. Durando, *Lettere famigliari inedite di Silvio Pellico* (Milan: Guigoni, 1879), 415. On the occasion of this exhibition were published the *Notizie storiche del SS. Sudario esposto alla pubblica venerazione, addì 4 maggio 1842* (Turin: Schiepatti, 1842) and the *Cenni sulla Santissima Sindone* (Turin: Fontana, 1842). Reports of the exhibitions are in AAT, Fondo dei cappellani palatini, 42, and in Gasca Queirazza, "Devozione alla Santa Sindone," 5–10; a reproduced lithograph can be found in *Sindone nei secoli*, 119.

140 S. Donaudi, *Pio esercizio di divote riflessioni e preghiere per venerare la Sacratissima Sindone* (Turin: Paravia, 1842); cf. Zaccone, *Sindone: Storia di una immagine*, 224–26.

141 On some aspects of this period, see M. G. Bosco, "Carlo Alberto e Maria Cristina di Borbone-Napoli di fronte ai temi della devozione," in Comoli and Giacobello Bernard, *Potere e la devozione*, 97–109; on the rituals of the royal chapel, see P. Gentile, *Alla corte di re Carlo Alberto* (Turin: Centro Studi Piemontesi, 2013), 41–49, 123–51; about the transformation of the chapel into a mausoleum, cf. Scott, *Architecture for the Shroud*, 276–91.

142 Cf. A. Bosio, *Alcune memorie sulla Sacratissima Sindone* (Turin: Artigianelli, 1868); *Atto verbale dell'apertura e del nuovo chiudimento dell'urna contenente la S.S. Sindone, e della esposizione di questa preziosissima reliquia* (AAT, Fondo dei cappellani palatini, 81, folder "1868"); *Variazioni che occorrono nelle ordinarie funzioni*, April 23–28 (ACT, Addenda 77).

in front of which the uninterrupted flow of the faithful could pour in. Clearly the role of the royal family now began to wane in importance: after 1865 Turin was no longer the capital of the kingdom and the king no longer dwelt in the palace, and thus the role of the archbishop of Turin began to wax prominent in the administration of the sacred relic. Once royal control had become more flexible, the local bishops also had greater freedom to reimagine the function of the dynastic celebration of the relic and to reframe its veneration to be more in the field of pastoral care and of liturgy celebrated by the diocese of Turin.[143] In this same year the office of the bishop grand almoner of the Palatine Chapel was abolished and replaced with a senior chaplain, no longer a bishop, who was joined by a guardian chaplain of the Shroud.

The decrease in public occasions to revive the cult of the Shroud went hand in hand with a generally more rationalistic orientation toward the cult of relics, as many of them were by then openly branded as false and deceptive. We have already mentioned the work of the Parisian canon Nicolas-Sylvestre Bergier, to which one can juxtapose the work of the priest Adrien Baillet, who in his ponderous *Vies des saints* gives no credence to the shrouds scattered about in churches all over Europe (one of the reasons, most likely, that led to his works being placed on the Index).[144] In Turin in 1723, for fear of similar criticism, a history of the Shroud by the abbot Giuseppe Pasini, although it was commissioned by Victor Amadeus II, the Duke of Savoy, was not printed because a commission appointed by the sovereign judged that it would not be appropriate "so soon to expose this work to the censure of modern critics, who would like everything to be proven by a series of facts and undisputed documents."[145]

In the years 1821 and 1822, Jacques Collin De Plancy, in his three-volume work entitled *Dictionnaire critique des reliques*, attempted

[143] For the exhibitions of the eighteenth and nineteenth centuries, see Pugno, *Santa Sindone che si venera a Torino*, 254–302 (with many documents); Fossati, *Sacra Sindone*, 192–229; and Scott, *Architecture for the Shroud*, 248–302. On the exhibitions of 1842 and 1868, see P. Gentile, "The Old Piedmont Becomes the New Italy: The Ostensions for the Nuptials of the Crown Princes Vittorio Emanuele and Umberto (1842–1868)," in Cozzo, Merlotti, and Nicolotti, *Shroud at Court*, 297–312.

[144] A. Baillet, *Les vies des saints et l'histoire des festes de l'année*, vol. 4, pt. 1a, *L'histoire des festes mobiles* (Paris: Nully, 1703), coll. 259–65.

[145] Quoted by Merlotti, "Holy Shroud between the Court of Savoy," 149–50.

to inventory all relics of which he had knowledge, even the most unlikely of them.[146] In the meantime, the first steps were taken for a historical study of certain categories of relics. That study did not necessarily depend on a declaration of authenticity: for example, one thinks of Charles Rohault de Fleury's book on the relics of the passion, as well as that of Paul Riant on the relics of Constantinople.[147] With regard to the Shroud, no one in Italy followed in the footsteps of the French. Shroud literature, although quantitatively much less than in the previous century, thus continued to tread the same path as in the prior centuries.[148] The apologetic tones are, at most, perceived as increasingly alarmed by the advance of Enlightenment thought and by critical thinking about relics and the popular cult attributed to them. On the other hand, the Shroud was then still, and would remain, the relic par excellence of the royal house; denial of its authenticity would certainly have been interpreted as a direct attack on the reigning family. Because of such a close connection, there was no dearth of encomia toward the Piedmontese dynasty, deserving protector of (and itself protected by) the holy relic. Such encomia grew more frequent after the restoration of the Savoy kingdom following the Napoleonic domination. Rather than focusing on history, speakers and writers treating the Shroud preferred to emphasize the devotional, dynastic, social, and civil aspects of the relic, and the tone of their work became increasingly aggressive toward the forces opposed to Christianity and toward modernity in general. For this reason, the metaphor most used in this period is that of the Shroud as the ensign of Christ's victorious triumph over death and evil, and at the same time as the flag or military tent that symbolizes patriotism and accompanies the army of Christians against the enemies of the faith.[149]

146 The section on shrouds: J. Collin de Plancy, *Dictionnaire critique des reliques et des images miraculeuses*, vol. 3 (Paris: Guien, 1822), 99–106.

147 C. Rohault de Fleury, *Mémoire sur les instruments de la Passion* (Paris: Lesort, 1870); P. Riant, "Des dépouilles religieuses enlevées à Constantinople au XIIIe siècle et des documents historiques nés de leur transport en Occident," *Mémoires de la Société nationale des antiquaries de France* 36 (1875): 1–214.

148 To provide but one example, Giovanni Bernardo Vigo, professor of rhetoric, composed in Latin a poem on the Shroud, based on Pingon's account: G. B. Vigo, *Ad Carolum Emmanuelem Sardiniae, Hierusalem, et Cypri regem, de Sindone Taurinense* (Turin: ex Typographia Regia, 1768).

149 See A. Dordoni, "Aspetti della devozione sindonica dall'Aufklärung cattolica alla crisi modernista," in Zaccone and Ghiberti, *Guardare la Sindone*, 161–80.

The House of Savoy never tolerated any attempt to diminish the importance of the cult of the Shroud, to the extent that the relic's veneration continued to execute its political function of dynastic legitimacy. The concern of the sovereigns in this regard can be understood from their prompt reaction to a decision by Pius VI in 1786, when the pope reduced the number of the holy days of obligation in the Savoy dioceses. For the days so demoted, he revoked the obligation to abstain from work. Since the provision was also going to cancel the Shroud festival on May 4, after only one month the Senate of Turin, at the request of Victor Amadeus III, rendered the papal provision ineffective, proposing that "in memory and veneration of the precious relic of the holy Shroud, by which it was pleasing to divine Providence to decorate and protect the royal house and these States, it be allowed to continue even in the present system to have its festival solemnized."[150]

After 1860, when the Savoy region was annexed to France, the Italian sovereigns engaged deeply in a clash that opposed them to the French, who also claimed control of the Church of the Holy Shroud of Rome, considering it an original Savoyard institution. In response, the king of newly unified Italy proposed for the church a fresh start and restoration, which had been necessary for a long time. It is not widely known that in 1869 John Bosco, already famous in Turin for his charitable works, asked that he or one of his priests of the Salesian congregation be appointed the church's rector. But instead, perhaps because of his capacity as a historian, Joseph Croset-Mouchet, of Savoyard origins and canon of the cathedral of Pinerolo, obtained the commission. In fact, Croset-Mouchet collected historical documentation about the church and the confraternity, asserting the importance of the church and demonstrating its character as a Piedmontese national church at Rome, against the claims of the French.[151]

[150] Epistle *Paternae caritati* of May 27, 1786, and Senatorial Manifest of July 29, 1786; F. A. Duboin, ed., *Raccolta per ordine di materie delle leggi, provvidenze, editti, manifesti, ecc. pubblicati dal principio dell'anno 1681 sino agli 8 dicembre 1798 sotto il felicissimo dominio della Real Casa di Savoia*, vol. 1 (Turin: Davico e Picco, 1818), 40–44 (citation here is from p. 43).

[151] He himself recounts it in G. Croset-Mouchet, *Dello stato presente della R. Chiesa del SS. Sudario in Roma* (Rome: Regia tipografia, 1872); to understand the climate of that epoch, compare it with J. Mailland, "Les Savoyards et l'église

3.2.2. *Lazzaro Giuseppe Piano*

In this period of relative decline in the public function of the Shroud, a notable development can be seen in the commitment of a scholar who still today can be read with profit. Lazzaro Giuseppe Piano, a member of the Order of the Minims, was a professor of philosophy and dean of students of the Royal University. His imposing work, in two volumes, significantly entitled *Comentarii critico-archaeologici sopra la SS. Sindone* (*Critical-Archaeological Commentaries on the Most Holy Shroud*), was intended to analyze the Shroud in as complete a fashion as possible. One fairly substantial part of the work has theological, paraenetic, and encomiastic intentions; the other part, in my opinion the most innovative, is one in which he sets the praiseworthy goal of reconstructing a history of the relic based on critical opinion, correcting the numerous errors of his predecessors.

> The lack of documents from the first centuries of the Church relating to our precious relic and the ardent desire to praise it, especially whereby our writers have been particularly animated with the aim of promoting with all their ability its devotion in the souls of others, caused some people to have too easily confused it with other shrouds, and many events have been attributed to our Shroud by those writers, events that occurred in the spans of time mentioned above and could not in fact be attributed to the relic itself.[152]

Piano's deep commitment to finding the truth stands out. Thanks to his own research, he could convincingly refute some of the historiographical reconstructions that were then in fashion, beginning with explanations provided by Pingon and Adorno in 1578: the Shroud could not have been given to a Savoy named Amadeus by the grand master of the Hospitallers in appreciation for having saved Rhodes from the siege of the Turks, because neither Amadeus V nor Amadeus VI, the Green Count, was ever in Rhodes; it could not have been left as an inheritance to the Savoys by Charlotte of Lusignan, queen of Cyprus; it could not have been sold by an Egyptian woman in exchange for the release of her captive husband; finally, Marguerite

---

du Saint-Suaire—Rome," *Mémoires de l'Académie des sciences, belles-lettres et arts de Savoie* 9 (1902): 355–456.

[152] Piano, *Comentarii critico-archeologici*, 1:113.

de Charny was not a relative of the Cypriot sovereigns.[153] The Minim priest of Turin knows the writings of Chifflet and Camuzat, and he has at hand all the published documentation available at the time and knows the events surrounding the Shroud in Lirey. Thus he undertakes the task of furnishing a portrait of Geoffroy I de Charny, and, in response to those who hold certain documents of the period when the Shroud was in France to be false, he defends their authenticity and even republishes some of them.[154]

At this point, having cleaned up of the previous historiographical reconstructions, Piano finds himself facing the usual lack of documentation for thirteen centuries. He is convinced of the authenticity of the Shroud, which belief ultimately leads him to repeat the error of his predecessors: he starts to invent. His "new" history of the relic is as follows: after being in the tomb in Jerusalem, the Shroud, initially kept by Nicodemus, remained hidden in Palestine until the First Crusade; this explanation forces him to deny the oft-asserted identification of the Shroud of Turin with the shroud that Bede the Venerable mentions. Piano prefers to consider Bede's shroud the same as the shroud of Cadouin—which, however, as stated above, is an Islamic fabric. After the First Crusade the Shroud would fall into the hands of the Hospitallers in Jerusalem, and their grand master, Raymond du Puy, would then make a gift of it to Amadeus III of Savoy (1095–1148). After the death of Amadeus in Nicosia, the capital of Cyprus, the Shroud must, according to Piano, have remained in the possession of the Greeks. In 1240 Gregory IX ordered the Latin archbishop of Nicosia to exclude all Greek priests who had not sworn obedience to the Holy See from sacred celebrations. Abandoning Cyprus to escape from this restriction, they supposedly repaired to Armenia, bringing the precious relic with them. At this point Piano inserts the figure of Geoffroy de Charny, imagining that he undertook the trip to Armenia to fight the infidels. The occasion was identified with the clashes that in roughly 1330 put the sultan of Egypt in conflict with Hugh IV of Lusignan, king of Cyprus, and Leo V, king

153 Piano, *Comentarii critico-archeologici*, 1:204–38, 293–302.

154 Piano, *Comentarii critico-archeologici*, 1:239–84. On pages 250–60 he defends the authenticity of a document of Louis I of Savoy, refuting an opinion, written in 1821, of an author whose name he does not mention. I have identified the author and the text; the author is the archivist Pietro Datta, whose handwritten observations are at the AST (Benefizi di qua da' monti, file 31, no. 3).

of Armenia. Piano recounts that the ambassadors of the two sovereigns, accompanied by the Latin patriarch of Jerusalem, had gone to Pope Benedict XII in the same period in which Marie, daughter of Louis of Bourbon, Count of Clermont, married (by proxy) Guy, son of Hugh.[155] In reality, Geoffroy did not have anything to do with these events. At the time, he was most likely to be found in Morea with his father and brother Dreux. Further, we have no evidence of his participation in any battle against "the infidels." Nor was there a French expedition for the liberation of Armenia, as at that time there was a truce of fifteen years enacted between the patriarch of Armenia and the sultan of Egypt.[156] Even this explanation will therefore have to be abandoned. For everything else, like his predecessors, unfortunately Piano continues to trust Pingon: the arrival of Marguerite in Chambéry, the theft of the relic, the miracles, the celestial sign through the pack animal, and the free gift of the Shroud to the Savoy family. What can be salvaged from all this is the discussion about the year in which the transfer to the Savoys happened: Piano discovers that the year 1452, a date that he reads in the Pingon's treatise and is repeated by all his emulators, is wrong (due to a minor printing error), and it must be replaced by the year 1453.[157] For the period that follows, one characterized by the existence of documents, Piano turns out to be a very rich source of firsthand information; sometimes he is repetitive, sometimes innovative. In certain cases, such as when he tries to demonstrate at great length that the bulls of Clement VII of 1390 are inauthentic, he is utterly wrong.[158] He dedicates a great deal of space to the miracles accomplished by the Shroud, some already told by Pingon, others new.

[155] Piano, *Comentarii critico-archeologici*, 1:171–91, 280–84. [Melano], *Notizie storiche*, 18–20; and Lanza, *Santissima Sindone del Signore*, 39–40, also follow this explanation; the latter, however, confuses Guy with his father, Hugh. On this marriage, see O. Troubat, "La France et le royaume de Chypre au XIVe siecle: Marie de Bourbon," *Revue historique* 278 (1987): 4. Rohault de Fleury, *Mémoire sur les instruments de la Passion*, 241, even says that Geoffroy claimed to have received the Shroud from Hugh of Lusignan, which is inaccurate.

[156] Cf. T. S. R. Boase, *The Cilician Kingdom of Armenia* (New York: St. Martin's, 1978).

[157] Piano, *Comentarii critico-archeologici*, 1:293–315.

[158] Piano, *Comentarii critico-archeologici*, 2:272–88.

FOUR

The Shroud and Modernity

4.1. Science and History

4.1.1 The Exhibition of 1898 and the Photographs

Along the lines of the grand industrial expos of the time, the city of Turin, recently deprived of its role as capital of Italy, was called upon in 1898 to host an *Esposizione Generale Italiana*, an exhibition of Italian industry and culture, that coincided with festivities celebrating the fiftieth anniversary of the Albertine Statute. Strengthened by their recent success in local elections, which came in a period of political turmoil between Catholics and *laici*,[1] the Catholics of Turin requested a grand "Exhibition of sacred art, Catholic missions, and works of Christian charity"[2] that would parallel the *Esposizione Generale Italiana*. The occasion for the Catholic-themed expo was justified by a series of anniversaries, including the fifteen hundredth anniversary of the Council of Turin of 398, the four hundredth anniversary of the construction of the cathedral, and the three hundredth anniversary of the Confraternity of the Holy Shroud, that of Saint Rocco, and of the solemn exhibition of the relics of Saint Walric. The expo's executive committee worked under the chairmanship of Baron Antonio

[1] In politics the *laici* claimed an absolute independence and freedom of choice vis-à-vis the Catholic Church.

[2] Well described by G. M. Zaccone, "L'esposizione d'arte sacra del 1898 a Torino tra religione e politica," *Studi Piemontesi* 25, no. 1 (1996): 71–102; as a supplement, see Zaccone, *Torino 1898: L'ostensione della Sindone e l'esposizione d'arte sacra* (Turin: Gribaudo, 1998); and P. M. Prosio, "Torino 1898," in Zaccone, *Immagine rivelata*, 31–45 (images on 142–52). The epistolary exchange between the cleric of Piedmont, the organizing committee, and the Holy See is reported in ASV, Segr. Stato, an. 1902, rubr. 12, fasc. 13.

Manno, a deeply religious historian and genealogist on good terms with the House of Savoy.[3] The two expos were adjoining but officially independent; the areas for the two exhibitions were separated by a road, the Corso Massimo d'Azeglio, which, however, to allow for the movement of visitors, was surmounted by a bridge, immediately christened the "Bridge of Concord," a symbol of the will to overcome the ideological divisions, with a view to collaboration for the good of the city.

These important initiatives were accompanied by a new exhibition of the Shroud, which Giovanni Battista Ghirardi—promoter of the event and key representative of Catholicism in the region—wanted to put into play immediately:

> You recall that the town council of Turin during the siege of 1640 sent the municipality's flag depicting the Shroud onto the field, so let us make the Shroud our flag, waving it to the sun of our freedoms.[4]

Officially, the festivities surrounding the wedding of Prince Vittorio Emanuele of Savoy and Elena of Montenegro provided the impetus for the exhibition of the Shroud, although it was deferred until two years after the wedding had taken place.[5] The request for the exhibition, however, had come not from the royal house but rather from the diocese of Turin; despite being authorized by the king, the event was managed by the diocese through an organizing committee. Scheduled for May 11–19, the opening a mere two days prior was postponed until May 25 after riots hit many Italian piazzas, which culminated, sadly, in the famous suppression during the Four Days of Milan, when General Bava Beccaris turned his cannons upon the crowd of demonstrators.

The exhibition was held entirely inside the cathedral. The Shroud was fastened to a supporting apparatus with thumbtacks and had to

[3] Cf. G. Monsagrati, "Manno, Antonio," in *Dizionario Biografico degli Italiani*, vol. 42 (2007), 113–16.

[4] Cited in Zaccone, "Esposizione," 83.

[5] A description of the exhibition is in Sanna Solaro, *S. Sindone che si venera a Torino*, 135–40, 148–50; various reports occur in different issues of the journal *Arte sacra: Rassegna illustrata dell'Esposizione d'arte sacra indetta a Torino*, afterward reprinted in a volume (*1898 Arte sacra* [Turin: Roux Frassati, 1898]); the official minutes are in AAT, Fondo dei cappellani palatini, 81, folder "1898."

be displayed in a gold frame on the high altar. When the cloth was being readied for exhibition, a concern arose since the supporting apparatus and the gold frame were shorter than the fabric they were meant to accommodate. The problem was caused by an error during the transcription of the measurements of the Shroud; someone had reversed the numbers! It was too late to fix, and so the cloth had to be folded a bit at the bottom of the two short sides to make it fit, therefore partially obscuring from view the area of the feet of the human image.[6] Over the following days, from five o'clock in the morning until seven o'clock in the evening, without interruption the faithful went silently in a line past the Shroud. Whoever wanted to venerate the Shroud more closely could purchase a "special ticket" that permitted him to remain in the church for about half an hour. At the end of the exhibition, on June 2, over the course of nine days, eight hundred thousand visitors were counted, half of whom came from outside Turin.

For the first time the presence of the House of Savoy was truly negligible. The highest-ranking member of the family in attendance at the exhibition was the Duke of Aosta, the king's cousin; not even spouses took part. And yet the queen, Margherita, credited the Shroud with protecting her husband, Umberto I, from attacks by anarchists in 1878 and 1897, which he fortunately survived; on both of those occasions he had two large silver medallions hung in the church, ex-voto, and bearing the meaningful inscription *Domine, salvum fac regem* ("Lord, keep the king safe"). Unfortunately, he was denied the opportunity to hang a third medallion, since Umberto could not escape an attack at Monza in 1900: the anarchist assailant Gaetano Bresci announced that he wanted to avenge the victims of the incident in Milan, after seeing the authors of the massacre in May 1898 rewarded rather than hanged.

A small miracle, however, was proclaimed by a certain Anna Lerda of Cuneo, who claimed to have recovered her vision, which had grown weak, after praying and looking upon the Shroud. A second miracle happened upon her return home, as the lady reported that

6 See the detailed report edited by G. M. Zaccone, "Le 'Memorie' del cerimoniere arcivescovile Carlo Franco sull'ostensione del 1898," *Sindon* 12 (1999): 33–71. In 1868 the linen again had to be folded because the frame was too short: see Bosio, *Alcune memorie*, 20.

when she opened a small box where she kept her linens, she discovered that one of the cloths had the image of the Shroud impressed upon it. All this was published in the newspapers and was sworn to before the religious authorities, who, however, found it of little interest.[7]

The photograph is a nineteenth-century invention, and naturally someone decided to photograph the Shroud.[8] In 1842 an attempt was made to photograph an exhibition using a daguerreotype, but it was unsuccessful.[9] In April of 1898, however, after more than a little effort to obtain permission from the king, a subcommittee for the official photograph of the relic was formally established. The photographer chosen for the task was Secondo Pia,[10] a lawyer from Asti. Despite the experience and recognition he had attained, he considered himself an amateur, but in the best sense of the word; he lacked neither the finest instruments nor the technical capability, and the tangible and appreciable proof of his ability—a series of striking photographic prints of the monuments of Piedmont—was displayed in one of the pavilions at the expo. Beyond his undisputed competence, Pia provided certain guarantees. He worked entirely at

[7] Cf. A. M[alabocchia], "Una grazia miracolosa dall'ostensione della SS. Sindone," *Lo stendardo: Corriere della provincia di Cuneo*, August 23–24, 1898, 1; AAT, 14.14.93: declaration of the woman's daughter given May 25, 1939; AAT, Fondo dei cappellani palatini, 81, folder "1933: Ostensione della SS. Sindone": reports on the issue of the two miracles, in an envelope addressed to the canon Michele Grasso.

[8] Zaccone, *Immagine rivelata*, is largely dedicated to this topic.

[9] L. Capello di Sanfranco, "Un cenno sulla SS. Sindone," *Museo scientifico, letterario ed artistico* 4 (1842): 190: "Mr. Jest, an engineer at R. University, conceived the idea to make a gift for us by depicting the image of the Holy Shroud using a daguerreotype from the side facing east during one of the exhibitions that took place in the morning, but his attempted experience was unsuccessful, because the sun did not dare to shine with all its brilliance at the time of the exhibition, seeming to desire to respect the new light that the Holy Linen was emitting for us, and so because of lack of light, rising fumes, and dust from the ground, and even more because there was too little time during the exhibition, it was not to be that Mr. Jest depict the image he so craved."

[10] Some think that the first to put forth a request to the king was the Salesian Noël Noguier de Malijay; but he himself reports that he raised the issue with Baron Manno during the sacred art expo, therefore after May 1, when the subcommittee's negotiations were already in process: cf. L. Fossati, "Autografo inedito di don Natale Noguier de Malijay in merito alla ripresa della sacra Sindone nel 1898," *Salesianum* 45 (1983): 113–27 (in particular 117–18). B. Bellardo, *La Sindone di N. S. Gesù Cristo* (Turin: SEI, 1945), 43, believes the same thing.

his own expense, he gave up proceeds from the rights to the photographs, and he donated profits from the printing to charity.

Pia had never seen the Shroud, and he had little time in which to work.[11] An initial photographic session was held in the afternoon of May 25, but Pia, deeming the plates less than satisfactory, reported that the two test plates on which he had made exposures were unsuccessful. On May 28, he held other sessions, this time with great success, and many people rushed to see the images. Secondo Pia's home, however, soon proved insufficient to accommodate all those who were curious. It was decided, therefore, that as part of the Exhibition of Sacred Art, a hall would be prepared in which the first media "exhibition" of the Shroud would occur; in the hall, once visitors had entered in small groups, the lights were turned off and it was possible to admire the sole plate of the Shroud, resting on a cloth and strikingly illuminated.

Secondo Pia's photograph immediately became an object of wonder when he noticed that the photographic negative produced an image of the man of the Shroud that was visible in a way never before seen. The photographer would later report having a strong emotional experience when he saw the image of the man's face appear on the plate while developing the picture. Giuseppe Enrie subsequently describes that moment:

> He [Pia] devoted himself to a more attentive observation; and, there, in a few moments, as he sensed something extraordinary, an image formed and was there on the plate, unmistakable; but instead of a negative image, it was the positive shape and characteristics of a man, with a face clear as if it were a portrait, amazing, never seen, magnificent, the true face of Christ. That same photographer and those who assisted him recounted that he nearly fell ill, and his hands, trembling and awkward in the difficult manipulation of the large glass plate, which became slippery through contact with the bath, did not allow it to fall or strike harmfully against any object while maneuvering it to the soft, reddish glow of the laboratory. Only by great self-control did Pia succeed in

[11] Pia himself describes his own operations, which are commented on by G. Pia, "La prima fotografia della SS. Sindone," *Sindon* 5 (1961): 33–58; G. M. Zaccone, "La fotografia della Sindone nel 1898," *Sindon* 3 (1991): 69–94, supplemented by G. M. Zaccone and E. Ferraro, "Alcune note sul riordino e la consistenza dell'archivio Pia," *Sindon* 8 (1995): 91–98.

bringing the process of developing the image to an end and place the plate in the fix bath to relinquish it safely.[12]

Yet one could legitimately wonder whether it was strange that a photographer so skilled did not immediately notice the "negative" character of the shroud-image of the cloth and discovered it only at the point of developing the photographic plates; perhaps he wanted to convey a feeling of amazement to validate a sort of "proof of authenticity" established "on purely emotional bases"?[13] Pia's writings, in truth, are sober enough, and it was others who indulged in amplifying the impact of that moment. Certainly, at least on one level the accounts of the photographer were reticent: the test plates from May 25, which he had declared unsuccessful, were in truth only underexposed, as could be ascertained in 1991 when they were recovered. Perhaps Pia wanted to keep them hidden until the second photo session had confirmed what was already seen in the first tests; and later he decided that it was no longer necessary to speak of it. In any case, it is no longer possible to believe in the story of the wholly unexpected amazement he felt in the darkroom on May 28.

The photographs went around the world. The requests for copies were so numerous that it was immediately necessary to regulate the management of the proceeds and to create a special committee: the king, who held the artistic ownership, authorized Baron Manno to use those proceeds to cover possible expenses that might come from the budget of the sacred art expo; thereafter, as stated, everything had to be donated to charity.[14] To that end a Charitable Works of the Holy Shroud (*Opera di Beneficenza della SS. Sindone*) fund was created, to be managed by the Salesians. Two copies of the photographs were sent to Leo XIII; Cardinal Rampolla, secretary of state, prepared the letter of thanks. Initially, in the draft that I found, he wrote that the pope welcomed the gift and "had words of praise for the meritorious amateur photographer, the knight Secondo Pia, who succeeded in reproducing with such vividness and precision the image of the adored body of the Redeemer." He later reconsidered, since the

[12] Enrie, *Santa Sindone rivelata*, 17. This story has been recounted several times: see, for example, J. Walsh, *The Shroud* (London: W. H. Allen, 1964), 10–21.

[13] V. Pesce Delfino, *E l'uomo creò la Sindone*, 2nd ed. (1st ed. 1982; Bari: Dedalo, 2000), 32.

[14] CSS, Fondo Pia, 3.1.1.75 and 127: letters of the king's secretary.

wording amounted to an implicit declaration of authenticity; he therefore deleted the reference to Christ and replaced it with an innocuous and prudent formula: "the image of that most precious relic."[15]

The photograph began to be considered as proof of the authenticity of the Shroud. The case was made with particular insistence in France by Arthur Loth: to think that the Shroud is a human product, wrote Loth, "it would be necessary to admit that many centuries before the invention of photography—which alone has brought to light that it is a negative—a pious, brilliant forger, predicting what only experience could teach, anticipating all the modern discoveries of physics and chemistry, had an extraordinary idea, inconceivable, to paint a negative image on the Shroud." Since the Shroud contains just such an image, rather, "it is a true photographic plate," the result of which, according to Loth, is that it "is incontestably the original, and an original that could not have been made by any human hand." Whatever the origin of the images, natural or not, the Shroud became "witness of the death and resurrection of Christ, guarantor of the truth of the Gospel."[16]

In truth one cannot say that the Shroud is a "true photographic plate" or that the human hand is incapable of imprinting an image of this sort on a sheet. Photography simply restored the chiaroscuro inversion of what everyone had always seen on the Shroud, that is, the result (or the attempt to depict the result) of an imprint. However, one can say that 1898 is the year in which the scientific study of the Shroud began, on the wave of emotion provoked by the photographs: it makes a certain impression that the impetus came from the misunderstanding over the negative, which, as will be seen below, is an issue based on nothing.

4.1.2 Historians to the Rescue

Predictably, in 1898 many new publications came out, among which it is useful to recall the book by Giovanni Lanza, royal chaplain of the Shroud.[17] The historical information on the relic was still presented in a particularly confused and legendary way. Rarely did someone

[15] ASV, Segr. Stato, an. 1902, rubr. 12, fasc. 13, ff. 153–54 (draft); CSS, Fondo Pia, 3.1.1.65 (the final text that was sent).

[16] A. Loth, *Le portrait de N.-S. Jésus Christ* (Paris: Oudin, 1900), 45, 50, 47, 57.

[17] Lanza, *Santissima Sindone del Signore.*

record with precision the history of the prohibitions, excommunications, and condemnations from the Lirey period:[18] at best some brief, incomplete mention of it was made that drew upon the work of Lazzaro Piano, perhaps mixing it with the legends of Pingon.[19] In general, the events pertaining to the relic in the first millennium were invented or treated by sources that were too late. According to the anonymous author of an article published in the *Bollettino salesiano*, for example, the holy cloth was collected by the apostles and Mary Magdalene, taken to the home of Joseph of Arimathea, and given to Nicodemus, who took it with him to his uncle Gamaliel's house. Both Nicodemus and Gamaliel were martyred, and the Shroud ended up in the hands of Saint John, then of Simeon, second bishop of Jerusalem. Hidden until the peace of Constantine, it would reappear in the Jerusalem cathedral, where it remained at least until the time of the coming of Godfrey of Bouillon. The Shroud was given by the Order of Hospitallers to Amadeus III of Savoy, who took it to Cyprus; running the risk of having it fall into Muslim hands, Geoffroy de Charny secured it in France, in his castle in Lirey. At last, in 1461, it finally ended up in the hands of the Savoys after Marguerite de Charny gifted it to them following miracles and divine presages.[20] An equally unlikely story was also recounted in a pamphlet intended especially for visitors of the sacred arts expo. That pamphlet was the work of the canon Guglielmo Ramello, who, however, correctly provides at least the possible date that it was given to Savoy: March 22, 1453.[21]

Not everyone was unaware of the improper way in which the history of the Shroud was being handled, but whoever knew something preferred not to rock the boat. The Jesuit Giammaria Sanna Solaro, for example, declared that since 1898 he had noticed the presence, in many publications, of "not a few things that seemed not to hold up under criticism." Sanna Solaro, however, decided to remain silent at least until the exhibition had ended, in order to avoid openly

[18] For an exception, see "Pious Frauds," *Catholic Layman* 4, no. 38 (1855): 16.

[19] For example, *Cenni sulla Santissima Sindone*; G. Berta, *Della Sacra Sindone di Nostro Signor Gesù Cristo* (Turin: Reycend, 1842).

[20] *Bollettino salesiano* 22, no. 5 (1898): 114–15.

[21] G. Ramello, *L'omaggio dei secoli alla Sacra Sindone evangelica venerata nella chiesa metropolitana di Torino* (Turin: Marietti, 1898), 12–21; this is a translation from the original in Latin: *De Sancta Sindone evangelica quae in regio sacello apud ecclesiam metropolitanam Taurinensem servatur et colitur* (Turin: Tipografia subalpina, 1898).

contradicting what was said by others and causing confusion among "the common people who do not reason."[22]

But relative to the last exhibition the times had changed, and one could no longer hope for unanimous acceptance. An initial attack on the Shroud came from Pietro Caviglia, socialist city councilor for Turin, who denounced as impossible that a body could leave such an imprint on a fabric, noting also the inexplicable silence of all the ecclesiastical writers for fourteen centuries.[23] In response to Caviglia, the periodical *La Civiltà Cattolica* took the field with an article by Eugenio Polidori; declining to take a position regarding the Shroud, Polidori limited himself to confirming the legitimacy of devotion to relics but recognized also the need to investigate their historical plausibility, insisting on the fact that the authentication (or not) of the relics does not affect the infallibility of the Church. The possible veneration of a false relic, Polidori claims, is theologically a mistake that is, all things considered, negligible, as it does not disturb any principle of faith and does not invalidate the value and efficacy of the act of worship directed to God.[24] The *Revue du clergé français* immediately repeated and expanded upon the same observation.[25]

It was one of the harbingers of the dispute that was exploding between the Shroud's adorers and critics; and it could seem strange that this conflict later reached its most extreme point not in the opposition between believers and nonbelievers but rather within the Catholic world, very often among priests. On the side of the critics were the most renowned proponents of a tendency toward innovation that had swept all the fields of religious studies, from biblical exegesis to ecclesiastical history; such innovation was reliant upon an intellectual elite. These priests were often entrenched in the academic world, and their word garnered respect even in spheres far from Catholicism. They looked with suspicion on the appearance of a "popular" Christianity that was expressed through the mediation of objects, such as relics and sacred images, which in their opinion

[22] Sanna Solaro, *S. Sindone che si venera a Torino*, v–vi.

[23] [P. Caviglia], *La Santissima Sindone: Realtà o mistificazione?* (Turin: Tipografia cooperativa, 1899).

[24] E. Polidori, "E se una reliquia fosse falsa?," *La Civiltà Cattolica* 50, no. 5 (1899): 18–33.

[25] A. Boudinhon, "Et si ce n'était pas vrai?," *Revue du clergé français* 22 (1900): 241–63.

posed the risk of falling into idolatry. These same priests detested even more the apologetic attitude of those brothers in the priesthood who sheltered behind the defense of all the beliefs received from past centuries. On the other side of the field, many rushed to the defense of the Shroud: generally—but not always—they were less learned and capable but motivated by a sincere faith in the authenticity of the relic or afraid that renouncing certain religious practices would end up disorienting the faithful. Many among them received the arrival of methods of criticism and science in the sphere of religion with skepticism and saw therein the seeds of heresy. What happened with the Shroud was only one of many cases of the Catholic Church's internal opposition (one might think about the contemporary and equally incendiary discussions on the method of historical criticism in the study of the Bible) in a period that was characterized by the modernist crisis; modernism would be seen by the Catholic hierarchy as a danger to be combatted in the strongest possible terms and would be confronted with defensive and repressive measures. To understand properly the discussions that animated the debate over the Shroud in these years, therefore, it is necessary to keep in mind the cultural and religious context of the period, which on its own was already too heated.

4.1.3 Charles Lalore and Ulysse Chavalier

Charles Lalore (1829–1890), canon of the cathedral of Troyes, prolific scholar, and editor of numerous medieval documents that related to his diocese,[26] began the new historiographic phase. In 1877 he published a summary of the history of the Shroud of Lirey-Chambéry-Turin, which he based on many documents that were already published or cited in the preceding centuries, in particular by Chifflet, but which had been largely ignored. It was a meritorious and necessary project: let it suffice to know that at the time not even the archbishop of Turin had the least idea that his own Shroud had ever been in Lirey.

[26] Cf. A. Babeau, "M. l'abbé Lalore," *Mémoires de la Société académique d'agriculture, des sciences, arts et belles-lettres du Département de l'Aube* 54 (1890): 355–59, with bibliography preceding.

Lalore's article drew some immediate criticism: it was the first sign of the conflicts of the following years.[27]

The echo of the exhibition of 1898 and the rumor that photographs of the Shroud had been made reached the ears of Ulysse Chevalier (1841–1923), canon of Romans-sur-Isère. At the time Chevalier was already one of the most renowned historians of the medieval period and was associated with the major academies and cultural organizations of Europe, and the work that made him most famous, the *Répertoire des sources historiques du Moyen Âge,* even though over a century old, still retains its usefulness. Chevalier's first written work on the Shroud dates to 1899.[28] Its motive is discernible from the first lines: the learned canon wanted to react against whoever wanted to do without historians and sacrifice them on the altar of a supposed incontrovertible "scientific" reality, one worthy of modern times, exemplified by the amazing photography of the relic. An anti-historical attitude could seem seductive and unbeatable to the public, who were offered journalistic information such as this:

> The Man-God, desiring to leave the image of his person on his own sheet, took some precautions against the objections, the quibbles of men, not leaving anything other than a negative image that required photography to appear some day in its reality, in order to be enhanced. Such is the characteristic of divine work, the certificate of origin that banishes far and away all the papers, all the diplomas, and the manuscripts of scholars. What need have we to know the whole history of the relic venerated in Turin?[29]

Chevalier accepted the challenge. He responded as a historian, appealing to vilified documents and repeating *verbatim* the study of canon Lalore, enhancing it with some personal notes. He intended to hold the discussion in the sphere of the historical sciences, but the first significant reaction to his writing came from an expert in canon law:

[27] C. Lalore, "Historique de l'image du Saint Suaire de Jésus Christ primitivement à Lirey (Aube) et maintenant à Turin," *La Revue catholique de Troyes* 14 (1877): 120–24, 133–36, 328–32 (where on p. 329 one finds a quotation from a letter by Luigi Fransoni, archbishop of Turin until 1862, but in exile in Lyon since 1850).

[28] U. Chevalier, *Le Saint Suaire de Turin est-il l'original ou une copie?* (Chambéry: Ménard, 1899).

[29] M. Raboisson, in *La verité,* July 28, 1898, 2, cited in Chevalier, *Saint Suaire de Turin est-il l'original,* 7.

Emanuele Colomiatti, pro-vicar general of the diocese of Turin and president of the committee for festivities for the exhibition of that year (he delivered in the cathedral the formula of excommunication for whoever had dared to touch the Shroud without permission). Colomiatti was dean of the Department of Law of the seminary of Turin; in the area of historiography he was already distinguished, negatively, for his attempt to describe as miraculous a non-supernatural event that had happened in Turin in 1640. Here he used history for his own personal neo-Guelfist purposes, which were averse to the city's anticlerical party.[30] His writing against Chevalier was published with an introduction by Msgr. Albert Pillet, who immediately touched upon a crucial point: Chevalier is a priest, and as such—Pillet writes—he ought to have known that the authenticity (or not) of relics must not be announced in pamphlets to feed public opinion, which is absolutely incompetent in the matter, but must be discussed before the religious authorities of the Holy See, in particular the Congregation for Indulgences and Relics. Colomiatti also concentrated particularly on Chevalier's faithfulness to ecclesiastical authority: by giving credence to the document of Clement VII from 1390, the French canon was appearing to give the same level of authority to "the acts of the true popes and the acts of the antipopes," which "coming from a Catholic and a priest" seemed unacceptable to him.[31] The issue of pontifical authority was a matter that remained a particular concern for the Piedmontese canon, who had organized all his legal work around the celebration of the absolute primacy of the pope.

Colomiatti saw another danger looming on the horizon: if the absence of ancient documents was able to engender doubt about the authenticity of the Shroud, what about the authenticity of many other relics of Christ's passion provided for the veneration of the faithful, such as the nails, the crown of thorns, the spear, and the holy stairs? The abbot François Chamard was also posing the same question to himself; as for the shrouds, he took at face value the legendary accounts that pertained to them, and sometimes he had added to them himself (for example, when, wrongly, he attributed the first

[30] E. Colomiatti, *Miracolo del Santissimo Sacramento avvenuto nella chiesa del Monte di Torino* (Turin: Derossi, 1894). On the event, see L. P. G. Isella, *Il Monte dei Cappuccini e Filippo d'Agliè* (Città di Castello: Nuovaphromos, 2012), 115–18, 321–25.

[31] Colomiatti, *De l'authenticité*, 407–19, 502–22 (the quotation is from p. 504).

explicit mention of a shroud on which a representation of Christ was reproduced to the end of the seventh century).[32] These concerns may be able to make a twenty-first-century reader smile, but one must not forget that in the second half of the nineteenth century, Catholic authors could still be found who defended the authenticity of much more improbable relics, such as the holy foreskin of Jesus.[33]

According to Colomiatti, to demonstrate the authenticity of a relic there was no need for any physical or metaphysical certainty; rather, it was sufficient to have moral certainty, supported by the authority of the ancient accounts, of miracles performed through the intercession of the relics, of the approval of the highest pontiffs, and of the liturgical texts (criteria that, if applied, would render *all* the shrouds listed in the first chapter authentic). Where the authority of the Church was involved, he believed, the historical moment in which the approval of devotion of a relic happened was irrelevant and, at any rate, never untimely.

Chevalier answered immediately and in the same journal; others also encouraged him to do so, among whom was the great Benedictine scholar of patristics Germain Morin.[34] His response was that many events in the sacred history of the past, while approved by the pontiffs and included in official liturgies, had been revealed to be false beyond the doubt of anyone. As for the Shroud, so far no one had succeeded in producing evidence for it that antedated the fourteenth century, "and it is infinitely probable that it would never be found." In matters that touch upon neither dogma nor morality it was necessary then to allow the faithful their freedom: "*in dubiis libertas*, provided that this freedom is exercised with kindness and respect." But since the authenticity of the Shroud of Turin was "purely a question of historical criticism," the French canon proposed to Colomiatti that the question be referred to a "competent tribunal": the Bollandist fathers of Brussels, or three members of the Académie des Inscriptions et Belles-Lettres of Paris chosen by Colomiatti himself. The conclusion was therefore a challenge, because Chevalier stated he "[did] not want

[32] Chamard, *Linceul du Christ* (see p. 30).

[33] See *Narrazione critico-storica della reliquia preziosissima del santissimo prepuzio di N. S. Gesù Cristo* (Civita Castellana: Pietro Del Frate, 1861). On this curious and miraculous relic, see T. Ceravolo, *Il prepuzio di Cristo* (Soveria Mannelli: Rubbettino, 2015).

[34] Letter of January 3, 1900, to Chevalier; Nicolotti, *Processo negato*, 91.

to claim victory without combat"; and as a first move he pledged to publish all the medieval texts, including the unedited ones, that pertained to the issue.[35]

The fuse was by now lit. On June 6, 1900, Chevalier presented to the Sorbonne his *Critical Study of the Origin of the Holy Shroud of Lirey-Chambéry-Turin,* which was delivered and later published in French.[36] The study opened with the citation of a passage that appeared in the same year in the journal of the Bollandist fathers, who were at the time considered the most competent scholars in the subject of hagiography; in that passage they called to the reader's attention the medieval excesses that resulted from the cultivation of relics: such cultivation "neglected, on the majority of occasions, the most basic laws of prudence," having recourse to any means to satisfy the demand for holy memorabilia, thereby even creating the opportunity for illicit acts in order to get hold of them and so mixing false relics with authentic ones. The Bollandists' recommendation was to question the authenticity of *all* relics, especially "those which, without prior attestation, appeared on a specified day and place, in the period ranging from the ninth to the fifteenth century."[37] Paul Riant, founder of the Société de l'Orient Latin and noted expert on relics, believed that to be able to consider a relic authentic and display it for the veneration of the faithful, one should at least establish a continuous and uninterrupted chain of written testimonies dating to the time of the presumed origin of the object in question—even more so when there was a question of multiple competing relics, that is, relics contemporaneously present in different places.[38] No description was more suitable for the Shroud.

The historical part of Chevalier's volume has proved to be indispensable still today, particularly for the appendix of documents of the fourteenth to sixteenth centuries; the author was challenging his opponents to find contemporary or more ancient documents

[35] U. Chevalier, "Réponse aux observations de Mgr. Emmanuel Colomiatti," *Revue des sciences ecclésiastiques* 81 (1900): 73–80 (quotation from 78 and 80).

[36] Chevalier, *Étude critique.* It was subsequently supplemented by Chevalier, *Autour des origines du Suaire de Lirey.*

[37] Anonymous review of *Osservazioni critiche sulla vita di San Longino martire,* by F. Nodari, *Analecta Bollandiana* 19 (1900): 46–47.

[38] P. Riant, "Le Saint Suaire de Cadouin," *Revue des questions historiques* 8 (1870): 231.

that could repudiate his reconstruction, but no one up to now has been able to find any. The part of the book dedicated to the issue of photography, however, is unusable. Chevalier, not being skilled in the art, asked advice from his friend Hippolyte Chopin and published his response: his reply, however, was mistaken, because Chopin questioned the accuracy of the rendering of Pia's plates. One certainly cannot accuse Chevalier of carelessness: before he published his work, he submitted Chopin's report to the authoritative Gabriel Lippmann, the physicist who had just invented a technique for obtaining color photographs that would carry him to the Nobel Prize. Only after obtaining confirmation was Chevalier convinced that the photographs were an "immense falsification." But all three were mistaken in their conclusion, and as a result Lippmann, when it was possible for him to see a contretype on glass taken from the original, concluded that the photography of the Shroud had been carried out entirely properly.[39]

Chevalier's book would have an excellent reception in academic circles, and the author even received a gold medal of 1,000 francs from the Académie des Inscriptions et Belles-Lettres. Naturally the news was not well received by the supporters of authenticity. A Jesuit of Turin, Giammaria Sanna Solaro, hastened to respond. He was a figure of the highest level in the promotion of the veneration of the Sacred Heart of Christ and the cult of the Eucharist, and some years before he had already dealt with miraculous events. His training, however, was not as a historian: he was a professor of natural science and author of studies on plant diseases, the atmosphere, hailstorms, and earthquakes. Even this author, therefore, "clearly was not prepared to deal with a work of that sort," as the Bollandist Hippolyte Delehaye said:[40] the result was a book that, despite its elegant typographic appearance and wealth of content, lacked a critical perspective.

Where Chevalier insisted on the absence of certain information about the Shroud before the fourteenth century, Sanna Solaro invented his own history, which was completely linear and concordist: the Shroud was taken from Jerusalem to Constantinople by Saint Helena's hand at the beginning of the fourth century, or in any case

[39] The account is reported by Loth, *Photographie du Saint Suaire de Turin*, 10.

[40] H. Delehaye, review of *Le St. Suaire de Lirey-Chambéry-Turin*, by U. Chevalier, *Analecta Bollandiana* 21 (1902): 213.

before the sack by Khosrow II in 614. Therefore the Jerusalem shrouds described by Bede and Arculf are false. On the contrary the shroud of Besançon is authentic, being made of bands that came from Christ's tomb and were sewn together; but the image on the bands is not him, because someone painted it later (!). The Shroud of Turin ended up in Constantinople, where there was already another shroud without an image, equally authentic, which was split up to make various relics that were spread throughout Europe from the time of Charlemagne.[41] By multiplying the shrouds the author tried also to save the other competing relics.

With regard to the arrival of the cloth of Turin in the West, the Jesuit did not forego inventing his own personal theory. He knew that in 1204, in the days of the sack of Constantinople by the crusaders, many relics were amassed under the keeping of Garnier de Traînel, bishop of Troyes. According to Sanna Solaro, Garnier had two sisters, "Gille and Hélissente; his father, who himself had the name Garnier, gave Gille in marriage to Hugues, Lord of Vergy; and so he was Garnier's grandson. The other sister, Hélissente, was married to Clarembaud de Chappes; Garnier was therefore his brother-in-law." Moreover, among the "friends and relatives" of the bishop there certainly *had* to be also Guillaume I de Champlitte, second husband of Élisabeth de Mont-Saint-Jean, sister of the great-grandfather of Geoffroy I de Charny. The conclusion is easy to imagine: somehow, someone, probably Guillaume, would have taken the Shroud from the pile of Garnier's relics and brought it into France.[42]

The unlikelihood of these "hereditary" conjectures can be easily demonstrated (as is evident from the genealogical tree in this book's front matter). Gille and Hélissente de Traînel indeed had a brother by the name of Garnier, but he was Garnier III, husband to Agnès de Mello. The bishop, in fact, belonged to another branch of the family and was cousin to Gille's father. As far as Guillaume de Champlitte is concerned, after 1200 he was divorced from Élisabeth

[41] Sanna Solaro, *S. Sindone che si venera a Torino*, 1–23.

[42] Sanna Solaro, *S. Sindone che si venera a Torino*, 25–27. The theory was proposed again by M. Hernández Villaescusa, *La Sábana Santa de Turín* (Barcelona: Henrich, 1903), 109–12; and by Pugno, *Santa Sindone che si venera a Torino*, 49–50 and 88. The idea that the relic had been brought by Guillaume came from Dunod de Charnage, *Histoire de l'église*, 409 (Sanna Solaro [*S. Sindone che si venera a Torino*, 27, n. 1], because of an oversight, mistakenly quotes him as André Du-Chesne).

de Mont-Saint-Jean, ancestor of Geoffroy de Charny, to begin a third marriage, this time with Eustachie de Courtenay-Champignelles. This indicates that during and after the sack of Constantinople (1204), the time of the presumed theft of the Shroud by the crusaders, Élisabeth was no longer Guillaume's wife. Therefore the two links that would justify the relic's passage between Guillaume de Champlitte and the Charnys are tenuous.

At this point Sanna Solaro goes on to fantasize about the arrival of the Shroud in the collegiate church of Lirey; according to him, in the year 1353, the Shroud "was brought to that church with great pomp and a gathering of clerics and people of every stripe." Of the gift of the Shroud to the House of Savoy, he repeats that it happened at Chambéry (instead of Geneva) and concocts that it was even authorized by the pope.[43]

The Piedmontese Jesuit dedicates the better part of his book to the refutation of Ulysse Chevalier. The gross error of the French canon, according to him, is that he brought up medieval documents against the authenticity of the Shroud, thereby resurrecting the 1877 work of the canon Lalore "from under the dust of the libraries where it ought to have remained eternally buried." Still worse was to have spread it "to the four winds at a time in which all of Christendom is being sweetly moved by the honors paid to the Holy Relic, on the solemn feast-days of Turin, and while the venerated Image obtained from the photograph is being requested for devotion by all quarters of the earth." It would have been better if the Memorandum of Pierre d'Arcis and the bull of Clement VII had remained "forever buried in oblivion, because they are shameful for their authors and because they are not a credit to whomever wished to bring them to light."[44]

Sanna Solaro's book is more useful in the section that pertains to the modern history of the Shroud, from the sixteenth century forward. Some of his ideas are very curious and would be rejected by other sindonologists. He probably found those curiosities in old treatises, such as the one by Chifflet:[45] that Jesus was not crucified naked but clad in a loincloth (that he also sees on the Shroud), and that the Shroud was used only to transport Jesus' body from the cross to the

[43] Sanna Solaro, *S. Sindone che si venera a Torino*, 28, 32–33.
[44] Sanna Solaro, *S. Sindone che si venera a Torino*, 71, 78.
[45] Chifflet, *De linteis sepulchralibus*, 40–49, 145–50, 195–96.

tomb, before the body was washed and buried with other linens. He deems all of this incontrovertible and, what is more, confirmed by the visions of Saint Bridget, to whom he ascribes evidential value, the same value that he confers on the accounts of all the miracles that happened through the intercession of the Shroud as reported by Pingon. Where Sanna Solaro appears competent, however, is in the area of photography: his refutation of the part of Chevalier's book written by Chopin is correct.[46]

As for Chevalier, if the relic had been criticized by some "Judaic-Masonic journal" he would have been able to understand it, but that a cleric such as Chevalier was doing so seemed unbelievable to him.[47] Sanna Solaro's thinking was typical of a certain intransigent culture of the time, one oriented toward perceiving in society the fateful presence of Masonic conspiracies inspired by the Jews.[48] But this same zeal had already led him astray once, when he supported the unsuccessful case of the forger Léo Taxil.[49] Therefore, when his book on the Shroud appeared, someone did not miss the opportunity to reproach him for the gullibility and incompetence that he was slipping into for the second time.[50]

[46] Sanna Solaro, *S. Sindone che si venera a Torino*, 113–22, 128–29, 146.

[47] Sanna Solaro, *S. Sindone che si venera a Torino*, VI.

[48] His efforts to spread a society "for the social kingship" are described by D. Menozzi, *Sacro cuore: Un culto tra devozione interiore e restaurazione cristiana della società* (Rome: Viella, 2001), 175–210.

[49] Taxil was an ex-Mason and anticleric who, in 1885, after an ostentatiously false conversion to Catholicism, caused the ranks of the anti-Masons to swell. He spread a series of horrifying alleged revelations from an imaginary repentant "priestess," who was also an ex-Mason, by the name of Diana Vaughan. The case resonated with people, and Catholics were divided between those who, despite never having seen her, believed Vaughan's chilling revelations and made great use of them in anti-Masonic propaganda, and those who instead considered those revelations nothing more than a fraudulent invention by Taxil. Those who were wrong had allowed themselves to be deceived by the falsehoods of a woman who, perhaps, never even existed. Among the more zealous anti-Masons was Sanna Solaro himself, who at the recommendation of the archbishop of Turin supported steadfastly the empty case of Taxil-Vaughan before the Holy Office. On the whole event, see G. M. Cazzaniga, ed., *La massoneria* (Turin: Einaudi, 2006), 220–36; G. Wright, *Notable or Notorious? A Gallery of Parisians* (Cambridge, Mass.: Harvard University Press, 1989), 86–147; M. Introvigne, *Satanism: A Social History* (Leiden: Brill, 2016), 158–226.

[50] "It is a shame that a scholar of natural science did not remain in his field but sought to interfere in a historical matter, even though in the past he had already been deceived by his critical mind in the affair of Taxil-Diana Vaughan"

We might well wonder why it was not possible, among the clergy of Turin, to do better in responding to a giant like Chevalier than these two priests who were not very qualified on the subject. In fact, among the professors of the Department of Theology, there was at least one who was able make such a response, canon Giuseppe Piovano, professor of ecclesiastical history. But he did not write anything, because he sided with Chevalier.

4.1.4 The Debate over Chevalier

In the defense of his work, Ulysse Chevalier was anything but submissive; he was caustic in his style and disinclined to compromise, and he did not spare from any blame that Piedmontese Jesuit who had questioned his capacity as a historian and interpreter of documents.[51] First he mocks the incompetence and numerous errors of his opponent; then he focuses on the crucial point: Sanna Solaro proceeds "with a series of affirmations, not one of which is based on the shadow of a text, and with the continual transformation of initial conjectures into incontestable certainties," in this way arriving at his evidence "after having bridged the void of history with imagination."[52] These passages are important because lack of competence, work on second-hand sources, misuse of the historical method, and recourse to convenient conjectures still today comprise the majority of written work dedicated to the Shroud.

In his slender book Chevalier cites ample excerpts of opinions from many Catholic scholars who appreciated his scholarship. The Jesuit Bollandists, experts in hagiography, published in two reviews from the well-known Hippolyte Delehaye an unconditional approval "for the scientific campaign courageously undertaken by Ulysse Chevalier against the claims of those who persist in presenting the Holy Shroud of Turin as an authentic relic, despite the evidence."[53] The list of his supporters is long: I limit myself to mentioning in France

(P. M. Baumgarten, "Das 'Grabtuch Christi' von Turin: Ein Bericht," *Historisches Jahrbuch* 24 [1903]: 332).

[51] U. Chevalier, *Le St. Suaire de Lirey-Chambéry-Turin et les défenseurs de son authenticité* (Paris: Picard, 1902), 13–41.

[52] Chevalier, *St. Suaire de Lirey-Chambéry-Turin*, 17–18.

[53] [H. Delehaye], review of *Étude critique sur l'origine du St. Suaire de Lirey-Chambéry-Turin* and of *Le Saint-Suaire de Lirey-Chambéry-Turin*, by U. Chevalier, *Analecta Bollandiana* 19 (1900): 215–17 and 350–51 (the quotation is from p. 350).

the Benedictine Henri Leclercq, who in the renowned *Dictionnaire d'archéologie chrétienne et de liturgie* fully accepted the thesis of the relic's inauthenticity; in England the famous Jesuit Herbert Thurston, who some years after would do the same in the *Catholic Encyclopedia;* and in Germany the priest Paul Maria Baumgarten, scholar of papal diplomatics and the history of the Roman curia.[54]

And in Italy? In November of 1901 the Piedmontese historian Luigi Cesare Bollea admitted to Chevalier that "he had found in this free [!] Italy neither a journal, nor a daily newspaper, even among the outspoken liberals, that was willing to make mention of your learned publication, only in order not to attract ire."[55] Bollea himself would be the one to break the silence by publishing a note in the prestigious *Rivista storica italiana*, where he did not fail to confirm the existence in Italy of a "conspiracy of silence."[56] Salvatore Minocchi, director of a journal that some years later would be shuttered by an accusation of modernism, also added some thoughts.[57] From Rome the Jesuit Angelo De Santi, while announcing that he was in agreement with Chevalier, let him know that the Jesuit journal *La Civiltà Cattolica* was not able to address the issue because of "the considerations imposed on us."[58] Privately Chevalier received news of what was happening in Turin from the lawyer Francesco Invrea, a lively representative of the democratic-Christian side of the city (along with the canon Giuseppe Piovano, of whom I have already spoken and will again later).[59] But in Turin neither Christian Democracy nor the critical approach that

[54] H. Leclercq, "Suaire," in *Dictionnaire d'archéologie chrétienne et de liturgie*, vol. 15, bk. 2 (Paris: Librairie Letouzey et Ané, 1953), coll. 1718–24; H. Thurston, "The Holy Shroud and the Verdict of History," *Month* 101 (1903): 17–29; Thurston, "The Holy Shroud as a Scientific Problem," *Month* 101 (1903): 162–78; Thurston, "Shroud," in *The Catholic Encyclopedia*, ed. C. G. Hebermann et al., vol. 13 (New York: Encyclopedia Press, 1913), 762–63; Baumgarten, *Das 'Grabtuch Christi' von Turin*, 319–43.

[55] GBEI, R9089: postcard to Chevalier from November 1901.

[56] L. C. Bollea, review of various books on the Shroud, *Rivista storica italiana* 20, no. 2 (1903): 11–18, 429–30 (quotation is from p. 16). Unfortunately, even Bollea allowed himself to be misled by the unfounded photographic criticisms of Chopin. On Bollea, see M. Chiaudano, *Luigi Cesare Bollea* (Bene Vagienna: Vissio, 1936).

[57] S. Minocchi, "La S. Sindone di Torino, il Vangelo e la Scienza positiva," *Studi religiosi* 2, no. 6 (1902): 567–71.

[58] GBEI, R9089: letter by Angelo De Santi from November 26, 1902.

[59] On Invrea, see A. Zussini, *Franco Invrea: Un "patrizio Genovese" nella Torino giolittiana* (Alessandria: Dell'Orso, 2007).

could be suspected of modernism enjoyed the approval of Agostino Cardinal Richelmy, Archbishop of Turin, nicknamed "the hammer of the modernists." Whoever was not afraid to displease the archbishop in regard to the Shroud was afraid of displeasing the king, and, being caught between the two authorities, Italian scholars preferred to keep their mouths shut. But it was clear that the majority of the most renowned Catholic scholars had accepted Chevalier's thesis: the Shroud was not an authentic relic, even if it was better not to say so too forcefully.

4.1.5 Toward Censorship

Many of Chevalier's adversaries, unable to counter him on the level of history, set themselves the task of faulting him on theological and ecclesiastical bases. They chided him for having placed undue faith in medieval documents that emanated from Clement VII, since these came not from a pope but rather from an antipope.[60] The objection is without value, because the fact that the pope was or was not legitimately elected in no way changes the level of credibility of his writings, the contents of which must be treated in the same way as those of any other document. Many legitimate popes, on the other hand, have endorsed the authenticity of patently false relics; and this should not amaze even a faithful Catholic, since in this context the pope's infallibility cannot be brought up. Also, the category of "antipope" ought to be used with greater caution: as Chevalier himself replied at the time of the dispute over the Shroud, "there was no true pope and one or more antipopes: each of the opposing pontifices was deemed the authentic pope among those who obeyed him."[61] Sometimes not even his contemporaries were able to clarify the legitimacy of each pontifex. In this case the two opposing popes—Clement VII of Avignon and, first, Urban VI, followed by Boniface IX of Rome—fought by any means necessary to ensure their preeminence, while Europe was divided into those who obeyed one and those who obeyed the other. At that time, Clement represented

[60] This is a recurring objection among Catholic sindonologists, already hurled against Charles Lalore in 1877 and still repeated today. It can be found, for example, in A. Monti, *La S. Sindone di Torino, la S. Casa di Loreto e la critica del Can. Ulisse Chevalier* (Genoa: Tipografia della gioventù, 1907), 54–60.

[61] Chevalier, *Saint Suaire de Turin est-il l'original*, 18.

in France the sole supreme ecclesiastical authority recognized by the king, the bishop, the canons, and all those who could have any connection to the question of the Shroud. No one among them could imagine that, in the future, he would be considered an antipope. Clement was simply called upon to decide about a question that was within his jurisdiction, and his decision is an authoritative testimony pertaining to the facts.

Chevalier was also accused of having affirmed that the authenticity of relics is a historical question, not a theological one, which therefore ought to be submitted to the examination of scholars and not of ecclesiastical authorities. Today, these methodological premises are peacefully achieved, but at the time they were subject to strong resistance by those who opposed the introduction of the method of historical criticism in the religious sciences; the resistance was exasperated by the fact that the same premises were one of the basic demands of the modernist movement.

By leveraging these elements, at the beginning of 1900 Emanuele Colomiatti, on behalf of Cardinal Richelmy, archbishop of Turin, denounced Chevalier at the tribunal of the Holy Office with the following accusations: that he refused to submit to the judgment of the Holy See on the matter of relics, that he corroborated the writings of an antipope, and that he bypassed ecclesiastical censorship and propounded false doctrinal principles. Colomiatti thought that at least three papal congregations could intervene against Chevalier: the Holy Office (previously known as the Inquisition, also known as the Congregation for the Doctrine of the Faith), the Congregation of the Index of Prohibited Books, and the Congregation for Indulgences and Relics.

The Holy Office thought that the question was not worthy of being addressed and responded that the matter could eventually be judged by the other two congregations. The Congregation of the Index declared, however, that Chevalier's work was not censurable. At this point Cardinal Richelmy himself contacted the Congregation for Indulgences and Relics, asking them to act in order to "put an end to the audacity of such a priest, whose example could be an inducement to wickedness for others." The congregation took the case in hand, named a committee of experts, and for some months devoted itself to examining the Shroud.

Nothing is known of these measures, which were taken under pontifical secrecy. Chevalier, for his part, continued to publish responses at a fast pace, until, in December of 1902, two French newspapers made public the existence of the committee and reported that it had taken a position favorable to Chevalier: the Shroud, therefore, was a fake. Both newspapers added that the awkward verdict had already been referred to Leo XIII, but that it would probably never be published in an official way, on account of the delicacy of the matter. Among the names of those involved in the case, that of the noted historian Msgr. Louis Duchesne, director of the École française de Rome, comes to the fore.[62] The same news also reached Chevalier: the happenings in Rome came to him through Msgr. Albert Battandier, who in turn was informed directly by one of the consultors to the committee formed by the Congregation for Indulgences; Chevalier in this way found out that even the pope was convinced of the committee's verdict. The canon felt heartened, and in January of 1902 he allowed an article to go to press in which he confirmed what was written in the newspapers about the negative position on the Shroud taken by the committee: the authenticity of the Shroud did not stand up (*non sustinetur*). But he immediately adds: "The delicate relationships of the Roman court with the House of Savoy could make it hesitate to comment on an issue where national honor plays an important role."[63]

Perhaps the circulation of this news contributed to causing events to rush in the opposite direction of the committee's ruling. Despite the fact that the assembly of experts in Rome had reached the firm belief that the Shroud was not authentic, neither the king nor the archbishop of Turin, and probably not even the pope, could accept that the verdict of the committee had become official and operative. Not only did nothing come of this verdict, but Chevalier was hit, under pressure applied by Richelmy and the House of Savoy, with an order that forced him to stop publishing on the Shroud of Turin. A little before this, his most renowned supporters, the Bollandist fathers, had prepared a new written work that was favorable to him;

[62] Don Giuseppe, "Le Saint-Suaire de Turin," *La Croix*, December 19, 1902, 3; Don Alessandro, "Lettre de Rome," *Le XXe siecle*, December 28, 1902, 1.

[63] U. Chevalier, "Encore le Saint Suaire de Turin," *L'université catholique* 42 (1903): 127.

but it too was blocked by the ecclesiastical censorship to which they were subject, and it was not published. And so, a mortal blow was inflicted upon the deniers of the relic's authenticity, leaving the field open for the other faction instead. Chevalier, who up to that point had written almost frenetically on the issue,[64] had to interrupt his own research and did not write another line on the Shroud for the rest of his life.

The canon must have suffered more than a little in seeing his opponents going to so much trouble to deny the existence of the committee's verdict, almost leading one to believe that he had invented it himself.[65] In the following years the *non sustinetur* was even described by some sindonologists as "a falsehood produced by the canon Chevalier."[66] This regrettable situation ended only in 2015, when I published part of Chevalier's letters and the documents of the Congregation, preserved in the Vatican Secret Archives.[67]

Regarding the committee's position on the Shroud, according to the words of the abbot Luigi Nicolis di Robilant, those members who during the committee's deliberations relied only on the historical argument would later change their minds, because they were impressed by the value of a "chemical argument."[68] If this was truly

[64] A list of his publications on the topic can be found in *M. le Chanoine Ulysse Chevalier: Son œuvre scientifique* (Valence: Céas, 1903), §§ 106–25.

[65] For but one example, see A. Loth, "Rome et le Saint-Suaire de Turin," *La vérité française*, March 30, 1903, 1.

[66] L. Fossati, "Su una pretesa risposta di Roma contro l'autenticità della Sindone," *Sindon* 2 (1960): 7.

[67] Nicolotti, *Processo negato.*

[68] CSS, Fondo Pia, 3.1.1.198: letter from October 15, 1903, to Baron Manno: "What do they think about the Holy Shroud in Rome? Some hours before I put this question to the good Father Franco, who came to visit us in the villa. 'They are inclined toward its authenticity,' Fr. Grisar's associate answered. The chemical argument made a great impression on that commission, which three years ago, induced by the weakness of the historical argument, had issued its *non sustineri*. On the other hand, Chevalier in the meantime was recognized as a small man, not profound, who offered nonexistent documents as true and did not know how to recognize the value of those that were authentic. If the judgment were now, I believe that it would turn out very differently." But it seems to me difficult to believe that similar judgments on the critical capability and honesty of Chevalier were passed by someone competent in the matter. As for the Father Grisar who was cited, in the years preceding he had expressed his ideas that the sindonic image dated clearly to the fourteenth century (D. Zähringer, "Das Grabtuch von Turin," *Benediktinische*

so, it was not a good idea: the chemical argument, proposed in those years by Paul Vignon, would be revealed to be mistaken.

At this point Turin did not fail to react anew against Chevalier, nicknamed "the Achilles of the adversaries," in the person of the canon Giuseppe Giacomo Re, professor of Hebrew in the seminary's Department of Theology. He applies still less of the spirit of criticism than did Sanna Solaro, except when it is a matter of criticizing some weakness of his opponents, but much more biting, almost offensive, his prose is addressed against those whom he calls the "sudarophobes" and in general against those who doubt relics (including the Bollandists). For him, the tradition clearly proves both the existence of the Shroud from antiquity to the medieval period, and its authenticity as well as the speciousness of whoever believes the contrary.[69] For the public at large the canon Re also published a history of the Shroud in the form of a "popular historical account," beginning from the point when it was entrusted to Malchus, servant of the high priest, until its arrival in Turin. The whole work scorns the sudarophobes, who are considered guilty of having roused a "bitter war for the sacrosanct relic" "under the influence of malevolent spirits," by putting forth arguments "that are completely worthless, because they were founded on grounds that are laughable and false."[70] Giuseppe Re went on to mock as well the famous *non sustinetur,* in which he did not believe, and in which he saw the hand of the devil, who showed "the horns that betray him." One can easily understand why, after reading it, Paul Maria Baumgarten described the canon Re's work as "a fanatical writing," and was not surprised that Re, owing to his intransigence, was a member of the diocesan council for monitoring modernism.[71]

But Chevalier was no longer able to respond. His exit from the stage and the antimodernist repression slowly extinguished the fiery debate. Thereafter and until now, among sindonologists, Chevalier was known to history as a person of "little serenity and much acrimony"

Monatsschrift 26 [1950]: 154; CSS, Fondo Pia, 3.1.1.130: letter from Ulysse Chevalier to Antonio Manno from December 1, 1899).

[69] G. Re, *Dizionario di erudizione biblica,* vol. 4 (Turin: Paravia, 1900–1908), 109–31, 153–64.

[70] Re, *Santissima Sindone* (quotation is from pp. 18, 21, 22).

[71] Re, *Dizionario di erudizione biblica,* 161–62, 348; Re, *Santissima Sindone,* 23; Baumgarten, *Das 'Grabtuch Christi' von Turin,* 332.

and characterized by "anti-Italian and antisavoyard animosity." In sindonologists' opinion, Chevalier's work was an expression of "confused involvement at the emotional level" or "of the partiality, passion, and preconceptions of its author."[72] On the contrary, even today it is impossible to deny that Chevalier was absolutely one of the most competent and brilliant people dedicated to the historical study of the Shroud.

4.2. The Fragility of the Hard Sciences

4.2.1 Chiaroscuro and the "Negativity" of the Image

Beginning with its first photograph in 1898, we have grown accustomed to looking at photographs of the Shroud printed as a black and white negative, where the white image of the man's body is silhouetted on a dark background (fig. 4.1). That depiction is preferable, since the image on the negative is depicted much more clearly than the positive image, in which—exactly as happened on the original as well—the pale color that outlines the body tends to blend with the pale background of the fabric. But the habit of viewing the Shroud not as it is, but as it is reproduced on the photographic negative, also causes some problems: the inversion of tonal values, the reduction to white and black, and the accentuation of contrast through photographic techniques (contrast filters, orthochromatic plates of varying sensitivity to different colors, and so on) obscure the actual balance between the colors and render an image that does not accord with reality. There is, then, a fundamental point that merits clarification: from the time when the Shroud was first photographed, word spread that it was a negative photograph. This observation is obsessively repeated but is incorrect.

A photographic negative in black and white is an image on a transparent support (at the time, a glass plate) that, relative to the subject it reproduces, has undergone a chiaroscuro inversion, by which the bright parts of the object (the lights) turn out more or less dark, opaque, while the dark tones (the shades) appear more or less clear, transparent. Normally viewing a negative proves unpleasant

[72] A. Caviglia, "Il profilo religioso di Emanuele Filiberto e la SS. Sindone," in *Emanuele Filiberto* (Turin: Lattes, 1928), 384; M. G. Siliato, *Il mistero della Sindone* (Casale Monferrato: Piemme, 1989), 79; P. Baima Bollone, *Sindone e scienza all'inizio del terzo millennio* (Turin: La Stampa, 2000), 205.

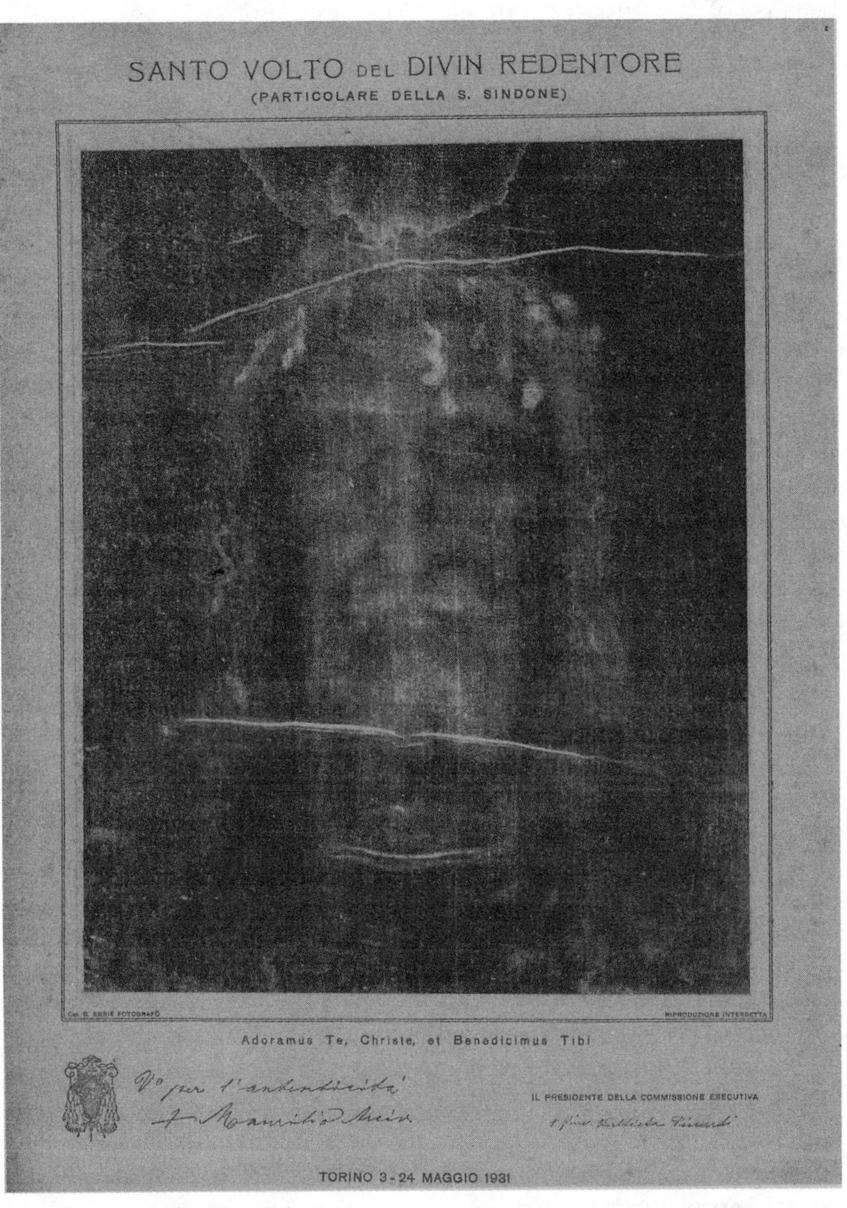

FIGURE 4.1 *Holy Face of the Divine Redeemer,* for the exhibition of the Shroud in 1931, photograph by Giuseppe Enrie

because of the unnatural inversion of light and dark, and only the subsequent process of developing the plate returns them to the same state as in the original that was photographed. For the Shroud, however, the contrary is true, because the original itself in respect to the corporal image already contains an inversion of lights and shades relative to the appearance of an actual body, for which reason viewing the negative image is more feasible and pleasant than viewing the positive or the Shroud itself.

Consider a human body bathed in natural light. When seen from the front and exposed to the light source, certain parts that are more prominent reflect the light more and therefore appear clearer, while other parts are darker because they are more in the shadows, darker in color, or set at an angle. The reality of the image on the Shroud is the exact opposite: if one observes the parts of the body that appear in greater relief on the cloth, that is, the ones that ought to be exposed more to the light, he will see that they are darker, while those that are less prominent are clearer. The point of the nose as well as the eyebrows, the cheekbones, and the moustache are darker than the eye sockets, for example, when in reality the illumination would be reversed. And so we feel more comfortable viewing the negative image of the Shroud, because the inversion of lights and shades on the plates renders the figure more normal in appearance and our brain decodes it in a way more familiar, as if it were lighted correctly.

Why is everything on the cloth inverted? Because the image of the man on the Shroud is not meant to be the representation of a body exposed to light, as in a normal painting, but is intended to show the effect brought on by a corpse, soiled with blood, sweat, and spices or unguents, that has come into contact with the cloth and was able to stain it. It is easy to understand that the more prominent parts of the body—that is, those that came into more contact with the cloth—left a greater coloration relative to those that remained farther away or were subjected to a lesser contact pressure. The final effect is that of an *impression*. The effect is somewhat comparable to that of a stamp, whose more prominent parts are the ones that leave color on the page. Therefore it is in no way strange if the negative plate seems more natural than the original: that is the case because it renders in bright color the points that came into contact with the cloth (that is, those parts that in reality are dark) and no longer creates the imprint but creates its opposite, namely, a human image that looks like an actual body exposed to light.

When in 1898 the first photographs were taken, this simple evidence was neglected and attention was focused on the fact that the photographic negative returned a positive human image; the conclusion drawn was that the image of Christ on the Shroud, or even the Shroud itself, was a photographic negative. Therefore, the following deductive fallacy was proposed:

> The concept of a negative became known only through the invention of photography in the nineteenth century. No artist of any earlier period could have conceived the idea of producing a picture in negative.[73]

This notion of a presumed non-falsifiability of the Shroud's image—which would be evidence in favor of its authenticity—is repeated up to the present day and is also put to whoever goes to visit the cathedral of Turin;[74] yet it is mistaken because it confuses the photographic negative with the effect of the impression, which was well known for centuries before the invention of the photograph (one might think about stamps, seals, drawing with *frottage*, molds, or any natural phenomenon in which an object leaves an image formed through contact). The only novelty of the photograph of 1898 was the ability to invert the shading and restore on the negative plate a likeness, as regards the distribution of light, of the figure that made the image. It is truly incredible, however, that such clear evidence is ignored still today: there is nothing strange or supernatural about it. Even before the invention of the photograph, everyone could calmly understand the effect of a mold; in fact it has long been thought that the Shroud's image was actually produced in that way—that is, through contact between the cloth and the body of Christ covered in sweat, blood, and spices used for the burial. To cite only three proponents of that idea: Cardinal Louis de Gorrevod in 1534, Philibert Pingon in 1581, and Lazzaro Piano in 1883.

[73] P. M. Rinaldi, *It Is the Lord* (New York: Vantage Press, 1972), 64. For another example, see N. Balossino, "La ricerca informatica sulla Sindone," in Barberis and Zaccone, *Sindone: Cento anni di ricerca*, 233.

[74] "It cannot be the work of any human hand because the images of negative character that it bears were already impressed on it many centuries before the difference between negative and positive was discovered" (December 2018).

It would not even be correct to say only that the *image* on the Shroud has the characteristics of a photographic negative. A characteristic of the image of the Shroud is its monochrome nature, consisting of a certain shade of yellow: there is no difference between the color of the skin and the hair, for example. But in a true photographic negative of a human body, the difference between the colors is discernible. On the old black and white plate, the matter was less evident because the differences in color and illumination of the subject were both reduced to shades of grey of varying intensities. But everything changed with modern color photographic negatives, which present images chromatically inverted into their complementary colors with respect to those of the subject (blue becomes yellow, green becomes magenta, red becomes cyan, and so on). If the image on the Shroud were a photographic negative in color, we would have to deduce from it that the man depicted had, in reality, skin and hair of the same color, namely a shade between violet and blue.

4.2.2 Geometry of the Image and Blood Stains

It is, however, impossible to think that the image of the man was formed merely through contact with a body soaked in a coloring agent. First of all, it lacks a sharp outline, degrading on the edge and fading until it blends into the coloring of the background of the cloth; on the contrary, the red spots corresponding to the bloody wounds have a definite contour and were clearly established by a different method.

The anthropomorphic impressions on the Shroud, then, are geometrically inconsistent. They appear as the result of an orthogonal projection of the image of a human body on a flat surface. The result is similar to an image seen in a mirror, a sort of projection at a right angle that lacks depth, enjoying only width and height.

This is certainly not a recent discovery. Already in the seventeenth century, Chifflet had realized that the image of the Shroud could not be an impression obtained by simple contact with a three-dimensional body, because of the missing distortion of the image.[75] In 1833 Lazzaro Piano requested to prove it experimentally:

[75] Chifflet, *De linteis sepulchralibus*, 198–99.

> By way of an example, let the face of a statue be dyed with color and let a white cloth be applied to it; if, after having pressed it a bit by hand, the cloth is removed and spread out, one will see on it a distorted image, much wider than the face itself.[76]

Both concluded that the image of the Shroud, which could not possibly be of natural formation, was the result of a miracle.

In fact, if a three-dimensional object capable of leaving an impression were wrapped in a cloth, once the cloth was spread out the result would be a deformed image. To put it another way, it is as if one were to use a flat map to cover a globe. To demonstrate this experimentally, various authors have performed tests with human models covered in coloring material, thereby showing that contact between a body and a sheet leaves impressions that are misshapen in width, distorted, discontinuous, and very far from the precision that one sees on the relic, especially in the fineness of the facial features.[77]

Therefore, if one wishes to assume that the image was formed while the Shroud held a corpse, one must conclude that at the time of the formation of the image the cloth was in a flat position either above or below the body, like two parallel plates, and that it received the image even at points where it was not in contact with the body. If this could be understandable for the back of the body by imagining that it was spread supine on a sepulchral slab, it is not at all applicable for the front of the body, where the cloth could not be stretched taut, but rather fell and sagged onto the corpse. As things are, the dorsal and ventral impressions present the same vividness; this indicates that the weight of the back of the body in contact with the sheet did not influence the process of the formation of the image: otherwise, the weight that laid on the cloth would have left a stronger mark. On the Shroud, moreover, there is not a single indication of the natural displacement that would be expected from the weight of certain parts of a body spread over a rigid surface. The buttocks and calves, for example, present a roundness of shape that lacks compression. The position of the hair is also unnatural because, contrary to the law of gravity, it does not lie on the ground but is pushed upward toward the sheet.

[76] Piano, *Comentarii critico-archeologici*, 2:312.

[77] To cite two pioneers: [Caviglia], *Santissima Sindone*, 8–13; and Vignon, *Le Linceul du Christ*, 49–51 (English translation: *Shroud of Christ*, 131–33).

In conclusion, everything points away from the possibility that the image of the Shroud was formed naturally and entirely through contact with a corpse spread out over a flat surface in the tomb. The difficulties can be resolved if one considers some devices used by the creator who fashioned the Shroud, who made it in such a way as not to produce a deformed and fuzzy image; those difficulties, on the other hand, remain insurmountable for whoever believes the Shroud to be authentic, forcing him to have recourse to explanations that generally flow into the supernatural. For example, Giulio Fanti fantasizes that the hairs are raised in their unnatural position due to a sudden electrical discharge,[78] while others suggest that, when Jesus was resurrected, he imprinted the Shroud while floating in a vertical position, after being raised into the air in the tomb.[79] Another idea is that the two edges of the Shroud could have been lifted and stretched perpendicularly in the air by angels to allow for the orthogonal impression of the image.[80]

The "blood" spots are just as problematic. How is it possible that the Shroud is not entirely stained with blood but has only very specific spots in correspondence to the wounds, which in some cases come to reproduce the shape of the wounds themselves (as in cases of scourge blows)? Everyone knows that the contact between a fabric and a bloody wound does not reproduce precisely the contours of the wound or the exact shape of the blood during the process of coagulation on the skin, but causes absorption into the fibers of the fabric, producing indistinct and jagged spots. Repeated flagellations would cause the skin to be completely drenched in blood, flowing beyond the wounds proper; scalp wounds, even small ones, bleed copiously and stain a large surface, because the area is very vascularized. The man of the Shroud, instead, has "perfect" bleeding, with precise and well-defined outlines, on a substantially clean background. Moreover, if the spots were due to contact, it would be quite strange that they

[78] Cf. G. Fanti, *La Sindone: Una sfida alla scienza moderna* (Rome: Aracne, 2009), 86–87.

[79] Cf. N. Mosso, "Le perizie sulla Sindone," *Osservazioni alle perizie ufficiali sulla Santa Sindone, 1969–1976* (Turin: Centro Internazionale di Sindonologia, 1977), 117; and G. R. Lavoie, *Unlocking the Secrets of the Shroud* (Allen, Tex.: Thomas More, 1998), 127–83.

[80] Cf. N. Cinquemani, *Le doppie immagini della Sacra Sindone* (Rome: Kappa, 2004), in particular 13, 94–97.

moved on the fabric without leaving any smudge, as if the alleged bloodied body had been put in contact with the fabric without making any movement or any adjustment, not even by the smallest measurements: the task of burying someone, however, forces the body to be manipulated in various ways.

The position of the blood spots is artistic but not credible. The flow of blood that runs along the arms is completely unnatural, and so is the stain on the forehead in the form of the Greek letter ε.[81] The signs of the scourging would make one think of a body that was struck by ropes at whose ends were fixed metal or bone balls; it is often repeated that this was the typical form of the scourges in Roman times, but this is false:[82] rather, the marks are in the form of the scourges that in the Middle Ages could be seen both in the artistic representations of the scourging of Jesus and on the streets of France, which in the middle of the fourteenth century, during the Great Plague, was crossed by flagellants who whipped themselves with ropes at whose ends there were knots with metal points.[83]

It is equally absurd that on the Shroud the spots occur not only on the skin of the face but also outside it—that is, on the hair where

[81] Experiments on actual human bodies demonstrate that the flow of blood on the skin does not occur in such a way, notwithstanding certain bold attempts to find explanations (for example, that the ε form is due to wrinkles in the forehead). The most recent work on this issue is M. Borrini and L. Garlaschelli, "A BPA Approach to the Shroud of Turin," *Journal of Forensic Sciences* 64 (2019): 137–43.

[82] Cf. A. Nicolotti, "The Scourge of Jesus and the Roman Scourge: Historical and Archaeological Evidence," *Journal for the Study of the Historical Jesus* 15 (2017): 1–59; a summary is in A. Nicolotti, "What Do We Know about the Scourging of Jesus?," *Ancient Near East Today* 6, no. 12 (2018), www.asor.org/anetoday/2018/12/What-Do-We-Know-About-Scourging-Jesus.

[83] As happened in 1349, when there appeared in France "individuals who were striking themselves with scourges made with three cords, on each of which there was a knot that had four points like needles. The needles intersected within the knot and appeared outside on a side of the knot itself. And they were making themselves bleed by striking themselves" (*Les grandes chroniques de France*, vol. 9 [Paris: Champion, 1937], 323–24); H. C. Lea, *A History of the Inquisition of the Middle Ages*, vol. 2 (New York: Harper, 1887), 382: "and scourged themselves at stated times, the men stripping to the waist and using a scourge knotted with four iron points, so lustily laid on that an eyewitness says that he had seen two jerks requisite to disengage the point from the flesh." Cf. É. Delaruelle, "Les grandes processions de pénitents de 1349 et 1399," in *Il movimento dei disciplinati nel settimo centenario del suo inizio*, ed. L. Scaramucci (Spoleto: Panetto & Petrelli, 1962), 109–45.

it falls away from the face. Yet when hair collects the blood coming from the underlying skin it absorbs it, becoming a thickened clump and certainly not having well-defined superficial blood swirls like those depicted on the Shroud.

All of this confirms that, exactly as in the case of the corporal image, not even the bloodstains can be explained through natural contact of the cloth with a cadaver. They must have been put there deliberately in an artificial way, probably with a brush, without the artist being able to or desiring to pay attention to the "scientific" verisimilitude of their form or position. Therefore it makes no sense that forensic science should consider the wounds of the alleged cadaver on the basis of these alleged bloodstains, as if this were all due to a natural occurrence.

The flow of blood from the hand, which is presumably due to the nail from the cross, deserves particular attention. The stain that one sees on the Shroud occurs not at the point where the nail would have entered the hand but rather where it emerged from it; the Romans likely hammered the nail in from the side of the palm. Even granting that there was a nail there (which I do not believe), one cannot deduce where the nail was positioned, but only where it emerged. The point of exit, however, is not precisely identifiable for two reasons: first, the imprint of the hand is blurry, and contours of the arms cannot be discerned with exactitude; and, second, the form of the bloodstain is distended, slightly cleft on one of its sides, and the exact point from which the blood would have flowed cannot be known. Typically sindonologists believe that the nail passed through the wrist, not the palm (the medical doctor and sindonologist Pierre Barbet spoke of an interosseous space between the bones of the carpus, calling it "Destot's space," an expression not in use among anatomists).[84] They think that the passage of the nail between the bones of the carpus had a precise reason, since the nails had to support the entire weight of the crucified man because the palm, being too fragile to do so,

[84] Especially in his book: Barbet, *Passion* (English translation: *A Doctor at Calvary: The Passion of Our Lord Jesus Christ as Described by a Surgeon* [New York: Image Books, 1963]). Many of his theories have been refuted, even by another sindonological doctor: F. T. Zugibe, *The Crucifixion of Jesus: A Forensic Inquiry* (New York: M. Evans, 2005).

would have been torn: both claims, however, are false.[85] It is much easier to believe that the bloodstains were drawn in an approximate position, as occurred for the rendering of the hair; and one cannot exclude the possibility that the Shroud's artist wanted to represent the visions of Saint Bridget, according to whom Jesus' hand had been pierced not in the palm, as one sees in stigmata, but rather "where the bone was hardest."[86] Thus the apparent contradiction with traditional iconography is also explained.

4.2.3 Unreliable or Falsified Photographs?

In 1898, the whole discussion over the Shroud's authenticity sprang up in response to the provocative elation induced by what seemed to be incontestable scientific proof—that is, the negativity of the photographic image. The canon Chevalier reacted by publishing and interpreting unpublished or neglected documents; in other words, reaffirming the primacy of the historical sciences. At issue was not only the authenticity of a sheet but also the positioning of the different disciplinary purviews; the great historian Ernst von Dobschütz opined that what was happening was "almost comical," namely, "an unusual division of roles in the battle for belief in miracles" in which the historians proved more reticent than certain representatives of the world of the hard sciences.[87] The Shroud, in the meantime, had become what today is termed "an object of interdisciplinary investigation."

The situation, as regards the "scientific" purview, was aggravated by a quite particular difficulty: the Shroud was not and still

[85] We know that the bodies of those crucified had to be supported on the cross not only with nails but also with ropes, or in any case by making use of a support under the feet or buttocks; otherwise the death would have been too quick. Therefore it does not make sense to wonder whether or not the palms of the hands were able to support the whole weight of a body, since to do so was not necessary. In any case, experiments were performed on different occasions with twenty or so fresh cadavers, demonstrating that the palm of a hand pierced by a nail is fully able to support a body without being torn, even if sindonologists insist on repeating the contrary.

[86] Birgitta Birgersdotter, *Revelaciones* 1.10.22: "Manum ipsam ex ea parte perforabant, qua os solidius erat"; 7.15.7: "Perforabant eam clavo per illam partem, qua os solidius erat."

[87] E. von Dobschütz, "Das Leichentuch Jesu," *Monatsschrift für Gottesdienst und kirchliche Kunst* 14 (1909): 321.

today is not freely accessible to scholars who seek to study it. The first adverse consequence of this happened at the point when the quality of Secondo Pia's photographs had to be determined without the possibility of checking the object with the naked eye. The Shroud, in fact, remained closed in its box until 1931. This great stumbling block, combined with a certain antisindonic prejudice, was the source of endless discussions that often, exactly as happened in the area of the historical sciences, revealed mere conjectures that were unable to hold up to verification.

Many reacted against the enthusiastic announcements about the photographs and the negativity of the image—and above all against the conclusions that it was claimed could be drawn from it—with unfounded criticisms of the process the photographer used.[88] One of the first detractors was the anonymous author of a brief article that appeared on June 15, 1898, in *Norddeutsche Allgemeine Zeitung*,[89] after which it was the turn of the famous photographer Léon Vidal.[90] In fact, to raise doubts about the accuracy of the process, some newspapers erroneously claimed that Pia had used photographic equipment "brought in for this occasion," and "with compounds of his own invention that were sensitive to the yellow tint of the cloth";[91] in all likelihood, the cause of this inaccuracy was a misunderstanding, since the journalists did not know how to explain the fact that the photographer had placed a yellow filter over the lens (a normal technique that only had the purpose of enhancing the contrast—that is, to emphasize the tonal separation of black and white). The fact that they circulated unofficial prints of the photograph of the Shroud that differed widely in the tonality of the colors generated confusion and uncertainty. Secondo Pia, moreover, did not think about publishing a detailed technical report. The reaction of some was to deny the reliability of the images, and some went to such extremes as to accuse the photographer of having falsified the plates. It is necessary

[88] I have thoroughly recounted the entire history of the photographs and the debate that accompanied them in A. Nicolotti, "Le fotografie della Sindone di Secondo Pia (1898) e di Giuseppe Enrie (1931)," in *Santi in posa: L'influsso della fotografia nell'immaginario religioso*, ed. T. Caliò (Rome: Viella, 2019), 239–72.

[89] Reprinted in Zaccone, *Immagine rivelata*, 174.

[90] *Le moniteur de la photographie* 18 (1898): 285.

[91] According to F. Crispoldi, "Una rivelazione," *Il cittadino di Genova*, June 13, 1898.

to recall that at the time, many photographs were in circulation that depicted alleged phantasms and other spiritual entities; the images were obtained with tricks and photomontages, which were not always easy to expose.

The first well-devised attack came from the expert in photography called in by Chevalier, Hippolyte Chopin. In his first contribution, which was published in Chevalier's book, Chopin put forward a series of observations that strongly called into question the value of Pia's photographs. Chopin's observations were technically correct, in a general sense; but in the particulars they were completely out of place. When Chopin asserts the possibility of obtaining in the darkroom a direct positive photographic image from a negative plate, he is correct. It is also true that there existed photographic negatives that gave the impression of being positives, due to the particular nature of certain colors associated with the type of plate used; yet certain photographic plates subjected to particular treatments provoked the inversion of colors. These things were technically possible but did not pertain to Secondo Pia's photographs.[92] The same sort of considerations, with much greater elaboration, were proposed by Alphonse-Louis Donnadieu, professor of the Catholic University of Lyon; the conditions under which the photographs were taken, the uncertainty over the monochrome or polychrome nature of the image, the incomplete technical reports, and the impossibility of verification using the original cloth prompted him to doubt that anything—the artificial illumination, in particular—was able to alter the fidelity of the colors on the photographic plate. He provided ample proofs of this, demonstrating how the photographs of certain designs carried out in specific colors (red on a yellow background, for example, as one could imagine was the case for the Shroud) gave rise to negative plates with bright images that seemed positive on a dark background. And that is why Donnadieu saw a need for a new photographic campaign that would take place under better conditions and with the help of a spectroscope to clarify the colors of the original and the level of actinicity of the light, which produced a different chemical effect on sensitive photographic material. To whoever said that the images of the Shroud were negatives and that a man could not ever have made them in that way, Donnadieu responded: "It has

[92] Chopin's letter was published by Chevalier, *Étude critique*, 50–55.

not been proven that they are not positive, since it is necessary to study the cloth to know this; and even if they were negatives, a man would in any case have been able to make them even in that way."[93] Chopin and Donnadieu, in conclusion, made conjectures, nor were they able to do otherwise; and even the famous heliographer Paul Dujardin joined with Lippmann in declaring the appropriateness of the criticisms levelled by French photographers.[94]

In 1902 Chopin and Msgr. Charles-Félix Bellet proposed a new theory to explain the negativity of the image, a theory inspired by reading the report of the Poor Clares of Chambéry written in 1534. In that report the nuns speak of the left hand being crossed over the right and of a spot of blood on the left side of the brow; such a description seems inverted relative to what one can see (but everything depends on the perspective one takes when indicating what is right and what is left, seeing the image from the viewpoint of the observer or from that of the human figure that left the imprint). Chopin and Bellet's erroneous conclusion was that the Poor Clares, when the Shroud was being restored, had covered the *recto* of the Shroud with a lining, leaving the *verso* uncovered, which Pia would later photograph.[95] Again for the reason of a presumed right-left inversion, a certain individual even came to deny that Pia's plate was truly a negative.[96]

Another misleading explanation for the "negativity" of the man of the Shroud was the argument of overexposure: it was, in fact, known that by greatly increasing the time of exposure for the plate to the action of light, one could create the phenomenon of an inverted image during development ("effect of solarization"); instead of a negative,

[93] A. L. Donnadieu, "Étude scientifique sur le 'Linceul de Christ' de M. Paul Vignon," *L'université catholique* 40 (1902): 209–41; Donnadieu, "Les hypothèses scientifiques relatives au Saint Suaire de Turin," *L'université catholique* 41 (1902): 481–99; Donnadieu, *Le Saint Suaire de Turin devant la science* (Paris: Mendel, 1903), 22–82. Quoted by Donnadieu, "Réplique à M. Vignon," *L'université catholique* 40 (1902): 395.

[94] In a letter reported by F. de Mély, *Le Saint-Suaire de Turin est-il authentique?* (Paris: Poussielgue, 1902), 29–30.

[95] C.-F. Bellet, "Le Saint-Suaire de Turin: Son image positive," *L'université catholique* 41 (1902): 47–62; H. Chopin, *Le Saint-Suaire de Turin photographié à l'envers* (Paris: Picard, 1902); Chopin, *Le Saint-Suaire de Turin avant et après 1534* (Paris: Picard, 1902); Chopin, "Le Saint Suaire de Turin," supplement, *Le XXe siècle*, November 2, 1902, 1.

[96] Cf. H. de Barenton, "Dernière note sur le Saint Suaire," *Études franciscaines* 8 (1902): 536–39.

a positive image turns out on the plate.[97] In truth, to disprove this it is enough to look at a photographic overview of the altar and the frame of the Shroud, which shows that all the outlines of the cloth's objects had the correct color and were in no way inverted; not everyone, however, had the images available, and not everyone took the trouble to find them. In 1905, Ferdinand de Mély announced that he had obtained a photograph that contradicted what was visible on Pia's plates; that photograph was obviously not credible and was not subsequently made available.[98]

All these objections arose from a fundamental error: none of those who opposed Pia's photographs knew that the image of the Shroud had inverted lights and shades because it was presented as an impression. All likely remained prisoners of their idea that the image of the man of the Shroud was the work of a forger who had painted it with brushes in keeping with natural shading. All these disputes, therefore, went in search of a cause that explained how a positive image could transform into a negative. It has also been noted that in certain pictures it has happened that colors have been inverted by a phenomenon of chemical deterioration: an example is Cimabue's *Crucifixion* in the Upper Basilica of Assisi, which at a glance looks effectively like a photographic negative. This happened due to the deterioration of the white lead used in the painting. But even this explanation, which does not apply to the Shroud, suffers from the same error underlying the criticisms of Pia's detractors: Cimabue painted with the intention of representing real people, not an impression on cloth!

Arthur Loth and Paul Vignon (though not alone) took on the task of responding to all the objections of a technical nature.[99] Secondo Pia, in February of 1901, drew up a report on his work and submitted it to Benedetto Porro, a professor of chemistry, who confirmed its

[97] Cf. P. Lajoye, "Note sur le Saint Suaire de Turin," *Études franciscaines* 5 (1901): 640–44.

[98] "Séance du 3 février," *Comptes rendus de l'Académie des Inscriptions et Belles-Lettres* (1905): 56.

[99] The treatment by Loth, *Photographie du Saint Suaire de Turin*, 1–39 and 63–68, can be considered the final word on the skeptics' criticisms. Many of Vignon's objections are also correct (Vignon, *Linceul du Christ*, 15–41 [English translation: *Shroud of Christ*, 108–25]), even if he goes too far in his conclusions. For a summary of the whole matter, see Hernández Villaescusa, *Sábana Santa de Turín*, 159–251.

accuracy;[100] but only after a considerable delay was a report published in France, in 1910.[101] Therein Pia underscored that he used normal procedures. Any remaining doubt was dispelled by the second photographic session held in 1931. What critics, however, were never able to accept—and this time rightly—was the notion that the negativity of the image was in itself a demonstration of the authenticity of the Shroud and was sufficient to disprove any human intervention in the production of the image. Arthur Loth was the strongest supporter of this authenticist perspective; his books made a great impression, and in Italy they were also a source of inspiration for certain writings of the famous poet Gabriele D'Annunzio.[102]

4.2.4 Paul Vignon and Vapography

I have already mentioned Paul Vignon (1865–1943), who can be considered the father of modern sindonology. Having completed his degree in natural science, he became *préparateur* of zoology at the Sorbonne; afterward he became a professor in the Department of Philosophy at the Catholic Institute of Paris. More brilliant than Arthur Loth, he was no less tenacious a defender of the authenticity of the relic, so much so as to become the canon Chevalier's most visible adversary. Using photographs of the Shroud, which he analyzed in a quite thorough manner, he was able to propose a scientific explanation—mistaken, unfortunately—of the means by which the image on the Shroud was formed. An explanation such as his, which was elaborated with help from René Colson, a physicist from the École Polytechnique Militaire of Paris and an expert in photographic plates, is known as "vapographic theory."[103]

While excluding any attempted forgery, use of bas-relief, or other techniques, Vignon departs from the notion that the images of the Shroud are imprints formed in Jesus' tomb. He must therefore attempt

[100] The correspondence by letter was published by Pia, "Prima fotografia della SS. Sindone," 55–58; English translation in "A Letter from Secondo Pia," *Shroud Spectrum International* 18 (1986): 8–11.

[101] Cf. Loth, *Photographie du Saint Suaire de Turin*, 17–21.

[102] Cf. P. Scotti, "La Sindone nelle opere di D'Annunzio," *Atti della Accademia ligure di scienze e lettere* 19 (1962): 248–58; R. Bettica-Giovannini, "La Sindone nelle opere di Gabriele D'Annunzio," *Sindon* 11 (1967): 34–43.

[103] Fully outlined in Vignon, *Linceul du Christ*, 52–97 (English translation: *Shroud of Christ*, 137–70); Vignon, *Saint Suaire de Turin*, 5–7, 22–30, 197–206.

an explanation that allows him to reconcile the presence of a real body, the absence of distortion in the image, and its characteristic orthogonal projection onto a flat surface: the image must, therefore, have been the product of some intervention on the cloth apart from the body.

Vignon began by considering two types of actions from a distance, examined by his friend René Colson, that could affect photographic film: irradiation and the action of gas or vapors.[104] The first possibility was discarded (it would be revived decades later), and Vignon, together with Colson, engaged in some experiments: he sprinkled zinc dust onto a plaster relief of the face of Christ, placed a photographic plate over it, and, after leaving them in the dark for forty-eight hours in a light-proof box, obtained on the plate a vague image, "negative" and faded, where the points of contact with the plaster were darker than those that were merely close, with the darkness being proportional to the plate's proximity to the plaster. The theory that was reached was that the body of Christ had behaved like the mold and the Shroud was like the emulsion of the photographic plate.

But there is no zinc on corpses, and the sheet is certainly not a plate. So, then, this is what happened in Jesus' tomb, according to Vignon: once they removed the body from the cross, Joseph and Nicodemus covered it (without wrapping it) in the Shroud, which had been soaked in a mixture of myrrh and aloe. The sheet made contact with the protuberant parts of the body and remained at a greater or lesser distance from the rest. Jesus, covered thus, was set down in the tomb. His skin was covered in sweat that was particularly rich in urea; the fermentation of the urea generated ammonia carbonate; the ammoniacal vapors reacted with the aloetine contained in the aloe, causing oxidation and therefore a darkening of the surface of the cloth. The result on the Shroud was a reproduction of an image of the body, darker in places in contact with the body, and progressively lighter in places at an increasing distance, fading proportionally until it disappeared into the color of the background; the parts of the body that were too far away did not leave a perceptible impression. The same vapors also dissolved the fibrin, a protein essential to the

[104] R. Colson, "Revue des actions à distance capables d'influencer les couches photographiques," *Bulletin de la Société française de photographie* 16 (1900): 481–90.

coagulation of blood, allowing the clotted blood to break down and dissolve and imprint on the fabric.

The theory of "vapographic prints" made a great impression but was extremely conjectural and, in practice, unworkable: sweat does not contain enough urea and evaporates quickly; its distribution on a body is insufficient and irregular; the conditions for its fermentation are not easily brought about; the ammoniacal vapors are extremely volatile, and the particles of which they are formed spread in all directions irregularly, not in parallel lines that would run perpendicular to a piece of fabric. It is impossible that such a hypothetical phenomenon could produce on a cloth an orthogonal image so well defined. The theory of vapography assumes, moreover, that the sheet was positioned with extreme care, spread out well, in a way suitable for avoiding distortions, contortions, fragmentation, and gaps in the image. This is impossible to imagine, and, according to the biblical scholar Primo Vannutelli, if the body was wrapped between linens and spices, as the Gospels say, "to wrap a corpse in a sheet without it taking on wrinkles, folds, and twists, is not possible."[105]

"If, in fact, the process was so simple, why then didn't they ever put a cadaver in a cloth, sprinkle it with aloe dust and demonstrate the effect?" asked the abbot Damasus Zähringer.[106] Vignon adduced practical difficulties in obtaining a suitable cadaver;[107] but it would have sufficed for him to use an anthropomorphic model, which he avoided.[108] His experiments on figures of shallow depth or little detail (like a plaster mold or the hand of a statue covered in *Peau de Suède*) in no way approximated the complexity of the details of a whole human body. In the areas of his figures not in direct contact with, but still in close proximity to, the cloth, the effect is too faded and conducive to uniform coloration. Moreover, he worked not with true ureic sweat but at most with ammonia solutions created for the purpose, not by reproducing the conditions of a sweaty corpse. It is true that already under these artificial conditions the results leave something to be desired, since the precision obtained from the images was

[105] P. Vannutelli, "La S. Sindone e gli Evangeli," *Palestra del clero* 18, no. 1 (1939): 307.

[106] Zähringer, "Das Grabtuch von Turin," 156.

[107] Vignon, *Linceul du Christ*, 96, n. 1 (absent in the English translation).

[108] For which he was criticized by R. Meldola, review of *Le Linceul du Christ*, by P. Vignon, *Nature* 67 (1903): 243.

too far from the clear picture of the man of the Shroud, especially the features of the face that appear in such detail on the Shroud. In the years to come, in spite of their intentions, Vignon and Colson did not ever succeed in reproducing their hypothesis on a body or an anthropomorphic face, even on a statue.

Vignon's studies, as one can imagine, provoked a heated debate. As Chevalier already had, Vignon also undertook to respond personally to all those who doubted the value of his research.[109] But his theory and his experiments proved unable to draw any conclusions regarding emanations from a corpse,[110] until, at the beginning of the second half of the twentieth century, the theory of vapography lost all its supporters.[111]

Vignon's explanation was, all things considered, natural, but that does not mean that the author ruled out divine intervention on the Shroud. Rather, as he himself revealed in a letter sent to a fellow sindonologist, he wanted to organize the apostolate of what he called "propaganda" of the Shroud according to a well-defined progression: the first matter was thoroughly to convince public opinion of the fact that the Shroud was not painted, second was to convince the public of the fact that it held a corpse, and only at the end, when "we have perceived that our explanations have run through everywhere," then would it be possible "to prepare to enter the realm of the supernatural."[112] The true pseudoscientific attitude of Vignon did not escape

[109] See, for example, the exchange between L. de Meurville, "Le Saint Suaire de Turin," *Le correspondant* 207 (1902): 546–52; and P. Vignon, "Le Saint Suaire de Turin," *Le correspondant* 207 (1902): 777–81.

[110] Cf. J. Braun, "Das Turiner Grabtuch des Herrn," *Stimmen aus Maria Laach* 63 (1902): 249–61 and 398–410; Donnadieu, "Étude scientifique," 221–41; P. Vignon, "Réponse à M. Donnadieu," *L'université catholique* 40 (1902): 362–83; Donnadieu, "Réplique à M. Vignon," 384–96; Donnadieu, "Hypothèses scientifiques," *L'université catholique* 41 (1902): 481–523; and *L'université catholique* 42 (1903): 22–63, 184–223; Donnadieu, *Saint Suaire de Turin devant la science*; S. Dezani, "La genesi della S. Sindone di Torino," *Gazzetta sanitaria* 12 (1933): 124–26; M. Eskenazy, *Le Saint Suaire de Turin devant l'histoire, la science et la médecine* (Paris: Menant, 1938), 101–34; P. Scotti, "Il primo convegno internazionale di sindonologia," *Salesianum* 13 (1951): 137.

[111] Consider how it is spoken of by G. Judica Cordiglia, *La Sindone* (Padua: Lice, 1961), 145–50.

[112] Letter to Antoine Legrand, 1937, quoted by Celier, *Signe du linceul*, 107–8.

the chemist Raphael Meldola, the attentive reviewer of Vignon's book for the journal *Nature*:

> Who is simply anxious to know the actual facts of the case, will probably come to the conclusion that Dr. Vignon is either the victim of credulity or that he has overdone his evidence to such an extent as to have damaged his own reputation as an expert scientific witness. . . . The magnitude of the conclusions based on such lame experimental evidence justifies the condemnation of the whole work as an *étude scientifique*. To the reviewer, it reads like an antiquarian dissertation ending in a pseudo-scientific anti-climax.[113]

4.2.5 Yves Delage at the Académie des Sciences

Let us now turn to the spring of 1902. At that time Paul Vignon was working in the laboratory of an older and more established zoologist by the name of Yves Delage. Having taken notice of the research of his young assistant, Delage offered to present it to the Académie des Sciences in Paris, of which he was a member. At a meeting on April 21, 1902, the theory of vapography as a mechanism for the formation of images on shrouds was therefore presented to the assembly of the illustrious academy.

In the report read to the assembly Delage presented the negative quality of the image of the Shroud and the anatomical and aesthetic perfection of the man depicted, showing in Secondo Pia's photographs the well-portrayed limbs and the head "so remarkable from an expressive point of view that, to judge from authoritative pictures, none of the heads of Christ depicted by Renaissance artists is superior to it." After dismissing the possibility that the image was the work of a forger, the zoologist's conclusion was that it was formed naturally, thanks to alkaline vapors from his sweat and in accordance with the process already described. Delage did not limit himself to these observations: as an addendum to his speech he proposed to identify the man depicted on the Shroud as the Jesus of the Gospels. The argument was as follows: the possibility that all the circumstances of the passion could be brought about in the same way for a man condemned to death other than Jesus seemed to him to be one in ten

[113] R. Meldola, review of *Le Linceul du Christ*, by P. Vignon, *Nature* 67 (1903): 242–43.

billion. "And if it is not the Christ, then it is some criminal. But how to reconcile that with the remarkable expression of nobility that one reads on the figure?"

Delage's report immediately triggered a bitter debate. When the speech was to be printed in the Académie's reports, the secretary Marcellin Berthelot refused to publish the whole text given to him by Delage. Only the technical-descriptive part detailing Vignon's experiments was printed, under an utterly neutral title and without any reference to the Shroud.[114] This greatly upset Delage, who then wrote an open letter to the director of *Revue scientifique,* in which he published what had been prohibited from publication in the reports, with some accusatory remarks:

> I want to reestablish the facts and therefore request accommodation from your journal. I would not have needed to do so if the secretary of the Académie had agreed to publish the explanations that I provided while presenting Mr. Vignon's work. . . . A religious issue that has excited spirits and distorted straightforward reason was unduly inserted into this scientific issue. If rather than Christ it was a question of a Sargon, an Achilles, or any pharaoh, no one would have found anything objectionable. . . . In treating this subject, I have remained faithful to the true scientific spirit, concerned only with the search for truth and without being troubled over whether or not this might have touched upon the interests of one or another religious camp.[115]

Thereafter this became a symbolic episode that is recorded in nearly all modern books on sindonology.[116] According to one interpretation, on one side there was Berthelot, an atheist and anticlerical, who refused to publish the results of a scientific study only because they pertained to Jesus and could support arguments in favor of the authenticity of his shroud; on the other side was Delage, an agnostic but consistent defender of the true scientific spirit, who was unafraid

[114] P. Vignon, "Sur la formation d'images négatives par l'action de certaines vapeurs," *Comptes rendus hebdomadaires des séances de l'Académie des Sciences* 134 (1902): 902–4; English translation can be found in "M. Vignon's Researches and the 'Holy Shroud,'" *Scientific American* 86, no. 21 (1902): 367–68.

[115] Y. Delage, "Le Linceul de Turin," *Revue scientifique* 17 (1902): 683–87 (quotations from 683, 684, 686, 687).

[116] For example, Wuenschel, *Self-portrait of Christ,* 25–28; Walsh, *Shroud,* 69–83; Rinaudo and Gavach, *Linceul de Jésus enfin authentifié?,* 79–89, 97–105.

to recognize the value of Vignon's experiments but was censured in contempt of the evidence of the facts. On this occasion, the Académie des Sciences behaved like a band of anticlericals who were willing to reject the objective results of a scientific experiment only because they favored the Catholic cause.

I do not share this interpretation. First of all, it should be noted that the reports of the Académie des Sciences in those years were often limited to printing basic summaries of the issues treated during the sessions, thereby leaving the scholar free to publish more thorough reports elsewhere. But, apart from that, it seems to me that the comportment of Berthelot and the other scientists was unexceptionable. In substance Vignon and Delage did not confine themselves to presenting the objective results of an experiment but claimed to describe the means by which the image of the Shroud of Turin was formed, on the basis of conjectures that, as already noted, were insufficient to prove it. The two zoologists speculated about photographs and were unable to examine the Shroud in person. They presented the effect of some alkaline vapors on photographic plates or on small fabrics soaked in aloetine but were not able to demonstrate that the sweat from a corpse was capable of doing the same on a sheet. In substance, they proposed an unverified theory. Despite Delage's complaints, there were serious obstacles of a scientific nature, even before any ideological ones, that made it necessary to adopt a healthy skepticism. In fact, the theory that the two zoologists wanted to publish in the reports of the Académie des Sciences was mistaken, the phenomenon of vapographic impression could never be replicated, and after a few years it was clear to all that the image of the Shroud was not formed in that way. Berthelot was right, while Vignon and Delage were wrong; rather than criticize him, it would have been better to praise his foresight.

Vignon's experiments, however, were promulgated by other less scrupulous means, and this had a disruptive effect. It seemed to many that "scientific" arguments put historical arguments to flight, to the shame of Chevalier and his followers:

> It seems to us that a scientific thesis, based on the very nature of the things and their intrinsic characteristics, possesses a different authoritativeness and an incomparably greater probability of being true compared to a historical thesis based on documents

> extrinsic to the thing itself, and on human testimonies whose veracity is sometimes so difficult to determine; its interpretation lends itself to many errors. In short, it is of little importance that any texts deny the authenticity of the Holy Shroud, if the Holy Shroud bears on itself the certain proofs of its own authenticity.[117]

The epistemological perspective is clear: the "hard" sciences are superior to the "soft" sciences. But what escapes the author of these words is that even "a scientific thesis, based on the very nature of the things" is still an interpretation of reality that does not avoid the possibility of errors. The scientist is not merely an irrelevant spectator of the events and results of his experiments but is sometimes their author, the one who must correctly perform and interpret them. He can be wrong, and sometimes makes mistakes, just as in this case. Nevertheless, in 1902—exactly as happens still today with any new presumed "scientific" discovery on the Shroud—it seemed to many that science had issued its irrevocable verdict.

4.2.6 The Iconography of Vignon

A further field of study that Paul Vignon pursued was iconography. He began to take an interest in it to rule out the possibility that the image of Christ visible on the Shroud corresponded to a well-known iconographic canon, since he wanted to highlight the uniqueness of the Shroud. As a result, though partially contradicting his initial aim, he investigated the possibility that Christian art was influenced by the image, starting, therefore, with a search not for differences but for similarities.[118]

Vignon's conclusion was that the face of the man of the Shroud bears some details, even seemingly negligible ones, that are also found in many artistic representations of Christ beginning in late antiquity. The model that inspired the artists was a painting made, according to Vignon, by observing the Shroud very closely—the portrait known as the Mandylion of Edessa—without intending to produce a faithful copy; instead, certain details in the painting were modified, concealing the funereal character of the original image by

[117] "Le Saint-Suaire de Turin d'après le travail de M. Vignon," *L'ami du clergé* 24, no. 27 (1902): 587.

[118] Vignon, *Linceul du Christ*, 163–92 (English translation: *Shroud of Christ*, 84–107); Vignon, *Saint Suaire de Turin*, 115–91, 211–25.

omitting the blood and accidentally transforming certain marks on the Shroud into anatomical characteristics (fig. 4.2).

The theory is highly conjectural and lends itself to being applied as one pleases, because anyone can see something on the Shroud and imagine also finding it completely transfigured in some way on a painting. For example, the locks of hair in two or three points that are found at the center of the forehead in some portraits of Christ have been considered an erroneous transposition of the stain in the form of an ε that is on the forehead of the man on the Shroud; or, in certain icons of Christ, his right hand at chest height, positioned in a pose of blessing, has been described as a mistaken interpretation of the patch of blood on the Shroud at the level of the ribs on the image. There has since arisen in sindonological studies a current that puts into practice what Gian Marco Rinaldi has termed the "theory of iconographic sindonocentrism," carried to its extreme by the Jesuit Heinrich Pfeiffer.[119] Computers have simplified enormously the process of bringing more or less reliable comparative analyses to bear on the search for "common features confirming the uniqueness of the image of Christ handed down through the centuries," in order to "lead one to consider very probable the hypothesis that the face of the Man of the Shroud was the prototype on which Christian iconography is based, at least from the sixth century."[120] The applications are infinite and uncontrollable, and have reached the point of recognizing hundreds of alleged points of correspondence between nearly all the images of Christ endowed with a beard and the sindonic image, even pushing the analysis onto minute representations incised on coins, focusing on details on the order of a tenth of a millimeter in size and coming to conclusions that are excessive (for example, that the engravers of certain Byzantine coins with the face of Christ had

[119] Following all the lines of this theory would be a lengthy endeavor. I therefore will limit myself to noting some publications: H. Pfeiffer, "The Shroud of Turin and the Face of Christ in Paleochristian, Byzantine and Western Medieval Art," *Shroud Spectrum International* 9 (1983): 7–20; 10 (1984): 3–19; L. Coppini and F. Cavazzuti, eds., *Le icone di Cristo e la Sindone* (Cinisello Balsamo: San Paolo, 2000); B. Frale, *La sindone e il ritratto di Cristo* (Vatican City: Libreria Editrice Vaticana, 2010); E. Marinelli, "The Shroud and the Iconography of Christ," pro manuscripto (online), 2014, https://www.shroud.com/pdfs/stlemarinellipaper.pdf.

[120] Balossino, "Ricerca informatica sulla Sindone," 83–84.

FIGURE 4.2 Face of the man of the Shroud as the foundation of Christian iconography, according to Paul Vignon

a very low probability, one in a quintillion, of obtaining that result without having seen the Shroud).[121]

The theory assumes that the Shroud is older than all the other iconographic depictions of Christ. The argument is obviously circular, and the exact opposite could be affirmed, namely, that the Shroud was made on the model of the iconography of Christ. The question is complicated by the fact that the same Christian iconography is quite variable[122] and only after the end of the late antique period did it assume certain stylistic features that could be compared in some measure with the image of the Shroud; that fact forces the supporters of authenticity to conclude that the sindonic face had remained unknown or hidden throughout all the preceding centuries, and therefore it could not be replicated.

Aside from being arbitrary, the alleged iconographic correspondences have been drawn from observations of modern photographs of the Shroud in which the contrasts have been enhanced and the imprint rendered particularly visible. Nevertheless, the same sindonology, as an argument that would preclude the intervention of a craftsman, insists on the fact that the sindonic imprints are very ephemeral and visible only when positioned at a certain distance from the sheet, which would prevent an artist from observing the details up close. In certain cases, the comparisons are carried out using photographic negatives in black and white, which is an anachronism, because no one before the invention of the photograph would have been able to see the image with inverted lights and shades, which create a very different figure from what can be seen on the original.

Even judgments on the correspondence of the sindonic image to a specific historical period have been diverse, and sometimes contradictory.[123] Moreover, it is difficult to establish a meaningful parallel

[121] Cf. A. Whanger and M. Whanger, *The Shroud of Turin: An Adventure of Discovery* (Franklin: Providence, 1998); G. Fanti and P. Malfi, *Sindone: Primo secolo dopo Cristo!* (Tavagnacco: Segno, 2014) (English translation: *The Shroud of Turin: First Century after Christ!* [Boca Raton: CRC Press, 2016]). I examine these works in Nicolotti, *From the Mandylion of Edessa*, 173–82.

[122] An argument already put forth in the time of de Mély, *Saint-Suaire de Turin est-il authentique?*, 47–86.

[123] Cf. Zähringer, "Das Grabtuch von Turin," 154 (for the opinion of H. Grisar); G. de Jerphanion, "Le Sainte-Suaire de Turin," *Orientalia christiana periodica* 4 (1938): 570; V. Viale, "Se il tipo sindonico corrisponda ai caratteri della pittura gotica e se la S. Sindone possa essere opera di pittore piemontese del primo Cinquecento,"

between the art of a certain historical period and the face of the Shroud, because the latter is neither a painting, nor a mosaic, nor a statue, but rather a monochromatic imprint, which does not provide a good subject for a serious comparison with such different styles.

The argument for iconic sindonocentrism, in any case, is fundamentally weak, as can be inferred by observing those paintings that, beginning in the sixteenth century, undoubtedly derive from the Shroud. The dozens of copies of the Shroud of Turin that are spread throughout the world are rarely faithful and are often almost unrecognizable in their grotesque appearance: nevertheless, we are sure, they were recopied directly from the original. If none of these painters was capable of rendering a faithful copy, how is it possible to expect Byzantine icons and coins to depict a face of Christ that would overlay that of the Shroud perfectly to the tenth of a millimeter?

4.3. Between Monarchy and Republic

4.3.1 Exhibitions of 1931 and 1933, and Denied Examinations

The marriage of Crown Prince Umberto to Maria José of Belgium (January 8, 1930) was the occasion for a traditional exhibition of the Shroud. However, it was postponed because the episcopal see was vacant; it took place later the following year, in the presence of the new archbishop, Maurilio Fossati. It was the last matrimonial exhibition for the House of Savoy.[124]

It was not entirely to be taken for granted that a new exhibition would go forward: opposition from scholars and representatives of the clergy, and all the serious debate from Chevalier's time, had diminished the image of the Shroud in the eyes of many. Even in the ecclesiastical sphere of Turin opinion was not unanimous, although today it is difficult to measure how much it differed: in fact, in general the

in *Santa Sindone nelle ricerche moderne*, 167–69; C. Cecchelli, "Rapporti fra il Santo Volto della Sindone e l'antica iconografia bizantina," in *Santa sindone nelle ricerche moderne*, 153–65; F. Sühling, "Neuere Literatur über das Grablinnen des Herrn," *Theologische Revue* 38 (1939): coll. 5–6. Limiting oneself to the essentials, it is also useful to consult P. A. Gramaglia, *Le ultime "scoperte" sulla Sindone* (Turin: Claudiana, 1981), 63–72; Gramaglia, "Ancora la Sindone di Torino," 97.

124 The ten prior matrimonial exhibitions are described by E. Ferraro, "Elenco e bibliografia delle ostensioni della Sindone in occasione di matrimoni in casa Savoia," *Sindon* 19–20 (2003): 101–9, who supplements information from Fossati, *Sacra Sindone*.

disagreement of the clergy in regard to the veneration of the Shroud or the practice of exhibitions is not disclosed to the public, for reasons of prudence, opportunity, caution, or fear of damaging the Church's image or attracting personal antipathy. It is an approach that recalls the Nicodemism adopted in the early twentieth century by various sympathizers with certain tenets of the modernist movement.[125]

An interesting case that I came across is that of Giuseppe Piovano (1851–1934), canon of the cathedral of Turin, a leading figure of the clergy of Turin who, in the last years of the nineteenth century, had played a fundamental role in the birth of the Christian Democracy movement. As a professor of church history in the Department of Theology he concerned himself with establishing his own teaching on the use of the method of historical criticism, proving himself "the most effective professor and most open to the cultural issues of the times." But in 1911, in the midst of antimodernist persecution, he seemed suspect to the eyes of Giovanni Pelizzari, an apostolic visitor to Turin, who requested his removal from teaching and the substitution of a professor who was willing to give the discipline "a direction that was more educative of piety and the supernatural." Deprived of the chair of church history, Piovano remained in any case a professor in the seminary's faculty of law, of which he was also the dean.[126]

Among his numerous writings,[127] there was one, unpublished, on the Shroud, of which I have found a copy. It is not a completely innovative work but a theological, historical, and scientific compendium of the arguments expressed by those who, especially in France, had contested the authenticity of the Shroud, beginning with Ulysse Chevalier. If it had been published, it would have been one of the most unusual studies in the Italian language conceived from this point

[125] Nicodemus, a Pharisee, was secretly a follower of Jesus. By "Nicodemism" today one means the attitude of those who out of fear or convenience do not dare exhibit their beliefs in public life.

[126] Cf. G. Tuninetti, *Facoltà teologiche a Torino* (Casale Monferrato: Piemme, 1999), 177–83 (quotation from p. 10); see C. Valente, "Piovano, Giuseppe," in *Dizionario storico del movimento cattolico in Italia*, ed. F. Traniello and G. Campanini, vol. 3, bk. 2 (Casale Monferrato: Marietti, 1984), 669–71; B. Gariglio, *Cattolici democratici e clerico-fascisti* (Bologna: il Mulino, 1976), 157–62.

[127] An incomplete bibliography can be found in E. Dervieux, *I miei trovanti* (Turin: Tipografia Anfossi, 1940), 96–100.

of view. It was finished in 1930 and sent to the archbishop Maurilio Fossati with an accompanying letter:

> Your Most Reverend Excellency,
>
> I have sent Your Excellency my study on the matter of our Shroud. I undertook this study about thirty years ago, when the conflict for and against authenticity was seething everywhere; and I began with the sole aim of defending it. But after making an accurate examination of a great number of works rich in new, conclusive documents, I reached the conclusion that it is not authentic, a conclusion shared by all Catholics who, adhering to the canons of historical criticism, have made such a study.
>
> My numerous remarks have slept for almost thirty years, but new circumstances have led me to review them and arrange them in a substantially complete study. My only goal was to purge the Church of the accusation of deceiving the people with the endorsement of an inauthentic relic; to make it clear, the authenticity of the relic is an issue that belongs to historical criticism; it is not a doctrinal issue, much less an ecclesiastical declaration.
>
> Your Excellency will see from a reading that I do not intend to oppose the exhibition—which shall serve to extinguish the enormous debt that still burdens the archbishop and the chapter, debt that other offering of the faithful will not quench, given the general discontentment left by the manner of the restoration; but I intend only to elicit from the proper authority full, clear, and public instruction regarding the veneration and invocation of the Saints and pertaining to the worship of relics and images of our Lord and the saints. In those matters there is much ignorance among the laity, and not a little carelessness among one part of the clergy. I beg Your Excellency not to take important, definitive positions before having seen and heard in person, not some who came before, but all, at least those of the chapter of the cathedral. I personally renew my congratulations and good wishes, and I kiss with reverence the hand of the superior sent to me by God.[128]

One can conclude from the letter that not everyone in Turin was in favor of exhibitions. As for the restoration of the cathedral, carried out between 1926 and 1928, the cost was around 1,692,000 lire (which

[128] AAT, 14.14.93B.

is roughly equivalent to 1,426,000 euros today).[129] Despite appeals, donations to cover the expenses did not come; it was necessary to go into debt, and work had to be interrupted earlier than expected due to lack of funds, leaving a debt of 500,000 lire. Piovano alludes to the fact that such restoration, because it had considerably modified the appearance of the church, was not met with favor by many people of Piedmont, and the prior archbishop had intervened many times to press for the generosity of the faithful.[130]

Fossati received Piovano's work and responded to him by recommending "highest prudence"; and so the work was never published. The two individuals did not have much in common: Fossati's love for the Shroud was truly great, to the point that in his official portrait as archbishop, he wanted to be depicted with a small Shroud in his hands. Fossati's merits, which were many, did not include a propensity for study: "a man fasting from strong theological studies and of scant culture in general"—as one of his canons describes him[131]—he had "a certain fear or perhaps distrust of cultured clergy." In the first years of his bishopric at Turin, the theology department, of which Piovano was a professor, was closed; the department for years had found itself in a grave crisis, and the archbishop did not undertake to save it.[132] It was natural that this predominantly historical, exegetical, and theological work was unable to gain traction with him.

"Highest prudence" was counselled to anyone who was not convinced of the Shroud's authenticity, but the same prudence was not required of anyone who continued to tell the faithful a history of the Shroud that completely ignored what medieval documents, published for decades by now, allowed us to know. There is a short work from 1930, published on the occasion of a Savoyard wedding, which provided a history of the relic replete with fantasy and

[129] According to the rates of monetary revaluation provided by Istat (Istituto Nazionale di Statistica).

[130] Cf. G. Gamba, "La parola del Cardinale Arcivescovo," *Il Duomo di Torino* 2, no. 8 (1928): 1–3; E. Olivero, "Il restauro del Duomo torinese e la critica," *Il Duomo di Torino* 2, no. 8 (1928): 4–9; "Appello per i restauri del Duomo," *Il Duomo di Torino* 2, no. 12 (1928): 35–36; cf. Momo, *Duomo di Torino*, 167–261; L. Borello, *Il Duomo di Torino e lo spazio sacro della Sindone* (Ivrea: Priuli & Verlucca, 1997), 77–82.

[131] S. Solero, *Ricordi di un prete-soldato* (Lanzo: Società storica delle Valli di Lanzo, 2001), 181.

[132] Cf. Tuninetti and D'Antino, *Cardinal Domenico Della Rovere*, 227.

historical errors, such as the preservation of the relic in Jerusalem, its discovery at the time of the First Crusade, its safekeeping under the grand master of the Hospitallers, the gifting of it to Amadeus III of Savoy, its stay in Cyprus until 1240, the transfer to Lirey by Geoffroy de Charny, and how it was granted to Savoy on March 2, 1458 (*sic*), in Chambéry (*sic*) after the miraculous event of the reticent quadruped.[133] Others were insisting on the "undisputed" credibility of stories about different shrouds mentioned in sources beginning in the sixth and seventh centuries, perhaps taking advantage of the false medieval account of the shroud of Besançon as a replacement for the documentary silence regarding the Shroud of Turin. There was even talk of a transfer of the Shroud to the House of Savoy in 1452 (*sic*) attested by "authentic letters" that in fact do not exist.[134]

As for the exhibition of 1931—the same archbishop, Fossati, gives an account—it met with some opposition. He believed the opposition was unfounded, "stifled by the unanimous consensus of the learned after the photograph of Commander Pia had worked the miracle of revealing to an astonished humanity the divine features of Christ." Fossati says as well that some Catholics (but he does not name anyone) had drafted a memorandum written to advise against the exhibition, relying on the danger of exposing Catholic religion and worship to attack and the mockery of Protestants, "who would have willingly taken advantage of an argument that provided an open flank, easily exploited, in the form of the gap in the historical documents." It seems that this memorandum, which "was brought into the hands of the influential," had some effect, if the cardinal received from above "principles of prudence that could also assume the appearance of counsel for an abeyance." Does this perchance allude to Piovano's work, which, though unpublished, may have had a limited circulation?

[133] *La SS. Sindone spiegata al popolo nella sua realtà e attraverso la storia* (Turin: Terzetto, 1930), 6–9. Others were content to repeat all the historical conjectures without inclining one way or another, such as F. Facta, *La SS. Sindone* (Turin: Arneodo, 1930), 20–29.

[134] Cf. C. Lovera di Castiglione, "Da Gerusalemme a Chambéry," *La festa* 10, no. 232 (1931): 443–44; C. Borla, "La pietà dei Savoia verso la S. Sindone," *La festa* 10, no. 232 (1931): 445; E. Oberty, "Anna di Cipro e Margherita di Charny," *La festa* 10, no. 232 (1931): 459–60.

At this point, however, the pope intervened to settle the doubts of the archbishop. In a meeting with Fossati, Pius XI in fact uttered a remark that remains famous:

> Rest assured: we speak at this time as a scholar and not as pope. We have followed personally the studies on the Holy Shroud and are persuaded of its authenticity. Some oppositions have been raised, but they do not hold up.

For Fossati, any doubt was removed:

> One can easily imagine what sort of sensation such words produced in my mind! I entered the meeting with the fear of one who sees clouds gathering on his horizon; I left there with a comforted and serene heart, just like when all of a sudden and in an unexpected way, a delightful sun follows the clouds that threaten a storm. It seemed to me at that moment that every difficulty had disappeared and every obstacle was surmounted. Therefore, I presented myself to His Majesty the king to ask for the great honor of exhibiting the Shroud.

The pope's role was also felt in the years that followed. Pius XI put himself at odds with the request to submit the Shroud to some scientific tests, including exposure to rays of ultraviolet or infrared light: "The Holy Shroud, as history tells us, was exposed to too many vicissitudes, including the test of fire and water. Under these conditions it would not be possible to provide all the elements necessary for a scientist's research." Conversely, the pope thought that the photographs were sufficient in and of themselves: "This photograph is worth more than any study!" But what Fossati considered "the paean of the Holy Shroud sung by the Pope" was an address delivered in 1936, when Pius XI spoke of that "object still mysterious, but certainly not of human manufacture (this can be said to have been demonstrated previously) that is the Holy Shroud of Turin." Certainly, the fact that the pope was "a fervent and enthusiastic devotee of the Shroud" gave the sindonological cause a formidable boost and made it riskier for Catholic skeptics to maintain a contrary view.[135]

[135] M. Fossati, *Pio XI e la Sindone*, in *Santa Sindone nelle ricerche moderne*, 15–20. The pope's speech is quoted in "Il pellegrinaggio mariano," *L'Osservatore Romano*, September 7–8, 1936, 1.

The exhibition of 1931 took place from the third to the twenty-fourth of May, in correspondence with the liturgical feast day of the Shroud. In preparation a novena was held that concluded on Saturday, May 2. The exhibition opened with all the bells of the diocese sounding for half an hour. In Turin five cardinals and forty-five bishops gathered for the event, and for the first time a motion-picture film was made. The ceremony was organized on behalf of the court by Count Federico Ricardi di Netro,[136] and compared to the exhibition of 1898, the Savoyard presence was greatly felt: the prince, Umberto, attended the ceremonies of the exhibition (at the time he resided in Turin). In the Palazzo Madama, which had served as a theater for exhibitions in the preceding centuries, a historical display of objects and documents relating to the Shroud was held; everything was later collected in a nice commemorative volume with numerous illustrative plates, of which a thousand copies were printed.[137]

From an economic standpoint, things went as well as possible for the diocese: it received an income of 1,388,364 lire (in current terms, 1,316,000 euros) against expenses totaling 490,720 lire. The higher revenue was assured by the income from railway tickets and the sale of "special entrances" to the cathedral that allowed the holders to linger near the Shroud. When the exhibition was over, the chapter of the cathedral immediately sent to the cardinal their hope "that the unforgettable celebration, beyond the great spiritual benefit bestowed on the faithful, is able also to eliminate the grave debt still resulting from the restoration of the cathedral." Thus, 330,000 lire were used to pay off the outstanding debts from the restoration—as Piovano had expected—while the majority of the assets were put in the bank (558,000 lire); of the rest, some were donated to the Municipal Guard and the Red Cross, some were put under the control of the archbishop,

[136] *Cerimoniale per il corteo reale che dal real palazzo si recherà nella real cappella della SS. Sindone per l'apertura dell'urna contenente la SS. Sindone e per la processione dalla real cappella in duomo nella domenica 3 maggio 1931 alle ore 16* (Turin: Bona, 1931); see also R. Ricardi di Netro, "Note sul cerimoniale dell'ostensione del 1931," *Sindon* 12 (1999): 11–18.

[137] *L'ostensione della S. Sindone.*

and 3,000 lire were given to the Jesuit Pietro Righini's Organization for Workers' Retreats.[138]

The exhibition of 1931 was the occasion for a new photographic session. This time as well a renowned photographer from Turin was called upon, Giuseppe Enrie,[139] to whom was entrusted the task of reproducing the photographs of 1898 under better conditions. To avoid a recurrence of the unjust accusation levelled against Secondo Pia, a notary's report was drafted declaring that the photographic plates were absolutely free of any retouching or other artifice.[140]

At the end of the exhibition, many voices hoping for the establishment of a committee for scientific investigations on the sacred relic made themselves heard. In 1901 Baron Manno and Paul Vignon, bolstered by the support of Cardinal Richelmy, had already made such an attempt; they had contacted the Holy See, proposing a series of studies, thanks to which Richelmy was hoping that "it would be granted to the people of Turin to see reduced to silence, for once, the stubborn adversaries of one of our greatest glories." Everything had to happen "with the greatest secrecy," but after initial negotiations that elicited some optimism, Leo XIII decided that it was better "to let the matter drop," and nothing more came of it.[141]

Thirty years later the matter of scientific examinations was again put forward. The archbishop Fossati consulted the Franciscan friar Agostino Gemelli, the founder of the Catholic University of Milan. Gemelli proved hesitant but believed that a possible committee of study

> should not have restrictions, namely it ought to be able to perform all the tests that it believes appropriate to determine the authenticity of the Holy Shroud. Of course, the committee ought not to begin from doubt about its authenticity, but however must establish itself, if it wishes to be scientific, on grounds that are openly and clearly scientific.

138 AAT, 14.14.93B: Ostensione SS. Sindone: Rendiconto; AAT, 14.14.40, folder "Metropolitana: Restauri e amministrazione": letter from the chapter to the cardinal, June 8, 1931.

139 Cf. I. Zannier, "Enrie, Giuseppe," in *Dizionario Biografico degli Italiani*, vol. 42 (1993), 774–76.

140 *Ostensione della S. Sindone*, 45. Fully described in Enrie, *La Santa Sindone rivelata*, 21–26, 77–92. See also Nicolotti, "Fotografie della Sindone."

141 ASV, Segreteria di Stato, an. 1902, rubr. 12, fasc. 13, ff. 182–97.

Fossati was even more hesitant, especially since he knew that the relic was the property of the king and that it would be difficult to obtain permission to examine it; furthermore, he thought that "the beginning of new studies could easily provoke dangerous discussions, with great damage to the faith of much of the population that came in such a rush the previous year to venerate the Holy Cloth."[142] The king, Vittorio Emanuele III, for his part, was completely against any scientific investigation:

> I distrust certain critics, who come obsequiously to ask permission to study the Holy Shroud and then write against it. When a thing is venerated by so many people and for so long, it is hardly decent to come to stick a finger in the eye.[143]

In effect, despite numerous requests advanced by scholars, even those who favored authenticity, the king—with the full support of his senior chaplain—never granted a close examination of the relic. Instead, that same chaplain believed that in 1931 the cardinal Fossati had conducted an improper desecration of the Shroud by allowing some scholars the opportunity to observe it up close.[144] It was a matter not only of distrust but of the king being fully aware of the sacred, symbolic role that the Shroud had performed for centuries as the property of the House of Savoy. Fossati was not late in being informed of this, and this unpublished declaration of intent, which came to him confidentially from the royal palace, is abundantly clear:

> The Royal House has always responded negatively to all those who, and among them those professors of the university and specialists, sought to obtain permission to be able to conduct studies, examinations, take photographs, etc. of the Most Holy Shroud, not only during its next exhibition, but during those of the past as well. The Royal House thinks that by granting such permission, it would be almost to admit doubt, or some shadow of suspicion

[142] AAT, 14.14.93B: letter by Gemelli, July 2, 1932; and the response by Fossati from July 25.

[143] *Le Saint Siège et la guerre mondiale: Novembre 1942—décembre 1943* (Vatican City: Libreria Editrice Vaticana, 1973), 118 (meeting with the apostolic nuncio Francesco Borgongini Duca).

[144] ACS, Real Casa, Chiese e cappelle palatine, Chiesa del SS. Sudario, 5 ter, fasc. 2: letter from October 2, 1939, by Msgr. Giuseppe Beccaria, senior chaplain to His Majesty, to General Emilio Gamerra.

> about the authenticity and historicity of that noted relic, which, having been passed down to it for centuries as authentic and having been recognized as authentic even by the supreme pontiffs and, to the glory of the August Family, having been venerated for so many centuries with the most solemn worship, must remain so as far as the House is concerned, and must be handed down in the same way. Is it therefore possible that the House authorize and permit these studies, even to the praiseworthy end of proving and demonstrating even better its authenticity, without implicitly admitting that it was also possible to have been keeper of something false, and that this false object had even received and is still receiving so much worship and veneration? Whoever wishes may say so, but certainly the Royal House, owner of the Most Holy Shroud, cannot be the very one to provide the material for discussion in one sense or another, which for the House must logically be above suspicion and remain inviolable.[145]

This letter explains why the request to study the Shroud that the Salesian Noël Noguier de Malijay put forth was rejected.[146] Even a harmless examination, like the observation of the fabric with a lens, could arouse concern; Professor Oscarre Giudici, a famous expert on textile technology of the Turin Royal School of Engineering, was denied the opportunity to examine the cloth to avoid what was interpreted as a "desecration" of the relic.[147] Later, Virginio Timossi, secretary of the fascist union of financial traders, was able to examine it, but unfortunately he proved less than competent.

The exhibition of 1931 was swiftly ended when an occasion arose that prompted a request for another exhibition: in 1933 the Holy Year of the redemption was celebrated, nineteen centuries after Christ's death.[148] Pius XI had shown his desire that the most notable relics of Jesus'

[145] AAT, Fondo dei cappellani palatini, 81, folder "1933: Ostensione della SS. Sindone": letter of September 15, 1933, by Msgr. Giuseppe Beccaria, senior chaplain to His Majesty (Rome), to the canon Michele Grasso, custodian of the Shroud (Turin), with the recommendation that it be referred to the archbishop.

[146] ACS, Real Casa, Chiese e cappelle palatine, Chiesa del SS. Sudario, 5 ter, fasc. 2: correspondence between Msgr. Giuseppe Beccaria and the minister of the royal house, April 1930.

[147] AST, Casa di Sua Maestà, 8553: letter from August 17, 1933, from Professor Giudici; and the reply from the minister of the royal house on September 12.

[148] It was traditional to believe that Jesus was born in AD 1 and died at the age of thirty-three.

passion and death be exhibited for the anniversary, and of course, the Shroud was not left out from his appeal. This was no dynastic occasion but an exclusively religious anniversary to which the king assented willingly. On June 20, 1933, an invitation to participate in the event was sent "to the diocesan councils and parish priests of Italy" on behalf of the committee for the exhibition, taking advantage of the railway system (which offered a 50 percent or 70 percent discount off the price of tickets to Turin) and declaring that "the studies recently performed by scientists on the latest photographic evidence, among which scholars Paul Vignon of the Académie of Paris must be mentioned, have even dispelled the final doubt about the authenticity of the precious Cloth."[149] Studies were undertaken on the photographs precisely because access to the original remained prohibited even to Vignon himself, who in the meantime had attempted fruitlessly to obtain permission to submit the relic to true examinations.[150]

The exhibition lasted from September 24 until October 15, and access to the cathedral remained opened from 4 am until 10 pm (fig. 4.3). On the closing day of the exhibition, the Shroud was removed from its frame and carried onto the steps of the cathedral so that the people, who were held back by two cordons of soldiers, could admire it out in the open. An oddity should be noted: before the Shroud was returned to its coffer, there was a short ceremony in which a copy of the relic was briefly brought in contact with the original, as was customary to do with Renaissance copies. Beginning on September 14 and for the entire period of the exhibition, it was possible to visit Piazza San Giovanni and see a "Holy Diorama," a plastic and pictorial version of the passion of Christ in ten scenes, with 450 figures and 3,000 m^2 of painting. On this occasion also, as previously in 1931, a plenary indulgence was granted to pilgrims.

The exhibition ended with a profit of about 241,000 lire (250,000 euros); this time the greater income was assured by the tickets for entrance to the Diorama, since the percentage obtained from the railway tickets was much lower.[151] As previously in 1898, some even claimed to have received a miracle, but this time as well the

149 AAT, Fondo dei cappellani palatini, 88.

150 AST, Casa di Sua Maestà, 8553: letter from September 20, 1933, by the minister of the royal house.

151 AAT, 20.4.1, accounting folders; in AAT, Fondo dei cappellani palatini, 88, there are some train tickets, receipts, and invitations from the time.

FIGURE 4.3 Exhibition of the Holy Shroud in the Cathedral of St. John the Baptist in Turin, 1933

ecclesiastical authorities did not pursue the matter.[152] A contrary note was sounded by Tito Signorelli, pastor of the Italian Methodist Church and freemason of the Scottish Rite, who wrote a booklet against the authenticity of the Shroud using historical and theological arguments, many of which were based on the work of Chevalier.[153] But all in all the two exhibitions of 1931 and 1933 were unprecedented successes, far superior to the rallies organized by fascist authorities of the time; the fascists, though they took an active part in the organization of the two events, remained on the sidelines, since all the propaganda and rhetorical symbolism of the exhibitions and their paraphernalia were principally centered on the Church and the House of Savoy.[154] This occasion as well was followed by the publication of a commemorative volume, whose historical section was edited by Carlo Lovera di Castiglione. In that volume, his account of the first millennium was conjectural, and when he tried to recover the testimonies of various ecclesiastical authors, he unfortunately mixed up information about the Shroud of Turin with details pertaining to the relic of Besançon.[155] Count Lovera—aristocrat, member of *Azione cattolica*,[156] sincere fascist, mild anti-Semite, and firm anti-Mason[157]—played a leading role in the organization of exhibitions and sindonological meetings in these years.

Exhibitions, as we have seen, for centuries had been the exclusive expression of the will of a ruling house eager, among other things, to promote the veneration of a relic that it owned and that provided a source of prestige for the dynasty. Some scholars perceived a growing effort by the ecclesiastical authorities of Turin, beginning with the exhibitions of 1898, 1931, and 1933, to weaken this dynastic link by assuming greater control over the management of the relic and

[152] AAT, Fondo dei cappellani palatini, 81, folder "1933: Ostensione della SS. Sindone": envelope addressed to the canon Michele Grasso with the account of a woman whose stomach was miraculously healed.

[153] T. Signorelli, *La Santa Sindone: Studio critico-storico* (Turin: AGI, 1933).

[154] Cf. G. Graglia, "Le due esposizioni della SS. Sindone (1931–1933) e la sacralizzazione della politica nel Ventennio," *Annali della Fondazione Luigi Einaudi* 46 (2012): 333–59.

[155] Cf. G. Pozzi, ed., *L'ostensione della SS. Sindone: Torino 1933* (Turin: Giachino, 1933); see especially 13–24.

[156] "Catholic Action" is a widespread Roman Catholic lay association in Italy.

[157] There are some hints in F. Piva, *La gioventù cattolica in cammino* (Milan: Franco Angeli, 2003), 114–16.

by insisting much more on the purely religious aspect of the exhibitions. In these years, too, a religious "sindonic pastoral," which was not as closely bound to traditional dynastic celebrations, was in its infancy. By that point, certainly, the Church and sindonologists had replaced the Savoys in promoting the propaganda of the Shroud; but it would be a mistake to go on to imagine that the function of the royal house was reduced to simply permitting exhibitions as soon as they were requested by the clergy. It is true that the distance between Turin and the new Roman capital had partially broken the link that connected, even visually, the Shroud to its owners; Vittorio Emanuele III, moreover, was not religious and did not have a particular interest in the relic, nor did he ever go to see it. But that does not mean that the Savoys thought it possible to leave the Shroud in the hands of the Church. Rather, their opinion ran in the opposite direction; the king had always refused the opportunity to perform any scientific examination on the Shroud, since he thought that to do so might bring doubt upon its authenticity and its role as a "heavenly" dynastic legitimator. He himself considered the exhibition of the Holy Year of the redemption—an exclusively religious event that was proposed to him by the cardinal—as an exception, not, of course, as the beginning of a new trend. Vittorio Emanuele made this quite clear to Fossati in a meeting held in March of 1938, in which he let him know that from then on he would no longer authorize exhibitions until the next marriage, that of the new crown prince (his grandson, who had been born the previous year). These indications allow us to recognize how closely bound the king still was to a traditional conception of the Shroud, one inherited from his predecessors. Fossati, on the other hand, had no intention of pressing the matter. In his own words, for the final exhibition of 1933, "the troubles brought upon me were such that I promised never again to repeat a similar event."[158]

In 1938, a French petition with the aim of requesting a new exhibition gained the signatures of six cardinals, ten archbishops, and twenty-one bishops, but nothing could be done.[159] In the same year, the cardinal Ildefonso Schuster, archbishop of Milan, wanted symbolically to repeat the pilgrimage of his holy predecessor Charles

[158] AAT, 14.14.93B: draft of a letter by Cardinal Fossati to Cardinal Maglione, secretary of state for the Vatican (April 5, 1939).

[159] AAT, 14.14.93B: petition sent to the secretary of state.

Borromeo; he was welcomed with pomp at the gates of Turin, but no exhibition followed, not even a private one. Even after the fall of the monarchy, Fossati expressed his view against a request for an exhibition as part of the Holy Year of 1950, and he did the same for the National Eucharistic Congress of 1953.[160] In 1962, on the occasion of the opening of the Second Vatican Council, the prospect of a possible exhibition was proposed to John XXIII, but the issue was considered "convenient" neither by Fossati nor by the pope.[161]

4.3.2 First Conferences of Sindonology, War and Postwar

Under the episcopate of Maurilio Fossati, at a remove of nearly forty years from the great conflicts between supporters and deniers of the Shroud's authenticity, the apostolate of sindonic worship and veneration expanded vigorously. In 1936, within the Confraternity of the Most Holy Shroud of Turin and with the approval of the cardinal, the society of the *Cultores Sanctae Sindonis* was founded with the aim of coordinating studies on the Shroud at the international level. A corresponding French branch of the society immediately opened in Paris (which, however, did not meet with the approval of Paul Vignon).[162] In 1939, a pavilion set up for the International Expo, which was still in Paris, hosted a historical-artistic display of the Shroud, where a life-size photograph of the relic was exhibited.[163]

The first significant achievement of the Italian *Cultores* was the organization of a national conference in Turin.[164] For the first time, a group of scholars interested in the relic gathered and held a series of multidisciplinary presentations in the fields of history, archaeology,

[160] AAT, 14.14.85, folder "Anno Santo 1950 e Giubileo 1951": correspondence from January–February of 1949; AAT, 14.14.63, folder "Cappella S. Sindone": correspondence between Fossati and Giovanni Battista Montini, pro-secretary of state for the Vatican.

[161] AAT, 14.14.26, folder "Segreteria di Stato anni 1946–1962": secretary of state to the archbishop of Turin, prot. 75852 from February 5, 1962.

[162] AAT, 14.14.93B: letter from December 10, 1936, to Cardinal Fossati and from December 27, 1936, without a recipient (I believe it was intended for Bernardo Bellardo of the *Cultores* of Turin).

[163] Cf. "Il padiglione della S. Sindone all'Esposizione internazionale di Parigi," *L'Italia*, May 29, 1937, 5, and November 21, 1937, 4.

[164] See the report by F. Trossarelli, "Convegno nazionale di studi sulla S. Sindone," *La Civiltà Cattolica* 2136 (1939): 521–34. The proceedings: *Santa Sindone nelle ricerche moderne*.

medicine, chemistry, photography, theology, liturgy, and anthropology. I believe that this was a critical moment in the development of what Pietro Scotti, eclectic Salesian scholar and editor of the proceedings of the conference, had the insight to denote as "sindonology."[165] "The problem of the Shroud became a scientific problem," as the canon Cesario Borla, president of the *Cultores*, affirmed in his introductory address: "to gather anatomical, physiological, chemical, and physical data generated by the studies of these scientists and to make it known in order to explain the wondrous document, that is one of the reasons for the current conference." Agostino Gemelli, who in the meantime had become president of the Pontifical Academy of Sciences, assumed the presidency of the colloquium. This conference was the first installment in what would become an uninterrupted tradition of sindonological conferences.

The overall scientific value of this first experience was doubtlessly superior to that of many other similar undertakings held subsequently. Various prestigious names belonging to diverse disciplines took the floor, even though two significant obstacles weighed down the entire project: the impossibility of directly examining the object and the authenticist leanings of all the organizers. It is clear that for various reasons neither the king nor the archbishop nor the *Cultores* would have welcomed the participation of anyone who denied or challenged the authenticity of the relic. A quotation from the archaeologist Carlo Albizzati is bitter and sarcastic:[166]

> In the spring of '39, I was invited to a scientific conference, to be held in Turin, to address in various ways the issue of the authenticity of the Most Holy Shroud. A gentleman there, who is a member of the committee, wrote to me with every courtesy, informing me, however, that because of the sacredness of the topic and because of other concerns, it would not have been permitted to discuss it, and that no one would have been able to examine the distinguished relic. I responded in this way: "If there are concerns to avoid discussion, and if there are other reasons not to allow the object under discussion to be viewed, it is useless to attempt a rationalistic procedure, which is not suitable to the event. Because,

[165] He recounts it himself in P. Scotti, "La Sindone: Spunti quasi autobiografici," *Ministero pastorale* (June 1977): 347.

[166] On this individual, see A. Stenico, "Albizzati, Carlo," in *Dizionario Biografico degli Italiani*, vol. 2 (1960), 17–18.

as a Towering Religious Authority seems to have said,[167] the matter concerns a relic that is not a human work, so its authentication must also be supernatural. Therefore, I await the Almighty's direct intervention, thereby saving miserable sinners, such as us, some wasted time."[168]

The conference had been successfully concluded for a few months when, on September 1, 1939, Germany invaded Poland, an act that would inaugurate the Second World War. At the time, Italy was a nonbelligerent nation, but some immediately thought about the security of the Shroud. The problem had already been taken into consideration during the First World War, at which time the king ordered that the relic be sheltered in the Royal Palace. To that end a hidden underground chamber had been acquired in connection with the so-called "Staircase of the Airs"; the fabric remained hidden therein from May 6, 1918, until October 28, 1919.[169] This time, however, a different decision was made, and with amazing speed. Five days after the invasion of Poland, the Shroud was secretly removed from its chapel and on the following evening, September 7, was loaded onto a train to Rome with an escort of two priests traveling in a normal passenger compartment. It was the king's intention to hide the relic in the Vatican, but the pope informed him that it would not have been very secure there. At this point the secretary of state, Cardinal Luigi Maglione, suggested it be brought to the abbey of Montevergine, near Avellino. And so again in utter secrecy the Shroud was transported there by police car, delivered to the abbot and the prior (very few monks were informed of the transfer), and placed under an altar (the altar of the "little choir of the night"). The war ran its course, and no one ever came to know that the Guarini chapel was empty.

[167] Albizzati alludes to the pope here; he uses intentionally vague language so as not to provoke the Holy See.

[168] C. Albizzati, "Tre casi insigni," *Athenaeum* 19 (1941): 64–65. The article continues with some considerations against the authenticity of the relic, using arguments that could not all be supported today.

[169] Cf. A. Barberis, "Capitolo inedito della storia recente della S. Sindone," *Sindon* 1 (1959): 37–40; G. Moretto, "6 maggio 1918—28 ottobre 1919: La Sindone allogata nei sotterranei del Palazzo Reale di Torino," *Sindon* 12 (1999): 73–84. A number of interesting documents that concern, among other things, the distribution of the altar keys, are collected in ACS, Real Casa, Chiese e cappelle palatine, Chiesa del SS. Sudario, 5 ter.

Only in 1946, after the end of the war, was it decided to return the Shroud to Turin, and this time the operation was performed in the presence of the archbishop himself. Fossati arrived in Montevergine on October 28, having previously obtained authorization to grant a private exhibition in honor of those monks who for seven years had lived next to the Shroud without knowing it. After a stop in Rome, the Shroud was again loaded onto a train bound for Turin, where it arrived on the morning of October 31. Among the members of the small group that had accompanied the cardinal should be noted the name of the geneticist Luigi Gedda, a prominent figure in the *Azione Cattolica* organization and future president of the civic committees of 1948, which Pope Pius XII wanted to direct the 1948 electoral campaign against the communists.[170]

The Shroud returned and took its place in its chapel in Turin, but in a completely new position. Events during the war had driven Vittorio Emanuele III to abdicate in favor of his son Umberto II; and a little later, following the referendum that led to the formation of the republic, Umberto also had to leave Italy forever. Umberto's exile brought the issue of the Shroud's ownership back under discussion, since the new Constitution of the Republic of Italy, which came into force on January 1, 1948, contained this provision:

> Access and sojourn in the national territory shall be forbidden to the ex-kings of the House of Savoy, their spouses and their male descendants. The assets, existing on national territory, of the former kings of the House of Savoy, their spouses and their male descendants shall be transferred to the state. Transfers and the establishment of royal rights on said properties which took place after 2 June 1946, shall be null and void.[171]

There were no doubts about the confiscation of the Royal Palace, along with the annexed Chapel of the Shroud: since 1850 both had

[170] Cf. M. Fossati, "Lettera al clero," *Rivista diocesana torinese* 23 (1946): 146–50; L. Gedda, "L'ostensione della Sindone a Montevergine," *Tabor* 1, no. 1 (1947): 40–47; A. Barberis, "Nuovo capitolo inedito della storia della Sindone," *Sindon* 9 (1965): 8–11; Pugno, *Santa Sindone che si venera a Torino*, 327–42; G. Mongelli, *La Sacra Sindone a Montevergine e la sua ostensione il 28–29 ottobre 1946* (Montevergine: n.p., 1973); C. Moriondo, "Viaggio clandestino a Montevergine e ritorno," in Moriondo and Piazza, *Torino e la Sindone*, 103–9.

[171] XIII, transitory and final provision.

been classified as forming part of the so-called *Dotazione della corona* ("civil list of the King"), that is, those goods belonging to the patrimony of the state allowed to be used freely by the king. The Savoys were unable to put forward any claim over them, and these goods remained property of the Italian state. What about the Shroud? During those months, it remained in Montevergine. In a letter dated June 10, 1946, only three days before departing into exile, Umberto II wrote the following to Cardinal Fossati:

> Current events have led me today to communicate to Your Most Reverend Eminence that—while it is my intention that the precious Relic remain the sacred and inalienable heritage of my House—I forthwith give my full consent that it again find its original placement in Turin, in the chapel that bears its name.[172]

Until that moment, the three keys to the grating on the altar that held the box were kept by the palatine chaplains of Turin. After this letter, Cardinal Fossati, who felt invested by the royals' will with a responsibility for the relic, ordered Paolo Brusa, the guardian of the Shroud, to surrender two of the three keys; one should be for himself, and the other was to be given to the chapter of the cathedral. Brusa offered some resistance, somewhat offending Fossati; eventually, the cardinal agreed to be content with only one of the keys, leaving the other two with the palatine chaplains, who, after their service to the royal house had ended, came into the employ of the president of the Republic.[173] From that point the religious authority in the person of the archbishop of Turin assumed in practice an active role in securing the relic. But with whom did its ownership lie?

For the moment no one posed the question. On the contrary, since it was kept in the chapel and was the object that gave the chapel a reason to exist, the Shroud could most immediately be considered the property of the new republican state, which substituted for the monarchic state. If, however, the Shroud was not a good included as a

[172] ACS, Real Casa, Divisione III, miscellanea, 499, folder "Custodia della SS. Sindone a Montevergine."

[173] The institute of the palatine clergy was only formally abolished in 1986; cf. T. L. Rizzo, *Il clero palatino tra Dio e Cesare* (Rome: Rivista militare, 1995). For the issue of the keys: correspondence of November 6–19, 1946, between Msgr. Giuseppe Beccaria and canon Paolo Brusa (ACS, Real Casa, Chiese e cappelle palatine, Chiesa del SS. Sudario, 5 ter, fasc. 6).

Dotazione della corona but the personal property of the king (*Spettanza di Sua Maestà*, "Concern of His Majesty"), we must conclude that it became the property of Umberto II on May 9, 1946, at the moment when he assumed the crown, when his father Vittorio Emanuele abdicated the throne. But the result is the same, since in this case it would have been included among the goods confiscated by the state according to constitutional norms. The third possible interpretation, even if somewhat improbable, is that the Shroud had to be considered the personal property of Vittorio Emanuele, and remained such even after his abdication; it should be considered, then, that at his death on December 28, 1947, three days before the constitution that deprived him of all his goods on Italian soil came into effect, his property passed to heirs.[174] There were five heirs: four daughters and Umberto. That means that in this case, in accordance with the confiscation of the goods of male descendants, the Italian state would in any case have inherited a fifth of the Shroud, namely, the part belonging to Umberto.

Therefore, there are well-founded reasons for believing that at the advent of the republic, the Shroud became, along with the chapel that held it, part of the patrimony of the new Italian state, or according to the most restrictive and improbable hypothesis, that the state had confiscated a fifth of its ownership. From a legal standpoint, in any case, there seems to be no legitimacy to the approach of Umberto II, who even in exile always continued to manage the Shroud as his personal property. I believe that Umberto II's bequest of the Shroud to the pope in his will of 1981 is void, since he was in no condition to make such a bequest. On the basis of these challenges, which were not entirely new,[175] in 2009 two Italian parliamentarians sought the

[174] As regards the retroactive annulment of the transfers after June 2, 1946, established by the constitution, the law limited it to only acts of passage of rights among the living and not also to cases of succession by cause of death; see the decision with commentary in *Temi: Rivista di giurisprudenza italiana* 7 (1952): 553–62.

[175] Cf. A. Martucci di Scarfizzi, "Condizione giuridica della reliquia della S. Sindone di Torino," *Il diritto ecclesiastico e rassegna di diritto matrimoniale* 89 (1978): 603–20 (quotation from the conclusions on 611–12: "After the institutional change from June 1946 . . . moreover, any sort of claim of royal rights to the relic remains invalid for Umberto II, and also, since it is not a question of goods passing in succession after Vittorio Emanuele III, it is not possible to recognize any claim to it by the heirs of the female line of the House Savoy and their descendants"); G. Galeazzi, "La Sindone è dello Stato," *La Stampa*, May 26, 2009 (interviewing the

reaffirmation of the Italian state's ownership of the Shroud, ownership that "can and must signify above all the possibility for new independent scientific studies, without conditions, on the origins of the sheet."[176] No response was made to this demand. For a variety of reasons, I would not consider appropriate the removal of the Shroud from its usual placement in the cathedral of Turin; but free access to the Shroud for scientists, who are currently impeded by those who manage it, was and remains a serious problem.

So, following World War II, the Shroud returned to the darkness of its chapel. Not long after, however, a momentous event would to some extent overshadow the Shroud's prominence in the collective consciousness of the citizens of Turin. On May 4, 1949, the day of the liturgical feast of the Shroud, tragedy struck the city: the Torino Football Club, called at that time the "Grande Torino" because of its many lauded successes, boarded a plane to return home from Lisbon after a friendly match; perhaps because of bad weather or a faulty altimeter, the plane crashed into the Basilica of Superga, on the Turin hill, which was wrapped in a thick fog. The entire team and reserve players perished. Even today, the date of May 4 in Turin is remembered not for the Shroud but rather for that tragic accident.

The next year the *Cultores Sanctae Sindonis* decided to hold a second sindonological conference, which took place in 1950, on the occasion of the Holy Year, in two separate cities: Rome and Turin. The conference's organization was overseen by the *Cultores*, with central roles given to Pierre Barbet, French doctor and sindonologist, and Luigi Gedda. The inaugural session in Rome was a solemn affair: six cardinals were present, as well as various bishops and superiors of religious orders; ambassadors from Italy, France, and Spain; and a prince. Seventy-four members comprised the Honorary Committee of the conference, including many clergymen, diplomats, and university rectors. One man was absent who, because of his scientific merits as a historian of antiquity, would have been one of the most prestigious members, Gaetano de Sanctis. Cardinal Fossati invited

---

jurist Francesco Margiotta Broglio, president of the two governing committees for Church-State relations).

[176] Parliamentary written question number 4–01563, from the radical senators Marco Perduca and Donatella Poretti, presented to the minister of cultural heritage on March 9, 2009.

him, but he, confirming his already well-known independence,[177] preferred to decline:

> Most reverend Eminence, I have received from the presidency of the central group of the *Cultores Sanctae Sindonis* an invitation to take part in the Honorary Committee of the international conference on studies of the Holy Shroud according to the instructions given by Your Eminence. I am always happy to attest publicly my Catholic faith and my devotion to the Holy See. But on the present occasion, while I am most grateful to Your Eminence and the organizing committee for the distinguished proof of the respect that you have sought to afford me, I am very sorry that I must decline the invitation. In fact, I ought to state that the careful study of ancient and recent argumentation about the authenticity of the Shroud has convinced me that it is not authentic. Moreover, being eager to avoid any scandal, I have always kept silent about the issue and I wish to keep silent about it still today, which would clearly be impossible if I were to participate in the conference. Therefore, I trust that Your Eminence, in Your high spirit of understanding and charity will wish to find my refusal justified and avoid it offering an opportunity for scandal.[178]

Giving this quotation from De Sanctis' letter, as well as the previous quotation from canon Piovano, seems necessary to me not because I wish to elevate those who do not accept the authenticity of the Shroud but rather simply to reestablish equilibrium. There were many more names of those who, unlike De Sanctis, agreed to take part in the Honorary Committee, and among those were even distinguished scholars of recognized expertise; but while adherence to the authenticist cause was publicly attested and made known to all, the same could not be said, in the overwhelming majority of cases, for adherence to the opposite view. But for a few exceptions, in the sphere of Catholic non-authenticists—and this letter clearly demonstrates the point—it was preferable to remain silent rather than provoke "scandal." It is a situation that, above all among the clergy, endures still today and deserves to be brought to light; otherwise, one risks committing an error from a historiographical

[177] He was one of about fifteen Italian university professors (out of a total of 1,225) who in 1931 refused to sign an oath of loyalty to the fascist regime and was then fired.

[178] AAT, 14.14.93B: letter to Cardinal Fossati, Rome, April 2, 1950.

perspective by concluding that in the world of Catholicism, the scarcity of contrary voices is proof of an almost unanimous adherence to the belief in authenticity.

The quality of the conference was inferior to that of its predecessor; no proceedings were ever published, but only a summary.[179] A biting criticism was made by a Catholic historian from France of undisputed renown, Henri-Irénée Marrou:

> The partisans of authenticity must first undergo a qualifying exam before the tribunal of historians, and I see that they have never been able to explain from where and how this imprinted fabric came in the middle of the fourteenth century to the collegiate church of Lirey, in the diocese of Troyes, a place and time very far from the Palestine of the Gospels![180]

The same arguments had already been offered at the end of the previous century. Conference participants' claim that they were studying the Shroud in accordance with a scientific perspective (though without being able to see it), by emphasizing not so much its religious significance as the argument over authenticity, could not but rekindle the debate.

Among those who sent messages to the secretary of the conference of 1950, there was a certain Kurt Berna (in reality Hans Naber, also known as John Reban). He was a mentally unstable individual who believed that he had received a vision of the passion of Christ; he claimed that Jesus, while he was in the tomb, was not dead and had left on the Shroud traces of uninterrupted cardiac activity, which were detectable from the hemorrhages that had soaked the fabric.[181] Berna tried to give weight to his theories by flaunting support, which in fact did not exist, garnered from distinguished scholars or clergymen.[182] It is an extreme case, but this episode can be considered the first sign of a process that would become unrestrainable: sindonology, by

[179] *La Santa Sindone nelle ricerche moderne: Primo convegno internazionale* (Turin: Lice—Berruti, 1951); cf. Scotti, "Primo convegno," 136–46.

[180] H.-I. Marrou, "À propos du saint suaire," *Le Monde*, June 23, 1950, 2.

[181] K. Berna, *Das Linnen: Ein Bericht nach Entdeckungen und Ereignissen im 20. Jahrhundert* (Stuttgart: Naber, 1957).

[182] Cf. W. Bulst, "Heretical Phantasies of a Visionary: Kurt Berna," *Sindon* 4 (1960): 19–40; R. K. Wilcox, *Shroud* (London: Corgi Book, 1978), 59–73; D. Willis, "Did He Die on the Cross?," *Ampleforth Journal* 74 (1969): 27–39; Ricci, *Holy Shroud*, 219–37.

that time having proclaimed itself an autonomous and independent science dedicated to the study of a potentially miraculous object, began to attract eccentric individuals, who were inclined to the use of unchecked fantasy (as happens somewhat in all areas of the so-called "parallel" or "unconventional" sciences).

Kurt Berna's delirious request to the pope for permission to perform examinations on the Shroud met with a terse refusal.[183] Berna, however, was not the only one hoping to be able to approach the Shroud, since Vittorio Emanuele III's death and Umberto's exile could, perhaps, open up new possibilities in that regard. But among scholars of the Shroud, consensus was lacking about whether direct scientific investigations should be performed. In May of 1950, when the *Cultores Sanctae Sindonis* privately gathered the opinions of some of their number, a plurality of views emerged. Agostino Gemelli was against such testing, for example, while others were in favor of it. The opinion expressed by a person inclined to scientific examinations is noteworthy:

> Carlo Lovera di Castiglione believes that, after the two conferences, the thorough examination of the Shroud is necessary, despite recommendations against it. He does not believe a public examination is advisable. It ought to be performed by the religious authorities under the greatest secrecy by a few well-chosen experts versed in chemistry, exegesis, and archaeology. Religious men who are consulted should belong to different congregations. The examination could be held in Rome and arranged with a secret meeting of the examiners. If the results were favorable, the news ought to be made public; if unfavorable, no more would be said of the examination.[184]

Among those who pressed harder for scientific examinations was the Jesuit Werner Bulst, who can be considered the founder of German-language sindonology.[185] Through his Benedictine confrère Cyryl

[183] The exchange is reported by M. Centini, *Breve storia della Sindone* (Casale Monferrato: Piemme, 1998), 167–69.

[184] AAT, 14.14.93B: Cultores Sanctae Sindonis, ed., *Riassunto delle risposte pervenute da alcuni studiosi della S. Sindone* [. . .] *circa nuovi diretti esami sul Sacro lenzuolo*, pro manuscripto, May 1950.

[185] He is the author of W. Bulst, *Das Grabtuch von Turin: Forschungsberichte und Untersuchungen* (Frankfurt am Main: Knecht, 1955); English translation: *The Shroud of Turin* (Milwaukee: Bruce, 1957).

Korwin-Krasiński, member of a princely Polish family connected by marriage to the House of Savoy, he succeeded in obtaining Umberto II's consent. Bulst communicated the approval to Father Agostino Gemelli, offering support for the establishment of a committee for Shroud studies, and often pressed both the archbishop of Turin and the *Cultores* without ever meeting with a satisfactory response.[186] Cardinal Fossati did not even allow the Shroud to be filmed with a television camera.[187] On the contrary, it is clear that Umberto had freely granted everyone permission.[188] If previously it was his father, the king, who did not want scientific examinations to be performed, now it was the archbishop. For the House of Savoy, the Shroud had ceased its proper function of legitimizing the dynasty, since the kingdom was no longer in their hands.

Bulst was tenacious. Ignored by Turin, in 1956 he directed his efforts toward the Holy See by approaching it with a project of scientific studies together with the previous authorization of Umberto, which also allowed for the possibility of a new exhibition. Bulst proposed to include some scholars in the examinations, among whom were Mario Ponzio of Turin, Boris Rajewsky, Ferdinand Wiethold, and Friedrich Dessauer of Frankfurt am Main, as well as two Italian sindonologists, Pietro Scotti and Giovanni Judica Cordiglia. An international scientific conference to be held in Turin in 1957 provided a good opportunity for the project. The Holy See was not against it in principle, but Cardinal Fossati put forward "almost insurmountable difficulties" due principally to the need to maintain the utmost secrecy and to find a discreet location to bring the Shroud in order to examine it. Agostino Gemelli provided this opinion:

> It seems to me that it is neither agreeable nor useful to remove the Holy Shroud from the sacred area. Your Eminence once mentioned to me the possibility of taking the Holy Shroud to the Royal Palace: this would be the most, in my view, that could be granted.

186 This epistolary correspondence is found in AAT, 14.14.93B.

187 AAT, 14.14.93B: letter from Rudolf Hynek on January 4, 1948; and from the Astra Cinematografica society on September 20, 1957.

188 In 1969 Umberto II authorized an exhibition with scientific examinations, upon consent from the ecclesiastical authorities, even to an "assembly of Catholic graduates from the province of Pordenone" (message from Count Dino Olivieri, personal assistant to Umberto, from June 15, 1969, in response to a telegram from Giacomo Ros, mayor of Pordenone). Nothing came of it.

> I, however, would be of the opinion that you absolutely must not take it to a scientific institute of the university, and above all on the occasion of an international conference. We do not know what the outcome of these examinations would be; if the result were negative, in what sort of situation would the Holy See, the diocese of Turin, and the same high Patron find themselves? It seems to me that, at least, any publicity is to be avoided, because we do not know the Christian character of all those who, according to Father Bulst's project, ought to participate in the examination or assist with it.

The experts, according to Gemelli, "ought to be scientists, yes, but able to keep a secret, therefore faithful to the Church." He thereby excludes the possibility of making use of Ponzio and Rajewsky. As for the others, his judgment is merciless: "Prof. Dessauer is a man of modest scientific worth; Prof. Scotti, a Salesian, is not a scientist, but a popularizer; Prof. Judica Cordiglia is an excellent Christian, but he, too, is not a scientist." It must be noted that Scotti and Judica Cordiglia, at the time, enjoyed high regard among Italian sindonologists. The former edited the proceedings of the 1939 conference, and the latter would for many years be the director of the Center of Sindonology of Turin. And so the examinations of 1957 also came to nothing.[189] In this matter the ecclesiastical authorities appeared to be thinking along the same lines as Vittorio Emanuele III, since they feared the damage to their image that a possible unfavorable result from the tests would have inevitably provoked. Secrecy and the assurance of being able to keep the experts under control were nonnegotiable conditions. Clearly, there would have been every interest in promulgating the results, if they were favorable; conversely, it was possible to impose silence.

Meanwhile, sindonologists encouraged the spread of devotion to the Shroud throughout the world, always connecting devotion with the requirement of accepting its authenticity. To these years, for example, belongs the indefatigable work of Edward Wuenschel, who disseminated information about the Shroud in English-speaking

[189] AAT, 14.14.40, folder "Real capella": correspondence among Werner Bulst, Vittorio Prunas Tola, Angelo Dell'Acqua, Maurilio Fossati, Agostino Gemelli (April–July 1956).

countries.[190] In those years some interest was raised in the matter of a possible miracle involving Josephine Woolam, a ten-year-old English child with osteomyelitis. When the child seemed to be dying, her mother kissed the image of the Shroud and the child showed improvement. Therefore, she was hoping that contact with the authentic relic could lead to a complete healing. The highly decorated Captain Leonard Cheshire, one of two English pilots who assisted in dropping the atomic bomb on Nagasaki in 1945, took charge of the matter. Having converted to Catholicism after the war, Cheshire, through the intervention of Umberto II of Savoy, succeeded in obtaining permission to have the ailing girl touch the relic. On July 7, 1955, young Josephine and Cheshire reached Turin. The Shroud's box was opened, without, however, removing the relic, and the girl was permitted to put her hand on the bundle that surrounded it.[191] A few years later, Woolam and Cheshire wrote a book.[192] A similar request also came to Cardinal Fossati from a Greek official, but he was denied permission, perhaps because he lacked the recommendation of King Umberto.[193]

In October of 1958, John XXIII was elected pope. Some months later, on February 16, 1959, a delegation of the *Cultores Sanctae Sindonis* was received at the Vatican and offered to the pope a gift of books, short works, and photographs of the relic. An account has been passed down that on that occasion, the pontifex proclaimed these words: "Here is the finger of God," and later still: "Truly, at first, I had some doubt about the veracity of the relic, but then I realized how sacred

[190] Wuenschel, *Self-Portrait of Christ*. To allow him to dedicate himself fully to the Shroud, his superior exempted him from all teaching duties; see AAT, 14.14.93B: letter of June 27, 1938.

[191] Cf. AAT, 14.14.93B: letter from Umberto on July 3, 1955, which announces that Cheshire is coming "to accompany there the 'miraculously cured' Josephine Woolam, who hopes to be able to venerate the Most Holy Shroud of Our Lord"; AAT, Fondo dei cappellani palatini, 81: minutes from July 7.

[192] Cf. L. Cheshire and J. Woolam, *Pilgrimage to the Shroud* (London: Hutchinson, 1956); there is a brief account in Humber, *Sacred Shroud*, 160–63. In 1978 Josephine returned to Turin for an exhibition of the Shroud and gave an interview: J. Woolam, "Il commosso 'grazie' di Josie," in "Speciale Sindone," supplement, *Avvenire* 233 (September 23, 1978), v. See also C. Foley, "More than I Went to Ask For," *Shroud Spectrum International* 15 (1985): 13–21; and on the figure of Cheshire in general, see R. Morris, *Cheshire: The Biography of Leonard Cheshire* (London: Viking, 2000).

[193] AAT, 14.14.63, folder "Cappella S. Sindone": supplication of Dimitrios Tsiantis, captain of the Greek army, submitted to the archbishop by the secretary of state for the Vatican, June 23, 1956.

and real a thing it is."[194] In that same year at Turin, after contentious discussions within the Confraternity of the Holy Shroud that led to the resignation of Bernardo Bellardo, president of the *Cultores*, a new structure was agreed upon. An organization was created to replace the *Cultores*, the International Center of Sindonology, which had the aim of spreading knowledge and coordinating studies, research, and initiatives pertaining to the Shroud. The appointment of the Center's director was entrusted to the executive council of the confraternity, with the first director being the above-mentioned forensic examiner Giovanni Judica Cordiglia. One year later, in Vercelli, the Center held its first regional conference.[195]

4.4. The Postconciliar Period

4.4.1 The Episcopate of Michele Pellegrino and the Examinations of 1969

In 1965 Archbishop Maurilio Fossati died. He had governed the diocese of Turin with a steady hand for no less than thirty-five years, sponsoring two exhibitions, surviving a difficult period of the war, assisting in the transition from the monarchy to the republic, and participating in the elections of three popes. His successor, Michele Pellegrino, however, was a man who had made culture his reason for living; he had three degrees and, at the time of his appointment to the episcopal see, was professor of ancient Christian literature at the University of Turin; for some years he was also professor of the history of Christianity, just where I have the same role today. While participating in the last session of the Second Vatican Council he delivered two significant speeches to the assembly, one on the freedom of research in the Church, and the other on the culture of the clergy.

It is natural that the new archbishop would not take the same approach to the Shroud as his predecessor. Pellegrino was the first bishop of Turin who avoided insistent declarations of the relic's authenticity. We do not know whether he ever dealt in depth with the historical and exegetical problems connected with it, but certainly,

[194] Quoted by L. Fossati, *Breve saggio critico di bibliografia e di informazione sulla Sacra Sindone: Dal primo Congresso nazionale di studi (1939) al secondo Congresso internazionale (1978)* (Turin: Bottega d'Erasmo, 1978), 145, § 822.

[195] *Atti del I convegno regionale del Centro Internazionale di Sindonologia*, ed. Reale Confraternita del SS. Sudario.

as a scholar of the first order, he could not ignore them. More than anything else it seems that he doubted the credibility of the sindonologists. Franco Bolgiani, a student of Pellegrino and in turn professor of the history of Christianity at the same university, recalls of him "that he was personally very suspicious of a phalanx of exalted sindonologists and supposed scientists."[196] Whatever his thoughts, which were not necessarily monolithic, Pellegrino did not hinder devotion to the Shroud, but neither did he do anything to increase it. His most innovative contribution was the creation, formalized on March 23, 1969, of a commission of experts who proceeded with a reevaluation of the cloth. The members chosen by Cardinal Pellegrino—as was explained at the closing press conference—were scholars "who did not hold, not even in their subconscious, positions for or against the Shroud."[197] This excluded the sindonologists, contact with whom was in any case guaranteed by Giovanni Judica Cordiglia, director of the Center of Sindonology.

From the sixteenth to the eighteenth of June 1969, the Shroud, after being moved to the chapel of the crucifix in the cathedral and arranged on a vertical frame, was examined using the naked eye, a microscope, and ultraviolet and infrared light. Giovanni Battista Judica Cordiglia, Giovanni's son, took a series of new photographs, including the first color photographs and the first using ultraviolet light.[198] He, too, was famous among the general public because, together with his brother, Achille, he was interested in listening for radio transmissions from space, and among other things claimed that he had heard and recorded voices of Soviet cosmonauts lost in space.[199]

[196] F. Bolgiani, "Tanti giochi sulla Sindone," *La Repubblica—Torino*, January 22, 1995, I.

[197] *Osservazioni alle perizie ufficiali*, 12.

[198] Described by Cordiglia himself: G. B. Judica Cordiglia, "Come si è proceduto alla ripresa fotografica della SS. Sindone," in *S. Sindone: Ricerche e studi*, 93–101 (English translation: "The Procedure Adopted for Photographing the Holy Shroud," in *Report of Turin Commission on the Holy Shroud*); Judica Cordiglia, "Ero solo con l'immagine di Cristo," in Moriondo and Piazza, *Torino e la Sindone*, 189–93; Judica Cordiglia, "Tra le luci e le ombre della fotografia appare il Cristo sindonico," in *La Sindone: La storia; La scienza*, ed. Centro Internazionale di Sindonologia (Leinì: Centrostampa, 1986), 151–59.

[199] Cf. A. Judica Cordiglia and G. B. Judica Cordiglia, *Dossier Sputnik* and *Dossier Sputnik* 2 (Turin: Edizioni Vitalità, 2007 and 2010).

The scholars ascertained that the sindonic cloth was in excellent condition, and they hypothesized, for the future, the potential to consider a new method for the preservation of the object, which would be no longer rolled up but stretched between two pieces of glass. Moreover, they proposed the following procedures: dating of the fabric using an archaeological investigation and available physical and chemical means, ascertainment of the nature of the different imprints and the weight of the Shroud, optical investigations over various bands of wavelengths, and examination of the fabric. For the moment the only operational requests made to the authorities were the detachment of the Holland cloth that had completely covered the back of the fabric since 1534 and the removal of very small samples of sindonic cloth that would undergo further examinations. The experts promised to bring afterward, in writing, other substantive proposals.[200]

The entire operation had to remain secret, at least initially. But it is quite difficult to keep secrets for long when they are of such import and, simultaneously, of such interest; and therefore, some information leaked out and came to the attention of the wrong person, Hans Naber (also known as Kurt Berna), the fanatic previously mentioned. He immediately committed all his effort to disseminating alarmist reports in various newspapers, imagining a plot by the Church to destroy or alter the Shroud in order to hide evidence of the fact that Christ did not die on the cross. All of this provoked a series of reactions, sometimes exaggerated, that were aimed at both the Holy See and the archbishop of Turin; at first, there were unofficial denials, then weak confirmations given in the difficult situation of having to justify the secrecy of the examinations. The most forceful protests came from the sindonologists to whom it seemed incredible that they had to learn of the existence of the commission from a raving mythomaniac like Naber.[201]

At that time, the role of the Italian-American Peter M. Rinaldi was growing. In the United States, where he lived, Rinaldi worked in close contact with the Redemptorist priest Adam J. Otterbein, president of

[200] Minutes published in *S. Sindone: Ricerche e studi*, 7–11 (English translation in *Report of Turin Commission on the Holy Shroud*).

[201] See for example, D. Willis, "False Prophet and Holy Shroud," *Tablet*, June 13, 1970, 567–69.

the Holy Shroud Guild.[202] In a letter sent to Turin's Catholic weekly *Il nostro tempo*, but not published, Rinaldi declared his frustration as follows:

> Regretfully it must be said that the cause of Christianity's greatest Relic has for years suffered by the difficult-to-understand reluctance on the part of the Church authorities to act or even speak on the subject. If not actually obstructive, theirs have been dilatory tactics that are perplexing and exasperating to serious students and devout admirers of the Holy Shroud throughout the world. . . . How can a relic of such tremendous significance be kept locked and sealed for decades at a time? And when finally brought to light, why is it examined secretly?[203]

Rinaldi found it "incomprehensible" and "hardly justifiable" that the authorities of Turin did not grant authorization to display and study the relic, and he wondered what they were waiting for to do so.[204] A few weeks later, Cardinal Pellegrino, in an interview published in the same weekly, spoke for the first time publicly about the commission of experts, declaring that the principal aim of their investigations was to verify the state of preservation of the fabric. It was also an opportunity to respond to Naber's accusations and to express his hope that there might emerge new arguments useful for ascertaining the authenticity of the relic, since "from the historical point of view, documents are very, very sparse."

> It is a historical and scientific issue. Logically, if a Christian believes in the authenticity of this Relic, it is quite natural that he would expect an attitude of veneration before the Holy Shroud, but he is completely free to doubt or deny its authenticity (we know that there are many Catholic scholars, as well as priests, who do not accept the authenticity of the Shroud at all). The Church has no reproach for such a posture.[205]

[202] The Holy Shroud Guild was canonically established and approved by Cardinal Francis Spellman, Archbishop of New York, in 1951. On sindonology in the United States, see M. Minor, "La sindonologia in America," in Zaccone and Ghiberti, *Guardare la Sindone*, 399–409.

[203] P. M. Rinaldi, *The Man in the Shroud*, 2nd ed. (London: Futura, 1978), 97–98.

[204] P. M. Rinaldi, "What Are We Waiting For?," *Sindon* 20 (1974): 40–44.

[205] P. Gilles, "Un mistero chiamato Sindone," *Il nostro tempo*, February 15, 1970, 5.

The times had truly changed: seventy years earlier a predecessor of Pellegrino had brought Ulysse Chevalier to trial before the Holy See until he had reduced him to silence precisely because Chevalier had made this very claim, namely that the authenticity of the Shroud was a question of a historical and scientific nature that did not touch upon the patrimony of the faith.

4.4.2 The Televised Exhibition of 1973

In May of 1972 a weekly publication of the diocese of Turin published a letter in which a group of women expressed their desire to see the Shroud again after forty years. The director of the periodical, Father Carlo Chiavazza, responded to their letter, offering his thoughts that "the great uncertainty concerning the exhibition of the Shroud originates from doubts about its authenticity," and that in any case it "could no longer be approached as in the past amid incense and solemn ceremonies." In response, the following week that same periodical published a letter from an "astounded" sindonologist, who did not understand how a Catholic newspaper could doubt the authenticity of the Shroud; Chiavazza, however, held to his view, because "we cannot impose as absolutely certain that which is not such."[206]

This exchange provides some indication of what the situation was like in the 1970s, when there was a certain hesitation among various Catholics not only toward the Shroud but more generally over the appropriateness of continuing to encourage devotion to the relics. The Second Vatican Council had dedicated only a few words to these issues: "The Church, in accordance with its tradition, venerates the saints and honors their authentic relics and their images."[207] The Council speaks of "authentic relics" specifically, but did that include the Shroud? Interest in the Shroud remained strong among sindonologists, that is certain, but it cannot be said that the relic was an object of grand popular devotion independent of events occasioned by rare exhibitions. Chiavazza himself claimed that the Feast of the Shroud "draws more interest outside of Italy than in Turin itself." The object was not visible, and the Chapel of the Shroud was certainly not one of the preferred pilgrim locations in the city.

[206] "La Sindone sconosciuta," *Il nostro tempo*, May 7, 1972, 2; M. D. Fusina and C. Chiavazza, "Sacra Sindone e l'autenticità," *Il nostro tempo*, May 14, 1972, 7.

[207] Constitution *Sacrosanctum Concilium* (December 4, 1963), § 111.

In those years the Shroud was quite far from being one of the most venerated relics of the Christian world. But the situation was destined to change radically just in the years immediately following, thanks to powerful propaganda that made the Shroud known everywhere and brought the scientific aspects of the study of the relic to the fore, as had previously happened in 1898, by presenting those aspects from the perspective of authenticity.

First, let us consider the exhibition. Pellegrino did not remain indifferent to requests to grant a new exhibition, which would be the first to take place since the fall of the monarchy; but he did not want it to be performed as exhibitions had been in the past. The archibishop wrote, "I reflected that, for the diocese of Turin and for me, such an exhibition would involve the paralysis, for a time, of other grave and urgent activities and that, after all, following the liturgical reform, it could not be carried out in the traditional ways and methods." Therefore, the choice was made of a format using "a televised exhibition clearly of a very short duration" to be conducted not in the cathedral but in a hall in the Royal Palace. Immediately apparent is the desire to erase any trace of a traditional exhibition, the way it was conceived for centuries, which, in the archbishop's opinion, "bears with it serious inconveniences"; the palace, a secular place, had to replace the church.[208]

On November 22, 1973, at about noon, in a press conference at the Royal Palace, Cardinal Pellegrino explained to those present the reasons that had led him to authorize the broadcast of the exhibition that was to take place the following day. Among those in attendance was Ian Wilson, who had become one of the most influential English-speaking sindonologists in the world, and who later said he perceived in the archbishop a "reluctance" to the idea of displaying the relic publicly. When the press conference ended, amid a very informal atmosphere, the attendees were moved into the Salon of the Swiss, where the Shroud was hanging from a wall in a simple frame, illuminated by the broadcaster's lamps brought in by RAI (the national broadcasting network of Italy). Beginning with the position of the

[208] Extracted from G. Tuninetti, "Pastorale sindonica nell'azione degli arcivescovi torinesi," in Zaccone and Ghiberti, *Guardare la Sindone*, 199. Useful "official" commentary of the time is that of J. Cottino, "Perché la Sindone in televisione?," *Rivista diocesana torinese* 55 (1973): 404–7.

Shroud on the wall, hung vertically, no longer displayed horizontally, everything indicated a break with the past. A vase with flowers was present, but not a single candle; there was no priest clothed in vestments, but rather the context was extraliturgical, recalling a room in a museum. For the first time after so many years—and still the most recent even today—a group of "ordinary" people was able to approach the Shroud freely, to photograph it from close by, and to touch it with their fingers—there was no protective glass—almost as if they were experiencing a work of art.[209]

On the following evening, the relic was visible to millions of people on their televisions. In the room of the palace, in addition to the archbishop and the palatine clergy, thirty people were admitted who were invited to honor the Shroud "almost as a representation of the People of God." The broadcast, produced by the author and playwright Fortunato Pasqualino, was accompanied by a message from Paul VI, a speech by the archbishop, and a moment of prayer. In his message, the pope avoided pressing too far the topic of authenticity, directing his reflections to the contemplation of Christ's features:

> Whatever historical and scientific judgment that able scholars will wish to express concerning this amazing and mysterious relic, we cannot refrain from vowing that it is useful in conducting visitors not only to a rapt viewing that perceives the exterior, mortal features of the marvelous figure of the Savior, but it can also usher into them a more penetrating vision of his recondite, fascinating mystery. . . . Ought we resign ourselves, with the tradition attested, for example, by Saint Irenaeus and Saint Augustine, to confess that the human appearance of Jesus is completely unknown to us? Well then, we have great fortune, if this alleged surviving effigy of the sacred Shroud allows us to contemplate some authentic feature of our Lord Jesus Christ's physical form, which is deserving of adoration, and if it truly helps our thirst, so inflamed today, to be able to recognize his form visibly! Gathered around so precious and pious a keepsake, the mysterious allure of Him will grow in us all, believers or nonbelievers, and in our hearts will resonate

[209] Cf. Wilson, *Turin Shroud*, 3–9; "Sindone in TV: L'annuncio del Cardinale," *Stampa Sera*, November 22, 1973, 5; R. Cobo [P. Coero-Borga], "Spunti di cronaca dell'avvenimento," *Sindon* 19 (1974): 36–40. The official minutes are in *S. Sindone: Ricerche e studi*, 12–18 (English translation in *Report of Turin Commission on the Holy Shroud*).

> the evangelical admonition of His voice, which then invites us to seek Him there, where in human shape He still lies hidden and allows Himself to be discovered, loved, and served.[210]

Although in his message the pope used the expression "renowned relic," Cardinal Pellegrino chose to limit himself to the terms "image" and "keepsake" and opened the way to a devotion of the Shroud that was more detached from the assessment of authenticity because it was based on the contemplation of the image of suffering:

> If one can doubt—as some doubt—that the image we piously venerate is truly the imprint left by the body of Christ on the new sheet in which Joseph of Arimathea wrapped him, one thing is certain: the face of Christ is imprinted on that of the brothers, His and ours, as many as have neither face nor voice.[211]

Despite all of this caution, there was no want of critics, driven by a variety of motivations. Critics were even to be found in the Catholic world. The exhibition provoked Vittorio Messori to make his voice heard; in the years to come he would touch upon the issue of the Shroud many times.[212] It is difficult to strike a balance: the exhibition, due to how it was organized and the fact that the televised images were rendered in black and white, did not elicit much enthusiasm. Of those with whom I had the opportunity to speak, many who were

[210] "Messaggio di Paolo VI per la prima ostensione televisiva della Sindone," *Rivista diocesana torinese* 55 (1973): 465–66.

[211] M. Pellegrino, "Miracolo eloquente," *Rivista diocesana torinese* 55 (1973): 467.

[212] V. Messori, "La Sindone-TV," *Stampa Sera*, November 24, 1973, 1: "Last evening's television broadcast on the Shroud has brusquely set us back twenty years. Close-ups of nuns with coif and wimple; 'innocent' children in a posture of prayer; a speaker with broken voices as a devotional highlight for the context; prayers intoned by monsignors with firm countenance. The perfect illusion, an environment masterfully arranged: we have returned to the postwar period of the pilgrim Madonnas, of mystic visions revealed to magazines at a high print run. An embarrassing 'sermon' more than half an hour given to the usual twenty thousand television viewers. . . . An apologetic move instead of a moment of reflection, acceptable to all. In a society that calls itself pluralist and secular, such as ours, is it permissible to occupy a channel of a television monopoly with a broadcast of this type of Catholicism?" Vittorio Messori later clarified this idea in "È convinto della Sindone non della TV," *La voce del popolo*, December 9, 1973, 6.

interested in the Shroud recalled the exhibition as a disappointing experience.[213]

Again in 1973 the Shroud had to undergo another act of "desacralization." The liturgical reform instituted by the Second Vatican Council obligated each diocese to review and translate into Italian its own liturgical texts; in Turin attention had to be given as well to the liturgy of the Holy Shroud, which was still the one approved in 1506 and revised at the end of the seventeenth century. In 1966 an Italian translation of the *Proprium* of the mass had been published,[214] and in 1973 the work of a special Piedmontese liturgical committee began, concluding in 1976 after a complete restructuring of the texts. The Liturgical Office of the diocese of Turin went further, proposing also to abolish the traditional Feast of the Shroud on May 4 and to merge it with the celebrations of Holy Week. The proposal came up against strong protests and was shelved but provides a good indication of how suspiciously the relic was viewed even in certain circles of Turin's clergy. In any case, the office of the Shroud was downgraded from "Double of the First Class" to simply "Memorial." Its liturgical texts were dramatically diminished and modified, and the hymns entirely removed; in the new text, references to the Shroud are minimal and take great care to avoid any declaration, even implicit, of the authenticity of the relic. Despite Rome's requests, an official Latin version was not even prepared.[215] This episode is a significant indication of a theological orientation that was anything but favorable to the veneration of the Shroud. Only in 2006, in a profoundly different situation, was the "Memorial" elevated to the rank of "Feast."

4.4.3 The Results of the Pellegrino Commission

The day after the televised exhibition, November 24, was set for the removal of samples from the Shroud for examination.[216] Umberto of Savoy consented to these withdrawals on the condition that the material be returned after the examination and placed in the reliquary. The

[213] Franco Peradotto, director of the diocese of Turin's weekly, speaks of "failure" ("La TV ci può offrire immagini migliori," *La voce del popolo*, December 2, 1973, 3).

[214] *Proprium missarum archidioeceseos Taurinensis cum interpretatione italica* (Turin: Marietti, 1967), 17–20.

[215] Cf. Savarino, "Sviluppo della liturgia ufficiale," 217–21.

[216] Minutes in *S. Sindone: Ricerche e studi*, 19–25 (English translation in *Report of Turin Commission on the Holy Shroud*).

results were not published until 1976, but they were not in accordance with the expectations many had. Three forensic pathologists from Modena conducted different investigations on the fibers that were taken (microscopic examination, tests of reactions to the benzidine, micro-spectroscopic examination, thin-layer chromatography), but those tests were negative for blood; however, they left open the possibility that the typical characteristics of blood could not be further identified on so ancient an artifact.[217] The microscope, however, could not detect the presence of corpuscles that could be identified as red blood cells.[218] One of the most debated questions was the possibility of subjecting the fabric to C14 examination. The destructive nature of the removal of additional material from the Shroud, however, hindered the study; dating the Shroud required sacrificing part of the fabric, and at the time the amount needed was substantial.[219]

Noemi Gabrielli, an art historian, released a much-debated report in which she attempted to identify the means by which the corporeal image could have been imprinted on the cloth. Gabrielli thought that a template of a human figure had been designed by an artist on a wet cloth, which was then placed in contact with the Shroud and pressed with a padded weight to transfer the color from one fabric to the other. The Shroud was a masterpiece of figurative art; it was the creation of a great artist active near the end of the fifteenth century and the beginning of the sixteenth century, who used Leonardo da Vinci's sfumato technique. Gabrielli therefore denies that the present Shroud is the same one that appeared in Lirey in the fourteenth century and believes that it is a version from about 130 years later, after the 1532 fire in Chambéry (providing an argument to those who believed that the current shroud was a replacement for the one that

[217] Cf. G. Frache, E. Mari Rizzati, and E. Mari, "Relazione conclusiva sulle indagini d'ordine ematologico praticate su materiale prelevato dalla Sindone," in *S. Sindone: Ricerche e studi*, 49–54 (English translation: "A Definitive Report on the Haematological Investigations Carried Out on Material from the Shroud," in *Report of Turin Commission on the Holy Shroud*).

[218] Cf. G. Filogamo and A. Zina, "Esami microscopici sulla tela sindonica," in *S. Sindone: Ricerche e studi*, 55–57 (English translation: "Microscopic Investigations on the Shroud," in *Report of Turin Commission on the Holy Shroud*).

[219] Cf. C. Codegone, "Sulla datazione di antichi tessuti mediante isotopi radioattivi," in *S. Sindone: Ricerche e studi*, 31–38 (English translation: "Concerning the Dating of Ancient Fabrics by Means of Radioactive Isotopes," in *Report of Turin Commission on the Holy Shroud*).

burned). In contrast with others issuing reports that were more open-minded despite the negative results, Gabrielli declared the Shroud a fake.[220]

The report by the Egyptologist Silvio Curto was perhaps the most complicated. He admitted that extant historical information did not permit a proven identification of the Shroud of Turin with that of the Gospels. He believed that some traces of color had been artfully added. He denied that the image was the result of a natural imprint made by contact with a cadaver, or a painting made with a brush; he did not consider impossible the theory proposed by Gabrielli but added another to it that dealt with an unspecified photographic process. It seemed to him that the subject depicted on the fabric was a living person in the pose of someone deceased rather than someone truly deceased. In conclusion, Curto was inclined toward the hypothesis of artistic fabrication.[221]

A flaw in some of these experts' reports lies in the choice to intervene in issues already amply discussed in the preceding decades, without being aware of the debate. One can equally speak of certain conjectures and certain encroachments into some fields that did not fall within the experts' competencies. The best reports, in their complexity, were those of a technical nature.

The reaction to the publication of the findings of the commission was very swift. The International Center of Sindonology—substantially excluded from the examinations—ten months later sent to press a small volume of *Observations* on the experts' reports.[222] Giovanni Judica Cordiglia, who had also been a member of the commission, lamented that the scholars' reports did not allow any decisive step forward and that

[220] N. Gabrielli, "La Sindone nella storia dell'arte," in *S. Sindone: Ricerche e studi*, 87–92 (English translation: "The Shroud in the History of Art," in *Report of Turin Commission on the Holy Shroud*).

[221] S. Curto, "La Sindone di Torino: Osservazioni archeologiche circa il tessuto e l'immagine," in *S. Sindone: Ricerche e studi*, 59–73 (English translation: "The Turin Shroud: Archaeological Observations concerning the Material and the Image," in *Report of Turin Commission on the Holy Shroud*).

[222] *Osservazioni alle perizie ufficiali*. Other sindonologists prefer to ignore these studies; Frank Tribbe, for example, dedicates a chapter to the Turin Commission but does not say even one word about the results: F. C. Tribbe, *Portrait of Jesus? The Shroud of Turin in Science and History* (St. Paul: Paragon House, 2006), 107–20.

they could instead lead to distorted beliefs.[223] Father Luigi Fossati criticized the work of nearly all the experts and insisted on the idea that the somatic images were imprinted on the cloth by way of the awesome presence of the glorious Christ. He lamented the absence of theologians, biblical scholars, and forensic pathologists from the commission, thereby demonstrating that he did not understand that the commission was not called to approach the Shroud in the style of the sindonologists—that is, as if its authenticity were already a determined or probable fact. He concluded by declaring that he was disappointed and convinced that "for the Holy Shroud, more and better could and ought to be done."[224]

It would take too long to summarize every response. It can be said that Gabrielli's theory was most criticized, and many requested that Gabrielli provide a practical demonstration of the technique that she conjectured, which she did not do (and which perhaps she did not even have the equipment to attempt). In general, however, the sindonological publication did not escape the usual temptation to amass discussions and theories heterogenous in character and value, connected only by the thread of faith in the authenticity of the object. Various renowned sindonologists participated in writing the volume; some discussions, however, fell outside the volume's scope, were inconclusive, or clearly were not equal to the task. There was also a paper from a painter as well as one from an architect, who did not fail to propose a new theory on the formation of the image: Jesus imprinted the image by emitting light from his blood in the instant that he rose again and went up to heaven.[225] Some just criticisms directed toward certain weaknesses in the official report, therefore, ended up being overwhelmed by the flaw of the volume's perspective and by its inadequacy in handling the complexity of such a response. Evidently the Center was not able to draw meritorious scholars, and it cannot be ruled out that this was one of the reasons why the cardinal decided not to make use of it.

[223] G. Judica Cordiglia, "Osservazioni critiche sulle ricerche e gli studi perseguiti sulla S. Sindone dalla commissione di esperti tra il 1969 e il 1976," in *Osservazioni alle perizie ufficiali*, 19–29.

[224] L. Fossati, "Considerazioni sulle relazioni degli esperti che hanno esaminato la Santa Sindone nel 1969 e nel 1973," in *Osservazioni alle perizie ufficiali*, 31–65.

[225] Cf. Mosso, "Perizie sulla Sindone," 116–17.

FIVE

The Creation of a Myth

5.1. A Rebirth

5.1.1 The Shroud and Sindonology

The year 1976 marked a new beginning for the Shroud. Although the Pellegrino Commission had not provided encouraging results, for the first time the Shroud had been made available to scholars. From that point on there was significant growth in scholarship and scientific examinations of the Shroud, whether merely proposed or actually undertaken. For many, these studies held the promise of authentication of the relic through various experiments. As had been the case at the time of the first photograph, the fields of history, exegesis, and philology, none of which could provide decisive support for authentication, were relegated to the background. We are now in what has been defined as the "second stage" of sindonology: the first, after 1898, had focused on investigating the alleged torture of the man of the Shroud; the second aims increasingly at demonstrating the miracle of the resurrection scientifically.[1]

Yet the history of the Shroud cannot ignore the ever-increasing progress of sindonology; indeed, one could say that for the last forty years the history of the Shroud has been, to a large extent, a history of sindonology. The historical investigation also accounts for this development, which to those not directly involved with research is the most readily perceptible and best-known aspect of the study of the Shroud.

[1] Thus J. Eslava Galán, *El fraude de la Sábana Santa y las Reliquias de Cristo* (Barcelona: Planeta, 2005), 63.

After the Pellegrino Commission, the Shroud was subjected to scientific examinations carried out on only two other occasions: in 1978, with an orchestrated program of studies, and in 1988, but then only for radiocarbon dating. The 1978 scholarly commission was created with criteria opposed to those of Cardinal Pellegrino, because that commission was assembled and led by those who had previously investigated the Shroud with the inclination to authenticate it. Its responses have often been challenged not so much for the results themselves but for their subsequent interpretations. Some members of this commission continued for the rest of their lives to occupy themselves with research on the Shroud. The radiocarbon examination of 1988, which was conducted with the best methodology and in the best laboratories then available, dated the fabric to the late Middle Ages. The result was incompatible with the authenticity of the relic but in perfect agreement with the surviving historical documents. The negative result was not accepted by the overwhelming majority of the sindonologists, who continued to propose alternative explanations and behave as if the radiocarbon dating had never happened.

Since the end of the eighties until the present time, sindonology has continued to produce studies that have grown exponentially, even without access to the Shroud. This situation can be easily understood inasmuch as the greater part of the scientific community has little or no interest in the relic. Almost all the material that has been produced is the work of those who are predisposed toward a particular outcome and are thus readily satisfied with conjecture about an object that they have never examined. Furthermore, at present it does not seem that those who control access to the Shroud have any intention of alleviating this situation.

The Shroud is obviously for some an important faith-affirming religious object that to them bears witness to or is a consequence of the miracle of Christ's resurrection. As such, the Shroud becomes the object of clashes where very often logic leaves space for partisanship, regardless of the personal position of those involved. As a consequence, the level of much of the literature on the Shroud, whether historical or scientific, is very low, and those who are sufficiently skilled to deal with it generally refrain from doing so in order to avoid making an argument that is controversial and unmanageable, scientifically speaking. The vacuum created by the absence of qualified research projects has created an avenue for intentional dilettantism.

The result is an impressive amount of scientific studies on the Shroud, the majority of which, however, are less than credible.

Sindonology in the last century has been organized as a discipline that has drawn a great number of Shroud fans and unfortunately has adopted the characteristics typical of pseudosciences.[2] Although it is concerned with the Shroud in all respects (historical, archaeological, artistic, medical, palynological, etc.), sindonology has, in recent years, sought to garner the most public attention possible, especially as concerns studies aimed at understanding the nature of the image impressed upon the fabric. In this regard sindonologists are united in the shared belief that the Shroud cannot have been made by an artificial method, but only in a way incomprehensible, extraordinary, or miraculous, and incapable of being replicated by human hands. This fundamental assumption is an indispensable one for them, without which the field of sindonology cannot stand.[3] Internally, contrary voices do not exist.

> Perhaps the biggest difficulty in dealing with the science of the Shroud is that sindonology does not have one of the most important checks common in science to prevent sincere scientists from presenting wishful thinking as data. There are no opposition scientists—no experts with an alternative theory to defend who would work just as hard to disprove the original theory. Perhaps it is just lack of interest, although some may have been put off by the knowledge that critics would never actually get to the Shroud.[4]

Since the scientific community generally does not consider the Shroud an object of scientific study except when those charged with keeping it issue certain requests for scientific examinations (which virtually never happens), the field of investigation is utterly uncluttered and has been taken over by sindonology, organized in associations that "publish" mainly through postings on the Internet, books, and self-referential and self-managed conferences, where one finds,

[2] As previously observed by S. Schafersman, "Are the STURP Scientists Pseudoscientists?," *Microscope* 30 (1982): 232–34.

[3] I examine these claims in A. Nicolotti, "La Sindone: Banco di prova per esegesi, storia, scienza e teologia," *Annali di storia dell'esegesi* 33, no. 2 (2016): 459–510.

[4] J. Hanlon, "Christ under the Microscope," *New Scientist* 1124 (October 12, 1978): 98.

predictably, the absence of the normal checks and balances of the international scientific community. The dissemination of the tenets of sindonology is also vouchsafed by publishing, television, and the widespread network of ecclesiastical institutions (dioceses, parishes, various associations) that, even if in theory they do not officially support authenticity, in practice clearly favor it.

Human curiosity about mysterious subjects, the superficiality of the press, and the strength of sindonological organizations have created the false impression among the general public that the Shroud is an object widely studied by science and is now definitively recognized as incapable of being deciphered. Precisely because of this misplaced trust and also, above all, because the ecclesiastical authorities have accepted unquestioningly what sindonologists advance as science, which consequently has the aura of objectivity and infallibility, the fortune of the Shroud in the modern era has proved to be far better than it was from the Middle Ages to the beginning of the twentieth century. The "scientific" response thus provides support apparently founded on what often remains substantially an apologetic impulse or an inclination toward interpreting reality in paranormal terms.

What follows is what I have been able to conclude after having read hundreds of sindonological studies and, when necessary, having turned my attention back to competent persons in each specific field (with great difficulty, as scientists generally shun any association with pseudosciences and prefer simply to ignore them). A sufficiently detailed discussion of all topics related to this theme, accompanied by an appropriate commentary, would occupy hundreds of pages. Therefore, it will be sufficient here to summarize briefly the events of recent years, reducing to a minimum the essential references in the notes and privileging the historical-narrative aspect over the scientific-analytical. I will defer for now a more thorough explanation of some aspects.

5.1.2 The Pollen Study of Max Frei-Sulzer

On October 4, 1973, the Shroud was removed from its box for a technical television test. This offered the opportunity to compile and have notarized a report on the photographs taken in 1969 by Judica Cordiglia in order to certify their authenticity, their correspondence with the Shroud, and the absence of any manipulation. To make the inspection and to perform the appraisal, the custodian of the Shroud, Msgr. Pietro Caramello, accepted the advice of Father Piero Coero-Borga of the International Center of Sindonology and turned over the responsibility to Aurelio Ghio, a technical consultant of the Turin tribunal; Ghio in turn put forth the name of one of his colleagues, Roberto Spigo, and of Max Frei-Sulzer.[5] Max Frei had been the founder and director of the laboratory of the Zurich scientific police; he had recently resigned from his post following a judicial scandal in which he had been involved because of a flawed report, which had led to life imprisonment of an innocent man. The commission that judged his work retained the right to affirm that his mistake could not have been accidental.[6]

On March 20, 1976, a few days before the publication of the expert reports from the Pellegrino Commission, in the newspaper *La Stampa* an article authored by Pier Paolo Benedetto appeared. Its title was unequivocal: "The Fabric Dates Back to the Times of Jesus."[7] The article quotes Max Frei, saying that he had been authorized in 1973 to take some samples of dust present on the Shroud and that he had identified plant pollens that were "present exclusively in the area of Palestine and alive twenty centuries ago."

This announcement startled those who followed the fortunes of the Shroud, because Frei had been called to authenticate some photographs, not to examine dust. In the meticulously documented minutes there was no trace of the samples. Had they been removed without permission? At this point contradictory statements alternated in the newspapers, but after some hesitation, it was stated that the samples were withdrawals that were gathered at night, with permission asked and obtained at the last minute from a palatine

[5] Report in *S. Sindone: Ricerche e studi*, 26–30 (English translation in *Report of Turin Commission on the Holy Shroud*).

[6] The history is recounted by G. Ciccone, "La truffa dei pollini: Il dossier completo," http://sindone.weebly.com/pollini1.html. On this and other events that involved Frei in those years, cf. H. M. Sutermeister, *Summa Iniuria: Ein Pitaval der Justizirrtumer* (Basel: Elfenau-Verlag, 1976).

[7] P. P. Benedetto, "Il tessuto risale ai tempi di Gesù," *La Stampa*, March 20, 1976, 5.

chaplain, while keeping the official commission in the dark.[8] For the second time in the span of a few years, the ecclesiastical authorities found themselves in the embarrassing position of having to justify the secrecy of certain operations.

The controversy concerned not only the semi-clandestine character of taking samples but also the scope of the analysis. According to the press release, Frei had identified "grains of fossilized pollen of plants existing only in Palestine twenty centuries before." He would also affirm with certainty that "the fabric dates back to the time of Christ and was displayed in Palestine, Turkey, France and finally in Italy in Turin," precisely in those places where, according to information that the Center for Sindonology had already provided him, Frei believed the Shroud had been kept in previous centuries.

Obviously similar statements, disclosed just before the publication of the report of the official commission, perpetuated the debate and partially cast a shadow over its reported results. Yet for various reasons some of the statements were nonsensical: pollen cannot be dated, and the plants that Frei claimed to have identified were not extinct and could not even be said to have come exclusively from the region in or near Palestine or Turkey. It was pointed out immediately, too, that any attempt at dating pollen on the Shroud was futile; but at that point Frei denied that he had ever entertained the possibility. Some blamed the journalist, accusing him of having put in his mouth phrases that he had never spoken. The reporter had, however, cited the words of the Swiss expert with quotation marks and explicitly mentioned a written report dated March 8, 1976. I have obtained a copy of this report, albeit with a slightly different text from what was published. It is not clear whether Frei put into circulation two versions of the same document, or if he made some statements verbally that he was then forced to retract to avoid criticism, or if Pier Paolo Benedetto falsely attributed the words to Frei. Two years later, Benedetto became a member of the inner circle of sindonology, coauthoring a book with Pierluigi Baima Bollone, who at the death of Judica Cordiglia in 1980 was named director of the Center for

8 Cf. P. G. Accornero, "L'autenticità della Sindone," *La voce del popolo*, March 28, 1976, 1; M. Bertola, "La Sindone interessante e misteriosa," *Il nostro tempo*, April 4, 1976, 5; P. Coero-Borga, "È polline del Golgota?," *Il nostro tempo*, April 4, 1976, 5; P. Caramello, "La S. Sindone e il prof. Frei," *Il nostro tempo*, April 11, 1976, 2.

Sindonology.[9] This consideration is not trivial, because from that point on sindonologists began to disseminate the notion that Frei had dated the Shroud to the first century thanks to the discovery of pollen from extinct plants. As a consequence, this information is still disseminated today. The first sounding board of the false report was the volume of observations on the reports by the Pellegrino Commission, published in 1977 by the Center for Sindonology, where the false statement twice appears.[10]

5.1.3 The 1977 Conferences and the New Exhibition

Following in the footsteps of the devotion to the Shroud exhibited by Saint Francis de Sales, the Salesian congregation has had among its members a good number of Shroud scholars and, since the time of Chevalier, has been recognized as the organization that has most widely disseminated knowledge of the relic "in the two worlds."[11] The Salesian who in the second half of the twentieth century exercised the greatest influence was the already-mentioned Father Peter Rinaldi. The 1974 meeting of Rinaldi and Otterbein, who were respectively vice president and president of the Holy Shroud Guild, with the twenty-eight-year-old American physicist John Jackson was fraught with consequences. Ever since childhood Jackson had dreamed of working on the Shroud, as he himself recounts:

> I was introduced to the Shroud by my mother when I was 13 or 14 years old. She told me that she had a picture of Jesus. She showed it to me. And my first experience with the Shroud was that I didn't recognize the image. Suddenly it dawned on me that I was looking at the face and the face was looking right at me. And it was that moment of interaction, that encounter, that little did I know at that point that it was going to change my life. . . . When I arrived back at Colorado State University, I had every intention of

[9] Baima Bollone and Benedetto, *Alla ricerca dell'uomo della Sindone*.

[10] Mosso, "Perizie sulla Sindone," 116: "He discovered that it was pollen fossilized from plants that existed exclusively in Palestine twenty centuries ago." J. L. Carreño Etxeandía: "Un año ascensional para la SS. Síndone," in *Osservazioni alle perizie ufficiali*, 136: "pollen from Palestinian plants, today extinct, that flowered precisely in the time of Christ."

[11] Chevalier, *Étude critique*, 55. A profile of some Salesian sindonologists is in E. Valentini, "Settant'anni di ricerche e studi sindonologici," *Sindon* 12–13 (1968): 13–27.

> finishing up my Master's degree in Physics there. I told my professor that I would like to do a project, a thesis, on the Shroud of Turin. Of course, he had no idea what that was. When I explained it to him, I think he didn't know whether to laugh or to cry.[12]

At one point he contacted the Holy Shroud Guild of Esopus, offering his expertise in the service of the Shroud. Soon his colleague Eric Jumper joined him. Both airmen and professors of physics and aerodynamics, respectively, at the United States Air Force Academy in Colorado Springs, they sought out further members from a Catholic discussion group based also in Colorado Springs. Later, members of other institutes were added (e.g., Los Alamos, Air Force Weapons and Jet Propulsion laboratories). After finding interested individuals, they made a proposal to the Holy Shroud Guild to organize a conference on the Shroud. That conference took place behind closed doors in March 1977 in Albuquerque, New Mexico.

The lectures that were published as conference proceedings range from history to theology, to medicine, to ecumenism. Germane to the current study are the lectures that sought to create a three-dimensional image of the man on the Shroud using computer technology. Other lectures treated the possibility of studying the fabric with X-ray fluorescence, infrared thermography, and radiocarbon dating, as well as microscopic observation. One hypothesis that is often pointed out is that the image of the man of the Shroud could have formed due to radiation. In the absence of the object, the researchers had to be content to work on the photographs that for the first time were proffered for electronic investigations.

Captain Kenneth Stevenson, as editor of the conference proceedings, concluded the volume with the testimony of his own belief that, during the months of the studies, the hand of God had effectively operated among scholars. He declared that he was certain that all the published proceedings had a single purpose: "to bring the Shroud, and with it the Gospel, to the world."[13] In September of the same

[12] J. Rinaudo, "Shroud of Turin: Shroud Experts & Original STURP Team Members Gather at Shreveport's Cathedral of St. John Berchmans for Special Panel," *Catholic Connection*, September 28, 2018, www.thecatholicconnection.org/?p=8407.

[13] K. Stevenson, ed., *Proceedings of the 1977 U.S. Conference of Research on the Shroud of Turin* (New York: Holy Shroud Guild, 1977), 242.

year a symposium was also held in England, during which the British Society for the Turin Shroud was inaugurated.[14] The relic began to achieve great fame: a story was invented regarding the death of Elvis Presley . . . that in August of 1977 he supposedly died while reading a book about the Shroud!

The "discovery of three-dimensionality" merits a brief consideration. In 1976, John Jackson and Eric Jumper attempted to subject a photograph of the Shroud to an electronic device, the "VP-8 Image Analyzer," which was used, among other things, to analyze images of the moon's surface sent by space probes. The device allowed the different levels of intensity (from brightness to darkness) of a two-dimensional image to be transformed into corresponding elevation levels to achieve an apparent three-dimensional relief that could be displayed from different viewpoints. For the human figure of the Shroud, it happened in practice that the computer screen displayed the representation of a three-dimensional body.[15] Sindonologists then proposed anew the argument already used in the period when the negativity of the Shroud was "discovered" by Secondo Pia in 1898: how could one possibly think that a medieval forgery would have been capable of incorporating into the image of the Shroud three-dimensional information that would only be discernible in the future using a sophisticated computer?

This time as well, however, the argument was fallacious: if a painting or a photograph is subjected to analysis by the computer, one does not obtain a three-dimensional result, but if instead one uses an imprint (as in the case of the Shroud) one is able to recreate the "three-dimensional" effect. In fact, where the imprint is darker, in correspondence to the areas that project out more and that have most touched the cloth, the computer creates a bas-relief, returning the three-dimensional character of the model.

A professor at the University of Turin, Giovanni Tamburelli, wanted to improve the three-dimensional development that the Americans had obtained. The Centro Studi e Laboratori Telecomunicazioni (CSELT) of Turin put a device at his disposal, as well as

[14] The proceedings were not published: the program is taken from the brochure *Symposium on the Shroud of Turin, 16th and 17th September 1977: Provisional Program.*

[15] Principally, see J. Jackson et al., "The Three-Dimensional Image on Jesus' Burial Cloth," in Stevenson, *Proceedings of the 1977 U.S. Conference*, 74–94. There are other essays in the volume connected to the argument.

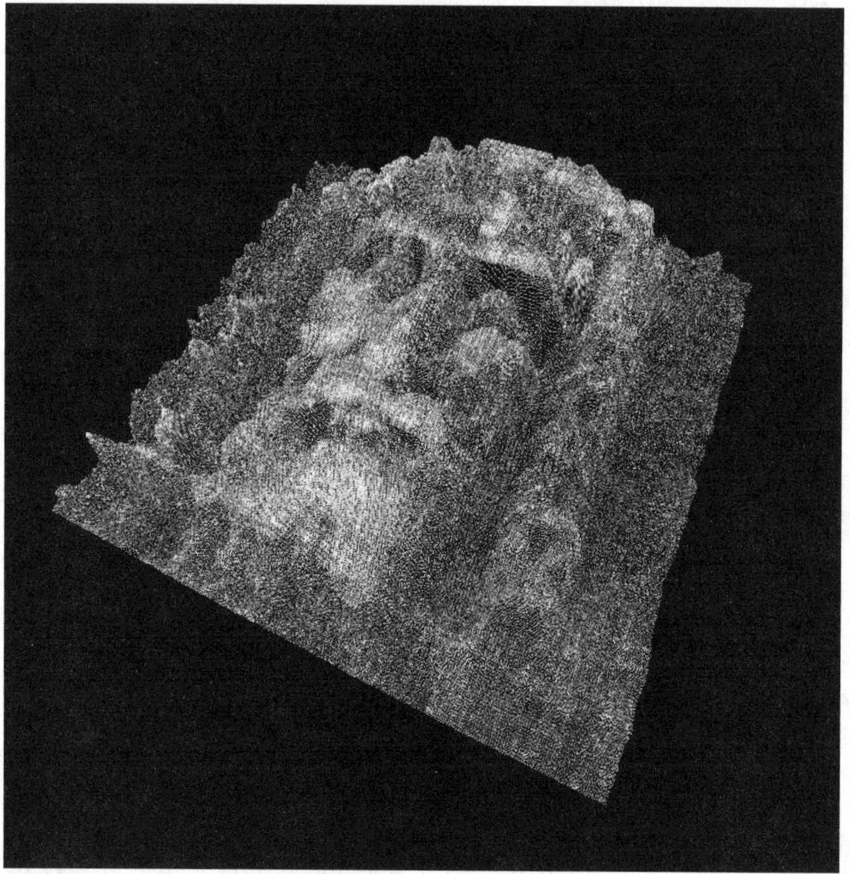

FIGURE 5.1 3D reconstruction of the image of the face imprinted on the Shroud

those with the necessary expertise to use it. The engineer Giovanni Garibotto of CSELT programmed the computer to obtain a three-dimensional image of only the face of the man of the Shroud, adding further improvements.[16] In fact, Garibotto explains,

> the low contrast of the picture and the saturation effect of some picture-elements in the digitized image caused the appearance of

[16] Cf. G. Garibotto and L. Lambarelli, "Fast On-line Implementation of Two-Dimensional Median Filtering," *Electronic Letters* 15 (1979): 24–25; G. Garibotto and R. Molpen, "A New Approach to Half-Plane Recursive Digital Filter Design," *IEEE Transactions on Acoustics Speech and Signal Processing* 29, no. 1 (1981): 111–15.

> irregular structures and sharp discontinuities, which made the image reconstructed by the American team quite "unpleasant." To improve this result we adopted some new techniques of image processing and digital filtering which allowed us to remove the most significant spikes of noise as well as to smooth out the reconstructed surface of the body, and we achieved a more realistic shape of the human being displayed on the Shroud.[17]

The images thus obtained became famous throughout the world (fig. 5.1).[18] In this case as well there was nothing miraculous: Garibotto himself, at my request, has subjected to the same process photographs of faces obtained from a cloth that was heated or colored after being placed on a bas-relief. The result, a few differences notwithstanding, is comparable to that of the Shroud (fig. 5.2). "I believe that the 3D reconstruction alone cannot constitute a sufficient reason to assert the supernatural exceptionality of the sindonic image"—the engineer continues—"which remains moreover a singular object and one of great interest. One of the reasons that explains the great difficulties encountered by whoever has tried to reproduce it artificially is certainly the issue of the process of natural aging, prolonged over time, which made the picture on the cloth rather smooth and of quite low image contrast. And it is this very characteristic that has made the processes of three-dimensional digital reconstruction possible."[19]

In the meantime, in Turin on August 1, 1977, a new archbishop had been appointed, the Carmelite Anastasio Ballestrero. Unlike his predecessor he immediately accepted the proposal for a new exhibition in a form very similar to the traditional one, without tailoring it to a televised audience. The opportunity arose at the four hundredth anniversary of the translation of the Shroud from Chambéry. Accordingly, he returned to the notion of displaying the Shroud inside the

[17] Personal correspondence from December 21, 2018.

[18] G. Tamburelli and G. Garibotto, "Nuovi sviluppi nell'elaborazione dell'Immagine sindonica," in Coero-Borga, *Sindone e la scienza*, 173–84, 354–62; G. Tamburelli, "Some Results in the Processing of the Holy Shroud of Turin," *IEEE Transactions on Pattern Analysis and Machine Intelligence* PAMI-3 (1981): 670–76; idem, "Reading the Shroud, Called the Fifth Gospel, with the Aid of the Computer," *Shroud Spectrum International* 2 (1982): 3–11. Tamburelli recognized in the image all the marks of blood, the wounds, and the swellings of Christ's passion, and even coins; Giovanni Garibotto assures me that these interpretations were held by Tamburelli alone.

[19] Personal correspondence from December 21, 2018.

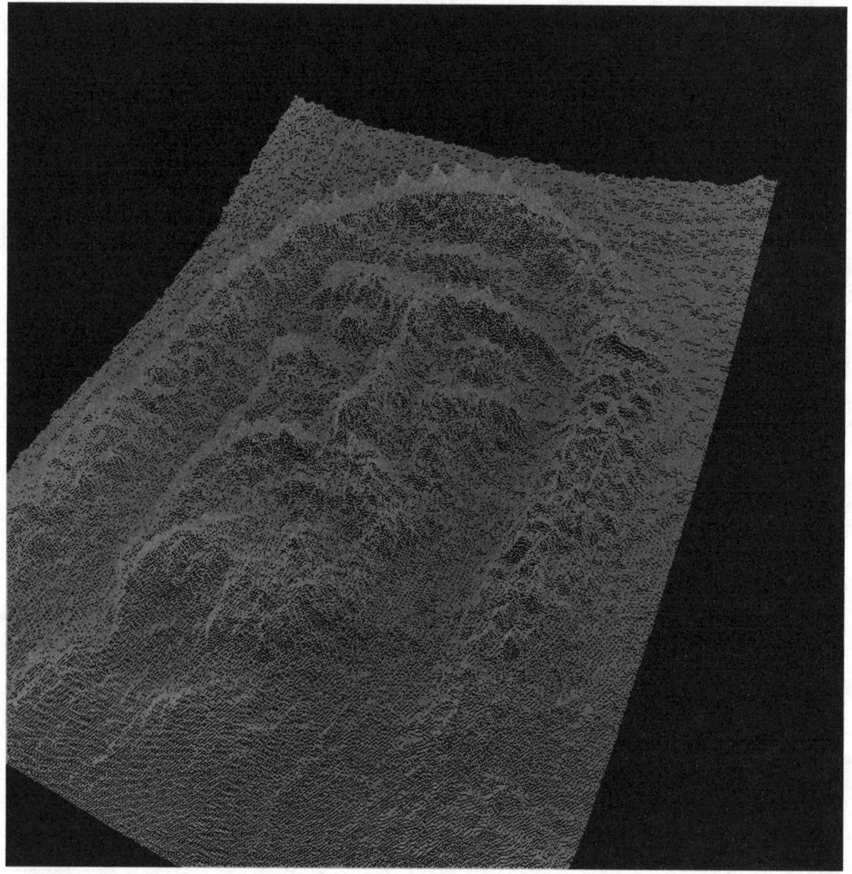

FIGURE 5.2 3D reconstruction of the image of a face imprinted on a linen cloth, obtained by *frottage* on a bas-relief

cathedral, though obviously not in the precious golden frame bearing the Savoy coat of arms: the new arrangement for preservation of the object consisted of a case made of crystal and bulletproof steel, with controlled temperature, humidity, lighting, and atmosphere.[20] The exhibition lasted for forty-three days, from August 27 to October 8, 1978. At the solemn eucharistic celebration of the opening on August 26, about twenty bishops were present; on the same day in

[20] Cf. V. Ferro and F. Faia, "Caratteristiche tecniche dell'impianto di protezione della Sindone durante l'ostensione del 1978," *Sindon* 31 (1982): 51–54.

Rome the conclave elected John Paul I, who died the next month, just before the exhibition had come to a close.

Inside the cathedral a platform was constructed to allow visitors to walk in front of the display case. From 7:30 am, after the celebration of Lauds, to 8:30 pm, before the mass, pilgrims were able to process before the relic. There was no possibility of purchasing a ticket to have closer and longer access to the relic, as had happened in the displays in the past. Before entering the cathedral the pilgrim could view an exhibition set up in the cloister of the seminary, which contained a "pre-reading" of the relic that provided the visitor with a better understanding of the object. Among the pilgrims at that time, the most illustrious were Cardinal Karol Wojtyła, then archbishop of Krakow, and Nikodim, metropolitan bishop of Leningrad, who some days later died from a heart attack in the midst of a meeting with the pope.

Thanks to the wide distribution of newspapers, radio, and television, the mass media played a fundamental role in broadcasting information about the event. Conversely, the Waldensian Protestant community, strongly rooted in the Piedmont area, reacted negatively, publishing through their own Claudiana publishing house two books very critical of the Shroud and the exhibition: the first was the work of a Catholic priest from Turin, Pier Angelo Gramaglia, with an appendix by Carlo Papini, director of the publishing house itself.[21] The second was the work of Pastor Ernesto Ayassot and Franco Barbero, who at the time was a Catholic priest.[22] Ironically, the name of the Claudiana publishing house is derived from Claudius, bishop of Turin at the beginning of the ninth century, who had expressed his opinion against the cult of images. Many more publications of that time were, of course, favorable toward the Shroud's authenticity. *La Stampa*, the daily newspaper of Turin, tried to provide space not only to the authenticists but also to the critics; among the latter was the historian Luigi Firpo, who summarized in a few words the

[21] P. A. Gramaglia and C. Papini, *L'uomo della Sindone non è Gesù Cristo* (Turin: Claudiana, 1978); followed by Gramaglia, *Ultime "scoperte" sulla Sindone* (Turin: Claudiana, 1981).

[22] E. Ayassot and F. Barbero, *La Sindone: Radiografia di una prova* (Turin: Claudiana, 1978). Barbero founded the Christian Base Community of Pinerolo. In 2003 he was dismissed from clerical status.

questions that many representatives of the more progressive wing of Catholicism were asking at the time:

> But in truth, the believer must ask himself—whether the relic is real or fake—is this what today's Christianity and our own human civilization needs? What meaning can the cult of relics, surrounded by ostentation and superstitious emotion, have in the Church of the living God? Does the Church of the Immaculate Conception and the Virgin Mary received into heaven, of the rosary and the Sacred Heart, of Lourdes and Fatima, truly answer the expectations and the needs of man today, with his sufferings and fears, which await words of life, gestures of brotherly solidarity, and not devotional expedients and "proof" of illusory reality? Non-Catholic Christians, Orthodox Catholics and the Roman Catholic priests themselves who are involved in evangelizing the downtrodden and the suffering say that a Church of believers in the Resurrected cannot loiter in the necromantic atmosphere of the tomb. The angel told the pious women: "He is not here."[23]

The 1978 exhibition was also the subject of a systematic sociological investigation from which, among other things, it turned out that 92.4 percent of those who went to see the Shroud were believers and that the better part of them did not go to put their devotional approach into practice (with prayers, requests for grace, veneration) as instead typically occurred in pilgrimages to other relics or sanctuaries, but rather they seized the opportunity to reflect on their own Christian identity.[24]

At the close of the exhibition, after overhead expenses, the diocese grossed a surplus of 141,639,539 lire (in today's currency, approximately 450,000 euros). This sum does not include some 18,205,560 lire that were separately earmarked for Third World charities; the profit would ultimately be allocated to the financing of renovations of the

[23] L. Firpo, "Man Stands before the Shroud," in "La Sindone," supplement, *La Stampa*, August 27–October 8, 1978, 28.

[24] F. Garelli, *Il volto di Dio: L'esperienza del sacro nella società contemporanea* (Bari: De Donato, 1983). There is a summary in idem, "Il tempo straordinario della manifestazione del sacro: Alcuni risultati di una ricerca sulla visita alla Sindone," *Schema: Rivista di storia economia società politica* 8 (1981): 45–70.

cathedral and other charitable and social works at the discretion of the archbishop.[25]

5.1.4 The Congress, STURP, and the Examinations of 1978

The International Center of Sindonology announced that it was organizing a new congress, parallel to the 1978 exhibition, to be held in Turin on October 7 and 8. The event received the patronage of the Ministry of Cultural Heritage, and its direction was entrusted to the rector of the University of Turin. There were twenty-five scholarly presentations, in addition to which thirty-three more were published as an appendix of the proceedings. The range of topics allowed the congress to assume a truly interdisciplinary character: history and art, medicine, science and technology, as well as biblical exegesis and theology. Many of the participants from the conference in 1977 also took part in the conference of 1978; some were already known as sindonologists, while others appeared for the first time. Harry Gove and Walter McCrone's communications, which were proposing radiocarbon dating for the Shroud, also arrived; these two names should be kept in mind, since some years later theirs would be strong voices against authenticity. None of the experts of the Pellegrino Commission, however, offered any contribution. Generally speaking, the conference papers were oriented toward the argument for authenticity.

Some essays are worthy of interest and still retain their value. Others, on the other hand, are not very useful, and some contain rather bizarre proposals: one hypothesis was that Jesus' sperm allegedly escaped at the time of death and was present on the Shroud; it even compared the sperm, on some mystical level, to the fragments of eucharistic bread. Another theory postulated an imaginary loincloth on the Shroud that was invisible to everyone else. There were also more esoteric papers on the possibility that the paranormal experiences of psychics could shed light on the Shroud—on the "self-resurrection" and ubiquity of Christ and on other topics similarly esoteric—such as a proposal to convene a team of "people equipped with a super-sensitivity" to evaluate the energy field present in the

[25] The events of the exhibition have been recounted, with an appendix of the expenses incurred, in "Ostensione della S. Sindone," *Rivista diocesana torinese* 55 (1978): 411–19.

"living organic cells" that remained on the Shroud after the atomic explosion of the resurrection, since "during one meditation that would lead them to contemplation of the Holy Shroud, they would be able to detect the bio-plasma irradiation that is highly luminous to the eyes of a competent psychic." Yet the rector Giorgio Cavallo had asserted that the congress was to be such that "only facts with scientific basis" would be discussed![26] Instead, the inexorable pseudoscientific drift of sindonology was evident. Beyond the papers themselves, the ability of the Shroud to attract the interest of people unable to comport themselves according to the normal rules of critical reasoning was palpable at the congress. One witness to this mindset, which was exceptional for its objectivity, was Msgr. Giuseppe Ghiberti, who would himself, in the years to come, be called upon to hold the highest office in the diocesan commission on exhibitions:

> The responses to the lectures made in the hall were frighteningly off-topic. Every sort could be heard: private revelations, mystical experiences, professions of faith, theological absurdities and many, many confessions of people who had found the safe and definitive solution to problems of all kinds. Strange fate, that of the Shroud: everywhere it was spoken of with an incredible passion. Prior to this autumn, I had never seen such a vast overview of phenomenology pertaining to religious behavior. The Shroud has constituted a great appeal to the faith, but it has also unleashed unreasonable, irrational reactions among more than a few among the Christian fringe. It is strange that this happened on an occasion of a deed absolutely secondary to the Christian life. Yet, perhaps because the discussion was declared very permissible, many felt touched to the quick and perhaps put in danger. Many felt, too,

[26] R. P. Côme [F. Tanazacq], "Le detail le plus atroce de la passion du Christ," in Coero-Borga, *Sindone e la scienza*, 424–27 (the presupposition of the author is that the hanging might have provoked the erection of the penis and an emission of sperm, a presuppostion that is erroneous; cf. G. Umani Ronchi and G. Bolino, *Asfissie meccaniche violente* [Milan: Giuffrè, 2006], 32–33); E. Garello, "Di quale fascia e cintura lombare fosse avvolto l'uomo della Sindone," in Coero-Borga, *Sindone e la scienza*, 525–33; D. Vaughan, "The Shroud and the Resurrection," in Coero-Borga, *Sindone e la scienza*, 461–67; A. Montagna, "La resurrezione di una persona e l'autoresurrezione di Gesù," in Coero-Borga, *Sindone e la scienza*, 475–77; O. Coltro, "O exame científico do Santo Sudário," in Coero-Borga, *Sindone e la scienza*, 534–37; G. Cavallo, "Saluto del Presidente del Congresso," in Coero-Borga, *Sindone e la scienza*, 15.

> a secret desire to revoke even that freedom, which instead was authoritatively recognized. For more than one person the congress offered an occasion to attain and take away a sense of certainty. And since one could not impose such a sense of "certainty" on scientific experts, they were, instead, with much greater fury and conviction imposed on those of religious studies. Philological problems were now proclaimed to have been resolved above all doubts; faith, hypothesis and imagination could come together as one. Affirmations, sometimes delusional, were pushed even closer to hallucination when they were expressed in the brilliant and accurate language of those beyond the Alps.[27]

I can only add that in the subsequent sindonological conferences voices such as these often came not only from the audience but also from the pulpit.

The most significant event of 1978 was the new campaign of investigations conducted on the relic. Father Otterbein and Father Rinaldi were the inspiration for these examinations, who obtained permission to study the relic thanks to their repeated contacts with Umberto of Savoy, with the archbishop of Turin, and also with the pope. The main study commission was made up of those American scholars who for some years had been associated with the Holy Shroud Guild and had attended the Albuquerque convention; once they had organized into an association, this group gave rise to the Shroud of Turin Research Project (STRP or STURP). They undertook a series of studies on the Shroud once the exhibition and the conference had ended. In addition to STURP, others were also authorized to work on the Shroud with their own research program; chief among them was Pierluigi Baima Bollone, on behalf of the Turin Center of Sindonology, who, unlike the Americans, had the opportunity to undertake some sampling of the fabric.

For the occasion a genuine and appropriate workshop was set up in the hall of the Royal Palace known as the "hall of the library." At midnight of October 8 the Shroud was taken from the cathedral and transported to the salon and made available to researchers up to midnight of October 13. The total time allowed was 120 hours, and the Shroud was studied continuously through each day and night, with

[27] G. Ghiberti, "Il secondo congresso internazionale di sindonologia," *Parole di vita* 23 (1978): 455.

scholars alternating so as to make the most of the time granted. The studies were organized with great attention to detail and vigorously undertaken; the hours passed with great excitement and intensity for those who had dreamed for years of having the opportunity to lay their eyes on the Shroud.

The first to avail himself of this arrangement was Max Frei, who proceeded to collect new dust samples—this time surely with official permission—with common adhesive tape, to continue the investigation of the types of pollen that remain trapped between the fibers. Next Baima Bollone took a turn, withdrawing a dozen thread samples from different places, and then the technician Giovanni Riggi, who investigated the back of the Shroud, unstitching the Holland cloth that was covering it in some places in order to make some photographs and to aspirate the dust. The following morning, the Americans began their work: infrared, visible, and ultraviolet spectroscopy; reflectance spectroscopy; X-ray fluorescence; ultraviolet fluorescence; X-ray radiography; thermography; transmitted light photography; raking-light photography; micrography; macrography; microscopy; microchemical tests; and sampling of surface dust by adhesive tape.[28] A group of scientists from Turin took colorimetric measurements.

Each of them busily examined the collected data in different manners and at different times. Max Frei claimed to have identified other pollens useful for the reconstruction of the different changes in the Shroud's location. Baima Bollone, along with others, examined the samples taken and came to the conclusion that aloe, myrrh, and human blood (with type AB identifiable) were present on the Shroud. STURP members also elaborated and published in different journals the result of each of their studies. In 1981, they released a joint statement that gathered their conclusions:

> No pigments, paints, dyes or stains have been found on the fibrils. X-ray fluorescence and microchemistry on the fibrils preclude the possibility of paint being used as a method for creating the image. Ultra violet and infra red evaluation confirm these studies. Computer image enhancement and analysis by a device called a VP-8

[28] There is a brief summary in E. J. Jumper and R. W. Mottern, "Scientific Investigation of the Shroud of Turin," *Applied Optics* 19, no. 12 (1980): 1909–12.

image analyzer show that the image has unique three dimensional information encoded in it.

Microchemical evaluation has indicated no evidence of any spices, oils, or any biochemicals known to be produced by the body in life or in death. It is clear that there has been a direct contact of the Shroud with the body, which explains certain features such as the scourge marks, as well as the blood. However, while this type of contact might explain some of the features of the torso, it is totally incapable of explaining the image of the face with the high resolution which has been amply demonstrated by photography. The basic problem from a scientific point of view is that some explanations which might be tenable from a chemical point of view are precluded by physics. Contrariwise, certain physical explanations which may be attractive are completely precluded by the chemistry. For an adequate explanation for the image of the Shroud, one must have an explanation which is scientifically sound, from a physical, chemical, biological and medical viewpoint. At the present, this type of solution does not appear to be obtainable by the best efforts of the members of the Shroud Team. Furthermore, experiments in physics and chemistry with old linen have failed to reproduce adequately the phenomenon presented by the Shroud of Turin. The scientific consensus is that the image was produced by something which resulted in oxidation, dehydration and conjugation of the polysaccharide structure of the microfibrils of the linen itself. Such changes can be duplicated in the laboratory by certain chemical and physical processes. A similar type of change in linen can be obtained by sulfuric acid or heat. However, there are no chemical or physical methods known which can account for the totality of the image, nor can any combination of physical, chemical, biological, or medical circumstances explain the image adequately.

No carbon 14 measurements have been done. Unless and until permission is given to use part of one thread of the Shroud, such an essay must wait.[29]

Thus, the answer to the question of how the image was produced, or what produced the image, remains, now, as in the past, a mystery.

We can conclude for now that the Shroud image is that of a real human form of a scourged, crucified man. It is not the product

[29] The part that I italicized, and only that part, was removed from many books and Internet sites that quote the text in full.

of an artist. The blood stains are composed of hemoglobin and give also a positive test for serum albumin. The image is an ongoing mystery and until further chemical studies are made, perhaps by this group of scientists, or perhaps by some scientists in the future, the problem remains unsolved.[30]

When part of the examinations had concluded, a STURP delegation, accompanied by Fathers Otterbein and Rinaldi, went to Europe to deliver the results to Cardinal Ballestrero, to Umberto of Savoy, and to the pope. The meeting with the pope was supposed to take place on May 13, 1981, the anniversary of the appearance of the Madonna at Fatima; there was no way, because that was the day of the assassination attempt against John Paul II. One of the members of the delegation offered these words:

> We had the impression that really those forces of evil that the seers of Fatima glimpsed and that brought them fear and suffering, had wanted that the Pope not see the fruit of our work, which reproduced the features of that which for us, as for millions of faithful, is the face and body of Christ.

This, according to Vittorio Messori, is the testimony of "a positive scientist, far from any mystic temptation" (!).[31]

With the exception of the 1988 radiocarbon dating, the examinations of 1978 are on the whole still the most sophisticated tests that have been performed on the Shroud. Never since has anyone had such access to the Shroud to study it so closely. Still, not everyone welcomed the conclusions that STURP came to. In fact, there were and still are scholars who acknowledge the value of many measurements and analyses performed by the STURP technicians (moreover, there are no other such studies in existence for comparison), but they interpret them differently and would like to repeat those studies to subject them to strict verification.

[30] A summary of STURP's conclusions, pro manuscripto; distributed to press agencies October 8, 1981. A summary article of widely published material is that of E. J. Jumper et al., "A Comprehensive Examination of the Various Stains and Images on the Shroud of Turin," in *Archaeological Chemistry III*, ed. J. B. Lambert (Washington, D.C.: American Chemical Society, 1984), 447–76. The complete bibliography of STURP is reported at the end of J. H. Heller, *Report on the Shroud of Turin* (Boston: Houghton Mifflin, 1983).

[31] V. Messori, *Ipotesi su Maria* (Milan: Ares, 2005), 200.

A recurrent critique of the STURP experts is that they did not constitute a group of scientists selected on the basis of their competence for analyzing the object, as usually happens in such cases, but they were people who offered themselves spontaneously to undertake the task. Under normal circumstances there would be no problem; but in this case the effect was that, essentially, the proposals for analyses came almost exclusively from sindonological organizations. Several were engaged with the Shroud and were generally convinced of its authenticity (a dozen members of STURP had already taken part in the congress of 1977).[32] STURP operated under the aegis of a sindonological organization led by two priests. Some of its members were so interested in this line of inquiry that they met the expenses of those investigations by drawing on their personal funds or by collecting offerings. In practice this group of scientists was, from its origin, generally uninterested in the guidelines established by Cardinal Pellegrino, who in 1969 had garnered the attention even of people who never had been concerned with the Shroud and who thus had no particular interest in it, as they were not themselves sindonologists. The two prominent figures of STURP, Jackson and Jumper, both military men (USAF), had recruited several others from the armed forces to their sindonological gatherings. That group did not, however, have any experience with paintings, blood, images, or the coloring of cloth. Some of them continued throughout their lives to concern themselves with the Shroud, in certain cases reaching rather outlandish conclusions; Jackson, for example, opened a research center on the Shroud in Colorado, and, regarding the origin of the image of the Shroud, he arrived at this conclusion: the man's body wrapped in it at a certain moment became radiant and mechanically transparent; then the Shroud collapsed due to gravity, and the body that was vanishing passed through it while "radiation emitted from all points within that body discolored the cloth so as to produce the observed image."[33] Since corpses in nature do not emit radiation and then disappear, it is clear that Jackson has in mind the resurrection of Christ (which, even if it happened in this way, being

[32] There are some firsthand reports in D. Sox, *The Shroud Unmasked: Uncovering the Greatest Forgery of All Time* (Basingstoke: The Lamp, 1988), 44–56.

[33] J. Jackson, "An Unconventional Hypothesis to Explain All Image Characteristics Found on the Shroud Image," in Berard, *History, Science, Theology, and the Shroud*, 325–44 (I quote from 339).

miraculous and irreproducible, escapes any scientific check). Jackson, together with his wife, propagated the curious notion that the Shroud was not only the funerary cloth of Jesus but also the tablecloth used at the Last Supper. One can well understand why, given such premises, some of the members of STURP may not provide the best guarantees of objectivity.

The group could not reach a convincing answer on the origin of the Shroud image also because it took as its starting point a series of assumptions that are not necessarily true. For example, that the cloth wrapped the body of a real corpse was never put into doubt: the supposition that this was the case, however, conflicts with the fact that the image and the bloodstains of the Shroud are not compatible with normal contact between a piece of cloth and a wounded human body. There are other ways to explain certain oddities (the precision of the image, the lack of deformation, the strange shape of the bloodstains, and so on), but these avenues exclude the notion that the image and blood are imprinted on the Shroud in a more or less natural way, and by contact with a true human body. To deny the presence of that body or accept the possibility of human intervention, however, would be to attempt to deny the authenticity of the relic, and this is not a road that the sindonologists believe traversable. In practice, rather than looking for alternative explanations able to solve all the difficulties, STURP preferred not to abandon the initial presumptions, thus remaining subject to them; in light of those same presumptions, then, they were at an impasse. It is clear that—despite certain prevarications and tacit assumptions that tend to prove the contrary—for years part of the group was already predisposed to consider it probable that the image was produced by some phenomenon, possibly supernatural, connected with the earthly ministry of Jesus. One can understand why science looks at STURP's studies with great suspicion or even with an inclination toward rejection. Though they act in good faith, sometimes scientists are able to find what they look for because they eagerly want to find it.

Accordingly, we should note that on some points agreement was lacking between the same scholars. For example, STURP excluded the presence of aloe and myrrh, which Baima Bollone claims to have identified on the threads excised from the fabric. Then there is the sensational case of Walter McCrone, a highly respected Chicago microscopist who had collaborated with the group since

1977.[34] Unlike others, McCrone was accustomed to working with canvas, and his laboratory was renowned for its authentication of paintings. Precisely because of this competency, Ray Rogers, one of the members of STURP, delivered to him pieces of adhesive tape with material taken from different areas of the cloth; but he did not expect the results to be completely opposite of those expected. After two years of microscopic investigation, McCrone concluded that the figure of the man of the Shroud was painted by applying red ochre in a very diluted animal-collagen tempera; the faint residual coloration visible today in the form of an image of a body would have resulted both from what was left of the ochre and from the yellowing of the tempera superimposed on the fibers. The so-called bloodstains would instead have been created with vermilion, in addition to red ochre and tempera. The fact that the image was weak and free of gross encrustations of pictorial material would have been the consequence of the use of a very diluted tempera. McCrone, who initially complied with the order of silence to which all members of the group had subscribed, sought at first to convince others of his theory; in the end, however, his relationship with STURP members deteriorated to such an extent that it was impossible for him to remain part of the group. Though he had to return the samples that had been gathered with tape, until his death he continued to insist on his own results and the incapacity of the STURP group to accept an explanation that put in doubt the authenticity of the relic; he published a book with an unequivocal title, *Judgment Day for the Shroud of Turin*, dedicated to Father Peter Rinaldi and the experts of the Pellegrino Commission of 1969, which, according to him, had already provided excellent bases to unmask falsification of the relic.[35]

[34] It seems that he was excluded from participation in the research at Turin because he had indisposed some members of STURP by attempting a unilateral step toward Umberto II in offering him the radiocarbon date; thus I. Wilson, *The Evidence of the Shroud* (London: Guild, 1986), 61. Maria Elisabetta Patrizi recounts these meetings with Umberto in the capacity of an eyewitness (M. E. Patrizi, *De Sindone: Nova et vetera* [Todi: Tau editrice, 2018], 348–62; these are the only useful pages of this book, which is otherwise rather poorly done).

[35] W. McCrone, "The Shroud of Turin: Blood or Artist's Pigment?," *Accounts of Chemical Research* 23 (1990): 77–83; idem, *Judgment Day for the Shroud of Turin*, 2nd ed. (Amherst: Prometheus Books, 1999).

The sindonologists have produced other studies aimed at neutralizing McCrone's conclusions or to furnish alternative explanations (for example, that the vermillion had been involuntarily transferred to the Shroud when the relic was placed in contact with painted copies); but this is not the place to discuss chemistry and microscopy. Rather, what concerns us here is the contradictory results. For example, where the experts of the Pellegrino Commission were unable to find blood, the sindonologists found it and even established the blood type, while McCrone only saw the vermilion dye. Such a discrepancy should at least have been a cause for alarm. Proper authority over the relic should have brought about new examinations, properly conducted, made by other scholars who were chosen not on the basis of their personal interest in the Shroud (an interest that McCrone, too, may have felt) but only on the basis of competence in their specific fields. Further, the extracted material, the strands or dust samples taken, should have been made available to the scientific community and not, as occurred instead, kept as private property by those who could obtain them. If the original is practically inaccessible, the same can be said of these samples.

The McCrone affair has always remained a thorn in sindonology's side. He was not the only one in STURP who did not follow the prevailing trends: there were discussions between various members about a manmade origin of the Shroud. For example Joseph Accetta came to believe that the Shroud was printed from a medieval bas-relief. But since Jackson and Jumper were the principal spokesmen for the group, their opinions were interpreted by the press and others as a group consensus. Afterward there was no real collaboration between the Italians and the Americans: to wit, when STURP asked to examine the samples taken from Baima Bollone, Baima did not consent.

Cardinal Ballestrero had named as his own scientific advisor Professor Luigi Gonella of the Polytechnic University of Turin, to act as the person responsible and the intermediary for the study of the Shroud.

Relations between Gonella and the Turin Center of Sindonology, represented by Baima Bollone, were tense: Gonella held deep contempt for most sindonologists, especially those connected to the Center. In addition, Giovanni Riggi, who was initially brought in by Baima Bollone, eventually broke with the Center, developed a close relationship with Gonella, and finally formally adhered to STURP. A trail of veiled controversy also turned up in the press.[36]

The criminologist Max Frei-Sulzer, for his part, working independently, enjoyed the full confidence of the Center of Sindonology. With the money made available by television producer David Rolfe and from the Center itself, he made a number of excursions (France, Cyprus, Urfa, Istanbul, and the Holy Land) to collect pollen samples to compare with those from the Shroud. For the very successful documentary on the Shroud made by Rolfe, he shot some scenes dedicated to pollens.[37] He continued to claim to have identified, amidst the dust deposited on the Shroud, pollen typical of Palestine, Turkey, France, and Italy. In the last years of his life he had expanded his scope of investigation to other relics, taking samples from the crown of thorns kept at Notre-Dame in Paris, from the Sudarium of Oviedo, and from the tunic of Christ in Argenteuil. He could not get the support of STURP members or of Riggi, who in turn attempted to examine their dust and their samples but were unable to secure a positive identification of the pollen; they were right, but it was said that this failure was due to their incompetence in the matter.

Over the years, however, many criticisms have emerged, whether regarding the methodology of his work or his identifications. Frei maintained that it was possible, by observing just one pollen sample, to identify the species of the plant that produced it and, consequently, to know the place whence the object came. But this is false.[38] And even

[36] For example, in the newspaper of the diocese of Turin, certain circles within the Turin Center of Sindonology described the members of STURP as sensationalists and scientifically unprepared (P. Soldi, "Due monete sugli occhi di Cristo: Una scoperta da ridimensionare," *Il nostro tempo*, July 6, 1980, 7). Gonella came to their defense, counterattacking the Center in turn (L. Gonella, "La Sindone potrebbe essere vera occasione ecumenica," *Il nostro tempo*, July 20, 1980, 2). Therefore the director of the Center responded, confirming the criticisms previously expressed and extending them to Gonella himself (P. Baima Bollone, "Gli studiosi americani, p. Filas e la Sacra Sindone," *Il nostro tempo*, July 27, 1980, 2); Gonella replied in turn, describing the situation as "an increasingly absurd diatribe" (L. Gonella, "La Sindone e gli scienziati: Opinioni che si contrastano," *Il nostro tempo*, August 3, 1980, 2.

[37] First in the Turkish desert, though pretending to be in Palestine; then in London, in a bogus laboratory set up in a room.

[38] In palynology, in most cases, the determination of grouping stops at a lower level: groups of species, genus, or family. The identification, moreover, is complex: it requires the use of precise "palynological cards" that Frei did not have, and it

if it were possible to identify on the fabric two-thousand-year-old pollen, which is doubtful,[39] it is necessary to deal with the contamination that occurred with more recent pollen types, as well as the issue of them coming from distant regions: for the question of location it is important to know not only the kind of pollen but also the percentage of occurrence on the fabric, something that Frei did not take into account. In opposition to what Frei claimed, a single pollen found on the Shroud does not prove anything,[40] and there is no way to affirm that the pollens on the Shroud demonstrate that it came from the ancient Near East. An accusation against Frei was lodged by a sindonologist who was a friar and who had gained close knowledge of the photographs of the magnified pollens that Frei used to show during his lectures. The friar correctly asserted that the photographs did not portray pollens of the Shroud, as was believed, but modern pollens of the species declared to be present on the Shroud. This gave rise to suspicions of fraud.

Frei died suddenly in 1983. He closed his career badly, with another scandal. He used his expertise to declare sixty-two famous diaries by Hitler purchased from the magazine *Stern* to be authentic,

---

entails different instruments and the evaluation of various parameters. Frei did not want and perhaps was not able to create a pollen spectrum; i.e., an evaluation of the relative abundance of each type of pollen present in the material that he examined. His methods of sampling and analysis were unorthodox and insufficiently documented, and his deductions were methodologically rash.

[39] Pollens can be preserved for a very long time in archaeological sediments, in acid substrates and not exposed to the air: on the contrary, basic and oxygen-rich environments can favor the decomposition of their outer shell, so caution is needed before declaring a pollen's age as being over a thousand years. This is especially true inasmuch as pollens are continuously present in the air, and new ones continually take the place of the old ones. The Shroud has been preserved in an aerobic environment and often spread, rolled up, rolled out, handled, and even dusted with feathers and combed over with a thick bristle brush to remove dust (this in fact was done, at the end of each exhibition, until the 1930s).

[40] In controlled environments, such as a laboratory, it has been discovered that it took only a few hours for more than 80 percent of the slides to be contaminated by foreign pollens. In addition to the hands and lips of those venerating the Shroud, objects and fabrics were regularly placed on the Shroud variously to create relics by contact. We know of flowers, handkerchiefs, holy cards, stamps, even souvenirs that had previously been placed in contact with relics in Jerusalem or came from the holy places. It is strange that those who believe they can find on the fabric pollen of the first century AD may be the very same people who declare the impossibility of dating the Shroud by radiocarbon because of subsequent pollution.

but they were not. His slides containing the samples of dust from the Shroud, initially promised to the Turin Center of Sindonology, were sold by his widow to a member of an American sindonological association, who in turn gave them to another sindonologist. When the samples gathered by tape were shown to some other palynologists, a series of denials began, especially regarding sure identification of the plant species. Despite the initial plans and declarations of those newly in possession of the data, neither the preparatory manuscript of the complete Frei study, which has never been published, nor other accurate palynological studies have appeared in print since then. Almost forty years have passed since Frei's death. Nonetheless, the entire process of pollen identification continues to remain only in the initial stages. The tape samples are private property and are not available for open verification by other scholars (in any case, by now the very idea that those bands truly contain material from the Shroud has been called into question). No further sampling of this kind has been allowed to be performed on the Shroud. In any case, it would be useless because, as a palynologist has well explained,

> Frei, perhaps taken by enthusiasm, with little reference material and not being an expert in archaeo- and paleo-botanical surveys, was not able to structure his research work from the scientific point of view, thus incurring a series of errors of evaluation that he was not able first to foresee, then to correct. . . . With current knowledge in the field of palynology, we are not able to obtain data usable for establishing the Shroud's authenticity or lack thereof. The Shroud's material is not suitable for traditional palynological studies, at least as they are carried out today. In fact, it has not even been preserved in a closed environment that prevented contact with pollens diffused through the air, not to mention other possible mishaps.[41]

The following conclusion presents itself: beyond the judgment about the person himself—some have attributed to Frei a deliberate manipulation of the results; others accuse him only of lacking particular competence—the pollens taken by the Swiss criminologist are of

[41] M. Mariotti Lippi, "Riflessione sulle analisi palinologiche condotte sulla Sindone di Torino," *Collegamento pro Sindone Internet* (September 2011), www.sindone.info/MARIOTTI.PDF, 5–6.

no use for establishing the antiquity of the Shroud or evaluating its movements.[42]

Returning to the discussion of the findings by STURP, the mass media emphasized the most spectacular aspects of the matter, even if none of the papers that were published in the scientific journals made any outlandish claims. The authority of scholars from the United States made a particular impression in Italy, and often the false news that the tests performed by STURP had been managed by NASA experts was repeated. The publication of a book that Kenneth Stevenson—former editor of the proceedings of the 1977 conference, engineer, and official spokesman of STURP—wrote together with Gary Habermas, an evangelical Christian and teacher of apologetics and philosophy of religion, made a great splash, and it was later translated into several languages. The book presented the results of STURP's investigations as the scientific demonstration of the resurrection, or at least as a very particular archaeological testimony about the burial of Jesus. The other STURP members did not agree with the contents of this book and brought a lawsuit against the authors; this did not prevent the book from being circulated and from being considered almost a semiofficial publication of scientific opinion.[43]

At the beginning of the 1980s this was the situation: according to STURP the human image on the Shroud that is visible today was due to a change in the color of the linen fibers, not owing to a pigment; the canvas had wrapped a bloody corpse of a crucified man, and it carried signs of blood; the body had left traces of blood and its own image because of some mechanism for which it was not possible to give an adequate explanation. Conversely, according to McCrone, the cloth had not contained a body, while the image and the blood were due to red ocher, tempera, and vermilion. In the wake of these competing ideas, the hypotheses developed by the authors of the past were now completely abandoned, this time with strong consensus: the image of the Shroud could not be

[42] I mention only two studies, the first somewhat skeptical, the second completely adverse: S. Scannerini, "La questione dei pollini," *Sindon* 9–10 (1996): 77–90; Ciccone, "Truffa dei pollini."

[43] K. E. Stevenson and G. R. Habermas, *Verdict on the Shroud: Evidence for the Death and Resurrection of Jesus Christ* (Ann Arbor: Servant Books, 1981). See, for example, how the book was received as authoritative in C. M. Mazzucchi, "La vera storia della Sindone," *Litterae communionis: Rivista mensile di Comunione e Liberazione* 11, no. 4 (1984): 54–55.

the result of direct contact between the fabric and a human body soaked with aloe and myrrh, or with sweat and blood; nor could it have been created by the diffusion of gases or vapors of any kind produced by the body; nor was it a painting made with standard brush techniques.

Also, out of a desire to affirm the conclusions of STURP, attempts have been made to reconcile them with the hypothetical work of a forger. One of the first to advance this notion was Vittorio Pesce Delfino, an anthropologist from the University of Bari. Using a flat metal bas-relief heated to a certain temperature (220–230°C / 428–446°F) and put in contact with a cloth, he showed that it was possible to darken fabric in order to reproduce some characteristics of the Shroud, including pseudonegativity, the uniformity of the color, and the lack of deformation of the figure. He therefore imagined that the Shroud had been so rendered in the Middle Ages through contact with a large metal anthropomorphic bas-relief heated to the right temperature. In fact, however, it seems that the fabrication of a shroud with a double imprint of a body with this methodology would be very complex, almost impractical, with regard to the difficulty both of obtaining the suitable material and, above all, of putting it into practice: to obtain a coherent image it is necessary to find an exact point of balance between time of contact with the sheet and the heat of the metal; moreover, this technique does not manage to reproduce the same finesse and the same detail in the image as that of the Shroud. Beyond the proposed technique, which can be improved, Pesce Delfino's book is particularly important for its distinct methodological approach, for it demonstrates the inconsistency of many axioms of "sindonological common knowledge" that tend to insist on the impossibility of replicating the Shroud while more or less openly pointing to the conclusion that there is no natural explanation for the formation of the Shroud's image.[44]

Outside Italy, the Shroud attracted the interest of CSICOP (Committee for the Scientific Investigation of Claims of the Paranormal, now known as CSI), an American organization founded with the explicit purpose of encouraging the critical investigation of alleged paranormal phenomena. CSICOP's intervention was natural, since the publication of the results of STURP observed the usual peer-reviewed scientific criteria, but, because of the conclusions, could be considered, in their

[44] Pesce Delfino, *E l'uomo creò la Sindone.*

eyes, a case of pseudoscience. The first reaction from CSICOP came in 1982 with the publication of some articles in the committee's journal, *Skeptical Inquirer*, by a physicist and paleontologist. The skeptic investigator Joe Nickell proposed a system of reproduction of the Shroud image through a bas-relief to be used not to heat the fabric, as Pesce Delfino proposed, but to color it. The following year Nickell came out with a book entirely dedicated to the Shroud: he was preoccupied, among other things, with unmasking paranormal phenomena and was interested in methodology of forensic investigation with the precise purpose of authenticating objects (he would be the author of a famous treatise on inks). As a member of CSICOP he could draw on a series of experts in various disciplines, which is why his book took into consideration the opinions of other scholars (a forensic pathologist, a photographer, an expert in hematology, a historian, an expert in criminological laboratory analysis, a physicist, and an artist).[45]

As one can imagine, the various conclusions of these scholars ran entirely contrary to the authenticist point of view (the hematological expert, for example, considered the presence of blood to be unproven, etc.). What engendered the most outrage, however, was the system of reproduction proposed by Nickell: inspired by a common practice that nearly everyone has tried at least once in childhood (i.e., producing an image by rubbing a pencil over a piece of paper on a coin or some other convex surface), he revealed the possibility of replicating an image with similar characteristics to those of the Shroud: the inversion of light and shadow, the appearance derived from an impression, the encoded three-dimensional information, and the blurred edges of the image. Nickell made his reproduction in such a way that the cloth he used adhered to a bas-relief, and, instead of using a pencil, he rubbed the fabric with a cloth-over-cotton dauber, experimenting with different ingredients (from the mixture of aloe and myrrh to red ochre powder). This system, which would later be further refined by certain Italians, at that moment afforded significant advancement in consideration of the Shroud's image. One can imagine that the bas-relief used for the face of the man of the Shroud was not so different, for instance, from an example found on the portico of All Saints Church in Wighton, England, which reproduces a face similar to that on the Shroud, with the hair likewise sticking out toward the top and a protuberance

[45] Nickell, *Inquest on the Shroud of Turin*.

under the neck that could leave a mark like that which one sees on the Shroud (fig. 5.3).[46] It has been observed that the height, position, and general characteristics of the man of the Shroud fairly closely resemble Christ's figures sculpted in stone in monumental medieval tombs.[47] An example, though with respect only to its position, is the *Transi* of Guillaume de Harcigny of 1394 (fig. 5.4).[48]

Meanwhile the sindonologists, organized in increasing number and growing enthusiastic about the revelations of the scientific tests, held national conferences in Bologna, Trani, and Syracuse.[49] Some studies were also published that described and commented on the examinations of 1978.[50] The film by David Rolfe on the Shroud's authenticity was broadcast in several languages and gave rise to a book.[51] This film was written by Rolfe himself along with Ian Wilson and Henry Lincoln, writer of esotericism and supporter of the theory of the marriage of Jesus with Mary Magdalene, ideas that were later used as the basis of Dan Brown's novel *The Da Vinci Code*.[52] Between 1980 and 1982 at least three new journals or newsletters for sindonology were created, paralleling the old *Sindon* founded in 1959 in Turin. These were *Shroud Spectrum International*, the *British Society for the Turin Shroud Newsletter*,

[46] The object dates to the years 1494–1497: see P. Cattermole and S. Cotton, "Medieval Parish Church Building in Norfolk," *Norfolk Archaeology* 38 (1983): 273.

[47] S. Aballéa, *Les saints sépulcres monumentaux du Rhin supérieur et de la Souabe (1340–1400)* (Strasbourg: Presses universitaires de Strasbourg, 2003), 19; I. Raviolo, "L'étincelle de l'âme et la cavité à l'endroit du cœur du Christ dans les Saints sépulcres monumentaux," *Revue des sciences religieuses* 88, no. 1 (2014): 66, n. 5.

[48] Laon, Musée d'art et d'archéologie, inv. 61.226.

[49] See Coppini and Cavazzuti, *Sindone: Scienza e fede*; Coero-Borga and Intrigillo, *Sindone: Nuovi studi e ricerche*; S. Rodante, ed., *La Sindone: Indagini scientifiche* (Cinisello Balsamo: San Paolo, 1988).

[50] I mention only G. Riggi, *Rapporto Sindone 1978–1982* (Turin: Il piccolo editore, 1982); idem, *Rapporto Sindone 1978–1987* (Milan: 3M edition, 1988); Heller, *Report on the Shroud of Turin*.

[51] *The Silent Witness: An Investigation into the Holy Shroud of Turin*, directed by David W. Rolfe, written by Ian Wilson, Henry Lincoln, and David W. Rolfe (Screenpro Films, 1978); P. Brent and D. Rolfe, *The Silent Witness* (London: Futura Publications, 1978).

[52] Henry Lincoln (born Henry Soskin) is one of the coauthors of the 1982 bestseller *The Holy Blood and the Holy Grail*. He put forward a hypothesis that Jesus married the Magdalene, and their descendants immigrated to southern France. Once there, they intermarried with the noble families who would eventually become the Merovingian dynasty, whose special claim to the throne of France is championed today by a (fake) secret society called the Priory of Sion. Lincoln concluded that the legendary Holy Grail is simultaneously the womb of Mary Magdalene and the sacred royal bloodline to which she gave birth.

FIGURE 5.3 Head of Christ in the porch of All Saints Church, Wighton (fifteenth century)

and the Australian *Shroud News*. The criticisms of Pesce Delfino and Nickell were generally ignored and in some cases misunderstood or ridiculed. From the sindonological point of view, the only blemish on the case for authenticity was the situation of the Reverend David Sox, from the British Society for the Turin Shroud; having allowed himself to be convinced by McCrone's theory, Sox began to publish increasingly unbalanced writings in favor of non-authenticity.[53]

But, in these years of profound upheaval, what was the role undertaken by the historical disciplines?

[53] H. D. Sox, *The Image of the Shroud* (London: Unwin Paperbacks, 1981).

FIGURE 5.4 *Transi* of
Guillaume de Harcigny, 1394

5.2. The Invention of a Story

5.2.1 Free Conjectures

Despite multiple efforts, no one was yet able to rediscover historical documentation for the Shroud dating to before the dispute between the canons of Lirey and the bishop of Troyes of the second half of the fourteenth century. In the absence of such documentation, the silence of fourteen centuries is one of the stronger arguments in the hands of skeptics. To use the words of the biblical scholar Josef Blinzler, "more than a thousand years of qualified silence renders utterly unlikely, if not impossible, the hypothesis that the Shroud of Turin was kept safe since the apostolic era and preserved over the centuries."[54] This is frustrating for the sindonologists, who are convinced that the cloth is really ancient and therefore necessarily must have left some trace of itself in history. They therefore strive to fill the void with conjectures based upon yet other conjectures, a practice in violation of the rules of historical criticism but, in a fascinating and effective way, capable of creating an appearance of credibility in the eyes of nonspecialists. The audience for these conjectures is not in fact the community of specialists, which generally ignores them, but the general public. More than a century since the story of the canon Chevalier, the problems generally remain the same: the relationship between faith, critical thinking, and scientific method; public use of history; the distorted use of "scientific" evidence; and the dignity and independence of the historical sciences.

In fact, in the course of the Shroud's history, each advocate for authenticity has offered separate theories and legends about the Shroud's ancient origins to describe stages of the Shroud's journey that never occurred: after the resurrection of Jesus the garment could have ended up in the hands of Nicodemus and Gamaliel, or perhaps of Malchus, servant of the high priest Caiaphas, or of Mary, the mother of Jesus.[55] Or it might have even been in the room where the risen Christ appeared, then in a cave on the banks of the Jordan, where some place it to accord with the tradition of the anonymous author from Piacenza having seen it; others claim it

[54] J. Blinzler, "Zur Diskussion um das Turiner Grablinnen," *Klerusblatt: Zeitschrift der katholischen Geistlichen in Bayern und der Pfalz* 35 (1955): 157.

[55] Cf. Judica Cordiglia, *Sindone*, 44–46.

was in Pella in the Decapolis, then in Beirut in Lebanon (to mingle with the legend of the icon of Berito), and, finally, in Edessa.[56]

Another presupposition is that it was with the Essenes, who would welcome Christians fleeing from Jerusalem together with their treasures, and who perhaps would have hidden the Shroud in a clay jar like the ones used to keep the manuscripts of Qumran.[57] As for the silence of the sources, it is maintained that it would have been primarily necessary so as not to offend the sensibilities of the Jewish Christians who would have deemed the Shroud to be unclean. Other purported explanations suggest that those who knew about the Shroud kept silence to escape persecutions and to act in obedience to the "Discipline of the Arcane," or to keep hidden a relic that would have been too useful or too damaging for the supporters of opposing christological doctrines, or to escape from the iconoclasts.[58] But the same freedom of conjecture can also be used by those who do not believe that the Shroud of Turin is that of Jesus: Robert Drews, for example, thinks it is a portrait of Christ, the so-called *forma Christi* of which Irenaeus of Lyons spoke. The Shroud, therefore, would not be at all miraculous but would be created by Gnostics (perhaps the Carpocratians).[59]

When, however, the conjectures do not agree with the overall reconstruction taken for granted by sindonologists, as in the case of Drews' hypothesis, they are criticized or removed. The outcome has been the same in the case of the art historian Thomas de Wesselow, who believes in the authenticity of the Shroud and naively accepts all

[56] Cf. Zaninotto, "Mille anni di congetture," 35.

[57] Cf. Siliato, *Sindone*, 151–65; M. Loconsole, *Sulle tracce della Sindone* (Bari: Ladisa, 1999), 18; Guerreschi and Salcito, "Études sur les brûlures," 30–45; Frale, *Templari e la sindone di Cristo*, 134–35 (English translation: *Templars and the Shroud of Christ*).

[58] Cf. J. L. Carreño Etxeandía, *La Sábana Santa* (Mexico City: Don Bosco, 1981), 48; Ricci, *L'uomo della Sindone è Gesù*, 20; J. C. Iannone, *The Mystery of the Shroud of Turin* (New York: Alba House, 1998), 97–98.

[59] Irenaeus Lugdunensis, *Adversus haereses* 1.25.6: "They style themselves Gnostics. They also possess images, some of them painted, and others formed from different kinds of material; while they maintain that a likeness of Christ was made by Pilate at that time when Jesus lived among them." "Orthodox" Christians, on the other hand, would have seen the Shroud as an obstacle to their conception of the resurrection of the body of Christ, which had replaced the original belief in the immortality of the soul. See R. Drews, *In Search of the Shroud of Turin* (Totowa: Rowman & Allanheld, 1984), 97–111.

the alleged scientific evidence produced by sindonology, but diverges from it on one essential point: he thinks that Jesus' body was left to rot in the tomb, while the discovery of the Shroud with its imprint deceived Jesus' disciples, leading them to believe that he had risen. Thus, all of Christ's appearances recounted in the New Testament and in the original professions of faith would have been none other than distorted memories of exhibitions of the Shroud. The author, therefore, has abandoned a mistaken theory in order to espouse one that is even more mistaken.[60]

In addition to making conjectures, sindonologists have a tendency to construct a history for the Shroud by blending unrelated accounts: they look for ancient sources that speak of fabrics, whether they are shrouds or otherwise, and identify them with that of Turin. It is a pernicious habit already mentioned by Lazzaro Giuseppe Piano as far back as two hundred years ago.[61] I have gathered here some so-called historiographical examples, not because they are part of the true story of the Shroud that I have already told, but because they are a part of the mythological construction of the sindonology of the twentieth century.

5.2.2 Palestinian and Spanish Witnesses

One inappropriately cited testimony is that written by Epiphanius, bishop of Salamis, dating back to the year 393. During a journey he tells of having arrived in a village called Anauthà (Anablata) and having gone to the church there. "Entering to say a prayer," says Epiphanius, "we found a canvas on the door, painted, in which something like a picture of a man had been depicted, with a look that suggested idolatry. They said perhaps that it was the image of Christ or one of the saints—in fact I do not remember what I saw."[62] Epiphanius, scandalized by the danger of idolatry that he viewed as

[60] T. de Wesselow, *The Sign: The Shroud of Turin and the Secret of the Resurrection* (New York: Penguin, 2012).

[61] Piano, *Comentarii critico-archeologici*, 1:113.

[62] Epiphanius, *Epistula ad Ioannem Hierosolymitanum*: εἰσερχόμενοι δὲ τοῦ εὐχὴν ἐπιτελέσαι εὕρομεν βῆλον ἐν τῇ θύρᾳ βαπτὸν ἐν ᾧ ἐζωγράφητο ἀνδροείκελόν τι εἰδωλοειδές, ὃ ἔλεγον τάχα ὅτι Χριστοῦ ἦν τὸ ἐκτύπωμα ἢ ἑνὸς τῶν ἁγίων—οὐ γὰρ μέμνημαι ἐγὼ θεασάμενος (P. Maas, ed., "Die ikonoklastische Episode in dem Brief des Epiphanios an Johannes," *Byzantinische Zeitschrift* 30 [1929–1930]: 282; Latin version in Hieronymus, *Epistulae* 51.9).

inherent in that painting, tears it and delivers the torn cloth to those present, speaking of using it to cover someone who died in poverty.

Some would like to see in this story an ancient testimony for the presence of the Shroud of Turin in Palestine,[63] without bothering to explain why it would end up in that village or why Jesus' sepulchral linen would have been used as a canvas to hang on the door or why Epiphanius was not able to recall having seen the image of the body of Jesus crucified, instead confusing it with a generic-looking idolatrous image or with the figure of a saint. Also, if that fabric was dyed and painted, and if Epiphanius ripped it, how can we think of the Shroud, which is not dyed and is intact? Conjectures get even more daring from here, such as one suggesting we can find on the Shroud traces of the tear carried out by Epiphanius, which, however strangely, would have preserved exactly what had to be torn out—that is, the image itself.[64]

Moving from Palestine to Spain, we find that in a letter written around 650 Bishop Braulio of Zaragoza discusses the possibility that traces of the blood of Christ have remained on earth. That possibility, however, is not recorded in any of the Gospels. The bishop writes:

> At that time many things could have happened that were not written, as for example concerning the linen and the shroud with which the body of the Lord was wrapped, of which we read that it was found but do not read that it was preserved; I really do not think that the apostles would have neglected to guard relics and other similar things from that time for the future.[65]

[63] Hypothesis already refuted by Gramaglia, "Ancora la Sindone di Torino," 92–95.

[64] Cf. G. Zaninotto, "L'enigma della striscia cucita sul bordo laterale della Sindone," *Collegamento pro Sindone* (May–June 1986): 13–14 and 17–18; G. De Nantes and B. Bonnet-Eymard, *Le Saint Suaire à l'âge de Jésus ressuscité* (Saint-Parres-lès-Vaudes: Éditions de la Contre-Reforme catholique, 2000), 3–4. P. Baima Bollone, *Sindone: La prova* (Milan: Mondadori, 1998), 205, manipulates the source and speaks of an "image of Jesus impressed on a fabric." Frale, *Sindone e il ritratto,* 15, with various arbiters of translation changes the sense of the story to make it compatible with the Shroud; see also Ciccone's criticism of Frale in G. Ciccone, "Commento a Barbara Frale, *La sindone e il ritratto di Cristo,*" http://sindone.weebly.com/frale6.html.

[65] Braulio Caesaraugustanus, *Epistulae* 49.98–102: "Illo tempore potuerunt fieri multa quae non habentur conscripta, sicut de linteaminibus et sudario quo corpus Domini est involutum, legitur quia fuerit reppertum, et non legitur quia fuerit conservatum: nam non puto neglectum esse, ut futuris temporibus inde reliquiae

From this testimony we find that Braulio does not, in theory, deny the possibility that someone collected and preserved certain relics, although the Gospels do not mention them: Jesus' blood, his sweat, the column of the scourging, his sepulchral linen, and more. But, of course, one cannot deduce from the above citation, as some sindonologists have done, that Braulio was informed about the fact that a shroud existed somewhere, and even less that that should be the very one today preserved in Turin.[66]

Other texts wrongly invoked are found among the formularies of the Spanish eucharistic liturgy.[67] For example, there is a prayer in which it is said that the faithful come "to the terrible throne of the altar, O almighty Father, kissing with tears the feet of the living Lamb, offering libations of ointments and tears."[68] There is no talk at all of sepulchral ointments and vestiges left by the risen Christ in the linens of the tomb, but of a celestial throne, on which the Lamb is seated, whose feet (*vestigia*) the faithful want to kiss and sprinkle with tears and perfumes, just like the sinful woman in the Gospel of Luke, who obtains remission of her sins after having bathed Jesus' feet in tears and, dripping with fragrant oil, anointing them, kissing them, and drying them with her own hair.[69] Thus it is useless to speculate

---

ab apostolis non reservarentur, et caetera talia" (L. Riesco Terrero, ed., *Epistolario de San Braulio* [Sevilla: Católica Española, 1975]).

[66] So believe Savio, *Ricerche storiche*, 68; and Chamard, *Linceul du Christ*, 26–28. Even Scavone, *Shroud of Turin*, 76, says that Braulio saw these cloths "in Jerusalem." The letter of Braulio has been contextualized well by Gramaglia, *L'uomo della Sindone*, 62–64.

[67] Cf. Savio, *Ricerche storiche*, 69–70; Carreño Etxeandía, *Sábana Santa*, 28–29; Guscin, *Burial Cloths of Christ*, 14–17. It is a question of misunderstandings that even the sindologists Vignon and Dubarle have recognized: Vignon, *Saint Suaire de Turin*, 100–103 and 233–34; and Dubarle, *Histoire ancienne du linceul*, 1:130–31.

[68] J. Janini, *Liber missarum de Toledo* (Toledo: Instituto de estudios visigótico-mozárabes, 1982), § 637: "Ad terribilem thronum altaris cursu concito, Pater omnipotens, properantes, vestigia agni viventis cum lacrimis osculantes, unguentorum ac fletuum libamenta offerimus."

[69] Luke 7:38. The act of prostrating oneself at the feet of Jesus often appears in the Gospels; e.g., Matthew 28:9. *Vestigia* recurs with a more generic meaning in another prayer: "Peter went with John to the tomb, and recognizes in linen the recent vestiges of the deceased and the resurrected" (Janini, *Liber missarum*, § 679.30). This is essentially a paraphrase of what is written in the Gospel of John; i.e., that the apostles entered and noticed that the newly resurrected man had left behind his sepulchral linen, which could be viewed as evidence of what had happened. This

about someone who went to the East in the sixth or seventh century, may have seen the Shroud with its bloody image, and then, after returning to Spain, had some mention of it inserted into the liturgy. The authors who put their hands to the liturgy in Spain were many, and it is useless to want to attribute to this or to that one the writing of these lines.[70] Nor are we sure that the texts cited, preserved in a manuscript dated to the eleventh or twelfth century, were already in use in the seventh century or even before that.[71]

5.2.3 Byzantine-Slavic Witnesses

What happened with the Spanish liturgy also happened with the Byzantine one, when the Salesian Antonio Cojazzi believed he found therein descriptive traces of the Shroud of Turin. But his deductions did not seem "sufficiently proven," not even to the editorial staff of the journal *Salesianum*, which published the article.[72]

In the same vein, it is useful to consider another extreme conjecture. Russian art typically represented the crucified Jesus with a sloping ledge to support his feet (the *suppedaneum*) (fig. 5.5). According to some sindonologists, this feature is due to the belief that Christ was lame, a notion derived from the artists' incorrect interpretation of the fact that the man represented by the Shroud seems to have legs of different length.[73] Thus, it has been repeated endlessly that the

---

is not enough to make us think that in these few words an allusion is hidden—one that would have been incomprehensible to the listener—to the traces of the image left by the body of the crucified on the fabric of the Shroud of Turin, traces of which are mentioned neither here nor elsewhere.

[70] I call to mind, among others, Leander of Seville, Peter of Lérida, John of Zaragoza, Conancius of Palencia, Braulio of Zaragoza, Eugene, Ildefonsus, and Julian of Toledo.

[71] On the sacramentarium from which the prayers are drawn (Biblioteca Capitular de Toledo, codex 35.3) and, in general, on the Hispanic liturgy and its authors, see J. Pinell, *Liturgia ispánica* (Barcelona: Centre de pastoral litúrgica, 1998), 42–44 and 71–135. For the changing nature of these texts, see A. Nicolotti, "Sul metodo per lo studio dei testi liturgici," *Medioevo Greco* 0 (2000): 143–79.

[72] A. Cojazzi, "La Sindone nella liturgia bizantina," *Salesianum* 14 (1952): 394–98.

[73] Cf. A. S. Barnes, "The Holy Shroud: A New Suggestion," *Universe*, March 22, 1932, repurposed in idem, *Holy Shroud of Turin*, 64–69; in Italian, it is reported by A. Cojazzi, "Il Redentore era zoppo?," *Rivista dei giovani* 13 (May 15, 1932): 263–70; also D. Raffard de Brienne, *Enquête sur le Saint Suaire* (Paris: Claire Vigne, 1996), 33–34.

FIGURE 5.5 Russian orthodox cross

sloping *suppedaneum* offers a clue about the dependence of Russian art on the Shroud's image.

But the Russian Orthodox tradition in fact presents different explanations, such as that it is simply a device to create perspective or even that it recalls a hymn (a "tropary") of the Byzantine liturgy of the ninth hour, which reads as follows: "Between the two thieves, your cross is revealed to be a balance of justice; one thief was dragged down to Hades by the weight of his blasphemy, while the other was unburdened of his sins by his knowledge of divine things."[74] The foot beam hangs low on one side, pointing toward hell, and on the other side points upward toward heaven.[75] To confirm this hell-heaven metaphor it should be noted that very often the foot supports on crucifixes depict on the lower portion old Jerusalem with the veil of the temple torn asunder by the death of Christ, while on the upper section, the new celestial Jerusalem is portrayed.

The faulty notion, derived from viewing the Shroud, that Jesus was lame has also been brought to bear on the depiction of the curvature of the body visible in some Byzantine crucifixes. This curvature was understood not as a sign of spasmodic suffering but as another way to represent that Jesus was lame. In reality, the curvature of the body is not a Byzantine detail that owes to the fact that the Greeks knew the Shroud but is one also found in the West beginning in the eleventh century; one can compare, for example, the crucifixion depicted in the Gospel of Judith of Flanders, decorated in England in the years 1060–1070.[76] Both of these explanations supporting the idea that Jesus was lame are so bizarre that even Edward Wuenschel, a strong authenticist, recognizes their absurdity.[77]

[74] Ἐν μέσῳ δύο λῃστῶν, ζυγὸς δικαιοσύνης, εὑρέθη ὁ σταυρός σου, τοῦ μὲν καταγομένου εἰς ᾅδην, τῷ βάρει τῆς βλασφημίας, τοῦ δὲ κουφιζομένου πταισμάτων, πρός γνῶσιν θεολογίας. Cf. Job 31:6. A similar concept is adumbrated in the Latin hymn *Salve crux, arbor vitae preclara*, in the line *Crux est nostrae libra iustitiae* ("The cross is the balance of our justice").

[75] Cf. L. A. Uspenskij and V. Lossky, *The Meaning of Icons* (Crestwood: St. Vladimir's Seminary, 1982), 181; M. Evdokimov, *Light from the East: Icons in Liturgy and Prayer* (Mahwah, N.J.: Paulist, 2004), 9.

[76] Pierpont Morgan Library, MS 709, f. 1v. Cf. P. Thoby, *Le crucifix des origines au Concile de Trente: Étude iconographique* (Nantes: Bellanger, 1959), 74.

[77] E. A. Wuenschel, "The Truth about the Holy Shroud," *American Ecclesiastical Review* 129 (1953): 100–103.

It often happens that the sindonologists do not care to consider the consequences of what they say. In fact, these two theories would only make sense if one could imagine that iconographers had been able to gaze upon the legs and feet of the man of the Shroud. And yet, as we shall see in a moment, this possibility in open contrast with a theory that they largely supported, according to which the Shroud was kept hidden for at least a millennium, closed in a box that left visible only the face.

We should therefore instead think that someone, for reasons unknown, broke the code of silence and secretly showed or told some painter that in the box the whole image of a body was hidden in the folds of the fabric, and that one leg of this body was shorter than the other, which could make one think that Christ was lame; and these painters would have continued to tell no one about it except their colleagues, all of whom would have conformed to this new pictorial style of these privileged observers of the concealed Shroud.

5.2.4 Arrival in France

The situation is no less rosy for those trying to understand how and by whose hand the Shroud appeared in the collegiate church of Lirey. Sindonologists have made several attempts to identify where and when Geoffroy I de Charny would have taken possession of the Shroud (granting, though it is not certain, that it was "acquired," and again, that Geoffroy was one of its owners). According to Pietro Savio, since several members of the House of Toucy had visited the Orient during the thirteenth century, "it will not be straying far from the truth to see the depositary of the Shroud in Guillaume de Toucy who at that time would have given it to his nephew, Geoffroy de Charny, as a gift."[78] But since such "straying" is open to a vast array of possibilities, someone else has instead speculated that Geoffroy himself obtained the Shroud in Smyrna.

As already mentioned, Geoffroy de Charny was in Smyrna, but perhaps not when he is usually believed to have been; thus, we do not know if he took part in the first expedition (1344–1345) or the second (1346) guided by Humbert II, Dauphin of Viennois. It is therefore not correct to focus attention exclusively on the period of the second expedition. In particular, we usually wonder whether Geoffroy actually

[78] Savio, *Ricerche storiche*, 122.

fought in a battle that is said to have happened on June 24, 1346; this date is strongly suspect, perhaps mistaken.[79] It is fruitless, therefore, to speculate about how and why Geoffroy wanted to and could return so quickly to France (on August 2, he was in Port-Sainte-Marie) when we do not even know if there ever existed a battle in Smyrna on June 24, or in what year he arrived in the East.

The questions about Geoffroy at Smyrna are of particular interest for those who conjecture that he obtained the Shroud in that city, perhaps receiving it as a reward for his actions in battle or, as Paul de Gail thinks, accepting it from the Templars or from the Knights Hospitaller.[80] This idea was taken up by Carlo Papini, according to whom Geoffroy thus received the Shroud, which, however, was only understood as a copy of Christ's shroud, a kind of souvenir that only after his death was passed off as authentic by the canons of the collegiate church.[81]

In reality there is no evidence that Geoffroy obtained a shroud in Smyrna. Moreover, it is completely irrelevant, with respect to the question, to know in which battles Geoffroy participated (in a crusade that, generally speaking, failed and was characterized by long periods of inactivity that Geoffroy despised). When he returned to France, his priority was not to come quickly home with a shroud but rather to engage in the then-raging French–English conflict. There is also a variant of this theory, according to which Geoffroy would have obtained the Shroud not in the East but from the hands of the king of France at the time of the division of the presumed spoils of that same crusade.[82]

[79] The source is a letter attributed to Hugh IV of Lusignan, king of Cyprus, and is preserved in various languages and editions. It describes a victorious battle, with hyperbolic tales and miraculous excesses, attributing that event to June 24, 1345 or 1347, not 1346; some believe the report to be credible, at least in substance, and thus are compelled to correct the date; for others, the letter is completely apocryphal and the event does not exist. Cf. N. Iorga, "Une lettre apocryphe sur la bataille de Smyrne," *Revue de l'Orient latin* 3 (1895): 27–31; idem, *Philippe de Mézières (1327–1405) et la croisade au XIVe siècle* (Paris: Bouillon, 1896), 51–56; Faure, *Dauphin Humbert II*, 196–99; Setton, *Papacy and the Levant*, 201–2.

[80] De Gail, *Histoire religieuse du Linceul du Christ*, 137; recently reevaluated by R. Romano, "Una vecchia ipotesi da rivalutare circa il passaggio della Sindone da Gerusalemme a Lirey? La pista di Smirne," *Porphyra* 21 (2014): 101–20.

[81] Papini, *Sindone: Una sfida*, 45–52.

[82] Cf. Pisanu, *Storia e la Sindone*, 236–37.

Smyrna aside, others believe that the Shroud arrived in Paris in 1247, sold by Baldwin II, the Latin emperor of Constantinople, to Louis IX (assuming that the Shroud was at the time in Constantinople). It would then be the "holy canvas inserted in a *tabula*" mentioned in a document of sale dated June 1247.[83] One should ask why an official document would have called the shroud generically a "holy canvas," when instead all the other relics sold on that occasion are accurately described using their specific names. Such a generic description—and proposed justification—according to proponents of the theory would be due to the fact that nobody had opened the reliquary and thus no one had noticed that the canvas was a shroud. The subterfuge of justifying the incapacity, out of ignorance, to describe the relics for what they were, on the assumption that no one there looked carefully at them even at the time of purchase and transfer, is heavily exploited by sindonology. In this case we find an additional difficulty—that is, that the "holy canvas" sold in 1247 was not a shroud but rather the famous Mandylion of Edessa, a cloth depicting the image of Jesus' face; the proof is that on the same bill of sale a piece of shroud is also mentioned, as a distinctly different object. Even if we accept the notion that the Shroud came to the king of France in 1247 (which is not true), in what way then could it have wound up in Lirey in the following century? The idea is in itself impossible, for we have evidence of the fact that the "holy canvas" mentioned above remained in Paris uninterruptedly until the eighteenth century and was later lost.[84]

Some have availed themselves of a document dated after 1525 that states that the canons of Lirey hung in their church a placard warning visitors of the injustice they had suffered when the Shroud had been taken from them. In it is stated that Philip VI of Valois gave Geoffroy de Charny "the holy shroud of our Lord, savior and redeemer Jesus Christ, with a beautiful portion of the true cross and many other relics" to place in the church of Lirey.[85] The document has long been known, but it has never been considered reliable

[83] "Sanctam toellam tabule insertam." *Tabula* can mean "table," "panel," "frame," "box," "case," "reliquary."

[84] On this transfer and the placement of those relics, see Nicolotti, *From the Mandylion of Edessa*, 188–202.

[85] H. Leynen, "Het mandilion nader beschouwd," *Soudarion* 5, no. 1 (1992): 2–9; 5, no. 2 (1992): 2–7; Leynen and Dubarle, *Histoire ancienne du linceul de Turin*, 2:71–98,

because of the numerous historical errors and the miraculous stories that it contains. Yet if it were deemed credible, it would still remain necessary to justify how Philip obtained a shroud, as there is no proof that he did; and why, after his predecessor Saint Louis had spent huge sums to buy relics of the passion and place them in his Sainte-Chapelle, he would have chosen to deprive himself of this shroud for the sole purpose of giving a gift to one of his own subjects to deposit in a country church. If, in the end, this was the true origin of the Shroud, then the documents would not have failed to report it; and the canons themselves or Marguerite de Charny would have remembered it when they were involved in the various judicial cases in which each one claimed for himself the right to possess the Shroud. We should not forget that in 1389 the Parliament of Paris produced an order of the king of France whereby the Shroud was declared a fake; the sovereign would have acted differently if he had something to do with a relic donated to Geoffroy by one of his predecessors.

Daniel Raffard de Brienne chooses to trace the Shroud's origin to the East, and he does so starting from another personal conjecture. Geoffroy de Charny would have made friends during the Hundred Years' War with Gautier VI de Brienne, titular Duke of Athens (and ancestor of the same Daniel); in 1346 Geoffroy would go to the East with the specific purpose of searching for the relic about which his friend Gautier had so often spoken. For this reason Raffard denies that in that year Geoffroy was in the East for the crusade against the Turks, and thinks he returned to France in a hurry because he had the Shroud with him.[86] But who could have told him where this alleged Shroud was? Why would he have been in Athens? Gautier had been born and raised in Europe, and when in 1331 he had tried to recover the duchy of Athens, which his father had lost twenty years earlier, he did not succeed. If the Shroud had been in Athens, why should someone have given it to Geoffroy, if not even Gautier had managed to keep it for himself?

113–38, with the publication of the document known by the name *Pour scavoir la verité* (citation on p. 129).

[86] D. Raffard de Brienne, "Les ducs d'Athènes et le Linceul," in *Acheiropoietos: "Non fait de main d'homme": Actes du IIIeme symposium scientifique international du Cielt* (Paris: CIELT, 1998), 171–72; idem, "Geoffroy de Charny's Journey to the East," *Sindon* 13 (2000): 427–30.

Jack Markwardt, by contrast, applies the evidence to the French Cathars of Languedoc; they would have obtained the Shroud from the "Greek dualists" of Constantinople in 1204; the relic would end up in the hands of Esclarmonde de Foix, in the Cathar fortress of Montségur, to serve as their palladium. The survivors of Montségur would have then kept the relic until 1349, when it was confiscated. It then wound up in the hands of de Charny. The pope came to know of everything but imposed silence on Geoffroy, so as not to have to send the Shroud back to the Greeks.[87]

From this list of places posited as the source of the Shroud only Palestine was missing: a document, today lost, that came into the hands of a canon of Villersexel in 1725 affirmed that the Shroud had "been brought from the Holy Land in 1253 by Geoffroy de Charny, knight of Burgundy." Unfortunately, however, in 1253 Geoffroy had not yet been born.[88] In 1997 a self-styled Kathrin of the dynasty of the Hohenstaufen claimed to have discovered that the Shroud had been in the hands of Frederick I Barbarossa, who would have hidden it in the Lorch monastery; the "discovery" reached the pages of the national newspapers.[89]

5.2.5 Othon de la Roche

I have already mentioned that in 1714 an anonymous clergyman of Besançon wrote a story of the shroud of his city and that he, having falsified some documents of the historian Jules Chifflet, fabricated a medieval yarn for his relic.[90] I have been able to identify the anonymous forger of the documents as the Jesuit Pierre-Joseph Dunod, a rather extravagant character. According to his fabricated account, the French knight Othon de la Roche took the Shroud from the emperor of Constantinople during the Fourth Crusade of 1204; then he sent

[87] J. Markwardt, "Was the Shroud in Languedoc during the Missing Years?," in *Acheiropoietos*, 177–82; idem, "The Cathar Crucifix: New Evidence of the Shroud's Missing History," in Marinelli and Russi, *Sindone 2000*, 2:409–22.

[88] Published in A. Lombatti, "La provenienza della Sindone in un documento inedito francese," *Approfondimento Sindone* 5, no. 1 (2001): 47–48.

[89] For example, P. G. Liverani, "La Sindone a casa Hohenstaufen," *Avvenire*, February 14, 1997, 19.

[90] *Dissertation sur le Saint-Suaire de Besançon*: BMB, MS 826, ff. 1–49, published with commentary in Nicolotti, *Saint Suaire de Besançon*.

it to France as a gift for his father, Pons, who would then donate it to Amédée de Dramelay, bishop of Besançon.

The false medieval history of the shroud of Besançon has nothing to do with the events surrounding the Lirey-Chambéry-Turin Shroud, except for the fact that the first is probably a copy of the second, painted in the sixteenth century; yet someone at the beginning of the twentieth century thought to exhume it from oblivion and accept it as an authentic story, proposing the curious hypothesis that the two shrouds were one and the same. The responsibility for this connection lies with François Chamard, abbot of Saint-Martin de Ligugé, who in 1902 wrote a booklet in which the legend of the Besançon manuscript comes into play, stating incredibly that "all the elements of that tradition are historical."[91] In the *Conquest of Constantinople*, Geoffroy de Villehardouin writes that, after the sack of the city of 1204, the treasures had all been amassed for just distribution, but someone had taken advantage of the opportunity, keeping something for himself.[92] This was enough to fuel the fantasy of Chamard so that immediately, without any proof, he jumped to the conclusion that Othon de la Roche had kept the Shroud for himself.

How did the Shroud arrive in France? According to Chamard it was brought by Ponce de Lyon, the emperor's treasurer, who once visited Othon. There is no proof of this: we only know that on another occasion Ponce de Lyon was commissioned by the emperor to transport some other relics to the bishop of Lyon, and this was enough for the abbot to deduce that he could have done the same with the shroud of Othon, carrying it to Besançon. At this point, this shroud would have been donated to the bishop of the city. But on the occasion of the fire of 1349 that destroyed the cathedral, the relic would have disappeared for a certain period, only to be found later (such a reappearance is a thoroughly traditional way to explain the failure of a relic to be destroyed during a fire). Fifty years after the Lirey-Turin Shroud was defined by the bishop of Troyes and by the pope as a "figure or representation of the shroud of Christ," and Bishop Pierre d'Arcis claimed that it was a portrait, Abbot Chamard had a stroke of genius:

[91] Chamard, *Linceul du Christ* (citation on p. 38).
[92] De Villehardouin, *La conquête de Constantinople*, §255.

> One and only one solution presents itself: there has been a fraudulent replacement after the fire of 1349. Instead of returning to the metropolitan church of Besançon the shroud that was brought from the East by Ponce de Lyon at the request of Othon de la Roche, who had taken it from Constantinople, one copy is returned, which the canons of Besançon took or pretended to take for the original that once had been honored in their church. And who was the author of this replacement? It was Geoffroy de Charny, or rather his wife or someone of his own family.
>
> Between 1349 and 1357 a skilled painter is entrusted with reproducing as accurately as possible the front of Christ on a canvas quite similar to the ancient one, so that the piety of the canons was deceived, as were the faithful of the metropolis of Burgundy. The painter, who had returned the original along with the copy to those who had ordered his work, believed, in good faith, that the shroud presented by the Charnys for the veneration of the faithful was none other than his own copy.[93]

Here we find a masterpiece of gross misconceptions and subterfuge, evoking the plot of the libretto of an eighteenth-century opera. And it is all rather farfetched, not least the idea that to deceive the canons of Besançon, Geoffroy had the Shroud copied by a painter using a canvas half the necessary length, and only the front.

The astonishing theory of Abbot François Chamard did not enjoy good fortune among serious historians, but the solution was too convenient to be abandoned. And so, believing that the shroud of Besançon had a history more ancient than that of Turin—in fact a mere illusion, as this story of 1714 is a falsification—a bevy of sindonologists accepted this idea, along with other possible explanations: Chamard's theory gives the freedom to imagine that the Shroud was stolen during the Besançon fire by Geoffroy de Charny, or his wife, or a relative, or Philip of Valois.[94] The theory of the Shroud's move-

[93] Chamard, *Linceul du Christ*, 69.

[94] Cf. Eschbach, *Saint Suaire de notre Seigneur*, 16–21; Noguier de Malijay, *Saint-Suaire de Turin ou le Saint Linceul*, 7–9; Tonelli, *Verso l'ostensione della Sindone*, 535–44; Barnes, *Holy Shroud of Turin*, 54–55; Wuenschel, "Holy Shroud of Turin," 441–72; Enrie, *Santa Sindone rivelata*, 168–69; G. Judica Cordiglia, *La Sindone contro Pilato* (Turin: Lice–Berruti, 1944), 35; Barbet, *Passion*, 32; D. C. Scavone, "The Turin Shroud from 1200 to 1400," in *Alpha to Omega: Studies in Honor of George John Szemler*, ed. W. J. Cherf (Chicago: Ares, 1993), 187–225; A. Piana, *Sindone: Gli anni perduti* (Milan: Sugarco, 2007), 55–95; Tosatti, *Inchiesta sulla Sindone*, 65–78. One has come to the

ment from Besançon, of course, stands in contrast with the theories developed by other sindonologists: as Tito Signorelli once grinningly affirmed, "the writers of the curriculum vitae of the Shroud of Turin contradict each other."[95]

5.2.6 Ian Wilson

The effect that the writer Ian Wilson has had on Shroud historiography is second only to that which Emmanuel Philibert Pingon, the historian of the House of Savoy, had upon it in the sixteenth century. The young Ian began to deal with the Shroud in 1966, at the age of twenty-five and during the period of his university studies, when he spent three months researching in the reading room of the British Museum. Wilson had undertaken studies in modern history at Magdalen College, Oxford, where he then obtained his degree. Those three months of research allowed him to develop innovative theories about the history of the Shroud that would make him famous.[96] Since then, beyond the Shroud, he has dedicated himself to various miraculous and esoteric topics (like life beyond death, reincarnation, stigmata, a biblical flood, and Nostradamus). In 1978 Wilson published a book in which he proposed to demonstrate the following historiographical theories: the Shroud would never have been mentioned in antiquity and in the High Middle Ages not because it did not exist but because it was known by a different name, that of the Mandylion of Edessa. Having come to Constantinople in the tenth century, it would later be stolen during the Fourth Crusade (1204) and kept secretly by the Order of the Templars until that order's suppression. Finally, after some vicissitudes, it would come into the hands of Geoffroy de Charny.[97]

With such a labyrinthine history, Wilson, in the eyes of sindonology, has had the merit of having responded to those who insist upon the absence of any documented evidence for the existence of the Shroud before the fourteenth century. One can understand how

point of imagining that Geoffroy would have even declared that he had received the Shroud from Philip: Carreño Etxeandía, *Sábana Santa*, 49.

[95] Signorelli, *Santa Sindone: Studio critico-storico*, 13.

[96] The account is from an interview with S. McCowen, "Sceptic Gives 'Resounding Yes' to Truth of Shroud," *Catholic Weekly–Sydney*, May 20, 2010 (www.catholicweekly.com.au).

[97] Wilson, *Turin Shroud*.

intolerable this dearth of evidence was for Wilson, as he himself has recognized, explaining his methodological assumptions that, unfortunately, instead of starting from premises, begin with conclusions:

> A significant part of the mystery of the Shroud is the fact, that, like an iceberg, most of it's [*sic*] history lies beneath the surface and unknown. . . . Now if from all the independent scientific evidence we believe the Shroud to be genuine, we are bound to back the "murky past" theory, and this is where the going gets very rough.[98]

Nevertheless, thanks to Wilson, such an impasse becomes quite traversable, and it presents itself as "the only reconstruction of the Shroud's history that seems to account for the otherwise inexplicable silence about the relic's history pre-14th century."[99] And, after forty years, this remains true: without the theories of Ian Wilson the Shroud would be, in the eyes of sindonologists, still deprived of its history. This explains why there is so much resistance to abandoning Wilson's explanations although they have proved to be largely conjectural, fallacious, and even rash. For too many years sindonology has been engaged in the diffusion of books, brochures, documentaries, and television programs in which "Wilson's history" is presented as established and is thus passively welcomed by everyone. The documentary *The Silent Witness*, produced in 1978 by David Rolfe, referenced previously, served as a powerful means of its diffusion. Yet in reality Wilson's account is far from well established: the opinion of the most renowned experts on the history of the relics of the Byzantine world and of the Order of the Templars opposes it, even if today there is still an attempt to gain more followers of the sindonological cause and so to obtain what is most coveted—that is, academic recognition. This undertaking, except in certain isolated cases, has almost always failed; yet many years of persistence have had the effect of confusing public opinion and forcing scholars to make an extra effort to separate sindonological from scientific literature.

Even some supporters of authenticity realize to what degree Wilson's explanations are the result of his imagination. But since at

[98] I. Wilson, "The Shroud's History before the 14th Century," in Stevenson, *Proceedings of the 1977 U.S. Conference*, 31, 36.

[99] I. Wilson, "The History of the Turin Shroud," in Coero-Borga, *Sindone e la scienza*, 22.

the moment they have nothing else to replace them with, they are faced with an inconvenient choice: to accept them, or else to reject them but then also to be obliged to delete from their books all those chapters concerning the history of the Shroud prior to the fourteenth century. Because this is perceived as extremely risky, many prefer to continue to sustain Wilson's theories, though occasionally inserting here or there some element of doubt by using such expressions as "charming," "suggestive," "promising," or "worthy of further study." Such worthy study has continued but has failed to confirm Wilson's claims; after forty years, surely the time finally has come to stop prevaricating.

5.2.7 The Mandylion of Edessa

As we have already seen, the often-exploited procedure of attributing to a relic an ancient history that it lacked involved taking hypothetical events attributed to a different relic and applying them to the other relic's story. Sometimes this even led to claims that the two relics were in fact the same. An example of this has already been seen in the story of the shroud of Besançon, which some have made to coincide with that of Turin, exploiting its (false) medieval history.

It is difficult, however, to reconstruct the first millennium of the shrouds, since they all appeared late and there are not many legends on which to draw. Yet there are some older stories that concern acheiropoieta images—that is, images "not wrought by human hands," fabrics on which the image of Christ would be impressed by a miracle. One of them is the so-called *mandylion*—that is, the "handkerchief" or "towel"—of Edessa. The legend about this towel originates between the fifth and sixth centuries as an appendix to another apocryphal legend, already known in the previous century, which encompassed an epistolary correspondence between Jesus and Abgar V, the king of Edessa in Osroene. The association of Christ with the beginnings of Osroene's evangelization provided a way to ennoble the kingdom.[100] A reference to the image of Christ appears for the first time in a written document known as the Doctrine of Addai, in which it is said that King Abgar had sent a messenger to Jesus, who not only gave him a letter but also painted a portrait of him, thenceforth

[100] Eusebius Caesariensis, *Historia ecclesiastica* 1.13.2–5.

kept at Edessa.[101] Toward the middle of the sixth century the legend was further modified, and, instead of the color painting, it began to include mention of a miraculous image: on seeing the incapacity of the messenger to portray him, Jesus supposedly washed his face and cleaned it with a towel; and on that fabric, it was said, the image of his face was miraculously impressed.[102]

Although the visitors and pilgrims who had gone to Edessa until then had never seen any image of the face of Jesus (because the legend had not yet been invented), from the time the legend of the towel arose the story began to be told that the portrait had always remained in the city since the days of Abgar, preserved in a reliquary framed with gold. And soon the problem of justifying replicas was born, as there were different and competitive examples of the same towel: incredibly, in the middle of the tenth century, three of the same relic were attested in Edessa, in the possession of three churches belonging to different religious denominations. One of these three copies was ceded in 944 to the Byzantine emperor Romanos Lekapenos. Having arrived with great pomp in Constantinople, it was placed in the emperor's personal chapel of his palace, along with other relics. From that moment, pictorial reproductions of the Mandylion multiplied throughout the Byzantine world, and still today, every year on August 16, the translation of the image is commemorated. Though it survived the sack of Constantinople in 1204, eventually all the imperial relics of Constantinople were sold, in 1247, to Louis IX, king of France; he placed them in a specially built royal chapel, the Sainte-Chapelle in Paris. The Mandylion remained there until the French Revolution: the last report concerning it before it disappeared dates to the end of 1793, when it became a victim of the revolution's destructive fury.

It is clear that there is no relationship between the Shroud and the Mandylion: the Shroud is a sepulchral linen almost 4.5 m long and slightly more than 1.1 m wide; it bears the double monochromatic image, front and back, of the whole body of a bloodied corpse; his eyes are closed, and he bears the marks of many wounds; this object

[101] *Doctrina Addai* (ed. Phillips, 4–5).

[102] *Acta Mar Maris* 3; Ioannes Damascenus, *Expositio fidei* 89; idem, *Orationes de imaginibus tres* 1.33; *Acta Thaddaei* 2–5; *Epistula trium patriarcharum* 7.1a–b (ed. Munitiz); and numerous other subsequent sources.

is, from the middle of the fourteenth century, attested in Lirey, then in Chambéry, and then finally in Turin. The relic of Edessa, by contrast, is a small cloth, the size of a towel; on it is depicted the physiognomy of the face of Jesus alone, perhaps in color; Jesus is alive, his eyes are open, his face shows no wounds; there were many representations of the Mandylion, but the one considered most "authentic" remained in Constantinople from 944 to 1247, then in Paris until the end of the eighteenth century.

We have already seen that, for Paul Vignon, the Mandylion was a copy of the Shroud. Ian Wilson believes instead that the Mandylion and the Shroud are the same thing, thus advancing the possibility of considering both together and allowing the story of the Shroud to span from the sixth to the thirteenth centuries.[103] The main element of his argument derives from the fact that since the seventh century some sources have applied to the towel the adjective τετράδιπλον (*tetrádiplon*)—that is, quite literally, "folded in four." Wilson imagines that folding the Shroud four times could obtain this result: a folded fabric in overlapping layers, which on the upper part leaves visible only the head and part of the depicted man's upper torso. With the Shroud being so displayed, fixed to a table of wood and hidden inside a golden reliquary, anyone would have had the impression of having a small cloth in front of him bearing the image of the face of Jesus alone, unaware of the fact that lying beneath was the image of an entire corpse hidden in the folds (fig. 5.6).

This theory, initially accepted with suspicion, has gained increased credibility among sindonologists. They are committed to the search for artistic representations and ancient texts that could somehow corroborate the identification of the two objects. It is an almost desperate enterprise, as all the sources that mention or depict the Mandylion exclude any relationship with the sepulchral cloth of Jesus; but over the years dozens of conjectures have been developed that trend toward this desired outcome, not infrequently forcing a certain interpretation upon the texts and employing an indiscriminate use of fantasy in consideration of individual, often irrelevant, details and often losing view of the proper context. On the foundation of a predetermined explanation and disdain for contrary

[103] Wilson, *Turin Shroud*, 86–153.

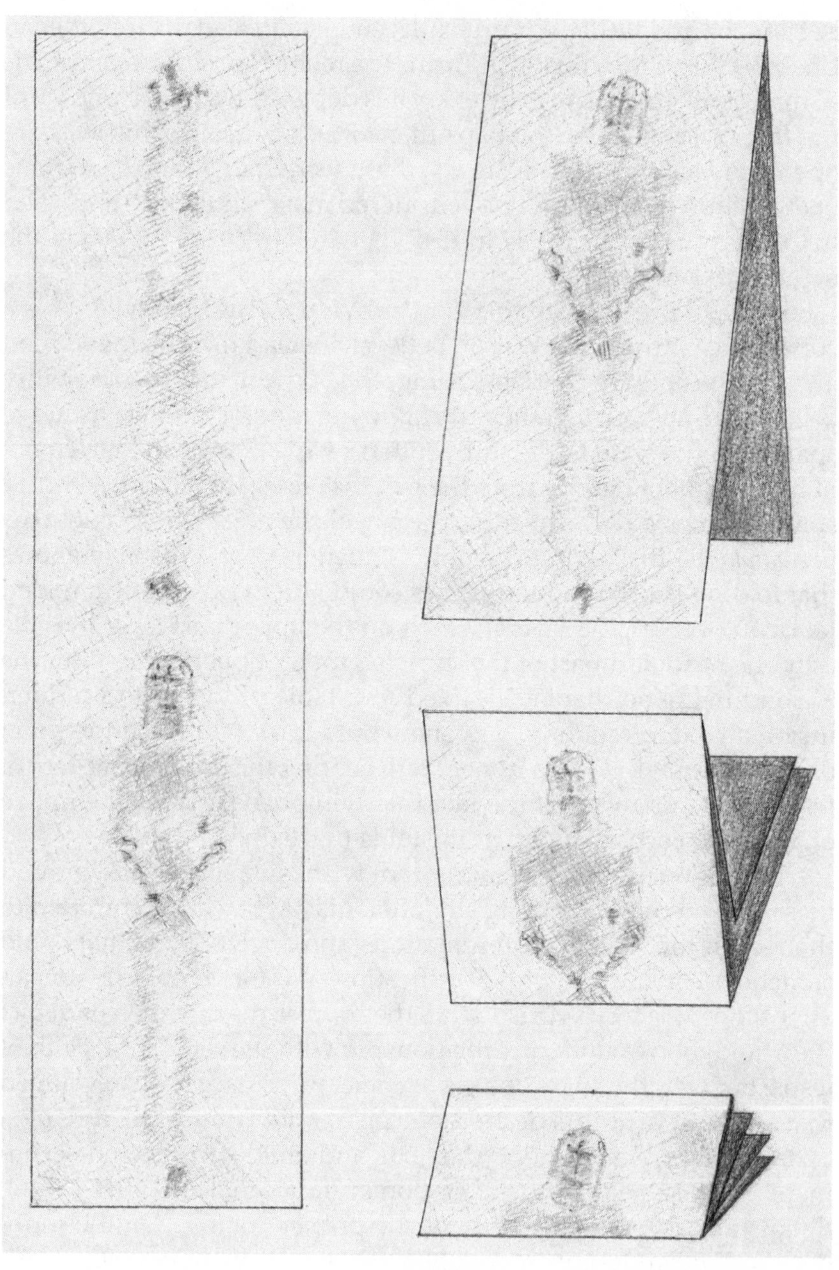

FIGURE 5.6 The Shroud as folded Mandylion, according to Ian Wilson, drawing by Claudio Votta

evidence, a fortress of alleged data has been constructed to buttress this interpretation.

For a reconstruction of the history of the legend of Edessa and for an examination of the totality of theories regarding the identification of the Shroud with the Mandylion, I would refer to one of my previously published books.[104] For the present argument, it is enough to point out the improbability of the theory, which is founded, among other things, upon a series of contradictions: the Mandylion would be the Shroud that someone would have voluntarily hidden, folding it, so as not to let anyone know its true nature; but why? This Mandylion supposedly deceived the faithful for centuries, because no one was able to recognize it for what it was; for almost a millennium everyone supposedly confused an image of a bloody deceased man with that of a living one. Yet at the same time the sindonologists believe that many were aware of the real identity of the Mandylion but were unable or unwilling to disclose it; and they also pretend to discover, both in documents and in iconographic representations, scores of references from which to derive clues about the form and image of the Shroud. This coexistence of knowledge and ignorance, of evidence and secrecy, is in itself contradictory but allows its supporters to adopt the interpretation that best befits any given occasion. Moreover, such a contradictory coexistence is founded on the presumed credibility of a series of improbable and shifting legends that claim to go back even to the age of Christ. Finally, it should be noted that different descriptions of the relics of Constantinople speak of the Shroud and Mandylion as two different objects, present in the same city; and we can trace, for the two objects, two parallel but distinct paths leading to two distinct places.

Daniel Scavone added a detail to the already weak theory: according to him the Western legends of the Holy Grail are influenced by the Mandylion (i.e., by the Shroud); but, inasmuch as the so-called legends speak of a coming of the Grail to Britain following Joseph of Arimathea, Scavone conjectures that there was a confusion of the names and that "Britannia" stands for *Britio Eddessenorum*, which

[104] Nicolotti, *From the Mandylion of Edessa*. The most recent attempts to support the theory are presented in Dietz et al., *Das Christudbild*; I have commented on them in A. Nicolotti, "Nuovi studi sulle immagini di Cristo: Fra Oriente e Occidente," *Medioevo greco* 18 (2018): 299–350.

according to him is Edessa.[105] Thus the Shroud would, in one fell swoop, become three things at once: itself, the Holy Grail, and the Mandylion. According to a variant on this theory proposed by Noel Currer-Briggs, the Grail would be not the Shroud but rather the box that contained it.[106]

In reality there is at least one thing that unites the Mandylion and the Shroud—the mechanism that was believed to create the image on the fabric: that is, the imprint, in one case left thanks to water and the power of God, in the other case engendered by blood and burial ointments. The same mechanism acted on the Veil of Veronica, which was said to have borne the imprint of the bloody face. For the creator of the Shroud of Turin, the idea of the imprint of the face of Christ was not a novelty, and that is why he decided to make his imprinted image as he did.

5.2.8 The Templars

The Shroud/Mandylion identification would explain the silence of some centuries of "darkness" but does not explain how the Shroud, no longer disguised as the Mandylion, would have come from Constantinople to Lirey. Wilson is forced to bypass the fact that the Mandylion ended up where it really ended up—that is, in Paris. At this point it was necessary, however, to find someone who could bring it to France.

The point of departure for formulating a new theory is the assumption of Wilson and his followers that in 1203–1204 the Shroud was in Constantinople. To justify this assumption reference is made to the testimony of the aforementioned Robert de Clari on the "Shroud"

[105] D. C. Scavone, "The Influence of the Edessa Icon on the Legend of the Holy Grail," in *Acheiropoietos*, 141–45; idem, "Joseph of Arimathea, the Holy Grail, and the Edessa Icon," *Arthuriana* 9, no. 4 (1999): 1–31. Pierluigi Baima Bollone also talks about the Grail in a confusing chapter of his book *Sindone: Storia e scienza* (145–59), in which he sides with the identification of the Chalice of Valencia with that of the Last Supper of Jesus. That *Britio Edessenorum*, indicated by a source as a burial place of Judas Thaddaeus, is Edessa and not Beirut is a hypothesis taken by Adolf von Harnack, who wanted to solve a textual problem in the *Liber Pontificalis* ("Der Brief des britischen Königs Lucius an den Papst Eleutherus," *Sitzungsberichte der Königlich Preussischen Akademie der Wissenschaften* [1904]: 909–16).

[106] N. Currer-Briggs, *The Holy Grail and the Shroud of Christ* (Maulden: Ara, 1984); taken up by P. Baima Bollone, "Graal e Sindone di Lirey-Chambéry-Torino," in *Verso la scienza dello spirito*, ed. P. Giovetti (Rome: Edizioni Mediterranee, 1991), 82–89.

and use it as a basis upon which to construct such a theory.[107] To Wilson, once it had been established (albeit without evidence) that the Shroud of Constantinople and that of Turin were one and the same, all that remained was to discover how it arrived in the West.[108]

The idea that the Templars are responsible for its transport goes back to Vivien Godfrey-White but only became public knowledge after Wilson tried to substantiate it through a series of conjectures: whoever collected the relic in Constantinople and kept it hidden until the middle of the fourteenth century must have vouchsafed a certain continuity of possession. Thus one ought to think of a group of owners rather than one individual. That group must have possessed considerable wealth, for it never felt the need to sell the relic. It must have had the means to hide it and guarantee the relic's safety. It must also have had some connection with Geoffroy de Charny. Thus does Wilson introduce the theme of the Templars: they were rich, they were distinguished by their intrepidity, and they had built a series of practically impregnable fortresses both in Europe and in the East, excellent places to hide such a relic. One may ask, however, why, if all this were true, one should think about a group of unrelated people and not, for example, a family; or why it would have gone to the Templars and not to the Hospitallers. On the basis of pure conjecture, one can affirm just about anything, and indeed someone has theorized, with just as much inconsistency, that the Shroud was in the hands not of the Templars but of the Spiritual Franciscans.[109]

The tangible link between the Templars and Geoffroy de Charny is based on the similarity of de Charny's name with the name of the last preceptor of Normandy, burned at the stake together with the grand master Jacques de Molay, who was called Geoffroy de Charnay (or Charney). It was therefore deduced that the Shroud should belong to the same Geoffroy de Charny's family, which, however, has never been demonstrated. In France, there are ten or more locations that have a name compatible with "Charnay" and "Charny,"

[107] The testimony of de Clari has been described earlier in the pages of this book, as a summary of Nicolotti, *Una reliquia costantinopolitana*.

[108] Wilson, *Turin Shroud*, 153–73.

[109] So A. Friedlander, "On the Provenance of the Holy Shroud of Lirey/Turin: A Minor Suggestion," *Journal of Ecclesiastical History* 57 (2006): 457–77.

and there is no proof of a connection between the two Geoffroys.[110] Even if there was such a connection, it is not clear why a preceptor of Normandy and not the grand master would have had to keep the Shroud; why the Shroud did not stay together with the other relics of the Order, which at the time were found in Cyprus; why, unlike his brothers who were arrested suddenly and without being able to save their property, this Geoffroy would have had time to leave the Shroud with his relatives before being burned at the stake. As for the Shroud itself, it is never named anywhere. As previously for the Mandylion, the solution adopted is that of conjecturing that no one ever spoke of it because it was kept hidden and was shown but rarely.

It is known that the Order of the Temple was the subject of a campaign of discredit by Philip the Fair, king of France. That campaign reached its climax on October 13, 1307, with the arrest of all the knights of the kingdom. After those arrests, Philip instituted an inquisitorial process founded on a long series of infamous accusations and trumped-up charges, culminating in 1312 with the suppression of the order. Among the numerous accusations addressed were those of heresy, sodomy, idolatry, blasphemy, and worship of an idol. Some of the Templars under interrogation left descriptions of this alleged idol; the discrepancies about the nature and shape of the object, however, are many: it was variously described as a human head, whether embalmed or not; a head made of bone, wood, silver, or gold; an object with two or three sides; a painting on a table; a bearded head with or without a cap, with or without horns; an idol of an entire human figure with male or female features. Sometimes it is said that the idol speaks; other times it is accompanied by black cats and veiled women who appear and disappear suddenly. Historians have long doubted the credibility of these descriptions, mostly extracted from the Templars under torture, corresponding to the well-known inquisitorial imagery of the thirteenth century.[111] Yet Wilson does not hesitate to recover this material, though it is characterized by

[110] Even Dietz denies this relationship. See K. Dietz, "Die Templer und das Turiner Grabtuch," in *The Templars and Their Sources*, ed. K. Borchardt et al. (New York: Routledge, 2017), 323–59.

[111] The most complete study on this idol is A. Nicolotti, "L'idolo/statua dei Templari: Dall'accusa di idolatria al mito del Bafometto," in *Statue: Rituali, scienza e magia dalla Tarda Antichità al Rinascimento*, ed. L. Canetti (Florence: SISMEL—Edizioni del Galluzzo, 2017), 277–333.

accusation and witchcraft, as well as contradiction. His intention is to apply it to the Shroud, identifying the idol (which sources sometimes call Muhammad or Baphomet) with the head of the folded Shroud that the Templars would have venerated. Supporting the strange theory that the Templars were indoctrinated into the cult of the Shroud—something not illegal in any case—Wilson would have us believe that they refused to reveal it, preferring to keep the secret of the Shroud even to the point of enduring the capital charge of idol worship.

As in the case of the history of the Mandylion, Wilson's proposal is founded on numerous misunderstandings, forced assumptions, errors, and imaginative conjectures. Among the presumed supplementary evidence for this theory, at least one item deserves to be mentioned. There is a fourteenth-century wooden panel, found in a woodshed of the English village of Templecombe, in the county of Somerset. This panel bears the image of a bearded face that, according to sindonologists, resembles the face of the Shroud of Turin. Based on this similarity it has been deduced that the panel belonged to the Templars and that the Shroud was known to the painter of the face, or even that the Shroud spent a period in England. Apart from the resemblance of the two faces, however—something that is itself entirely disputable—there is no evidence that the panel is of Templar origin; in fact the evidence rather suggests otherwise. A further proof would be the alleged uniqueness and particular use of certain seals by some Templar Masters of Germany, which left the impression in wax of the face of Christ crowned with thorns. I have already given a comprehensive account of this elsewhere.[112]

The trail of the Templars has obviously aroused the imagination of many. One commentator has even advanced the idea that the Shroud wrapped not the body of Christ but that of the last great Templar master, Jacques de Molay.[113] The film director Pupi Avati has put on stage the saga of some knights who in 1271 tried to recover for the king of France the Shroud, kept by the Templars at

[112] A. Nicolotti, *I Templari e la Sindone: Storia di un falso* (Rome: Salerno, 2011). The most respected expert on the case of the Templars has already responded negatively: M. Barber, "The Templars and the Turin Shroud," *Catholic Historical Review* 68, no. 2 (1982): 206–25.

[113] Cf. C. Knight and R. Lomas, *The Second Messiah: Templars, the Turin Shroud and the Great Secret of Freemasonry* (London: Century, 1997).

Thebes.[114] Among those advancing charming theories involving the Templars, the anthropologist Keith Laidler perhaps most deserves the palm for originality. Laidler believes that Jesus belonged to a royal lineage that goes back to the pharaoh Akhenaten, who, at his death, was ritually beheaded, and whose head was embalmed. It would be precisely this embalmed head that the Templar knights would rediscover in Jerusalem beneath the Temple of Solomon: this was the aforementioned Baphomet that, it is said, was the object of their cult. For Laidler, the Shroud of Turin is therefore at once false and authentic: a medieval creation, having been obtained with a rudimentary, proto-photographic technique, it bears the imprint of the true head of Christ associated with the body of some other man.[115]

No serious documentary support for any of the different variations of Templar theory, however, has ever been found. Only in 2009, when Barbara Frale announced she had discovered a French manuscript containing the proceedings of the trial of the Templars of Carcassonne, did any mention of the famous "idol" occur, in this case with the specification that it was an image of a man impressed on a cloth. This sensational news was shown to be false, however, when it appeared that the manuscript spoke instead of an idol of wood and that, in general, Barbara Frale had translated the text of the trial in an erroneous and tendentious manner.[116] At this point, following a certain untoward incident,[117] even Wilson himself disavowed Frale's claims.[118]

[114] *The Knights of the Quest*, a film directed by Pupi Avati (Duae Film, 2001); see P. Avati, *I cavalieri che fecero l'impresa* (Milan: Mondadori, 2000).

[115] K. Laidler, *The Divine Deception* (London: Headline, 2000).

[116] I have published and commented on the contents of the manuscript in A. Nicolotti, "L'interrogatorio dei Templari imprigionati a Carcassonne," *Studi medievali* 52, no. 2 (2011): 697–729.

[117] Like Frale, who, claiming to have acted in such a way in agreement with her publisher, il Mulino—which, however, has offered no confirmation—has been cast into a posture of self-defense and has suffered disqualification at the hands of her critics by publishing an article in support of herself under a false name; she did so, however, so clumsily that she could be easily unmasked: A. Nicolotti, "Quale l'antigrafo e quale l'apografo? Giovanni Aquilanti e Barbara Frale, 'Mysterium Baphometis revelatum,'" *Giornale di Storia* 3 (2010): 1–12 (https://www.giornaledistoria.net/wp-content/uploads/2017/03/Copia2diAquilanti.pdf).

[118] I. Wilson, "The Shroud, the Knights Templar and Barbara Frale," *British Society for the Turin Shroud Newsletter* 73 (2011): 39–44.

It must be added here that Wilson, no longer so convinced of his Templar theory, has moved on to new conjectures. Recently he introduced a new character, Édouard de Beaujeu, who was a comrade-in-arms of Geoffroy de Charny. When, at the time of the Crusades, en route back from Smyrna to France, Édouard and Geoffroy would have been found together, someone, he supposes, gave them the Shroud to bring to France for safekeeping.[119] As we have seen in the cases of Wilson's other theories, there is no proof; but it should be noted that this new version is incompatible with the previous one, because the Templars have nothing to do with Édouard de Beaujeu. A history for the Shroud can be invented or destroyed with similar ease.

5.2.9 Theodore's Letter

Between 1983 and 1985, three sheets were published of a nineteenth-century transcription of an alleged cartulary—that is, a collection of documents—of the De Angelis family of Collesano, in Sicily (hence the name *Chartularium Culisanense*). One sheet contains a letter of Theodore (Angelus) Komnenos Doukas to Pope Innocent III; the second one is a list of the dotal properties of Margaret (Thamar) Komnenos Doukas of Epirus, daughter of the despot Nicephorus I, who in 1294 married the Neapolitan Philip of Anjou; the third is the account of the transferal of a convoy of corpses of martyrs from Otranto to Naples that occurred in 1481.[120] These three documents are the only ones that survive, because they were copied from the original cartulary, which is said to have been destroyed in 1943 during the Second World War. Each of them contains a reference to relics: the martyrs of Otranto, the stones of the Holy House of Loreto (mentioned as Margaret's dowry), and a shroud (mentioned in Theodore's letter). The letter in the cartulary that most interests us is dated August 1, 1205. In it Theodore, half-brother of Michael,

[119] I. Wilson, *Discovering More of the Shroud's Early History*, www.shroud.com/pdfs/wilsonvtxt.pdf; idem, "Geoffrey de Charny, Edward de Beaujeu and the First Battle for Smyrna in 1344–5," *British Society for the Turin Shroud Newsletter* 74 (2011): 29–42.

[120] Cf. P. Rinaldi, "Un documento probante sulla localizzazione in Atene della Santa Sindone dopo il saccheggio di Costantinopoli," in Coppini and Cavazzuti, *Sindone: Scienza e fede*, 109–13; G. Santarelli, *Indicazioni documentali inedite sulla traslazione della Santa Casa di Loreto* (Loreto: Congregazione Universale della S. Casa, 1985), 97–99.

Lord of Epirus, asks the pope to request that the crusaders return the relics stolen during the sack of Constantinople in 1204; he names only one in particular, the Shroud, stating that at that time it was kept in Athens.

I have already explained why I believe this document is a modern forgery:[121] it is enough here to recall the essential reasons. First, the form of the writing, which betrays a recent origin through the name used by the sender, the dating system, the style, and the use of formulas.[122] A Greek original is lacking, other copies of certain provenance are lacking, and even the cartulary from which it is drawn is lacking—the kind of source that in itself, moreover, would not offer a complete guarantee of accuracy. When one then turns to examine the origin and the context of the cartulary, things get even more complicated.

This tome was in fact considered to be the diplomatic codex of the Constantinian Angelic Order of Saint Sophia, a chivalric institution allegedly created on June 22, 1290, by the despot of Epirus, Nicephorus I Komnenos Doukas; there is no doubt that the origins of such an order are false, as in other analogous cases, because it is entirely anachronistic to think that a Byzantine despot of the thirteenth century founded a chivalric order. The De Angelis family of Collesano that kept the cartulary presented itself as descended from Nicephorus, and carried as proof of this another document, dated to 1452, taken from the same cartulary, in which the line of descent of the grand masters of the order was indicated. This document, however, is also clearly false and manipulates the ancestry dramatically in order to ascribe to the De Angelis family a noble lineage that it did not have.

[121] Nicolotti, *Templari e la Sindone,* 104–13; idem, "Su alcune testimonianze del Chartularium Culisanense, sulle false origini dell'Ordine Costantiniano Angelico di Santa Sofia e su taluni suoi documenti conservati presso l'Archivio di Stato di Napoli," *Giornale di storia* 8 (2012): 1–17 (https://www.giornaledistoria.net/wp-content/uploads/2017/03/NicolottiChartulariumCulisanense.pdf), to be supplemented by R. Romano, "Confirmatio di Costantino XI Paleologo Dragazes per Costantino II Angelo Comneno," in *Auctor et Auctoritas in Latinis Medii Aevi Litteris,* ed. E. D'Angelo and J. Ziolkowski (Florence: Sismel, 2014), 971–77.

[122] It is also the opinion of two recognized experts on this kind of writing whom I interviewed: Luca Pieralli of the Vatican School of Palaeography, Diplomacy and Archive Administration, and Otto Kresten of the University of Vienna.

The surviving sheets of the alleged cartulary comprise a nineteenth-century transcription sponsored by the grand master of the order, Epifanio De Angelis (1836–1888), endorsed by Msgr. Benedetto D'Acquisto, archbishop of Monreale and grand chancellor of the same order. Naturally, the absence of the true cartulary, whose existence cannot be securely attested, requires us to take Epifanio at his word. Yet accounts of Epifanio[123] do not make him appear to have been a very trustworthy person: to this self-styled scion of Byzantine lineage are attributed improbable facts and nonexistent domains. On March 25, 1859, he would appear to have been in Kefalonia. He was even crowned king of the Ionian islands, in a context that finds no correspondence with the true history of those islands in the nineteenth century. Last but not least, the possession of a princely palace in Collesano was attributed to him, which at the time was a convent and was never a private palace. Everything leads us to think that, as happened on many other occasions with other presumed nobles, the Sicilian family of De Angelis (which has nothing to do with the Angelo Komnenos of Byzantium) created a false Constantinian order (which has no recognition, and today has virtually disappeared) and also manufactured false documents to give it credibility. Accordingly, it seems very risky to believe that such counterfeiters could have possessed a cartulary containing authentic medieval documents intermixed among false documents.

There is great resistance to accepting the falsehood of these documents, because doing so would threaten the credibility of the events narrated about the relics referred to therein.[124] The movement of a particular shroud to Athens can give the aura of authenticity to events conjecturally reconstructed pertaining to the Shroud of Turin (even if in the alleged letter of Theodore there is no element that permits

[123] In T. Li Pira, *Breve istoria della Despotal Casa Angelo, o de Angelis, di Epiro* (Palermo: Camilleri, 1939).

[124] Barbara Frale responded to my arguments with a long article in which she insists on the authenticity of the letter, skipping over the context in which the cartulary was produced and rejecting the opinion of the two Byzantinists interviewed by me; moreover, denying the evidence, she excludes the possibility that Benedetto D'Acquisto was involved with the creation of a false Constantinian order; finally, she attributes to me conclusions that I have never written or even thought ("*Redeat nobis quod sacrum est*: Una lettera sulla presenza della Sindone in Atene all'indomani della quarta crociata," *Aevum* 2, no. 86 [2012]: 589–641). In the future, I will take up the issue afresh with new evidence.

us to establish identity between the two shrouds). Some connect this stop in Greece with the Templars,[125] others with the false legend of the shroud of Besançon.[126] A further element of confusion was introduced by Antoine Legrand, who just after the "discovery" of Theodore's letter confused the names of the characters and reported the discovery of a letter attributed to the emperor Alexios V Doukas, called Mourtzouphlos. This letter, however, never existed; and immediately Daniel Scavone, without ever having seen it, included it in his list of sources favorable to the Turin Shroud. It is an example of how even today, new fakes are created, sometimes involuntarily, merely by sloppiness in the use of sources.[127]

5.2.10 The Pray Codex

One of the arguments most repeated in recent decades to support the existence of the Shroud before the fourteenth century concerns a miniature contained in the so-called Pray Codex, a liturgical manuscript preserved in Budapest.[128] It consists of the grouping of two originally independent, though almost contemporary, manuscripts. One of them comes from a Benedictine abbey (perhaps Boldva) and can be dated to 1192–1195. A bifolio with four drawings in pen and ink was bound between the two of them not later than 1210; they are among the first Hungarian copies of miniature books, which evidences a Salzburgian influence.[129] It is not possible to pinpoint

[125] Frale, *Templari e la sindone di Cristo*, 191–92 (English translation: *Templars and the Shroud of Christ*).

[126] Most recently, Barbet, *Othon de la Roche*, 31–37; see my review of this book in *Rivista storica italiana* 125, no. 3 (2013): 890–99.

[127] A. Legrand, "Du nouveau pour le Suaire de Turin: Une lettre de l'empereur Alexis V," *Historia* 433 (bis) (1982): 106–9, who speaks of a letter "discovered in the Vatican Archives at the Library of Santa Caterina in Fornielo [*sic*] in Naples," which naturally never existed; and also D. C. Scavone, "Besançon and Other Hypotheses for the Missing Years: The Shroud from 1200 to 1400," www.ohioshroudconference.com/papers.htm.

[128] Országos Széchényi Könyvtár, Budapest, *MNy* 1. Described by P. Radó, *Libri liturgici manuscripti bibliothecarum Hungariae et limitropharum regionum* (Budapest: Akadémiai Kiadó, 1973), 40–76.

[129] At ff. XXVII–XXVIII: Jesus on the cross; the deposition; the burial and the discovery of the empty tomb; the enthroned Christ. Cf. E. Hoffmann, "A Nemzeti Múzeum Széchényi-Könyvtárának Magyarországon illuminált kéziratai," *Magyar*

whether the drawings were executed during the binding or at some time previously.[130]

The interest of sindonologists focuses on the miniature on the second page, which contains two connected scenes (fig. 5.7): the higher of the two depicts the wrapping of Jesus in the sepulchral fabric and his being anointed in the tomb by Joseph of Arimathea, Nicodemus, and John; below is the coming of the women bearing myrrh (Mary Magdalene, Mary the mother of James, and Salome) on Sunday morning, their discovery of the empty tomb, and the encounter with the angel. The idea is that, since the miniature contains a series of elements in common with the Shroud, it was necessarily designed by an artist who had seen the Shroud (assuming that at the time it was in Constantinople).[131]

Many figurative elements that can be found in hundreds of other artistic specimens and lend themselves to all kinds of variations are presented by sindonologists as particular to this miniature; these, they say, owe to the artist's observation of the Shroud. In truth the differences are greater than the congruences. In the upper scene Jesus is lying on a large cloth, long and apparently not completely unfolded; both Joseph (left) and John (right, with the hand touching the face) are fitting the cloth over him, holding part of the fabric in their hands while another part falls upon the shoulders. Whereas the actual Shroud appears to be a long and narrow sheet that has been turned over the head of the corpse longways, and only on one side, here the sheet is depicted as being deployed crossways, turned over the body and passing over it on the side and at the two ends, not on the head.

It does not even seem certain to me that there is a single sheet; rather, there may be two, for at the height of the buttocks we see a strange curl that could suggest an overlapping of different cloths.

Könyvszemle 34 (1927): 2–3; I. Berkovits, *Illuminated Manuscripts in Hungary* (Shannon: Irish University Press, 1969), 19–20, with tables.

130 Cf. E. Poulle, "Le Sant Suaire et la datation du codex Pray," *Revue Internationale du Linceul de Turin* 25 (2003): 6–19; E. Poulle and E. Madas, "L'organisation des cahiers du Codex Pray," *Scriptorium* 57, no. 2 (2003): 238–52, credible for codicologic analysis but not from the sindonological perspective.

131 By title, for example, Dubarle and Leynen, *Histoire ancienne du linceul de Turin*, 2:47–57; A.-M. Dubarle, "L'icona del 'Manoscritto Pray,'" in Coppini and Cavazzuti, *Icone di Cristo*, 181–88; Guscin, *Burial Cloths of Christ*, 24–30; M. De Stefano, "Rivisitazione del Codice Pray," in Marinelli and Russi, *Sindone 2000*, 309–18; I. Wilson, *The Shroud* (London: Bantam, 2010), 183–84.

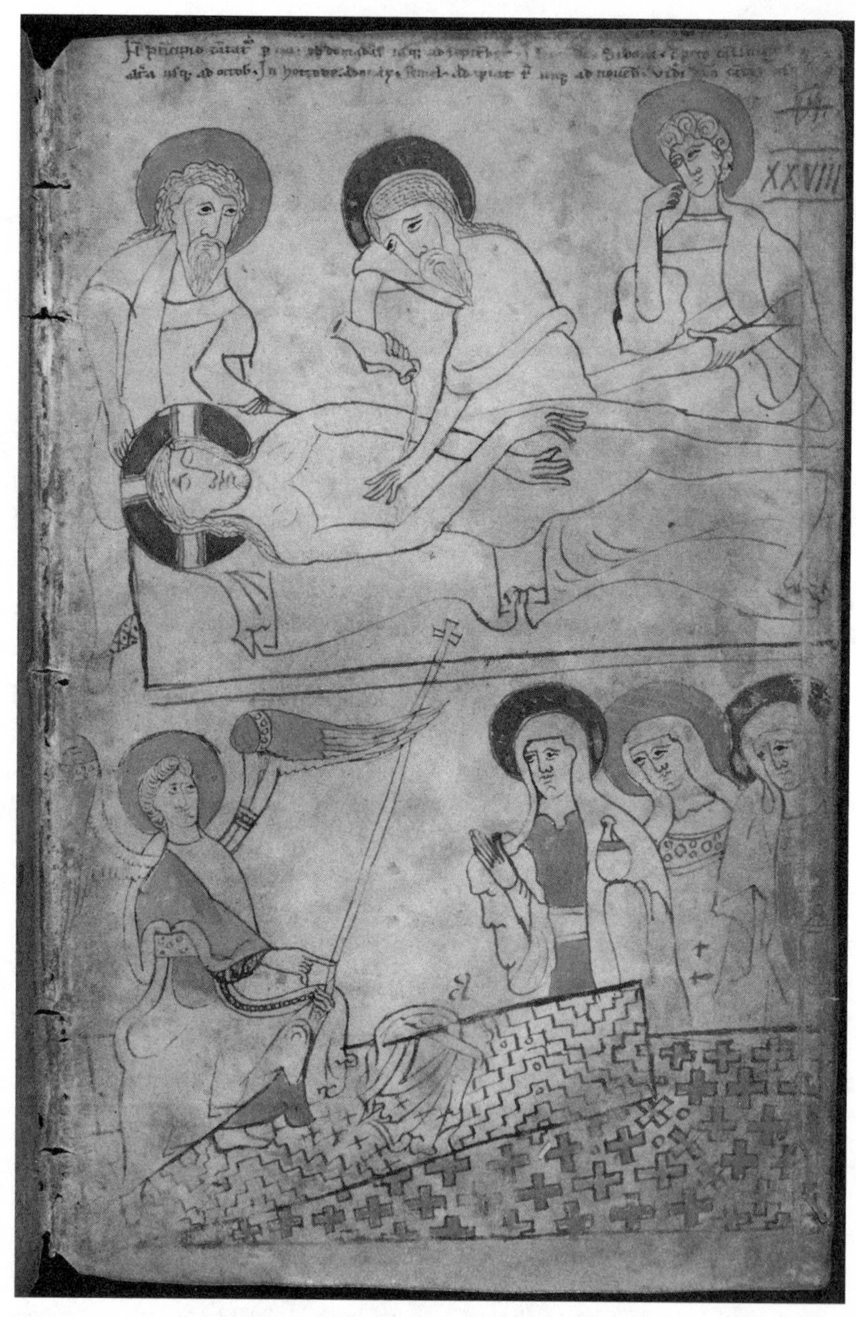

FIGURE 5.7 Anointing and visit to the tomb of Jesus, miniature from the Pray Codex, circa 1192–1195

The forearms of the corpse in the miniature are crossed, while the man of the Shroud crosses his hands, not his forearms. Those who aver the connection insist that Jesus' fingers are elongated and the thumb is not visible, as on the Shroud; yet the fingers of the other characters in the drawing are no shorter than those of Jesus, and also Nicodemus and John have a hand where the thumb cannot be seen: it depends on the position. In any case, it is quite natural for a hand resting on a level surface that the thumb remain hidden from the other fingers; that is, it is retracted (as happens on the Shroud, without that having anything to do, as is said, with a lesion of the median nerve caused by the nails that pierced the hands).

The body is naked both in the miniature and on the Shroud, but this is not anything strange (it has been said, wrongly, that in the artistic representations of the time, nudity is very rare). On the forehead of Jesus, above the right eyebrow, there is a small dark sign made to correspond to the trickle of blood in the form of an epsilon, which is also seen on the face of the Shroud. But that marking is an indistinct smudge, which is not similar to the epsilon in terms of its shape or its position (on the Shroud it is at the center of the forehead).

Furthermore, when the miniaturist wants to represent the bloodstains, as he does in the enthroned Christ on the next page, he uses another color, bright red, the same that he uses for haloes. Other discordances are more obvious: Jesus has neither a long beard nor a mustache like the man of the Shroud, and the part in his hair is not in the middle but moved to the left side of the forehead. On his body the wounds of nails, scourges, and lance are missing, which on the Shroud stand out because of the evident flow of blood.

In the lower figure we see the three women who go to the tomb with the spices and, instead of the body of Jesus, find an angel. Sindonologists believe that the two vaguely rectangular objects under the feet of the angel and at the height of the knees of the women are the Shroud, folded in two, with a cloth placed on top. Some regard this cloth to be the sudarium; others, the last section of the Shroud itself, wadded up.[132] They see a decisive proof in nine small circles

[132] One can see grotesque attempts to reproduce all the folds geometrically in J. Lejeune, "Étude topologique des Suaires de Turin, de Lier et de Pray," in *L'identification scientifique de l'homme du Linceul Jésus de Nazareth*, ed. A. A. Upinsky (Paris: Guibert, 1995), 103–9.

on the two flaps of the hypothetical Shroud, four above (in the form of an L) and five below (roughly in the form of a P). These circles are supposedly the exact representation of some holes on the Turin fabric, known as poker holes, and caused by an ancient charring. As this burn happened while the Shroud was arranged in a four-layered manner, the overlapping folds of fabric would all have to have been pierced simultaneously, layer by layer, and all symmetrically. The sindonological explanation, however, is inadmissible. As regards the miniature, only in *one* case are the small circles in a position vaguely similar to one of the four on the Shroud (in the case of the L-shaped holes). In the other case (the P-shaped holes) the correspondence is simply not there. On the Shroud the burns are repeated four times, while here in the Pray Codex there are only two groups of circles, which are not very comparable; on the Shroud the burns are lateral, while in the codex the burns are in the middle. Finally, we know that the poker holes of the Shroud already existed in 1516, because they were painted in a copy of that era. We have no proof, however, that they existed in the early years of the thirteenth century (or that the Shroud itself existed before the fourteenth century). An alleged conjectural resemblance based on two other conjectural presumptions cannot prove anything.

Everything else on the shroud in the painting has even less to do with the Shroud of Turin. What do the geometric patterns and red crosses have to do with the Shroud? Sindonologists respond that the decoration of the upper half of the fabric, in the form of geometric pyramids, would remind us of the intertwining "herringbone" weave of the Shroud textile, and that the one below is a lining decorated with red crosses. Inasmuch as the lining is an invention out of thin air, it is useless to discuss it. It ought to be mentioned that the herringbone pattern of the Shroud does not look anything like the miniature shroud's pyramids, which, moreover, are not repeated in parallel and perpendicular bands as in the twilled Shroud; rather, they are concentric, converging toward a central point. To the sindonologists, it does not seem strange that the miniaturist wanted to create (if badly) the millimetric herringbone design based on a weave that can only be seen by the naked eye if one is very close to the fabric of the Shroud. To do so, one would have to enlarge it dozens of times. Further, it does not seem strange the artist would faithfully have reproduced the burn circles—the largest is about 3 cm in diameter, on a Shroud of 4.5 m—but would somehow have neglected to draw the most important thing of all: the image impressed on the cloth and the bloodstains, elements that anyone who had seen the Shroud would certainly not have overlooked. Then there is one insurmountable contradiction between the fabric depicted below and the fabric portrayed in the figure above, which is completely white, without geometric patterns or crosses: what sense would it make to depict the same fabric in two different ways in the same miniature?

The whole sindonological argument collapses when the medieval iconography of the women at the tomb is taken into account. The standard depiction comprises the three women with the spices and the angel on an uncovered and empty tomb, which is depicted as a sarcophagus with its lid overturned and placed crosswise.[133] That iconographic composition is so customary and widespread that it merited a place in the famous manual of painting of the Byzantine monk Dionysius of Fourna:

> An angel, having appeared to the spice-bearers, announces the resurrection: a tomb is uncovered and seated on the lid [of the sarcophagus] is an angel dressed in white who, in one hand, carries a spear and, with the other, points out the linen cloth and the shroud in the middle of the tomb; and in front of him the spice-bearers hold the perfumes.[134]

A duplicate miniature resembling that of the Pray Codex, made in precisely the same period, is found in the Psalter of Ingeborg (fig. 5.8). As in the Pray Codex, the tomb is depicted as a sarcophagus, and the reverse of the uncovered upper plate is different, in terms of color, from the other plates. The angel is on the lid because, the Gospel of Matthew says, he sat on the stone; but since the Gospel of Mark says that the angel was sitting not on the stone but within the tomb, there are other

[133] Cf. G. Millet, *Recherches sur l'iconographie de l'Évangile,* 2nd ed. (Paris: Boccard, 1960), 517–40; N. C. Brooks, *The Sepulchre of Christ in Art and Liturgy* (Urbana: University of Illinois, 1921), 15–17, 24–25; W. W. S. Cook, "The Earliest Painted Panels of Catalonia," *Art Bulletin* 10, no. 4 (1928): 322–65; F. Rademacher, "Zu den frühesten Darstellungen der Auferstehung Christi," *Zeitschrift für Kunstgeschichte* 28, no. 3 (1965): 195–224.

[134] A. Papadopoulos-Kerameus, Ἑρμηνεία τῆς ζωγραφικῆς τέχνης (Petropolis: ek tēs typographias tēs agiotatēs sunodou, 1900), 114 (ch. 3.100).

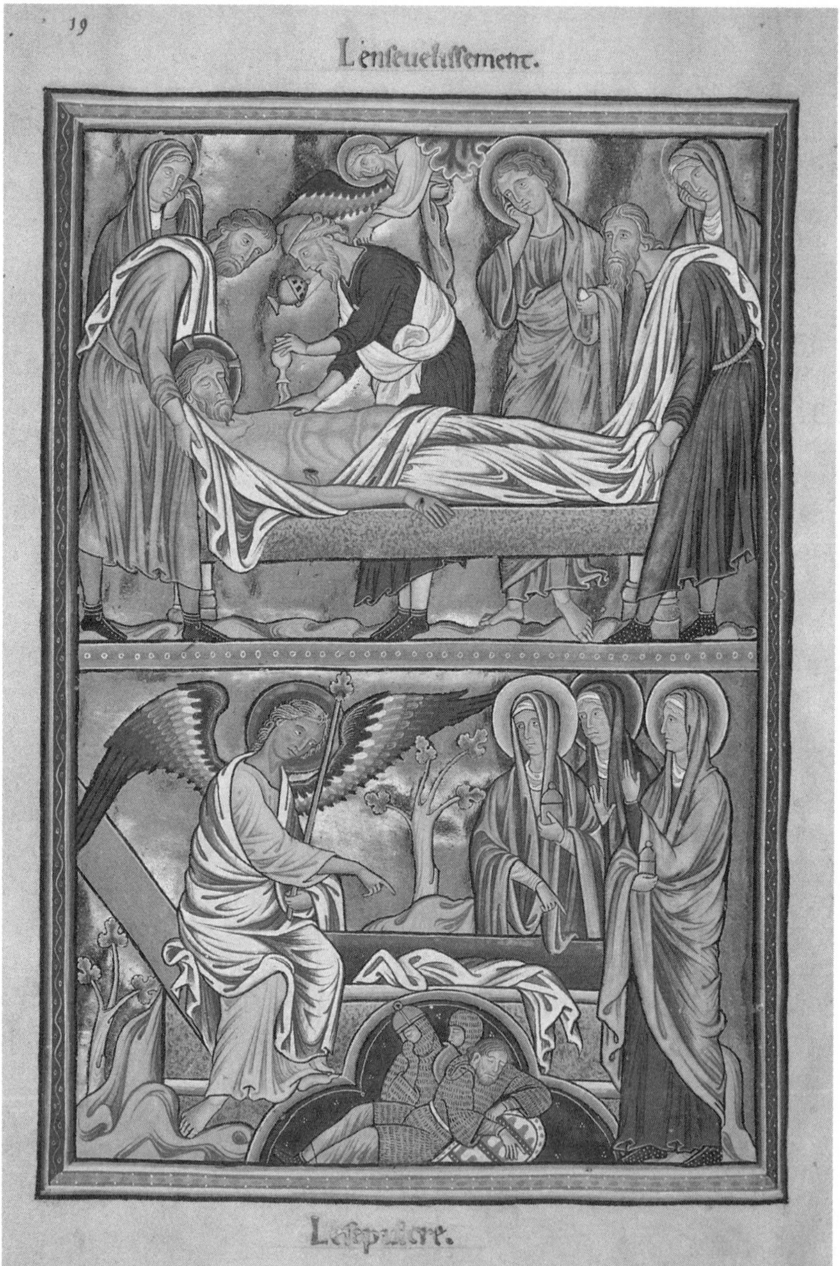

FIGURE 5.8 Anointing and visit to the tomb of Jesus, miniature from the Psalter of Ingeborg, circa 1200

possible variations, too, of harmonization (e.g., an angel standing or sitting on the burial bench with his feet on the lid of the sarcophagus).

Returning to the Pray Codex, we see that the contours of the stones are rigid, not flowing, as in the fabric that is in the design of the upper scene. In its simplicity, the diagonal line of the red crosses is most likely a primitive attempt at perspective to convey one of the corners of the sarcophagus. The geometric motif is purely decorative and also serves to suggest the grain typical of certain stones, such as marbles and onyxes. The same goes for the circles, which are likewise found in certain stones; here, however, the circles are everywhere—for example, on the belt and on the wings of the angel and on the dress of one of the women, serving as simple embellishment. They are also found, scattered here and there, in the miniatures of the other pages of the same codex. Were one to seek a historical parallel, one could hypothesize that the red crosses on the stones might recall those engraved by the crusaders on the walls of the Holy Sepulcher of Jerusalem, still visible today. The circles could recall the three round windows (the *oculi*) from which one could see the stone bank where it is supposed that the body of Jesus was deposed. These three round openings, in different sizes, recur on numerous medieval representations of the sarcophagus.[135] It is not necessary, however, to insist rigidly that these three designs represent the *oculi*, as there are many alternative explanations: embedded gemstones, tears shed by women, drops of perfumed ointment, or, as has already been mentioned, random decorative motifs. One can make a comparison, for example, with the small circles placed on the stone of the sepulcher represented in a miniature of the sacramentarium by Robert de Jumièges; as in the Pray Codex, they are also repeated on the characters' clothes, without any apparent meaning save that of pure decoration (fig. 5.9). All that, however, is unimportant, since there has never been any doubt, not even among Hungarian art historians, that in the Pray Codex we see the stone slab of the sarcophagus, decorated

[135] The hegumen Daniel speaks about this between AD 1104 and 1109: "As soon as you enter the little grotto through the small little doors, on the right there is a bench carved in the stone of the little grotto, and on this bench laid the body of our Lord Jesus Christ. Now that holy bench is covered with marble slabs. On one side three round windows were fashioned, and from them we can see that holy stone; there all Christians used to kiss it." G. Prokhorov, ed., "Хождение игумена Даниила," in Библиотека литературы Древней Руси, ed. D. S. Likhachev, vol. 4 (St. Petersburg: Наука, 1997).

FIGURE 5.9 The angel meets the women at the tomb, miniature from the Sacramentary of Robert de Jumièges, circa 1020, detail

in a manner evoking Byzantine style, and not a shroud. The shroud is also featured in the drawing: it can be clearly seen wadded up atop the lid of the sarcophagus, which is itself placed sideways facing the beholder.[136] A simple iconographic study of the motif of the three Marys at the tomb would be sufficient to see that the ways of depicting and decorating a slab of a sarcophagus are virtually endless: circles, rhombuses, squares, reticulation, dots, crosses, flowers, lozenges, colored veins, combinations of various colors and figures, with *oculi* or openings, even more than three of them. David Montero has collected an impressive series of examples.[137] Finally, what sense would it make to depict the scene of the women at the tomb . . . without the tomb?

The discussion on the Pray Codex is useful for recognizing how cavalierly sindonologists use the iconographic argument. When they find a detail in a representation that is, according to them, similar to that of the Shroud, they declare the dependence of the former on the latter; conversely, when one calls their attention to a discrepancy, they appeal to the bad memory of the artist or to his failure, in a given case, to copy the model exactly.

5.3. The Era of Radiocarbon

5.3.1 Finally, Radiocarbon Dating

In 1983 Umberto II, the last king of Italy, died. The Vatican secretary of state warmly accepted the gift of the Shroud bequeathed in his will and delegated its safekeeping to the archbishop of Turin, *pro tempore*.[138] Also in 1983, the pope indicated that it would be an extraordinary Holy Year; a rumor circulated that there was a desire to take advantage of the occasion by transferring the Shroud from Turin to Rome, and immediately a petition was generated bearing the signatures of 66,622 Piedmontese who opposed the idea.[139] Most likely, however, the rumor was baseless.

[136] Cf. W. Tünde, "Perugiai Bernát kódexe és a Pray-kódex helye a középkori magyar könyvfestészetben," *Ars Hungarica* 3 (1975): 202.

[137] See http://sombraenelsudario.wordpress.com/2014/08/10/las-santas-mujeresen-la-tumba-vacia-imagenes. See also H. Farey, "The Pray Codex," *British Society for the Turin Shroud Newsletter* 84 (2016): 17–31.

[138] Documents assembled by L. Fossati, *Sacra Sindone*, 269–72.

[139] AAT, 20.4.29. Signatures presented by Tino Zeuli.

The 1980s were very successful years for sindonology, which rode on the wave of emotion caused by the results of STURP. Meanwhile, everything seemed to presage an increase in the number of scientists or those presumed to be scientists who claimed to have found, by various means, further evidence of authenticity. There is not space in this book to consider all of the wild Shroud theories. There were those who magnified and manipulated old black and white photographs of the Shroud, who began to fantasize about the meaning of the chiaroscuro and were convinced that they could see on the fabric traces of Roman coins, inscriptions in Latin or Hebrew, flowers, and any other kind of object dating back to the time of Jesus. Others claimed to have identified traces of aragonite on the Shroud, a substance found in the tombs of Jerusalem (though not in them exclusively); once they found the aragonite, they suggested that it was partially responsible for the impression of the image on the cloth, imagining that the body of the deceased Jesus warmed up all the way to 46°C. For its part, sindonological medicine, which had played a fundamental role in Shroud studies between the 1930s and 1970s, went beyond the usual medical-legal investigations. These medical doctors believe that it is possible to conduct proper autopsies on the image visible on the Shroud, assuming that such image was imprinted by a human body which left behind traces that can be examined. Through these examinations, sindonology grew closer to arriving at unexpected results, such as the identification of the DNA of Christ. Several requests arrived in Turin for access to the Shroud for further examinations, presented by sindonological associations. Between 1984 and 1986 at least four arrived in Turin, one of which was presented by STURP.

But the most desired and expected procedure, even by those very sindonologists, was the measurement of the radiocarbon content (isotope C14), the single test able to establish the date of the fabric. This dating system had been conceived in 1945 by Willard Libby.

The rumor circulated among sindonologists that Libby was against applying the method that he had invented to the Shroud. Of this, however, I have found no proof; instead I found proof that at least twice he stated precisely the opposite, declaring his own interest in performing the study himself.[140] Excellent results had already been

[140] The judgment is cited by Wilcox, *Shroud*, 147–48. According to Pierluigi Baima Bollone, Libby asked for a piece of cloth from the Shroud in order to date it (P. Baima

attained for other false relics, such as the chair of Saint Peter in the Vatican and fragments of the cross of the Stavelot Triptych.

Until the mid-eighties, the test had always been postponed, first because it was not considered sufficiently tested yet, and later because of the amount of cloth that would have to be sacrificed (the procedure is destructive). But by the mid-eighties, C14 was universally considered a fully reliable system of dating, and it was regularly used to date antiques. For some years now, then, a new procedure (compared to the traditional beta-counting method) known as the AMS (accelerator mass spectrometry) method has been available that allows the investigator to date even very small fragments. One of the inventors of this new system, the physicist Harry Gove, did not even know what the Shroud was when, at the end of the 1970s, he was contacted for research by Reverend David Sox of the British Society for the Turin Shroud. After that, Gove began to keep the sindonologists aware of his progress.

Also, Cardinal Ballestrero and his scientific advisor, Luigi Gonella, were now in favor of performing the dating procedure. An equally favorable reaction came from the vast majority of sindonologists. They were now universally used to the idea that science could give rise to results increasingly favorable to the argument for authenticity. The less-than-encouraging results of the Pellegrino Commission had been buried in oblivion. The expected result was confirmation of the sindonological interpretation of the other studies—that is, that the Shroud dated to the first century of the Christian era. This in itself would not have been sufficient to support with certainty the claim that the fabric had been associated with Jesus of Nazareth rather than another person crucified at the time, but it would, nonetheless, have been a most encouraging result.

With the benefit of hindsight, we can say that the undertaking of radiocarbon dating was handled abnormally from an organizational point of view. The best thing, probably, would have been to have treated the Shroud in the same manner as any other object to be so investigated: it would have been sufficient to choose one or more equipped laboratories and send a sample of fabric in a sealed envelope, without declaring its illustrious provenance, then to have

---

Bollone, "Perché la Sindone non è stata datata con il radiocarbonio?," *Stampa sera*, September 17, 1979, 5).

waited comfortably for the response that would have come with a simple letter. Already at that time every testing facility received hundreds and hundreds of samples from museums, universities, art galleries, archaeological societies, and even churches; no one would have noticed the Shroud's specimen among so many samples of cloth, and it would thus have been treated like any other object. Instead it was decided to proceed otherwise. A commission was established involving several select individuals, which created some hard feelings because many others wanted to take part and some had been left out. Several C14 laboratories offered to perform the trial gratis, imagining that the examination, whatever its result, might bring them much publicity. Harry Gove himself, mentioned above, wanted to remain involved, hoping that the Shroud could be dated with the new method he had invented, possibly even in his Rochester laboratory. Among nonspecialists, all of these preparations and discussions created the false impression that the radiocarbon dating of a piece of cloth necessitated special precautions, when instead it was a routine operation. Furthermore, the various discussions, procedures, steps, and personalities involved were all to the detriment of the simplicity of the operation, and they would in the future become the basis for endless contestation of the C14 results. Hundreds of pages have been written on the radiocarbon dating of the Shroud. In this case, too, I limit myself to setting forth the main facts, leaving aside the examination of every detail. Insistence on the details risks losing sight of the essential point—that is, the result of the radiocarbon testing.

Once Cardinal Ballestrero, who was not the relic's "owner" but only charged with the Shroud's protection, had made the decision to proceed, he asked for the support and approval of the Holy See. The Pontifical Academy of Sciences was invested with the responsibility to oversee all operations. For the first time in its history, the papal academy was presided over by a scientist who was not a priest, the biophysicist Carlos Chagas Filho (who was also busy, at the time, leading the scientific section of the commission on the Galileo case). Even the opening step was fraught with difficulties because it was clear that certain managers of the radiocarbon laboratories and Gove himself had little regard for STURP or other scientific sindonological associations. The scientists' desire was to date the Shroud and nothing more, and they did not want the sindonologists to take part in the procedure. This desire for autonomy engendered reactions that were, one might say, somewhat vitriolic, since the sindonologists had hoped to manage the radiocarbon dating themselves. From the beginning Chagas took the side of Gove. Chagas had a negative report on STURP's proposed study prepared and sent to the Vatican secretary of state; that proposed study was dropped. He sought to marginalize the sindonologists, virtually blacklisting them vis-à-vis their further participation in any research, including dating, which, because of their poor scientific value and their biased authenticist perspective, he argued, would make the entire operation suspicious in the eyes of the scientific community. Chagas only granted them the right to remove the fabric (which anyone could have done). Thus began the headaches and cross-vetoes, which occurred not only among scientists but also within the Church. Gonella and Ballestrero found themselves having to mediate between everyone. Moreover, this awkward task had to be carried out in front of those who accused the Church of interfering with the examination for fear of undesired results. The Turin Center of Sindonology remained, at least officially, at the margins of the whole operation.

The commission's first operational meeting was convened in Turin on September 29, 1986, after a series of postponements led to a yearlong delay from its original projected date. These were engendered by the various interested parties' continuous conflicts, which the Vatican secretary of state tried to iron out. Those in attendance were the archbishop, Gonella, Chagas, Gove, some of the members of STURP, Michael Tite (director of the research laboratory of the British Museum), representatives of the seven laboratories who had offered to take the exam, and various other experts and technicians. If it had been up to Gove and Chagas, the day of the meeting would have been the same as that on which the fragments of the Shroud to be dated would have been cut. Turin refused and resisted, however, claiming a fundamental role in the operation and hoping that there would be room for STURP's proposals, too.

The discussion about the collection of samples hinges upon several points. In particular, to Gonella, STURP, and others, the request supported by Gove and Chagas to take seven samples for the seven laboratories seemed excessive: normally there would be only one sample and one laboratory—in rare cases two—while the involvement of seven laboratories was without precedent. The request was seen as a way to avoid displeasing any of the seven candidates, and it could serve to impress the public that had no knowledge of technical questions, creating the impression that the large number of laboratories involved would strengthen the credibility of the results (though the radiocarbon method would have long since been abandoned if it were always the case that each laboratory produced different results). The laboratories themselves also proposed the attractive notion of resorting to the contextual dating of control samples; that is, samples of cloth whose age and provenance are known but not communicated to the lab, in order to effect a "blind" determination of the date. In the end, however, no decision was reached regarding the question about the collection of samples. An intervention by the textile expert Mechthild Flury-Lemberg (who was then brought in by Chagas and would later become a trusted expert of the diocese of Turin) pointed out that it would be useless to take samples from different parts of the fabric because the Shroud was woven together on the same loom and therefore every part is representative of the whole. Thus it was decided to proceed in such a way as to minimize the mutilation of the cloth.

The meeting continued with difficulty for two days; no agreement was reached. Even the final document, drawn up by a representative of the Pontifical Academy, could not be agreed upon because Gonella considered it to be invalid, as not everyone signed it and, according to him, it contained some false statements. To be certain, the only solution was to resort to transcribing the tape-recorded discussions, which occupied seven hundred typewritten pages. The money spent for this first meeting alone (travel, board, and lodging) had already surpassed the cost of normal radiocarbon testing.

In the months to follow, after various vicissitudes involving letters, telegrams, phone calls, denials, declarations, and various quarrels, a solution was painstakingly reached. The Vatican's secretary of state and the representatives of Turin agreed to supply no more than three samples, which were more than enough. Turin chose three of the seven proposed laboratories: those at the University of Arizona in Tucson, the University of Oxford, and Zurich Polytechnic, because they had the most experience in dating small archaeological fragments. The Rochester laboratory, directed by Gove, was notably excluded. Despite being directed by the one who had invented the new system of radiocarbon dating, Rochester was a research lab, not one designed specifically to provide dating on request. Gove was greatly discomfited by this exclusion but later was allowed full access to the testing process, at least as a spectator.

On January 22, 1988, another meeting took place between Tite and Gonella and representatives of the chosen laboratories, where it was agreed that each should receive about 2 cm^2 of fabric. It was decided not to withdraw the idea of carrying out a blind test, even if it was clear that to do so would have been superfluous, because by then everyone knew the Shroud's type of weaving and even by the naked eye would have been able to recognize it immediately: the other specimens were, in practice, meant simply to serve as control samples. They would be procured and certified by the British Museum and would have to go back to the temporal span hypothesized for the Shroud—that is, the first to the fourteenth centuries. The extraction of the cloth would be executed at a certain place on the Shroud and by the hand of someone chosen by the archbishop. The representatives of the laboratories were to complete their measurements within three months and send them for statistical analysis to Tite and an institution of Turin, the Gustavo Colonnetti Institute of Metrology, without divulging the result of the radiocarbon test until the end: the disclosure would be the purview exclusively of the archbishop himself.

April 21, 1988, was the day chosen for the extraction. Those who did not want the sindonologists to be present had managed to exclude them, and Turin had not thought it opportune to insist on this point. The sole exception was Giovanni Riggi, who had entered sindonological circles in 1978 thanks to Baima Bollone and was now aligned with STURP; to him Cardinal Ballestrero decided to entrust the operation of cutting the cloth. Riggi took the matter very seriously and did not employ merely a pair of scissors but used a whole repertoire of instruments, like surgical tools, including operating-room lights and wireless microphones. In addition, he organized a team, including a photographer, a video operator, and a dozen assistants ready for every eventuality. The assignment of this task to Riggi would, however, unfortunately give rise to subsequent problems. The archbishop designated Franco Testore, professor of textile technologies at the Polytechnic University of Turin, as a textile expert. He was joined by Gabriel Vial of the Textile Museum of Lyon, one of the greatest experts in the world of ancient fabrics. Others present were Michael Tite and a priest representing the Pontifical Academy of Sciences (who later would become famous for quite another matter);[141] five representatives of the laboratories; Gonella, consultant to the archbishop; the archbishop himself; and other priests.

The textile experts observed the fabric and discussed the best place to make the withdrawal; after excluding the presence of material that could interfere with the dating, they decided to take a strip from one of the corners, in the same place in which a sample had already been taken for examination by Gilbert Raes at the time of the Pellegrino Commission. Riggi had the task of dividing the strip into pieces and of delivering a sample to each of the three laboratories. Some leftover pieces remained from the piece cut out, which Riggi and Gonella held separately. All of the cloth fragments were measured and weighed on a precise scale before being inserted into cylindrical containers and then sealed. This operation was entrusted to Testore and Riggi. The control samples would be inserted into identical containers. The procedure was performed under the scrutiny of over thirty people and filmed in its entirety, except when the cardinal left with Tite and Gonella to render the containers unidentifiable. At the end of the procedure the representative of each of the three laboratories departed with his own samples, without knowing which of the cylinders contained the cloth of the Shroud.

Now there was nothing to do but wait for the results of the laboratories. Gove insisted that he, along with his Arizona colleagues, be permitted to attend the radio carbon testing at the University of Arizona, a request that was granted. On May 6, he came with his collaborator Shirley Brignall, who was not allowed to enter the laboratory; but immediately afterward Gove informed her of the result. Reverend Sox somehow also came to know of the first results, and he proceeded to communicate these to Father Peter Rinaldi. At this point it is impossible to reconstruct the chain of whispering: in a short time the stipulation of silence was broken, and rumors of a medieval result began to circulate and then made their way to the ears of a certain journalist. This is the third time, in the recent history of the

[141] It was Msgr. Renato Dardozzi, who made sure that after his death the proof of the involvement of the bank of the Institute for the Works of Religion (IOR = Vatican Bank) in money laundering operations was disclosed: G. Nuzzi, *Vaticano S.p.A.* (Milan: Chiarelettere, 2009).

Shroud, when attempts to keep something hidden about the object proved unsuccessful.

Turin, which had to await the official communication, was placed in the difficult situation of having to manage a growing uncontrolled news leak. Gonella came to know from Tite on July 1 that the results of Arizona's examination yielded a medieval date and communicated this news to the cardinal and no one else. In the meantime he released interviews to newspapers that revealed his palpable anger with the laboratories. Soon the first unjustified suspicions that the Church wanted to hide the results began to spring up; but the archbishop could do nothing but wait until all controlled operations were duly performed. Finally, Tite communicated the results of the radiocarbon tests of all the samples. At this point a press conference in Turin was called for the morning of October 13 in which the archbishop would read this communiqué, agreed upon with the Holy See:

> In a dispatch received by the Pontifical Custodian of the Holy Shroud on 28 September 1988, the laboratories of the University of Arizona, of the University of Oxford and of the Polytechnic of Zurich which had conducted the tests for the radio-carbon dating of the cloth of the Holy Shroud, have finally communicated the result of their tests through Dr Tite of the British Museum, the coordinator of the project. This document states that the cloth of the Shroud can be assigned with a confidence of 95 per cent accuracy to a date between AD 1260 and 1390. More precise and detailed information concerning the result will be published by the laboratories and Dr Tite in a scientific review in an article which is in the course of preparation. For his part Professor Bray of the 'G. Colonetti' Institute of Metrology of Turin, which was charged with the review of the summary report presented by Dr Tite, has confirmed the compatibility of the results obtained by the three laboratories, whose certainty falls within the limits envisaged by the methods used. After having informed the Holy See, the owner of the Holy Shroud, I make known what has been communicated to me. In submitting to science the evaluation of these results, the Church confirms her respect and veneration for this venerable icon of Christ, which remains an object of devotion for the faithful in keeping with the attitude always expressed in regard to the Holy Shroud, namely that the value of the image is more important than the date of the Shroud itself. This attitude disposes of the gratuitous deductions of a theological character

> advanced in the sphere of a research which had been presented as solely and rigorously scientific. At the same time the problems about the origin of the image and its preservation still remain to a large extent unsolved and will require further research and study. In regard to this the Church will show the same openness, inspired by the love of truth which she showed by permitting the radio-carbon dating as soon as she was presented with a reasonable and effective programme in regard to that matter. I personally regret the deplorable fact that many reports concerning this scientific research were anticipated in the press, especially of the English language, because it also favoured the by no means objective insinuation that the Church was afraid of science by trying to conceal its results, an accusation in open contradiction to the Church's attitude on this occasion also when she has gone ahead resolutely.

Later a scientific report would be published in the world's leading multidisciplinary scientific journal, *Nature*.[142] On the day immediately following the announcement of the results, Reverend Sox, who had been informed before the results were officially disclosed, would publish his book on the subject, which he had evidently already prepared. In subsequent years, Gove, Gonella, and Riggi would also put their thoughts about the whole operation in writing, the study of which is useful for ascertaining the point of view of each of them.[143]

5.3.2 "It's Medieval": The Reactions

For all those who already expected the medieval result, this announcement was little more than a confirmation. The dating coincided perfectly with the first historical documents concerning the Shroud. For the sindonologists, however, it was an intolerable blow. After a few moments of hesitation, they began a campaign to discredit the results, which necessarily could not leave the representatives of the diocese and of the Holy See untainted. Ballestrero and Gonella found themselves under friendly fire, because fringes of the Catholic world blamed them for mishandling the operation. The famous Catholic journalist Vittorio Messori allowed only three days to pass

[142] Damon et al., "Radiocarbon Dating," 611–15.

[143] Sox, *Shroud Unmasked*; H. E. Gove, *Relic, Icon or Hoax? Carbon Dating the Turin Shroud* (Bristol: Institute of Physics Publishing, 1996); L. Gonella and G. Riggi, *Il giorno più lungo della Sindone* (Milan: Fondazione 3M, 2005).

before he began publishing contributions extremely critical of them in the columns of the Catholic newspaper *Avvenire*.[144] Ballestrero became "the guardian who did not guard." John Paul II, responding to a question from a journalist adhering to sindonology who asked him whether the Shroud was an icon or a relic, responded that "it is certainly a relic," and from that point began a war against those Catholics who wanted to abandon the previous definition of the Shroud as a "relic" in favor of the term "icon" that Ballestrero had used.[145]

Both Gonella and Ballestrero were very disappointed by the "internal" criticism. In 1989 Ballestrero had to leave the diocese due to its retirement age limitation; in Rome it was decided to keep him for a certain period in the office of Papal Guardian of the Shroud even after retirement, to show that he enjoyed the pope's favor. But the following year his deteriorating health compelled him to pass this assignment on to his successor as archbishop, Giovanni Saldarini. Expressing appreciation for Gonella and those who had worked with him up to that point, and advancing particular reservations about the International Center of Sindonology, Ballestrero recommended that Saldarini continue to study the Shroud. Saldarini, who had little respect for Ballestrero,[146] chose the opposite course, however, dismissing Riggi and Gonella, and from that moment he followed the advice of the Center. These decisions were not without consequence because, after the fall of the monarchy, the archbishop had become the decision-making authority for everything pertaining to the Shroud. His support for the sindonological cause is essential, even more decisive than that of the pope, who deals only indirectly with the management of the relic and essentially defers to Turin.

Ballestrero, on the day when he had communicated the result of the radiocarbon dating, said:

[144] Articles later collected in V. Messori, *La sfida della fede* (Cinisello Balsamo: San Paolo, 1993), 139–58, 428–31.

[145] Cf. O. Petrosillo, "Il tabù della Sindone come reliquia: Note critiche di pastorale sindonica," *Collegamento pro Sindone* 8 (September–October 1999): 15–30.

[146] Cf. G. Caviglia and P. Alciati, *Un'ombra che non fa ombra* (Rome: Edizioni OCD, 2013), 207: "It was clear and one could see that the new archbishop was biased enough against both Father Ballestrero and the diocese that had been entrusted to him." Ballestrero's secretary, Giuseppe Caviglia, revealed to me that in subsequent years, Saldarini changed his opinion of Ballestrero and asked his pardon for his prior attitude.

> I think that it is not the case that the Church should call these results into question. . . . I do not believe that we, the Church, should trouble ourselves to quibble with highly respected scientists who until this moment have merited only respect, and that it would not be responsible to subject them to censure solely because their results perhaps do not align with the arguments of the heart that one can carry within himself.[147]

The sindonologists, instead, decided to reject the result of the medieval dating as, according to them, it conflicted with what they already knew about the Shroud. A response, however, came from top-tier scientific institutions at the international level. The weight of their judgment seemed beyond question, and at any rate could not simply be ignored. The Catholic press chose to react by giving voice to the opinion of the sindonologists, who parroted the usual argument according to which the Shroud is an inexplicable object, full of mysteries, which had already passed too many tests to be forced to capitulate to a single piece of incompatible evidence (in reality there was no proof in favor). Those inclined to accept the scientific response sought to find a reconciliation with the theories of the sindonologists, going on to speculate about what bloody corpse in the Middle Ages could have left such an impression or who the extraordinary artist was who could have made it. There would also be several fantastic suppositions, including the idea that the Shroud was made by Leonardo da Vinci, using his own face and a corpse that he happened to have at his disposal, and making a photograph through a method he invented, rendering the fabric discernible with a special photosensitive substance.[148] The theory of the photograph produced by da Vinci has been proposed again and tested by the art historian Nicholas Allen. He took a mannequin and exposed it to the sun for a few days in front of a large "dark room" (a primitive photographic machine); inside the dark room he extended a sheet coated with photosensitive substances that were available or could have been fabricated in the medieval period (silver sulphate or silver nitrate). The light passed through a quartz lens (rock crystal); in this

[147] Conference on October 13, 1988 (audio transcription).

[148] L. Picknett and C. Prince, *Turin Shroud: In Whose Image?* (New York: HarperCollins, 1994).

way he succeeded in obtaining an image impressed on the cloth,[149] which, however, does not match all of the characteristics of the image of the Shroud.[150] The idea that Leonardo da Vinci was the artist of the Shroud has been taken up by others, with the proposal of other techniques, such as a red hot iron being passed over the cloth.[151]

The basis of many theories remains the conviction, with roots in the sindonological environment, that the image of the Shroud could not have been made by a manual process within the capacity of a human being. The reactions to the radiocarbon dating test were unhinged and amateurish, with some having recourse to the most unlikely pretexts. Although up to this point none of these observations had ever convinced C14 experts, the naysayers' persistence, the support of various ecclesiastical authorities (at least unofficially), the media bombardment, and the publication of hundreds of contributions on the topic all gave rise to the widespread opinion that the result of the C14 test was completely unfounded. The remainder of this section is dedicated to examining at least the most recurrent justifications that have been advanced for such a response.

The first opportunity to contest the result was provided by the Turin officials themselves who had cut the material. The sample of cut-out cloth had been divided into parts, but no one had thought it necessary to write a report with the official description of the subdivisions and the weight of each fragment. There were, however, footage and many photographs, which would have been more than sufficient documentation on a typical occasion. The lack of a written report became problematic the following year, when a French sindonological association organized a conference requesting that Riggi and Testore give a lecture; they sent two reports that described differently the subdivision of the cloth sample for the laboratories

149 N. P. L. Allen, "Is the Shroud of Turin the First Recorded Photograph?," *South African Journal of Art History* 11, no. 1 (1993): 23–32; idem, "An Overview of the Photographic Hypothesis for Image Formation as It Applies to the Shroud of Lirey-Chambéry-Turin," *Approfondimento Sindone* 2, no. 1 (1998): 25–42; idem, *Turin Shroud: Testament to a Lost Technology* (Saarbrucken: Lambert Academic, 2017).

150 Cf. M. Ware, "On Proto-Photography and the Shroud of Turin," *History of Photography* 21, no. 4 (1997): 261–69.

151 V. Haziel [pseudonym of Maria Consolata Corti], *La passione secondo Leonardo* (Milan: Sperling & Kupfer, 1998).

into fragments.[152] Someone then pointed this out to Testore, who appended a correction to the text he had already sent. Riggi also later withdrew his first version and presented a second, then a third and, in 2005, a fourth.[153] The blatant contradiction of the reports opened them to fierce criticism. To this one can add that on the day of the cutting, Riggi and Gonella had set aside a fabric sample for later use. In 1992 they returned it to Ballestrero; but there remained other shreds, of which, in 1994, Riggi, though unauthorized by Ballestrero's successor, would imprudently use to try a new C14 test proposed by an American scholar. The day of the Riggi cut (under the watchful eye of Gonella and many others) had also seen withdrawals of small fragments, including small bits of dried "blood," that would have the same fate. Due to the lack of a written report, a large controversy was born, one that eventually ended in charges of embezzlement.

These episodes did nothing but provide further confirmation to those who had always considered the intervention of a sindonologist in any study of the Shroud to be harmful. Nevertheless, such problems have had no bearing upon the result of the radiocarbon test. The footage, photographs, and notes that Riggi, Gonella, and Testore took are sufficient to reconstruct correctly the sequence of events. But above all, the way in which a piece of cloth was cut out in multiple places is information that is negligible in and of itself, and that could also be completed without being detailed verbally (especially since the operation was filmed). Each laboratory, before proceeding to the examination of the object, subjected its sample to cleaning and further weighing operations. The laboratories simply dated what they received, and it is a separate issue whether in Turin no precise report of the samples was produced or if there was confusion about the numbers.

Criticism of the behavior exhibited during the sample gathering became an opportunity for some to make accusations of deliberate fraud. The champions of the fraud theory were two French priests, Georges de Nantes and Bruno Bonnet-Eymard. They were members

[152] Published in *Actes du symposium scientifique international de Paris sur le Linceul de Turin*, vol. 1, *Le prélèvement sur le Linceul effectué le 21 avril 1988 et études du tissu* (Paris: OEIL, 1990).

[153] A clear description of all these discrepancies is in G. M. Rinaldi, *La Notte della Sindone: Il documentario di Francesca Saracino*, § 9, viewable at http://sindone.weebly.com/articoli.html.

of a reactionary Catholic group repeatedly subject to disciplinary measures by the religious authorities; de Nantes had even been forbidden to celebrate the Eucharist. Both priests, obsessed as they were with Masonic conspiracies, were convinced that the C14 dating was the result of a vast conspiracy against the Church ordered by Michael Tite with the agreement of all the laboratory authorities. The confusion that Riggi and Testore had made in reporting the results served Bonnet-Eymard as he constructed a very convoluted explanation that, so he said, sorted out all the contradictions. According to Bonnet-Eymard's theory, Tite essentially would have fraudulently swapped the samples of the Shroud with the control samples of medieval cloth, exchanging the containers. Then, in the second instance, he would have personally intervened to convince the laboratories to provide altered data even for the replaced sample. All these ruminations (of which there are two different versions, because the first at some point seemed too unbelievable) were printed in various languages by a publishing house owned by the friars themselves, bearing the significant name *The Catholic Counter-Reformation in the Twentieth Century*.[154] De Nantes and Bonnet-Eymard did not hesitate to pin blame on the archbishop of Turin and even on John Paul II, to whom both attributed the characteristics of the Antichrist. To substantiate the accusations, other false rumors were added, such as, for example, that the radiocarbon laboratories had refused to deliver the "raw data" of the measurements; but the truth is that they sent the data to the relevant authorities, not to whomever asked for it.

The charge of a colossal conspiracy, despite coming from a questionable source, was welcomed by many and received a lot of attention in the Catholic press; there are still those who maintain it, as it seems to have been recycled by others with some variations (I only mention here the Jesuit Werner Bulst, who is considered the father of German-language sindonology).[155] Some began also to insinuate the

[154] For example, de Nantes and Bonnet-Eymard, *Saint Suaire à l'âge de Jésus ressuscité*, 30–42 (English translation: "Holy Shroud Is as Old as the Risen Jesus," *Catholic Counter-Reformation in the XXth Century* 330 [2000], https://web.archive.org/web/20080323083940/http://www.crc-internet.org/may00.htm); see also B. Bonnet-Eymard, "The Crime Committed against the Holy Shroud," *Shroud News* 95 (1996): 10–27.

[155] W. Bulst, *Betrug am Turiner Grabtuch: Der manipulierte Carbontest* (Frankfurt am Main: Knecht, 1990).

doubt that the laboratories had been paid to alter the results. It goes without saying that even Ballestrero could not help but be brushed by suspicion of fomenting the conspiracy: both he and Gonella had been witnesses of the moment in which each sample was inserted into its container.

Others preferred to deny the validity of the method of radiocarbon dating as such. Sindonology had by now assumed the character of pseudoscience, and it is not surprising that it drew not only on the ruminations of the traditionalists but also on the war chest of creationist and fundamentalist literature. The method of radiocarbon dating is in fact used to date objects up to fifty thousand years old, which stands in contradiction to the idea of those who believe that the world and the life in it were created only a few thousand years ago. What follows from such creationist convictions is the wholesale rejection of radiocarbon measurements, as well as the rejection of more popular scientific explanations of the origins of the universe, the existence of the dinosaurs, human evolution, and so on. To combat such modern scientific theories, then, creationists and fundamentalist Christians had already prepared a whole list of alleged errors in the method of C14 dating, which was promptly copied in the books of sindonology (the authors conveniently forgetting that the proposal to date the Shroud with radiocarbon came from sindonologists). The alleged errors generally concern cases of objects of a known age that, it is claimed, would be given a date by C14 testing that was off by several hundred or even a thousand years. But a careful evaluation of these so-called errors (which, however, are always cited in a generic and approximate manner) demonstrates that they do not exist, or that they go back to an earlier epoch in which the dating system had not yet been refined, or that they concern materials that do not lend themselves to radiocarbon dating but whose concentration of carbon 14 is measured for purposes other than those concerned with their age. To take but one example: a freshly killed seal was C14 dated to be thirteen hundred years old. These cases, the few times that they are genuine, are well known in scientific literature; for example, it is known that for a while there were difficulties with bone dating, and that certain living organisms, such as ocean-dwelling creatures, cannot be dated at all because in the ocean the concentration of carbon

14 is lower than it is in the atmosphere.[156] This is not the case with fabrics, however, which are a type of material that responds very well to radiocarbon analysis.

The creationists' arguments have fared well among sindonologists, particularly in France, especially because the president of the newborn CIELT (International Center for Studies on the Shroud of Turin) was Daniel Raffard de Brienne, an anti-evolutionist. CIELT also hired another scholar of a similar ilk, Marie-Claire van Oosterwyck-Gastuche. Early in her career, she presented herself under the pseudonym of Michaël Winter. Sindonologists for a long time regarded her, erroneously, to be a (male) expert on radiocarbon dating.[157] In Italy the sindonologists also drew on the writings of Giuseppe Maria Pace, a Salesian traditionalist and creationist.[158]

Other sindonologists less inclined to the cause of creationism preferred to discredit the C14 dating by resorting to the notion of contamination of the samples. The dating method is based on the fact that all living organisms possess a certain quantity of radiocarbon (isotope C14), which gradually begins to decay from the moment of their death. Because we know the speed of this decay, by measuring the radiocarbon concentration residue it is possible to know fairly accurately the moment in which an organism died—in the case of the Shroud, when the flax plants were cut. The sindonological pollution hypothesis claims that through the centuries the Shroud picked up deposits of more recent elements which would, therefore, contain a greater quantity of carbon; the radiocarbon dating, having been performed on a linen so contaminated, would thus have produced an erroneous result. Candidates for the role of pollutants are many: the smoke of candles, the sweat of the hands that touched and held the fabric, the water used to extinguish the fire of 1532, the smog of the sky of Turin, pollens, oil, and much more.

[156] A review of examples is in G. M. Rinaldi, "Gli 'errori' del C14," *Scienza & Paranormale* 81 (2008): 48–55 (also available at www.cicap.org); idem, "L'elmo vichingo (con le corna) di Barbara Frale," and idem, "L'esperimento fantasma sulla mummia 1770," both to be found at http://sindone.weebly.com/articoli.html.

[157] M.-C. van Oosterwyck-Gastuche, *Le radiocarbone face au Linceul de Turin* (Paris: François-Xavier de Guibert, 1999).

[158] Cf. G. M. Rinaldi, "Un travaso creazionista in un articolo di Giuseppe Pace," http://sindone.weebly.com/pace.html.

This approach gains traction among those who do not know how C14 dating works; in reality, however, it is untenable. Indeed, if a bit of smoke and sweat were enough to produce a false result, the measurement of carbon 14 would have already been declared useless and one could not understand why it is still used today to date thousands of finds every year. The truth is rather that the system is not significantly sensitive to such pollutants. Let us suppose that we were to admit that the fabric of the Shroud dates back to the thirties of the first century; we also admit that the Shroud has suffered exposure to strong pollution, for example, around 1532, the year of the Chambéry fire. To distort the C14 dating by up to 1,300 years, it would be necessary that for every one hundred carbon atoms originally present in the cloth, another five hundred dating to 1532 be added by contamination. In practice, in the Shroud, the amount of pollutant should be several times higher than the amount of the original linen, which is nonsense. Things get even worse if we assume that pollution did not happen all at the same time in the seventeenth century, but gradually over the previous centuries. In this case there is no mathematical possibility that pollution having occurred before the fourteenth century—even if tens of times higher than the quantity of the original material—could give a result of dating to the fourteenth century. It should be added, moreover, that all samples, before being radiocarbon dated, are subjected to energetic cleaning treatments able to remove the upper patina that has been in contact with outside contaminants; this procedure was also undertaken on the Shroud. Indeed, each of the three laboratories used a different cleaning procedure. To use Vittorio Pesce Delfino's expression, not even an unwashed cover of a garbage truck could have been contaminated enough to provide so misleading a result. Those who believe that the Shroud was an object that could not be dated because it was subjected to numerous vicissitudes during the centuries evidently do not know that often C14 dating laboratories work on materials in much worse condition, whether coming from archaeological excavations or from places where they have been in contact with various contaminants. For a radiocarbon scientist the Shroud is a very clean object.

In 1990 the fifth national congress of sindonology was held in Cagliari, significantly entitled "Dating of the Shroud," featuring for the first time papers critical of the value of radiocarbon dating. The insistence on this theme became even stronger in the conference held in Rome in 1993.[159] On this occasion what would become the most famous application of the pollution theory was established. Some had already tried to attribute the alleged carbon enrichment to the effects of the fire on the Shroud in Chambéry in 1532; this was Msgr. Giulio Ricci's idea[160] as well as that of Oosterwyck-Gastuche, mentioned previously.

Through another creationist, Guy Berthault, in 1992 the idea reached the ears of a Russian scientist, Dmitri Anatolievich Kouznetsov,[161] on the occasion of a symposium of English creationists. He had already contributed to the cause by publishing, some time earlier, certain studies in which he claimed to have found evidence against the Darwinian theory of evolution and against all dating of the skeletal remains of the dinosaurs proposed by palaeontology. Indeed, Kouznetsov was somewhat suspect, not only because of his pseudo-scientific intentions. One of his studies, the most famous, had indeed come into the hands of a biologist from Uppsala who, after analyzing it carefully, discovered that most of the references in it directed the reader to nonexistent articles and studies. In short, it was a case of scientific fraud.

Kouznetsov and the creationists who supported him would be mocked for this fraud in the *Skeptical Inquirer*, that same journal that had previously published some criticisms of the studies of STURP; by that point even the greater part of the creationists now wished to get rid of him.

Returning from that bad experience, Kouznetsov fell back on sindonology, and in a short time he made it known that he had succeeded, together with his colleague Andrey Ivanov, in experimentally demonstrating the theory proposed by Oosterwyck-Gastuche. He was immediately invited to speak at the sindonological convention in Rome and generated enthusiasm even from the moment that he arrived, as he was there to say exactly what the attendees wanted to hear. He claimed that the cellulose of a fabric could, under certain conditions, incorporate "young" carbon coming from the

159 Cf. Ladu, *Datazione della Sindone*; Upinsky, *Identification scientifique*.

160 Ricci, *Sindone contestata difesa spiegata*, 226–35.

161 Sometimes his name is transliterated as "Dmitry Kuznetsov"; in Russian his name is Дмитрий Анатóльевич Кузнецов.

environment and therefore enrich its component of isotope 14, invalidating the result of a radiocarbon test. Kouznetsov said that this effect was produced by the conditions that occurred in the silver box that held the Shroud, which was heated up by the fire of 1532 to the melting point. To this he added further ruminations on a particular biofractionation of carbon isotopes in the flax plant. The Russian claimed to have experimentally measured these rejuvenations by radiocarbon dating fabrics of the first century comparable to the Shroud.[162]

Yet this explanation could not convince the physicists. Gonella himself several times revealed his skepticism, and the experts on C14 replied that the theory was groundless, that Kouznetsov's work was "clearly flawed in several respects," and that their experimental reproduction of what he described had not been successful.[163] Others also tried to repeat Kouznetsov's experiments, but they did not obtain any rejuvenation.

But the sindonologists were not in a position to understand that Kouznetsov was making them into a joke, and they long continued to invite him to intervene in their symposia (especially in Italy, where Kouznetsov enjoyed the encouragement of the members of a Roman association of supporters of the Shroud, the *Collegamento pro Sindone*, as he made the rounds of numerous conferences).[164] Even worse, they continued to give him money that he claimed that he used for his experiments. Later, even John Jackson, the leading figure in STURP, lent scientific and economic support to Kouznetsov. It seemed beyond belief that a Russian scientist, who declared himself non-Catholic, could serve the cause of the Shroud. Yet the advocacy of Kouznetsov was dear to sindonologists, because the adherence to the cause by

[162] Amidst the various articles, which, however, in large part are repetitive, I cite only that of D. A. Kouznetsov, A. A. Ivanov, and P. R. Veletsky, "Effects of Fires and Biofractionation of Carbon Isotopes on Results of Radiocarbon Dating of Old Textiles: The Shroud of Turin," *Journal of Archaeological Science* 23 (1996): 109–21.

[163] A. J. T. Jull, D. J. Donahue, and P. E. Damon, "Factors Affecting the Apparent Radiocarbon Age of Textiles: A Comment on 'Effects of Fires and Biofractionation of Carbon Isotopes on Results of Radiocarbon Dating of Old Textiles: The Shroud of Turin,' by D. A. Kouznetsov et al.," *Journal of Archaeological Science* 23 (1996): 157–60; R. E. M. Hedges, C. B. Ramsey, and G. J. Van Klinken, "An Experiment to Refute the Likelihood of Cellulose Carboxylation," *Radiocarbon* 40, no. 1 (1998): 59–60.

[164] See for example, E. Marinelli, "Dmitri Kouznetsov in Italia," *Collegamento pro Sindone* (March–April 1996): 49–53.

a Protestant or an atheist or agnostic, or better still a Jew, is always emphasized as an element that guarantees greater credibility. But this outlook was not universal, and, in any case, eventually some began to wonder where all the money that Kouznetsov pocketed ended up. In 1997, the Russian was arrested in the United States for a scam linked to the collection of false checks. In 2002, after a meticulous investigation, the Italian physicist Gian Marco Rinaldi, a member of the CICAP (Italian Committee for the Investigation of Claims of the Pseudosciences), demonstrated that Kouznetsov's studies on the Shroud were a serious scam based on reports of experiments never performed, with invented archaeological materials, in a nonexistent laboratory, and supported by false publications.[165] But nothing happened. Rinaldi signaled disappointedly four and again five years later that the most distinguished personalities of international sindonology continued to propagate the value of the experiments of the charlatan, despite having been informed of his fraud.[166] In the meantime, Dmitri Kouznetsov switched targets and more recently has begun to swindle biochemists.[167]

The year 1993 was fruitful, because at the Rome convention another character appeared who proposed yet another variant on the pollution hypothesis. This was Leoncio Garza-Valdés, a Mexican pediatrician and microbiologist living in Texas. Observing some findings under a microscope, Garza was convinced that they were covered with a very thin patina produced by a microscopic fungus, known as *Lichenotelia*, that grows on rocks. Having obtained from

[165] G. M. Rinaldi, "Lo scienziato immaginario," *Scienza & Paranormale* 43 (2002): 20–33; idem, "L'uomo che salvò la Sindone," *Scienza & Paranormale* 43 (2002): 23; idem, "Dossier Kouznetsov," *Scienza & Paranormale* 43 (2002): 34–64. The first and last articles have been translated into English and updated at http://sindone.weebly.com/kuznetsovspecial.html ("Dmitry Kuznetsov, the Imaginary Scientist"; "The Kuznetsov Dossier: Fraud in Experimental Reports").

[166] Rinaldi, "Quello strano silenzio sulla frode di Kuznetsov," *Scienza & Paranormale* 65 (2006): 6–8; idem, "Scotta ancora il caso Kuznetsov," *Scienza & Paranormale* 74 (2007): 5–7. All Rinaldi articles are also available at www.cicap.org and at his own personal page at https://independent.academia.edu/RinaldiGianMarco.

[167] Again discovered by G. M. Rinaldi, "Inconsistencies in a Series of Papers by Dmitry Kuznetsov and Co-workers," http://sindone.weebly.com/kuznetsov-special.html; cf. also K. Grens, "Accused 'Fraudster' Heads Two Journals," *Scientist*, July 2, 2013, www.the-scientist.com/daily-news/accused-fraudster-heads-two-journals-39072.

STURP one of the adhesive tapes that was placed upon the Shroud in 1978, he purported to see significant traces of the same "bioplastic coating," nevertheless having to admit that "such coatings have not been previously observed nor confirmed by other investigators."[168] And so he immediately reached the conclusion that the patina could be responsible for the more recent radiocarbon date, conjecturing that the bacteria responsible for the coating could draw sustenance from carbon dioxide in the air and thus would have absorbed recent carbon 14. Garza claimed that certain apparent discrepancies observed in other radiocarbon datings confirmed his theory, but he has never been able to provide acceptable proof.[169] The theory in this case is also untenable because the thickness of the bioplastic coating on a cloth that would be necessary to produce a loss of thirteen centuries would be not of microscopic proportions but even greater than the thickness of the linen itself. Harry Gove, who was brought in by Garza, for a time gave attention to the hypothetical coating and to the theory of rejuvenation, but he was presumably prudent enough never to take it up himself or to apply it to the Shroud except in a hypothetical way, while he waited for someone to prove the theory experimentally (and also because he was well aware of the amount of pollutant that would be necessary).[170] This proof, however, never came.

But in the meantime Giovanni Riggi came back into play, who was enthusiastic about the theory and thought he had something useful for Garza. As has already been stated, he had some material that he had cut from the Shroud locked in a safe. Riggi was out of the field by now, because the new archbishop had decided no longer to take any of his advice or that of Gonella. In November of 1994, he decided to deliver his own samples to Garza, who proposed performing a new radiocarbon dating after separating the flax cellulose from the polluting bioplastic (hoping, of course, to have a result compatible with the era of Jesus). As soon as the testing was done, it came to

[168] H. E. Gove et al., "A Problematic Source of Organic Contamination of Linen," *Nuclear Instruments and Methods in Physics Research B* 123 (1997): 505.

[169] See the reports by Rinaldi, "'Errori' del C14," 52–55; and Rinaldi, "Esperimento fantasma," http://sindone.weebly.com/marinelli-garza.html.

[170] The article that Gove wrote with Garza clearly states that "it would be premature to draw any conclusions about the true age of the Turin Shroud from these measurements" (Gove et al., "A Problematic Source," 507). See also Gove, *Relic, Icon or Hoax?*, 308.

be known in Italy, and the ecclesiastical authorities declared that it was an unauthorized experiment, on noncertified material whose immediate return was requested. Things went badly for Garza and Riggi: the pediatrician, who evidently was not up to the task of processing the samples, used an unsuitable chemical solution that caused contamination that changed the carbon 14 value for the samples. It did so to such a degree that it placed the date not in the first century but a few millennia before Christ. He thus sacrificed unnecessarily a quantity of fabric that could not be replaced. Leoncio Garza-Valdés has continued in vain to hope to get new material, but in the meantime, he has never been able to prove the existence of his bioplastic patina, which was clearly of his own imagining. Garza published a book on the subject in which he speculated about whether it were possible to extract the DNA of God from the Shroud and described a new bacterium he had discovered on the Shroud, which he baptized *Leobacillus rubrus* ("Leo" from his own name, "Leoncio"). This bacillus, he argued, would be capable of producing the plastic coating and also a color responsible for the human image of the Shroud.

Unsurprisingly, Garza fell out of circulation without being able to demonstrate a single one of his theories.[171] In fact, microbiology does not recognize any bacterium capable of doing that which Garza would have us believe, and no one has ever confirmed the existence of the *Leobacillus* that, were it real, ought to have significant effects on all radiocarbon dating and would be an interesting object of study, even lending itself to some practical applications. Instead the mythical microorganism has gone unobserved, and there exists not even a description of it published in a scientific journal. Simply put, it is a fantasy.

Even after Kouznetsov and Garza's vain attempts, John Jackson continued to think that the hypothesis of carbon enrichment due to the fire of 1532 was the best road to achieving the result he sought. He therefore began looking for a capable substance on his own, too, even if present only in a very small quantity, that could produce contamination able to move the dating by thirteen fateful centuries. At one point he imagined that this substance was carbon monoxide released during the fire. After incubating samples of linen fabric in

[171] L. Garza-Valdés, *The DNA of God?* (London: Hodder & Stoughton, 1998).

an atmosphere rich in carbon monoxide, he sent them to the Oxford radiocarbon laboratory, then under the direction of Christopher Ramsey. However, the examination showed that the carbon monoxide did not cause any change in the dating.[172]

In returning the result to Jackson, in March 2008 Ramsey wrote a statement in which he explained why the theory could not work and why at that moment "there is no direct evidence . . . to suggest the original radiocarbon dates"—that is, the result of 1988—"are not accurate." He then concluded with an open exhortation that addressed, in a purely hypothetical way, the difficulties expressed by Jackson:

> There is a lot of other evidence that suggests to many that the Shroud is older than the radiocarbon dates allow and so further research is certainly needed. It is important that we continue to test the accuracy of the original radiocarbon tests as we are already doing. It is equally important that experts assess and reinterpret some of the other evidence. Only by doing this will people be able to arrive at a coherent history of the Shroud which takes into account and explains all of the available scientific and historical information.[173]

Of course, Ramsey, as a physicist, would not necessarily ascertain the true value of the alleged contrary evidence, which the sindonologists obviously have presented to him via their own perspective. Ill-informed newspapers and television stations, rather than divulge the weakness of Jackson's hypothesis, began to noise abroad that Professor Ramsey had admitted that the radiocarbon examination of 1988 could be blatantly wrong.[174] Having already published an article that included a reappraisal of Ramsey,[175] a journalist for the Turin

[172] See also A. Long, "Attempt to Affect the Apparent 14C Age of Cotton by Scorching in a CO2 Environment," *Radiocarbon* 40, no. 1 (1998): 57–58.

[173] Cf. http://c14.arch.ox.ac.uk/embed.php?File=shroud.html.

[174] A collection of journalistic launches is in G. M. Rinaldi, "Sindone: Datazione da rifare?," *Scienza & Paranormale* 78 (2008): 64–70; and idem, "Caso Ramsey: Disinformazione a oltranza," *Scienza & Paranormale* 81 (2008): 56–61, also viewable at the site www.cicap.org/n/articolo.php?id=273769. On the same topic the BBC produced a documentary (*Shroud of Turin: Material Evidence*) constructed according to the common authenticist stance and directed by the same David Rolfe who had produced the 1978 film *The Silent Witness*.

[175] V. Sabadin, "Esami forse sbagliati: Sindone, giallo senza età," *La Stampa*, January 26, 2008, 37.

newspaper *La Stampa* wrote the professor requesting an interview; but Ramsey, having read what was attributed to him, reacted by condemning the newspaper article as "very irresponsible." He even asked for it to be removed from the Internet site of the newspaper and demanded a written correction, stating that that description did not represent his opinion in any way. He thus concluded: "I consider it very unlikely that the original radiocarbon measurements made in 1988 are incorrect in any significant way."[176] But this denial was not taken into account at all.

A more curious variant of the pollution theory suggests that the radiocarbon dating was performed on a sample that was repaired with more recent threads. This would force us to imagine that two widely recognized textile experts were unable to notice that they had cut a piece so repaired, despite the fact that they had observed the fabric carefully for hours; to distort the result by thirteen centuries the threads employed in the mending would have had to have been more numerous than the threads of the part to be mended. The idea, however, was ingenious and, in a sindonological congress held in the year 2000, was resurrected by a former Benedictine monk, Joseph Marino, and his wife, Sue Benford, a former nurse and a weight lifter, expert in crop circles, pyramids, and other oddities, who believed that she spoke with Saint John and Jesus Christ.[177] Marino, who, having abandoned the priesthood, felt invested by God with responsibility to study the Shroud, founded, along with Benford, a Spiritual Science Institute that features alternative medicine, care of the body through spiritual energies, and mystical-paranormal themes. Benford, for her part, claimed that one day in March of 1997, she heard the voice of Jesus, which invited her to turn on the television, which just then was airing a program on the Shroud; she later claimed that Christ instructed her with regard to the false result of the radiocarbon dating.[178] For the benefit of sindonology, the two spouses reproposed the mending theory, but this time as "invisible." They advanced the notion, based on the observation of certain photographs, that in

[176] Christopher Ramsey, e-mail message to Vittorio Sabadin, January 26, 2008.

[177] Cf. Marinelli and Russi, *Sindone 2000*, 57–64. Now see J. G. Marino, *Wrapped up in the Shroud: Chronicle of Passion* (St. Louis: Cradle, 2011).

[178] See the interview with Benford conducted by R. Boswell, "A Fresh Attempt to Prove Shroud of Turin Is No Fake," *Ottawa Citizen*, August 21, 2002, 1. It is useful to read Benford's own book *Strong Woman: Unshrouding the Secrets of the Soul* (Nashville: Source Books, 2002).

the modern era the Shroud had been patched so perfectly that not even textile experts could distinguish the new fabric from the old one. But the invisible mending, unfortunately for them, does not exist.[179]

Nevertheless the idea took hold, and today the notion has developed to the point of some believing that the piece subjected to C14 dating was modern and was attached to the rest of the Shroud in an "invisible manner," to cover a hole. At some point the theory won the favor of one of the STURP chemists, Ray Rogers, according to whom some fibers of the Shroud that he was able to examine, coming from the section of fabric that was radiocarbon dated, would not be chemically consistent with the other fibers that came from another point on the fabric, and they even would have been aptly colored with a dye. Rogers even developed a personal dating method on the basis of the kinetics of vanillin loss: as he was not able to detect vanillin on his Shroud fibers, he concluded that the fabric is between thirteen hundred and three thousand years old. This method was in turn immediately criticized, even by Jackson himself and Gonella.[180]

One of the fundamental problems with Rogers' study is that he wanted to demonstrate the dissimilarity between fibers coming from different points on the Shroud (points where the fibers were original and others where the fabric was presumably mended); but in his study he used samples that were not comparable, inasmuch as, not having access to the Shroud, he had to make do with using fibers extracted by different people at different times, some of which were altered, being immersed in an adhesive and then cleaned again with an organic solvent (xylene), while others were not. It is completely normal that fibers treated in different ways would yield different results during

[179] As far as being well made and hidden, mendings can be seen on the front with careful attention but above all on the back of the fabric (an example can be found in H. Farey, "Invisible Weaving," *British Society for the Turin Shroud Newsletter* 82 [2015]: 13–17). If they were truly "invisible," then we ought to deduce that while making the repair, the one doing the mending saw his work disappear before his eyes!

[180] R. N. Rogers, "Studies on the Radiocarbon Sample from the Shroud of Turin," *Thermochimica Acta* 425 (2005): 189–94; criticized by P. Berger, "'Suaire' de Turin: Comment Ray Rogers a trompé ses lecteurs," www.zetetique.ldh.org/suaire_rogers .html#1; and by G. M. Rinaldi, "Medievale era il rattoppo?," *Scienza & Paranormale* 59 (2005): 11–14; on the reaction of Jackson and other scientific papers, cf. A. Lombatti, "Indagine critica degli studi recenti sulla Sindone di Torino," *Scienza & Paranormale* 62 (2005): 30–41, also viewable at www.cicap.org/n/articolo.php?id=102011.

analyses. Moreover, in the only instrumental analysis reported (pyrolysis mass spectrometry), conducted on threads extracted from the radiocarbon-dated sample, Rogers seems to have ignored the presence of a contaminant clearly present on the surface of the fabric, erroneously attributing a diagnostic value to the indications caused by such contamination. This led other scholars to conclude that not only were Rogers' samples not comparable but also that if they perhaps could have been comparable, instrumental analysis could provide no evidence of a chemical difference between them.[181]

All this disappointed the experts of Turin, who continue to insist that there are no repairs on that part of the Shroud, whether visible or invisible. In 1997 the archbishop had pulled out of the safe the reserve sample, a piece cut from the larger sample extracted for the radiocarbon dating, and submitted it to the analysis of a textile expert. Also on that occasion no repair work was found.[182] The textile conservator

[181] The same journal in which Rogers' essay appeared also published a forceful criticism of his work: M. Bella, L. Garlaschelli, and R. Samperi, "There Is No Mass Spectrometry Evidence that the C14 Sample from the Shroud of Turin Comes from a Medieval Invisible Mending," *Thermochimica Acta* 617 (2015): 169–71; a response to this criticism came from M. Latendresse, "Comments on the Mass Spectrometry Analysis of a Sample of the Shroud of Turin by Bella et al.," *Thermochimica Acta* 624 (2016): 55–58; which was in turn answered in M. Bella, L. Garlaschelli, and R. Samperi, "Comments on the Analysis Interpretation by Rogers and Latendresse regarding Samples Coming from the Shroud of Turin," *Thermochimica Acta* 632 (2016): 52–55, which demonstrated that Latendresse's interpretation of the mass spectra was mistaken. Given the absence of instrumental details in the analysis that Rogers carried out, it is not possible to establish with certainty the nature of the contaminant; certain elements might lead one to suspect that it is a matter of oligomers of polyethylene from the plastic package in which the sample of the radiocarbon-dated section had been wrapped.

[182] Vercelli, *Sindone nella sua struttura tessile*. Recently a Portuguese sindonologist in one of his books cited, without providing the source, phrases of Umberto II of Savoy that would have been heard by the writer John Mathias Haffert during an interview held in Fatima in 1967. Umberto would have talked about the House of Savoy's practice of detaching pieces of the Shroud to make relics and would have remembered that the cloth was periodically mended in the damaged edges. The author is a collector of relics and claims to be in possession of some relic belonging to the House of Savoy that would contain some fragment of the Shroud (C. Evaristo, *The Untold Story of the Holy Shroud* [Fatima: Regina Mundi Press, 2011], 110, 217–18, 268–88). The book is unreliable, full of errors, and naive; I do not even know how accurately the author has reported the words of Haffert, who in turn interviewed Umberto. However, the argument is irrelevant, because the piece cut for dating was

(an authenticist) who worked on the Shroud in 2002 has affirmed that "there is no doubt that the Shroud does not contain any reweaving" and that regardless "this process will always be recognizable as mending and in any case visible on the reverse of the fabric."[183] To eliminate any doubt, the University of Arizona in 2010 reexamined a trace of fabric leftover from the radiocarbon dating in 1988, concluding:

> We find no evidence for any coatings or dyeing of the linen. . . . Our sample was taken from the main part of the shroud. There is no evidence to the contrary. We find no evidence to support the contention that the 14C samples actually used for measurements are dyed, treated, or otherwise manipulated. Hence, we find no reason to dispute the original 14C measurements.[184]

Among the various attempts to invalidate the radiocarbon procedure, there is also one based on an examination of the statistical analysis by the laboratories that carried out the C14 tests; it is a less common objection, as it is mathematically complex, but this would also prove to be inconclusive, as "it seems evident that the sindonologists have not understood what the methods of statistical analysis used were."[185]

Recently, some sindonologists have maintained that certain "raw data" determined by laboratories and kept secret until now have revealed problems with the dating of the Shroud.[186] In fact, these dates have been in circulation for some time now and do not pose any problem that might invalidate the medieval date. The three laboratories obtained twelve results for the date of the Shroud's fabric, of which seven are within fifty years of the mean, another four are within one hundred years, and only one is scarcely over one hundred years from the mean. This outline is clearly compatible with the level

---

not on a margin but some centimeters further in, where there were no mendings. The mendings that are truly there are easily identified even by the naked eye.

183 Flury-Lemberg, *Sindone 2002*, 60.

184 R. A. Freer-Waters and A. J. T. Jull, "Investigating a Dated Piece of the Shroud of Turin," *Radiocarbon* 52, no. 4 (2010): 1526.

185 The topic was put back in play by Tosatti, *Inchiesta sulla Sindone*. Gian Marco Rinaldi in 2012 dedicated a sizeable study to the question: "La statistica della datazione della Sindone," http://sindone.weebly.com/uploads/1/2/2/0/1220953/nature_statistica.pdf.

186 T. Casabianca et al., "Radiocarbon Dating of the Turin Shroud: New Evidence from Raw Data," *Archaeometry* 61, no. 5 (2019): 1223–31.

of precision that one would expect of tests conducted in the 1980s, a time when dating using AMS had been in use for only a few years. Some sindonologists have subjected these twelve results to statistical tests of homogeneity, but even if they do not pass such a test, that does not mean that the dating is mistaken, but at most that the confidence interval may be widened so that the change to the final result is negligible. This issue is completely irrelevant in any case, because the twelve results are concentrated at a period around AD 1300 and not around AD 30, as the sindonologists would like.

It is interesting to note that, as Dominican Father Jean-Michel Maldamé wrote, "the disputes over the carbon 14 dating do not come from individuals who are competent in the subject of dating."[187] The scientific journals that concern themselves with this technology, *Radiocarbon* being preeminent among them all, would certainly be interested in publishing some serious studies on the matter, if any existed. Rather, a publication concerned with the use of radiocarbon in archaeology, released in updated form in 2014, dedicates an entire chapter to the dating of the Shroud and to the various criticisms put forth by sindonologists to discredit it. The conclusion states:

> For those whose interest in the Shroud is dominated by a belief in its religious or devotional function, it is virtually certain that any scientifically based evidence, including any additional 14C-based data, would not be compelling—unless, of course, it confirmed their beliefs.[188]

Some believe, I think optimistically, that to put all objections to rest it would be sufficient to take other samples or use the reserve sample and repeat the radiocarbon dating (which in fact could be done at any time and with insignificant expense). With regard to this possibility, there is a declaration that seems to me particularly alarming. Bishop Marcelo Sánchez Sorondo, chancellor of the Pontifical Academy of Sciences, explained that

> in order to do something scientific, another test should be carried out, but since the institutions that carry out these tests are rather

[187] J.-M. Maldamé, "À propos du Linceul de Turin," *Connaître: Revue éditée par l'Association Foi et Culture Scientifique* 11 (1999): 64.

[188] R. E. Taylor and O. Bar-Yosef, *Radiocarbon Dating: An Archaeological Perspective*, 2nd ed. (Walnut Creek: Left Coast, 2014), 169.

> anticlerical, the PAS currently thinks that it would not be prudent to reopen the matter until other scientific identification systems are devised.[189]

Such a statement would be acceptable if it were just the personal opinion of a bishop, whose qualifications are theological rather than scientific. The problem is that Bishop Sánchez Sorondo is a high Vatican authority who, in 2014, seemed to believe that all the C14 laboratories in the world (more than fifty with the method of AMS, about one hundred with the method of beta-counting) are managed by anticlerical—therefore, in his view, automatically dishonest—technicians ready to fake a relic test to spite the Church. This means that the movement of certain Catholic factions toward apologetic and conspiracist, and therefore antiscientific, positions has waxed more than slightly. Msgr. Sánchez Sorondo, however, has nothing to worry about, because even a new radiocarbon dating that provided a medieval result would probably be ignored like the previous one; in fact there is the example of the Sudarium of Oviedo, which already has been dated to the Middle Ages four times but continues to be presented as authentic by Spanish sindonologists, with growing support from the local ecclesiastical authority. The tunic of Argenteuil has been C14 dated twice to the Middle Ages, but there are sindonologists who nonetheless consider it authentic, and the French Church in recent years has been focusing renewed attention on it; some do the same with the *titulus crucis* of Rome, thrice dated to the Middle Ages.[190] One must ask, of course, why radiocarbon never seems "to work" when certain ancient relics are dated.

The final possibility raised against C14 dating falls within the sphere of the supernatural. As the radiocarbon present in the Shroud is excessive relative to the hopes of sindonologists, a German chemist, Eberhard Lindner, explained at the 1990 sindonology convention that the resurrection of Christ caused an emission of neutrons that

[189] M. Sánchez Sorondo, letter dated January 28, 2014, to Hugh Farey, director of the *Newsletter of the British Society for the Turin Shroud*, which he himself published on the Internet.

[190] Cf. A. Marion and G. Lucotte, *Le linceul de Turin et la tunique d'Argenteuil* (Paris: Presses de la Renaissance, 2006); and M. L. Rigato, *Il titolo della croce di Gesù* (Rome: Pontificia Università Gregoriana, 2003). Essential reading for the *titulus* is A. Pontani, "Note sull'esegesi e l'iconografia del *titulus crucis*," *Aevum* 77 (2003): 137–86.

enriched the Shroud with radioactive isotope C14.[191] The list of all those who have queued up to support the hypothesis of the neutron emission is too long to include here; I mention only the priest and biophysicist Jean-Baptiste Rinaudo and the attorney Mark Antonacci.[192] A very economical solution proposed by the former—and one must bear in mind the longstanding scholastic admonition that *non sunt multiplicanda miracula sine necessitate* ("miracles must not be multiplied unnecessarily")—advances the notion that the resurrection involved a nuclear reaction that produced not only neutrons capable of distorting radiocarbon measurements but also protons capable of creating the image on the sheet. According to Antonacci, it would be necessary to search the Shroud for the isotopes chlorine-36 and calcium-41, which would be proof of the occurrence of neutron irradiation. In the meantime Mario Moroni carried out tests in a laboratory by irradiating different fabrics with very high doses of neutrons and raising the content of carbon 14 in the fabrics to hundreds of times the original.[193] On one occasion he came to a gross exaggeration: with a cloth of 2000 BC he actually obtained a date forty-six thousand years in the future, with the effect, however, of damaging the instruments of the radiocarbon dating laboratory, polluting it with too many carbon 14 atoms coming from his simulated resurrections.

Miraculous explanations can be constructed with scientific jargon, but they have no chance of being scientifically tested (as there is no availability of bodies that have come to life from the dead and emit protons or neutrons). They are, however, extremely convenient because they are able to solve any problem without having to submit to the laws of nature. Thus the sindonologist would seem always to have the advantage over the serious scientist, who would never resort to supernatural explanations.

[191] The idea had already occurred to T. Phillips, "Shroud Irradiated with Neutrons?," *Nature* 337 (1989): 594.

[192] M. Antonacci, *The Resurrection of the Shroud* (New York: Evans, 2000); idem, *Test the Shroud: At the Atomic and Molecular Levels* (Ashland: Forefront, 2017); Rinaudo and Gavach, *Linceul de Jésus enfin authentifié?*

[193] The conclusions of years of experiments were presented at the Ohio Sindonology Convention in 2008: F. Barbesino and M. Moroni, "Effects of Neutron Irradiation on Linen Fibres and Consequences for a Radiocarbon Dating," www.ohioshroudconference.com/papers/p03.pdf.

5.4. A Revival in the Third Millennium

5.4.1 New Fire and New Exhibitions

The decade after 1988 was decisive for the future of the Shroud. At the end of the period of radiocarbon dating, which had been undertaken at the behest of the sindonologists themselves and the ecclesiastical authorities, three different possibilities presented themselves: first, there could have been an abandonment of the veneration of the Shroud; second, the Shroud could have been preserved for veneration in a mitigated form, more focused on the value of the image as an icon of the passion, along the lines advanced by Cardinal Ballestrero; and, third, a counterattack and defense of authenticity could have ensued, to the bitter end. Msgr. Victor Saxer, rector of the Pontifical Institute of Christian Archaeology and president of the Pontifical Committee for Historical Sciences, sought to guide the Church toward the first option:

> To bring the matter to a head quickly and dispense with any nostalgia, the ecclesiastical authorities should have the courage to make a decision about the Shroud of Turin such as had been made for that of Cadouin: to remove it forever from the veneration of the faithful. But they often excel more in the art of compromise.[194]

At the time, it would probably not have been too traumatic an event for the faithful, since devotion toward the Shroud was substantially enacted on the occasion of exhibitions. Though it was decided officially to take the path of "compromise," in practice the two archbishops who were Ballestrero's successors, Giovanni Saldarini and Severino Poletto, decided to favor the faction that declared the radiocarbon examinations invalid and accorded to the sindonologists their full confidence. This attitude was also passed on to the lower clergy and to the Catholic-inspired systems of information, with the tendency to insist on authenticity. Thus the same situation that had provoked the reaction of the bishop Pierre d'Arcis six hundred years earlier arose again: although "in public it is not claimed to be the true Shroud of Christ, nevertheless in private it is asserted and proclaimed, and so it is believed by many." At that time (1990s), a well-known forensic pathologist, Pierluigi Baima Bollone, who was then at the

[194] Saxer, "Suaire de Turin," 50.

helm of the International Center of Sindonology of Turin, published a book that managed to mix traditional authenticist arguments with most of the criticisms of radiocarbon, irrespective of such criticism's source. Thus a new literary genre was born intended to discredit C14 dating.[195] The voice of the sindonologists in Italy was amplified in the newspapers, especially by Vittorio Messori and Orazio Petrosillo. Their meeting with Emanuela Marinelli generated the idea for a book intended for the general public. That book could be considered the summative repository of groundless accusations addressing the results of the radiocarbon dating.[196] Marinelli would become one of the most famous sindonologists in the world, publishing about twenty propagandistic books in various languages (the books are not very reliable and are often recopied one from another)[197] and holding more than three thousand conferences, especially in religious and parish contexts. In the meantime, attempts to invalidate radiocarbon dating were variously multiplied. For example, it was

[195] P. Baima Bollone, *Sindone o no* (Turin: SEI, 1990); all subsequent sindological publications are of a similar ilk, rarely offering any extra caution: Centini, *Breve storia della Sindone*, 32–49; Iannone, *Mystery of the Shroud of Turin*, 159–75; A. Cherpillod and S. Mouraviev, *Apologie pour le Suaire de Turin par deux scientifiques non croyants* (Paris: Myrmekia, 1998), 67–82; Antonacci, *Resurrection of the Shroud*, 155–210; Fanti, *Sindone*, 166–91; B. Barberis and M. Boccaletti, *Il "caso Sindone" non è chiuso* (Cinisello Balsamo: San Paolo, 2010), 190–95; Baima Bollone, *Sindone: Storia e scienza*, 275–302; D. de Matteis and A. P. Bramanti, *Sacra Sindone* (San Giorgio Jonico: Servi della Sofferenza, 2010), 141–78. Almost every argument can be found among these: possible fraud, wrong weights, polluted area, carbon growth, mending, and even the bioplastics and the lies of the Russians treated as if they were valid theories. The journalistic authors of books on the subject recycle the same arguments, handling them with superficiality and lack of competence, so as to make them even worse: for example, Tosatti, *Inchiesta sulla Sindone*; and A. Tornielli, *Sindone: Inchiesta sul mistero* (Milan: Gribaudi, 2010).

[196] O. Petrosillo and E. Marinelli, *La Sindone: Un enigma alla prova della scienza* (Milan: Rizzoli, 1998) (English translation: *The Enigma of the Shroud: A Challenge to Science* [San Gwann: Publishers Enterprises Group, 1996]); see also E. Marinelli, *La Sindone: Testimone di una presenza* (Cinisello Balsamo: San Paolo, 2010), 153–211. Similar considerations apply to a book by the pediatrician Sebastiano Rodante, the Sicilian delegate to the Turin International Center of Sindonology, *La scienza convalida la Sindone: Errata la datazione medievale*, 2nd ed. (Milan: Massimo, 1997); and to a pamphlet of F. Barbesino and M. Moroni, *L'ordalia del carbonio 14* (Pessano: Mimep-Docete, 1995).

[197] See, for example, the analysis in A. Nicolotti, "Novità sindoniche riciclate," *Historia magistra: Rivista di storia critica* 23 (2017): 153–67.

again proposed that writings and coins from the time of Pontius Pilate—first only one coin, then two, then three—were visible in the photographs of the Shroud; in reality, these do not exist and are not visible. The recent use of electronic enhancements could lead the reader to believe that the pareidolic interpretation of the marks on the Shroud has a scientific character; however, by examining both the photographs, whether real or manipulated with a computer, and the various identifications of figures, letters, and marks put forth by sindonologists, which change continuously and contradict each other, we realize that *in every case* it is a matter of fantasies, if not of willful manipulation of the evidence.[198]

Gonella for several years found himself in the difficult situation of wanting simultaneously to defend Cardinal Ballestrero, himself, his colleagues, and the value of the results of the experiments. In a declaration to the press he stated:

> It is only they, the so-called "sindonologists," who lash out against C14. In the scientific, physical, chemical fields, there is no one who has the least doubt. Nor do I. The Shroud dates back to the Middle Ages.[199]

[198] Initially, only one coin was identified on the eye of the man on the Shroud, on the right eye, as reported by the Jesuit Francis Filas in 1979, while a coin on the left eye was seen very slightly; but that theory had not even succeeded in convincing the STURP technicians. On July 8, 1996, during an episode of the television program *Mixer*, Pierluigi Baima Bollone and Nello Balossino announced that they had discovered another coin, no longer on the left eye, but on the left eyebrow. On the question of the coins I recommend, after the groundbreaking study by Gramaglia, *Ultime "scoperte" sulla Sindone*, 41–52, the valuable work of G. M. Rinaldi, "La farsa delle monetine sugli occhi," *Scienza & Paranormale* 81 (2008): 28–47, which can also be found at www.cicap.org/n/articolo.php?id=273767, and from which one can conclude that the presumed coins are actually a "farce." It must be said that in recent years, recourse to discoveries of writings and coins has diminished, in part because the number has increased of individuals who see new and unusual things, such as, for example, the signature of Giotto, which comes with the risk of providing arguments against authenticity (L. Buso, *Giotto firmò la Sacra Sindone* [Casella d'Asolo: Acelum, 2011]). On pareidolia in general, and also with respect to the Shroud: R. G. Capuano, *Bizzarre illusioni* (Milan: Mimesis, 2011); on pareidolia in the religious sphere, see J. Nickell, "Rorschach Icons," *Skeptical Inquirer* 28, no. 6 (2004): 15–17.

[199] L. Gonella, "Così ho riaperto il giallo della Sindone," interview by G. Bazoli, *Epoca* 19 (July 1996, 30).

The expert in ancient fabrics Gabriel Vial, who was among those present at the extraction of the fabric samples, had already reached the conclusion, based on textile considerations unrelated to radiocarbon, that the Shroud should be dated to the Middle Ages; yet he quickly ducked out of the controversy. The experts from the C14 laboratories were overwhelmed with questions and protests, which seemed to them to be specious, groundless, or amateurish; they declined all invitations to sindonological conferences, which only strengthened the sindonologists' conviction that they had something to hide. They became convinced that the sindonologists were a guild of irreducible fanatics and thus stopped acknowledging them.

Once the work was done, they returned to their occupations and almost never concerned themselves with the topic. Anyone outside the sphere of sindonology who might have been curious lost interest in the object after it was given a medieval date. In any case, it is improbable that a respected scientist would start to discuss an object that no one is able to see. Among the few exceptions are scientists belonging to some associations that concern themselves with examining claims about the paranormal, who are not so much interested in the Shroud itself as the pseudoscientific claims that pertain to it.

The interdisciplinary study project of STURP, temporarily shelved at the time of the radiocarbon dating, was now definitively discarded. The same happened with all the other projects that, at the time and even later, were presented by various sindonological agencies and organizations. Despite certain statements by the archbishops who succeeded Ballestrero, from then on, the ecclesiastical authorities no longer authorized any type of research that was not intended solely for the preservation of the artifact. Access to the Shroud, to its photographs, and to the extracted fragments was shut down. Only certain Turinese and a few others have periodically had the opportunity, granted them by the curator for various reasons, of access to the fabric. Such selective access has fomented tensions, clashes, and envy among the sindonological associations, problems that have only increased in the last few years.

It should be noted that the factions in the various camps of sindonology are more complex than it is possible to describe here. When I use the expression "the sindonologists" (affectionately known as "Shroudies"), it is obvious that I do not mean to refer to any particular individual among them, but I am rather speaking generally.

One must keep in mind that under the umbrella of sindonology there are different ideas—sometimes irreconcilable—and there are indeed many people on opposite sides. All this, for the nonspecialist, however, can be distilled into a consistently coherent position, summarized thus: the Shroud is a special object that cannot be duplicated, and it is practically impossible that it is not authentic. Aside from their interest in the religious and devotional aspects of the relic, almost all the activity of the sindonologists is oriented toward disseminating knowledge of the Shroud and finding arguments in favor of its authenticity or at least toward minimizing those that oppose it. Of course, some scholars (albeit a minority) show a greater capacity to be reasonable than others, as they are aware of the unbalanced environment in which they are operating and also find the label "sindonologist" unattractive. Unfortunately, however, these distinctions are not readily apparent to the external observer, for there is a certain tendency within sindonology itself to tolerate even rather extreme positions when they contribute to the common cause. Thus, it is almost impossible to make distinctions within the field of sindonology. Therefore, the impression is that all sindonology falls entirely into the category of pseudoscience, influenced as it is by a predetermined agenda, and that those involved make no effort to disassociate themselves from the pseudoscience.

It is now time to turn our attention back to the Turin cathedral. At the beginning of the nineties it became very apparent that the Guarini chapel needed a restoration that could no longer be deferred. It could no longer be visited beginning on May 4, 1990. To allow for the work to be carried out conveniently, on February 24, 1993, the relic box was temporarily moved to a lower position, behind the main altar of the cathedral. A completely transparent case was built for the occasion: this was a glass case at the center of which was the precious relic's casket, held up and protected by armored glass.[200]

On the evening of April 11, 1997, when the restoration then underway had come to a close, due to an electrical system not built according to the legal code on the building site, a short circuit gave rise to a slow fire, which itself was fed by the flammable material and

[200] Cf. A. Bruno, "Il viaggio più breve della Sindone," *Sindon* 5–6 (1993): 7–14, 66–74; G. Moretto, "La S. Sindone cambia provvisoriamente sede," *Sindon* 5–6 (1993): 15–20.

the wooden scaffolding in the chapel. When the fire alarm system went off, a custodian made a superficial check and did not notice the fire, which, if caught at that time, could have easily been controlled. After an hour, the flames that had been allowed to grow unchecked exploded ferociously and became visible outside. Firefighters, having assembled straightaway, verified the extreme gravity of the situation and planned a swift intervention to rescue of the Shroud. Failing to activate the mechanism to open the glass of the Shroud's case, they decided to break the panes by hitting them with a bat. The Shroud was recovered at approximately 1:15 am, taken into possession by the state police, and whisked away to safety; after its integrity had been verified, it was taken and hidden somewhere outside the city, where it remained until April 15 of the following year. During the hours and days to follow, the shutdown and the securing of the unsafe chapel was undertaken.[201]

At that time, conjectures ran rampant. Some thought the fire to have been malicious, set by terrorists. Others regarded it as an attack. Others suggested a satanic ritual, recalling some strange events that had occurred in 1972, when someone had repeatedly slipped into the Chapel of the Shroud by passing through the roof, leaving curious traces. Already at the time there had been certain fanciful allegations, such as that there had been encrypted warnings or black magic rituals, but in the end only a deranged person was taken into custody.[202] At the time a novel was even written based on the events, and the same thing happened in the case of the fire.[203] But the reality was more prosaic: simple negligence. In 2004, those responsible for restoration operations were convicted, as was a

[201] A precise technical report and some testimonies are found in L. Vidal and A. Marangoni, *The Fire and the Holy Shroud: The Last Fire* (Bologna: Timeo, 2000).

[202] Beyond the journal articles of that period—among them are V. Messori, "Riti di magia nera?," *Stampa Sera*, December 4, 1972, 3; G. Bensi, "È un maniaco acrobata il 'nemico' della Sindone," *La Domenica del Corriere*, November 7, 1972, 33–35; idem, "Volevo bruciare la Sacra Sindone perche Gesù non mi aiuta," *Gazzetta del Popolo*, January 2, 1973, 4—see "Realtà e fantasia negli avvenimenti alla cappella della S. Sindone," *Sindon* 17 (1973): 42–43.

[203] I. de Rolandis, *Attacco alla Sindone* (Turin: SEI, 1978); L. Mancinelli, *Attentato alla Sindone* (Turin: Einaudi, 2000). My favorite novel on the Shroud, in which there is an attempt to clone Christ from the blood of a thread of the Shroud stolen after the fire, is L. Foster and E. Lupieri's *Il patto: Un thriller teologico* (Reggio Emilia: Diabasis, 2005).

custodian; the retrial, stemming from an appeal, came to naught because it extended beyond the statute of limitations.[204]

The rescue of the Shroud from the fire of 1532 had been described as having miraculous features, and it is said that toward the end of the sixteenth century, a thunderbolt, generated by demonic force, had fallen near the altar of the Shroud in Turin but had left the relic unharmed.[205] So also in the fire of 1997, divine intervention is invoked, thanks to which a courageous fireman summoned the strength to smash the bulletproof glass plates with a bat. Mario Trematore, who played a role in breaking the case and saving the relic, from that day has had dozens of interviews, all of them rife with supernatural details.[206]

The fire also aroused great concerns because in 1995 it had already been decided to offer two new exhibitions: one in 1998, celebrating the sixteen hundredth anniversary of the Council of Turin, the five hundredth anniversary of the consecration of the cathedral of Turin, and the centennial of the first photo taken by Secondo Pia; and one in 2000, on the occasion of the Holy Year.

At the general assembly of the Episcopal Conference of Italy in May of 1996, Cardinal Saldarini, archbishop of Turin, delivered to the other Italian bishops a file with information on the future exhibition. As for the historical and scientific side of things, the texts had been written by sindonologists who presented the facts in their own way: a sindonic image not made by human hands, pollens, Roman coins,

[204] Cf. M. Ponte, "Processo senza colpevoli," *La Repubblica–Torino*, April 12, 2007, 2.

[205] So told the canonical theologian Giacomo Baldesano; cf. Ricuperati, *Storia di Torino*, 3:519–20.

[206] See, for example, M. Trematore, "È toccato proprio a me salvare la Sindone dal fuoco," in *Grande libro della Sindone*, 113–16; and "Saving the Shroud," in *The Shroud of Turin: Unraveling the Mystery; Proceedings of the 1998 Dallas Symposium*, ed. M. Minor (Alexander: Alexander Books, 1998), 363–68, where Trematore recounts the emotions he felt and that he was persuaded that the Shroud changed his life. In other subsequent papers he has argued that without a celestial help it would not have been possible to break the same glass and that it would have withstood, some moments before, the attempts made with a clamp of "12 tons of breaking thrust"; then he recounts that during the journey to the outside of the cathedral he did not feel the weight of the case or the floor under his feet, and that he heard the cry of a child coming out of the case. One should not forget that there were a dozen firefighters that night who took turns at trying to break the glass.

human blood, and so on. The results of radiocarbon dating, it was affirmed, "are today called into question within the same scientific community."[207] The same archbishop inaugurated a magazine with information on the Shroud, which was released in a few issues and presented the ideas of some sindonologists as if they were established fact.[208] Some small volumes written by sindonologists connected to the Turin Center of Sindonology were recommended to and distributed by the Diocesan Committee for Exhibition.[209] In practice the new archbishop had definitively abandoned the impartial air of his two predecessors, choosing to maintain and promote, with all the authority and means at his disposal, the authenticist line of sindonology. His two successors would continue to do so as well, in increasing measure. There have been few priests since then who have dared to take a public position against authenticity: among these few are Pier Angelo Gramaglia, Jean-Michel Maldamé, and Francesco Pieri, all of whom are university professors on theological faculties; one is even a member of the Pontifical Academy of Sciences.[210]

After the fire, nothing in the program was changed, since the movements necessary for the exhibition would not have affected the rooms damaged by the fire: the first exhibition took place between April 18 and June 14, 1998, twenty years after the previous one. Among the novelties of that year, a noteworthy one was the introduction of a convenient gratis reservation system for those who wished to venerate the Shroud, which afforded an effective regulation of the flow of traffic into the cathedral. Along the route of approach for visitors to the relic a moment of "pre-reading" was arranged that consisted of the projection of a film that guided the interpretation of the visible signs on the Shroud. Over the course of the fifty-eight days in the cathedral, some 2.4 million pilgrims filed in (among them the highest authorities of the Italian state). Pope John Paul II was able to

207 *Ostensione Sindone: Comunicazione alla Conferenza Episcopale Italiana*, enclosure 4b.

208 *Informa Sindone*, supplement to the diocese's weekly publication, *La voce del popolo*.

209 The series, in seven volumes, is entitled *La Sindone di Torino*.

210 J.-M. Maldamé, "Encore le Saint Suaire de Turin," *Bulletin de littérature ecclésiastique* 97 (1996): 280–87; idem, *Que penser de . . . ? Le Saint Suaire* (Namour: Éditions Fidélité, 1997); F. Pieri, "La Sindone di Torino e il suo culto," *Vetera Christianorum* 53 (2016): 205–19. I provided the bibliography on Gramaglia below.

venerate the cloth during a private exhibition on his first visit to Turin on April 13, 1980; he returned for the exhibition, and in his homily for the Shroud offered the fortuitous expression "challenge to our intelligence." So far as concerns authenticity, according to the pope:

> Since it is not a matter of faith, the Church has no specific competence to pronounce on these questions. She entrusts to scientists the task of continuing to investigate, so that satisfactory answers may be found to the questions connected with this Sheet, which, according to tradition, wrapped the body of our Redeemer after he had been taken down from the cross. The Church urges that the Shroud be studied without pre-established positions that take for granted results that are not such; she invites them to act with interior freedom and attentive respect for both scientific methodology and the sensibilities of believers.[211]

The pontifical exhortation to face the study of the Shroud has not been followed, because the relic was never again made available to scholars. But, following the words of the pope, who could the scientists deserving to "find satisfactory answers" be? If one were to scroll through the list of participants in the international sindonology conference that was celebrated that year in Turin, entitled "Shroud and Science," there would be no hope of finding such scholars.[212] Among those at the conference was one Eberhard Lindner, who had theories on the physics and chemistry of the resurrection. There was room for miraculous flashes of light, and for the theory of protons and neutrons, for describing radiation with heating components consisting of infrared and microwaves that left traces on the Shroud, for explaining how the body of Jesus had emitted X-rays from within and electric discharges from its surface. The American psychiatrist Alan Whanger came to describe what he saw on the photographs of the Shroud: flowers and coins from the era of Pontius Pilate, Hebrew amulets, a nail, a spear, a crown of thorns, a sponge, a cloak, a pair

[211] John Paul II, "Celebration of the Word and Veneration of the Shroud" (homily, May 24, 1998).

[212] Acts published by P. Baima Bollone, M. Lazzero, and C. Marino, eds., *Sindone e scienza: Bilanci e programmi alle soglie del terzo millennio*, pro manuscripto. Some interesting things that do not appear in the proceedings are described by R. Morgan, "The 3rd International Shroud Congress, Turin," *Shroud News* 108 (1998): 2–21; 109 (1998): 2–23; 110 (1998): 2–23.

of tongs, and two Roman flagella.[213] The historiographic theories related to the Mandylion of Edessa, the Mozarabic liturgy, the Holy Grail, and so on were reintroduced. There was also reference to other relics, such as the Veil of Manoppello, a modern painting of the face of Christ made on linen (and not, as it is said, on sea byssus), that had been recently transformed into a miraculous image similar to that of the Shroud, triggering a competition over which of the two was more significant and extraordinary but meeting considerable resistance from more "orthodox" sindonologists.[214] Garza-Valdés, the inventor of the bioplastic coatings, observed under a microscope the crust of blood supplied to him by Riggi. Based on that, Garza-Valdés said that he had been able to establish that Jesus' cross was made of rough, unfinished oak wood. The fact that the conference was organized by the Confraternity of the Holy Shroud and by its offshoot, the International Center of Sindonology, with the blessing of the cardinal of Turin (and inaugurated in the presence of the president of the republic and the rector of the university), suggests that for them this was the "science" to which the pope referred, under the aegis of which the Shroud should be studied.[215]

The exhibition organized two years later, in the year of the Jubilee, was the longest of the century, as it lasted for seventy-two days (from August 12 to October 22, 2000) and yielded over one million visitors.

213 It has all been described quite well in their book: Whanger and Whanger, *Shroud of Turin*.

214 This veil, of which almost nothing was known until a few years ago, since it was rediscovered by the Jesuit Heinrich Pfeiffer (the champion of the iconographic "sindonocentrism" of which I have already spoken) has become the subject of an incredible and growing propaganda. According to some, the veil should even outclass the Shroud, because it would contain the image of the Christ irradiated at the moment at which he is resurrected. On the birth of the interest in the object, see G. M. Rinaldi, "Il Velo di Manoppello," *Scienza & Paranormale* 62 (2005): 20–29; idem, "La leggenda del colore che non c'era," *Scienza & Paranormale* 74 (2007): 62–64; idem, "Leggende di Manoppello," *Scienza & Paranormale* 75 (2007): 56–63. The most bizarre theories are in S. Gaeta, *L'altra Sindone* (Milan: Mondadori, 2005); idem, *L'enigma del volto di Gesù* (Milan: Rizzoli, 2010); P. Badde, *La seconda Sindone* (Rome: Newton Compton, 2007). To see how some sindonologists who believe in the Shroud attempt to discredit the Veil of Manoppello, see some contributions in K. Dietz et al., *Das Christudbild*; I have made a summary of them in Nicolotti, "Nuovi studi sulle immagini," 299–350.

215 In the same year, another conference was held in Dallas, and one was held in Nice in 1997: Minor, *Shroud of Turin*; and *Acheiropoietos*.

This time, along the access path to the Shroud, three stations intended for meditative pauses were installed, dedicated respectively to the coming of Jesus to Jerusalem, his suffering, and his resurrection. This exhibition was accompanied by two sindonological congresses, one in Turin and the other in Orvieto; four cardinals and six bishops sat on the honorary committee of Orvieto.[216] In Turin, where the quality of the scholarly presentations was, on average, superior, two experts in radiocarbon dating, Robert Otlet and Jacques Évin, presented lectures at the conference. The opinion of Évin was particularly significant, because he had been long convinced of the authenticity of the Shroud; for this reason he had also been allowed to be present for the collection of samples in 1988, as director of the radiocarbon laboratory at the University of Lyon and a member of the French sindonological organization CIELT (Centre International d'Études sur le Linceul de Turin). Once the results suggesting a medieval date had been published, Évin examined them. Though he accepted those results reluctantly, he did so without casting doubt upon them, seeking in vain to convince the other members of CIELT. At the Turin conference he once again revealed his reasons, but his presentation was followed by that of the Russian counterfeiter Andrey Ivanov, the colleague of the counterfeiter Kouznetsov, who had obviously reached opposite conclusions.

In the first days of November a new campaign for photographing the Shroud was undertaken.[217] It even included an electronic scan of some portions of the front side and of numerous portions of the back, achieved by inserting a scanner between the relic and the Holland cloth. It was concluded that on the back of the fabric the image of the man is not visible.[218] The photographs and scans in their original

[216] Cf. S. Scannerini and P. Savarino, eds., *The Turin Shroud: Past, Present and Future: International Scientific Symposium* (Cantalupa: Effatà, 2000); Marinelli and Russi, *Sindone 2000.*

[217] That is, by Gian Carlo Durante, who on June 25, 1997, had taken some color photographs in the Most Holy Shroud Church, where the Shroud was moved for a single day from the place where it was kept starting from the night of the fire: cf. B. Barberis, "La prima ostensione della Sindone nella chiesa del SS. Sudario," *Sindon* 11 (1999): 75–78.

[218] A description of the exhibitions of 1998 and 2000 and of the photographs of the cloth: G. M. Zaccone, ed., *The Two Faces of the Shroud: Pilgrims and Scientists Searching for a Face* (Turin: ODPF, 2001). The operations were directed by Paolo Soardo.

definition remain inexplicably inaccessible to those who request them for study and research purposes.

5.4.2 The Shroud under Inert Gas, the 2002 Restoration, New Photographs, and Skeptics

Beginning in 1992, the Shroud's custodian expressed his wish for the institution of a commission to be responsible for identifying the clearest means for optimal preservation of the fabric. From 1998 on, the custom of preserving the Shroud in a roll on a cylindrical wooden pole that was covered with cloth was discontinued, as that system was shown to be inappropriate and to have caused folds on the fabric hazardous to its preservation. The relic, which had been removed from the baroque altar of Antonio Bertola in 1993, now found its definitive resting place in a space below the royal tribunal, an eighteenth-century structure located on the left wing of the transept of the cathedral. Since the turn of the millennium the Shroud has been preserved in a horizontal and extended position in an airtight case of light aeronautical alloy whose upper face consists of multilayered glass.[219] Preservation under inert gas (argon) in electronically controlled climatic conditions serves to protect the Shroud from all manner of pollution and to slow down, to the extent possible, the natural process of the yellowing of the linen, and so prevents the faint image of the man from becoming less distinguishable from its background.

During the months of June and July 2002 the Shroud was subjected to a significant restoration. The purpose was to free the cloth from all the other fabrics and linens that surrounded and enveloped it, including the Holland cloth on which it was fixed, as well as all the patches and the repairs that had been added over the centuries since 1532. With all the fabrics removed, using a small aspirator with filters and tweezers, someone even proceeded to remove the free material that had accumulated in certain points and that was found loosely attached to the edges of the burned areas. Microscopic and photographic studies were then performed, as were scans and fluorescent photographic (UV-Vis) surveys; recordings of Raman, UV-Vis, and reflectance spectra; and sample extractions done by suction and

[219] Cf. P. Savarino, "New Conservation Techniques," in Zaccone, *Two Faces of the Shroud*, 143–48.

adhesive tape. Some other bits of thread were also extracted. The material removed and the results of the measurements were delivered to the archbishop of Turin, intended eventually to be made available for further research (something that has not yet happened, as far as we know, and if it has happened, we do not know the results). The careful process of restoration and its unpublished results were entirely managed by the Turin commission.[220]

The non-Turin sindonologists did not know anything about it and were disconcerted to learn of it after the fact. Relations between the various "schools" of sindonology were already tense: a few years earlier, Emanuela Marinelli, one of the most famous sindonologists operating in Rome, had complained about what she perceived as a "disgraceful personalism of those who consider themselves masters of the Shroud and make it stand for self-promotion while they try to silence, even with denigration and slander, those who are unwilling to submit to their Stalinist methods."[221] Soon reactions to news of the restoration turned up in the newspapers, starting in Rome.[222] The question of restoration also exposed the tensions of previous years. There were those who for some time blamed the International Center of Sindonology of Turin for hindering the other sindonologists and of perhaps not being sufficiently explicit in the support of the case of authenticity (Baima Bollone could be considered exempt from such an accusation; in 2002, however, he was replaced as the director of the Center by Bruno Barberis).

The accusations and the polemics reached unheard-of levels, because some claimed that the long, thoughtful restoration had been improvised, self-managed, amateurish, and harmful to the Shroud. In the opinion of those critics, it seemed clear that the process had been decided upon by a small group with no title or claim to do so; these critics felt slighted because they had not been consulted, though they thought themselves equally entitled to participate. Turin reacted strongly, defending itself from every accusation. The

[220] The documentation is published in Flury-Lemberg, *Sindone 2002*.

[221] Preface to Loconsole, *Sulle tracce della Sindone*, 7–8.

[222] Cf. O. Petrosillo, "Sindone, nuovo mistero: Trenta rammendi spariti," *Il Messaggero*, August 9, 2002, 8; see also, for example, "Scontro sulla Sindone restaurata," *La Stampa*, September 24, 2002, 37.

aftermath of these battles was long and not lacking for even personal offenses.[223]

We must bear in mind the 2001 publication of a long-awaited Vatican document dedicated to popular piety, the fruit of thirteen years of consultations. In it appears this instruction:

> The faithful deeply revere the relics of the Saints. An adequate pastoral instruction of the faithful about the use of relics will not overlook ensuring the authenticity of the relics exposed for the veneration of the faithful; where doubtful relics have been exposed for the veneration of the faithful, they should be discreetly withdrawn with due pastoral prudence.[224]

The fact that the Shroud is treated in practice as a relic, but officially as a sacred image, can exclude it from this requirement. Tension remains, however, between what is said and what one is allowed or led to believe: at Turin the authenticity of the relic is forcefully maintained, and there is a clear desire to increase devotion toward it. As every anthropologist who concerns himself with these issues knows, behind mass devotion "there is always a desire that, through specific practices, this devotion is allowed to spread or, on the contrary, disappear."[225]

In January 2008 an impressive campaign of photography of the Shroud was carried out by the Haltadefinizione company of Novara, Italy, which specialized in high-definition photography of famous works of historical and artistic heritage.[226] New images would allow a close observation of the cloth with unprecedented ease; they would

[223] Again in 2005, at the Dallas conference, polemics were resumed and the archaeologist William Meacham—who had been dealing with the Shroud for many years—came to accuse the organizers of the conference of fascism, when Baima Bollone described him as paranoid (P. Baima Bollone, *Il mistero della Sindone* [Milan: Mondolibri, 2006], 156–59). Meacham even wrote a book to denounce what for him is the "devastation" of the Shroud: *The Rape of the Turin Shroud: How Christianity's Most Precious Relic Was Wrongly Condemned, and Violated* (n.p.: Lulu, 2005).

[224] Congregation for Divine Worship and the Discipline of the Sacraments, *Directory on Popular Piety and the Liturgy*, § 237.

[225] F. Sbardella, *Antropologia delle reliquie* (Brescia: Morcelliana, 2007), 168.

[226] The entire surface of the cloth has been recorded through 1,649 photographs, each of which captures an area of the cloth measuring a few square centimeters and allows it to be distinguished clearly, even to the single threads that make up the cloth.

also allow us to avoid incautious use of old photographs, technically less reliable, in order to find writings, coins, signatures, and various objects. Unfortunately, these images are not available because the archdiocese of Turin, which holds the property, does not grant the use and free consultation of them. For a few years the only way even to get a vague idea about the photos was to consult some prints;[227] finally, in 2013, an app was released for the iPhone and the iPad that has allowed us to appreciate the beauty of these images on electronic media, but with a disruptive transparent watermark and without the ability to access the original high definition. It is not the best that can be done, but at least it is a step in the right direction. Unfortunately, the apps do not work after recent iOS updates.[228]

In the years since the radiocarbon dating, both skeptical scientific organizations and independent researchers have shown increased interest in the Shroud (or rather in sindonology). In France, Paul-Éric Blanrue[229] and Henri Broch are leaders among skeptical scholars;[230] in Spain, Juan Eslava Galán,[231] Félix Ares,[232] and David Montero;[233] in England, Hugh Farey, former director of the *British Society for the Turin Shroud Newsletter*.[234] In Italy, after the aforementioned Father Pier Angelo Gramaglia, Vittorio Pesce Delfino, and Carlo Papini,[235] one

[227] For example, a very expensive limited edition, *Sindone* (Turin: UTET, 2010).

[228] *Sindone*, v. 2.0 (Haltadefinizione, 2013). See also the website www.haltadefinizione.com.

[229] Blanrue, *Miracle ou imposture?*; idem, *Le Secret du Suaire: Autopsie d'une escroquerie* (Paris: Pygmalion, 2006).

[230] H. Broch, *Le paranormal: Ses documents, ses hommes, ses méthodes* (Paris: Seuil, 1989), 43–73; and some essays at http://webs.unice.fr/site/broch/articles/index.html.

[231] Eslava Galán, *Fraude de la Sábana Santa*.

[232] F. Ares, *La sábana santa ¡vaya timo!* (Pamplona: Laetoli, 2006).

[233] On his website at http://sombraenelsudario.wordpress.com.

[234] H. Farey has published several essays between issues 78 and 84 of the *British Society for the Turin Shroud Newsletter*, available at www.shroud.com/bstsmain.htm; and two essays titled "The Medieval Shroud," available at http://independent.academia.edu/HughFarey.

[235] Gramaglia, *L'uomo della Sindone*; idem, *Ultime "scoperte" sulla Sindone*; idem, "La Sindone di Torino: Alcuni problemi storici," *Rivista di storia e letteratura religiosa* 24 (1988): 524–68; idem, "Ancora la Sindone di Torino"; idem, "Giovanni Skylitzes, il Panno di Edessa e le 'sindoni,'" *Approfondimento sindone* 1, no. 2 (1997): 1–16; idem, "Il problema della mentoniera," *Approfondimento sindone* 2, no. 1 (1998): 15–23; idem, "Panni funerari"; idem, "I cimeli cristiani di Edessa," *Approfondimento sindone* 3,

should mention some other scholars generally related to CICAP: Gian Marco Rinaldi, the discoverer of the fraud of Kouznetsov, who has dealt mainly, but not exclusively, with scientific aspects of the Shroud and is the author of some fundamental studies;[236] Luigi Garlaschelli, who specialized in investigations and experiments on the paranormal and on the miraculous, and who attempted a reproduction of the Shroud by artificial methods; Gaetano Ciccone, who dealt mainly with the medieval history of the Shroud and other similar relics, and who led a long study on the pollen issue;[237] and Antonio Lombatti, who was more oriented to historical-archaeological questions and to the popular aspect.[238] Their production, numerically insignificant compared to the quantity of authenticist publications, should not be neglected by one seeking to form a balanced judgment.[239] The skeptical voices are very few, in no small part because studying the Shroud and hundreds of sindonological publications is tiring and takes a great deal of time, time that generally only those who believe in the Shroud are willing to sacrifice; one also encounters the frustration of never being able to approach the object of study directly.

Garlaschelli is also responsible for the design and execution of an experiment to make a scale reproduction of the Shroud. The method is partly derived from Nickell's proposal to use the *frottage* that, better than the experiments using heat did, is able to create pseudonegative images on cloth, images that are shaded, adirectional, superficial, halftone, with blurred edges, not fluorescent under ultraviolet light, and containing three-dimensional

no. 1 (1999): 1–51; idem, "Reliquie palestinesi"; idem, *Reliquie cristiane a Gerusalemme*, 3–39; idem, *La discontinuità* (Turin: Tipografia saviglianese, 2012), 605–70; Pesce Delfino, *E l'uomo creò la Sindone*; C. Papini, *Sindone, un mistero che si svela: Il verdetto americano non conferma l'autenticità* (Turin: Claudiana, 1982); idem, *Sindone: Una sfida*.

236 His studies are published in the CICAP magazine *Scienza & Paranormale* (many of them online at www.cicap.org), between the pages of http://sindone.weebly.com, or on his personal page at https://independent.academia.edu/RinaldiGianMarco.

237 Ciccone and Sturmann, *Sindone svelata*; Ciccone, "Truffa dei pollini."

238 He founded a magazine called *Approfondimento Sindone* and directed it for some years.

239 Much material has been collected at http://sindone.weebly.com. See also L. Garlaschelli, *Processo alla Sindone* (Rome: Avverbi, 1998); and the monographic issue of *MicroMega* of the year 2010 entitled *L'inganno della Sindone*. For further information in English, cf. www.freeinquiry.com/skeptic/shroud.

information. According to STURP, the image of the Shroud does not reveal a significant presence of pigments, but that is due to superficial yellowing of linen fibers (a disagreement between STURP and McCrone on the presence or absence of coloring material remains). An attempt was made to come up with a system that, initially employing pigments, might provoke a yellowing of the underlying fibers that could remain visible even after the removal of the color.

Perfecting Nickell's experiments, which were limited only to the reproduction of a face, Garlaschelli used as a model a living human body and a bas-relief for the head (to get around the problem of deformity). An ingredient was added to the dye, to make it slightly acidic (as, one can imagine, it could have been in the Middle Ages). The dye was then distributed with a dauber. The essential idea is that the acidity of the pigment over time has yellowed the underlying fibers; even if the pigment on the reproduction is artificially removed to simulate the Shroud's natural degeneration over the centuries, yellowing remains visible in the shape of a human being, though very weak and blurred, as on the Shroud. The process of yellowing the fibers, which ought not to happen immediately, was artificially simulated by aging the fabric inside an oven.[240]

Garlaschelli's reproduction is more satisfactory than those previously undertaken,[241] even if not entirely identical to the original and therefore discredited by sindonologists. Here, however, a few thoughts about methodology are necessary. No reproduction can claim to replicate the Shroud exactly down to the microscopic level, and none can be asked to do so: every handmade rendering is unique, and to approximate a given rendering, one would need to know each ingredient accurately and the means used to make it (such as pigment, with its components and effects on that particular fabric). Even natural aging of the cloth can be simulated but not recreated by

[240] L. Garlaschelli, "Life-Size Reproduction of the Shroud of Turin and Its Image," *Journal of Imaging Science and Technology* 54, no. 4 (2010): 1–14; idem, "Perché la sindone è un falso," *MicroMega* 4 (2010): 27–48.

[241] Publication of a book that proposes the use of tannic acid and iron sulfate is planned for the future: G. Vikan, R. Morton, and R. Hoppes, *The Shroud of Turin: Mystery Solved*. I await the publication to evaluate its results.

artificial means.[242] The experiments of skeptics do not seek to prove exactly how the Shroud was made, which at the moment one cannot know with definite certainty for various reasons (and especially due to the impossibility of studying the Shroud itself); they simply seek to demonstrate the inconsistency of the fundamental affirmation on which sindonology is based, that is, that the Shroud is authentic because it has characteristics that are humanly irreproducible. *Frottage* is a mechanism simply able to account for the formation of the image and its main characteristics. It cannot be ruled out that, at some point in the future, alternative mechanisms will be developed or that, perhaps, the technique used to create the Shroud will never be discovered (it would not be the such first case in archaeology or in the history of art). Not even a Stradivarius can be reproduced exactly in all its features, yet this does not make it an "impossible" or miraculous object.

5.4.3 The Twenty-First Century: Exhibitions, Earthquakes, a Laser, Lightning Bolts, and the Big Bang

The most significant Shroud event of the new century has been the exhibition of 2010, where for the first time since the restoration the Shroud was shown in public. Over two and a half million visitors attended this exhibition, which lasted forty-four days (April 10–May 23). The culminating event was the visit, on May 2, by Pope Benedict XVI, who, while standing in front of the Shroud, offered a meditation on the passion of Christ inspired by the Shroud image. Though not addressing the issue of authenticity per se, he offered conclusions derived from sindonology: that the Shroud once wrapped the true body of a scourged corpse, crowned with thorns, crucified and wounded in his flank, and that the bloodstains came from that body.

With this exhibition, one can say that the Turin episcopate of Cardinal Severino Poletto also symbolically came to an end.[243] No formal convention of sindonology was held, but during the period of

[242] Pierluigi Baima Bollone failed to understand that the oven was used only to simulate aging, and so doubts that in the Middle Ages there existed a stove capable of maintaining a constant temperature: *Sindone: Storia e scienza*, 278.

[243] A volume was published in memory of the 2010 exhibition: *Icona del Sabato Santo: Ricordi dell'ostensione della Sindone* (Cantalupa: Effatà, 2011).

the exhibition, the Center of Religious Sciences of the University of Turin sponsored a non-sindonological conference dedicated to the tradition of "acheiropoieta" images—that is, those "not wrought by human hands"—in different religions.[244] In the same time frame, a public display of objects constituting the so-called "Treasure of the Shroud," including vestments, relics, and sacred furnishings, was also undertaken.[245] David Rolfe, already a controversial figure in 1978 for the production of a film on the Shroud, was in charge of preparing the official documentary for the exhibition (*Shroud: Passio Christi, Passio Hominis*). Two years later, a documentary was released that gathered all the worst allegations of fraud directed at dating laboratories, taking up the theme of the Masonic conspiracy.[246] On this topic, various sindonological books quote some phrases attributed to Cardinal Ballestrero, from which it would seem that, once retired, he attributed to freemasonry some influence on the medieval result of the radiocarbon dating; but it is a matter of the erroneous interpretation of an interview in which he was speaking not of the laboratories and scientists but rather of some authenticist sindonologists who were freemasons.[247]

On March 30, 2013, the new archbishop, Cesare Nosiglia, achieved his desired global transmission of an exhibition on television. In 1973 the same undertaking had fallen short of viewers' expectations, but this time the public could see well-defined color images. This broadcast was entirely different from that of 1973: the Shroud remained in the cathedral (without being removed from its new chapel), and the exhibition was presented as a part of a liturgical celebration with prayers, testimonies, and meditations. As had been done in 1973, a papal video message was also displayed, this time by the new Pope

[244] Cf. A. Monaci Castagno, ed., *Sacre impronte e oggetti "non fatti da mano d'uomo" nelle religioni: Atti del Convegno Internazionale–Torino, 18–20 maggio 2010* (Alexandria: Dell'Orso, 2011). Also available on Google Books.

[245] The catalog: D. Biancolini et al., eds., *Il Tesoro della Sindone* (Turin: Daniela Piazza, 2010). See also L. Facchin, "Il tesoro della Sindone tra XVII e XVIII secolo," in *Le forme della meraviglia*, ed. E. E. Barbero (Chieri: Gaidano & Matta, 2014), 71–81.

[246] *The Night of the Holy Shroud*, directed by Francesca Saracino (Medusa Film, 2012). Gian Marco Rinaldi reviews it unpleasantly at http://sindone.weebly.com/uploads/1/2/2/0/1220953/notte_complottopart_1.pdf.

[247] I demonstrate this in Nicolotti, "Sindone: Banco di prova," 492–95; and Giuseppe Caviglia, personal secretary to the cardinal, has confirmed it for me orally.

Francis. The approximate number of spectators was 2,134,000.[248] The meditations given during the liturgical ceremony were more explicit than in the past regarding identifying the imprints and bloodstains of the Shroud with those of the body of Christ.

The most recent traditional exhibition took place in 2015, only five years after the previous one, and was held in an extraordinary form as part of the celebrations for the second centennial of the birth of Saint John Bosco; moreover, the exhibition occurred, as previously in 1898, in conjunction with an international exposition, the Milan Expo, and lasted more than two months, from April 19 until June 24. There were over two million visitors. The effort on the part of the diocese of Turin and the Italian Church to spread the veneration of the Shroud and to encourage pilgrimages to Turin was impressive, with the use of a significant amount of propaganda at every level. All over the world the practice of acquiring life-size photographic copies of the Shroud to be displayed in churches grew ever more widespread and was encouraged by the diocese of Turin, which holds the rights to all photographs.[249] Not far from the cathedral a large bookstore with a huge quantity of books and audiovisual materials dedicated to the Shroud was set up; the present book, published in Italian a few weeks before by the largest publisher in the city, was deliberately kept off the shelves.

On June 21 and 22, Pope Francis visited Turin and, among other things, went to see the Shroud. Compared to his two predecessors, the time and attention he dedicated to the Shroud were rather limited: during his speeches he mentioned it only in passing and did not offer any homilies in front of it, nor did he kneel down before it (fig. 5.10); various sindonologists expressed their disappointment over this. To the contrary, the archbishop of Turin, Cesare Nosiglia, came to the point of publicly embracing the sindonological argument according to which the Shroud "cannot be a medieval forgery"[250] and has many times openly taken authenticist positions: this represents a step backwards to the preconciliar period.

[248] Cf. L. Misiti, "L'ostensione straordinaria della Sacra Sindone di Torino del 30 marzo 2013," in Ciola and Ghiberti, *Passione di Gesù e la Sindone*, 129–32.

[249] For more on this, see P. Cozzo, "Dall'immagine copiata all'immagine fotografata: Evoluzione del culto sindonico fra XX e XXI secolo," in Caliò, *Santi in posa*.

[250] C. Nosiglia, "Sindone, resta un enigma per la scienza," *Il nostro Tempo*, June 21, 2015, 2.

During the exhibition, an international conference that I conceived and organized along with Paolo Cozzo and Andrea Merlotti took place at the Department of History of the University of Turin and the Palace of Venaria; that conference concerned the relationship between the Shroud and the courts of Europe.[251]

On September 27, 2018, after being closed for twenty-eight years, the Chapel of the Shroud was reopened to the public, newly restored to appear as it was before the fire of 1997. For this occasion, as previously in 1931, a display of objects related to the Shroud was held in Palazzo Madama.[252]

It is not possible to offer a very brief account of the progress of sindonology in recent years. Despite the fact that access to the Shroud remains forbidden, the number of sindonological publications has increased. Sindonology tries to make inroads with children through comics, animated authenticist cartoons, and, in school, scholastic books, generally exploiting the presence of professors of religion who, in Italy, are named by the bishops. Beginning in 2001, the Turin Center of Sindonology has organized conferences held by sindonologists in schools to indoctrinate students; already more than thirty thousand schoolchildren have been involved in these conferences from the elementary level on. For adults, the Pontifical Athenaeum Regina Apostolorum, in collaboration with the Turin International Center of Sindonology and the Diocesan Center of Sindonology of Rome, inaugurated a diploma of specialization in Shroud studies.

Sindonologists have not made much progress in the field of history, where the repetition of historiographical hypotheses of Ian Wilson or some variant of it seems still to suffice. The only newsworthy event has been the release of the work of Barbara Frale, of which I have already spoken, on the connection of the Shroud with the Templars and on certain Greek, Latin, and Hebrew writings that she, drawing variously on the authors who preceded her, claims to have read on the electronically manipulated old photographs of the Shroud.[253] Frale claims that a trace of ink has remained on the fabric after bleeding through some papyrus strips

[251] Cozzo, Merlotti, and Nicolotti, *Shroud at Court*.

[252] Catalog of the show: Arnaldi di Balme, *Sindone e la sua immagine*.

[253] Frale, *Templari e la sindone di Cristo* (English translation: *Templars and the Shroud of Christ*); idem, *La sindone di Gesù Nazareno* (Bologna: il Mulino, 2009) (English translation: *The Shroud of Jesus of Nazareth* [Dunboyne: Maverick House, 2011]).

FIGURE 5.10 Pope Francis stands in contemplation before the Shroud during the 2015 exhibition

that contained, in excerpts of different languages, some sentences taken from a certificate of Jesus' death that was glued to the Shroud by an official Roman mortician. Of course none of this is extant, neither the ink on the Shroud nor the papyrus strips.[254] At this point the theory seems to have been abandoned even by authenticists.

As far as concerns scientific considerations, however, there has been an almost "pathological" proliferation of studies.[255] University of Padua professor and mechanical engineer Giulio Fanti sought "some trace of the resurrection still imprinted in the relic," integrating scientific data with the Holy Scriptures and the visions of some mystic. In his opinion "the Man of the Shroud became mechanically transparent in respect to the coverlet and emitted a flash of energy,

[254] Cf. A. Nicolotti, "Barbara Frale e le scritte sulla Sindone di Torino," available in two parts at www.christianismus.it; in abbreviated form, idem, "La leggenda delle scritte sulla Sindone," *MicroMega* 4 (2010): 67–79.

[255] According to the Nobel Prize winner for chemistry Irving Langmuir, scientific "pathology" comes about when certain scholars become so attached to the object of their research or to the explanation they propose that they are no longer able to act according to common sense, and the scientific methodology breaks down: I. Langmuir, "Pathological Science," *Physics Today* 42, no. 10 (1989): 36–48.

which would be the cause of the formation of the body image," which means that "Jesus of Nazareth arose after having been wrapped in that sheet."[256] According to Fanti the sindonic image was generated by an intense electrostatic field within Christ's tomb that would have given rise to the so-called "corona discharge"; he conducted various experiments on this theory in his university's laboratory, using fabrics and mannequins similar to the man of the Shroud, and subjecting them to electric fields generated by a tension up to three hundred thousand volts. The theory of the corona discharge had already been proposed by Allan Mills in 1981;[257] the energy needed to imprint the Shroud, according to some, could have been due to ball lightning formed inside the tomb or, as Fanti prefers, to a sort of brief, intense lightning bolt of unknown (or supernatural) origin. The notion of the lightning bolt was presumed to be corroborated by the visions of Maria Valtorta, a twentieth-century Italian mystic (whose writings, however, have been condemned by the Church).[258] She recounts that she relived the scene of Christ's resurrection, when "a shining meteor going down, a ball of fire of unbearable brightness, followed by a trail" descended from heaven and entered the tomb.[259] Fanti also advances the concepts of resurrection and special phenomena of environmental ionization similar to those which, according to him, were measured during the apparitions of Our Lady in Medjugorje,[260] and he believes that the Shroud has also something in common with the sacred fire of the Holy Sepulcher in Jerusalem.[261]

Recently Fanti also said he had developed new methods for dating individual linen fibers: a mechanical multiparametric dating method, Raman spectroscopy, and attenuated total reflectance-Fourier transform infrared spectroscopy, which would be capable of providing a date

[256] Fanti, *Sindone*, especially pp. 343–91 (citations on pp. 344, 351, and 376).

[257] A. A. Mills, "A Corona-Discharge Hypothesis for the Mechanism of Image Formation on the Turin Shroud," *Proceedings of the British Society for the Turin Shroud* (Summer 1981): 14–21.

[258] G. Fanti, *Sindone: La scienza rafforza la fede*, 2nd ed. (Padova: Edizioni messaggero, 2015), 63–64.

[259] M. Valtorta, *L'evangelo come mi è stato rivelato*, vol. 10, 4th ed. (Isola del Liri: Centro Editoriale Valtortiano, 2001), § 617.3.

[260] G. Fanti, "Hypotheses regarding the Formation of the Body Image on the Turin Shroud," *Journal of Imaging Science and Technology* 55, no. 6 (2011): 6–7.

[261] G. Fanti, "Is the Holy Fire Related to the Turin Shroud?," *Global Journal of Archaeology & Anthropology* 10, no. 2 (2019): 1–6.

for the Shroud compatible with the era of Jesus. The archbishop of Turin, on his own behalf and that of the pope, immediately denied value to these studies, because they were conducted on noncertified material,[262] but it seems that the problems with Fanti's dating methodology are far more significant than the questions related to certification.[263] In fact these examinations are unusual; they do not constitute a scientifically recognized system for the dating of fabrics and have evidently been designed and put forth for the sole purpose of being able to date the Shroud near the first century.

It is important to consider the ideological presuppositions of Professor Giulio Fanti, who for twenty years has tried everything to authenticate the Shroud and seems to be a dominant figure in modern sindonology. He himself revealed that in 1988, when the result of the C14 was announced, he heard an "internal voice" suggesting to him that the result of the examination was not reliable. Therefore, during an exhibition he directed a prayer at the man of the Shroud—the text of which Fanti himself has provided for us[264]—so that the man might reveal his identity to him; he received a positive "internal response."

[262] Declaration of the pontifical custodian of the Holy Shroud, Msgr. Cesare Nosiglia, dated March 27, 2013: "Since there is no degree of certainty about the possession of the materials on which these experiments would be carried out pertaining to the Shroud, the Propriety and the Custody declare not to be able to recognize the results of such alleged experiments to be of any serious value."

[263] Initially in a book written with a journalist, G. Fanti and S. Gaeta, *Il mistero della Sindone: Le sorprendenti scoperte scientifiche sull'enigma del telo di Gesù* (Milan: Rizzoli, 2013); and then in greater depth, no longer with a journalist but with one of his students: Fanti and Malfi, *Sindone: Primo secolo dopo Cristo!* (English translation: *Shroud of Turin: First Century after Christ!*); cf. the criticism of G. M. Rinaldi, "Sindone: Le 'datazioni alternative' di Giulio Fanti," www.queryonline.it. The tests were performed on linen fibers with a diameter of ten- to twenty-thousandths of a millimeter. Since he has never been allowed to study the Shroud closely, Fanti used very small bits of material extracted from the filters of an aspirator of air used on the cloth by Giovanni Riggi in 1978, therefore from threads possibly already detached and in poor condition and mixed with fragments from the Holland cloth to which the Shroud at the time was stitched, as well as with other fragments of every kind and of different origins that happened to be present on the linen. Fanti vaunted having been able to distinguish the Shroud fragments from all the others that came from various pollutants; yet this is difficult to verify.

[264] "O Jesus, I have so much material to study pertaining to your Holy Shroud. I do not want to lose several years of studies and research on this subject if this were just a medieval icon. Accordingly, if you, O Jesus, are truly the Man of the Holy Shroud, let me know by giving me a sign."

The author said that he perceived "a so-called 'sense of infinity,' that is, a strong internal attraction toward that Holy Sheet, which it seemed was calling his soul inside the Holy Sheet itself." From that point "before making important decisions about undertaking or not particular analyses on material coming from the Holy Shroud, the author decided to put a question of confirmation to the Mother of God," receiving the longed-for celestial consent afterward during a journey to Medjugorje, through "an 'internal voice' that suggested to him to continue the planned analyses." According to the author, "perhaps all of this clearly corresponds to a divine plan"; and he cares to let us know that for his studies—which he evidently subjected to a sort of "peer review" by Christ and the Madonna—he spent tens of thousands of euros taken from public funds of the Italian public university system.[265] In one of his articles most widely publicized by the press, Fanti, along with others, believed that he had demonstrated the existence, on the Shroud, of the blood of a tortured man; but after some verifications the article was withdrawn by the same journal in which it had been published due to problems "about the validity of the conclusions and the reproducibility of the results."[266]

Giulio Fanti is not the only one to attempt research on materials presumed to have been taken from the Shroud. In France, Gérard Lucotte obtained from Giovanni Riggi a triangular scrap of a bit of adhesive tape that had been applied to the Shroud, 1.36 mm in height with a base that was 0.614 mm wide; naturally, on this trifle Lucotte found pollens and spores, red blood cells, skin, and a fragment of a hair, from which he deduced that Christ was blond or had red hair and shaved with a copper blade.[267]

[265] G. Fanti, *La Sacra Sindone di Gesù Cristo* (Tavagnacco: Segno, 2015), 227–28, 230. The author completely confuses science and faith in this book: Fanti sets experiments and theories alongside mystic visions, prayers, prayer beads, a Way of the Cross, and a diorama of the Shroud.

[266] E. Carlino et al., "Atomic Resolution Studies Detect New Biologic Evidences on the Turin Shroud," *Plos One* 12, no. 6 (2017), https://doi.org/10.1371/journal.pone.0180487.

[267] G. Lucotte, "Exploration of the Face of the Turin Shroud: Pollens Studied by SEM Analysis," *Archaeological Discovery* 3 (2015): 158–78; idem, "Red Blood Cells on the Turin Shroud," *Jacobs Journal of Hematology* 2, no. 1 (2015): 1–14; idem, "Skin Debris on the Face of the Turin Shroud: A SEM-EDX Analysis," *Archaeological Discovery* 4 (2016): 103–17; G. Lucotte and T. Thomasset, "Scanning Electron Microscopic

A different hypothesis that tries to explain the formation of the Shroud's image, always resorting to corona discharge, assumes that an electrostatic field was created by the release of piezoelectric energy caused by mechanical stresses produced by some earthquakes that disturbed the Holy Sepulcher of Jerusalem in the year 30 or so. The link between the earthquakes recorded in the Gospels[268] and the Shroud, already proposed in 1982 by Graeme Coote,[269] has been taken up by Professor Francesco Lattarulo of the Polytechnic of Bari: inside a tomb with a high level of ambient ionization, which was caused by the accumulation of radon gas, an electric discharge, originating from an earthquake, may have occurred; such a discharge would have been capable of impressing the image of the corpse on the Shroud.[270] Giovanna de Liso—an opera singer who before this had experience with crop circles and said that she had been abducted by aliens on more than one occasion—has shown her readiness to testify to the effectiveness of radon. She claims to have experienced such a gas buildup in the cellar of her own house (which she then renamed the "Seismic Precursors Study Center") and to have tested the effects on fabrics soaked in solutions containing aloe and myrrh and placed between two rock plates acting as electrical capacitors.

Theories can also be mixed; if an earthquake produces electric fields, it can also disintegrate the deuterium present in the body and

---

Characterization and Elemental Analysis of One Hair Located on the Face of the Turin Shroud," *Archaeological Discovery* 5 (2017): 1–21.

[268] Ignorance of the exegetical literature on the subject leads to an imprudent, literal reading of the Gospels. According to the majority of biblical scholars, the "quakes" of which only the evangelist Matthew speaks in correspondence with the death and resurrection of Jesus (Matthew 27:51 and 28:2) are not real earthquakes but symbolic, apocalyptic signs referring to Old Testament motifs (especially Ezekiel), indications of a theophany, of a direct intervention of God in human affairs; cf. J. Gnilka, *Il vangelo di Matteo*, pt. 2a (Brescia: Paideia, 1991), 686–87, 695–96, 719–20; and G. Scaglioni, *E la terra tremò: I prodigi alla morte di Gesù in Matteo 27,51b-53* (Assisi: Cittadella, 2006). Also, in Acts 16:26 an earthquake is mentioned that opened the doors of the prison. N.b. also that Matthew 8:24 uses the same Greek term (*seismós*) to designate a storm.

[269] Cf. R. Morgan, "Word from New Zealand on Electrical Discharge Image Formation," *Shroud News* 29 (1985): 7–8.

[270] Cf. F. Lattarulo, "Electrostatic Imaging for the Turin-Shroud Man," *MATEC Web of Conferences* 36 (2015): 1–15; V. Amoruso and F. Lattarulo, "A Physicochemical Interpretation of the Turin Shroud Imaging," *Scientific Research and Essays* 7, no. 29 (2012): 2554–79.

favor the emission of proton and neutron fluxes, necessary (according to Jean-Baptiste Rinaudo) not only to form the image but also to take the blame for the "false" radiocarbon dating. Alberto Carpinteri, an engineer at Turin Polytechnic best known for announcing the discovery of nuclear fission reactions within granite blocks submitted to high pressures, contributed to these discussions. Carpinteri thinks that in Jerusalem, during an earthquake approaching nine on the Richter scale (which would nearly have destroyed the city—but of which we have no trace), "piezonuclear" reactions able to provoke neutron fluxes were created.[271] Meanwhile, his piezonuclear research, whose existence did not convince anyone, cost him the loss of the presidency of the National Institute of Metrological Research,[272] and twelve of his articles, including that on the Shroud, were withdrawn by the publisher for irregularities. An examination of his articles demonstrates significant errors, of a historical and interpretative nature.[273]

Not everyone uses electrical agents external to the body: August Accetta, for example, believes that it is incorrect to resort to external causes and that it is enough to imagine that the image was caused by energies coming from inside the body of the crucified man; to prove this, Accetta tried to offer his own evidence using a scintigraphic process and injecting his body with the medical radioisotope known as metastable technetium-99.[274]

A new field of investigation has been suggested by some scientists of the ENEA Research Center of Frascati, led today by Paolo Di Lazzaro. Wanting to identify the processes that may have led to

[271] A. Carpinteri et al., "Piezonuclear Neutrons from Earthquakes as a Hypothesis for the Image Formation and the Radiocarbon Dating of the Turin Shroud," *Scientific Research and Essays* 7, no. 29 (2012): 2603–12; A. Carpinteri et al., "Is the Shroud of Turin in Relation to the Old Jerusalem Historical Earthquake?," *Meccanica*, published online in February 2014, but retracted by the publisher in 2015 "due to conflict of interest reasons" and "as the editorial process had been compromised." It is a very serious action.

[272] As a result of his alleged discovery of the "piezonuclear," which is considered to be unfounded, 1,200 physicists signed an appeal to the minister in 2012 to call for his resignation. The institute was put under administration through an external commissioner; subsequently, a new president was appointed.

[273] Gian Marco Rinaldi is preparing a list of these errors.

[274] A. D. Accetta et al., "Nuclear Medicine and Its Relevance to the Shroud of Turin," in Marinelli and Russi, *Sindone 2000*, 3–6.

the formation of the image of the Shroud, they used impulses of light in the vacuum ultraviolet spectrum emitted by an excimer laser. An extremely short (less than fifty-billionths of a second) laser pulse in a very narrow range of irradiation parameters demonstrates a tool suitable for replicating some features of the Shroud's coloring. To reproduce the entire image of the Shroud with a single flash of light, they add, would require fourteen thousand lasers firing simultaneously.[275] The choice of the vacuum ultraviolet, a radiation in a wavelength strongly absorbed by oxygen in the air, solved the chiaroscuro problem of the Shroud's image by supposing that the farther the cloth was from the body emitting radiation, the less intense was the yellowing of the fabric. Another sindonologist, Bernard Power, had ventured to calculate mathematically the degree of damping and colorization on the fabric, but with microwaves instead of ultraviolet light.[276] However interesting such experiments may be (even if they could be criticized to some extent),[277] there still remains the problem that the laser and microwaves obviously did not exist at the time of Christ or in the Middle Ages. These tools are at best useful for creating copies of the Shroud, not for explaining the creation of the original. Though Di Lazzaro prudently did not offer any definitive conclusions, the former head of his laboratory, Giuseppe Baldacchini, who was the first at ENEA to have the idea of undertaking the study, has expressed his own belief that the body of Jesus vanished from the Shroud through a matter-antimatter annihilation process, provoking a "superfluorescence" by means of an "emission of a burst of coherent and directional Vacuum Ultra-Violet light," while at the same time neutrons were released in sufficient measure to distort the dating of the C14. Christ's resurrection, says Baldacchini, was like a little Big Bang in which "the body dematerialized into the Shroud

[275] P. Di Lazzaro et al., "Superficial and Shroud-Like Coloration of Linen by Short Laser Pulses in the Vacuum Ultraviolet," *Applied Optics* 51 (2012): 8567–78. There is much more material at www.frascati.enea.it/fis/lac/excimer/sindone/sindone.html.

[276] B. A. Power, "Image Formation on the Holy Shroud of Turin by Attenuation of Radiation in Air," *Collegamento pro Sindone Internet* (March 2002), www.sindone.info/POWER1.PDF.

[277] Cf. Nicolotti, "Sindone: Banco di prova," 495–502.

and instantly materialized again in another place" to appear to the disciples.[278]

In May 2010, ENEA organized a convention on sindonology with Di Lazzaro as chairman. Among the speakers were Giulio Fanti, the singer Giovanna de Liso, the attorney Mark Antonacci, a biologist to talk about history, a physicist and a natural science graduate to talk about iconography, and a philosopher who explained "the dynamic interface between thought, light and matter." The Vatican newspaper *L'Osservatore Romano* ran the headline "Science comes face to face with the impossible" with an article whose summary stated, "The conclusions of the tests conducted with carbon 14 in 1988, which indicated a medieval dating for the Shroud, today turn out to be even more weakened by the results, albeit partial, of ENEA's research."[279] The logic here eludes reason but nonetheless offers a way of understanding once more what some people would seem to mean when they talk about the kind of "science" that should study the Shroud. Since then, Paolo Di Lazzaro has been rewarded with the position of vice director of the Turin International Center of Sindonology and also has taken up a series of lectures refuting the value of radiocarbon dating.

In 2014, shortly before the completion of the Italian edition of this book, a conference was held on the Shroud at the Polytechnic of Bari, also sponsored by the University of Bari and the International Center of Sindonology of Turin. The speakers and theories are always more or less the same for all the conventions; here the false history of the shroud of Besançon and research on the Sudarium of Oviedo were proposed yet again. There was also a report from the palynologist Marzia Boi, a candidate to be a possible replacement for Max Frei as scholar of pollen for the Shroud. Boi described Frei's research as imprecise, erroneous, inconclusive, and unscientific (as was already known); soon after, however, she herself undertook the identification of other pollens, falling into the same errors of those she had criticized. Never having observed any actual grain of pollen from the Shroud or even the original slides of Frei's samples—which are kept strictly under lock and key—Marzia Boi had to be content

278 G. Baldacchini, "Religions, Christianity and Shroud," *Collegamento pro Sindone Internet* (February 2013), www.sindone.info/BALDAKI2.PDF.

279 M. Bonatti, "La scienza a tu per tu con l'impossibile," *L'Osservatore Romano*, December 29, 2011, 5.

with examining photographs that she presumed Frei had obtained from pollens on the Shroud. The outcome was singular: Frei's and Boi's results are in full contradiction and cancel each other out, but sindonologists combine them as if both sets of results constitute proof of authenticity.[280]

References to earthquakes, to corona discharges, to lasers, and to sacred fires of the Holy Sepulcher did not obscure the news of the discovery of a new type of special energy. Indeed, Dr. Valery Shalatonin of Belarus reported on the "dynamical and biological properties of the electrical field about the Shroud of Turin replica" revealed by placing some jars with wheat seeds at different distances from a modern photographic copy of the Shroud; he noted that the seedlings grew better in the jars closest to the copy. The electromagnetic field of the room, he asserted, changed even if someone introduced a sheet of paper with an Our Father written on it.

Such, it would seem, is the triumph of sindonology in the twenty-first century.

[280] A synthesis of the new claims can be found in in M. Boi, "Palynology: Instrument of Research for the Relics of the Shroud of Turin and the Sudarium of Oviedo" (2015), www.shroud.com/pdfs/duemaggioBoiENG.pdf.

Index of Names

The general order of the index is alphabetical by last name followed by abbreviated first name (e.g., Presley, E.). The names of sovereigns and members of the highest nobility are indexed by proper name (e.g., Umberto I of Savoy, king of Italy); nobles are indexed by surname (e.g., Savoy, Louise of). Names dating back to ancient and medieval periods, when use of the surname was not yet established or univocal, are given in full (e.g., Charny, Geoffroy de) or with an explanatory note (e.g., Claudius, bishop of Turin). The following are not included in the index: names of God, Jesus, and Holy Mary; names included within the titles of books, book chapters, or articles from the footnotes; names of places, buildings, etc. (e.g., Church of Saint Peter).